HAWTHORNE'S REDEMPTION

HAWTHORNE'S REDEMPTION

The Mystery of The ScArlet Letter

An Analysis of
Nathaniel Hawthorne's Tale

As presented by
GARY P. CRANFORD, Editor
(for and in behalf of
Daniel K. Bayinhund)

authorHOUSE®

AuthorHouse™
1663 Liberty Drive
Bloomington, IN 47403
www.authorhouse.com
Phone: 1-800-839-8640

Published by AuthorHouse   10/08/2012

ISBN: 978-1-4772-7015-8 (sc)
ISBN: 978-1-4772-7014-1 (hc)
ISBN: 978-1-4772-7013-4 (e)

Library of Congress Control Number: 2012917057

"A writer of story-books!
What kind of a business in life,—
what mode of glorifying God,
or being serviceable to mankind
in his day and generation,—may that be?"
Nathaniel Hawthorne

*   *   *

"A little learning is a dangerous thing;
Drink deep, or taste not the Pierian spring:
There shallow draughts intoxicate the brain,
And drinking largely sobers us again."
Alexander Pope

**

"A little knowledge is a dangerous thing.
So is a lot."
Albert Einstein

ACKNOWLEDGEMENTS

This work, written for laymen by a layman, however pretentious, insular, or unprofessional it may appear to be in the eyes of the learned, stems from my faintest recollections and sketchy notes of an unknown student's analysis of *The Scarlet Letter*. While it is possible we may have been students at the same university, my acquaintance with him, however, is fairly limited to the contents of this book.

As his editor, I ascribe the entirety of this work to the unknown Mr. Daniel Bayinhund, if that be any likely identification, inasmuch as the papers I found bore this name, and may constitute one of the last of his academic adventures at our old alma mater. He may yet appear, unless he has gone the way of all flesh, and lay claim to all that to which he is rightly entitled, to which request his editor would gladly acquiesce. For that matter, how his work got this far should be credited more to the sagacity of others than to any of my own, for it has taken me years to drum up the nerve to impose Daniel's text upon the literary mind, or rather, upon the liberality of our higher educators, though I may stand in danger of even higher censure by those more conservative in thought. I have long since lost the papers from which I relate his ideas; and, fortunately, for his sake only, I have found a courageous publisher who has put his hunches a little ahead of his better sense in challenging Hawthorne's critics, however far under some of them, too, may be.

To Bayinhund give we the credit, or the blame, either for creating an innovative analogy where there was none, or for demonstrating a keen analytical insight that purports to resolve the mystery of Hawthorne's novel. We have done so in proper order to discharge oblations to an alter ego, to whom I made an oath years ago to bring Daniel's moment of genius to the public's view, if I could, however small and insignificant that effort might be, as it were, from the sepulcher of his faded mind. Today's students of fine literature, should they ever have the opportunity, may like to forage among the tidbits of Daniel's insight. No less, Mr.

Who may likewise have had in mind to delight in what commentary both friendlys and unfriendlys may pleasure in the matter. I myself have been torn between enthusiasm and reticence, between the pleasure I have derived from the experience of digesting that insight, and the qualms of transmitting it. In any case, it is with an easy trepidation I accept the challenge of an incessant conscience.

Ambiguous, obscure, and fanciful may sum the terms critics have used to describe Hawthorne's tale. But Bayinhund, in a fancy of his own, has dared to assume to have clarified Hawthorne's ambiguity, sounded the depths of his literary genius, and, lo and behold, perhaps unified the meanings of the allegory surrounding the scarlet letter. Or we may say, that he has done nothing of the sort, but created an elaborate scarlet letter all his own. But it is time for the general public to sharpen their teeth upon the matter as much as has Hawthorne's literary critics.

Since the time of my original discovery of Mr. Bayinhund's documents, I have had occasion to discuss his interpretations with only a few, one of which is a dear lifemate, who, may her name be praised, has patiently resisted them; and should they likewise fall hapless upon other less fortunates, who may likewise fear as I to be misaligned with them, I must credit her influence as most beneficial in whetting my appetite to present them and in inspiring my method of doing so. An English teacher, who is disinclined among the many to believe the essential premise of Bayinhund's analysis, and who has maintained little reticence as to her judgment thereof, she has nevertheless helped tremendously in ways other than simple grammatical suggestions, if no other than by the strength of her responses, in bringing this work to publication.

Her position is most tenable. Swamped in the lore and legend of Hawthorne's abstruseness, a teacher of such can do no less, unless some spark of intuition hold sway on such a repast, squelch the surface incrimination in his tale, stifle one's own intellectual whims, and look for some ray of sunshine from such a ghastly yarn. That is quite a sum of tasks for any student, especially to do so in the face of the respectable guardians of such a repast. Others, some of whom repute in the same academic field, seem to share a similar literary assessment, without so much as even a hint of daring to go intellectually further. In fact indeed, they are part of a majority, I have found, that has distinguished the singularity of the minority.

Perhaps such an in-depth, impersonal approach would require much more control over one's own presuppostions and prejudices than can be mustered at a particular moment in time. Perhaps the majority of democratic minds hinge on the whiff of what is the most popular at the time, and the uniqueness of the new may need more support from the few mavericks who prefer to air their views in the face of the common notion rather than to acquiesce for fear of censure.

Opposition to such a notion is therefore very understandable, for anything new on the subject might not only be questionable but, heaven forbid, sacrilegious to the old Bard himself, who apparently did not want to be fully understood by every casual reader anyway. The outshot of such dyed-in-the-wool largess may strongly mitigate against any change of mind in the literary field, but may nudge the appetite of the more free-thinking young student not so overwhelmed by past prejudices. To such, this exposition is dedicated, in memory of my own young unbiased mind, for they may be more inclined to take issue with established customs, yet perhaps wise enough to support or modify them when other forthcoming evidence outweighs the contrary.

For an academic review of Bayinhund's analysis, perhaps more to test the permeability of those waters than to confirm that larger sentiment, an attempt, however vain and misguided it may have been, was made to publish a short paper in the *Nathaniel Hawthorne Review*. Dr. Frederick Newberry, a professor at Duquesne University in Pittsburgh, Pennsylvania, and editor of the periodical, despite his colleagues' refusal to consider the text worthy of publication in their journal, was kind and professional enough to direct my misalliance to the works of Becker and Muirhead, both of which were apparently not available to Daniel Bayinhund at the time of his analysis, and one of which has been scrutinized carefully in an appendix because it strengthens Daniel's views. Methinks the professor was graciously condescending to make such a reference, especially in view of my half-hearted attempts to get Daniel's analysis published in his worthy publication, of which he may have had no close or large connection. It is highly a mark of exceptional integrity for a man of renown to aid the infantile efforts of a possibly contrary spirit.

However, in view of the lengthy and detailed list of his editors' objections to that feeble attempt, from a scholarly point of view, methinks they unitedly protested too much, thus reinforcing my eagerness for a second and more thorough review. Not having full access to Daniel's complete analysis, which only now is forthcoming, their position likewise is most tenable. Several other publishers, as publishers go, perhaps for lack of time and energy, would accept nothing from a nobody either, or the nobody's nobody.

So the analysis has sat, as on a moss-covered stone, far from the beaten path of common commerce, hemmed in on both sides by the dark forests of academia, for some long period of time, the interval of which has fixed my attention, from Daniel's perspective, to more details in Hawthorne's novel. Not that I have attempted most ardently to follow the modern customs of our scholarly scribes in presenting a more learned approach. That justifiably might require more authoritative quotation that I am want to provide, in order to speak with any more worthy substance; rather, I have simply advanced Bayinhund's ideas from his own intuitive interpretations, as best as I could from memory, in conjunction with this latter, more refined vigil, with as much enthusiasm as I could muster from my experience of his experience. Come what may, it is time to throw Daniel's ideas on the public mind, and leave to chance and reason what might become of it.

In view of advancing anything new and enlightening, I do so mindful of the difficulty others have entertained in a different but similar field, who, rather than subscribing to the academic standards of their day, instead addressed their public from their own impressions, in analogies and parables, like unto Hawthorne, which they also claimed to obtain directly from a higher authority. Time has proven those students' mark on society; and this purveyor, of something he deems bright and promising in Daniel's exposition, would hope, at the least, that his and Hawthorne's grandchildren might exult in his redemption, whether Hawthorne's, Daniel's, or mine.

Nevertheless, a contemporary of Bayinghund's, whose work has been more readily accepted among his kind, might also bear some witness to the soundness of this purveyance, and open the way for some consideration, if not acceptance, of what might be judged outrageously new on the subject. Becker's scholarly analysis has been weighed in the balance in Appendix 2 in order to show its relevance to Bayinghund's conclusions as a worthy academic foundation for his lofty ideas.

Becker may have done Bayinhund justice by taking his own analysis to the very brink of literary credibility. However, he appears perhaps to have been a little too academically cautious in advancing too far beyond the mien of obscurity, which apparently has been enshrined around Hawthorne's tale. He may have had substantial reasons for daring to go no further, for had he done so, some of his comrades in arms might not have hesitated to remind him of present-day literary protocol.

No less credit for this airing goes to Gregory Widman, a minister and friend of mine, who read pertinent portions of this book and rendered his concurrence that it might be fit for public consumption, as a Christian text. In his defense, I must admit that I do not know the extent to which he shared my own dubious judgment, or the reader might not now be entertaining himself possibly at my expense. I failed to ask for his literary opinion, perhaps because I had already obtained the more expert from closer quarters on that matter. I was willing to leave the summum bonum of that to the first publisher having the foresight and the courage to foist either innovation or enlightenment upon the public mind. I have had my own doubts concerning both regards; but then, again, I have felt compelled intuitively to make the attempt out of a fair, if not misdirected, conscience, and, hopefully, not too distant from the sound reasoning of mind perhaps a little better-ordered than in his youth.

I have presented Mr. Bayinhund's analysis in his stead, with the aid of a few references, in the first person, simply in the interest of identity. Since the question of source often first chances to cross the minds of those whose disagreement flourishes on cherished traditions, in all fairness to him, I must put myself in the more accurate position as only his half-hearted and posthumous editor. Inasmuch as it purports chiefly to reflect Bayinhund's own experiences with Hawthorne's novel, with only a squalid review of the few critics he may have studied, this book is not intended as meat for a scholar's table. Though his editor is still in the midst of studying Hawthorne's works, and, with less intensity, those of his critics, he would be most content should one or two of his descendants fondly peruse the ruminations of an ancient ghostwriter, point out the identify of Mr. Who, reverence the source of all truth, and credit the means whereby it cometh.

CONTENTS

EDITOR'S PROLOGUE

P lagiarism may not often come so delicately branded, or indiscretion feign to hide the embarrassment written well enough over most of its face. The editor does not mind the timidity of the latter in vouching for a fellow student—whom he really never met face to face in the flesh—nor speaking for him in his absence, or even doing so without his express permission. For this may very well be the only way to unearth him, thus giving him the opportunity of confronting his editor with the former, and claiming for himself what is rightfully his. This lackey most heartedly and upfront attests that the ideas presented in this volume are entirely Mr. Bayinhund's. Were he to come forth, or become readily known, and so accost the editor himself, he would surrender all credit, or blame, for the ideas he believes Daniel would have shared as openly as his humble footman. That should have to be the gracious case in point in order to redeem his indiscretion, or to prove otherwise.

It behooves him, therefore, but with no large measure of confidence in the enterprise, to attempt to relate the ruminations of a would-be scholar, if not to the interests of academia, at least to the curiosity of fellow students who would understand a masterpiece of American literature. Those who stand in awe of Hawthorne, and are still perplexed by all the failed attempts of our well-known and distinquished scholars to sort out the mysterious meanings of his most popular novel, may still wallow somewhat in the mire of ambiguity surrounding that tale, and fain would have some greater understanding of one of the most misunderstood works of art. At the same time, it least bothers the editor to speak in behalf of his friend, if I may speak personally, first to relate the circumstances surrounding his fate, who probably by now, if not so many years ago, has passed away in some obscure and equivocal ignominity. Death is probably too harsh a label for it, however, for he may very well be alive and kicking elsewhere still, perhaps even restored from the state whereof last evidence of his demise was found, which, as Daniel himself called it, seems to have been accomplished mostly by a kind of decapitation. Although it appears he likely became a nobody in his own mind, if losing one's academic head qualifies one so, I have come to gain a little more respect for the contents thereof, if not in perfect agreement therewith. I have had occasion to explore the ruminations of that appendage, after it took leave of absence, more carefully in the intervening years, and feel somewhat to say that I have been seduced, against my better senses, to follow suit, although at my age, *das macht nichts.*

Perhaps fewer students commit suicide, however, than succomb to the honorary halls of academia, over such a simple sin of which my friend, Daniel, was accused. Nevertheless, it is but that one ebb of scholastic life I feel bound to redeem, that one sin I am unmercilessly driven by something inside me to exonerate, however squalid the attempt might be.

Some forty years ago, while perhaps in my intellectual birth, and given to late night vigils at the library of one of the larger schools in one of the valleys of the Uinta Mountains, I came upon a large parcel of yellowish papers stuck in a copy of Hawthorne's novel, *The Scarlet Letter,* which I had found hidden away in back of a bust of the bard himself, in an out-of-the-way corner of the library's lowest level floor. I use the word, bard, loosely, in Bayinhund's behalf, as it was he who referred to Hawthorne as the Bard of Boston, because of the maze of metaphors and parables he cleverly twisted into a red and black tale of gloom and hope. Whether the book had been placed upon Hawthorne's head, and fallen off later, or purposefully lodged out of sight in its secure spot, was a question I was as apt to consider as any other, large or small, at that stuporous hour of the night. At the time I wondered if the experience was more of a dream than a reality, or if the reality of the find was merely an invention of its author.

At such a moment, when one's vigil comes in a package of several nights to meet some nearing deadline, the body and mind seem to cooperate in a kind of Pavlovian symbiosis, somewhat apart from one's own ego, which itself seems to float somewhat above its catbird seat, and passively observe what the interactions between the two may conjure up next. So I knew not whether I was in the body or out, or spaced half-way in some dream between one world and another, or hallucinating the whole event for lack of a sufficient state of mind, as it were some kind of coma induced by no less than an inexplicable impulse to escape the awful reality contriving it. Perhaps it is such a moment when intuition is loosened from the rational mind, and is able to transcend the boundaries often imposed upon it, thus working some wonder in search of what might be called, or alleged, as truth. Such vigils have awakened genius, so it seems, and students are ever so disposed to identify with it.

In this state of mind, or lack of it, I may have leaned against the wall, with my eyes closed or open, I cannot tell; but something inside me must have peeked down behind the smooth and rusty-red marble of the bust, upon which I had placed my left hand for support—the feel of which itself may have opened up that intuitive conduit—and spotted in the shadows a shape out of sorts with them. It was a book whose hard-bound binding, with a long tear down its thin scarlet cover, was black as pitch. I marveled that I could have even noticed it at all; but the mind had said, "Pick it up," and the body replied, "I did," and Mr. Who, who had taken a back seat to the whole enterprise, suddenly awoke and interjected sarcastically, "Please, let's just pretend that I've completely vacated the premises!" It was beyond all reason, for I had other things to do, and hours to go before I could afford the luxury of completely allowing such independent thought and action of my comrads.

The poor student, Brother Bayinhund, whose name was noted on an unfortunate package folded inside the book, mayhaps have been content to dispose of his genius so, without the slightest concern whether some other lackluster wit should stumble upon it, and, ignorantly so, chance another pass of it at some other discontented journeyman. One such evidently had seemingly had the lavish pleasure of marking the contents of the papers with almost as much indelible red ink as there was black thereon. A specific proscription limits how much carbon can be deposited upon a particularly sized sheet—perhaps for the reason of the same result thus obtained—and I would have to say, in all fairness to the average student, upon a more careful and unbiased examination, that there was considerably more red ink than black, as though that was the very intent or calculation for the restriction.

However, I do not wish to accuse myself of being unfair to the brighter professors of higher education. Though it may seem difficult for some students to surmise they have found one—to which difficulty Brer Bayinhund might readily attest—perhaps the more part of them might be really rather given less to distancing their genius from that of their students than to promoting their own. In my own regards, I have met many academians for whom I had utmost respect and admiration.

Inasmuch as students may be inclined to give only a superficial glance at other student's literary efforts, unless they are really hard up for individual thought other than their own—the sum of which is often wearisome at any hour of the night or day—I might have dismissed the event altogether, especially since the bundle was thick, containing two compositions, one with no bloody commentary, and the other sporting a gigantic red C that composed half the title page. For some unfathomable reason, Bayinhund had doodled a flowery design around the perimeter of his scarlet shame, as though he had plenty of idle moments thereafter to consider the effects of defeat.

As I say, I probably would have just rolled my eyes, had they not already been under the remote control of who knows who at such a transfixed hour, and had I not noticed the falling of a small square piece of memo paper from the contents thereof. I debated the worth of stooping to retrieve it, but since I was no longer the captain of my ship, I discovered that my fingers had already beat my consciousness to it. Slow motion often buffers the zone between sanity and unsanity, and I could scarcely tell whether I was still quite safe enough. But, as it so happened, moment adds to moment what next the eye takes unto itself, and the transformation thereby soon helped redeem me from past confusions.

Yet I must confess that it was not fellow pity, nor simply some curiosity of the mind, that bade me haunt that lonely corner, and absorb the shadows for the remainder of the night. What I am about to relate may cause the reader to question in disbelief, but must not accuse my mind of any invention; for I had no sooner clasped the small note as to drop it and leap back from the place, as though a red scorpion had bitten my finger, and, in the delusion of the hour, the poison spreading instantly over my entire soul and body. Or, like as it were, for a more logical conclusion, perhaps a sharp-witted pin in the note had pricked me, and the shock thereof had clothed my whole person, like the fearful premonition of an intimidating shadow in the back alley of a dead-end street. Be that as it may, the piercing affliction faded as instantaneously as it came, and I eventually ventured to examine the appendage to see if there were some insensitive demon on it laying claim to my precious blood. None such, however, was evidently lost, my finger still as smooth as the bard's head, and the memo actually pinless.

It was the mystery of the sensation itself though, and nothing else, that compelled my fingers cautiously and slowly to unfold the jaundiced sheets to seek some connection between the inexplicable pain I had experienced and the scribbling thereon. The sting seemed to awaken some searching part of my inner self, not the mind and not the body, none less pehaps than the inquisitive Mr. Who, whose impulsive nature, upon being roused from his ubiquitous slumber, finally jammed the rudder of my soul, and demanded my complete focus, howbeit still beyond all rational appeal.

The handwriting on the slip that caught my eye seemed to contain some message not obviously as simplistic as the topic indicated; and its distinctly indescript and illegible scribble must have challenged the curiosity of my languorous mind, or something like it, which moved my body out of its passive midnight mood. That I know, because I remember discovering it fumbling around on the floor just a little behind my fingers, which located before the rest of me where the scarlet slip had finally rested. I could barely translate but one sentence, something to the effect of questioning Brother Bayinhund's source of information, or where he got the crazy idea, or something else as impertinently as an unspoken reproof can be couched without the blatant stamp of rudeness.

In examining the manuscript from which the slip had fallen, and beholding the extent of comments carefully inscribed thereon, I discovered another small piece of paper lodged between its pages. Nothing appeared upon the memo at all, not a word or symbol, nor a mark of any kind to signal its purpose. Small, square, of the same dimensions as the memo, and as crimson as the large C flourished upon the manuscript, it likewise cast a mysterious spell upon the whole enterprise. However, I surmised that it was some kind of inferior classification used peculiarly by the professor to label his students, or the works thereof, and dismissed it from my mind as best as I could.

The other paper probably never obtained the eyes of the professor, as it was spared this red-gutted humiliation, perhaps because it was only Daniel's autobiographical reaction to the one stamped with his critic's genius, or to some other unfair and unsparing judgment. Or perhaps the bloodless manuscript was an attempt to salvage the remains of Bayinhund's graduate status after the red-stained other had met its apparent fiasco. Whichever document predated the other, had his personal defense been submitted, it would probably only have been regarded no more than the frustrated yelps of a puppy lost in his own back yard. Were these documents yet to be found and come forth unto the general public today, however unlikely the prospect, those yelps might be deemed erroneously, and similarly, no less than the baying howls of some abandoned and aging hound, awakening in the middle of a dream, and thinking that some crow or two were still in pursuit of him. Brevity bids me relate only the substance of this pure and undefiled document, though I am still in a quandary as to whether or not it should have been included along with Daniel's analysis. The student reader may choose to dismiss or ponder its relevance, for it may only serve as an insignificant analogy to the prospects thereof.

It must have been much later that I awoke to whispers and scuffling of other anxious vigils, my usual alarm for the last few mornings, and was about to accord the night's enrapture as merely a dream. But there on the table, by my left hand, lay the black book in its scarlet sleeve, with the tear half way down its front; and beside it, near my right, lay the black and red mosaic of Daniel's manuscript, and Prof. A. Pollon's handwriting thereon, with the muted argument placed beneath it, the crimson symbol and note weighing them both down before me. Then my mind flashed back the promise I had made earlier to Mr. Who, and the conversation previous thereto. "Pursue," said he, "and redeem the treasure lost to your brother. But beware," he warned me, "lest you account yourself with his merits and further his shame." And I remember answering, "Very well, if I have no choice in the matter," before losing everything to the refuge of slumber again.

As I said, that was some few years ago, and I regret to say, I have not kept that comatose promise as faithfully as I may have intended. Why the interval of my silence has been so long extended may have been what I deemed I owed myself and family first. Or maybe it was the sad visage of fellow Bayinhund assuring me that the professor was probably right, and any rudeness immaterial. Why I should now awaken and attempt a redemption may be due, to some measure, to having obtained relief from those demands upon my temporal focus. Or perhaps it was the spector of the professor whispering in my ear his eternal affront to the freshness of thought that kept provoking the mad man within me. I really cannot tell, but since I have as little to lose as our fellow student, I have wandered into the fray, or begun it, though not with as much enthusiasm perhaps as did Bayinhund before his disfranchisement. Be it as it may, any resulting ruckus may be attributed to a confusion of past and present prejudices, which customarily often come into play with the introduction of a new idea.

And yet, I should have had more admiration for his keen insights and not have been so reluctant to support them. Yes, from the pitch of his papers, wherein he was convinced he had evidenced a particularly venerable image in Hawthorne's gloomy tale, he sometimes seemed to have asserted the same a little too assuredly, and much too often, as though repetition were the better valor of persuasion, or brainwashing, as the more sensible may be inclined to call it. Perhaps I should have at least ventured with no less than a spoonful more of liveliness than his on the day he suffered the cutting edge of the professor's pen. Alhough I may have averted much abuse by the complete failure thereto, sad to say, I might otherwise have afflicted the public mind some several years earlier instead. Therefore, and nevertheless, being thus split over the matter, like the oneness of lifemates, I hazard the prospect of being fully understood.

It is to my credit or censure that I kept those maligned papers for some long time, probably out of the sense that someday I might in all honesty keep my oath to Mr. Who, who from time to time would hound me to forage my friends for affirmation of Bayinhund's ideas. Many an hour I would meditate upon the contents of Bayinhund's papers, after winning little in argument with my better half, before, alas, though perhaps all better for the transformation, I finally lost them. Nevertheless, trying with much effort to decipher the red hieroglyphic commentary in the margins, and in between the double-spaced lines, and on the back of each page, and, indeed, as it were, upon every space that once was pure and white as the bliss of ignorance, I came to conclude that the argument of one sounded just as reasonable as the other.

Perhaps Mr. Who would not have been so relentless had not the professor been so liberal and prolific with his merciless acrimony. So scorching at times in fact that, as I gazed often and intently upon the pulpy-red sheets, I thought I saw, or some part of me saw, a gist of smoke rising from their surface, like as from the glow of embers, as though the burning had no end of trying to consume the carbon script thereupon. The smoke seemed to fade toward and into the array of scholastic journals sitting idly upon the library's shelves. "Methinks the professor protests too much," Mr. Who seemed to say, mindless that the matter was no longer in his hand, and that he ought to butt out. Nevertheless, the more I pondered, the more I began to understand the mosaic patterns of Bayinhund's analysis, the style of which, to agree with the professor, may not have been, though digestible, the most appetizing.

I reluctantly relate the contents of his untouched autobiographical defense first, inasmuch as it may have some distant connection with the professor's commentary upon the other, the substance of which perhaps should also be addressed, though neither distinctly nor directly. Though I have taken the liberty of condensing the rather lengthy sketch of his graduate history—as it probably would be interesting to no one other than Bayinhund himself—the reader may wish altogether to bypass this background, and Daniel's lengthy essays in Section II, which may only prejudice the student's query, and move studiously to Daniel's analysis in Section III.

*   *   *

It appears that Brother Bayinhund was once selected for an assistantship while pursuing his graduate degree. Having obtained a fair grade point average in his bachelor's degree in psychology, with a minor in English, his apparent intellectual acuity, though now long time suspect, had come to the attention of one of his professors, Dr. Roy Bollings, a rather kind and fatherly type. A year or so later, this same professor had confronted Bayinhund with a question of whether or not he had pilfered or fabricated one of his papers. Sad this, in view of the basis by which Bayinhund had been selected in the first place as an assistant teacher. But then again, perhaps their judgment in that case was simply as cursory, with a greater reverse effect, for thinking themselves so taken in, as that which issued from his orals later. It appeared then that his graduate committee had apparently combined to rip him to shrewds unmercifully, as though debasement were a supportive companion to shallow judgment.

Apparently, in the case of presumed plagerism, the professor had told Bayinhund that the ideas therein were either couched in such intellectual terms that he had difficulty in following the train of thought, and was inclined to confirm his earlier appraisal of Daniel's intellect, or that such conceptual language seemed too far beyond the scope of Bayinhund's intellect to be his own. Not knowing whether to be pleased or offended, he had asked the professor what he meant, whereupon the latter had voiced his suspicions more clearly. So shocked and pondering was he with the clarity of the accusation, Daniel later wondered if his reaction of silence had been interpreted as a guilt reflex.

In the sudden face of it, Bayinhund, perhaps given to too much introspection, began to question himself also as to whether his method of analysis in his paper constituted a measure of piracy. In his defense, which intent seemed to have been the purpose for the autobiographical sketch, Bayinhund related that he had not denied the superficial accusation at the time because he was initially not sure what the professor was talking about, and then stunned when illuminated. It being elaborated, he, being a somewhat self-consulting person by nature, had tried to assimilate the accusation in terms of whether or not the process by which he had engineered the composition was indeed one that could have been not only suspect but dishonest. Albeit as honest and analytical as he was with himself, he likewise automatically assumed the esteemed professor to be as much or moreso, and felt instantaneous guilt when confronted with the suspicion of a superior mind.

Nevertheless, he knew that he had spent many hours analyzing the data he had researched, and could not see how the process could be considered a fabrication, since he had referenced his materials, documented them to his bibliography, and tried to use his own language in drawing his conclusions. Apparently, Bayinhund's quiet reaction was the furtherest extent to which Prof. Rollings went in checking out his assumptions, which he may have spent upon other faculty, as later was evidenced by the tone of his graduate committee. "Oh the evil that makes men suspect the minds of others," seemingly runs in many directions.

Perhaps his natural shyness, Bayinhund related, as much as his reluctance to refute the accusation—which refutation thereof might implicate the professor in a lie—was the reason this defense was never spoken to Dr. Bollings at the time; and thus his silence may have been construed as an admission. Bayinhund wondered if the suspicion was then allowed to ferment among the staff, without any of them taking the time to check out the bibliographical references to his paper.

Nonetheless, the fair-minded might ask, why should they have bothered to confirm or discount their suspicion? If professors, many of whom must either publish or perish, did not place a high premium upon their time, the halls of higher education might tumble upon the heads of far worthier students, for whom no such suspicions could be raised. Surely, on the scales of unquestionable justice, perhaps a little more to the left than to the right, the undiminished advance of the many justifies the unfortunate plight of the few.

As it stands, Bayinhund reported that it was not until he went before his committee later, in regard to his graduate research, that this fermentation seemed to climax in an attack upon his integrity and competence as a graduate student. Admitting being naive and trusting, he thought at first that the hostility of the committee was par for the course, as an adversarial design to test his confidence in and knowledge of his thesis. Yet it had been far more invective than he thought was necessary, and for which he was not prepared, and was stunned again into doubting his own worthiness, possibly as a further reflection of having been held highly suspect before.

In all fairness to this collection of noble judges, however, Bayinhund, prior to the oral examination, admitted having made a terrible, careless mistake in processing his research, the extent of which he was not fully aware until facing his graduate committee. In selecting the chairman of his committee, Dr. Hayes Allright, who was advantageously on sabbatical, or some other kind of leave, during the orals, Bayinhund unknowingly had picked one of the professors perhaps not as very knowledgeable in thesis writing as others, or so the committee openly implied, and had relied upon him to guide the process. In so doing, Bayinhund, in equal ignorance of the procedures, had never submitted a proposal to the chairman of the department for approval before beginning the collection of data. Alas, the chairman, familiar only with statistical designs, had never approved the use, in his department, of the experimental design Bayinhund had chosen, and thus would not accept his thesis.

Apparently, the better partner of the scientific method, known and utilized in other fields, had not climbed so high in this particular domain. Moreover, the findings of Daniel's thesis had established a question mark about the validity of certain courses offered in the curriculum, itself reason enough to discredit his long-labored study. That the chairman had not approved the design of the research, as a valid method to be used by his department, and thence had rejected his thesis, was also accorded an embarrassing throwback to the department as well, for the oversight had likely prejudiced the chairman's later acceptance of the design for use in other students' theses. This oversight, noted by the irate thesis committee members, coupled with a particular eye of suspicion likely already fixed among the staff—which should have been voiced among them, but was not—Bayinhund adduced, was apparently the primary foundation for the hostility of his committee, and his ensuing decapitation. Had the suspicion been voiced by his committee, howbeit such might admit collusion on their part, this issue might have been resolved, good feelings accorded, and Bayinhund, to both our good fortunes, would probably have had no need for a *post hoc* editor.

Due to other technicalities, perhaps stemming from the same misunderstanding, to make his long defense short, Bayinhund lost his status as graduate student, was not allowed to be reinstated, and apparently faded away into oblivion, from which post mortem state his editor herein now feels bound to attempt a resurrection of his honor.

As I said, Bayinhund's defense, presumably never submitted to his committee, may have no connection whatsoever with his slaughtered manuscript, which, to keep faith with myself, I present here, with several modifications. Just as I have ventured to keep myself far removed from Daniel's dilemma, neither, as far as I can rationally examine my own motives, does his argument seem to have anything to do with the publication of his analysis herein. They appear as things apart, and to have no direct connection whatsoever.

I have tried to locate from among the untouchable recesses of my soul, without too much success, the reasoning behind that force compelling me to bring into the light the peculiar and perhaps original thoughts contained in Bayinhund's red-smeared analysis. Whether it be by intuition or insanity, if they can be adduced as things apart, I will have to leave to the judgment of the apprehensive reader, who hopefully will perhaps give Bayinhund's work less a cursory review than his committee members gave him. Any more intensive study might reveal details that may return to haunt me.

To my best recollection, such was the substance of Daniel's defense in the undoctored document. The contents of the other, which had apparently been subjected to some other refuse, looked as if drops of blood had streaked down some of its pages, and gave the package the appearance of bleeding under the piercing thrusts of the professor's scalpel. These contents constitute in summary form, the essays of Section II, without so much as one thorn to pierce the departed forehead of Brer Daniel.

Needless to say, nevertheless, his analysis should become accustomed to the cutting edge of critical thinkers. Such is accorded the nature and intent of constructive criticism. It is like unto the skills of the adept surgeon, whose purpose is to heal and cure by cutting away that which he considers adversarial to health, such as an unwanted appendix or a set of tonsils, which, though the Creator deemed otherwise, are often disposed of for lack of evidence to the contrary. All in all, it is only for one's good, whether the criticism is sought for or needed, or even helpful. Moreover, it is expected that such a worthy become a most gracious recipient, with condescending gratitude, for any diminution of worth that may be granted by a more elevated mind. Such subjects should only nod in acquiescence and account themselves multiply blessed by the measure of time and ink spent in such an exudation.

Yet it was not the professor's commentary, nor the blood-streaked appearance of the document, nor its defensive companion, nor any combination thereof, that stood up and confessed responsibility for prompting my impulsive nature to attempt a restoration of Bayinhund's dignity. The culprit lay within the contents of his bleeding handiwork itself, and it was not until I had thoroughly digested them that I understood myself. I knew it had taken many hours of Bayinhund's scholarly time to extract, if not indeed to conjure up, the meanings of Hawthorne's dark and gloomy mystery; and it required of me, it seemed, no less time to fathom the significance of his ideas.

Perhaps the whole episode, from the moments of my midnight vigils to the printing of Bayinhund's divination, evidences the value of blind intuition, and should therefore be subject to the graciousness of the expert's logical scapel. The reader, just as did the publisher, will have to judge the quality of that value, either by subjecting it to the limitations of reason or, going beyond, allowing intuition likewise to take command of his senses.

Howbeit, fare thee well; I present all portions of Bayinhund's analysis, even those parts the professor may have slighted with acute justification, as best as my memory can serve me. Within the last few years or so, though Mr. Who would occasionally prompt my review of his work, which reviews may fairly account for my memory thereof, I have either lost track of where I stored its remains, or some unsympathetic part of my mind has dispatched it to a resting place deemed more suitable. Or perhaps, in some vengeful abandon, I may myself have tossed it to get rid of the baggage, at the unmitigated nagging of Mr. Who, and assigned it to a permanent grave at some dump on the outskirts of Hawthornian civilization. If like minds are inclined to wallow in the same mire, it may yet be that some enterprising and malnourished person, under the same circumstance and delusion, and not too little like Bayinhund himself, might someday venture to salvage its decaying soul, and thereby vouchsafe the authenticity of my edition, however unlikely the fare.

In no sense or fashion have I thought to include any portions of the professor's red commentary, merely the substance thereof; but true to form, instead, I have allowed my publisher plenty of room to vent his benevolent nature, whether to aid in the reader's digestion of its contents, or to carry out his own purgings thereof. I have urged him likewise to leave sufficient margins on each printed page for students and readers alike to join in the scholarly fray. Who knows but what scribblings may be fodder *ad infinitum* for other natural's discontent, whose own green and refreshing new ideas may need airing also, like all squeaky wheels in want of lubrication.

Bayinhund had entitled his paper, "*The Nazarene of The Scarlet Letter*," which approximates the subtitle his editor has given his book, in all due respect to Mr. Who's warning. No credit need be accorded the editor for his ideas, nor, dare I say, any blame, for all that comes to the reader is entirely a carbon copy of Bayinhund's analysis, with but a few palatable improvisations; and all responsibility should be laid squarely at his feet. My part is simply that which I am driven to do because of a moment of insanity, in the middle of a mindless night, and in the throes of some inexplicable notion to reverence Brother Bayinhund's pain, despite my opinion on the whole matter. His shame, symbolized so cryptically by the letter C, which he had embellished with such elaborate design upon his ill-begotten script, seems to burn still within me, as though some enigmatic kinship was formed years ago with some intractable part of myself.

The one frightening weakness, if we can call it so, in Bayinhund's fervid analysis, seems to be his audacity to think the bard's tale an allegory depicting Deity's relationship with humankind by identifying one particular character in Hawthorne's tale with a particular historical hero of the Christian faith, in absolute disagreement with more credible earlier critics. Be it as it may, I have innocently done my duty to Mr. Daniel Knotta Bayinhund, and faithfully have performed the office which Mr. Who has this long time exacted of me. If Bayinhund can posthumously only receive due credit, or, ironically, a second and widespread condemnation, then I would prefer Mr. Who be brought before the bar instead of any other. As a passive observer, not fully in accord with my own judgment in this matter, I disclaim any belief in the following ideas that may be associated with Daniel Bayinhund's creativity, and am only party thereto as a pale ghostwriter attempting to transfuse a corpse with a little more life blood of dignity than probably accorded justly heretofore.

Bayinhund's conclusions are fairly strong, but their chief weakness lies in their redundancy because of the various themes he has bundled together from the numerous tie-ins in Hawthorne's tale. He also appears at times to have exercised too much restaint in voicing them, as though his convictions might be offensive to others, or as though fidelity to his experience of Hawthorne, or his own religious views, needed an apology. On the other hand, such tentativeness might be considered only a contrary to dogmatism.

Although I have taken the liberty of dividing his composition into sections more suitable for publication, as a text for younger and brighter students to study, as was likely his intentions, I begin with Bayinhund's own preface and introduction to his analysis. To further sway the tide of plagerism, I must confess that the title given his handiwork is my own, for the one he had chosen might be considered too bold and too heretical, of its own accord, to be worthy of the greater audience Hawthorne saught. I admit to toning it down a little, to focus more on the redemption of the man himself; but the reader must feel free to assume, by logic or intuition, what is the true substance of the matter at hand.

I have also taken another liberty of guessing what Biblical text, or other similar thought, may have fancied Bayinhund's imagination of what he thought might have prompted Hawthorne's. Each quote might possibly frame the primary theme and general focus of each chapter; and placing it at the beginning, much as I have placed a quote of Hawthorne's at the head of this analysis, openly suggests what might have been the motive behind the veiling of his allegory in a mystery. The editor admits that the quotes may be his own fanciful imagination of Daniel's, and would like to marginalize the religious tones thereof, for the sake of our literary critics, who may have some reservations about Hawthorne's novel being considered a religious allegory. Out of respect for such reservations, he therefore has included a list of references to such quotes in an appendix, for those who may be unfamiliar with them. This is not to say, however, that, for the sake of avoiding offence to others whose sensitivities may reside at the other end of the continuum, that he likewise discredits the merits thereof by doing so. Those whose prejudices dwell in the middle may feel more at home as they peruse these pages.

SECTION I

Section I contains Bayinhund's own preface and introduction to his analysis, which is essayed in Section II. Both have been written in the first person, as though they were his own words, first, to disassociate the editor from the originality of his analysis, and, second, to distance him from the critics, who surely will make easy fodder of his text, like a hound gone beserk on a prized bird he was meant only to retrieve. At the same time, he gives these bird dogs advance notice that, in the absence of Bayinhund's manuscript, the style and language of the text could therefore resemble no other than but mine own. To advance the proposition that the use of the personal pronoun, or the similarity in style and language, suggests any agreement on the part of the editor with the author's speculations, may be as absurd as assuming Hawthorne's complicity with Surveyor Pue of the Custom House in originating the history of the tale itself.

The Preface postures a defense for his claim to have advanced a unique and definitive analysis of Hawthorne's novel. The Introduction prates about various aspects of *The Scarlet Letter*, its relevance to Hawthorne's time and ours, and examines a few of the criticisms leveled against it. Unlike the editor's preceding foreplay, Bayinhund's words themselves are recorded as best as he can remember them, and are substantially free of any commentary by his editor so that the reader may have no reason to confuse the two.

Perhaps a few suggestions to readers as to how to evaluate his analysis are in order. Students might choose to enjoy reading Hawthorne's novel through as least once before conducting a detailed study of it concurrently with *Hawthorne's Redemption*. Be they friend or foe, some may consider this one-time perusal a sufficient effort to probe the mind of one of the most respected and intelligent authors in America. However they equate their affinity with him, each should savor the richness of the mystery before examining the clues to its hidden allegorical meanings. The editor recommends a quick reading of Sections I and II before the more detailed parallel study of Section III, which analyzes each chapter of the novel. A cursory perusal of Sections I and II may prevent the reader from becoming embedded in any predisposition that might impede a more objective analysis of Bayinhund's interpretations of each chapter's contents in Section III. Section III's detailed contents serve only to vindicate or support the premises summarized in the previous sections, and perhaps should be examined upon their own merits.

Since the editor has undertaken to advance a dead brother's interpretation of Hawthorne's allegory that seems Christian in content, he has deemed it necessary to refer to the records of that faith, notably, the Kings James Version of the Holy Bible, at the beginning of most chapters, to elaborate on the possible allegorical theme focused therein. It is most fitting also on the bases that this version of sacred writ came to us at the hands of the Puritans; Hawthorne's own references to King James in his novel makes the selection of that Biblical text most appropriate; and the metaphorical contents of its language parallels the mystic subtlety of his own unique style. Quotations from Hawthorne's tale itself have been referenced to the Centenary edition by page only, which edition was not published at the time the editor discovered Mr. Bayinhund's text.

It is not likely that this literary license would be objectionable to Mr. Bayinhund; but should he rise from the ignominity of his academic demise to claim entitlement to this edition, his editor will take up the matter quite equitably with him then. At the present, there is not much better counsel available to him. Yet, were Daniel to emerge at any time and tell him differently, he might be most inclined to make a few changes. He might be hard pressed otherwise to consider any other request.

It is hoped that these liberties that have been taken with Bayinhund's text might accord with the spirit of his intended enterprise, be it what it may, just as he possibly hoped his interpretation of the tale was in accord with Hawthorne's intended purpose. Were Daniel's real ghost to appear at some future time, he would be no less frightening to this purveyor than was Hawthorne's reactions to the sagacious promptings of the ghost of Surveyor Pue.

PREFACE

In the beginning, I debated seriously what I should entitle my experience. Considering the times, it would have been perhaps more palatable had I called it, *Hawthorne's Mystery Unveiled*, or *Hawthorne Rediscovered*. It would have probably sparked more controversial interest had I named it *Heresy in The Scarlet Letter*, but to have done so would have been an injustice to the man. At the same time, to have labeled it, *The Christ of the Scarlet Letter* might be too bold an insult to both scholar and layman, who may have already formed fixed opinions on an otherwise abstruse mystery. And should I have ventured to entitle it *Hawthorne: Mind in Matter*, I am afraid I would have defeated one of its primary objectives and affrighted its intended public, for who in his right mind in these days relishes a probe into deep philosophy, even though that philosophy might be hidden within the mind of such a deep thinker as Hawthorne?

But similar to the machinery of an allegory, as I began to sense what Hawthorne was trying to communicate to fairly close friends, in full respect and admiration for Hawthowrne, I was compelled to label it simply as I have, and leave it to the reader to judge whether or not this layman wrote to the appeal of the layman. For having perceived of Hawthorne delicate qualities in his work—sensitivity, compassion, intelligence, introspection, intuition, and a penetrative inquisitiveness—below all that, if not the sum bonum and base, I also saw him as deeply religious, yet not in any formal expression, but in a most personal and private way, intent on reverencing his Maker, possibly even as a Christian apologist.

It has come to be the essential intent of this work to do that which I perceive might have been, if not the central purpose of Hawthorne's novel, at least a strong motivating factor behind his "autographical impulse." Perhaps at this late date, it would cause him little injury to invade his privacy by revealing, in the singular experience of this student, "the inmost Me behind its veil." Indeed, in seeking to unravel the mystery, it is his uppermost desire to honor him, if no more than to raise the eyes of his descendants once more to the grand old scribbler, as he may have secretly wished.

> It may be, however,—O transporting and triumphant thought!—that the great-grandchildrren of the present race may sometimes think kindly of the scribbler of bygone days, when the antiquary of days to come, among the sites memorable in the town's history, shall point out the locality of THE TOWN-PUMP! (45)

Let me be, if forever nothing else, witness to the fact that he was more than a writer of story books! His masterpiece should be compared to Milton's "Paradise Lost," for some of Milton might be in it. And one may sense, inside the pages of his novel, that he may have gazed upon the Creation scene by Michaelangelo, or heard a few notes from Handel's "Messiah," for the Nazarene haunts it. Like any work of art, it can be enjoyed mostly, if not only, by intuition and imagination, the one key that may unlock its meanings, though perhaps differently for each of its beneficiaries.

Perhaps the reader should begin this unveiling with the idea of a mystery that has captivated a wide audience, as seemingly was one of his objectives, then allow intuition to balance rationality in approaching the veil to "find out the divided segment of the writer's own nature." The mystery seems designed to intrigue a community of readers, even though Hawthorne's inmost self may have been meant to be disclosed "only and exclusively, to the one heart and mind of perfect sympathy" (3). To discover Hawthorne's inmost self, the reader may have to suspend all judgments and prejudices and allow his imagination to lead the way.

I admit that *The Scarlet Letter* has been an extraordinary obsession to me. From my first reading I was determined to analyze the symbols until I could understand their connections and relevancies. Without realizing it at the time, I had taken Hawthorne to task:

> there are few things,—whether in the outward world, or to a certain depth, in the invisible sphere of thought,—few things hidden from the man, who devotes himself earnestly and unreservedly to the solution of a mystery" (75).

It became a quest I could not shake. As I studied the novel intently, I was puzzled by many passages that I knew had some hidden meanings; but nothing made sense, until intuition, call it what we may, envisioned and focused upon Dimmesdale on the scaffold as an historical figure of eminent stature. But the mind cried, "How could that be if he were involved in, what was seemingly, a scandalous affair with Hester?"

Exhausting all other possibilities, in order to probe deeper into what their relationship might mean at a deeper level, I finally resolved to restrain my Puritan impulses. Like a stone cast into water, from that point in the center outward, I was compelled to elude every quasi-Puritanical premise in search for an explanation that would unify every image in the novel with that central theme. I began to understand the rippling effect of symbolic, near incredible meanings, and to make connections below the surface of the tale. I say incredible because the interpretations I have advanced herein may be considered, at the least, extraordinarily new and somewhat unique, if not beyond common credibility, and, at the most, perhaps even a fabrication of the grossest order.

The critical analyses of the elements of *The Scarlet Letter* that I have since read seem to sense something meaningful, though inexplicable, in Hawthorne's great mystery; and perhaps that it is why it is so popular. The fact that this tale has maintained its place among the most read novels may attest to both its intrigue and the reader's desire to understand it. However, none of the critical articles I have read have been fully able to identify the mystery, or to show the harmony and consistency of interplay between the symbols and representations of the main characters. [Notwithstanding, the editor recommends the reader's reference to Appendix 2 as one scholarly attempt which supports some of the foundation for Daniel's interpretation.]

However, should there be but one critic, none or many, who would concur with my interpretation, perhaps that may not really matter after all. If the interpretation I have advanced is entirely a creation of my own, much like Hawthorne claimed his tale was, despite what a few of his critics said, then perhaps that wouldn't matter either; for, in the field of literature, creativity is the rule, and speculation but fodder for futher analysis. Just as one could suppose it were possible, with only a little intelligence, for an author to metaphorize every moral truth he intended to project, one could equally suppose that it would require even less acuteness to contrive meanings where none were ever conceived. Though I may leave that call to each reader, perhaps only the critic, and the abstaining oblivious, may be more liable to defer to the honorary tradition of obscurity, although the former may be much more verbal about it.

A question that may inescapably be posed in the reader's mind is a puzzling one: have any others before now advanced an interpretation similar to that which I dare present? The answer may be that they very well may have, but may have been more discreet than myself, or may have been kept more at bay by the fixed opinions of others, or the better part of valor squelched from public consumption by the structure of things as they are. I have perhaps read enough to realize that there doesn't seem to be one as thoroughly clear and comprehensive, at least, in the public's eye; and that this submission may lead eventually to such a one. And that may really be all that matters.

I have thought to publish my interpretations of Hawthorne's novel so that those critics in the field of literature, who will, may have additional cause for which to expound their intelligence, either in trying to better understand this mystery, or to salvage the old cherished ambiguities by which the public brain is presently intoxicated. If I am correct in only a few of my impressions, hopefully the main ones, we shall have to reappraise Hawthorne as a literary prophet who hoped for and predicted a future time when the human family would look more favorable upon the human creation. His talent was focused at a time when he seemed to have been most discontent with the society of his day, especially with the religious roots from which he sprang, and particularly with its effect upon the character of his fellowmen. If Hawthorne was not posing himself as a Daniel of sorts, by some "prophetic instinct," in proposing his own phisolophy, as to the riddle of the nature of the mere mortal and the problems of mortality, then he surely was anticipating one: "Of a truth, friend, that matter remaineth a riddle; and the Daniel who shall expound it is yet a-wanting" (62).

Of a truth, Hawthorne did not believe that Puritanism had the answers, whose venerable stewards "were less capable of . . . disentangling its mesh of good and evil . . . and had no right . . . to step forth . . . and meddle with a question of human guilt, passion, and anguish" (64-65). Perhaps Hawthorne thought he had resolved the riddle of life, in his own mind, and used the allegory to share it with his sympathetic friends.

I am simply content to expose the mystery of a great American novel as I have experienced it. There is much more beauty and goodness in

Hawthorne's book than any seem ever to have guessed. Even though my explanations may be considered heterodoxical to both the literary critic as well as to the devout Christian, there is too much to appreciate that is positively edifying in his tale, either to let it alone, or to get sidetracked by any philosophical differences. It needs to be enjoyed by the layman as much as it is worshiped by its scholarly critics.

I am prepared to examine the evidence with the reader who has the time, the patience, and the interest to investigate a marvelous allegorical tale. However this study may strike one as an intellectual puzzle, it likewise may envelop him, as it did me, in a spiritual adventure that takes the reader to the edge of his/her faith, and perhaps a little beyond, without too much stretch of the imagination. And that may compose my greatest consternation, that the conclusions I claim the readers may find in Hawthorne's work could possible have an adverse effect upon one's own natural sensitivity to their belief system. I can assure my readers that the experience of writing this analysis has not diminished my faith in Christianity one iota. To the contrary, I believe that the adventurous hours I have spent laboring over the meanings of Hawthorne's allegory have been supportive, if not modifying, of my own spiritual insights, if only to a small measure, of a principle or two of Christian hope. For that, even if laid purely to bald imagination, I am indebted to Hawthorne for what some might call the *splendide mendax* of the experience.

It may be that those who think they understand Hawthorne's novel, because they are likewise familiar with Biblical concepts, may nevertheless dare not to venture sharing that understanding for the same reason Hawthorne was careful to conceal it, and for the same reason of which I myself have been somewhat reluctant to risk being accused a variegated harlequin. So, unless more light comes forth from elsewhere to unveil the mystery of this enchanting novel, hereafter, wherein I must give answer to those who disagree with less substance, I may be loathe to reject the interpretation that to me seems most natural. Similarly, I may be equally constrained, as Hawthorne, to continue to barter this sketch without the change of a single idea, though the wording might call for a proper and extensive overhaul.

The proof is in the pudding, if indeed there can really be any such thing as proofs of any kind in attempting to explain what has been obviously and adeptly hidden from the public mind for so long. I appeal to the consistency and unity of the ingredients, and hope that one's tastes may find my dish both literate and exciting. I predict that the initial reaction of readers may, at worse, be one of disgust, contempt, or disbelief. Then, after allowing their litmus minds a thorough cross-referencing between the incredible ideas herein and each page of Hawthorne's novel, they may find it more test worthy, and perhaps even palatable, like the allegory itself is designed to change the minds of its readers. If not so, then at least it might provide some sporting enterprise to those who, instead of carefully examining its merits, might prefer to throw it in my face. When an intelligent mind, like Hawthorne's, attempts to puzzle the minds of others, who consider themselves of equal intelligence, it seems only natural that it might indeed breed a form of criticism whose purpose may be primarily to cover up an unequal epitude. Such seems to have been a typical reaction to Hawthorne's novel.

Perhaps the most accurate criticism that could be leveled at this attempt might be—similar to those leveled by religionists at one another—that of reading things into the text, and this simply in order to prevent a departure from an heretofore established understanding, or misunderstanding. That I have read things into Hawthorne's work is not an impossibility. However, I maintain that it is more likely that my imagination was cued more by the symmetry of Hawthorne's symbols, to deduce his meanings, rather than a desire to create them.

On the other hand, though my interpretation be wholly a creation of my own, though that intent was never in my mind, that likelihood, in and of itself, would not be so much a fault as an outgrowth of the art, and perhaps the very essence of literary criticism. It would seem that its purpose, apart from providing some authors a source of amusement, is to dissect and recreate so as to explore possible meanings; and it seems fair play for anyone who appreciates good literature to indulge in the same. Self-expression is the game of life, whether in a book, a verse, a social chat, or, in our day and time, a simple twitter; and the audience of either might very well question the value of the other, perhaps simply for no other reason than as a matter of self-validation.

In the case of *The Scarlet Letter*, the game is also the discovery of what Hawthorne is trying not to say but is attempting to conceal from the lazy or unfriendly reader. This indictment of silence on Hawthorne's part is similar to the indictment of silence leveled against Dimmesdale, and one which my own conscience seems no longer able to harbor.

Perhaps the least approval of my text, if there should be any at all, might suggest that a configuration of sorts has pieced together a work of art whose richer meanings have too long been suspended in obscurity and ambiguity. My least concern might be getting no reaction whatsoever from a society whetted more on sensationalism and less on philosophical thought. Yet, there might be at least three or four small audiences for the material offered herein—the intellectual half-wits, the lost literary critics, the religious nuts, and The Scarlet Letter freaks—all of which, I must confess, I may have become somewhat all-in-one in the process of writing this expose.

I would rather my interpretations be enjoyed mostly for the candor of their ideas, for the delight of discovery, and for the newness of life they give to an old and splendid masterpiece. But I have also prepared this text, should it bypass the lowest expectations, as a definitive document for students who are apt to read Hawthorne, whether in high school or college, who might have the time to study its expositions in concert with their reading of The Scarlet Letter itself. Since the ideas contained in this text support the premise that Hawthorne's novel is indeed a religious book, I would hope that it should remain upon the shelves of school libraries, despite its religious premises, as an appropriate study for young minds who are interested in the art of composition, especially in aiding their understanding of an allegory so remarkable as Hawthorne's novel.

It would indeed be an act of irony were this piece of work to be censored from public consumption on the basis of its scholarship, or lack thereof, or its religious content. Whereas Hawthorne's novel was censored by some critics for its tasteless impropriety as a lurid sex novel, and thought it should not have been written, this interpretation of it might possibly likewise be censored because of its religious allusions, which censuring might be as sad a commentary on our times as well. Hopefully, and perhaps similarly as Hawthorne anticipated, the transformations of ideological thought over time may effect improvement in our communities, at least in the way of tolerance for the view of mavericks like myself.

Nevertheless, to be sure, we would hope that such a censorship of intolerance might do no less than raise the ghost of Surveyor Pue or Hawthorne himself, from the pipes of the Old Town Pump, to petition a better conscience. Were that to be the occasion, since our society seems more liberally open-minded than his, he might be much more favorably inclined toward his Puritan heritage.

Of what dubious worth this purveyorship may be permitted, the reader will be bombarded with numerous analogies, the effect of which will be a constant repetition of the themes that lie beneath the gloomy brilliance of his tale. This repetition is a necessary strategy to help certify the credibility of the purveyor's interpretations which he believes connect the allegorical meanings, and bind them together for some interesting and controversial conclusions. In relating the allegorical meanings to Hawthorne's figures of speech, his literary style, and the strategies he uses to clue the intent reader to these meanings, metaphor by metaphor, it is this editor's intent to show how these strategies correlate so as to corroborate the plausibility of his analysis. Since the meanings of each of the metaphors, etc. are related to the author's interpretations of the allegory, this repetitious nature may also be considered an overbearing necessity useful to the student who might find himself in a maze among so many analogies.

If nothing more, perhaps this interpretation can give a new perspective and fresh, additional thought to those who care to do more than perform a cursory reading and commentary on one of our earliest and perhaps greatest American novels. Hopefully, my efforts will go one step further in removing the ambiguity, obscurity, and confusion with which some critics may prefer zealously and guardedly to surround *The Scarlet Letter* still. Or, at least, I may provide fuel for a greater fire from which a purer refining may make Hawthorne's novel more understandable in time.

INTRODUCTION

What a piece of work is man! Preeminent of species! Transcendant prodigy! A paragon of power and beauty! Master of virtue or vice! In his earthly romance with the universal heart, Hawthorne seems secretly to clothe and echo but a hint of Hamlet's appraisal of the human being. Perhaps, on rare occasions, and in our best moments, we may peek beyond the impositions of reality, and sense an echo of our own that, arising from some intense meditation, testifies of the goodness of life, and prompts some measure of awe for the inexplicable that haunts us. We marvel at the vastness of life's complexity, delight in its sensations, and find glory in some promise that beckons its movement. Out of the midst of our life's pains and sorrows, the rare delights we find in ourselves and in life's wonders whisper of some goodness that lies at its mystical roots; and, like Hawthorne, we may be compelled to contemplate some better destiny for humankind.

The mind is such an amazing instrument, to ponder the wonders of its tabernacle, and to query its purposes. Who or what is its source? Its purpose or meaning? Its destiny? Is it art or happistance? As they challenge the philosophical urges of our greatest thinkers, these questions seem to lie at the threshold of the mystery of Hawthorne's great American novel. This introduction prefaces a mere attempt to remove that mystery so that the ideas herein may form, at the least, a new foundation for a more careful look at this classic, and, at the most, through that masterpiece, a broader understanding of the man. The interpretation of the symbols and the interrelated representations of his captivating tale, as proposed herein, may be considered provincial more to the literary society, than to the Christian community of our times, both for which I have had at various times mixed feelings of amusement, appreciation, and awe.

A MESSAGE FOR A FEW

Though the main characters in both Hawthorne's book and in Shakespeare's play have somewhat a dismal end, yet Hawthorne's gloomy tale, when fully understood, has a silver, or rather, a scarlet lining. The premise of this analysis is that Hawthorne's novel is first and foremost a philosophical or religious allegory that cleverly conceals a bright red message of hope against its gloomy perspective. The many references to Biblical texts are too numerous to dismiss the probability that this great work is essentially religious in nature, however cleverly Hawthorne may have disguised his own philosophical urges about the nature and destiny of the human family.

A careful analysis of the elements of the several parables, metaphors, similes, symbols and character representations, along with their sequences and connections, construct and consistently support Hawthorne's use of the allegory to contain a particular hidden mystery or message. This message or moral burns through Hawthorne's deliberations, as an Anti-Transcendentalist's romance about the nature of humanity, its origin, and its destiny. That message is very much like the scarlet letter burning upon Dimmesdale's chest from some mysterious urge and ache within. We might even suppose that Hawthorne had something mysteriously burning within himself, of which he was possessed to expound, but clever enough to conceal from all but sympathetic friends, in the tale and symbol of a scarlet letter.

That the message Hawthorne intended has been by many critics considered ambiguous or obscure perhaps illustrates a motive of the author to conceal this message from all but a few. As a religious fiction, Hawthorne's novel contains deeper meanings than its critics have supposed, meanings that may even be considered somewhat heterodoxical both to the Christian element and Hawthorne's literary heritage. For that reason, since he was counting very heavily upon his prized work being a success and establishing his reputation as a novelist, perhaps he chose the allegory as the vehicle to reach a wider audience than one that might only reach a selected few. Hawthorne's own introduction to his novel illustrates this point, and history attests to the fact that he achieved both objectives, probably beyond his expectations.

> The truth seems to be, however, that, when he casts his leaves
> forth upon the wind, the author addresses, not the many who
> will fling aside his volume, or never take it up, but the few who
> will understand him, better than most of his schoolmates and
> lifemates. (3)

Melville was absolutely right when he commented that Hawthorne was more sophisticated and complex than his public realized. Hawthorne was adeptly capable of being ambiguous, or concealing double meanings, though he despised deceit, by using tongue-in-cheek humor in a seemingly contradictory manner to camouflage his message, among a generation of many, and lead the readers to intuit their own choice.

Hawthorne, therefore, did not write his tale for the simple or narrow-minded only, or to be perused by the intellectual with only a cursory reading. No reader should presume to understand anything so complex with only a superficial effort. *The Scarlet Letter* is a philosophically challenging adventure, as much as it seems to be a treatise on religious themes, meant to be understood only by those of like-mindedness, whom Hawthorne probably would claim to be his friends. It appears, then, that Hawthorne realized that only a few would grasp the purport of his parabolic allegory, perhaps as planned, as he took pains both to reveal, without being too obvious, and to conceal, without being totally deceptive. It is much more than a simple romance or love story, if indeed the surface tale can be called such. It is my supposition that *TSL* is an allegory whose philosophical implications recant one of the most global and resonant explanations for life, as it may have been designed by Providence to be.

Hawthorne himself may have written his first novel as an extended parable combining ideas from his earlier short tales. In his frequent reference to Biblical text, one might be reminded of another great story teller, who apparently used the device of the parable to teach truths which he knew only a few were prepared to understand. Because Hawthorne's religious conclusions have been purposefully, cleverly, and wondrously hidden from the understanding of superficial readers, the preparation of the reader, then, becomes a significant intervening variable between the telling of a tale and the understanding of its intended message.

That the purveyor of these revealed messages may claim kinship to the spirit with which Hawthorne wrote this endearing tale does not mean that he entirely believes the conclusions implied in the allegorical ramifications. Nevertheless, those conclusions have reminded him again of the magnificence of the human species and our relationship with the Creator. This relationship of the human family with Deity seems to lie at the very heart of Hawthorne's novel, perhaps in much the same way as it does as a central theme of Dimmesdale's Election Sermon. In a remarkable fashion, *TSL* is an Election Sermon, retold in a different format to conceal the author's conclusions from all but similar minded folk.

A TIMELY DISCOVERY

The Scarlet Letter may be said to be a book written about our time. It seems to point to a time when humankind would look more favorably upon the tabernacles of flesh as noble works to be enjoyed and not to be utterly disdained. But it also addresses the foundation for that joy in the richness of the scarlet letter's subtle meaning of a better world through a more compassionate way of living. It is this context of the times that may make the revelation of the scarlet letter in our day more timely than it may have been in Hawthorne's, and, therefore, much easier to accept by the layman, unless he is philosophically tied to the scholastic boundaries that may forbid it.

True to that vision Hawthorne has encapsuled within the symbols of a tale, we live in a time today when the human family no longer looks scornfully upon the human body as a depraved instrument of some inexplicable and ignominious nature. Indeed, we may have supped at the other end of the extreme: we may worship this noble invention too much. We may have cast off not only the Puritan shadows, like a sable field, but also the substantial roots of its essential morality, like the faded etchings of red gules thereon. Having, for the most part, rid ourselves of Puritan vituperation, and no longer considering ourselves depraved and ignominious creatures worthy of condemnation, designed for a life of gloom, we may have shorn our conscience along with its insidious shadows. Like the narrow-minded perspective of our Puritan forefathers, we may have likewise forgotten the central message of Christianity, as we bask in the glow of the rediscovered human. In disclaiming our guiltiness, where even the mention of the words, sin and wickedness, so much the black text of Puritanism, are today social *faux pas*, we may have uprooted the very foundations of our moral society by easing our departure therefrom. At the same time, with or without the imprint of this continent's attempts at Christianity, Hawthorne's conclusions, as might be allegedly conjured herein, might also preferably be rendered too far left field.

A RELIGIOUS TEXT

In the final analysis, or summary thereof, Hawthorne's novel appears to be about the transformation of the human family along the continuum of hate vs. love. This spectrum of emotion appears to parallel the sensitivity of the inner senses to a spiritual dimension to which they are not thwarted by conflict with the intellect. Since the novel purportedly treats various religious or Christian themes, with many allusions to Biblical text, readers must have an understanding of these references in the book before they can decipher the literary figures and comprehend Hawthorne's private or autobiographical thoughts.

A literary knowledge alone may not equip critics to fathom the depth of meanings in this great work, nor may a knowledgeable familiarity with the Biblical text of itself be sufficient. To understand the burning within one of his main characters, Dimmesdale, or, for that matter, within Hawthorne himself, the reader must also be equipped with a broad familiarity with the Biblical records, as was Hawthorne, some measure of literary appreciation, and perhaps, to claim friendship with the old bard himself, share some similar kinship with the values contained therein. At the same time, readers must be open-minded to the connections between the representations of the characters, or their understanding will be impaled upon their own squeamishness, whether it be a shallow though authentic Christian disgust, or a literary critic's illiberal circumscription.

The reader must therefore be able to suspend judgment of its characters in order to put the pieces of the metaphorical puzzle together. For example, contrary to an earlier critique of this novel by Woodberry, who claimed hastily that there was no Christ image in Hawthorne's tale, Dimmesdale seems inescapably a humanized image of the historical Nazarene. Beyond any prepossession harbored by the reader, that image unlocks the mystery of the scarlet letter and unites all the symbolic rrepresentations presented in the tale; that is, of course, according to the author's interpretation, which he openly admits might itself be a creation of its own, but for the apparent preponderance of evidence therein that logically begs otherwise.

This premise is primary and essential to the interpretations proposed within this book. Readers must suspend their value judgment over the surface meaning of Dimmesdale's relationship with Hester in order to interpret the allegorical meanings between the representations of these two characters. To help the readers dissociate their first Puritanical impressions from their broader and purer meanings, perhaps to recall that Hester first had a relationship with Chillingsworth before Dimmesdale may provide the first of many epiphanies. Examining that relationship with Master Prynne reveals it to be the original source of Hester's fall, and not the one with Dimmesdale. The conclusions herein become evident in the consistency and unity among the numerous allusions to a level of meaning much deeper and more sophisticated than the simple surface tale.

EXAMINING THE CENTER

It is the task of this life to deal with its worrisome problems and challenges as best we can. We adopt or form a philosophy of life either to guide our actions or justify them. This task seems to have been a great concern for Hawthorne in his own Christian element; and if we are to understand him at all, we must understand the mainsprings of his religion as well as the questions he posed in his writings. We must sit beside the Thinker and ponder upon what we sense or intuit below the surface of the tale.

If we think we understand Christianity but only a little, whether Hawthorne's, mine, or the reader's, then we must comprehend the principle of saviorship centered within its very bosom. For a book to use many metaphorical allusions that are Biblical in content, speak essentially of compassion, or want of it, and at the same time overlook its centerpiece, would be as great an oversight as to overlook the sun as a central source of life-giving radiance in considering the mysterious growth upward of a blade of grass.

Missing the substance of Christianity, of which it appears to Hawthorne that his Puritan ancestors were guilty, a book on Christian thought would be vain and vapid, perhaps even dark and dreary, like the Puritan experiment in America was to Hawthorne. To overlook this centerpiece in *The Scarlet Letter* is to do so at the peril of understanding and fully appreciating the American masterpiece it is. It is the purpose of my analysis to show the relevance of the historical figure of the Nazarene in Hawthorne's allegory as central to the redemption of the characters in his tale as well as that of their author. At the same time, this figuration may structure a religious conclusion that could be considered heterodoxical. For these reasons, though Hawthorne's novel is both historical and psychological fiction at the surface level of comprehension, it is much more religious, "with a livelier effect of truth" (2) at the deeper allegorical level, than most realize. As a commentary on the contemporary religions of his day, Hawthorne's book becomes first and foremost an exposition on both prominant philosophical thought and religious themes central to Christian thought. To catch that perspective, the reader may be surprised to find that there may be at least three levels of understanding fused together in his tale to advance it.

DEDUCING RELIGIOUS MOTIFS

Since this purveyor has thrown caution to the wind and called Hawthorne's masterpiece a religious work, some may think that he may have as well added literary blasphemy to religious heresy by taking the liberty of quoting Biblical references at the beginning of each chapter of his book. Perhaps the thought or charge of blasphemy might first and best be quartered in the minds of those more in control of the premises to which higher education already heretofore has laid claim, one of which, silently but overtly upheld, might be a separation of religious and educational ideas, as though they were ethereal enemies. They were less so in Hawthorne's times than in ours, and we must judge this mingling from his perspective than from the present. These references, howbeit many that could be quoted, seem highly relevant to the basic motif of each chapter and may be considered somewhat the substance of Hawthorne's symbolic references therein.

In addition, considering his novel as a treatise on several religious themes, it behooves reason to delve into these motifs in order to explore somewhat the possible interior of Hawthorne's mind, which, to all but the congenial and apprehensive reader, he apparently camouflaged, but not without flags to guide the intuitive reader. Hawthorne tells us that there is a veil in his novel that separates his impersonal tale—the circumstances about which he prates—from the autobiographical revelations of his inmost thoughts, perhaps in order to prevent imposing or infringing upon the values of the reader.

It is scarcely decorous, however, to speak all, even where we speak impersonally. But—as thoughts are frozen and utterance benumbed, unless the speaker stand in some true relation with his audience—it may be pardonable to imagine that a friend, a kind and apprehensive, though not the closest friend [a reader?], is listening to our talk; and then a native reserve being thawed by this genial consciousness, we may prate of the circumstances that lie around us, and even of ourself, but still keep the inmost Me behind its veil. To this extent and within these limits, an author, methinks, may be autobiographical, without violating either the reader's rights or his own. (4)

In other words, the symbolism of his tale is the veil that benumbs his utterances and prevents him judiciously from revealing them so candidly. The reader who has a "true relation" with Hawthorne may have a genial consciousness, or intuitive insight, that will thaw or penetrate the native reserve which conceals the inmost thoughts that are frozen within the contents of his tale, separates the congenial from the critic by their understanding, and thus covertly offends neither.

Since this purveyor has declared his novel to be an expose on religious or Biblical themes, he has supposed himself to share a true relation with Hawthorne's intentions, and to have a somewhat congenial apprehension of those frozen thoughts, in undertaking how to thaw them out for the reader. He has therefore assumed the license to elaborate on these themes, out of a kind appreciation for Hawthorne's motives, so that the ordinary reader may understand Hawthorne's alleged references to them, and the possible interpretations thereof. It is not his intent to prelect any point of scriptural doctrine in referring to these Biblical themes, only to appreciate and somewhat elaborate or expand, the possible parameters of Hawthorne's allusions, to marvel at his ingenuity, and to laud the finesse with which he has hidden these impersonal themes. Hopefully, the reader will pardon any expanded appreciations in the event he doesn't share them; for, unlike Hawthorne, an open exposition, of necessity, nevertheless, "will find out the divided segment of the writer's own nature" (3-4), which, he admits, is congenial to that nature which he perceives in Hawthorne, if it be but only proximate thereto.

DEALING WITH THE HETERODOXICAL

We are often controlled by our philosophy of life; and, in the process of revealing or hiding that philosophy, no matter how cleverly we may do so, when that burden of thought departs too much from the society with which we identify, if only partially, we essentially step up upon a scaffold of our own in revealing it. Yet every human being eventually ascends a scaffold called honor, answers to conscience, and addresses the consequences for positions taken. Hawthorne stepped upon that scaffold very carefully, anticipated not being fully understood, and may have appreciated the lack thereof with some great measure of humorous relief.

Much like some of Dimmesdale's parishioners, many of Hawthorne's readers may have thought of his dark tale as an ambiguous parable, "to impress on his admirers the mighty and mournful lesson, that, in the view of Infinite Purity, we are sinners all alike" (Hawthorne 259). This particular passage is one of the four reactions of Dimmesdale's parishioners to his revelation of the scarlet letter, supposedly etched upon his chest, and may be described as one of the major reactions of critics to Hawthorne's novel. To those who can imagine a moral only from the surface level of the novel, perhaps this simple message is the only one they may glean from their misunderstanding of an obscure tale.

Unfortunately, in like fashion, whereas Hawthorne's philosophical conclusions might be considered unorthodox to the Christian element of his day, or perhaps even in our day, such a religious interpretation advanced herein may be considered by some to be inappropriate, or blasphemous, to the religion of secular humanism, or whatever it is now called, that forbids the intrusion of a religious context upon the arena of academic thought once considered exclusively its own. There are some pockets of our society, fortunately, that do not fear opposing the guardians of higher education, who may have laid so long a claim to the catbird seat regarding any analysis of thought contrary to their own. Apparently, Hawthorne had some fear of this chilling infant monster himself, as well as a strong distaste, as we shall see in the characterization of the educated Master Prynne. His type seems always around us, setting up shop to uproot the noble, inter his medicines in our bones, and thwart the good destiny; whether intentional or not may be beside the point, at least, until some future standard become more evident, as Hawthorne seems to have hoped.

Opposition to the inordinate, therefore, whether due to its unfamiliarity or extremity, often conjures up the catcall of "heresy," and having practiced its facial features first upon his friends, who are both religious and teachers of literature, this purveyor thinks he is fairly well set to brave the ideological controversy that may arise, should his pudding ever be menued to the taste of the general public. After all, he is posturing an interpretation in a field in which he may be considered, most graciously, a novice and, most obnoxiously, a fool. For a defense to, or relief from the focus of either, he begs for a better alternate exposition than his own, one which might propose a more complete analysis of Hawthorne's philosophical mystic than any of those he has studied heretofore. Indeed, he is still in the midst of a study of this great novel, and its critics, and is yet unable to find one who has offered a more harmonious interpretation of the allegory. [The one exception is the work of Becker condensed in Appendix 2, a study written concurrently, or after, Bayinhund's manuscript was discovered.]

The "heresy" alleged in Hawthorne's tale may be ascribed solely to this student's own invention, as well as every other analytical conclusion. Yet, heresy is a challenge of time and place that most thinking minds should be prepared to encounter, unless they are clever enough to conceal their ideas to all but their friends. Because he does not fear being pilloried, shackled, or ostracized in today's society by what he seeks to share, being somewhat over the hill, this student has less reluctance than Hawthorne might have had to divulge his hidden mystery. If he has taken the pulse of the American Christian community with any degree of accuracy, then his purveyance may even escape censure for the extremity of the view he alleges may lie well clothed within Hawthorne's beloved tale. His premise is that, in the hands of the solemn halls of academia, Hawthorne's novel has too long remained a mystery; perhaps it is time for the minions, who today may be constrained by neither religious zealotry nor literary haughtiness, to wrest the mystery from its hallowed grave, and perhaps give honor to its creator where it rightfully belongs, which may have been Hawthorne's more significant aspiration all along.

ANALYZING THE METAPHORS

Another freedom he has taken, with more caution, has to do with the extent to which a critic selects and analyzes the several possible elements of a parable or metaphor: a critical analysis belabors a metaphor when it seeks to apply all the elements of the metaphor to the moral or message intended. He therefore has also used license to use those main or central elements of Hawthorne's figures of speech that contrive the unified interpretations offered in this exposition. The objective is to present and justify an interpretation that is supported by both the numerousity and unity of the figures as well as by an allegorical characterization that threads them together, thus to reveal the possible private ruminations Hawthorne may have astutely concealed in his work. Why he was so abstruse about it may be yet another mystery that understandably may parallel the silence of Dimmesdale, or his reluctance to confess what is so obviously a necessity to the superficial reader. Those mysteries of abstruseness and silence center at the very heart of this analysis.

It must be said, again, that it is highly unlikely that anyone who has not made a thorough study of the Bible, or who has not thought long and deeply upon those religious subjects that similarly concerned Hawthorne, would be able to decipher the allegorical meanings and metaphors of his novel. Nor has it been so easy for one who has studied that text since his youth. Reading Hawthorne is like trying to read Isaiah of the Old Testament, another highly metaphorical work of art. And he seems to ask the same questions many students of life have asked: who or what am I, who is responsible for what I am, whence came I, whither do I go from here, and what is the purpose or meaning of life, if there is one? These are the metaphysical questions Hawthorne is alleged to have pulled out of his nature, as a Romantic, and placed into his novel, the answers to which he provides only in the relationships between the meanings of the symbolic figures and the allegorical representations of the four main characters. However, all the characters, as described in his novel, support the basic conflicts in the story of love vs. hate, and intuition vs. rationality.

HAWTHORNE'S HOPEFUL REDEMPTION

To all who are perplexed with the seeming paradoxes of life itself and the philosophical problems we have with its pains and unanswered questions, there is a better refuge from this wilderness of reason in Hawthorne's book than the early Americans thought they had found in Puritanism. Today we no longer live in a community, though founded in part by Puritans, that is dominated by the gloom of its joyless interpretations of life's purposes. Hawthorne's tale is the work of a man who reflected ill-content with his own society, especially with his Puritan heritage, and had a vision of a quality of life more rooted in compassion than in condemnation. One of its many themes addresses the idea of a transformation of religions that would allow the American culture to usher in a better world for humankind to enjoy, as we become a more merciful society.

Many critics have addressed the sin and the gloominess that dominate Hawthorne's work, but none have stepped forth to redeem him from the gloominess of his tale. His novel is much more than a dark tale of sin and gloom. It is more than the black background of the Puritan experiment. There is a scarlet letter sewn with threads of golden hope throughout the tale, with an explanation for that hope that redeems both Hawthorne and his characters. As it lies within the design of an allegory for the readers to reverse their view of the characters, so should the image of black in Hawthorne's tale be swallowed up in the image of red, like a letter which is boldly embossed upon a squallid and wanting background.

To Hawthorne, perhaps the better part of the ethics of Puritanism may have cultivated some moral restraint, but its lack of focus upon a life based on "sacred love" was not conducive to a "life successful" to the development of a happier state of life. Without that base, both religion and science would cultivate characteristics in the individual not as affable as original Christianity intended. To wit, perhaps to show the effects of both religion and science, without some close connection with the universal heart, the character of Chillingworth, knowledgable in both, was portrayed possibly as a backdrop to upstage Hawthorne's other heartless characters. One of such was the old Inspector, an official in the Custom House at Salem, who possibly epitomized the absence of both conscience and compassion, and symbolized Puritan ecclesiasticals for whom their moral code had no impact. Against this field, the force of the universal heart has an appeal that is locked inside the revelation of the scarlet letter.

Between these two opposing forces contended the characters of Hester, Pearl, and Dimmesdale, vying intuitively against logical speculations for some inexplicable mission that might redemn the human family in the end. Hester, despite her continual speculative weaknesses and vascilations, remained compassionate towards her fellow beings and loyal to her redeemer; Dimmesale, fighting successfully against his prime adversary, volunteered to ascend his cross upon the scaffold in fulfillment of his destined mission; and, Pearl confident of the future based on that redemption, consistently and successfully signaled to them both the necessity of fulfilling the office of the scarlet letter, and later seemed to bear the fruit of that destiny.

Hester's transformation, which may symbolize the transformation of humankind's nature, therefore, perhaps resides more in her child's future nature. To Hawthorne that transformation is perhaps transmuted by each generation's successful advancement toward a golden end, as assisted by some "magic touch to effect the transfiguration" (164). This, then, according to a purveyor of sorts, is Hawthorne's redemptive vision "thrown at large upon the wide world." To this student, Hawthorne hoped that Christianity would be transformed so as to create a humanity more sympathetic in nature. Though the generations of the Christian experience in America in his day, or possibly in ours, may not have as yet met his dim hopes for a balanced society that could be both prosperous and religious in their best dimensions, nonetheless, were his ghost to set foot in America today, his hopes for that transformation might either be crushed or vindicated, depending upon what pocket of our society into which he might descend.

Hawthorne's redemption, then, hinges upon a possible future redemption that may effect that transformation of society, wherein "Hatred, by a gradual and quiet process, will even be transformed to love" (160). Thus, his allegory is an open-ended, and perhaps prophetic, conclusion, as he so implied, "We shall see whether Hester Prynne were ever afterwards so touched, and so transfigured" (164).

SECTION II

This section comprises articles or essays dealing with issues of the analysis raised in Section I, but with a little more background central to understanding Hawthorne, as detailed in Section III. For the most part, the articles prepare the reader to understand and appreciate, depending upon their own philosophical bearings, Daniel's interpretation of the allegory that, in Section III, consistently threads together the figures of speech from chapter to chapter.

The first article depicts Hawthorne as an allegorist, and the second examines the ideological underpinnings or structural background that may account for Hawthorne's style of writing. The third relates the historical or Puritan setting of the tale itself, the sable field Hawthorne painted for his readers and his characters. The fourth discusses the problem of sin in early and present America as it relates to the mortal body, which Hawthorne seems to celebrate allegorically instead of condemning it, as did his Puritan forebears. The fifth seeks to explain the purpose of pain and misery as a beneficial earthly experience, as possibly projected by Hawthorne into the relationships between his characters. The sixth reviews how the relationships among the four main characters frame the hidden meanings of the allegory. The seventh presents the message that may have been cleverly and abstrusely reserved for sympathetic minds. The eighth explores Dimmesdale's confession as Hawthorne's peculiar statement of belief about Deity's relationship to humankind, or mankind, as used by Hawthorne, both terms and others being used synonymously throughout this analysis with reference to the human family. The ninth expounds upon why Hawthorne may have cast a code of silence upon his characters, as a metaphor itself, from which the readers must intuit the hidden message.

The editor presents Bayinhund's interpretations and comments in this section without any further elaborate commentary on his part. With as little effort as possible, he has squeezed as much passion out of Bayinhund's enthusiasm as manageable without choking the life out if it, or without choking himself upon it, in order to keep the specters of Daniel and Mr. Who at bay.

THE ALLEGORIST

P erhaps the first order of understanding Hawthorne would be to digest all that is known of the man. But that would take a scholarly study apart from that intended by this particular purveyor's notions. He has confined his analysis to his experience of *The Scarlet Letter* as a layman, and has begun with the purpose Hawthorne may have had in mind when he chose to use the allegory to convey his message. Neither is it intended to be erudite in the smallest measure, but simply as a reflection of the regard for the man this student developed in the process.

So perhaps the first order of business might properly be a definition of allegory:

> "1. The veiled presentation, in a figurative story, of a meaning metaphorically implied but not expressly stated. Allegory is prolonged metaphor, in which typically a series of actions are symbolic of other actions." (WEBSTER'S NEW COLLEGIATE DICTIONARY, p. 23)

Taken from an old dictionary, the face of which has almost faded away, and the details of the edition thereof gone the way of treasured books, crumbled and torn away by too frequent use, this definition should stand the test of time as well as any other. Though I have replaced this old friend with its universal edition, I still use it from time to time because of its ancient prejudices, and the particular attachment I seem to have to it. Perhaps its definitions are not that ancient, although they may be closer to Hawthorne's day than the larger version I peruse less often. In any case, when reading Hawthorne's novel, the reader might use this definition, or one like it, as a base around which to organize his deductions and intimations, mindful not to let one dominate the other until all are in place.

Perhaps the particular implication of the use of the allegory is to teach as well as to entertain; and that is what this reader has experienced in Hawthorne's marvelous tale. He believes he has heard, and felt, and seen, with long and intense meditation, what perhaps few have experienced from such a deep and hardly fathomable author. And though the surface tale, entertaining as it has been to many a reader, may have offended some of Hawthorne's public, yet the allegory, in the full estimation and calculations of this student, redeems Hawthorne as a master teacher as well as a master of the allegory.

Hawthorne's genius plays to the intuitive sensibilities of his readers. Perhaps one of the greatest gifts of an artist is to invoke new meanings that lie within their own experiences, to probe the depths of their own nature in response to what stimulates it, and perhaps even to identify its particular benefits. Hawthorne's art personalizes his meanings for his readers in the form of questions that seem aimed at reinforcing their self-discovery. As Hawthorne might ask, "What mode of glorifying God, or being serviceable to mankind . . . may that be?" (10)

With that question in mind, I would let my listeners proceed from hence to pay attention to Hawthorne's questions in his tale, to puzzle with the intimations of answers he may give in bits and pieces here and there, to deduce for themselves what meanings are conjured up in their own minds to meet their own personal whims, and to define, of their own accord, the extent of Hawthorne's allegory. For it appears that he has offered an array of possible meanings, perhaps to match the wide interests and predilections of his audience. This student only presumes to relate what meanings Hawthorne's allegory has disposed him to sense, as though he was lead thither by a knowledgeable teacher. Sad to say, however, that in thus doing so, he may have broken Hawthorne's code of penmanship by addressing his presumptions "to the one heart and mind of perfect sympathy;" and therefore his analysis may "find out the divided segment of the writer's own nature," as well as the reader's.

THE ALLEGORY AS A COMMUNICATIVE TOOL

Woodberry asserts that Hawthorne embodied the allegory artistically and most effectively to allow its definiteness to balance the mystery and vagueness in his work. "Hawthorne's art became always, not only more vividly symbolized, but more deeply moralized" (Woodberry, p. 143-146). He further states that Hawthorne was absorbed in the moral sphere of life and desired to express it in an allegory or symbol that out—valued the plot or characterization (*ibid.*, p 155-156). Woodberry, however, did not appreciate the extent to which the scarlet letter outvalues the simple plot of the allegory, argued against himself, and weakened his analysis when he claimed that there was no Christ image in Hawthorne's tale. His argument limped when he failed to explain what the symbolism of the allegory is after declaring what it is not. After all, there is really no justifiable recourse at all in stating what something is not if one cannot state what it may be. And to make such an audacious claim seems a last-resort measure to save face as a person of learning, or worse, to sidetrack a reader or student who might otherwise be led contrary to the critic's own predilections.

Hawthorne made superb use of the allegory, and metaphors and parables within the allegory, as tools to implicate double meanings so as to hide his inmost Me. This device suited his purposes, especially in concealing a message or conclusion that was religious in nature, and may have only been meant for only a few to understand.

> In an allegory the hidden meaning is easy to discover; indeed it is the allegory itself which superficially conceals it. The purpose of allegory is to strengthen, by an exercise of fancy, the received doctrine and the shared moral code. Symbols, on the contrary, put accepted meanings into doubt, introduce new ones, and finally create a radically different alignment of sympathies."
> (Kaul, p.13)

Though his meanings apparently were not so easy to discover, this reversal and realignment of sympathies was a strategy that Hawthorne employed very astutely in his tale, whether to assist those who were familiarly sympathetic with his views, or to confound those who were not. Hawthorne unraveled the message of the scarlet letter upon Hester's chest by creating confusion as to its surface meaning, then reversed the initial meaning to create a different view of the characters in the tale, and a "different alignment of sympathies" for them.

Hawthorne's tale at the surface initially prates of circumstances at a superficial level, while simultaneously developing another or different view of the main characters. Recreating the meaning of the scarlet letter to hallow Hester's relationship with Dimmesdale, Hawthorne used his allegory to introduce a radical meaning that eventually exonerates three of the four main characters, closing with a short essay on love and hate at the end of his tale that may even exonerate Chillingworth himself.

ROMANTICISM, ANTI-TRANSCENDENTALISM, AND PURITANISM

To understand the relationships between the symbols and the allegorical representations of the four main characters and other contextual clues, it may also be helpful to understand the movement of literary thought in Hawthorne's time, from a layman's point of view. Keen of intellect, but endowed with a Romantic heart and a Puritan conscience or heritage, Hawthorne was given to a literary style that has been labeled Anti-Transcendentalism.

SOURCE OF TRUTH

The Puritans seemed to believe that, although the Creator manifested himself in the physical world, the Bible was the source of truths that should regulate social, governmental, and personal conduct. Puritans therefore probably believed that their Creator not only was revealed through the physical world but also through the Bible. However, their moral lessons learned from nature may have been limited by their Biblical definition of Deity.

Not so for the Romantics of Hawthorne's days:

> The Romantics found in nature a far less clearly defined divinity; their experience is usually recorded as a more generalized emotional and intellectual awakening" (Anderson, et al., 119).

As a revolt against classicism, Romanticism seems to rely on passion and imagination, rather than reason, as a source of truth; freedom for the individual, rather than the constraints of social conventions and order; and a fusion of time and place, rather than the classical unities of time and place and action. Hawthorne seemed to have relied upon all of them.

DISCOVERING REALITY BY PRYING INTO NATURE

Romanticism is the idea that there is a greater spiritual reality that surrounds our physical reality, and that we can best access those spiritual elements by examining nature intuitively rather than by logical study alone. The Romantics' belief, perhaps known as native mysticism, that some Supreme Being was revealed through nature, might have been referred to by Hawthorne as the universal heart. Providence is good and works through nature. Alone in nature, the logical part of a human's mind may give way to allow direct visionary contact with the spiritual world. If we are separated from a direct, intuitive knowledge of this Deity, we are capable of evil. If we trust ourselves to know this Being directly, we realize we are a part of the Divine Soul. In other words, the world of humanity today may be mean, dull, and routine, unless humans respond to the divine within each of them, and those influences without, that transcend the realities of this world. The Romantic believed we make these discoveries about ourselves, and perhaps in the universe, in moments of contemplation by prying into or searching a natural world most accessible by intuitive insights.

> Prying farther into the manuscript, I found the record of other doings and sufferings of the singular woman, for most of which the reader is referred to the story entitled "The Scarlet Letter"; and it should be born carefully in mind, that the main facts of that story are authorized and authenticated by the document of Mr. Surveyor Pue. (32)

Of course, there was probably no real document; the actual facts of the surface tale were likely created solely in Hawthorne's mind, which is one and the same as Surveyor Pue's. We might say that Surveyor Pue is Hawthorne's alter ego while he was employed in the Salem custom house, unable to write, and "decapitated" when he lost the post. Hawthorne perhaps contrived the ideas while employed there, but the setting was not conducive to the intuitive solitude he felt he needed in order to compose those ideas. "I began to grow melancholy and restless; continually prying into my mind, to discover which of its poor properties were gone . . ." (39)

The idea of intuitive meditation, or "prying," is used by Hawthorne over and over, possibly to demonstrate to the reader the greater advantage of doing the same. The reader must pry intuitively in order to grasp the significance of the scarlet letter as a symbol with "some deep meaning in it, most worthy of interpretation . . ." (31) Therefore, perhaps the "y" in Hester's married name is meant to be pronounced as a long "i" instead of a short "i." Perhaps the focus of that particular pronounciation is the character of Master Prynne, the antagonist.

Transcendentalism, also opposed to the empiricism of Classicism, seems to be the idea that truth—the ultimate reality of the Supreme Being, self, and the cosmos—transcends human experience. The empiricism of science can only study the things it sees, hears, tastes, touches, and smells, despite the fact that the scientist's initial interest may have been intuitively sparked. Many a great discovery has resulted from the inexplicably persistent, intuitive, prying of the discoverer, be he scientist, Romantic, or perhaps even an arduous student.

Apparently Anti-Transcendentalism, as it is called, is the idea that there are dark and evil, as well as refined and enlightening, elements of truth in the spiritual dimensions, which, though they lie beyond the physical appearances of the known world, can yet be ascertained by one's introspective sensibilities. This bipolar dimension of the spiritual is seen in Hawthorne's novel as explaining humankind's nature and personality, and is explored at a deeper level to represent the relationship between the human family, nature, and the spiritual world. The interplay of light and dark in his novel, along with the color red, help structure these allegorical relationships and address the nature of humankind with respect to the origins of the human species and the destiny planned for them.

Hawthorne used intuition within his characters, therefore, not only to sense and evaluate the impact of these forces upon the human soul, but also to alert the reader to do the same in his novel. Whereas logic or reason is of the mind, intuition is of the heart; and separating them presupposes a tragic beginning. "Wherever there is a heart and an intellect, the diseases of the physical frame are tinged with the peculiarities of these" (124). Master Prynne is a prime example of these peculiarities at work:

Roger Chillingworth's aspect had undergone a remarkable change while he had dwelt in town, and especially since his abode with Mr. Dimmesdale. At first, his expression had been calm, meditative, scholar-like. Now, there was something ugly and evil in his face, which they had not previously noticed, and which grew still the more obvious to sight, the oftener they looked upon him. (127)

In Hawthorne's notes, as referred to by Specter, he expounds on the possibility of how the human soul begins its journey into committing the unpardonable sin, which appears to be the downfall of Chillingworth's character.

> The Unpardonable Sin might consist in a want of love and reverence for the Human Soul; in consequence of which, the investigator pried into its dark depths, not with a hope or purpose of making it better, but from a cold philosophical curiosity,—content that it should be wicked in whatever kind or degree, and only desiring to study it out.

> Would not this, in other words, be the separation of the intellect from the heart? (Spector, 251)

Hawthorne enacted the above idea in most of his characters, especially that of Chillingworth, who pried into the soul of Dimmesdale with the assumption there was some wickedness hidden there. He rejoiced in what he believed to be a confirmation of his expectation; but he was also horrified in seeing himself, but for a moment, for either the wicked being he had become, or his eventual destiny, by virtue of his hatred and revengeful passion. In what he considered a moment of triumph, he saw vanquishment and, as this student has proposed herein, the very hell of his own destruction. His prying mind, serving a vengeful impulse and yielding to no compassion of the heart, consumed him until he decayed spiritually and withered away.

WOMEN AS SYMBOLS

Hester's last name, Prynne, may be therefore symbolic of the Romantic's thirst to pry into nature for answers to its being. Hawthorne thus seems to believe we can find both good and evil, love and hate, compassion and hostility, in the intuitive process of investigating the nature of the world we live in. Hester seems to represent the principle of Nature itself brought about by the Fall, as well as a possible personification of an legendary historical figure, Eve, and her innocent but curious quest for knowledge.

It must also be noted that other writers, as well as the Romantics, have used women symbolically to represent the structures of civilizations and the impulse to domesticate. For example, the Biblical record, to which Hawthorne referred frequently, used women to symbolize institutions. Hawthorne may have used his women characters in *The Scarlet Letter* to represent certain features or principles of the world in which we live, as a reflection of those realities that transcend and relieve the present one. For another example, Hester experienced insight in the market-place, in the face of the harsh realities she experienced at the moment, which gave her a measure of relief therefrom.

> Possibly, it was an instinctive device of her spirit, to relieve itself, by the exhibition of these phantasmagoric forms, from their cruel weight and hardness of the reality. (57)

Both Hester and Pearl, as mother and child, may also represent three different generations, or spheres of life: Hester, the principles of both pre-mortality and mortality, and Pearl, the principle of post-mortality, as the offspring of its mother.

THE RATIONAL VS. THE INTUITIVE

As a reaction to classicism, the Romantics considered the intuitive sense superior to the rational in search for truth. Imagination, spontaneity, individual feelings, instinct, and nature were of greater value than reason, logic, planning, and cultivation (Anderson, et al. 118-9). Contrarily, today's civilization is mostly based upon the scientific or empirical approach to a discovery of truth and its application. Even some of our choices may be based more upon democratic logic than upon individual intuition. For example, one of the strategies used by the field of marketing is the appeal that "everyone's doing it." This rationalized response may thus justify and persuade the individual against an instinctive sense of personal rightness about the matter: "Why should I not buy it?"

In Hawthorne's novel, the value of intuition is foremost, which seems to verge on personal revelation, or communication from the spiritual dimension, and appears opposed or complicated by logical or speculative conclusions. It appears to be the person's intuitive self one must believe in and follow as a guide, rather than relying entirely upon one's logical conclusions. To the Anti-Transcendentalist, as well as to the Christian, one's juxtaposition in life between the neutral elements of the earth and the things of the spirit—where one is enticed by both good and evil dimensions of the spiritual realm—allows one's intuitive powers to come into interplay with both influences so as to foster a discipleship to one or the other.

It seems to Hawthorne that one's inherently individualistic nature, which has some connection with the universal heart, becomes the pivotal point in the development of his/her character and, therefore, his/her destiny. Hawthorne appears to project his objections to pure rationalism in his novel, and to argue for intuition as a more direct avenue to a discovery of the truth, as well as encouraging it of the reader. One's choice, therefore, seems based upon what one prefers to believe, and is willing to sacrifice for that preference, despite the absence of absolute knowledge. The use of reason in yielding to experience, rather than the use of intuition in yielding to spiritual impulse, seems to become the dividing line in Hawthorne's characterization of good and evil. Whereas intellectual speculation may serve as a barrier to intuition, one's intuition, nevertheless, can be influenced by the dark side of the spiritual realm as well the other. Hawthorne does not appear to address the relevance of how one can distinguish between an intuition from the dark side and one from the other—other than whether one's base of character is compassion or hostility—nor to indicate the obvious value of logical deduction.

In the pursuit of that finer reality which transcends the physical existence, Hawthorne's emphasis on passion and imagination demonstrates his Romantic impulse to rely on intuition. Passion occurs in his novel contrary to convention, and imagination exploits the ramifications of the consequences of passion. His heroic protagonists ambivalently challenge and yield to the order of their society at the same time they submit intuitively to higher realities. Their search for freedom from social constraints and intuitive submission to higher law conceals an allegorical plot that metaphorically fuses times and places in order to present to the insightful reader some moral intimation. He requires the reader to probe or pry into those intimations in order to understand Hawthorne's use of imagery.

As we note the swing of the pendulum from classicism to romanticism and somewhat back to empiricism, in view of Hawthorne's vision in his novel of the transformation of society, the question may form in the mind of the sensitive and apprehensive reader, "is there a real relationship between this transformation and achieving a balance between following the promptings of the heart and the prying curiosity of the rational mind?" As Hawthorne projects his Romantic hope towards the Christian's dilemma in a fallen world, it is this balance that seems to lie at the heart of Hawthorne's "successful life." Not satisfied with the past, Hawthorne looked to the future in that the present generation might be transformed into a better by succeeding generations whose sensibilities gradually became more intuitively compassionate to one's fellowmen.

THREE ANTI-TRANSCENDENTALISTS

Hawthorne, Melville, and Poe were considered Anti-Transcendentalists. Hawthorne and Melville believed in the Romanticism of Emerson that found reality in nature, but held that this reality may not be all good or benign. The great power of darkness in Hawthorne's work, Melville claimed, "derives its force from its appeal to that Calvinistic sense of innate depravity and Original Sin, from whose visitations, in some shape or other, no deeply thinking man is wholly free" (Anderson, et al., 186). They had imaginative vision essentially Romantic in that it stressed intuition, power of nature, and individual emotion. Whereas Emerson ignored the dark side of Puritanism, these other three developed ideas from the mystical and melancholy aspects of Puritan thought, and used symbolism as a technical strategy in their writing to deal with these aspects. In addition, Hawthorne and Melville's characters live simultaneously on two levels, as real people and as representatives of something larger (ibid., 186).

CONCLUSION

The object of my analysis is to focus upon these larger representations in his novel in order to discover what Hawthorne was teaching his studious readers at the deeper level of meaning, insinuated by his metaphors and played out by his characters. We find these Romantic and

Anti-Transcendental elements interlaced in Hawthorne's novel in such an ambiguous way as to be purposefully confusing, at a first or superficial reading. Besides the deeper analysis required by an intensive study of his work, an understanding of Romanticism, Anti-Transcendentalism, and the Judaic-Christian religion are essentially helpful in interpreting Hawthorne's novel fairly. That he was a student of the Biblical text is overwhelming apparent in *The Scarlet Letter*. Equipped with an appreciation of these three elements, the reader is prepared for an exciting adventure of discovery in one of the most mysterious tales in American literature, and perhaps one of the most shrewdest reflections of the greatest story ever told.

THE AMERICAN EXPERIMENT
AND BEYOND

As Hawthorne's readers come to understand the imagery of red on black in *The Scarlet Letter*, they begin to see that Puritanism, to Hawthorne, was like ancient Judaism in the days of the Nazarene. His primary aversion for Puritanism was its black spirit of condemnation born out of the concept of Original Sin and the depravity of the mortal's nature. Hawthorne perhaps pitied the gloomy aspects of his Puritan heritage that had its grasp upon the New World, perhaps similarly as the Galilian sorrowed for the Pharisaic perversions of the Mosaic law in Israel, and for their conventional death-like grip upon its adherents.

Yet Hawthorne seemed to retain a little of his Puritan consciousness as he focused upon the sensitivity of the individual and the value of goodness. He achieved this focus in a similar parabolic manner as the man from Nazareth used to instruct his followers, while retaining the spirit of Judaism. Hawthorne's metaphors and parables, knit together in an allegory with a Puritan setting, leave to the reader the task of intuiting deeper meanings therein. Wherein the Nazarene utilized the prophecies of his Jewish forefathers to restore, refine, and reveal these moral truths, Hawthorne from time to time, as the narrator, would insert commentaries to buttress more directly other allusions to moral meanings made by his characters, thus guiding the reader who might be sensitive to them. It is this sensitivity, love and reverence, as well as the want of it, that lies at the heart of his allegory, as well as a key for the reader to understand it.

RELIGIOUS TRANSFORMATIONS

Perhaps having witnessed changes in the Puritan experiment from its inception in America to that of his era, as well as being familiar with the history of Christianity, Hawthorne possibly foresaw continual and hopeful changes from generation to generation, in the religious orders of the day, and in their positive impact upon those individual who would be true to their finer sensitivities toward their fellowmen. He seems to hold out hope for a better world as the carekeepers of Christianity become more focused upon the compassionate and merciful acceptance of the sinner, or the spirit of the order, and less concerned with the condemnation of the sinner by the letter of the law. In that sense, Hawthorne may have been more in tune with our own time than his own, or perhaps, one far better, but just around the corner, and down the street a ways.

Hawthorne realized that the current or contemporary religious order in America, though an improvement in the world in his day over that of his Salem ancestry, was still possibly hung up on its Calvinistic origins. He "recognized that the effort to achieve a well-integrated community life in such a world must lead to tragedy" (Kaul, 20). Through the eyes of Hester and through the words of the story teller, he revealed a sense of the need for a change in the society of Puritanism that was heavily endowed with the Calvinistic concept of human nature as evil and depraved: "As a first step, the whole system of society is to be torn down, and built up anew" (165). Later, in the forest, Hester encouraged the divine to "[b]egin all anew!" (198) "The challenge to break away from organized society is there in Hawthorne." (Kaul, 15)

A NEW MORAL CONSCIOUSNESS

It is in the forest, close to nature, that truths emerge perhaps because the wilderness of the forest is not subject to the laws of organized society. One can break away from the conventional grasps of a lifeless society by merging with nature. The forest or wilderness in Hawthorne's tale seems to represent the raw, naked knowledge of good and evil that is not under the control of the society's religious order and is free for the taking.

> The lawless wilderness is thus lawless only insofar as it is beyond the reach of established law . . . a haven of freedom and the possibility of starting a new life . . . . To start a new life in the world there must first be born a new moral consciousness. (Kaul, 19)

It is this new moral consciousness of a better world, that doesn't view human nature as evil and depraved, to which Hawthorne addresses the moral of his novel. This better world is beyond the capacity of the Puritan experiment to produce. The new perspective he seems to advance looks upon the natural body as a noble work of the Creator, perhaps in the scheme of the Providential plan to bring about the immortality and eternal life of the human family. Hester had intuitively, and apparently unconsciously, elaborated the scarlet letter A as the one hope to effect that immortality. She would have it done her way (as in the case of Eve's rational decision); but Dimmesdale had a destiny of his own he was bound by Providential duty to fulfill, and without which that transformation could not be achieved.

> The one thought of 'this exemplary man,' wholly self-absorbed again, is to preach the Election Sermon so well that the world may say of him ever after that he left 'no public duty unperformed, nor ill-performed'" (Kaul, 19, quoting Hawthorne, 215).

Though Dimmesdale had briefly been thwarted from his intuitive instincts by Hester's rationality, his revised sermon, though not one word of it is recited, may symbolize, in brief form, the good news heralded during the dispensation of the carpenter from Nazareth on "the relation between the Deity and the communities of mankind" (249). Apparently, both Hester and Dimmesdale are Providential kingpins in the scheme of life, each seemingly not fully understanding the other's part, in bringing about this "transfiguration" for and in behalf of Pearl, "infant immortality" (91), or redeemed humankind.

Hawthorne would have the readers to pry into their intuitive nature to consider "whether Hester Prynne were ever afterwards so touched, and so transfigured" (164).

Perhaps Hawthorne believed, in his tragically hopeful tale, that that destiny or transfiguration would some day come about through a generational transformation in mankind's nature, perhaps aided by her experiment with Christianity, and alludes to that possibility in Pearl's prosperous relocation in some other clime. He seems to have expected that "at some brighter period, when the world should have grown ripe for it, in Heaven's own time, a new truth would be revealed" by some prophet or prophetess (263). Perhaps, if Hawthorne were to stroll down one of our streets in our own time, would he pry about to see if his prophecy of a better period were fulfilled, and look for such a prophetess?

THE PROBLEM OF SIN

Though a religious man, who was familiar with Biblical scriptures, Hawthorne seemed tied more socially and psychologically than he was intellectually or spiritually to his Puritanical heritage. As a Romantic, his definition of Deity seemed to be more generalized than the Puritan's Biblical concept; and his allegory indicated he was concerned with the problem of sin, its origin, inevitability, and consequences. At the same time, one or two of his conclusions on the relationship between Deity, humankind, nature, and evil, as abstrusely as they may be seen in his characters' representations, might have been considered heterodoxical in his day as well as they might in modern Christianity today.

THE PARADOX OF THE CREATION ACCOUNT

To those who consider and question the religious experience, there is a great paradox, an overwhelming contradiction, that frets the human mind when they ponder the origin of sin and the resulting problems of pain, especially the responsible parties involved. In all due respect, their perplexity seems to rests upon at least two or three harrowing question: how could a divine Being, who is purportedly caring, allow the horrible depravity which history evidences of humans as practicing upon their own kind due to the Fall? A corollary question to this paradox is also well made: how could an intelligent Being, who is all-knowing, have been so dim-sighted as to put the tree of knowledge of good and evil in the Garden of Eden, in the first place, without knowing that Adam or Eve would eventually bring about the Fall of human nature and the advent of sin? A third inexplicable, not often perceived: why, being barred from the boundaries of heaven, was Lucifer and his hord, according to the Biblical text, not banned from meddling with the Creator's new creation in the Garden of Eden? The Christian answers, somewhat confidently, and often without any clarity of reasoning, that it was not dim-sightedness on his part, but some well-designed plan, however abstrusely communicated: he perhaps foresaw the end from the beginning and had a reason for it. Nevertheless, that reason seems to have been withheld from mortals; and this silence of Providence seems another problem that presents another theme in Hawthorne's tale, begs the readers' query, but leaves them somewhat stranded to their own devices.

The problem of evil, pain, and misery this world heaps upon us from time to time might be too burdensome for many people, and a greater knowledge of world events may challenge one's philosophical self. Perhaps the most rational conclusion derivable for a purely thoughtful person is the position of an agnostic, who is honest enough to admit he really doesn't know and can't believe what he has not experienced. In an educated society, where the scientific method seems most successful in alleviating a few of earth's problems, that position might appear as an acceptable mind set.

Science, by definition, supported by the purely rational mind, and based solely upon what it can see, hear, smell, taste, and touch, can only purport that humankind is little more than a superior species of animal at the top of their food chain, whose mistakes are common to all. As far as any life beyond, if there be any, there are probably few demerits, if any at all, awaiting these mistakes, for lack of certitude on the matter. Having neither seen nor heard the Supreme Being in person, nor having the means to etherize him upon a table, or quantify him in a laboratory setting, science must of necessity, then, disregard the existence of Deity in its study of nature. The purely logical person can easily explain the world-wide notion of Omnipotent promises for relief as a psycological need in humankind to believe that such exists. They are simply the myriads of religious lullabies sung by the nations of the world in hope for a better. Thus, science mitigates against the plausability of a compassionate Cause in the universe. Marginalizing that Cause underminds absolute law, and allows situational ethics to fit the occasion when everything seems simply circumstantial. So all this agonizing over sin is, at best, only conjecture; at worst, pure nonsense.

Religion, on the other hand, compounding experience with an intuitive sense of the spiritual dimension, which presumably lies beyond and transcends known reality, proclaims that the human being is a divine being whose existence is destined for some better end, or perhaps worse. The instinctive nature of mortal beings worldwide senses intuitively some connection with some Omnipotent, and proclaims that connection in various formats, however dimly it may do so. Those myriads of lullabies springing from his children all over the earth may attest to some other numinous or sacred sense, which the Romantic might label intuition, or a sense of some emanations from some other dimension of life that speaks for some other better end of life. To the Christian, or for that matter, to most humans who hang their hat on such a hope, there seems to be sufficient evidence to accept life as it is, on the basis, first, that Providence has not seen fit to reveal any more detail other than that which purportedly has been revealed; and, second, that he has allowed us to use that sacred sense to guide us in quest for knowledge to better cope with life as it is.

Some sense a divine purpose in scientific knowledge to aid in that quest, and others do not. Of course, Hawthorne had somewhat a skewed view of both science and religion; but it seems he used religion, its adherents, and Biblical themes as the vehicles to explore his take on the destiny of the human race, leaving to his readers to deduce their own conclusions on the matter. He had questions about both religion and science; but it is clear that Hawthorne placed more value in intuition than in logical deduction in arriving at some plausible answers. Although Hawthorne comments on both perspectives in his allegory, he presumes the validity of Providence; and he juxtapositions the faith of the scientist, based on logic, side by side with the faith of the religious person, based on intuition. Hawthorne asks the reader questions, relies heavily on exclamation marks, uses "as if" scenarios, and injects several devices to cue the reader to intuit certain meanings beneath the contextual surfaces of his tale. His reliance on intuition in his novel places him perhaps closer to one alignment than the other, and his parley with religious texts and themes appears, on first impressions, to center him in a kind of Christian humanism.

However, the problem of the introduction of sin and depravity into the world by the Fall, and the life we therefore have to live, may not be as ominously foreboding in the twenty-first century, as it may have been to our ancestors, or Hawthorne's. One reason for the difference is that our society no longer shares the same social consciousness of the Puritans, its spirit of condemnation, or its deplorable attitude toward the human soul. Our prosperity may be a hugh factor in the change, and in his novel seems to be one connected to the destiny of one of his characters, Pearl. Indeed, in a unique way, Hawthorne appears to predict this change or transformation in his novel as in other writings. For example, in "Main Street," Hawthorne reveals explicitly his ambivalent feelings about the

American Puritans: "Let us thank God for having given us such ancestors; and let each successive generation thank Him, not less fervently, for being one step further from them in the march of ages" (Bloom, p, 6). At the same time, he might be shocked to realize how far successive generations have moved from that society.

WHAT AM I?

It is then by intutive insight, rather than by logical speculation, that Hawthorne appears to reveal his views on "the relation between the Deity and the communities of mankind" in regard to the problem of sin. Two themes seem to be cast opposite each other, as red metaphors on black, in Hawthorne's tale. Puritanism, as a derivative of Calvinism, had a gloomy slant on life, and Hawthorne spoke for a better perspective of it. While Puritanism conceived humankind more as a beast because of Original Sin, as Hamlet argues: "What is a man, if the chief good and market of his time be but to sleep and feed? A beast, no more" (Harrison I, 272: Hamlet, Act 4, Sc. 4), Hawthorne seems to implore his reader, through the characters of Hester and Pearl, to have a higher regard for the genus Homo, much as the same Hamlet earlier interjected amid his gloomy contemplations,

> What a piece of work is a man, how noble in reason, how infinite in faculties, in form and moving how express and admirable, in action how like an angel, in appreciation, how like a god: the beauty of the world, the paragon of animals!" (Harrison I, 254: Hamlet, Act II, Sc. 2)

Whereas Shakespeare's Hamlet is truly a tragedy in that Hamlet's perspective becomes darker and more depressed with the burden imposed upon him by his ghostly father, Hawthorne's novel, on the other hand, moves from the darkness of gloom to the dim brightness of a shadowed hope of what the human species might become. He plays one perspective against the other, mostly with the intent to reverse the first, as red projects from a background of black, to signal a conclusion he seemingly reached in his own reconciliations with the dilemma.

Wordsworth, an English Romantic who died the same year Hawthorne wrote his first novel, with whom Hawthorne likely was knowledgably sympathetic, also thought highly of humanity's origins and his relationship with the divine. He is quoted here to express openly what Hawthorne possibly sought to cloak:

> The child is father of the man . . .
> Our birth is but a sleep and a forgetting;
> The soul, that rises with us, our life's star,
> Hath had elsewhere its setting,
> And cometh from afar;
> Not in entire forgetfulness,
> And not in utter nakedness,
> But trailing clouds of glory do we come
> From God, who is our home . . .
> Heaven lies about us in our infancy!
> (Harrison II, 99)

Both of these philosophers may have been responding to their own soul inquiry, as a poet of old, with whom they might have sensed some affinity:

> When I consider thy heavens, the work of thy fingers, the moon and the stars, which thou has ordained;
>
> What is man, that thou art mindful of him? and the son of man, that thou visitest him?
>
> For thou hast made him a little lower than the angels, and hast crowned him with glory and honour.
>
> Thou madest him to have dominion over the works of thy hands; thou hast put all things under his feet. [1]

Many poets, writers, or philosophers desire to express their take on the meanings of life, to make some statement about the things that concern them most, or to sound the depths of nature which may personnally speak to their queries. Hawthorne was given no less to this propensity, though perhaps with less a bright and outspoken hope than his Romantic contemporaries. He takes his keenest readers on this quest, like a walk in the forest of life, in search for the answers or explanations he advances by way of the unified symbolism of his metaphors. Since the imagery in Hawthorne's tale has less an obvious meaning than in Wordsworth's poetry, perhaps the heaven that lay around Hawthorne was more clouded for him; or he may have been more inclined, as he intimated, to respect the reader, to whom both Hawthorne and heaven alike may have dimly concealed themselves, perhaps for different reasons, in order to appeal either to a larger or smaller audience.

WHITHER GO I?

In the bonding between Hester and Pearl, "infant immortality," Hawthorne seems to say that mankind's beginning may have some bearing on her destiny. Perhaps he is paraphrasing and echoing Wordsworth, "The child is mother of the woman," presuming that he was well aware of the English poet. Hence the questions asked the reader in the tale: Who is the father of Pearl? Of what is her nature derivative? What is the destiny designed for her? And at the allegorical level: Who or what is the father of mankind? Was she born of good or evil, and therefore inclined toward one or the other? Does the whence of that birth speak for its whither?

To Hawthorne, nature was the medium through which mankind might sense who she is, and whence she came, perhaps more accurately than through the Biblical derivations of the Puritan experimenters. Imbued with a glimmer of Romanticism, Hawthorne believed that one might discover divine truths when closest to nature in the woods or in the "wilderness;" yet, with a perspective peculiar to Anti-Transcendentalists, he believed these spiritual intuitions may emanate from a dark side as well as from a bright side. A person could be in touch with human nature and receive "light" from the greater reality of the spiritual dimension that transcends the physical or conventional one. To him, perhaps the dark side by contrast heightens or exposes the projection of light therefrom or thereabout. It is therefore perhaps ingenious of Hawthorne to leave the answers to these questions to the intuition of the reader rather than to elaborate on his conclusions. An open ended mystery makes for more interesting reading, appeals to a wider audience, and solicits perennial attention as long as it remains unsolved.

THE PROBLEM WITH SIN

As Hawthorne and others would have us believe, the definition of Original Sin seemed to have dominated the Puritan social consciousness; that is, because of Adam and Eve's transgression that resulted in a change from immortality to mortality and a loss of grace, eventuating in death, humankind inherited the tendency toward sin and depravity. To the Puritan, sin was evil, and the good life probably was simply appearing innocent of sin and restraining any expression of joy in a depraved world. Hawthorne seems to distinguish sin from evil. That which infringes upon or desecrates the human heart in consequence cultivates a disposition to hate and despize. To him, "the truest test of a life successful" was "showing how sacred love should make us happy" (262); and, probably the one and only sin, the lack of compassion, was a failure of that test.

The gloominess in Hawthorne's novel seems to derive from the excessive exaggeration with which the Puritans treated sin in view of their ill regard for the human body. Both civil and religious authority were combined in prosecuting sinners who broke Puritan law, and the attitude of the spectator in witnessing the so-called justice meted out was much like that of its carekeepers or magistrates, as though such an attitude was its owner's halo. Although the carekeepers of Puritanic doctrine received Hawthorne's greater aspersions, its followers were no less guilty.

> [T]here was very much the same solemnity of demeanour on the part of the spectators; as befitted a people amongst whom religion and law were almost identical, and in whose character both were so thoroughly interfused, that the mildest and the severest acts of public discipline were alike made venerable and awful. Meagre, indeed, and cold, was the sympathy that a transgressor might look for, from such by-standers, at the scaffold. On the other hand, a penalty which, in our days, would infer a degree of mocking infamy and ridicule, might then be invested with almost as stern a dignity as the punishment of death itself. (50)

Such a tendency on the part of Hawthorne's Puritans almost to revel in the sinner's punishment might cause one to suspect that envy or some other sinister motive was the thrust of their accusation moreso than righteous indignation. It might appear to those less possessed by this spirit of condemnation that such a reaction to the sinner is not really becoming the Christian, who should be mindful of following a more compassionate example, but is instead rather befitting Lucifer himself, who has been called an "accuser of our brethren."[2] Though condemning the sin can be done without condemning the sinner, and the condemnation reserved for some higher Judge, Hawthorne seems to have done neither, but allowed his characters to explore these positions. If he expressly condemned anything in his book, it was the Puritanic obsession with punishment for mortal weaknesses, without regard for that compassion that was supposedly centered in the very heart of Christianity.

A HAMLET IN PRISON

Perhaps, because of the Calvinistic concept of depravity in the early American religious experiment, Hawthorne may have felt himself a Hamlet imprisoned, like most Puritans, in a black and gloomy world. The Puritan consciousness seemed embedded in his genes, like a ghost haunting from the past, and may have supplied him the roots of his Anti-transcendentalism. Influenced by the dark side of the spiritual dimension, and thus unable to identify completely with the pure Romantics of his time, he may have wished for a deliverance, as did Hester, and may have posed some red roses from the bush beside the prison door, for himself as well as for his readers, to remind them of some moral message at the end of our prison tour. His hope for a brighter view may have seemed shrouded in shadows, like a black field, but, like stripes of red standing out against it, tasted like partridge-berries, "red as drops of blood upon the withered leaves" (204), growing here and there in his own moral forest.

Henry James has commented that the gloominess of his novel comes from Hawthorne's mood at the time of its inception. He proposed that several events in his life, while he was writing *The Scarlet Letter*, accounts for its tone of despair.

> His work has the tone of the circumstances in which it was produced . . . . It is densely dark, with a single spot of color in it . . . and it will probably long remain the most consistently gloomy of English novels of the first order. (James, p. 106).

It is true that his novel was written during a period following his mother's death, which affected him very much, and at a time when he had lost his political post and was unemployed. Yet the gloominess of his work may not be so much a reflection upon Hawthorne's mood as it was a true, and perhaps autobiographical, commentary on his perception of the dark and hopeless influence of the early American experiment with Puritanism, as an imperfect form of Christianity. Hawthorne said his novel was "a particularly hell-fired story into which I found it almost impossible to throw a cheering light" (Anderson, et al., 264); and it is therefore more likely that he purposefully painted this gloominess as a black field upon which to contrast his red metaphors, though lighted dimly by the hope of a brighter day, as a way of underwriting his philosophical urges.

ROSES BY THE PRISON DOOR

Perhaps Hawthorne felt that only the few who intuitively sense something better than this world seek for the answers to the seeming paradoxes of life. As a religious commentary, Hawthorne's novel cleverly conceals and reveals his conclusions with reference to several Biblical texts. It appears that one of those conclusions was that contemporary religion had such a strangle-hold upon the human's conscience that a long time might be required for humanity to redeem itself transitionally from such a hold in order for its better good to be advanced. This time-frame for the improvement of the ministry through the transformations of society seems to be embedded in his novel as one of the themes his allegory develops, as an escape from the current throes of humanity's view of its nature.

Hawthorne's commentary, as the narrator of his tale, and his allegorical ramifications, as seen by this friend, seem to implicate his Puritanic background, as accepting the problem of sin, in an explanation for the paradox of the Creation. But his views, based upon a higher view of humanity's nature, entail a brighter picture than perhaps he thought was cast by any Christian generation prior to or contemporary with his own. This vision may have precluded any reliance upon their customs or conventional practices, and rested purely upon his own intuitive sensitivities to the miseries of his fellowmen.

One of Hawthorne's essential differences with Puritanism is therefore symbolized by the red metaphor on the black field in his novel: there was a promise or a bright hope of a better community than the present, perhaps in some other quarter of the world, at some future time, as heralded by some significant action taking place, or having taken place in the past. That departure from his ancestral faith is like Hester beholding the rose bush as she exits through the door of the Boston prison. It may be reflected in his choice of certain pleasures, like playing cards, drinking wine at taverns, chewing tobacco, and avoiding intellectual company in favor of such (Anderson, et al., 263), as though passion was a function of life built into it by its Creator. Though the shadow of Puritan guilt etched in the order may seem to have darkened Hawthorne's life, perhaps he relinquished to his nature more as an expression of his philosophical beliefs than as either a means of defying established conventions or escaping periodically from his own reclusion.

THE PARADOX OF PAIN

Hawthorne's novel seems a treatise incognito addressing the problem of suffering in a mortal world, perhaps accepting it as a necessary content of some veiled Providential plan. He appears to justify the paradox of a world's "mesh of good and evil" in the disguise of the allegorical representations of the main four characters, whose performances, from the perspective of Hawthorne's philosophical urges, play out an apparent solution to the problems of sin and pain, in a world whose Creator is lauded as being All Good.

The rejection of a One-Cause philosophy or explanation of life is often based upon the seeming contradiction of a compassionate, all-knowing Being who created a world of suffering and misery for everyone in it. This problem with pain and sorrow in that creation is a great paradox to many, and has puzzled more than a few minds among our great thinkers. This apparent contradiction poses a philosophical problem perhaps more so for the Christian than the non-Christian, especially when either experiences harrowing depths of sorrow and despair. For those individuals who are concerned about the paradox of good and evil, pain and pleasure, love and hate, in a mortal world presumably created by a perfect Being, whereas the corruptible depravity of the flesh is pitched against that of a better world coming, there are observations today perhaps not so popularly available to the philosophical mind in Hawthorne's time.

For example, Hawthorne might have had more enlightened communion with C. S. Lewis than he had with either Emerson, the residents of Brooks Farm, his rowdy companions, or even his best friend, Horatio Bridge. Himself a philosopher who looked at life from both opposing views, Lewis, as a Christian apologist, gave us a more favorable concept of Deity in his book, The Problem of Pain. He explained how individuality and the agency of this world's creatures presuppose Hawthorne's "dark necessity" of pain in a physical world, and how pain and suffering may mold the elements of character, pity and compassion.

Hawthorne's allegory proposes a similar explanation that, in a peculiar way, relates this problem to its redemption. Out of the universal heart of Compassionate Mercy, suffering mortality is to be both redeemed and transfigured. Perhaps the message of that redemption composes the Deity's confession of his relationship with the human family, and his possible involvement in the creation of those "communities of mankind." These possible conclusions project a seemingly heterodoxical idea that may be entirely native to Hawthornian philosophy, and will be examined more thoroughly in a later essay.

It might appear encumbering upon this analysis to explain what wisdom or benefits derive from the fall into mortality, with all the attendant trials and tribulations that naturally befalls us; however, such was not the intent nor scope of Hawthorne's novel. He was making a simple connection between the actions of the Deity and the prospects of the human family: that the Deity's relations with his creations possibly includes a planned destiny, however inexplicable or dimly viewed the process might be. Whatever conclusions Hawthorne may have derived from his own meditations, he at least held out a better hope for the individual whose life, through sacred love," successfully "should make us happy." In the words of Dimmesdale,

> [A]ll intelligent beings . . . will stand waiting, on that day, to see the dark problem of this life made plain. A knowledge of men's hearts will be needful to the completest solution of that problem. (132)

In that legendary day, so to say, the problem of sin and wretchedness in mortal life, and especially the differences that a compassionate heart may make, may be more fully understood. It is perhaps a bold but subtle reference to the Christian's day of the Lord's judgment, at which time it is believed that every rational and intelligent being may plainly understand the role of sin and pain in mortality. The insinuations surrounding Dimmesdale's confession, death, and probable resurrection address this very subplot, and will be explored later.

THE PURPOSE OF PAIN

One of the implications, in what is presumed to be Hawthorne's take on the Christian view of the purpose of life, is an acceptance of life as it is on the basis of what it conditions us to become in the future. The Fall, brought about in the Garden through the knowledge acquired by Eve and Adam, brought about the experience of death, pain, and misery to human nature. This principle of advancement seems written into the character of Pearl, who, as a representative of that principle, and as a figure or symbol forecasting future humankind, perhaps needed grief as a redemptive measure to develop a compassionate soul. Speaking perhaps in behalf of this need, the narrator in the novel explains Pearl's one essential lack: "She wanted—what some people want throughout life—a grief that should deeply touch her, and thus humanize and make her capable of sympathy" (184). To Hawthorne, such a state of grief as mortality seems to be a "dark necessity" (174), and he addresses how this dark necessity apparently is to be resolved by a redemption from the Fall, as symbolized by Hester's ignominy; Dimmesdale's confession, death, and subtle resurrection; and Pearl's inheritance in a distant land.

Christian theology purports that God in Christ, out of compassion, voluntarily underwent the greatest pain and agony that a human might experience, that he compensated for the fall by overcoming it, and that he also bore the burden of its consequences by paying the penalty for the sins of the people. Why he would do that, for any other purpose than as an act of love, purportedly appears to be the centrally cloaked explanation enclosed in the allegory: it was an Act of Justice as well as Mercy.

However, part and parcel of this extraordinary Act of Passion is the irony apparent in the Christian appeal: joy is promised the world even though it revels in the misery of its sins. The connection between this misery and the joy is the link between Hester and Pearl, and Dimmesdale seems to be the vehicle of that connection. As Hawthorne demonstrated, pain and suffering, therefore, though their purposes may not be completely understood, can be accepted in patience in the hope that one's desires, faith, and love for goodly things will not only be vindicated, but that also the goodly life will have its own rewards here and beyond, "showing how sacred love should make us happy, by the truest test of a life successful to such an end!" (263) Hawthorne's take on that process, in comparison to the Biblical text, is of course less specific about the details of how a life of sacred love brings joy; but he at least may be saying that the pains of mortality were experienced by a commissioned representative of Deity, that he may have somewhat confessed some responsibility therefor, in order that a better day may in the end transmute all hate into love, and thus, by aid of some prophet or prophetess, then have rendered the problem of life more understandable.

A PLAUSIBLE CONCLUSION

To leave the reader, or the few inclined to understand the reasoning behind Hawthorne's conclusions, in the throes of a purported heterodox, without a clear understanding of the role of pain in the scheme of our alleged eternal immortality, would appear to be an act of indifference. Yet, as has been stated, Hawthorne's novel does not extend itself to treat the justification of mortality. To make our present state of existence palatable to the mind of the reader, thus to rescue Hawthorne from any accusation of "heresy" revealed herein, goes beyond the premises of this work. That heterodoxy, nevertheless, can become more plausible once we realize the crucial role that pain and agony may play in the creation of joy within the soul of the human being.

C. S. Lewis, in his book, _The Problem of Pain,_ explained how pain and suffering in this mortal world is simply a natural result of the existence of both individual identity and its separate agency, apart from being a compound in one with all other, and how mutually inclusive they are by the very nature of things. Referring to a Biblical text (Hebrews 2: 10), Lewis attempted to make the connection between pain and suffering and the purpose of life, which purpose appears to lie at the roots of Hawthorne's novel.

> I am only trying to show that the old Christian doctrine of being made "perfect through suffering" is not incredible. To prove it palatable is beyond my design (Lewis, p. 105).

It is likewise beyond the intent of this exposition to serve up suffering as a savory dish, or to place pain upon the menu in the eternal scheme of things. Whether or not the existence of pain and suffering seems justified perhaps becomes a matter of preferred opinion, in view of the dimness of our knowledge. The knowledge of whether or not their existence constitutes a "dark necessity" in the plan for the eternities beyond is another mystery for another Daniel to resolve.

THE EFFECT OF ONE'S FAITH

The Christians' basis for conduct in perfecting themselves, or gaining attributes of character like unto Deity, seems to be that these traits capacitate one to experience a greater degree of compassion and joy, if not fully on this side of the veil, at least on the other. Hawthorne addresses the development of this attribute of compassion, perhaps as a condition of future joy, in the descriptions of his novel's characters from the Custom House to the scaffold, in interplay with their allegorical meanings. It appears that this development is accomplished by believing in and following intuition, or the intimations perceived. These revelations of a sort correspond with the laws of universal nature, or some higher spiritual dimension, perhaps referred to more generally as the universal heart, upon which that growth is predicated. Such development presupposes the individual has some connection therewith. Hawthorne's "universal heart" may be the sum total of compassion that pervades the universe and centers in his "Universal Father" (84-85).

From the implications of his allegory, to Hawthorne, joy might seem to be more than a consequence of relief from pain, or experiencing the sweet because one has simply experienced the removal of the bitter. Perhaps the experience of mortality, flesh meshed with spirit, has an impact on its capacity to have joy by the very nature of its combination, a kind of symbiotic relationship in which the whole of the parts has a greater impact than the mere collective sum of each, and so much moreso when both are attuned to the universal heart. Be that as it may, Hawthorne's view seems to be that the body and all things physical in nature are not to be scorned as unholy and depraved, but to be seen as element that also somehow quickens the soul and tenderizes it by the woes it must endure here.

For Pearl, who represents a humankind that is intuitively more in touch with those transcendent spiritual dimensions, her sympathy seems developed by her association with Hester, whose experiences forebear Pearl's own sense of compassion. The grief of Dimmesdale's confession and death upon the scaffold appears to complete that sympathetic capacity in Pearl as her tears pledge that "she would grow up amid human joy and sorrow, nor for ever do battle with the world, but be a woman in it"

(256). In other words, if borne well, suffering helps develop compassion and enhances one's capacity to experience joy, in a day of maturity, when humankind may no longer battle with the throes of mortality, but be a fully developed, and perhaps consummated, generation.

This capacity to have joy seems unintentionally to have been denied by Puritanism. Joy in the Puritan was evidence of something wrong. Hawthorne therefore decried the gloomy effects of Puritanism's emphasis on the depravity of the flesh and the sin-inclined nature of mortality, perhaps because it detracted from the joy humankind could have otherwise been free to experience. Joy seems possessed by only one of Hawthorne's characters, Pearl, of whose future nature Hester was a necessary forebear. It seems that Hawthorne is paraphrasing Wordsworth, "The child is mother of the woman." The two appear to be one and the same, Hester as the present, and Pearl as the future, of the woman to be, one partaking of the experience of the other, and the other learning from the counsel of the one, a kind of unity of duality.

THE PROPHETESS

Hester, who hoped she might be a prophetess of a better world, as a harbinger of joy, assured those who come to her for comfort that

> at some brighter period, when the world should have grown ripe for it, in Heaven's own time, a new truth would be revealed, in order to establish the whole relation between man and woman on a surer ground of mutual happiness. (263)

That surer ground was not the sable field of Puritanism; nor perhaps contemporary Christianity; nor does it appear that Hester, brainwashed by its gloomy perspective, was that prophetess. If Hawthorne implicated in Hester's representation of mortality any premonition for the future, it might have been confined to his thematic proposition that her fall deservingly begs for a confession of a relationship with Deity, and a redemption or retransfiguration from the effects of that fall. An "angel and apostle of the coming revelation" would establish the real relationship between man (Dimmesdale) and woman (Hester or Pearl), upon a more knowledgeable ground, one not as dimly viewed as the present one. The reference to the "whole relation between man and woman" appears most singularly to be another symbolic reference to the central theme of Hawthorne's allegory—the connection between Deity (Dimmesdale) and the communities of mankind (Hester and Pearl). At the least, that surer ground was not contemporary religion, but another of a coming revelation, more refined and imbued with more of compassion and mercy. Hawthorne hoped for a transformation to take place beyond his own generation to bring about this surer ground.

To bring about this more stable environment or materiality, the prophetess—perhaps representative of a particular dispensation of some future civilization, or a refined and purified church, or perhaps another state of being (Hester's transformation?)—this prophetess

> must be a woman, indeed, but lofty, pure, and beautiful; and wise, moreover, not through dusky grief, but the ethereal medium of joy; and showing how sacred love should make us happy. (263)

Whether Hawthorne is using the figure of a woman to represent some principle or institution, similarly to that usage in Holy Writ in Revelations 12, is not very clear. He gives no clues, and therefore may have no express opinion, as to whether the woman prophetess symbolizes a church, a religion, a dispensation, a purified civilization, a holy city, or a glorified human family. Nevertheless, he apparently believed that some "coming revelation" would reveal a new truth by which the communities of mankind would then be able to demonstrate, through the medium of joy, and not through the dusky grief heralded by humankind's failed experiments, how a sacred love does produce eternal happiness. Hester's intuitive hope that she might be that prophetess, which she logically rejected, perhaps erroneously, seems to have some connection with the passage above.

Other Biblical references to the use of gender, as a symbol, cast woman as the bride of the King of Kings, a purified church, or a people being sealed (in marriage) to its Master. It is most probably a stretch of the imagination—that is, as the unfriendlys may say of the whole of this layman's exposition—to even hint that Hawthorne may have had in mind the Biblical parable of the marriage of the bridegroom to his holy city[1]. Whether the burial of Hester next to Dimmesdale bears any such suggestion, since it casts a further logical aspersion on their relationship at the surface level, is left for the reader to surmise, or, at least, to await further elucidation in any fulfillment of their prophetic representations. Hawthorne appears to leave the particulars of Hester's transfiguration as an open-ended future event.

THE NEW WORLD

Though "a woman stained with sin, bowed down with shame, or ever burdened with a life-long sorrow," a sorrow brought on by the Puritan's shadowy view of humanity's nature, yet, with the scarlet letter upon her bosom, Hester still intuits a hope for her transformation, perhaps a redemption of the human family foreshadowed in the character of Pearl. That Pearl might be that beautiful and joyful prophetess, who will inherit the New World, and reveal by her very nature the new truth of the race of man's relation to Deity, is a subtle implication one might also wrest from Hawthorne's allegorical novel. Or the prophetess of which Hawthorne spoke might be a voice coming from the generation of mankind Pearl might represent. In any case, Pearl lives in another clime, perhaps in another time as well as place, and apparently represents a healthier or more favorable opinion of humankind's nature than does Hester.

If Hester represents the best of the civilizations of the human family, despite their interpretations of the purposes of life that embody a life of gloom and despair, then Pearl may represent a new dispensation of that family which denies that dark label of life, promises a better or transcendent perspective that includes compassion and joy, and signals more clearly what the relationship is between God and humankind, between the spiritual elements and the physical elements, and between immortality and mortality. If Hester represents the best of the civilizations of mortality, perhaps produced through the generations of religious dispensations, then Pearl may represent the best of a second period of civilization for which her offspring may have hope. Pearl seems to become the metamorphed transformation of Hester. Pearl may also represent Hawthorne's hope for his daughter, Una, for whom he planned a different environment than Puritanism.

Thus Hawthorne appears to promote the promise of a day free from the pain and agonies of a mortal and sinful world. He unfolds symbolically some of the elements of Christianity that proposes Providence has laid out for the human family's progress toward a New World. But he does so in such a way as to cue the reader's intuition of that process, as would a Romantic, imbibing from nature some evidence of a spiritual reality transcending this present world. And he offers an explanation that, perhaps to him, justifies that search or prying into nature.

Hawthorne, of course, would perhaps make Romantics of all of us by directing our inward eye to a better world than this. Perhaps in his own peculiar way, he has attempted to be "serviceable to mankind" by glorifying his Maker with a parabolic allegory of his own creation. In any event, he has shown in almost all of his characters in his novel either an enhancement of the compassionate soul, or a diminishment of the uncompassionate one, relative to one's sensibilities. As we see Hester's inward beauty unfolding, while her outward diminishes, much like Dimmesdale's, we also see Chillingworth's ugliness becoming more repugnant and devilish and fading into oblivion. And we see Pearl bequeathed with "a considerable amount of property" on each side of the Atlantic, "the richest heiress of her day, in the New World" (261).

Other characters are described along a continuum between these two poles, and the description begins with the characters of the Custom House, to which we soon turn a detailed focus to begin a justification, metaphor by metaphor, page by page, and chapter by chapter, for the views expressed in this layman's opinion. These characters obstrusely interact to address a common Christian creed, beyond which Hawthorne may have come to some singular conclusions.

THE CHARACTERS
OF THE ALLEGORY

B efore a discussion can credibly reveal an allusion to the historical figure of the Nazarene in the novel, it must first advance the allegorical representation of the four main characters, Hester, Chillingworth, Pearl, and, then, Dimmesdale. These characters, along with the metaphors of red and black, form the framework for the delivery of the allegorical meanings. This article by no means seeks to account for this student's interpretations, but to proffer them in general as a preparation for that task, which is reserved for Section III.

LEVELS OF MEANING

There are two levels of meaning, possibly three, represented by these characters. The first level explicitly relates the tale of assumed adultery (although the word was never used in the book), and the relationships among the main characters, against a background of Puritan consciousness. The second and deeper allegorical level appears to relate the characters to historical figures inferred by the metaphorical allusions; and a possible third may relate the historical figures to principles that seem in operation among the representations of the characters, implicitly concealing Hawthorne's theological inferences concerning the Fall of Nature, and her Redemption. It is the summarial conclusion of this analysis, that when the passionate reader sounds the depths of Hawthorne's tale, the allegory at the bottom appears to represent the operation of at least three chief forces, or principles, as an explanation for the "mesh of good and evil" at play in the world we live in: the principle of human nature; the principle of Providential influence, by design and intervention; and the principle of adversarial hostility. Besides the conflicts that reside at each of the three possible levels of meaning, there is the conflict between intuition and reason that may decide the direction and destiny toward which one's passion drives a person.

HESTER PRYNNE

The tale of the scarlet letter begins at the surface level with Hester Prynne in jail, where she has given birth to a child, Pearl, some two and a half years after leaving her husband, Master Prynne. The assumption by the Puritan code (and the reader) is that she has committed adultery. Hester claims to be the mother, but will not identify the father. After all, it is common knowledge that children only come into the world by one common practice; she therefore is guilty of a reprehensible act, as seen by the self-appointed enforcers of the code. That Hawthorne has made no reference to a prior meeting of Hester and Dimmessdale to bring about the birth of Pearl, but has left little room for the logical mind of the reader to assume otherwise, has set the stage, in the first act, for a jaundiced view of Hester. However, since Hawthorne had already given the reader some reference to symbolism in his description of the rusted iron door of the prison, and the contrasting rose bush nearby, at the threshold of his tale, the reader has been alerted to wonder what Hawthorne may possibly have had in mind: to what similitude might he be alluding, or possibly, to what contrary.

Far be it from this purveyor to suggest that there are only two or three other ways by which the human family has been given life in this world; and we perhaps should pay little mind to Hawthorne's offhand statement at the time she emerged from the prison door, into the light of common day at the marketplace (56). But he might dare explore that later. For now, the assumption that she is an adulteress—although that assumption was never directly explored in his tale —must first grasp our mind, at least until compounded in a different light by other details that are revealed later. Like a Puritanic cloud, that notion dominates the surface tale.

At the second level, Hester may represent the view of mortal nature as condemned by Puritan theology, as well possibly as by some of their forebears and descendants. At the same time, she may possibly depict contemporary civilization dominated by a religious attitude for which Hawthorne had little affection. She may very well characterize the best of the Puritan community, in contrast to the description of other women in Boston. Hester's intuitive sense serves her better than her sisters or brothers, and more particularly, than her Puritan leaders, whose speculative conclusions form the basis for their dismal theology. And it appears she also may represent Eve, or Eve's beguilement, she who was deceived in the Garden of Eden by Lucifer, as strongly suggested in Hester's interview with the old physician. Hawthorne often speaks explicitly in places in his novel as the narrator, but somewhat more implicitly, though not exclusively, through Hester's intuitive activities. Nevertheless, the reader must differentiate between her intuitive ideas and her logical notions because she is intellectually confused about her own nature and the nature of her child by virtue of her Puritanic indoctrination.

To the Romantic, in this mortal world, nature is beautiful and pure. To the Christian, nature had a beginning that was even more pure and beautiful, until its mystical transformation. Hester seemingly represents both natures, before and after the Fall. Hawthorne has initially embellished Hester with a natural beauty, much as Hester has embellished the letter A, and her fall possibly denotes the Fall of humankind's nature up to the end of this mortal world. Hawthorne appears to believe that nature is neither depraved nor unworthy, but is impregnated with something of the divine. It is this divinity within nature the Romantic believes can be tapped, or perhaps pried into, in moments of intuitive contemplation, preferable in natural settings. At the end of the tale, Hester, though her beauty has waned unto death, is almost adored, and her letter A considered a mark of venerable distinction by the residents of Salem. This change is the trademark of the allegory, whereby one view is exchanged for another, to elicit in the reader either an elevated or demoralized perspective of the character. In Hester's case, this adoration signifies that the scarlet letter stands for something other than adultery. The change of view from one of condemnation to reverential admiration represents the change Hawthorne seems to have hoped will be realized at some future date, as foreshadowed by the hopeful embellishment of the embroidered scarlet letter.

> Hawthorne, in fact, uses the very symbol with which society identifies Hester, as a means of reversing its view of her.

> To the Puritans . . . the meaning of the A is clear. But not so to a humane critic of the Puritan view of life (Kaul, p. 13).

This interpretation of Hester, as representing the spirit of nature, reveals not only Hawthorne's strong sympathy but also an attitude of adoration for nature and refutes Woodberry's second logical declaration: Because Hawthorne condemned the characters, "There is no sympathy with human nature in the book" (Woodberry, p. 202). It is the position of this analysis that Hawthorne does not condemn but exonerates all but one of the main characters, Chillingworth.

In addition, Woodberry has failed to apply his own conclusion that the plot and characterization are secondary to their representations. Sympathy for human nature is revealed mostly at the second level of comprehension, which Woodberry acknowledged, but of which he could give no accounting. Such a comprehension seems structured by Hawthorne as attainable only with the use of intuitive insight, and almost contrary to logical deduction. But then, perhaps it is the novice that can afford to give more time to unraveling a mystery than can the critic, whose credibility needs little to maintain it, although there might be some other explanation to account for Woodberry's shallowness.

Hester's plight pleads for compassion and sympathy, if not for pity itself. It parallels and identifies with the same shared by her fellowmen. She intuitively embroidered and embellished the scarlet letter A upon her bosom, perhaps to signal that plea, and the hope for its relief, for which she seems to look to Arthur. It is as though her embroidery is a bright promise of a redemption from her dilemma. However, it also seems to cast an ominous spell that promises a destiny "gloomier than the shadow" of Puritanism which hangs over human nature, especially if there is no absolution. Hawthorne seems to have concluded that that absolution needed a confession.

Hester, as does Hawthorne, seemingly, preferred to believe in the celestial radiance of her letter A; but her contemporaries initially saw only the dusky and lurid glow. Nevertheless, as Hawthorne hopes that each generation from the Puritan experiment will advance toward a more compassionate and understanding community, he has the Puritan disciples of Boston, in their own generation, changing their attitude about Hester and her scarlet letter, from one of condemnation to one of veneration, from one of hate to one of love. She seems to embody the spirit and essence of the Christian belief under the oppressive burden of Puritanism, as she wears her scarlet letter with utmost humility. Throughout her lifetime, her meek and compassionate service heralds the scarlet letter as a token of triumph.

Besides compassion, this quality of meekness pervades the characters of both Hester and Dimmesdale. Both principles of character oppose the principle of prideful self-righteousness inherent in the show of Puritanic condemnation. Laboring in the gloom of mortality, heavy laden with the stigma of sin, these two characters exemplify in their nature the trait of meekness as though Hawthorne was exemplifying this principle as a requirement for a life to be successful for the attainment of joy. Each had a yoke, a burden, a destiny, the office which, if done well, would give them peace, and perhaps, unity.

The burdens laid upon the souls of Puritan followers by its masters were not light or easy, as evidenced by Hester's long pilgrimage of suffering. What ray of hope she may have harbored seemed squelched by the Puritanic perspective. But the grace she bestowed upon all her beneficiaries eventually won her the adoration of those she served, and seemed to help reverse the effect of Puritanism wherever she plied her services. Under the circumstances, and perhaps by contrast, her example may have been the best Hawthorne thought possible to emerge from that dismal era, and probably from the history of the dreary world.

HESTER'S NAMES

The Romantics, especially the anti-Transcendentalists, were concerned about the relationship between the divine, humanity, evil, and nature, and dealt with them in their writings. Hawthorne in particular seemed concerned about the origin of sin, its consequences, and its absolution. He used metaphors of light, at the first or explicit level of meaning, to betoken the presence of the greater reality of spiritual principles. These truths can be accessed more freely in certain settings, perhaps by some intuitive prying into nature, or into one's soul, for answers to questions or dilemmas posed by the harsher reality of life. By prying into his own nature and the nature of the world around him, as a Romantic, and by prying into the mysteries of Christianity, Hawthorne perhaps sought to gain spiritual insight about the meanings and purpose of life that transcended the realities of his world. And he seemed to have passed these insights on to the more serious readers of his novel through the symbols he used to signify these insights.

One of these symbols was Hawthorne's use of his characters' names. Hence, because of the tendency of some humans to pry intuitively into nature to understand their destiny, we might pronounce Hester's last name with a long "i," somewhat as a homonym with "prying," to denote this Romantic notion. A perverse master in this prying was Master Prynne himself, from whom Hester obtained her last name in a contract of marriage early in the time frame of the tale, and from whom she later fled. She sought redemption from her fall, apparently through her minister, Arthur Dimmesdale.

What spiritual truths did Hawthorne seek to discover by prying into his own human soul, or the nature of the world in which he lived, or perhaps even in the messages of Holy Writ? These questions are asked parenthetically several times in the novel, probably to provoke the inquisitiveness of the reader: Who am I? Who is responsible for sin in the world? What is my relationship to the divine?

Hester's first name rhythmically, and semantically, with the relocation of the letter "h," might also be associated with the historical figure of Esther, a woman who saved a generation of Jews in the days of their Persian captivity. Esther was willing to face the possibility of death to save her race from destruction. The generation that Hester symbolically seemed to save is that possibly represented by Pearl, her offspring. Hester cannot save herself from her ignominy, for she concedes to belong, against her better nature, to the Puritan consciousness, but she can save Pearl's by and through the suffering and the penance to which she submitted.

Hester's triumphant victory of enduring the ignominy of her mortality to the end, according to Hawthorne's intentions, as viewed by this student, deserved some new nebulous transfiguration, but her just deserts are left in an open-ended allegory for the reader to surmise. Hawthorne may have envisioned Hester's transfiguration as a symbol of the future resurrection, which the readers may or not conjecture, depending upon the "divided segment" of their own individual nature. Of course, it is not so much Hester's victory alone as Pearl's, for whose sake Hester reaps the benefits.

PEARL

The character, Pearl, has no surname because it is not publicly known who her father really was (Ragussis, p. 62). This unknown may signal and parallel the controversy between science, secularism, and religion as to who is the author of the human family. In other words, who is Pearl's author; therefore, whence her nature, and thence her destiny? Questions are posed by Hawthorne: Is she evil in nature, an impish demon from the dark, something divine in nature, or something that just happened out of thin air? Hawthorne debates Pearl's ancestry, with narrator and character leanings, but depicts her as the Pearl of great price. This metaphor is possibly a reference to a Biblical parable pointing, at the alligorical level, to a desired and divine destiny for humankind.

If Hester represents mortal nature, Pearl, as her offspring may represent the future destiny of mortality in its transfigured state. According to Christian theology, this pearl is presumably the greatest of the gifts promised to humankind by her Creator,

Who will render to every man according to his deeds:

> To them who by patient continuance in well doing seek for glory and honour and immortality, eternal life:

> But unto them that are contentious, and do not obey the truth, but obey unrighteousness, indignation and wrath,

> Tribulation and anguish . . . . [1]

In the Christian creed, the passage above refers to the singular effect of humankind's redemption by the Atonement of a Divine Being, or to the destiny of the human race without that effect, like the light or "lurid glow" of a two-edged sword that cuts two ways: either the Redeemer atones for the sins of the penitent, or the impenitent atone for their own sins. The attainment of this pearl of great price–immortality and eternal life–is worth the price of selling all of one's possessions to obtain, and seems to reside in the promising character of Hester and Dimmesdale's child. Pearl, like the scarlet letter itself, seems also to signal retribution for the heartless as well as to symbolize the promise of a brighter day for the compassionate.

Pearl therefore seems to represent a particular lineage or civilization of future humanity–"in this one child there were many children" (90)–and may represent later the children of the election, which might be the subject of the Election Sermon preached by the young minister near the end of the tale. That she facetiously claimed to be plucked from wild roses that grew upon the prison door is perhaps nearer to the allegorical truth than we realize when we consider the symbolic meaning of red in this story. She appears to become the personification of the promise reflected in the scarlet letter A. She may even be considered to be Hester's transfiguration in the New World.

That she also seems a facsimile of Una, Hawthorne's own daughter, presupposes that she is not intended to be Old Scratch's offspring. Hawthorne's notes concerning Una seem to be taken from the novel itself, although it appears the reverse it true.

> "Una, I think does not possess humor, nor anything of the truly comic . . . . Her natural bent is towards the passionate and tragic . . . . There is something that almost frightens me about the child–I know not whether elfish or angelic, but, at all events, supernatural. She steps so boldly into the midst of everything, shrinks from nothing, has such a comprehension of everything, seems at times to have but little delicacy, and anon shows that she possesses the finest essence of it; now so hard, now so tender . . . . In short, I now and then catch an aspect of her, in which I cannot believe her to be my own human child, but a spirit strangely mingled with good and evil, haunting the house where I dwell." (Spector, p. 251-252, quoting Hawthorne)

Hawthorne presents Hester's child, Pearl, as "a lovely and immortal flower . . . whose innocent life" was birthed

> by the inscrutible decree of Providence . . . . God . . . had given her a lovely child, whose place was on that same dishonored bosom, to connect her parent with the race and descent of mortals, and to be finally a blessed soul in heaven! (89)

In the above quote, Hawthorne, in very explicit terms and tone, emphasized by the exclamation mark, which almost always is a cue for the reader to study carefully, seems himself to be speaking, and not through any of the characters. Perhaps foreshadowing, and overshadowing all other passages so manifestly intoned, this passage connects perhaps most obviously with the central theme of the book, as revealed in chapter 23, "The Revelation of the Scarlet Letter."

One of Pearl's alleged parents was the divine, or young minister, a representative of Deity whose sermon on the Election was to reveal the relation between "the Deity and the communities of mankind" (249). Perhaps the parent to which Hawthorne made reference, at the allegorical level, is mankind's Creator, the Author of life. It appears evident that this "inscrutible decree of Providence" has destined his lovely creation to live in the same place on earth, though it was temporarily dishonored and thereby disconnected from its parent by the Fall of original nature. Although that creation descended into mortality, it seems intended be reconnected with her parent(s), and finally return as a blessed soul back into the Garden of Eden, or heavenly abode on earth.

But the parent may also be Hester, mortal nature destined to be connected with the race of man in her transfigured state. Since Pearl's soul was imbibed "from the spiritual world, and her bodily frame from its material of earth" (91), she might be the offspring of the divine (Dimmesdale), and the material element of nature (Hester). One of the themes of the novel seemingly is to connect mortality with its divine origins, and that more blessed state promised in the resurrection. What seems no less than Dimmesdale's allegorical mission to relate Deity to the communities or generations of humanity, it appears, in the Christian faith, that mankind, in her glorified state, evidences Deity's divine connection, or reconnection, with redeemed mortality.

At seven years of age, Pearl seems to represent the beauty and divinity of humans in mortality about to undergo a transition, or removal, during or after the millennial period of the earth's history, to a New World. Whether or not Pearl's removal to a place far from Boston represents Hester's hoped-for metamorphic transfiguration, is not all that clear. This removal of Pearl across the Atlantic, where she is more worthy of recognition, as a creation of divine origin, seems to project into the novel his hopeful prospects for his own children:

> My children have had other birthplaces, and, so far as their fortunes may be within my control, shall strike their roots into unaccustomed earth. (12)

As we later see Pearl playing peacefully with the animals in the forest, in seeming full harmony with nature at its best, we might conjecture in what unaccustomed earth Hawthorne may hope his children's future may be rooted. Perhaps that unaccustomed earth is at least free from the customs of degenerating religious institutions. And perhaps that place in Hawthorne's tale is a reference to humankind's "ultimate salvation":

> If the child, on the other hand, were really capable of moral and religious growth, and possessed the elements of ultimate salvation, then, surely, it would enjoy all the fairer prospect of these advantages by being transferred to wiser and better guardianship than Hester Prynne's (100-101).

Because Pearl at seven years–a time frame mentioned most inordinately in the tale–does not remain in Boston, but resides elsewhere in more well-to-do circumstances, this residence in an unknown land with great wealth implies Hawthorne's hope that the next generation, or some future generation, will perhaps be better off the farther it has removed itself from the Puritan experiment in America. That is possibly why Pearl is viewed as "the scarlet letter endowed with life," and why Hester is the mortal forebear of that "infant immortality that was committed to her charge" (91).

As "an abbreviated form of her father" (Ragussis, 65), it is only slightly possible that Hawthorne may also be suggesting an anthropomorphic resurrection, and possibly even an anthropomorphic view of Deity, which is contrary to some, but not all, Christian creeds. In chapter VIII, wherein Mr. Wilson is seeking to discover Pearl's creator, Ragussis may have suggested such an interesting analogy.

> When Mr. Wilson asks Pearl . . . "Canst thou tell me, my child, who made thee?" . . . (i)t is essentially the same question asked Hester, but now Mr. Wilson wants a different answer–not the earthly father, but the Heavenly Father. The child is viewed as the product of a mysterious and contradictory process in which her maker is either spiritual or biological, or–worse– indiscriminately both . . . . Pearl's refusal to name "the Heavenly Father" as her maker is, stated baldly, a refusal to name Him, the unnameable source of her being, that "Creator of all flesh,"

who is fleshless himself. The Heavenly Father here seems at once an idealized and ironic double of the earthly father who neglects to name Pearl. (Ragussis, p.62-64)

Such an anthropomorphic view of the resurrection, however, would seem contrary to the perception that the Romantics held a more general rather than a limited notion of Deity. It must be stated, nevertheless, that Hawthorne, more than did his Puritan ancestors–in his descriptions of Hester and Pearl, and in his rejection of the Puritan's view of the depravity of the mortal nature—seems to have valued the beauty of God's material masterpiece. At the same time, Hawthorne liked to review several points of view about a matter, and then leave it to his readers to intuit his philosophical inclinations within the allegory.

ARTHUR DIMMESDALE

The young divine, who is mysteriously but allegely the father of Pearl, seems to represent an emissary commissioned of Deity with a destiny he must fulfill. Hester's destiny also appears to be related to his relationship with her. The young minister's confession and death upon the scaffold may typify a redemption in kind, and imply an overdue revelation, wherein God expresses his responsibility for the Fall and makes recompense therefor. This latter implication, which will be given further elucidation later, is a unique and questionable theme not heretofore conceived even in the innumerable and varying creeds of Christianity.

It appears that, as the presumed father of Pearl (the Author of an infant immortality), Dimmesdale needs to confess his relationship with her, admit accountability in Pearl's creation, redeem her from the ignominity of unknown parentage, and perhaps lay claim of ownership thereto. Dimmesdale's character may therefore represent both the creative and redemptive acts of Deity. As a party responsible, in some inexplicable way, for the mortal nature of humankind, he must compensate for her fall, confess his responsibility in the matter, and thus fulfill the destiny Providence exacts of him as an act of Eternal Justice. The Election Sermon he delivers may represent the promise of eternal life to those for whom the Redemption effects that result; and the scaffold upon which he died following his Confession may typify the cross at Golgotha, whereon the Nazarene finished his mission and Atonement for the sins of humanity.

The unspoken sermon may also symbolize Hawthorne's hidden messages to his insightful readers.

His first name, Arthur, is homonymic to author and possibly signifies that the young minister represents the author of life, the Creator of the world, who was Christ incarnate, according to some interpretations of Christian theology. His last name, Dimmesdale, could refer to the idea that the Nazarene may not have had a detailed or clear view of how he was to fulfill his destiny. Or it may depict the dimness of understanding in which Deity has left mortals concerning the purpose of mortality. Or it may point to the near silence Deity has maintained concerning responsibility for mortality itself. Or it might relate to all three ideas. If Hawthorne intended to suggest additional meaning by the latter part of his last name, "dale," perhaps it might signify his mission of passing through the valley of death in order to fulfill his enigmatic destiny.

MASTER PRYNNE

Hester had earlier in some other residence and former life entered into a kind of contract of marriage with Master Prynne, in exchange for knowledge, although Hester had later rejected the contract and disappeared from her former life. Master Prynne is Nemesis to Good Master Dimmesdale. Perhaps he represents the Master or god of this world, the Prince of the Air, the archdemon, Satan, Lucifer, Apollyon, the angel of the bottomless pit, whose ambition is to stake his claim on those who willingly contract subservience under him. Or, at least, he represents the characteristic extremity of those who fall prey to his passionate hatefulness. He becomes the young divine's arch enemy and seeks to lay claim to his soul, through which claim he would possess Hester's and her child's. By focusing upon the destruction of Dimmesdale, Master Prynne apparently symbolizes Satan's attempt to thwart the plan of Redemption. He later saught to prevent Dimmesdale's confession-redemption upon the scaffold. That confession, which includes the revelation of the scarlet letter upon his chest, seems associated with its constant burning sensation, and appears to signify a kind of payment, and possibly even ownership. It may also be Hawthorne's explanation for Deity taking some subtle responsibility for the Fall and the fathering of humankind.

Master Prynne appeared later in the community as Roger Chillingworth, a scholarly consort with Indians and practitioner of medicine. He became a cold character, as chilling as the depth of the darkness he represents, in his torment of Dimmesdale, with a plan to destroy his soul. He is probably the Black Man of the wilderness (a Puritan belief), pretendingto be a captive of the Indians, while he appears to be their leader. As an emissary of the Devil, who is traditionally depicted as a red man with a three-pronged spear, his nature is deceitfully true to that of Old Scratch. The choice of his first name, Roger, is interesting inasmuch as its Germanic origin means "famous spear," or "renown for his sword." Though he initially appears to be an upright citizen, his shape, with one shoulder lower than the other, characterizes the crookedness and deformity of his inward person in his attempt to destroy Dimmesdale's soul and lay claim to Hester's and Pearl's.

We are told in the tale that Roger gave up a former life to associate with humanity, which relinquishment "Chillingworth wills for himself (without realizing the consequences) when he 'chose to withdraw his name from the roll of mankind'" (Ragussis, 64, quoting Hawthorne, 118). Some of the Biblical records indicate that Lucifer and his angels were forceably cast out of heaven, and that he became the tempter and tormentor of humanirty in seeking revenge for his exile. Chillingworth may represent, then, the evil or dark side of the spiritual world, or the worst effects of it, that, as the anti-Transcendentalists believed, can affect one's nature if one is not in touch with the divine or light side of the greater spiritual reality around us.

The young minister's fading health, under the care of Chillingworth, is believed by some of Dimmesdale's parishioners to be caused by the doctor's poisons, perhaps a kind of spiritual spear. One of the chief roles which Hawthorne gives this scholarly old gentleman is that of the physician learned in the crude practices of both Indian and civilized world, especially from "famous men,—whose scientific attainments were esteemed hardly less than supernatural" (121). Both he and Dimmesdale may also be allegorically figured as mortal incarnations from the spiritual dimension; the former embodying hate and the latter, love. Strangely, in a parenthetical essay on the two emotions, Hawthorne hypothetically considers that they may have come from the same source (260).

Witchcraft, as represented by Mistress Hibbins–who ironically is the sister of Governor Bellingham, a former Puritan ruler of the New England Colony–is associated with the Dark Man of the Forest. That witchcraft and Puritanism are relatives from the same stock may insinuate either

Hawthorne's general or humorous view of Puritanism in particular, or contemporary religion in general; or it may connote, at least, the customs, practices, and other conventional forms of institutional religion, any of which may have missed the mark. This relationship may allude to any form of Christianity that contains a mixture of elements opposed to each other, especially without focusing upon the significance of the redemption and the resurrection in addressing the problems of mortality. This combination might be symbolized in the novel by a shield that heralds red stripes embossed against a black motif.

SUMMARY

In the interchange between Hester and Roger, we have a reflection of a previous relationship between Eve and Old Scratch before the Fall. In this flashback, the reader learns that Hester (as Eve, representative of early humankind), at some former residence in some other part of the world, obtained knowledge from Roger (Lucifer), whose image is likened by Hawthorne unto a snake. That knowledge of itself seems directly related to Hester's fall. Hester remembered him in her former life before her fall with somewhat of a vague and distasteful recollection. Whereas Chillingworth may have caused her fall, it was not he who fathered Pearl. Hawthorne makes that very clear by putting the appearance of Hester in Boston two or less years after leaving Master Prynne, whether or not that has any relevance to the authorship of Pearl.

The vagueness and incompleteness of the flashbacks confuse the time element of the tale, but Hester, at some time, by implication only, also had an unspecified relationship with Dimmesdale, her minister, before or after having conceived a child by some unspecified manner or event. Arthur Dimmesdale (Deity incarnate) is insinuated in the tale as allegely fathering (authoring) Pearl (mankind), or has assumed responsibility for her condition as her minister.

That the scarlet letter may represent both the Atonement and the Author of humanity may link them together to show the relationship between "the Deity and the communities of mankind," one possibly as the Cause and the other as the consequence. This relationship may pose a question for the insightful reader: Is Hawthorne also saying that Deity, who has a keen sense of justice, holds himself responsible for the consequences of his actions, or the actions of his children who reside in a state of being for which creation they were no direct cause, as he likewise holds them responsible? This implication, were it intended by Hawthorne, underscores a possible philosophical conclusion or inference that is unique to the explanations proffered by Christianity for the quality of human life, and seems only intuitively deduced at best.

Thus Hawthorne remains true to his own position wherein he asserts that the value of intuition outweighs the value of unaided rational thought. In so doing, the reader becomes responsible for discerning what possible hidden messages may be contained in his mysterious tale.

THE HIDDEN MESSAGE

Hawthorne used the allegory seemingly as the means for advancing his observations as to the parties responsible for the Fall and the origin of sin. At a much deeper level than most critics understand, he may have concealed much more than his belief that the Redemption promises a more cheerful world which may gradually metabolize from the New World's experiment with Christianity. The metaphors of red on black symbolize this hope of change; the four main characters enact the events allegorically relevant to it; and the narrator's comments, in conjunction with that of the defensive repartee between the characters, infer a possible explanation justifying the whole of it.

Hawthorne provided contextual clues also to aid the reader in deciphering his meanings: "between the phenomenon and its reading stand the words 'as if,' which are, like the prison door, at once a passage and a barrier" (Carton, p. 110). Noted for ambiguity in his novel, Hawthorne's ability to double-speak is not only a means of cleverly disguising his religious conclusions but also a literary technique that seems to advance his Anti-transcendental orientations. But the allegorical representations of the four main characters and their underlying relationships form the basic structure of the second level of meaning, and perhaps a third, that becomes the central message Hawthorne attempts to both reveal and conceal, perhaps because of its questionable inferences.

However, the hidden message in Hawthorne's allegory is difficult to discern, unless one can grasp the representations of the characters, and also because it contains conclusions that some may consider heterodoxical in the context of Hawthorne's time, as well as perhaps in our own time. His symbols indeed demand that the reader suspend judgment, or develop ambivalence, about the circumstances of the tale until the reversal and realignment of sympathies intuitively occur. One must expect this reversal in Hawthorne's allegory to fully explore and understand the deeper level intended. If one cannot get past the presumed illicit relationship between

Hester and Dimmesdale, one cannot fully digest Hawthorne's message. He must also be as familiar with Biblical texts as Hawthorne was, as well somewhat knowledgable of the literary tools he used so adeptly.

For example, the commonly accepted reference of the scarlet letter symbol to adultery, at the first level of understanding, is not entirely connotative of the hidden meaning of the allegory. Instead, the scarlet letter A denotes a contrary meaning at the deeper level, and perhaps an Hawthornean inference that may be uniquely his own. The word, adultery, is never used in his book, possibly because that is not what the book is mainly about. Whereas it may be the Puritanical mind in us that seizes and closes upon this relationship, it may be the sensitive heart in us that suspends judgment and looks compassiontely deeper for its redemption.

Adultery is an obvious assumption Hawthorne left to the reader to surmise, as a first impression, possibly because the creation of Pearl gradually and more significantly connotes an allegorical relationship of a higher order contrary, and perhaps diametrically opposed, to that first impression. On the other hand, the word, unadulterated, is used, and only once (65), in reference to the sunshine that momentarily blinded one of Hester's judges. This "unadulterated sunshine" possibly represents a truth about Hester and its significance for humankind at the allegorical level that is not properly addressed by the Puritan code, and therefore not subject to judgment by it. Nor should any be so judgmental toward's Hawthorne novel until it is properly understood, which, of course, is the venture of this intervention, which purports that the birth of Pearl may be as mysterious as the birth of humankind.

If readers debase the relationship between Hester and Dimmesdale by imposing a Puritanic perspective upon it, they will disdain the likelihood of Dimmesdale representing the historical figure of the Nazrene, as perhaps most rational minds might, and therefore miss the opportunity to decipher the higher ordered meaning of his relationship with Hester. On the other hand, if readers suspend their inclination to be judgmental, they may more likely be able to apply their literary skills to decipher the deeper meanings behind that relationship and dramatically change their sympathies for the characters, even for Chillingworth. Those meanings hidden beneath the allegory come together piece by piece, page by page, chapter by chapter, in Section III, like the picture of a jigsaw puzzle that is imperfect until the last piece in place reveals an image within an image.

As Hawthorne's readers advance through the tale to the descriptions of its main characters, against a background of metaphorical analogies, they become aware that the scarlet letter A must symbolizes something more significant than simple adultery. Because that reference is neither consistent nor completely compatible with other impacting contextual imagery, they can cultivate greater sympathies for Hester and Dimmesdale, incur incredible awe over the work of a master artisan, and even feel a kind of reverence for Hawthorne's characters. Readers then begin to appreciate what a marvelous work *The Scarlet Letter* is, especially if they share a kind and genial apprehension of his meanings as well as his art.

DECEPTIVE REVELATION

Melville, an admirer of Hawthorne who met him in August of 1850, after he published his novel, "insisted he was immeasurably deeper than the plummet of the mere critic," that certain passages were meant to "egregiously deceive the superficial skimmer of pages," and that critics "can only speculate about why Hawthorne was impelled toward subversion" (Bell, p. 29-30, 54). This statement, made by an artist with whom Hawthorne felt kinship at one time, and likely discussed the implications of his novel, is a remarkable clue to anyone who might risk an analysis of this masterpiece. It is not likely, as has been the case, that one can digest the enigma of his tale without a profound and penetrative study. The messages are so cleverly disguised that any analysis must be regarded at best as speculative, including this one, for though it may appear to be definitive, it may yet only be a creation of its owner.

Critics are therefore more aware of this philosophical privacy than they are of the messages he intended. "The self-protective impulse that often prompts Hawthorne to conceal from his readers . . . is the most radical and real implications of his fiction" (Carton, p. 113). When it becomes clear that Hawthorne's religious conclusions might have been considered blasphemous in his day, if not even by many in our own, we can understand why he would attempt to be somewhat subversive. But because he loathed deceitfulness, he humorously made that deception both obvious and conspicuous out of a sense of fair play. Woodberry proposed that

Hawthorne had no fondness for mystery, secrecy, or darkness, and wished to be understood by those who could sympathize with his nature and penetrate his moral depths, not that he has a hidden message to relate, but an observation of what he considered "common to human nature" (Woodberry, p. 150-151).

Perhaps Woodberry completely missed the hidden moral depths of Hawthorne's tale because he simply could not or would not see Dimmesdale as an historical image of the Nazarene. Such a reaction is highly understandable from the viewpoint of any that do not undertake an in-depth study of his tale long enough to develop similar sympathies. Had Woodberry fully understood the purpose of the use of allegory, as did Kaul, and had he been able to apprehend its use in Hawthorne's novel, perhaps he would not have been so hastily assertive about that which he apparently knew little.

The failure to understand the particular allegory employed by Hawthorne in his tale seems to have been the fate of most of Hawthorne's critics. Nevertheless, Woodberry was insightful about Hawthorne's reluctance to use deception and his artistic use of the allegory. Hawthorne humorously did make honest tongue-in-cheek attempts to alert the reader to his deceptions and often would indicate his preference for the various ambiguous or multi-meanings he would juxtapose for his readers.

DISCURSIVE OR INTUITIVE

The obscurity of Hawthorne's tale may lie in the failure of the reader to understand and follow his method of revealing his inmost Me. Hawthorne coaches the reader to rely upon intuition and not logical speculation. His questions challenge the reader to confront his/her logical deductions with what intimations may be aroused. Intuition may often be held suspect, and the mind of the scientist may hold more sway upon our better senses; but to Hawthorne, as it perhaps was for Milton, intuition was a higher order of accessing truth more immediately. For example, in Paradise Lost, the angel Raphael, in giving account to Adam and Eve of the process of achieving heaven from their present corporal state, explains how the soul receives reason from the fruits of earth,

"whence the soul
Reason receives, and reason is her being,
Discursive, or intuitive; discourse
Is oftest yours, the latter most is ours,
Differing but in degree, of kind the same."
(Milton, in Harrison, Vol 1, p. 484)

Hawthorne's narrative and the discourses between his characters cue the readers to listen to one's intuitive sense, for it will not lead them astray, as will the tendency to rely solely on reason. He relates this reliance to the ease with which some people conform to the conventional regulations of society, and are therefore apt to be deceived, whereas intimations of the heart may lead to unerring conclusions.

> It is remarkable, that persons who speculate the most boldly often conform with the most perfect quietude to the external regulations of society . . . . (164) When an uninstructed multitude attempts to see with its eyes, it is exceedingly apt to be deceived.

> When, however, it forms its judgment, as it usually does, on the intuitions of its great and warm heart, the conclusions thus attained are often so profound and so unerring, as to possess the character of truths supernaturally revealed" (127).

Hawthorne has his characters encounter the obstacle of logical reasoning, show how moments of intuitive thought may partake of the supernatural, and serve as examples to the reader to do the same. Not only does Chillingworth, as mentioned earlier, intuitively sense his own defeat, but he persist in his own logical determination to destroy Dimmesdale. Likewise does Hester's curiosity, or thirst for knowledge, seem to be the initial cause of her fall, not an act of passion, or whatever their involvement was, between Dimmesdale and Hester. The reader is purposefully left without the very details of that initial relationship, and becomes surrounded by imagery figuring it other than what is initially projected into the reader's mind, who is left to his/her own intuitive assumptions about the nature of this event. It appears questionable at the surface level, but becomes venerable at the allegorical level. Perhaps even the mystery of Divine Maternity, which Hawthorne alludes to at the beginning of his tale, by comparing Hester, with her babe in her arms, to the virgin Mary, seems intentionally suggestive to the mind of the reader to help resolve the apparent conflict between the surface tale and whatever allegorical meaning Hawthorne is conjuring.

For another instance, Dimmesdale, though driven intuitively by an undefined destiny, is lost in a maze of bewilderment when he allows himself to be swayed by Hester's logic. But his awareness of his change in character rediverts him back to his inexplicable sense of duty to Deity.

AMBIGUITY AND THE CRITIC

Joel Porte, a professor of English at Harvard University, which was established by the Puritans, used the word "ambiguous" or "ambiguity" some eight times, and "obscurely" or "obscure" twice in fourteen pages of his introduction to a Dell publication. Porte's comments focus on the obvious or first level of meaning, offer little interpretation of the symbols, and indicate no representations of the characters, suggesting clearly he is possibly aware, but not confidently knowledgeable, of the double meanings. Since he offers no explanation either, it necessarily appears that he likewise, though more learned in the literary field than most of us, doesn't seem to understand the allegorical meaning of Hawthorne's tale. And this might be so because Porte's study of this tale was likely cursory also, or because there are some domains where literary angels fear to tread.

Henry James similarly seems to have given this novel only a superficial reading: "The faults of the book are, to my sense, a want of reality and an abuse of the fanciful element of a certain superficial symbolism" (p. 110). He intimated that Hawthorne's novel may have been a rehash of Gibson Lockhart, Adam Blair, by comparing the similarities between the triangular relationships in the two tales. Wherever from whence came the ideas, his novel does seem to be an artistically blended amalgamation of many of the themes of his short tales, such as "The Minister's Black Veil," "Endicott and the Red Cross," "The Bosom Serpent," "The New Adam and Eve," and "Roger Malvin's Burial." An analysis of this conclusion is another subject for some later discussion. But Hawthorne's novel was not conceived and written hastily just to meet some writer's deadline. He conceived of it and probably stewed over it for five years from the time of his employ in the Salem custom house to the time of its publication. The perceived superficiality of the symbolism may therefore not lie so much in the lack of intelligence of the perceiver as in the superficiality of the study given the novel by his readers and critics.

Whereas Woodberry has declared that "there is no Christ in this book" (Woodberry, p. 201), but has given no interpretation of the allegorical representations of the four main characters to support his claim, there are many who may very well line up behind, or in front of him, thus maintaining, by default or design, the shroud of obscurity that protects the mystery of Hawthorne's book. Perhaps it is the mystery itself that is worshipped by the lovers of his tale. However, it is only fair to say that Woodberry recognized the hint of absolution in the public confession on the scaffold. Likewise, Michael Ragussis came so close to identifying Dimmesdale as a Christ figure that I am surprised that no one has picked up on his particular analysis. Perhaps he was wiser than I to be intimidated by the experts. But I have no reputation whatsoever to lose and feel secure that Woodberry's ghost would have no grounds or substance with which to return and exact some redemption from me. [Becker may have had the same vision, but for similar reasons may have been scared off also.]

Other critics, perhaps having not even understood that Hawthorne's novel was designed to speak at a deeper meaning that its surface tale, have made hastier reviews.

Some have condemned the book as immoral. Several films have depicted various versions of the novel highlighting the single aspect of its presumed baseness. Perhaps few critics in Hawthorne's day have more scathingly failed insight than "Brownson's Review," quoted here in large part for several reasons.

> Mr. Hawthorne, according to the popular standard of morals in this age and this community, can hardly be said to pervert God's gifts, or to exert an immoral influence. Yet his work is far from being unobjectionable . . . . [I]t is a story that should not have been told. It is a story of crime, of an adulteress and her accomplice . . . . [Such crimes] are not fit subjects for popular literature, and moral health is not promoted by leading the imagination to dwell on them. There is an unsound

state of public morals when the novelist is permitted, without a scorching rebuke, to select such crimes, and invest them with all the fascinations of genius, and all the charms of a highly polished style. In a moral community such crimes are spoken of as rarely as possible, and when spoken of at all, it is always in terms which render them loathsome, and repel the imagination . . . .

The Christian who reads *The Scarlet Letter* cannot fail to perceive that the author is wholly ignorant of Christian asceticism . . . .

As a picture of the old Puritans, taken from the position of a moderate transcendentalist and liberal of the modern school, the work has its merits, but . . . we do not regard the picture as at all just . . . .

Their treatment of the adulteress was far more Christian than his ridicule of it. (Brownson, 272-274)

I would recommend a reading of the entire review because Mr. Brownson's criticism seems to reflect the Puritanic response of Hawthorne's time. According to the morality of his time, Brownson would have been absolutely correct in his condemnation of Hawthorne's looseness, were his allegory not addressing a higher Christian moral than the immorality of his characters—a moral more central to Christianity than the repugnance of sin, or the scorching rebuke of the sinner, as in the Puritanic view of life's existence. Were it not fowwr the higher meanings concealed in Hawthorne's allegory, Mr. Brownson's criticisms, to some pockets of our own modern society, would still be a viable and just commentary. However, far more objectionable literature, with no redeeming value whatsoever, is permitted in our society today; is meant to be explicitly understood; and, owing to the collective conscience of society, has fairly quartered its exposure and distribution to the public's divided segments.

Given the fact that the wording upon the gravestone over Hawthorne's famous novel seems to be chiseled in large letters, "Ambiguity, may it rest in peace," it is the opinion of this student that the multitude of Hawthorne's readers have been instructed by the few critics too long, and that it is time to appeal to those intuitions from their warmer heart. Perhaps it is time for its resurrection into a newness of life, that it may be seen and felt as it was intended.

Connection between "Deity and Mankind"

To undertake to write an explanation on the purpose of life and its problems, or to critique such, without regard to its origin and future, is like constructing an edifice without reference to its cornerstone or the purpose for which it was intended. That Hawthorne should attempt the same in *The Scarlet Letter*, and make no reference to that cornerstone, would debase the effort, the logic of which alone should prompt the critic to look deeper into Hawthorne's novel. To shut one's eyes to the role the Nazarene possibly played in the resolution of life's problems, and especially its sinfulness, from Hawthorne's point of view, would be a great oversight in trying to digest his tale. The various historical reactions of humankind to its own mortal weaknesses seem written upon its pages. And the symbols of red throughout whisper, if indeed they do not shout, against the blackness of man's puny interpretations to correct them, and recommend a a more worthy promise to the wary reader.

What Hawthorne seems to deplore most about Puritan heritage, which narrowly focused upon the sin of the sinner, the letter A on Hester's bosom, was that his ancestors seemed to have forgotten that one essential message of Christianity—redemption from sin by the Atonement—by not giving equal weight to its absolution by grace, mercy, and compassion. Those virtues, seemingly the intuitive purpose behind the beautiful and elaborate artifice embellished around the scarlet letter, were so characteristic of Hester, whose actions of community service portray paradoxically the intended office of the scarlet letter, that it is remarkable that the obvious seems to have been so adeptly overlooked. The mystery comes alive when we explore Hawthorne's philosophical self from the motive he so humbly embedded in his tale, to glorify his Maker, and therefore to be "serviceable to mankind" (10).

The connection between Dimmesdale, Pearl, and Hester appears to be the connection between "the Deity and the communities of mankind" (249), which is not only the very purpose of Dimmesdale's Election Sermon, but apparently the central theme of the novel. Whereas Pearl is the result of the connection between the other two, the transformed immortal appears to be the result of the connection between Deity and the communities of the human race; and Dimmesdale's image seems that very connection.

The very title of the sermon Dimmesdale preached, alone, suggests this connection. Whereas the Election sermon at the surface level refers to both the coming election of a new governor, and the sermon preached customarily during the festivities thereof, it also services the allegory. The fact that the text of the Election Sermon is not revealed in the slightest enhances the mystery; even the absense of a summary should perk the reader's curiosity. But to reveal the text of that sermon might unveil, or be, the very hidden message of the allegory itself.

Since Dimmesdale preached his Election Sermon on the eve of his demise, Hawthorne seems to play down the Christian doctrine of the elect in the climax to his allegory. Perhaps the brevity of his treatment intended only to highlight the connection between "the Deity and the communities of mankind," from the time of Adam and Eve to the millennium, rather than to insinuate the doctrine of predestination central in Puritanism. The doctrine of the Election, which purportedly unites a few with the Redeemer in the hereafter, may have been so monopolized by ecclesiastical interpretations that it seems highly sensitive of Hawthorne to give it brief reference.

To wit, perhaps it may have been the internalization of the doctrine of Election that induced the Puritan disciples to point their accusing finger so judgementally at the sinner, possibly with the subconscious motive: "The more I can exclude you from the inner circle of the chosen few, because your sins are now more public than mine, the more I am assured my chances of good standing, and being within that circle, at least in the eyes of those that matter." Or, "You're the sinner, and I'm the saved." Considering the number of churches in our times jockeying for an exclusive way to heaven, such an attitude among their members calls to mind Paul Harvey's tongue-in-cheek definition of a cult: "Your religion is a cult; mine's not." Most everyone wants to be a winner, to be on the inside, to be accepted. However, it is ironic, especially for the adherents of Christianity, that one's feeling of acceptance should lie in one's fanciful rejection of others, one of the aspects of religious hypocrisy Hawthorne seemed to decry.

If Hawthorne spoke for anything at all in his tale, he spoke for the unity of humankind, through a commom compassion, and for a graceful tolerance of our differences, until the day may come when we shall see eye to eye, and understand all things alike. He seemed to see that, in our present state of existence, we but dimly perceive what is going down, and stand in need of clarity, ironically.

THE CONFESSION

T he want of Confession, or acknowledgment of responsibility, with which some of the characters in the tale are distressed, centers around the question—who is responsible for the fathering of Pearl—and may represent the controversy of whether humankind was fathered by divine substance or its evil counterpart; thus whether it is basically good or evil in nature; and what destiny for it therefore may be prospective. On the surface, it might appear that societies are often somewhat less concerned about these philosophical ponderables than about economic security or leisurely enjoyment. But in each society there is a generation who fret their minds with such scientifically unanswerable questions, perhaps as a matter of identity, or concern about that destiny, or simply pure intellectual curiosity. Though much of our most popular fiction today is scientific in texture, or fantastic in theme, or sensational in appeal, where escape from reality harbors some comforting refuge, at the heart of our frantic dance with life there are those students who are given to ponder its unknowns.

As it was with Hawthorne. His novel appears to be a self-probing response, a covert expression of private meditations on the subject of life, perhaps a kind of public proclamation of those thoughts to those few who might understand and sympathize with them. We might even say, a type of confession, or self-revelation, as to where he leaned on certain subjects. He chose the allegory, colored with parables, metaphors, and as-if scenarios, as a vehicle to communicate those ideas. His devices might be weighed in view of his own sensitivities, his dimness caught in the need of a writer to seek an audience without being understood by every segment of its divided sentiments.

QUESTIONS FOR THE READER

Hawthorne asks provocative questions that point below the surface of the tale, seemingly for the purpose of whetting the reader's curiosity toward his allegorical meanings. The controversy as to Pearl's nature seems to reflect human society's controversary about our mortal nature, perhaps even to the extent of whether the material body is worthy of our being. Not too much thought has been given to the reverse of that question.

Hester, who may represent a civilization lost in religious exploits, does not seem to know whether Pearl is good or evil. Her intellectual confusion allows Hawthorne to raise questions in the mind of the reader who might be intuitively pursuing some deeper meaning to questions poised by his characters about her nature, and the principle it represents. Pearl and Hester may possibly also reflect Hawthorne's personal metaphysical beliefs (which refute a strong Puritan consciousness) about human nature and its association with Mother Nature. Hawthorne seems to want the reader to relate the divinity of Deity with the communities of humankind, perhaps to arrive at some allegorical conclusions similar to his own. In his novel, intuition upstages reasoning as a faculty more in tune with the spiritual domain and more accessible to its supernatural truths, and thus proffers a basic argument contrary to deism.

OUR CONNECTION WITH DEITY

If one will only pry into nature, so says the Romantic Hawthorne, he can discern truths of the greater spiritual reality. As humankind in general seems to sense some divine relationship with some Supreme Being, Pearl sensed something in Arthur Dimmesdale with which she felt some affinity. This relationship implies some destiny for the human family, the ultimate of which seems nebulous, and without too many specifics, even in the Christian's Holy Writ. The Christian community anticipates a time when some Almighty will begin some transition to a better world far removed from our own town, and, also perhaps, to Hawthorne, to explain his involvement in our present dilemma. To the Anti-transcendentalist Hawthorne, mortality is susceptible to influence from both dimensions of the spiritual world, as well as our own speculations about it; and this speculation appears to account for the shadow world of the Puritan consciousness. Without some manifest confession from our Creator—that some Goodness is the Author of our being, and that this mortal body may be ours to keep, perhaps as an instrument for some happy design—mankind, like Pearl, unless she yields to the intimations from the spiritual realm, is doomed to the throes of mere speculations about the purposes of life and its intended destiny.

The mortal, rational mind, influenced also by this black and dismal domain, according to the transcendentalist, may overwhelm the soul's intuitive awareness of its divine connections. Without a distinct insight or revelation of humankind's rooted connections with Deity, she seems bound to the despair of unenlightened and controversial religions. The dim Confession upon the scaffold by Dimmesdale appears to reveal somewhat that relationship at the allegorical level, and offers a hope for the future, though perhaps somewhat as dimly as Hawthorne projects it.

A CODE OF SILENCE

"The ban of silence lies on everyone in *The Scarlet Letter* . . . . The tale's center, then, lies less in the crime of sexual transgression than in the crime of silence" (Ragussis, p. 59). This ban on silence seems not only to hover over his novel, but seemingly also over any attempt to interpret it as a religious allegory.

Possibly Dimmesdale's silence closely parallels Hawthorne's "frozen and benumbed" thoughts cloaked in an imperspicuous allegory. Perhaps a little like Nickodemus, who was afraid to publicize his Christian faith, Hawthorne appears to have camouflaged, within his Romantic notions and literary style, his own religious beliefs, for only his sympathetic friends to understand. And perhaps, a little like Dimmesdale, who was fearful for his ministry's sake, he shrouded his inmost me in quasi-revelation to his own type of parishioners.

Dimmesdale justified his long silence on the basis that public knowledge of his responsibility for Hester's condition would negatively affect his ministry; that is, confession before the time would induce the tendency of human nature in his parishioners to shun their former allegiance to him, and lose confidence in what he taught, despite his fervid sensibilities. Neither does it appear, in the words of Dimmesdale, that Hawthorne believed that confession was necessarily a required function of retribution (131). Like Hester, on the balcony near the scaffold, for whom "it were wronging the very nature of woman to force her to lay open her heart's secrets in such broad daylight" (65), it seems that Hawthorne has somewhat justified Dimmesdale's silence on the matter.

Perhaps similarly inclined, the Biblical records do not contain any definitive statement as to any involvement with which Deity may accord itself in bringing about the Fall. There is little recorded to plainly declare that a plan was designed to set up the world so that there would be a Fall from immortality to mortality, that humankind's nature would be purposefully sinful, and that the consequences for those sins would be painful and miserable. It is likewise presumptive that Adam and Eve may have been placed in a double binded, impossible situation to bring about mortality in the Garden of Eden; that is, that they were given two commandments, one of which had to be broken in order to keep the other. That situation argues against unemcumbered agency, because they would not be free to choose obedience to both, and would be subject to direful consequences from the breach of one or the other.

However, the placement of the tree of the knowledge of good and evil in that Garden, rather than somewhere else on earth far from the reach of that Paradise, presupposes a plan for its use, like the sales strategy of impulse buying, by placing higher priced items, or unnecessary ones, within easy reach of the customer. Moreover, casting Lucifer out of heaven into the earth, rather than somewhere else in the universe, presupposes a similar purpose for his use later. In other words, given a First Cause, something about the mess the world is in implies design, or suggests that something is wrong about the whole matter, about which Hawthorne may have made at least one allegorical statement (84). (This statement is reviewed in detail in Section III.)

That the consequence of the Fall brought pain and misery, and may be good for us in the long run, is fairly openly stated in the words of Hester. In the indictment of all three in the fiasco, planned or not, the question of whether or not the Creator may have also held himself responsible somewhat for those consequences might have entered the mind of Hawthorne. Untimely confession for divine involvement in such a situation would have had self-defeating ramifications for Deity; silence therefor, therefore, seems justifiable on the basis that the outcome is good.

If the sensibilities of Deity, in the flesh, perhaps somewhat similar to those which Dimmesdale possessed, harbor such a sense of Divine Justice that begs such a universal and vicarious ordinance as the Atonement, then that act itself may speak, for Hawthorne, most effectively as a loud proclamation for accountability. In a keen sense of justice and mercy, wherein Deity may consider its involvement in the consequences of its actions, similarly as viable as he holds us accountable for ours, perhaps that Eternal Sacrifice of itself adjudicates Deity, if any is really needed. Perhaps Hawthorne thought that a confession of responsibility to the world of humanity may have been required for the setup in the Garden, and the consequence of mortality, even if it meant showing the "worst," or some inference of it (260).

That divine involvement in the creation of a mortal state of being, however, is only an implication by the props staged in the Garden of Eden. It seems purely an invented or intuitive conclusion possibly reached by Hawthorne, or, even worse, conjectured by the author of this analysis. However, the code of silence in his tale is broken by Dimmesdale's confession; coupled with his death, after an extended period of excruciating spiritual and physical pain, it appears additionally to be a redemption of some kind. At the allegorical level, the climax of Hawthorne's tale then appears to betoken the life, death, and Redemption of an Intermediary in behalf of the fallen nature of humankind.

Dimmesdale must therefore have remained a dim divine, and symbolically have foreborne giving this recognition or Confession as the Author of mortality, until a certain time, or else his ministry would have ended before its full effect. Indeed, in all reality, if Deity were to declare openly to the race of man that He was responsible for setting up the Fall of all nature, and the advent of corruptible and mortal flesh, before it was time for that revelation, perhaps that knowledge would have more of a disastrous that a beneficial effect upon humanity's ability to rationalize its behavior, or its institutions. (To Hawthorne, that tendency to rationalize, itself, may be responsible for the ineffectiveness of comtemporary religious institutions.) After all, what accountability would one assume for one's own mistakes if the Supreme Being were held responsible for the nature that led to them in the first place?

Perhaps his silence on this subject of responsibility for human nature has its justification in the fact that the mortal mind has its limitations, as well as its inclinations to rationalize its departure from periods of enlightenment. History, in repeating its social mistakes, appears to support that general propensity among nations. Perhaps Hawthorne accepted this silence, unlike past readers' rejection of Dimmesdale's, on the basis of faith in a perfect Omnipotent, who may have only laid a foundation sufficient for such faith, the ultimate end of which the details might not have been understood so clearly anyway.

A TABERNACLE OF FLESH

Hawthorne seems to justify Providential action, or the non-action of silence, on the basis of the assumed infallibility of Deity. When Dimmesdale bared his breast upon the scaffold, some saw the emblem of his suffering, some saw something else, and some saw nothing at all. This variety of different observations could represent the varying degrees of insight the residents of a community as large as the world may have toward the message of the Redemption, or the varying effects it has upon them, or both. He appears to imply that when the Redeemer (symbolized by the divine, Dimmesdale) wrought out the Redemption of fallen nature (Hester) upon the cross, he did it because he was the Creator or Author of "infant immortality" in its mortal form.

It seems that human nature, rational or otherwise, because of its tabernacle, chooses to believe what it prefers to believe, and that our preferences seem based upon our individual desires more than upon past or present enlightenment. To Hawthorne, intuition moderates the effect of those desires upon the mind and heart by the latter's ability to tap into supernatural radiations. In Hawthorne's novel, these radiations utilize Christian theology to cast a spell upon the reader to pry into his tale to catch a glimpse of his phisolophical urges.

To the Christian, the theology of the redemption apparently has two effects. Firstly, it removes the effects of mortality by promise of an unconditional renewal or return for all humankind to a previous state of existence, which is similar to the paradisiacal glory of the earth, like the Garden of Eden before the Fall. This is the better world to which perhaps Pearl has allegorically gone, a renewal of which is signified intuitively by the scarlet letter to Hester, Pearl, and Dimmesdale. Immortality was a gift taken away by the Fall, and a gift to be returned at the resurrection. The allegory of Hawthorne's tale allegedly retells the story of this Fall, hints at the renewal, arrays the different views about that story held by the "communities of mankind," and suggests Hawthorne's own possible meditations, as a hidden autobiographical appendage.

Secondly, in that creed, there is hope of a bright resurrection. For most Christians, it is the resurrection of the body that validates the significance of mortality, establishes the worth of the material body, and compensates the loss of deathless life in the Garden of Eden; and it is the redemption that determines the future state of existence for resurrected beings. It is perhaps Pearl's blessed state that justifies Hester's sacrifice for it, and it is perhaps symbolized by the sunken grave besides Hester's. Hawthorne seems to address symbolically the message of his novel to both of these future effects, against the gloomy background of his Puritan past. The scarlet letter becomes the key, or the focus, for the allegory to unfold a message that seems absent or missing in Puritanism, or perhaps all contemporary institutionalized religions. The Puritan concentration upon the depravity of mortal flesh, rather than upon the mercy and compassion of the Being that created it, and redeemed it, is the sable field for that crimson promise. Dimmesdale's confession and redemption seem to symbolize a kind of seal to that promise, as do the "armorial bearings" surrounding his and Hestor's grave site.

Thus the reader may sense something royal, lofty, and holy about Hawthorne's tale, and remain transfixed in a kind of wonderment that is serviceable to his most intuitive moments. Could not this wonderment alone, then, be Hawthorne's intent to glorify his Creator?

CODE OF SILENCE

Now that the reader may comprehend Hawthorne's concerns about the destiny of mortal existence, we have a groundwork laid to explore further the possible religious conclusions he has so silently concealed in his novel, perhaps because of their seemingly unorthodox nature. Perhaps a review or summary of the symbols of the scarlet letter in connection with certain moments of passion is first in order before we attempt to break that code.

MOMENTS OF PASSION

A question of heterodoxy might rear its ugly head in the supposition that Hawthorne allegedly may have accounted theologically for the mess, or the "mesh of good and evil," which the present world is now in, although it was initially created perfect and paradisiacal, according to the Biblical rendition. Whenever and whatever composed the passionate moment of Hester and Dimmesdale's first meeting might to the Romantic be analogous to the passionate epoch of the creation in which the divine invested itself in nature. Perhaps the mural by Michelangelo in the Sistine Chapel best illustrates pictorially this passionate moment of the creation of man and woman from the elements of the earth. Hawthorne may have conceived the creation of passionate bodies for Adam and Eve as possibly one of the two passionate moments for Deity, as mentioned in Hawthorne's tale.

Another passionate moment is the Act of the Redemption, in certain circles referred to as The Passion of Christ, the Nazarene. Dimmesdale makes his confession for his responsibility for Pearl in a moment of passion as the result of an apparent revelation given to him to be shared with his parishioners. As Dimmesdale thus had to fulfill the office of the scarlet letter, symbolically, Hawthorne has thus purportedly proposed that a heavenly confession was needed to account for the responsibility Deity may have had in engineering the Fall. That confession, however vague, ended the code of silence on the part of heaven, which, by voicing to the world, in an excruciating manner, the worst inferred by such, thus fulfilled its office. This confession was perhaps offered by his emissary, Dimmesdale, to symbolically implicate the act of the Redemption of mortal nature wrought out by the Christian's Nazarene.

There was a time set for this confession apparently, according to the time frame of the tale. That time frame corresponds to the meridian of time, when time was divided between B. C. and A. D., when the Creator met the demands of Justice in what may perhaps be accorded, in the annuls of Christianity, as the most merciful, passionate, and centrifugal moment in eternity. Dimmesdale's climatic passionate moment upon the scaffold may have been meant to reflect the agony of a redemption from the passion that resulted in the creation of Pearl, an "infant immortality," representative of humankind. The role of Creator and Redemptor seem essentially a compound in one, in which the latter was a consequential counterpart of the former.

THE SCARLET LETTER A

The scarlet letter A, in red stripes, upon Hester's grave stone, appears to herald the bright promise of her Redemption; has been necessarily attached to Hester, just as indelibly as the nature of the Fall; and is beautifully and hopefully embroidered upon her bosom to signify something more significant than some logical speculation. The effect of this Redemption, foreshadowed and contracted during the meridian of times, appears to be symbolically foreshadowed and contracted when Pearl was three years of age, at the time Dimmesdale made his midnight vigil. The effect of that Redemption would take place at the end of the earth's seven thousand years, that is, as symbolized by some time after Pearl left Boston in her seventh year. Though Hawthorne seemed to leave the allegory open ended, as to whether Hester and Dimmesdale were ever united again, following their burial, he twice made reference to Dimmesdale's sunken grave, perhaps to further cue the intuitive reader toward Hawthorne's own leanings.

The letter A gules upon the black field on Hester and Dimmesdale's tombstone possibly represent, more than anything else, the promise of a better world through a retransformation of mortal nature. It is perhaps displayed in the red roses upon the prison door that may herald some redemption for all who come forth from Puritan indoctrination, or similar "customs" and conventions. This promise seems figured in the beautiful scarlet letter embellished upon Hester's bosom, and in the like dress that Pearl herself wears, as though she is inheritly the owner of the promise. It may be reflected in the red roses in Governor Bellingham's garden that brighten the decaying mansion, the latter possibly symbolic of an ecclesiastical government in the throes of dissolution. The guarantee of its effects also appear symbolized in the red stripes of the bloody scourge with which Dimmesdale inflicts himself voluntarily, similarly as the Nazarene expected and accepted his scourging and crucifixion ("with his stripes we are healed"[1]). Eaten by Pearl, it is possibly tasted in the red partridge-berries, lying upon withered leaves, that, in a flood of sunshine, illumine the prospects of a resurrection from the grasps of death. So this promise is likely foreshadowed in the red gules or stripes on a black field embossed upon the gravestone at the head of "an old and sunken grave" (264). For all its promises, the scarlet letter A may also stand for the father of Pearl, the divine, the Author of life in the resurrection, as symbolized by Arthur's sunken, empty grave.

THE SUBJECT OF *THE SCARLET LETTER*

Hawthorne reveals rather directly the subject or objective of his allegory. That objective seems almost identical to the subject of Dimmesdale's Election Sermon. One line in Chapter 23, "The Revelation of the Scarlet Letter," reveals that "[h]is subject, it appeared, had been the relation between the Deity and the communities of mankind, with a special reference to the New England which they were here planting in the wilderness" (249). That relation between Deity and humankind might be the latter's creation and the Providential Plan of its Fall and Redemption, as absolution from the Fall's crimson effects. The special background reference to the black Puritan experiment with Christianity in early America, may symbolize all such speculative adventures void of a comprehensive compassion for the nature of the human mortal.

In summary, Hawthorne's message seems to suggest that the Redemptive promise is the one beautifully designed blood-ripe Act meant to be emblazoned on the compassionate heart as a ray of hope against the blackness of mortality as painted by his Puritanic fathers. Perhaps as red as the spilt blood of the Nazarene, in a world ruled mostly by darkness, the letter A also may signify an "ever-glowing point of light gloomier than the shadow" (264). Perhaps Hawthorne, as remnant of his Puritan heritage, envisioned contrary consequences for those not "showing how sacred love should make us happy," and for failing to pass "the truest test of a life successful to such an end!" (263) Perhaps their future state might not be too far from Salem, or far gloomier than any shadow cast by the black Puritan consciousness. However, in Hawthorne's short essay on love and hate in his last chapter, he seems to have modified this Puritan perspective with a more liberal cast on the future state of humankind, perhaps to redeem his own slight Puritan consciousness, when even its "earthly stock of hatred and antipathy [may be] transmuted into golden love" (261). If Chillingworth may have hope, then there is hope for the rest of the human family.

MUTUALLY EXCLUSIVE OBEDIENCE

With this review, the reader is now set to confront the same dilemma perhaps many deep thinkers have contemplated when considering the situation posed in the Garden of Eden. In that Garden, where the Creator put his new creation to dress and keep it, there seems to have been but two laws given in this state of paradise: multiply and fill the earth, but do not partake of the tree of knowledge of good and evil. In their state of innocence, could their obedience to one have excluded obedience to the other? Could they have kept the first injunction had they not transgressed the second? Could their act of transgressing the law, marked by an absence of a knowledge of good and evil, be considered a sin, in the Christian ethic, when they were innocently ignorant or incompletely aware of the full consequences of their choice? Was their agency free, or unencumbered without dire consequences, if a choice of obeying one commandment mutually excluded obedience to the other: was it really justifiable to place Adam and Eve in a Catch-22 situation? Reason alone, in considering the reasonableness and motives of the Creator in setting up the situation in the Garden as he did, might dismiss the Biblical text as a concoction without rational basis. Perhaps these questions, or similar, might have led Hawthorne to wonder if something went wrong there, or conclude some divine purpose in the degeneration that followed, and therefore have fostered his use of the allegory to conceal private thoughts about the matter.

If Adam and Eve had continued in the Garden, without any foul play from lower quarters, and begat other little innocents running about as gleeful as Pearl, the rest of us would probably have been just as content with the status quo; but, owing to subtlety and the thirst for revenge in the nature of some, Eve's curiosity, or discontent, beat down any constraints her innocence might have harbored. Consequently, in the Christian world, the wretchedness of this creation, which is probably one of the greatest stumbling block for the purely rational fellow, began at the time of the fall of nature into a state of mortality.

Familiar with the Biblical text, Hawthorne may have proposed some conclusions to deal with his own rational discontent: that the Creator of this mortal world was its Redeemer because he was also involved in its creation, and that a better world, because of the experiences of this one, is in the making to compensate for them. This conclusion—that the Creator of this world and the chief engineer of its fall into mortality may hold himself accountable for its present state of existence, and thus was the Chosen one to work out the Atonement—seems a natural consequence of the themes and questions Hawthorne has cautiously juxtapositioned in his tale. The explicit revelation of such in his time might have justified his Christian inclinations, but may have earned him far more scorn and rebuke than he received for allegedly authoring a "sex novel." How this conclusion may be considered in our own day and time remains to be seen, as heretofore no such statement has ever been publicly made, either in regard to the possible meanings of Hawthorne's allegory, or, to the knowledge of this purveyor, by any Christian apologist of which he is aware.

This seemingly heterodoxical conclusion that Hawthorne may be presenting under cover lies in the possibility that Dimmesdale's confession upon the scaffold may reflect part of the role and mission Providence had laid out for his Divine Emissary as a way of redeeming both Deity and humankind. As the admission of Deity's responsibility is dimly connected with that Redemption, so is Dimmesdale's confession upon the scaffold dimly connected with his redemption.

HERESY APPARENT

Perhaps then, Hawthorne may have given us a private interpretation of an additional reason for the Redemption; and private interpretations are allowable, at least until some higher standard or authority dictates otherwise, gives adequate reason therefor, and thus inclines us to accept their certitude without further regard for our own. Hawthorne's private ideas, then, of the Creator's particular sensitivity to our conditions here, his uncommon sense of justice, and therefore his own personal accounting for the fall, may lie at the bottom of Hawthorne's allegory. And to be true to himself, presumably in behalf of Hawthorne, his sympathetic friend has openly declared the possible worse, or at least, shown "some trait whereby the worst may be inferred!" But it also behooves him, insofar as it is in his power to do so, to redeem the both of us from the outcry of blasphemy by declaring it as only apparent.

To begin therewith, to wonder if the Christian Deity is responsible, even partially, for our earthly sorrows and inclinations, is not the same as declaring him irresponsible in the same. The latter would appear more obviously as profane, if the nature of a person were so inclined to venture it. To label any presumption associating Cause with some effect as suspect has not the same justifiable force as that against a statement of the same. Hawthorne appears to make few definite statements on anything, but seems only to insinuate or ponder such, and is therefore entirely off the hook. On the other hand, that the purveyor of this analysis may have knowingly unearthed, or created, what some might deem a sacrilege, from the depths of Hawthorne's burial place in his tale, might seemingly make him more responsible for its utterance than the presumption itself. Howbeit, as it is the objective of an allegory to reverse one's opinion or attitude toward its characters, it appears it was Hawthorne's intent, as it has been his friend's, to have his tale told, not to the defamation of, but to the glory of his Maker.

In addition, labeling anything heretical is a judgment call which should be measured against some standard of truth. Since there may be few, if any, Biblical statements to the effect that Providence was not involved in the fall of immortality into mortality, that Deity was not responsible in any way for that mortality, or that he had no such design in planning the progressive stages of humankind that included the necessity of mortality, technically Hawthorne's conclusion, if such were the case, cannot be rightfully declared a heresy: there is no standard by which to make such a judgment; and his opinion, or any other, including that of this exegesis, is as debatable as any. At worst, it is a logical speculation that might upset the reader's paradigm or configuration of Deity. At best, it might explain the paradox of life and define the Creator's compassionate sensitivity to our situation here; that is, until some additional documentation, or revelation by some "prophetess," is unearthed to confirm the contrary.

Since there technically is no definitive Biblical statement regarding whether or not Deity holds itself responsible for mortality, seemingly a conclusion contrary to his nature, and perhaps few bold enough to declare equal qualification to clarify the issue, it may be justly adduced a matter of conjecture, and left to what one chooses to make sense out of life's experiences. It does seems consistent, however, for the Christian in particular, to hold the view that the perfection of the Almighty forbids any weakness of judgment or absence of foreknowledge on his part: that he is granted to be all-knowing, all-powerful, and everywhere-present underlines the faith that no mistake was made in the Creation or the Fall. That view presupposes the necessity of the Fall, some inexplicable benefit of mortality in humanity's future destiny, and perhaps even the eternal significance of pain and agony in the scheme of his one eternal round.

It can perhaps be stated fairly that respect for another's opinion is probably as due as is reverence for Deity, no matter which God, non-god, or philosophy one may worship; and the appearance of blasphemy may rest solely in the mind of the beholder. If that mind is equal to the Supreme's, then this explicator bows to it; but he at least would like One as well as the other to stand in as witnesses for or against. That it may be considered heretical to state a cause and effect relationship between the Creation, the Fall, and the Atonement, may grow out of our ignorance of the Creator; and his thinking on the matter has been alleged to be a little higher than our own, save for the few who grant themselves equally gifted.

Therefore, a heresy may be only a state of mind when there is no authorized doctrinal standard revealed against which it can be measured, and becomes an epistemological matter of who does the defining. For that matter, since most cling to their beliefs as they cling to their lives, one regulating the other, perhaps some definitions are structured to suit what a particular audience is likely to choose to believe.

In any case, inasmuch as it is the nature of heresy to promote schism or dissension, although division can be created without it, this layman wishes to make it clear that it is not his intent to sow seeds of contention, nor is it his hope that this analysis will be interpreted as his own beliefs. Perhaps his greatest fear is that his conclusions, or the interpretations of an overworked imagination on his part, could be considered more that mere speculation on his or Hawthorne's part. It is not his desire to do damage to the public mind, but to redeem it from prior prejudices.

Nevertheless, the author of this analysis has labeled this one implication as heterodoxical for the purpose of diminishing in the mind of the reader the possible personal impact of such a conclusion. Rather the reader reject his analysis flippantly, capriciously or squeamishly, either a far better recourse, despite possible agreement with every other logical premise, than to let such a conclusion register as a truth, alter his/her happy life, and, thus, in some measure, disavow "the truest test of a life successful to such an end!" After all, in the long run, it may only be fodder for the critic or the curious student, a conversation piece at best, a red herring at worst.

As points to consider, but not in debate here, since we do not really know anything definite about the mind and motives of Deity, other than what is somewhat revealed in Holy Writ, we do not know if some prior or premortal existence compounds the question of what life is all about here. Insofar as everything existential may need vindication in a day so far removed from life's origins, the quandary, as it always has been, remains contingent upon our satisfactions with explanations of our existence. Neither do we know what pains Deity may endure for and in behalf of his creations, or because of them, or whether the law of vicarious sacrifice is either a temporary or an eternal law in the rounds of Deity. Indeed, we may know little or nothing at all, but what we think or believe we know.

Whether we are mere animals or children of a Supreme Creator, each vying for a better life in the sun, our differing beliefs appear to revolve around our inmost desires, our inmost Me. And Hawthorne's beliefs, however sacredly quartered, seem to hold fairer prospects for humankind that his readers have heretofore realized. Whatever our predelictions, as various as they may be—the evidence for which are the innumerable interpretations of existing Biblical documents, the various denominations that brandish them, and all other controversial philosophies to the contrary—Hawthorne would transmute them all to a more compassionate end than what the ever-flowing Puritan stream of consciousness, or their offshoots, may have conjured.

What perhaps matters most is the ultimate end. If, by design, this life being necessary to a better, though it entails a temporary life of misery and pain preparatory for such, then by its end the means used by Deity can be hallowed justifiable. To connect a Cause with the end, and to authenticate the end as beneficial, neither imputes ignorance nor malice to the one responsible for the cause. Indeed, on the other hand, it instead hallows and consecrates both the means and the ends. In the end, it exonerates the Cause, and makes it an object more worthy of loyalty, love, and devotion. However, we mortals might be very cautious in claiming right to this same standard. To concede perfection in the immortal Creator, in contrast with our own mortality, presupposes our inability to justify our means to some earthly end, both of which we may have conceived in our imperfections. Not knowing the justice of a perfect Being, by the means he uses to bring about an end better than its beginning, might render baseless any judgment call on the cause or causes of all our troubles.

The Christian conscience, fighting to maintain consonance with an appreciation of Hawthorne as a literary genius, perhaps moreso than the literary critic guarding the hallowed halls of Hawthorne's obscurity, might then need to be somewhat conditioned to suspend judgment on the matter, until more evidence is forthcoming. Perhaps other more arduous students of Hawthorne may suggest other alternative explanations, launch altogether different expositions of his mystery, and offer the reader a far more satisfying experience. It would appear that anything is better than maintaining a conundrum, or worse, consecrating his novel forever as enigmatic. There should be no sanctions on free thought, that is, until some apparition of Hawthorne, or more enlightened Daniel, should appear and set us all straight.

Favorable to this purveyor's perspective, then, is the prospect that Dimmesdale's confession, and possibly his redemption, underlies perhaps the central theme of Hawthorne's tale, that the nature of humankind, despite its harrowing pains and sufferings, has a significant destiny worthy of its continued existence, once it has undergone a transformation sufficient to achieve it. If the Fall can be seen as a blessing for humankind, rather than as a divine experiment gone awry, then Hawthorne's conclusions may not be viewed so narrowly, but as an explanation that implicitly hallows the purpose of mortality. Though a code of silence pales the shadow of Hawthorne's philosophical Me, the full impact of his allegory appears to do honor to his belief in the Creator of the human species.

Hawthorne's tale, therefore, seems to echo his possible faith in the plan of Providence to establish and resolve the purpose and plight of mortality. For any who may have entertained some measure of distaste in Hawthorne's tale, it is the hope of this layman that he or she may now have a redeemed view of Hawthorne. The burden of that redemption is left mainly to the chapter-by-chapter analysis of allegorical themes, which first needed to be properly quartered. Hopefully the proposed interpretations rendered by this purveyor's impressions will have, at least, little more than the stirrings of the reader's imagination, or, at most, a greater desire to explore the depths of Hawthorne's mysterious novel, as attempted in Section III. His explorations have heightened his regard for Hawthorne, given him a greater appreciation for his own Christian heritage, and transformed the twain into a pleasant sharing of them.

SECTION III

The previous essays have been centered on the interpretations Bayinhund has proposed as the meanings of the allegory, somewhat in relation to our time, of which Hawthorne seemed hopeful. In Section II, Bayinhund has referred to a few of the parables and metaphors without pinpointing their content in full detail. Section III contains Bayinhund's analysis of each allusion, chapter by chapter, and page by page, with reference to the Centenary Edition of *The Scarlet Letter*. Again we note that the analysis of each chapter is preceded by a quotation that could contain the essence of Hawthorne's thinking, around which each chapter might possibly pivot.

The use of the royal "we" throughout our text implies the measure of cooperation with which I have modified Bayinhund's wording of thoughts for this publication. It may no less include my recognition of Mr. Who, for whose incessant energy I am doubly grateful, inasmuch as something has helped my memory retrieve many of the details that may have been otherwise lost. Use of the first person, in Daniel's behalf, may only indicate that I did not wish to be particularly alligned with Bayinhund's declarations, the didactic nature of which and from which I have discretely tried to position myself some great distance, much like Hawthorne enjoyed disassociating himself from Mr. Surveyor Pue.

SECTION II.

THE CUSTOM HOUSE–INTRODUCTORY

Eat thou not the bread of him that hath an evil eye,
neither desire thou his dainty meats:
For as he thinketh in his heart, so is he.[1]

Having proposed an interpretation of Hawthorne's allegory that further unveils the hidden mystery of the scarlet letter, we now turn to each chapter to show how the imagery in Hawthorne's novel, page by page, supports an analysis of the religious themes he entertained in his allegory. Otherwise, it would be remiss to espouse an interpretation without attempting a detailed configuration of the many symbols and hints to justify such.

THE EFFECTS OF PURITANISM

Heart, crimson as scarlet, has everything to do with the themes woven into Hawthorne's tale, and having heart appears to differentiate among the characters the degree to which Hawthorne esteems their connection with the universal heart, the deep heart of Nature, "the universal impulse which makes likewise one vast heart out of the many" (250). Compassion and grace are also threaded into the central imagery of the scarlet letter, which is embellished and placed over Hester's bosom, fashioned upon Pearl's attire, etched upon the breast of Dimmesdale, and perhaps voluntarily self-inflicted in red gules upon his back.

Assuming the validity of our interpretation of the main theme of his tale, the characters in the custom house appear to be not only broad representations of cross-sections of Puritan humanity but also appear to show reflections and various manifestations of the effects of Puritanism upon its followers. On the wane, this impact appears to be the fading vestiges of that religious order established earlier in America,

> I was led to conclusions in reference to the effect of public office on the character, not very favorable to the mode of life in question. In some other form, perhaps, I may hereafter develop these effects. Suffice it here to say, that a Custom-House officer, of long continuance, can hardly be a very praiseworthy or respectable personage, for many reasons; one of them, the tenure by which he holds his situation, and another, the very nature of his business, which–though, I trust, an honest one–is of such a sort that he does not share in the united effort of mankind. (38).

The characters are described in relation to the center theme of compassionate redemption, and more than likely refer to no particular historical figure Hawthorne knew during his tenure as a surveyor for Uncle Sam in Salem, unless some of his associates there possessed attributes he wanted to embody in his characters, with "a few extra touches" (4), to represent those cross-sections. These officers of the Custom-House, as well as the main characters of his tale, were probably as much a product of Hawthorne's humor and imagination as the tale itself, wherein he allowed himself "nearly or altogether as much license as if the facts had been entirely of my own invention" (33).

The characters of the officers may reflect the various traits of character which the theology and practice of Puritanism possibly embodied in its adherents, especially its tenured ecclesiastical leaders. They were perhaps honest in their faithful execution of their harsh penalties for disobedience, but missed the mark if their efforts were not united with the universal heart of humankind. What form of personality and the attributes each of the characters possess seem, to Hawthorne, to be determined by what thoughts and motives lay in their hearts toward human nature, and toward their fellowmen, with whom they were not so well united in spirit. Dominated by the tenets of Puritanism, every officer, and probably many a devoted disciple, were fated to eventually engage in heartless practices, resulting in a joyless life, should their association with that faith continue for any extended length of time. The more compassionate the disciple, the more amenable to repentance, the more worthy of grace, and perhaps, the more evident of "the truest test of a life successful to such an end" of happiness (263).

> It is a pious consolation to me, that, through my interference, a sufficient space was allowed them for repentance of the evil and corrupt practices, into which, as a matter of course, every Custom-House officer must be supposed to fall. Neither the front nor the back entrance of the Custom-House opens on the road to Paradise. (12)

The gist of this quotation, with its preceding commentary on the characters of the custom house, seems to be that, because a heart without compassion is sullied by the blackness of Puritanic sovereignty, the custom house officers (Puritan leaders), and possibly its strongest adherents, will be hard pressed to enter the gates of heaven.

Hawthorne also appeared to view the younger generation of Puritan ecclesiasticals less contaminated by Puritanism that the older generation, "who ought to have given place to younger men, more orthodox in politics, and altogether fitter than themselves to serve our common Uncle" (13), or Uncle Sam. "Uncle" may possibly refer analogically to the Heavenly Uncle, whom the Puritan officials presumed to be serving. The orthodoxy of the younger generation, to Hawthorne, may be a refining improvement over the older, perhaps reverting back more identically to "ancient prejudices" than did the speculative adventure of Puritanism (164). This view probably paralleled Hawthorne's hope that the younger generations of Christianity would undergo a transformation for the better in the service of their Deity. Orthodoxy of religion seems also, then, though a major one for Protestantism in its attempts to reform its roots, to be a minor and corollary theme in his tale, and may correspond to his reference to "ancient prejudices."

Hawthorne, as a distant descendant further removed from his roots, perhaps viewed himself, in his capacity as surveyor, as a judge responsible to separate from employment those who were guilty of corruption. However, those who were inefficient but "excellent old persons," were allowed to remain, since they could do little harm. Hawthorne may then be seen as the circumspect hero, at least, of the Custom House.

Another Attempt, Another Failure

To Hawthorne, the American experiment in Puritanism, with its effect of gloom and despair, because of its depiction of mortal flesh as depraved and evil, was a miserable failure. His allegorical tale reveals his hopes that the future holds a better reformation for the welfare of the human family. This future might lie in the hands of these younger officials, or their progeny, who were "in their strength and prime, of marked ability and energy, and altogether superior to the sluggish and dependent mode of life on which their evil stars had cast them" (16). These younger coadjutors, possible contemporaries of Hawthorne, who inherited their Puritanism from the older ecclesiasticals, hopefully would not succumb to its parasitical lethargy as did the older officials, some of whom, to judge by way of Hawthorne's characterization in this chapter, had lost their spiritual depths.

Nothing Personal

It has been said that Hawthorne sought to castigate his fellow officers because he was bitter over losing his post as surveyor. Before writing his novel, Hawthorne lost his appointment as surveyor in the Salem Custom House as a result of a change in the national power structure. Critics have assumed he was bitter and reproachful with the citizens of Salem, who perhaps would have supported him had he taken a partisan course in his office and been more community-minded. The darkness and gloom of his tale is also assumed to reflect the death of his mother about this same time. It is certain he therefore finished his novel during a very dark hour in his life. Thus some critics have suggested that his attitude toward the officers of the Custom House was an overreaction to his bitterness towards them.

However, in his preface to the second edition, , Hawthorne expressed amusement with some of this criticism during his time, disclaimed any personal or political enmity or ill-feeling, and was "constrained, therefore, to republish his introductory sketch without the change of a word" (Preface, 3). Once the whole of Hawthorne's tale is views as an allegory, the characters in the Custom House seem to be only allegorical figures and not personal reflections. It is more probable that Hawthorne's descriptions of the officers are themselves allegorical representatives of Puritan degeneracy rather than of any particular acquaintances he really knew at the Custom House. Himself given the tendency to associate with a class of people seemingly out of his element, it is highly unlikely Hawthorne would blatantly and hypocritically have lied about his motives in that later preface. Since he purported to have liked all the Custom-House characters (15), probably with the exceptions of the ones he fired, his characters therefore bore no personal reflections to his former fellows Salem.

Moreover, the success of his novel, written after he lost the political post, would have been grounds enough for him to have been more honest about his motives in that preface. To him, the loss of the post was a Godsend, which he realized later, although at the time of the loss he did try to get his friends to salvage the position for him. Yet, Hawthorne refused to appease his critics perhaps because it was the allegory he was communicating and not just an historical or autobiographal sketch. As he said, "What I contend for is the authenticity of the outline" (33). That outline appears to be the allegory itself that refers to authentic historical events, for which he contended, though mysteriously, yet most eloquently, according to this purveyor.

FROZEN IN TIME

Hawthorne wrote meaning into the tale by "freezing" it in a mystical allegory. He explained his reasons for hiding himself in the pages of his book "when he [cast] his leaves upon the wind," and indicated he did not think it fit for writers to "indulge themselves in such confidential depths of revelation." Personal intimations may be too private to openly share with a public not inclined to receive them.

> It is scarcely decorous, however, to speak all, even where we speak impersonally. But–as thoughts are frozen and utterance benumbed . . . it may be pardonable . . . to prate of the circumstances that lie around us, and even of ourself, but still keep the inmost Me behind its veil. To this extent and within these limits, an author, methinks, may be autobiographical. (1)

Thus, Hawthorne's utterence of his philosophical ideas was properly benumbed by not revealing too much too openly about himself: he had something to hide, reasons for hiding it, and had devised an astute method of doing so, which required something on the part of the reader—"let us call it intuition" (124)—to melt those frozen thoughts.

It is noted that the narrator had not read the papers at the time he placed the scarlet letter upon his heart, much like the reader at this point of the narration has not yet finished reading Hawthorne's tale, and therefore could not yet interpret the deeper meanings. The implication seems to be that his first, rudimentary reading in the custom house, where his literary talents were dead, or frozen, could not fathom the deep meaning of the scarlet letter A that Hester had intuitively embellished so beautifully. Perhaps Hawthorne also is hinting that the reader may not be disposed to understand the deep meaning of the scarlet letter at first. There are many clues to the reader also that he may need a little intuition to sense something beyond the boundaries of normal intellectual sensitivity in order to transcend the realities to which the rational mind cleaves.

A PHILOSOPHICAL AUTOBIOGRAPHY

The "autobiographical impulse" Hawthorne refers to and explains in his introduction of his novel seems to deal more with his philosophical self than any description of his associates or real events that took place during his three years tenure in the Custom House. It seems that he was prating about the circumstances surrounding him, as an allusion to authentic history, and not about his real associates, to touch rather upon his philosophical or religious thoughts and conclusions than to embarrass previous acquaintances. To have softened or modified his character descriptions would have defeated or diluted the strength of his allegory. Hawthorne wished to reveal "the inmost Me behind its veil" (1), but seemingly only to his sympathetic friends, who may have had similar insights. Perhaps this motivation inspired his literary style in the use of the allegory to convey his own private meditations of "antique customs . . . going back, perhaps, to the days of the Protectorate" (29).

Hawthorne's tale presented his private or autobiographical thoughts, howbeit undercover, about the mode of life of Puritans, the impact their religion had upon their character, and the basis for his hope of a better, transformed society. He described that impact of gloom, despair, and joyless drudgery in contrast to that hope, beginning with a background of darkness, as perhaps reflected in the Custom-House, and building to a central point of light. The "few extra touches" he gives to his description may also refer to his humorous understatements pointing to this contrast.

> [I]t has appeared allowable, by a few extra touches, to give a faint representation of a mode of life not heretofore described, together with some of the characters that move in it, among whom the author happened to make one. (2)

It is very doubtful that the foolscap sheets of the posthumous papers, upon which Hester's story is purportedly written, ever existed in reality, and none but one of the characters, himself, was probably real. As the narrator of his tale, Hawthorne is referring to himself as one of the particular, second-person characters in the novel "he happened to make;" and that character is probably Mr. Surveyor Pue. Hawthorne identifies the Loco-foco Surveyor as a Democrat who, like himself, was swept out of office by political reform.

THE LOCO-FOCO SURVEYOR

Hawthorne covertly identified himself as the same person as the Loco-foco Surveyor in the beginning and at the end of his tale of the Custom House. He had written "The Old Manse" after emerging from that place, a short story about his life in the Old Manse, where he spent the beginning of his marriage, and yet was unsuccessful there in producing the novel he desired. Hawthorne again purported to write about himself after emerging from the Custom House, having met with the same failure there. There Hawthorne had conceived the ideas around which he wished to write *The Scarlet Letter*, but had been powerless to compose them (26, 34). Having lost the post of Surveyor with perhaps some slight trepidation, he was then able to write.

"Loco-foco" describes Hawthorne's political alignment as a Democrat among many Whigs in the Custom House. It also is an obsolete term meaning, "a friction match," perhaps posing the friction between Hawthorne's needing that post and not being able to write as a writer while he was there. In a sense, Hawthorne, "the inmost Me," and the Surveyor were a friction match.

He described the proper setting for a Romantic, or, more likely, an Anti-transcendentalist, to be able to easily capture the ideas and compose them, one aspect of which included moonlight instead of sunshine (35,36). The ideal writing circumstances included removing himself

> farther from the actual, and nearer to the imaginative. Then at such an hour, and with this scene before him, if a man, sitting all alone, cannot dream strange things, and make them look like truth, he need never try to write romances. (36)

The implication of this passage, and others, might be that his novel is a romance created from Hawthorne's own imagination and designed around some authentic historical source. Hawthorne's romance between Hester and Dimmesdale, as purported by the purveyor, is an allegory of the Creator's passionate romance with the elements, showing "a relation between the Deity and the communities of mankind" (249).

Hawthorne matched his experience in the Old Manse with his experience in the Custom House, and identifed the author of both as being one and the same person. In describing the office of the Old Surveyor during his tour in the Custom House, Hawthorne tells the reader that

> you might have recognized, honored reader, the same individual who welcomed you into his cheery little study, where the sunshine glimmered so pleasantly through the willow branches, on the western side of the Old Manse. But now, should you go thither to seek him, you would inquire in vain for the Loco-foco Surveyor. The bisom of reform has swept him out of office . . . . (8)

Surveyor Pue allegedly reported the story of Hester Prynne, which Hawthorne purportedly found in the attic of the Custom House; and the ghost of the decapitated Surveyor appeared to Hawthorne and extracted the promise from him to bring the story of Hester Prynne before the public (33, 43).

The ghost of Mr. Surveyor Pue seems to be Hawthorne's own consciousness, an alter ego or former state of mind, encouraging him to present the tale of Hester Prynne, her scarlet letter, and her associates, so as to prosper him in the stead of the custom house's position he had lost. Without any source of income, and upon the revival of his literary inclinations by the loss of his post, his mind naturally turned to writing again. Apparently, the ideas for *The Scarlet Letter* had been reflected upon during his tenure as a surveyor in Salem. Hawthorne may have been sidetracking the reader in posing a monetary motive for writing the tale, but the allegory message seems to be the underlying motive.

> "Do this," said the ghost of Mr. Surveyor Pue, "do this, and the profit shall be all your own! You will shortly need it; for it is not in your days, as it was in mine, when a man's office was a life-lease . . . . But, I charge you, in this matter of old Mistress Prynne, give to your predecessor's memory the credit which will be rightfully its due!" And I said to the ghost of Mr. Surveyor Pue,—"I will!" (33)

Hawthorne's ability to poke fun at himself is both subtle and complex. He said, in examining of the papers he purportedly found, he "found more traces of Mr. Pue's mental part, and the internal operations of his head, than the frizzled wig had contained of the venerable skull itself" (30). The ghost of Pue committed him to write the tale, which Hawthorne did just as he has described above, and considered calling his work "the POSTHUMOUS PAPERS OF A DECAPITATED SURVEYOR" (43).

Mr. Pue (the name may strongly suggest Hawthorne's disgust for his former post and character as a surveyor) conducted "researches as a local antiquarian, and other inquisitions of a similar nature" in writing the story of Hester's life (30). Here, Hawthorne may be implying that he himself was a student of ancient antiquity. One source of such antiquity is likely to have been the Bible, the text of which he referred to numerous times. In any case, Hawthorne states that "a portion of [Mr. Pue's] facts, by and by, did me good service in the preparation of the article entitled 'Main Street'" (30), which was meant to be published with his tale. Hawthorne's conversation with himself evidences his intentions to write again at some future time because he had lost his literary powers while employed by Uncle Sam; and at the end of his Custom House sketch, he identified himself as "the gentleman who writes from beyond the grave" (44).

NATURE'S RETURN

After being relieved of his post, true to his intuitive premonitions, he wrote the tale of *The Scarlet Letter*, which established Hawthorne as an eminent American novelist. Not only that, but his particular description and representation of the mode of Puritan life has won for Hawthorne the reputation of having written one of the earliest and gloomiest American novels, if not one of the most mysterious, and thereby, one of the most obscure.

Prior to losing his post, it appears that nature somewhat came out of hiding on the second floor of the Custom-House when Hawthorne, as he narrates, discovered the story of Hester. Hawthorne relates that Hester Prynne's story "was the subject of my meditations for many an hour" as he wearied the officials of the Custom-House tramping the floor late at night (34). The tale he relates appears to be a revelation of nature to him at a higher or second floor level of manifestation, or, at the allegorical level, where nature is spiritualized with imaginative delight, a central Romantic motive.

THE SOURCE

Hawthorne could have read Adam Blair's tale, according to Henry James, and used characters and symbols from that piece to serve his own symbolic purposes in his novel. But Hawthorne implies that he invented the so-called facts of his tale entirely by himself. Hawthorne regards himself as the editor of the tale he claims to have found on foolscap sheets recorded by one Mr. Surveyor Pue, a tale he confided, in an ambiguous way, as having been created at the promptings of what he might consider his alter ego,

> I must not be understood as affirming, that, in the dressing up of the tale, and imagining the motives and modes of passion that influenced the characters who figure in it, I have invariably confined myself within the limits of the old Surveyor's half a dozen sheets of foolscap. On the contrary, I have allowed myself, as to such points, nearly or altogether as much license as if the facts had been entirely of my own invention. What I contend for is the authenticity of the outline. (33)

In other words, the characters he created were intended to frame the outline for an allegory. He further stated that, if he had remained in the position of surveyor in Salem and had not been decapitated by the political turmoil of the times, the characters of the narrative would not be warmed and rendered malleable, by any heat that I could kindle at my intellectual forge. They would take neither the glow of passion nor the tenderness of sentiment, but retained all the rigidity of dead corpses . . . . In short, the almost torpid creatures of my own fancy twitted me with imbecility, and not without fair occasion. (34)

On the other hand, if Hawthorne did borrow some of the symbols or characters, it seemed to serve the purpose of contending for "the authenticity of the outline." The tale itself is a secondary interest: the primary motive of his novel, according to this student, was to unfold an authentic autobiographical philosophy of some religious conclusions, in the outline of an allegory, concerning the origin and resolution of sin and misery in a mortal world; and he did so in such a way that can only be deciphered by an in-depth study, and not by any superficial reading. The subtle revelation of his conclusions are found in the outline, or allegorical structure, and his contention is that his explanations for his perspectives are authentically his own, one of which may be controversially unique.

LOOSE CONNECTIONS WITH SALEM . . .

Interjecting a short autobiographical and humorous description of his affections for Salem, he restricts his feelings to the soil which contains his ancestors, from whose dust he is genetically connected, and which contains only his "sensuous sympathy of dust for dust." This affection possibly touches on his feelings for mother nature and himself as a "transplantation . . . better for the stock" (9). He seems to reflect no affinity for anything but the dust of Salem, which contains the dust of his ancestors, after whom he considered himself a descendant better off since his removal from the same grounds.

. . . BUT "SERVICEABLE TO MANKIND"

However, to show that his "sentiment has likewise its moral quality" (9), he sets up a contrast between the probable opinion of his ancestors–who would look questionably upon his idle occupation as a writer, and proclaim that his success would be deemed "worthless, if not positively disgraceful" (10)–and his own opinion or hope to the contrary.

He posed questions for the reader to ask, ironically in the words of those same ancestors: "What kind of a business in life,—what mode of glorifying God, or being serviceable to mankind in his day and generation,—may that be?" (10) Hawthorne is really not discrediting himself, but asking questions to cue the mind of the readers to discover a significant and serviceable message as they study his novel. What is the contribution of this particular work to humankind, what the moral quality, and how does it glorify his Maker? If such is the design of *The Scarlet Letter*, then, to fully appreciate Hawthorne, we must look at his tale from a religious point of view.

Perhaps Hawthorne may have conceived his religious conclusions to be somewhat controversial to the general public, but to friends symmpathetic to his views as proffering some benefit to the human family, if only in the future, and thus to the glory of Deity. He thus clothed the tale of the Custom House with a tongue-in-cheek hope that his great grandchildren at some future date would think more kindly of him when some student of antiquities would proudly point out where he once lived (45).

At the same time, he harbored "a prophetic instinct, a low whisper in my ear, that, within no long period, and whenever a new change of custom should be essential to my good, a change would come" (26). Dismayed with contemporary religion, is Hawthorne saying that his hope for a better world has been whispered to him as a kind of prophecy? Whether Hawthorne was speaking of expecting his removal from office for his own good, or whether he was referring to a change of religious customs for the better in time, are possible autobiographical implications of this prophetic instinct. This foreshadowed change of custom, and perhaps a change of custom houses, may also represent the change in religious perspectives Hawthorne anticipated would come to replace Puritanism, or to substantially improve the vestiges of it in some future time.

He concluded this portion of his autobiographical sketch of his roots by proclaiming that it is not progressive of humankind to be "transplanted" over and over again in the same worn-out soil. Though it was by instinctive connection with Salem that he was drawn to the spot, he proclaimed it unhealthy for him and his children to remain there, and was want to be replanted in unaccustomed earth. Wanting to be somewhere else, perhaps Hawthorne felt somewhat out of place and time, wondered what might be his particular purpose in life, and of what benefit to humankind he might be.

Human nature will not flourish, any more than a potato, if it be planted and replanted, for too long a series of generations, in the same worn-out soil. My children have had other birthplaces, and, so far as their fortunes may be within my control, shall strike their roots into unaccustomed earth. (11)

Thus Pearl, like Una, for allegorical reasons, shall not remain in Salem, but will strike her fortune in some other soil with different "customs." In other words, to interpret the metaphor of changing roots, just as the soil is depleted of its minerals by planting the same crop year after year, it is better for the generations of humankind to be planted in better religious soil from time to time. To Hawthorne, perhaps continual religious reformation would occur and transmute hate into love by means of some superior religious dynasty, the outgrowth of which might produce a better generation than the practices or customs of contemporary religion.

Hawthorne has Pearl relocated to another area away from Salem, presumably because the unaccustomed earth where Pearl goes, and where Hawthorne would prefer his children go, is probably a religious root other than Puritanism, that has more moral fiber of grace and compassion. His hope for Una and Pearl seems his hope for the mankind, which, if she can partake more of the compassionate center of Christianity, has promise of a glorious day, perhaps in some distant clime.

THE CAREKEEPERS OF PURITANISM

The Custom House, then, appears to represent the business of the Puritan church, which, presumably at the time of the writing of *The Scarlet Letter*, may have exhibited "few or no symptoms of commercial life" (4). The decaying trade or commerce (of saving souls) had gone to New York or Boston, perhaps symbolic of the dispersions of the Puritan faith into other denominations, and perhaps forecasting the transformation of society already taking place.

The custom house itself most likely represents the aged Puritan church as a civil institution, not particularly a governmental one, although both were closely connected. The American eagle with outstretched wings over the entrance of the Custom House possibly foreshadowed the mien and spirit of the Puritan fathers regarding the customs or tenets of their faith. It forecast "the general truculency of her attitude" to "fling off her nestlings,"

(5) or parishioners, with little tenderness. Even the growth of grass around the edifice probably evidenced Puritanism's sparse membership of young proselytes, whose attributes, we are told, have not degenerated as much as in their aged predecessors. It revealed little commerce of late, "a decaying trade" of religion, unlike that of earlier years of bustling Salem, now "scorned . . . by her own merchants and ship-owners" (6). It threatened "mischief to the inoffensive community" and protected the premises of Puritanism from other religious intruders (but without any great tenderness for her own brood). This description is metaphorically a burning rebuke of Puritan civil and religious domination of the early American conscience, and the heartless condemnation of its carekeepers, most of whom seemed without a large measure of compassion or pity.

Hawthorne focused the major text of this chapter of his tale upon a description of the officials of the Custom-House, and metaphorically ascribed the decadence of the Puritan ministry to its religious monopoly. He didn't seem to think too highly of a paid ministry either as he compared these officials to "the occupants of alms-houses, and all other human beings who depend for subsistence on charity." This comparison uses the simile, "like Matthew, at the receipt of custom, but not very liable to be summoned thence, like him, for apostolic errands" (7), possibly to infer a ministry lacking divine guidance, or character of any significant spiritual qualities.

To wit, using the metaphor of womankind, which often represents a more refined civilization, Hawthorne's description of the insides of the Custom House implies possibly that civility, or the gentle touch, was also lacking in the Puritan church. It was "a sanctuary into which womankind, with her tools of magic, the broom and mop, has very infrequent access" (7), as if to say their corruptive practices needed some cleaning up.

"TWOFOLD MORE THE CHILD OF HELL"[2]

As Hawthorne discusses the characters of the Custom-House officials, he makes interesting parenthetical interjections about Puritanism. The purpose of these characters and interjections, seems to be to show the effect of Puritanism upon its chief carekeepers.

Having stated that "[n]either the front nor the back entrance of the Custom-House opens on the road to Paradise," he implied metaphorically that the Puritan faith had an effect upon its ministers and parishioners that doomed them to a life of gloom on earth as well as perhaps in the afterlife. The Puritanic faith had no saving power because it produced a cold and heartless character void of compassion and grace, and diminished such over time in its converts.

Such a condemnation of Puritanism is reminiscent of the Nazarene's censure of the officials of Judaism when he claimed that they canvassed the earth for proselytes and made them more a product of hell after their conversion than they were before it. Indeed, the background of Puritanic influence on one's character remarkably parallels the background of Judaism. With such a backdrop, a curious reader might intuitively question, "Then what is front and center stage?"

He also interjected the use of the metaphor of light in contrasting the spiritual qualities of the custom house officers as a quality that, either gleams with the cheery aspect of real sunshine for all, or "resembles the phosphorescent glow of decaying wood" (16). This metaphor appears to reflect the anti-Transcendentalist's view that intellect is not a virtue in and of itself alone but only a means of imbibing either goodness or evil out of life and reflecting it upon others. It also sets the stage later for both a description of Lucifer in the form of Chillingworth, a knowledgeable doctor, and Dimmesdale, a young divine, as well as other Custom-House officers.

THE INSPECTOR

As we follow the theme of dark to light, from old to young, from the worst of Puritanism to its finest, the first character Hawthorne described was that of the "father of the Custom-House–the patriarch . . . of the respectable body of tide-waiters all over the United States . . . dyed in the wool, or rather, born in the purple" (16)–the permanent Inspector. The Inspector is a robust and cheerful person apparently without mind or soul who is motivated purely by the instincts of nature. He thus has not been affected from birth by either the good or gloomy aspects of Puritanism and was deemed by Hawthorne "most fittest to be a Custom-House officer" because he was incapable of suffering "moral detriment from this peculiar mode of life." In other words, Puritanism could not hurt him in the slightest because he was impervious to its doctrines, and perhaps lived at the lowest depths of humanity regardless of them.

[H]e seemed–not young, indeed—but a kind of new contrivance of Mother Nature in the shape of man, whom age and infirmity had no business to touch . . . . Looking at him merely as an animal,—and there was very little else to look at,—he was a most satisfactory object, from the thorough healthfulness and wholesomeness of his system, and his capacity, at that extreme age, to enjoy all, or nearly all, the delights which he had every aimed at, or conceived of . . . .

[He] possessed no power of thought, no depth of feeling, no troublesome sensibilities; nothing, in short, but a few commonplace instincts, which, aided by the cheerful temper that grew inevitably out of his physical well-being, did duty very respectably, and to general acceptance, in lieu of a heart . . . . My conclusion was that he had no soul, no heart, no mind; nothing, as I have already said, but instincts . . . . [O]f all men whom I have ever known, this individual was fittest to be a Custom-House officer. (17-18)

The short but near full description of the Inspector is given here possibly to contrast him with Hester. Governed neither by mental powers nor spiritual inclinations, he was given purely to natural instincts, perhaps mostly of a sensual kind, and might possibly representing 100% influence from the dark side of nature. If Hester, discussed after the characters of the Custom House, is Hawthorne's concept of Mother Nature, in the form of a woman beautifully embodying the best of spiritual essence, or embracing the best of the divine nature infused in her, then the Inspector is the opposite: he is the epitome of the animal devoid of anything divine and impervious to any of its influences, even what may still exist in Puritanism. If she is the representation of the best of civilization dominated by the worst of Calvinistic doctrine or contemporary religion, then the inspector represents the worse of that civilization upon whom even the best of Puritanism had no spiritual effect whatsoever.

THE COLLECTOR OR GENERAL

The description of the Collector, on the other hand, is praiseworthy. In terms of the effect of Puritanism upon the Collector, he seems to have features of integrity, native elegance, and benevolence that stubbornly endured Puritanism. He was remote and unattainable and "lived a more real life within his thoughts, than amid the inappropriate environment of the Collector's office" (23). Perhaps the Collector is partially redeemed from Puritanism not only because "he was as much out of place as an old sword" (24) in the custom house but also because

> there was light within him, and that it was only the outward medium of the intellectual lamp that obstructed the rays in their passage . . . .

> The heat that had formerly pervaded his nature, and which was not yet extinct, was never of the kind that flashes and flickers in a blaze, but, rather, a deep, red glow, as of iron in a furnace. (21)

Though "the framework of his nature, originally strong and massive, was not yet crumbled," (20) and his shapeless mound "overgrown, through long years of peace and neglect, with grass and alien weeds" (21), he had a "bloody laurel on his brow" and "seemed to have a young girl's appreciation of the floral tribe" (23). These images symbolize a heart touched by compassion and therefore may have hope of redemption in time. The imagery of red at any time in Hawthorne's novel apparently points to some redemptive hope to raise a compassionate people from the black and gloomy dominion of the Puritan experiment, "the black flower of civilized society" (48). To the vulgar, who demonstrates no such compassion of the heart, red may also symbolize a final and bitter state of being, which may be intuited with fear and horror, as did Chillingworth.

Nevertheless, whereas the Inspector was incapable of being affected by his tour in the custom house, the Old General had lost much of the heat and virtues of his youth.

> Many characteristics . . . must have vanished, or been obscured, before I met the General. All merely graceful attributes are usually the most evanescent; nor does Nature adorn the human ruin with blossoms of new beauty, that have their roots and proper nutriment only in the chinks and crevices of decay. (22)

This official, whose roots had been too long embedded in the decay of Puritanism, cannot hope to have Nature restore what has been lost. Apparently, the General, representing a Puritan ecclesiastical, was probably filled with light before his office; and in the process of administering the cold justice of its tenets, had lost the vigor of the noble qualities he once possessed. Thus we see through Hawthorne's eyes in these two personifications what effects the Puritanic religious and social system seem to have had upon the best of its stock, the General, and the worst, the Inspector. Having described two ends of the continuum, all other adherents of the faith apparently fall in between in terms of Puritanic effect upon them, relative to their measure of compassion for the unfortunate.

RECORDS IN THE ATTIC

The introductory context to the tale—a discussion of the Revolution, a dearth of records before, the Protectorate, and antique customs—seems highly metaphorical in intent also. The imagery is too consistent to ignore as a possible context for allegorical infusion. In other words, there was a dearth of Biblical records prior to the Reformation (Revolution), having been carried off or lost or kept from public consumption before the arrival of the printing press. Hawthorne may be expressing his regrets for their loss,

> for, going back, perhaps to the days of the Protectorate, those papers must have contained many references to forgotten or remembered men, and to antique customs, which would have affected me with the same pleasure as when I used to pick up Indian arrow-heads in the field near the Old Manse. (29)

Those lost records, going back perhaps to the days of the Protectorate, could have contained truths (antique customs or ancient prejudices) about life which would have delighted him as much as a Romantic gleans truth from nature. Though Hawthorne's mention of the Protectorate seems to be a reference to Cromwell's leadership of the Puritans at a time when England was struggling for some form of government, and Puritanism was at its heights in seeking religious reform, it may also be an allegorical allusion to the only bona fide Protectorate in the Christian faith, around which Holy Writ originated.

There are notably several lost records mentioned in the Bible that are not contained in this collection of Judaic-Christian traditions or "antique customs." For Hawthorne, perhaps the romantic notion of discovering arrow-heads (raw, spiritualized, and penetrating) in the wilderness of nature, or truths which reveal themselves to earnest seekers, is similar to discovering truths from meditative study of the Biblical records. To support the possible double-speak reference to Cromwell and the Christians' Nazarene, it may be mentioned that the King James Version of the Bible was perhaps the most notable achievement of the Puritan movement in its effort to reform the Church of England. Hawthorne seems to recognize the improvements brought about by the Puritans' effort to restore original Christianity, but to have thought it likewise a failure because of its inordinate emphasis upon the sinful and depraved nature of human flesh.

When Cromwell died, the political power the Puritan revolution achieved ended, and many Puritans came to America to shape religion, social life, and the government along the New England coast. The hope and promise of Puritan reformation in England had failed to bring the changes it sought, and came to America (India) to try its experiment here. It strongly appears from the allegorical meanings of the tale of the scarlet letter that Hawthorne believed that the American experiment, though bright with promise in its beginning, had its debilitating effects also. In its earlier days Puritanism seems to have held a brighter promise that it was the only way to heaven, much as India was thought to be the commercial Utopia, for which Salem may have been considered the closest outpost thereto, if not India itself.

"Poking and burrowing" into the remaining old records in the attic (is he reading in the Old Testament or retrieving memories from his mind?), Hawthorne has to exert himself from the spell of old Puritanism to think about earlier days "of the old town's brighter aspect, when India was a new region, and only Salem knew the way thither!" In so doing, he found a package wrapped in faded red tape, "with the sense that a treasure would here be brought to light" (29).

The total premise of this purveyor's interpretation of Hawthorne's novel rests upon the belief that it is a religious or philosophical allegory which treats the relationships between good, evil, and human nature. Hawthorne thus presents his explanation and perspective of human nature not as depraved and ignominious, as did the Puritans, but as a noble work of the Creator which was created to enjoy some future state of happiness and joy. It is plausible, therefore, to suggest that this package wrapped in tape may symbolize the scriptures, or some of Hawthorne's earlier short stories, or some inflamed memories or recollections of both, that he was mulling over in his mind in contemplation of writing again. The faded red tape may represent the promise of redemption that is the centerpiece of Christianity which threads itself beautifully throughout the scriptures and holds them together. Without the bright hope and the promise inherent in the sacrifice of the Nazarene, perhaps to Hawthorne life was practically doomed to the darkness and gloominess of its Calvinistic creed, like the prison of "the black flower of civilized society," outside of which nevertheless grew a wild rose-bush promising "some sweet moral blossom" (48), a sable field against which the promise of the scarlet letter A offers some raised relief.

"SOME DEEP MEANING"

Every analogy can only be carried so far, and there are only a few points the author wishes to make with his analogies. The reader has to judge the extent to which the author is taking them. It may therefore be an extreme extension of the analogy to assert that the parchment cover of the papers, a commission by the Governor of the Massachusetts Bay colony, may represent the King James authorized version of the Bible, the one good thing that came out of the Puritan revolution in England, and that the handwritten story itself is Hawthorne's own play on his version of its contents.

On the other hand, since the papers were written in the handwriting of Surveyor Pue, Hawthorne's alter ego or lesser self while serving in the custom house, we could also construe that the papers represent some of Hawthorne's earlier writings or short stories. Or perhaps the bundle represents a combination of both Biblical and earlier writings, which Hawthorne intended to fuse together, and purported he was impelled "to so pious a task" (31). A careful reading of his earlier works indicates that there is much imagery in them that is modified, molded, and integrated into his allegorical tale. The red tape could symbolize, in this case, the theme or faded promise of the bundle of papers into which he pried for some deep meaning in it, most worthy of interpretation, and which as it were, streamed forth from the mystic symbol, subtly communicating itself to my sensibilities, but evading the analysis of my mind. (31)

In this passage, Hawthorne seems to be alerting the reader to consider his tale of the scarlet letter as imparting some deeper meaning that evades intellectual reasoning and calls for some intuitive sounding for spiritual truth. A quest is thus introduced, and Hawthorne sets the stage, against its dark background, for an introduction of one of his main charactors, Hester Prynne.

THE SACRILEGIOUS MOTH

The ragged scarlet letter, which "for time, and wear, and a sacrilegious moth, had been reduced to little other than a rag" (31), and which was found with the papers, also suggests its purpose as a central theme to Hawthorne's novel. That the moth was sacrilegious implies that the scarlet letter A represents something more hallowed and deserving of reverence than the ill-repute presumably contained therein. It has been assumed by many that the letter stands for adultery, yet that word is found nowhere in his novel. The word, unadulterated, is used, however, in connection with the metaphor of light of day, or untarnished truth. The unadulterated truth revealed by the natural light of day, and by a deeper understanding of the complexity of Hawthorne's riddle, as proposed by this author's interpretations, leads one to accept the scarlet letter as a reference to the Atonement, and, as we have discussed, a recompense for the creation of mortal humankind. This creation possibly was the unadulterated act of the divine (Dimmesdale) infusing a portion of himself, or his children, into nature (Hester) to create mankind (Pearl). The act of creation alone, according to this purveyor's interpretation of Hawthorne, refutes the basic Puritanic tenet of the depravity of mortal flesh, and regards the body as having some purposeful destiny.

Then again, if not at the same time with multiple meanings, the scarlet letter, eaten by some sacrilegious moth, may refer similarly to the remaining investiture of divine, redemptive substance in Christianity that has not been completed digested by the latest Puritanic interpretations of the Protestant Reformation. Later, Hawthorne expands this possible allegorical concept to include the hope that other generations, transplanted in different and better soil, may in the ongoing religious revolution give birth to a new generation, perhaps even a civilization that is more compassionate and merciful than the Puritan attempt. This reformation may be analogous to Hawthorne's reference to Hester's transfiguration.

Another intuitive moment of this Romantic narration by Hawthorne occurred when he put the scarlet letter to his breast.

> It seemed to me,—the reader may smile, but must not doubt my word,—it seemed to me, then, that I experienced a sensation not altogether physical, yet almost so, as of burning heat; and as if the letter were not of red cloth, but red-hot iron. (38)

The premise this analysis states for the reader is that the symbols of red and heat, especially when combined, may represent the effects of the Redeemer's sacrifice and suffering for humankind. It likewise may signal the unholy suffering ordained for those indifferent, calloused, or scornful persons whose actions have not passed "the truest test of a successful life to such an end!" (263) This pain may depict the mystical meaning which the scarlet letter is communicating to the narrator through the intuitive sensations of burning heat, and may signal the same to sympathetic readers as they give the tale a more meditative and apprehensive study.

O, BUT TO WRITE!

Hawthorne had been successful as "a writer of tolerably poor tales and essays (38); but as a good Surveyor, when attempting to write, the materiality of his daily life pressed so intrusively upon him that "the impalpable beauty of [his] soap-bubble was broken by the rude contact of some actual circumstance" (37). The story fermenting in his mind about Hester would not unfold, and he mused that he might have chosen a different style of writing other than a romance, such as the humorous style of one of the Inspector's story-telling, or one with a more serious intent; but the style he preferred was too illusive while he was yet in the setting of the Custom House.

Hawthorne spent some four pages relative to what may have been required to create his characters, "where the Actual and the Imaginary may meet, and each imbue itself with the nature of the other" (36). His description of that style is probably the one he used, as soon as he was decapitated from the office of Surveyor, to write and diffuse his mystical meanings into his tale of Hester. It is probably insightful to the reader to understand this process so as to be able better to interpret the characters of the story, and to fathom its deeper import, but only a small portion pertinent to the mystery is presented here:

> The wiser effort would have been to diffuse thought and imagination through the opaque substance of to-day, and thus to make it a bright transparency; to spiritualize the burden that began to weigh so heavily; to seek, resolutely, the true and indestructible value that lay hidden in the petty and wearisome incidents, and ordinary characters, with which I was now conversant. The fault was mine.

> The page of life that was spread out before me seemed dull and commonplace, only because I had not fathomed its deeper import. (37)

The above passage is another marvelous manifestation of Hawthorne's ability to convey multiple meanings simultaneously. Perhaps thought and imagination were spread throughout the seeming reality of Hestor's story to spiritualize the burden she bore, the burden we all bear. Although perhaps not so brightly transparent, the moral value of the tale, "hidden in the petty and wearisome incidents, and ordinary characters" of the story, if indeed about the Fall and the Atonement, to Hawthorne, and to those who still cling to the vestiges of Christianity, would be "true and indestructible." That his characters are spiritualized, with a mesh of the Actual and the Imaginary, may account for the brightness of the tale, and its intimate appeal to the intuitive reader; but its moral messages were hidden so well that its deeper import is not so transparent. The physical world of element and nature, perhaps represented by Hester, who bore the burden well that weighs so heavily upon our own mortal nature, may be dull and commomplace to the readers as well, unless they spend moments of quiet comtemplation seeking to decipher the thought and imagination that spiritualize his tale and give it some true and indestructible value.

This message of brighter, deeper import is communicated through the ordinary characters and the petty and wearisome incidents surrounding the tale of the scarlet letter. The passage quoted above not so apparently double speaks about the two levels of meanings. By implication, Hawthorne may also be saying that readers may fathom the spiritualized, deeper import of the tale by placing themselves in those same meditative circumstances which are conducive to the Romantic's illumination.

THE PERSONAL TOUCH

When the narrator found the ragged scarlet letter and put it to his breast, he "experienced a sensation not altogether physical, yet almost so, as of burning heat; and as if the letter was not of red cloth, but red-hot iron." Hawthorne lets us know that he identifies with the meaning of the scarlet letter, as did Hester, Dimmesdale, and a few others later in the novel. His reaction is perhaps one of the first clues of some hidden value contained within his tale for his readers. This student pictures the symbol of red as a reference to the blood-ripe effects of the Redeemer's pain, to which, as Hawthorne delineates later, Dimmesdale's parishioners react differently, perhaps in proportion to their sensitivity to its effects. The story on the foolscap sheets are not so much then about an adulterous woman but rather about "the young clergyman," who was "a miracle of holiness," a "man of ethereal attributes, whose voice the angels might else have listened to and answered!" and who "gained from many people the reverence due to an angel"(142).

"Prying farther into the manuscript" (32), Hawthorne may be referring the reader to his story to learn other details of Hester's sufferings and doings. Perhaps he is expecting the reader of like-mind and sensibilities to pry into Hester Prynne's character and her relationships with other main characters to solve the riddle of the spiritualized tale, which has to do with the relationship between "the Deity and the communities of mankind," as stated in the chapter, "The Revelation of the Scarlet Letter," and may be the very subject of Dimmesdale's Election Sermon (249).

LIVING WATER FROM THE TOWN PUMP

Writers perhaps see themselves as harbingers of some truth. Each develops a style and chooses the material from which to pump some living water to satisfy the reader's thirst. Hawthorne seemingly envisioned himself as a particular herald from the town of Salem, the seed-bed of his ancestors. He devoted the last of the chapter on the Custom-House in autobiographical commentary discussing the environment and process which is required for a Romantic writer to compose his art, why the Custom-House environment did not facilitate this process, and how the fortunate experience of being relieved of his duty as Surveyor of the Customs allowed him to write again. He used a humorous analogy to refer to his desires to quit his post so that he could write again, which notions were, to his surprise, aborted by his being severed from it.

> My fortune somewhat resembled that of a person who should entertain an idea of committing suicide, and, altogether beyond his hopes, meet with the good hap to be murdered. (42)

This murder, of course, is the decapitation of Mr. Surveyor Pue, Hawthorne's loss of office, and the mentality he disdained while serving therein. Hawthorne delighted in this loss, for he was unable to write due to the confinements of the office, and was able to write thereafter.

> The moment when a man's head drops off is seldom or never, I am inclined to think, precisely the most agreeable of his life.

> Nevertheless, like the greater part of our misfortunes, even so serious a contingency brings its remedy and consolation with it, if the sufferer will but make the best, rather than the worst, of the accident which has befallen him. (41)

Hawthorne concludes this chapter on the custom house, a parable or analogy for the setting of the sable field, with the comment that his past is dead to him, that the old town of Salem "ceases to be a reality of my life. I am a citizen of somewhere else . . . . I shall do better amongst other faces (p. 44)". He appears to identify with some other region, perhaps another time or dispensation, perhaps like that into which Pearl later disappeared. His comments are reminiscent of Pearl's departure into another place for lack of identity with her birthplace. Hawthorne thereby possibly identifies himself also with this allegorical character and the concept she represents instead of his Puritan heritage. The town of Salem had lost "the genial atmosphere which a literary man requires, in order to ripen the best harvest of his mind" and shall become a memory, like a mist brooding over and around it, as if it were no portion of the real earth . . . with only imaginary inhabitants to people its wooden houses, and walk its homely lanes, and the unpicturesque prolixity of its main street. (44)

As Salem produced no life to inspire the "literary man," perhaps Hawthorne is saying at the allegorical level that its main street affairs of administering Puritanism offers no life to the Christian for lack of a compassionate fire or merciful light.

His closing reference to THE TOWN-PUMP seems, at worse, an utterly curious and out-of-place comment without relevant meaning; at best, a metaphysical conceit. Yet, interpreted in the light of his allegory, the choice of this relic, as a symbol of Hawthorne's worthy contributions as a writer, may bear a significant message to the reader who thinks he can decipher the riddle of images in his tale.

It may be however,—O, transporting and triumphant thought!–that the great-grandchildren of the present race may sometimes think kindly of the scribbler of bygone days, when the antiquary of days to come, among the sites memorable in the town's history, shall point out the locality of THE TOWN-PUMP! (45)

Though Hawthorne may purely only have been hoping that *The Scarlet Letter*, and possibly the other short tales and sketches he planned to publish along with it, would establish him as a well-known writer, the reference to the "antiquary of days to come" offers a signal of another possible hidden message. To Hawthorne's great grandchildren, perhaps some student of his ancient works, in praise of the man who produced them, will point out the residence of the Old Bard who siphoned some life-giving water from the depleted soil of his Puritan past.

In the passage above, "the antiquary of days" might refer to the Biblical prophecy of the Ancient of days (Daniel 7: 9, 13, 22), who would come in a day of judgment to usher in a better world for the saints. Hawthorne later made reference to the prophet Daniel (62), who might be needed to expound the riddle as to who was the father of Pearl. This reference might therefore relate to the "prophetic instinct," or whisper in Hawthorne's ear, that "a change of custom" soon would come for his good (26). This allusion may more likely refer to the spiritualized "true and indestructible value that lay hidden in the petty and wearisome incidents, and ordinary characters" of his tale. It may be a stretch of imagination to suggest that Hawthorne is saying, tongue-in-cheek, that a particular Ancient of days himself may come to vindicate the benefit he was to his fellowmen. If Hawthorne was referring to Daniel as the antiquary of days, then he may also be referring to the transformation of society, of which he spoke, as the fulfillment of that particular prophecy. In either case, antiquary or Ancient of Days, perhaps the Bard of Salem will "win [himself] a pleasant memory in this abode and burial place of so many of my forefathers" when the people of Salem will see him as having "some importance in their eyes" (44).

This antiquary highlights that possibility.

CHAPTERS 1 AND 2

THE PRISON-DOOR
AND THE MARKET-PLACE

> The religious builders have so distorted and deformed the
> doctrines of Jesus, so muffled them in mysticisms, fancies and
> falsehoods, have caricatured them into forms so inconceivable,
> as to shock reasonable thinkers . . . Happy is the prospect of a
> restoration of primitive Christianity. I must leave to younger
> persons to encounter and lop off the false branches which
> have been engrafted into it by the mythologists of the middle
> and modern ages.[1]
> (Thomas Jefferson)

These two chapters establish the setting of the tale consistent with the parabolic comparison with the custom house officers. They serve as a typical connection between the ministers of Puritanism and the effects the enforcement of their faith have upon their fervid adherents. In other words, they particularize the sable background, or the Puritanical attitude seemingly based upon a beast-like image of human nature.

A detailed analysis of the imagery of these two chapters, along with others of remaining chapters, will be integrated to show the internal consistency between the symbolisms of the novel and the interpretations proposed by this antiquary. One perhaps can somewhat evade the accusation of "reading into" a work if there are sufficient parallel interpretations between the parables and imagery within the allegory that run consistently throughout the work, and, chapter by chapter, point to the same possible meanings.

THE BLACK FLOWER OF CIVILIZED SOCIETY

The blackness of the Puritan consciousness and singular focus upon mortal depravity is likely figured by the field of sable painted on the tombstone above the graves of Hester and Dimmesdale. Blackness is the Puritan prison, "the black flower of civilized society" (48), from which Hester emerges with child. It may be the world into which humankind may emerge from the womb. Indeed, Pearl's birth in a prison, and her exit therefrom into the market-place, may allegorically represent the present world into which humankind has emerged from another. The field of sable also seems imaged by the shadows of the tall dark trees in the forest, where Pearl plays unaffected by the dismal scene, and which themselves appear to reflect the Puritan consciousness. The black field may represent as well the dismal era of life itself, or its pains and miseries.

Hawthorne notes in the novel that the prison and the cemetery were two of the first structures Puritans planned when opening up a colony in America, the "black flower," or the first fruits of that civilized society (47). The prison could signify their obsession with condemnation and sinfulness, as likewise exemplified by the pillory upon the scaffold, which "stood nearly beneath the eaves of Boston's earliest church, and appeared to be a fixture there" (55). Thus the dark prison seems to be a symptom of the effect of the Puritan religion, as Hawthorne saw it, perhaps even a symbol for the history of a transformed Christianity as Jefferson saw it. The market-place may typify the new world in which Puritanism panders its wares before sending its parishioners home to the grave.

The symbols of the prison and market-place may then serve as a microcosmic parable within the allegory itself about the world of Puritanism, or contemporary Christianity. The metaphor of the prison may symbolize the condemnation of human nature by the officials of Puritanism, and, perhaps for Hawthorne, may depict, besides all its disciples in Boston, other colonies under Puritan dominion as prisoners to that discipline. "Heavily timbered with oak, and studded with iron spikes" (47), the door of the prison possibly signifies the iron-braced boundaries of Puritanism from which none might stray without penalty and punishment, including those outside its grasps, as in the case of the "sainted Anne Hutchinson" (48). Along with the hardships the Puritans had to endure, their lives must have been quite bleak under the auspices of their eagle-like demeanor, "and the general truculency of her attitude" (5).

Hester's emergence with Pearl through the prison door, like the birthing of humankind from the womb, may represent, for the better part, the birth of mortal nature and humankind into a world dominated by the gloom and despair of Puritan or contemporary institutional interpretations. Her exit therefrom, and perhaps her mild punishment, though harrowing, in keeping with the theme of progressive transformation, might reflect a measure of relative growth toward a kind and sensitive heart, through the experience therein. The small measure of grace extended by the officials might reflect not only a thin movement in the right direction along the hate-love continuum but also a relaxation or waning of Puritanic dogmatism, according to this theme.

The market place in Salem may be that world of Puritanism into which the colonists of the American experiment are born. The pillory upon the scaffold, which was located beneath the balcony where the officials sat, may represent the suffering, or the cross, which straying adherents of Puritanism must bear under the scorching brow of the carekeepers of their faith.

The market-place could therefore represent a cross-section of the life of the Puritan character as well as perhaps of the world that has fed upon inadequate Christian merchandise, or the reformations thereof. The analogies of the prison and scaffold fade into a continuation of the main allegory itself, where the three main characters—Arthur, Hester, and Pearl—thematically struggle with the question of whether to run away from the problems of their life, or to stay and fulfill the duty of their office in preparation for a better world.

ON CIVILIZATION

The chapter on the market-place introduces the treatment by dominant Puritanism of those who depart from its tenets as well as those who shared religious ideas other than its own. The market-place is an interesting outlet from the custom house, as though, as an analogy, it is a fitting bartering place for the exchange of goods by customers thereto. Any customer not satisfied with the present customs of Puritanism might expect adverse treatment. For example, on a particular grass-plot in front of the jail, a crowd gathers.

It might be, that an Antinomian, a Quaker, or other heterodox religionist, was to be scourged out of the town, or an idle and vagrant Indian, whom the white man's fire-water had made riotous about the streets, was to be driven with stripes into the shadow of the forest . . . . In either case, there was very much the same solemnity of demeanour on the part of the spectators; as befitted a people amongst whom religion and law were almost identical, and in whose character both were so thoroughly interfused, that the mildest and the severest acts of public discipline were alike made venerable and awful. Meagre, indeed, and cold, was the sympathy that a transgressor might look for, from such by-standers, at the scaffold. (49)

The carekeepers of Puritanism, being both a civil and ecclesiastical order, had no tolerance for other belief systems in their community other than the customary, perhaps because civil and religious order was easier to maintain, by getting rid of the differences, rather than allowing freedom of choice in a matter. The passage above also seems to be an extension of Hawthorne's conclusion about the characters of the custom-house officials. The two-edged sword of Puritanism that fused both religion and law with equal severity for all infractions may have charged its adherents with a similar heartless character.

Therefore, should the custom house represent the Puritan institution or church, then the market-place may represent the socio-economic and political manifestations of American society, or a cross-section of it, at the time leading up to Hawthorne's generation. If the setting more broadly symbolizes the present condition of Christianity, as perhaps framed in the graphic words of Thomas Jefferson quoted at the beginning of this chapter, then Hawthorne's allegory may be a softer peddling of his similar antinomian wares. The comment by Jefferson was selected from similar opinions that have voiced this frame of mind to show that Hawthorne's allegory may have reflected identical sentiments less offensive to his public.

THE TIME FRAME OF THE ALLEGORY

An indication that the market-place might even symbolize a microcosmic representation of humanity in general is a reference to the time frame of the allegory uttered by the town-beadle, who "prefigured and represented in his aspect the whole dismal severity of the Puritanic code of law" (52):

> "Make way, good people, make way, in the King's name," cried he. "Open a passage; and, I promise ye, Mistress Prynne shall be set where man, woman, and child may have a fair sight of her brave apparel, from this time till an hour past meridian." (54)

The key symbol of the time frame is the use of the word "meridian." This symbol is used a few times in the novel, and will be referred to again later. While it defines midday, it also has another definition, the division of time between B. C. and A. D., at the time of the birth of the Nazarene. There is an inordinate number of references to the seven year period of the tale; and such may incline the mind of the reader, who is perhaps sympathetic with Hawthorne's inclinations, to think of its parallels in relation to the deeper import of the scarlet letter.

Besides the wearing of the letter A, Hester must also stand three hours on the scaffold as part of her judgment, holding her sin-born infant of about three or four months old, until "an hour past meridian." The number, three, is commonly used to denote the trinity of Deity; and the number, seven, which surfaces later in the story, denotes perfection or completion. One might ask, is there also a connection between the numbers three and seven? This connection is advanced later as other references are mentioned in succeeding chapters.

The time-frame of the novel consistently seems to represent the allegorical imagery, as rendered by the author's interpretation, and in keeping with most Christian theology, concerning the earth's destined seven thousand years of existence. The reader must configure what significance Hester's appearance, dominated by the scarlet letter, has to the time reference mentioned. That significance may come slowly by intuition as she stands upon the scaffold in the meredian of time, in conjunction with Arthur Dimmesdale's oracular midnight or visionary stand upon the same platform, then again when he completes his mission of expiation and confession, and finally seals his redemptive act with his death. Barring some loose Puritanical impulse, or contrary prejudice, the life, ministry, and death of the Nazarene, whose mission contained a memorial promise, may come to the reader's mind, especially in context with so many other

Biblical references thereabout, and remain somewhat in its uttermost recesses. Hester's brave apparel may therefore prefigure that promise of a time when mortality's problems may be resolved. Hester, however, is only intuitively tuned to that promise, and her rationality often clouds that picture, as may that of the reader not fully aware of Hawthorne's allegorical strategy, or wanting to consider it.

THE WILD AND RED ROSE-BUSH OF NATURE

Contrasting the "black flower of civilized society," is a rose bush lying near the threshold of the iron-studded oak door of the prison. The red rose bush seems to represent and herald the real centerpiece and promise of Christianity overlooked by the jaundiced eyes of Puritans, possibly principling the promise of a relief from an oppressive world, as in the grace and mercy of it future Redemption. For the prisoner entering and the criminal exiting the prison, the wild rose-bush might betoken that "the deep heart of Nature could pity and be kind to him" (48), despite the blackness of the background of life, as interpreted by Puritanism. Hawthorne depicted the rose bush as possibly springing up from the footsteps of Anne Hutchinson, whose antinomian ministry focused on grace.

One of its flowers is to be plucked for the reader to symbolize "some sweet moral blossom that may be found along the track, or relieve the darkening close of a tale of human frailty and sorrow" (48). Though Woodberry claimed that Hawthorne intended no moral in his novel, it seems Hawthorne himself thought otherwise. Experiencing the moral fragrance of that sweet blossom may strain the reader's imagination, at this point, but perhaps spark the intuitive challenge Hawthorne framed for his readers by his imagery and questions.

It is the firm position of this analysis that that moral is developed in the allegorical meanings and is symbolized by several metaphors of red. Like a relief, the rose bush stands out against the prison as a contrast to suggest some significant message. The rose that releases its moral fragrance begins to unveil the promise of a better world, perhaps through a perspective of life higher than that which either the Puritanism of Hawthorne's forefathers or the contemporary religion of his day could provide. Much like the scarlet letter A embossed upon a black field, the rose forecasts an enlightened meaning within a darkened tale of human misery, perhaps even the hope of a special dispensation that triumphs over a mortal nature condemned by Calvinistic doctrine, or the like.

> This rose bush, by a strange chance, has been kept alive in history; but whether it had merely survived out of the stern old wilderness, so long after the fall of the gigantic pines and oaks that originally overshadowed it,—or whether, as there is fair authority for believing, it had sprung up under the footsteps of the sainted Ann Hutchinson, as she entered the prison-door,—we shall not take upon us to determine. (48)

Perhaps the gigantic pines and oaks of the stern old wilderness, that overshadowed the rose bush, represent the former religious empire across the Atlantic that overshadowed the message of grace. Wherein the rose bush may symbolize either the survival of that message, despite the long history of failing ecclesiastical dominions, or the fresh revival of that compassionate message by certain antinomians, Hawthorne leaves somewhat to the reader to determine. Although the ministry of Ann Hutchinson brought her banishment from the Massachusetts' colony, yet Hawthorne might have believed that her emphasis on divine grace and love, without respect to church or minister, may have kept the *elan vital* of pristine Christianity from being completely extinguished in the early American experiment. The point Hawthorne seems to make is that the rose bush survived, and that its delicate gems still offered to each prisoner entering or emerging from the prison some token effusion of pity and compassion, perhaps despite the mythologies of current religious thought, or the common miseries of mortality. Perhaps, in the passage above, to Hawthorne, hope springs eternal, in the symbol of the red bush, as the remaining life-blood of the Nazarene's teachings that emphasized mercy over judgment and forgiveness over condemnation.

"The deep heart of Nature [which] could pity and be kind" to the prisoner (48), might describe the compassion of the Creator of Nature for those who suffer from the benighted machinations of humanity's justice, or the plight of mortalilty itself. The "fragrance and fragile beauty" of the roses are possibly the promise of this compassion for each prisoner who might be condemned for the smallest deviation from the Puritan society.

The rose bush, then, appears to be a symbol that introduces the reader to a tale of passion and compassion. "Finding it directly upon the threshold of our narrative" (48), Hawthorne apparently is proposing to the readers that they are about to cross a threshold into an act or tale of grace. At the moment Hester Prynne exits the prison door, Hawthorne begins to grace his sad story with a rose bush raised to greet Hester, and the reader, as a glimmer of relief from the dark tale of Puritan society in particular, and perhaps, in general, of like institution interpretations.

> [W]e could hardly do otherwise than pluck one of its flowers and present it to the reader. It may serve, let us hope, to symbolize some sweet moral blossom, that may be found along the track, or relieve the darkening close of a tale of human frailty and sorrow. (48)

The tale is indeed itself an act of grace characterized at the allegorical level by two of its main characters, Hester and her minister, the divine Dimmesdale. The roses on the bush, Hester's embellished scarlet letter, and, later, Pearl's attire, may also be blossoms to be picked from this dark tale, along the track of life, by those who sense something more than a sordid story. All symbols of red in the tale appear to allude to the relationship between the mortality of human nature, the problems of life, and redemption therefrom. But what seems most significant about this rose bush near the threshold of the prison door is that mercy, overshadowed and blighted by previous and/or current religious dominions, is still to be derived from the remnants of the Nazarene's ministry, despite the best or the worse efforts of its ordained or self-appointed carekeepers.

THE FEMININE WOMAN

Hawthorne seemed to use his women characters symbolically to represent successive civilizations, or improvements from one to the other, perhaps from before the reign of the man-like Queen Elizabeth to the current Puritan experiment. He portrayed the older women as more masculine and less graceful than their descendent daughters, possibly reflecting the less genteel side of earlier reformations; and he figured the younger as more lady-like, "after the manner of the feminine gentility of those days" (53).

> Morally, as well as materially, there was a courser fibre in those
> wives and maidens of old English birth and breeding, than in
> their fair descendants, separated from them by a series of six or
> seven generations; for, throughout that chain of ancestry, every
> successive mother has transmitted to her child a fainter bloom,
> a more delicate and briefer beauty, and a slighter physical frame,
> if not a character of less force and solidity, than her own. (50)

Hawthorne visioned the older Puritan women as ethically as coarse
as their temporal diet, "with a moral diet not a whit more refined" than
the beef and ale they commonly ate (50). Yet, Hawthorne seems to note
slight changes in his characters over time that imply some improvement.
The femininity of Hawthorne's women seems to typify those generations
of civilization that are advancing more toward a compassionate society
through the medium of more relaxed religious practices. Throughout
the novel, Hawthorne also rendered the more feminine women as more
tolerant in their view of human or mother nature (Hester), likely indicating
his hope for a future generation that has higher regard for our mortality
than did preceding generations.

A touch of Anti-transcendentalism also seems to embrace his
womenfolk: that part of womankind (civilization) that sees the flesh as
depraved is influenced by the dark side of the ethereal, and that part which
values its beauty and wonder has a more refined and sensitive nature,
as though it is influenced by the divine. The contrast in Hawthorne's
women between coarse masculinity and graceful femininity, then, seems
to symbolize the refinement of contemporary society through a more
gracious philosophical interpretation of Christianity, perhaps, of course,
aided more by intuitive insight, or revelation, than by logical deduction.

THE WOMANHOOD OF HESTER

Is humankind evil in nature or inherently noble? What does that
meaning portend for the value of mortality and the worthiness of flesh?
Hawthorne framed these questions in the minds of his readers around the
characters of Hester and Pearl to aid their intuitive quest. The answers to
these questions, asked directly upon the scaffold, are unfolded in the pages
of Hester's life thereafter, and are addressed as directly as golden silence
can best do so.

Perhaps Hawthorne uses characterization of the market-place crowd, as of the custom house officials, to contrast human nature, as affected by Puritanism, with unblemished nature, as perhaps the Creator intended it, or as Hawthorne saw it. Solemn, cold, equally merciless for either mild or sever departure from established prescriptions, the "Puritan character" was formed by a fusion of both the religious and legal codes of the time (50). Hester, on the other hand, appears to represent the beauty of mortality, as Hawthorne sees it, whose appearance over time becomes blemished and faded under the relentless and putative brow of Puritanim. As she stood in the market place, boldly facing the austere countenance of the women gathered around her, "never had Hester Prynne appeared more lady-like, in the antique interpretation of the term, than as she issued from the prison" (53). Even Hester's aging signals the eventual destiny of mortality itself, and the need for its transformation by some divine, golden touch.

So Hester's character, as mother nature, is depicted early as beautiful, charming, and graceful. She is more feminine and lady-like than any other woman character in his novel, and described in radiant elegance. Once readers envision Hester representing our mortal nature, they may begin to see Hawthorne's view of the natural body. When first we appreciate her beauty, we intuitively feel that there is something divine about it. Beginning with intuition, perhaps Hawthorne then is relying upon the reader's logic to support that intuition: perhaps, Providence would not have invested his time and creative powers in the creation of humankind unless there was some significant destiny in store, a more promising breed of humanity, particularly for the coming millennial era. Thus Pearl is fathered from a blend of earth and sky.

Pearl seems to represent that stage of mortality, or the beginning of a civilization, whose mother is of the elements of nature, but whose maker, or father, is unknown by the general populace. The divine Dimmesdale, as Hester's minister, seems to have assumed some responsibility for addressing, and possibly alleviating, her condition. Pearl thus may represent a generation of humankind, though raised on a sparcity of light, which hopefully will share a more advanced Christian philosophy not only closer to the original than its successors, but also far superior to the present.

When Hester stepped over the threshold of the prison with natural dignity, she did it "as if by her own free will" (52), as though unfettered, unashamed, and unabashed for the child in her arms, and proudly displayed the elaborate and splendidly embroidered scarlet letter. Hawthorne was not portraying Hester as a brazen hussy, but seemingly as a woman scornful of her treatment, as though the deed she had done had its merits; not as a coarse and indelicate strumpet, but as a standard of integrity symbolized within the moral fragrance of her inward beauty, as though her worthiness was neither understood nor appreciated; and not as an exemplary rude deviate of her society, but as an extraordinary emissary, as though her dignity heralded some hopeful tidings contemptuous of the ignominious facings of Puritanism. Some readers may take offense with Hester's attitude until they realize that the allegorical meanings whitewash the red stain of her infamy.

Just as much as the Puritan fathers discouraged extravagance of dress, the regulations of the Puritan fathers did not favor mercy for the wayward, though some of its adherents still had inklings of it. She could have covered the scarlet letter with a brooch, but chose instead to make a statement by elaborately embellishing it and stitching it with "fantastic flourishes of gold thread": the act which she had committed was nothing she was at heart ashamed of but should be regarded with splendor "greatly beyond what was allowed by the sumptuary regulations of the colony" (53). The symbol of gold here may suggest some royal or heavenly connection. She used golden threads to crown her deed as though the highest majesty had given it his stamp of approval. Hester expressed her contempt for the shortcomings of Puritanism, and intended to make "a halo of the misfortune and ignominy in which she was enveloped" (53).

Any shame Hester felt may have been a reflection of the shame of conjured depravity cast upon her by Puritanism. Or perhaps it reflects the shame of mortality for the nakedness humankind feels in the absence of Deity, whose presence, in Christian thought, has been described as clothed in the radiance of burning immortality. It is a shame from which she would have liked to escape, but which, she realized at the end, seems to identify her both as a product of her time and place, and as a precursor of another coming. She therefore bore her shame willingly, perhaps intuitively aware of eventual relief, as though she were, by the rites of her endured sufferings, the manifest harbinger of a better civilization coming

THE BRIGHT SUNLIGHT OF TRUTH

Perhaps darkness in his tale is the absence of light, or the light of truth. The winking of two characters in the light of the sun may be symbols consistent with the image of the sable shield, or the black effect of Puritanism. Pearl, as she comes forth from the prison in which she was born, winks perhaps because she has been weaned on darkness and is presently accustomed only to the "gray twilight of a dungeon" (52).

John Wilson, the oldest clergyman in the colony, whose study is that of benighted Puritanism, has gray eyes, that, "accustomed to the shaded light of his study," also winks, "like those of Hester's infant, in the unadulterated sunshine" (65). Unadulterated light seems to represent the pure truth of existence, too bright for the eyes of its present guardians. Conversely, shades of darkness, like gray, may be adulterated with a mixture of impure doctrine, or some contrivance of it.

Puritanism gloried in its version of truth, as most religions do, and perhaps should, since each claim, or should claim, to be the only true way to heaven, or else they perhaps cast beams of adulterated sunshine. Ironically, Hester intuitively sensed unadulterated truth, that humankind's nature is noble, as intended by its Creator, and destined for some glorious end. She apparently was not entirely a product of Puritanic indoctrination, but rather epitomized the best of human nature despite her brainwashing by it. She lived in the adulterated gloom of the Puritan interpretation of truths about the purpose of our mortal existence and its controversial sireship.

THE MAKING OF A NAME

The task of Hawthorne's allegory is to reverse the meaning of the scarlet letter in the minds of the reader by reversing the reader's views of his main characters. The manner in which Hester proudly flaunts the fantastically embroidered scarlet letter "illuminated upon her bosom" (53) appears to reflect Hawthorne's hallowed concept of human nature, a nature that is nevertheless punished by Puritanism because it is perceived as depraved and wicked. That the letter has an illumination may alert the perceptive reader to some moral truth hidden within the allegory that is designed to reverse our view of Hester. To effect this reversal of perspective, Hawthorne adds many other allusions as her story unfolds.

The scarlet letter, "having the effect of a spell," has perhaps been embellished for the purpose of also casting a spell of intuitive wonder upon the reader. Hester's nature and her signal attachment to the scarlet letter serve to classify her as an icon, "taking her out of the ordinary relations with humanity, and inclosing her in a sphere by herself" (54). As a principle to herself, perhaps with no extensive association with humankind, her destiny is confined and limited, like the nature of mortality, which has its own place and time for a season. Hester, therefore, shall remain in Salem, and not have an ordinary relation with Pearl (perhaps an extraordinary or spiritualized one instead), whose life in an unknown region, is rich with joy and prosperity. As mortality is the forebear of immortality, so Hester is the mother of Pearl.

Mortality may seem a misfortune to those who do not understand its purpose; but Hester has attempted to make a "halo" of its destiny, and has illuminated the scarlet letter to signify that the letter A stands for something more noble and promising than the ignominious hues cast upon it by Puritan definition. In the embellishment of the scarlet letter, Hawthorne ironically seems to throw his concept of human nature into the very face of Puritanism, in the words of the worthy gossips who witness Hester's rendering of the letter: "[W]hat is it but to laugh in the faces of our godly magistrates, and make a pride out of what they, worthy gentlemen, meant for a punishment?"(54) Hawthorne therefore seems to cast a spell upon the reader by trying to signify her as something greater than a woman taken in ordinary sin, with a meaning all her own despite her limited relations with all of humanity. Perhaps the singularity of the spell pinpoints the significance of the symbol as a meaning which can be sensed only intuitively.

> But the point which drew all eyes, and, as it were, transfigured the wearer,—so that both men and women, who had been familiarly acquainted with Hester Prynne, were now impressed as they beheld her for the first time,—was that SCARLET LETTER. (53)

The letter A is the centerpiece or kingpin of the allegorical tale, and is designed to focus the reader's attention to fathom its deeper meaning, especially as they identify with her compassionate service to others, even those who disdain and scorn her.

Transfigured thus, as a representation of something superior to Puritan consciousness, or its gloomy civilization, Hester, in the light of the scarlet letter, can be seen in a different perspective "for the first time" (53). As we see more clearly later, she appears to be a prophetic prototype of a future generation, neither everlastingly identified nor closely attached with the mortality of humanity, but transfigured into a sphere or state of existence far removed from it. Pearl, who imbibbed of all Hester's bitter experiences, also for some destined purpose, appears to be her better outgrowth by that very sharing.

To the Romantic, just as the ethereal or spiritual element of this physical world is a separate dimension that transcends and surrounds the reality of the physical world, and commutes some ray of sunshine thereto, perhaps the spell which the scarlet letter casts upon its observers, and its readers, may forecast aspects of the allegorical relationship between Hester and Pearl, and "the relation between the Deity and the communities of mankind." This rare view of Hester premonitions or begins the development of the allegorical theme of the better world possibly awaiting humankind.

In the light of all the contextual clues of this chapter alone, the label of the scarlet letter, being repainted and unfolding in the intuitive mind of the reader, cannot be clearly named Adultery. That is merely the initial image conjectured by the tale which the allegory is designed to reverse.

HESTER UPON THE SCAFFOLD

The scaffold is described in the market-place as the instrument of Puritanic shame used to purge out the evil tendencies of the depraved flesh. The pillory upon the scaffold was used to focus the sinner's consciousness on the shame of his/her human nature, and may represent the cross human beings carry by nature of their mortality. To Hawthorne, this simple device may represent the greatest single perversion of reality he levels at Puritanism. In the description of the pillory's use, Hawthorne, in his narrator's commentary, perhaps makes his most candid and emotional statement about the Puritanic view of human nature:

> There can be no outrage, methinks, against our common nature–whatever be the delinquencies of the individual,—no outrage more flagrant than to forbid the culprit to hide his face for shame, as it was the essence of this punishment to do. (55)

The scaffold, with the pillory, was regarded with a measure of reverence for the legal enforcement of Puritan law. For example, in referencce to a mock incidence of swordplay upon it, later on in the tale, "the town beadle . . . had no idea of permitting the majesty of the law to be violated by such an abuse of one its consecrated places" (232). But to Hawthorne, the pillory seems not only to exalt the concept of depravity but also to deny the divine essence of the human being that Hawthorne covertly seems to herald. It blasphemed the inherent dignity of humankind by public ridicule and exaggerated, if not utterly falsified, its debasement.

Mother nature is pure, Hawthorne seems to proclaim, and humankind, as a child of nature and the divine within, should be considered as the noble work of her Creator. So noble and beautiful a creation in fact that "the world was only the darker for this woman's beauty, and the more lost for the infant that she had borne," because her beauty, and the miraculous wonder of life, could not be appreciated through the dark lens of Puritanism. The gloomy and distorted perspective of this religion tainted "the most sacred quality of human life" (56), and the world is the more darker for its effect.

But how can the reader escape the Puritan consciousness within that reflectively clouds this appreciation with the logical assumption concerning the manner of Pearl's birth? Hawthorne offsets this cloud with a slight ray of sunshine, in this same paragraph, by comparing Hester on the scaffold, with Pearl in her arms, to an unlikely historical figure:

> Had there been a Papist among the crowd of Puritans, he might have seen in this beautiful woman, so picturesque in her attire and mien, and with the infant at her bosom, an object to remind him of the image of Divine Maternity . . . ; something which should remind him, indeed, but only by contrast, of that sacred image of sinless motherhood, whose infant was to redeem the world. (56)

We must pay no mind at all to this offhand statement. Surely it has no suggestive bearing whatsoever on the mystery clothed within Hawthorne's allegory. Far be it from this student to suggest that there are only two other ways by which the human being has been given birth, or that Hawthorne is referring to either of them. Let us persist to hold to the one view of Hester, at the surface level, and dare not suggest that there might be some other reference, at the allegorical level, to explain the relationship between Hester and Dimmesdale. We might likewise consider but wisely ought to leave Mary and Adam out of the equation of life altogether.

The use of the parenthetical phrase, "but only by contrast," is surely not in the least to be considered a sarcastic or facetious remark, but is intended completely as an apologetic remark on the part of Hawthorne to excuse his boldness in proposing such a reflection, although, however, he does use this technique quite often.

This comparison to Mary, the mother of God in the flesh (according to the Christian creed), is so glaringly a contradiction so early in Hawthorne's characterization of Hester that—marveling that it alone does not compel the readers to reconsider their image or view of Hester—this layman would instead prefer to defer their attention to two other chapters, "Hester at Her Needle," and "Another View of Hester," both of which unveal a little more of Hester's representation. To cast a holy aspersion in the face of blatant common sense, or conjecture, so early in the tale, is beneath the man, at least, at this point.

But since Hawthorne himself is the culprit of this controversy, it might be considered a literary sin to keep completely silent on the matter. Let us briefly indulge another fantasy that imagination may be guilty of harboring, but for some logic, for which we might be thankful, that forbids it. It would appear that Hawthorne seems very obstrusely to signal some contrast or reversal of imagery he is already beginning to weave into the reader's mind, a contrast that might relate to the mystery within the allegory. This purveyor faintly might suggest that this passage is probably his only direct or slight reference to the historical figure of the Redeemer of the human race. Is Hawthorne suggesting that, as some "Divine Maternity" of Hester, or offhand contrast within the allegory, she may be the mother of an advanced stage of humankind (Pearl), to be rescued by some redeemer in a divine suffering, in the which Hester (Nature) takes an allied and redeeming role? Squelch the thought! Forbid the audacity! Emphatically no!

Yet, Hawthorne possibly indirectly makes a possible second reference to another setting when he notes that the only element of shame missing from Hester's treatment was the absence of cruel ridicule by the market-place crowd, which "had none of the heartlessness of another social state, which would find only a theme for jest in an exhibition like the present" (56). That social state could, hush the thought, be primarily a reference to the Roman empire, whose soldiers, in thoughtless jest prior to his crucifixion, mocked the man of Nazareth for being considered by his followers to be King of the Jews. A platted wreath of thorns crowned this absurdity, and a purple robe jeered the crowd's claim of his Kingship. We might perish the thought that Hawthorne has made any significant allusion to both the birth and the death of such an historical figure.

Logic again cries out against such a comparison, doesn't it? Although it may signal some other moral meaning, this allusion may simply signal a premonition of the young divine's exhibition upon the scaffold to make his Confession about his relationship with Hester,. It also could be that, in the absence of an heartless mockery by the crowd, which "was sombre and grave," Hawthorne may again be implying that the human race is improving over time as it moves toward another significant period in the history of the world. Differences in the parishioners' reactions to his characters appear to signify shades of improvement from time to time in their attitude, perhaps as differences in the perceptions of his readers may signify an improvement in their measure of intuition. Far be it from this reader to disallow such differences, whether in Dimmesdale's parishioners, Hawthorne's readership, or mine.

CHILLINGWORTH AND THE CONTINENTAL CITY

Hawthorne's ability to develop in a few words multiple meanings from his symbols is extraordinary, but not unique, since some Biblical authors or prophets used the same strategy. Having possibly, though unlikely at this point, set up a foreshadowing of the Passion of Christ, Hawthorne next introduced Dimmesdale's Nemesis, Chillingworth, who, from numerous descriptions, is an apparent Satanic figure, whom no less by historical contrast might prefigure his counterpart. Satan, as Lucifer, was cast out of heaven into outer darkness by his Nemesis, and Chillingworth seems out to get revenge for it. Perhaps an analogy is intended to seize the reader's mind at this point, but let us not too soon worry about it; logic will surely make short work of it.

Nevertheless, in the closing paragraphs in the discussion of the market-place, Hester had a flashback to other scenes, other faces, of her subsequent life before she met Master Prynne. Hawthorne stated that "the scaffold of the pillory was a point of view that revealed to Hester Prynne the entire track along which she had been treading, since her happy infancy" (58). This "entire track" possibly represents the history of humanity up until the present.

Hester's allegorical life seems revealed in many metaphors alluding to the beginning of humanity's nature as a sentient being, first in Paradise, then again after the Fall. This fall was caused by a connection with another being, "with eyes dim and bleared by the lamp-light," Master Prynne, by name. Before she awoke from this memory trip to the rude reality of her present state of shame and infamy, Hester saw her past life almost as a destiny unfolding in connection with this other person "of the study and the cloister."

> There she beheld another countenance, of a man well stricken in years, a pale, thin, scholar-like visage, with eyes dim and bleared by the lamp-light that had served them to pore over many ponderous books . . . . This figure . . . was slightly deformed, with the left shoulder a trifle higher than the right. (58)

She remembered in a past association with this deformed person, not by the light of day but by lamp-light (a man-made light), the face of this man studying ponderous books dimly through bleared eyesight, a scholar-like person who can "read the human soul" (58). The reader discovers the identity of this scholarly character later as Master Prynne, next, as Chillingworth, and then possibly as the Black Man of the Forest himself. He is seen in a cloister, an edifice secluded from the world, in connection with "the Continental City," which seclusion may allude to Satan being cast out of heaven for rebellion, who since has been "a wanderer, sorely against my will" (61). Hester had a flashback of a former happy life upon which the misshapen scholar somehow effected a drastic change from one of endless life to one that dies by feeding upon itself (58); and this reflection may alllude to the Biblical role of Eve, as a possible immortal figure before the fall. In his role, Satan appeared to Eve in the Garden (Hester's former happy life) and shared his knowledge with her, which resulted in the fall of humankind's nature,

> where a new life had awaited her, still in connection with the misshapen scholar; a new life, but feeding itself on time-worn materials, like a tuft of green moss on a crumbling wall. (58)

Reference later to green moss growing upon fallen trees may connect with this analogy as well. Here, it seems to refer to the degeneration of mortality, and later, to the degeneration of Christian institutions. The Continental city might be a city as big as a continent and appears, in the first analysis, to be the Garden of Eden, or the world in paradisiacal glory, in a place and time in Hester's happy days. This "city" existed in a time that occurred before Chillingworth helped effect the fall of Hester into a life that could exist only by feeding on mortal element, like "moss on a crumbling wall." Hester remembered him before she saw the Continental City; and the transition from the memory of Chillingworth to the Continental City back to the present reality of Puritanism suggests a synoptic reference to the history of humankind, perhaps in some connection with Deity. We will learn more later about that future relationship with Deity.

As a possible correlary theme, just as mortality is a life that feeds upon other life, Puritanism itself may also be seen, from Hawthorne's point of view, as feeding gloomily upon the adulterated Calvinistic doctrine of the depravity of human nature. How Chillingworth is connected to this new life of mortality, that feeds upon itself, is depicted more thoroughly later in the tale.

As a Satanic figure, Chillingworth represents the dark side of the ethereal that has an effect upon human character because of his ability, as an old scholar, "to read the human soul," howbeit through blurred or distorted vision. His bleared visage, as a result of night-study, possibly highlights Lucifer's inability to see the truth by the light of common day, or that he is accustomed to sight only in the darkness of his sequestered abode. He has a difficult time both in discerning and in relating truth, as is developed in a later chapter when he and Hester discuss their past relationship, wherein he admits sharing his knowledge with her to some disastrous effect. As a principle, at a third level of meaning below the second level of his representation of an historical figure, Chillingworth may represent the extreme end of hostility on a continuum between love and hate, as reflected in Hawthorne's essay on love and hate, perhaps the major thematic conflict in his tale.

So Hester may represent the immortal nature of humankind before the fall and the mortal nature of a new life afterwards. The scarlet letter on her bosom possibly highlights the curse, as well as the Redemption, or her transformation later, in relation to the divine Dimmesdale, that may result in yet a better life in a time and place to come. She has been doomed to bear the burden throughout her lifetime, but has chosen to carry it embellished with this promise, or the hope of that transformation.

Chillingworth, it might be added parenthetically, is the name of an actual historical figure who argued strongly in favor of the English Anglican Church which the Puritans wished to reform. It is possible that Hawthorne chose this name for the character who was to be the antagonist opposite the Puritan minister, Dimmesdale, referred to as the young divine. As his Satanic character unfolds to the reader, the most likely candidate as protagonist in the novel ostensibly and perspicuously, though regrettably and incredibly to many a critic, seems to be, by analogical contrast, an image of the Nazarene, despite all we can logically conjure to the contrary.

CHAPTER 3

THE RECOGNITION

For such are false apostles, deceitful workers, transforming
themselves into the apostles of Christ.
And no marvel; for Satan himself is transformed into an angel
of light.[1]

This chapter begins to unfold the relationships between the main characters at the story level and also at the allegorical level. One of the least understood relationships in Hawthorne's novel is that between Hester and her husband, Master Prynne. As she stood upon the scaffold, his personage was the object of her curiosity that distracted her momentarily from the naked reality of her ignominy, and then filled her with terror and dread at her recognition of him. The reader might easily view this chapter as an introduction to the character of Chillingworth, whom Hester recognized as her ex-husband. However, at the surface level of seeking to identify the father of Pearl, it is a more subtle introduction, at the allegorical level, of an attempt to identify and recognize who the father of the human race might really be.

MR. AND MRS. PRYNNE

Hester received a second rude awakening from her recollections of her earlier childhood when she recognized that the object of her curious observations, an Indian's companion, is her husband, one of whose "shoulders rose higher than the other." This physical deformity, or imbalance, was the result "of a person who had so cultivated his mental part that it could not fail to mould the physical to itself, and become manifest by unmistakable tokens" (60). His association with the Indians, and his deformity, connote characteristics of an evil nature from whose presence Hester intuitively cringes, and his Indian consorts may represent those spirits which were cast out of heaven along with Lucifer. Rather than being one of their captive victims, their willingness to do Chillingworth's bidding suggests the contrary.

His "strange disarray of civilized and savage costume" or "heterogeneous garb" (60) probably represents Lucifer's influence upon civilized as well as upon uncivilized societies. That his heterogeneous costume is in disarray may imply deceptive disharmony and incongruence of character as well as a capacity to appear acceptable to both the Indian and Puritan cultures. It may also symbolize the double-minded nature of Satan, to appear as an honorable servant of the people, while at the same time he seeks to gather them into his "lonely and chill" cheerless heart (74). Chillingworth, as we will learn as the tale unfolds, perhaps represents the historical figure of Lucifer, Satan, the Black Man of the forest, in general, the dark side of life that has an ability to influence nature, as does the divine, according to the anti-Transcendentalists. He may also represent, at the far end of the continuum between hate and love, the epitome of hostility toward humankind in his penetrating belief that all are evil. He is an intelligent visage and master at prying into one's soul, and is bent on discovering some evil he anticipates in the father of Pearl so that he can secretly destroy him. He is the same character Hester remembered from the flashback of her happy past before her fall, which is associated with her prior relationship with him. She had rejected her contract of marriage with him, had fled from him, and apparently was lost in a fallen world seeking divine assistance.

INTIMATIONS OF THE TONGUELESS ONES

To the Romantic, the ethereal world does not trumpet its truths but reserves its revelations for those who draw close to nature and are in tune with the palpitations of its delicate heart. Similarly, Hawthorne requires the reader to sense intuitively a greater truth lying somewhere below the surface of his tale. The Puritan code, possibly under the influence from the dark side of the spiritual world, sees human nature (typified by the figure of Hester) as depraved, whose acts mostly are worthy of censure and punishment. Hawthorne, as a Romantic, sees nature as a mirror of spiritual truths from both realms of light and darkness, imbues Hester initially with beauty in form and character, but projects within her the conflict between logic and intuition.

At the very moment Chillingworth's penetrative insight beheld the significance of the scarlet letter on Hester's bosom, "A writhing horror twisted itself across his features, like a snake gliding swiftly over them, and making one little pause, with all its wreathed intervolutions in open sight." (61) That Hawthorne may have personified Old Scratch in Chillingworth's character seems to have been connoted in the simile of the snake that deceived Eve in the Garden of Eden. (Chapter IV, "The Interview," elaborates on this allusion.) This expression upon Master Prynne's face reflects the darkness of some "powerful emotion" that seems to convulse his features in contemplating some event that has some terrible fate in store for him. This momentary convulsion of horror, which happens again later in the tale, appears to be a precognition of some truth by which he is destined to be defeated in time. At this point in the tale, Hawthorne gives us no clues to explain this "writhing horror" which Chillingworth struggled to control, but he does later when Chillingworth beheld Dimmesdale upon the scaffold. It is the scaffold that connects Hester's scarlet letter with the scarlet letter on Dimmesdale's chest, the sight of which later strikes Chillingworth again with both delight and terror.

The image of the snake seems likely a reference to the seduction of Eve when Satan appeared to her in the form of a snake to deceive her into partaking of the forbidden fruit. A conversation between Hester and Chillingworth later in the story confirms the nature of Hester's seduction by him, and dates her fall by him, and not by the divine. This seduction forms the basis for the contract by which nature fell from immortality into mortality, flesh that to the Puritans was depraved and evil in nature, but that to Hawthorne seems associated more with the divine element. Though this simile may allude to Eve's association with the snake in the Garden of Eden, Hester, however, appears to represent, besides an allusion to a historical figure, a broader principle, the larger concept of humankind's nature, and that representation is not simply confined to the one individual.

After Chillingworth regained control of his intense feelings, when his and Hester's eyes have met, he invoked Hester's silence calmly from a distance, as he does later in his interview with Hester. There seems to be purpose in this appeal to silence, just as there is purpose in Dimmesdale's need for silence in his relationship with Hester. Whereas silence for Dimmesdale seems a precaution in Providence's plan to glorify humankind, like a well-kept secret, silence for Chillingworth seems a cloak for Lucifer's deceptive plot to claim the human race through the thwarting of that plan, like the disguise of a serpent. Silence in Dimmesdale's and Hester's case seems acceptable, though questionable to Hawthorne, for the reason given heretofore, but not so in Chillingworth's case. The silence he invoked from Hester is part of that vengeful plan. In Hester's case, in another sense, human nature, in of itself alone, cannot speak with too much certitude either for or against a creator, perhaps because of this conflict between reason and intuition.

Hawthorne's ambivalence about the question of silence on the part of Hester and the divine, if only for the sake of the reader at this point in the tale, perhaps is best demonstrated in Dimmsdale's request of her upon the scaffold:

> "Hester, though he were to step down from a high place, and stand there beside thee, on thy pedestal of shame, yet better were it so, than to hide a guilty heart through life. What can thy silence do for him . . . ?" (67)

In other allegorical words, it were better for the Creator to condescend to step down from on high and stand upon the scaffold himself, which Dimmesdale will symbolically do properly in time, thus admitting his involvement in the plan of mortality, than to keep its purposes a secret from humankind forever.

The question, "What can thy silence do for him?" stages for the reader the mystery of Dimmesdale's silence, which later he explains to Chillingworth in a hypothetical case. The passage above may be interpreted as a premonition of Dimmesdale making his dubious confession upon the scaffold at a time in better keeping with Providence's plans. Perhaps it may also signal to Hester what her cup ought to be at the present time, while Dimmesdale may be suggesting to her that his cup is due and yet coming.

To detail the allegorical implications further, the question Hawthorne may be framing for the reader, might be, "what compels the silence of heaven as to the accountability for the mesh of good and evil in mortality?" He is noted already as having stated "that it were wronging the very nature of woman to force her to lay open her heart's secrets in such broad daylight, and in presence of so great a multitude" (65). As Hawthorne has stated he deems it inappropriate for any author in indulge himself in such open revelation, he likewise is according Hester the same right. If it were wrong for Hester to divulge her inmost secrets, what good can her silence do for Dimmesdale? This question is addressed elsewhere in a discussion of Dimmsdale's silence; but in a nutshell, the implication rises from the tale that Diety, represented by the most divine on earth, answered the question of accountability for the birth of the human's mortal nature, in the Atonement, which paid for the wronged pains and and agonies of life, and offered humankind hope for an immortal nature refined elsewhere in the future. To have openly in the full brightness of daylight told the whole multitude of the world that Providence was responsible for mortality by design, might wrong the very nature of mankind by giving her excuse to justify her waywardness rather than to work it out through repentance, the process by which the nature of evil is transformed into goodness. Keeping the accountability muted favors the purposes of Deity in getting humankind to overcome evil rather than giving in to it.

So what good can the silence of human nature do for its Creator? Though nature may long for an answer from the divine as to its viable connections with Deity, only the voice of the divine can declare what those connections are. Though intuition and logic may vie for a word in the matter, only the Creator of humankind can vouch for what destiny is in store for it. In the meanwhile, Hawthorne seems to be intimating that the silence of heaven leaves it to the individual to believe what one chooses to believe, to listen to one's intutive sense for the tongueless intimations, or the more louder tongues of intellect and logic.

IN PURSUIT OF HESTER AND HER LOVER

In his conversation with a townsman, Chillingworth disclosed that he had been held by the Indians and had been brought into Salem to be redeemed out of captivity. This disclosure appears to be a bold lie, as he is free to move about, and the Indians seem to be doing his bidding, rather than the reverse. Since the subterfuge is no longer continued as a plot or subplot of the tale, the reader begins to realize that the character of Chillingworth is that of a liar. The Christian's concept of Lucifer is one of a revengeful deceiver and an "accuser of the brethren"[2], who intended to bring about their death. Chillingworth, as the antagonist, played this role in pursuit of his revenge upon the young divine and his Providential mission.

Master Prynne, unknown by that name in Boston, extracted the story of Hester from the townsman, who explained that Hester's husband is Master Prynne, a learned man or scholar who sent his wife ahead of him two years ago, that the father of the child is unknown, and that it will take a prophet like Daniel to expound the riddle: "Of a truth, friend, that matter remaineth a riddle; and the Daniel who shall expound it is yet a-wanting" (62). Though the Daniel mentioned here might also refer to the astute reader who can decipher and expound the riddle of the scarlet letter, this author's earlier disclosure of a symbolic reference to a prophecy by Daniel is not merely coincidental. Perhaps Hawthorne's reference has to do with Daniel's visions and dream interpretations dealing with the last days of the earth when, after other kingdoms have ended, the kingdom of heaven shall be established. This reference might be another allusion to one of the themes this purveyor casts as central to the allegory, that of the transformation of, or the transfiguration of, the civilizations of the world.

That Chillingworth is a learned man is consistent with the analogy that Lucifer tempted Eve with the idea of gaining knowledge to discern good from evil. In the townsman's reference to her fall, Hawthorne may be alluding to Chillingworth, who knew Hester first, instead of Dimmesdale:

> [T]his woman is youthful and fair, and doubtless was strongly tempted to her fall;—and that, moreover, as is most likely, her husband may be at the bottom of the sea" (63).

The bottom of the sea is a fit metaphor for Master Prynne's dwelling place, like the bottomless pit, in the Biblical text, is the proper abode for Satan.

We learn later that Chillingworth is seeking revenge in his efforts to claim the souls of the other three main characters–Hester, Pearl, and Dimmesdale, especially the latter. It appears that if he can lay claim to Dimmesdale's soul, the souls of the others are inclusive. Keeping his identity unknown, therefore, is crucial to this pursuit, which began with his discovery of Hester at the scaffold. He is determined to pry into the mystery himself for some evil he hopes to find, and to bring out the hellish hues thereof, proclaming, "he will be known!–he will be known!–he will be known!" (63) Though that is his primary quest, the reader will discover that Master Prynne changes his mind when he discovers who Dimmesdale really is.

THE JUDGMENT OF HESTER

The death penalty for adultery, as instituted under Mosaic law, and hypcritically enforced under Judaism, was harsh and unmerciful up to the meridian of time, that is, until the advent of the Nazarene, according to Christian theology. Hawthorne's use of the time span of three hours, perhaps symbolic of the first few thousand years before the meridian of time, may have reference to the practice of enforcing the law of Moses instead of the more compassionate teachings replacing it. Although the Puritan fathers did exercise some mercy in not putting Hester to death, the magistracy assembled to judge Hester are deemed by the narrator, Hawthorne, to be unfit or incapable of judging her. Their act of grace seemed insufficient to constitute the kind of compassion he felt should have been in effect in the Puritan code.

John Wilson, the eldest clergyman of Boston, "had no right . . . to step forth . . . and meddle with a question of human guilt, passion, and anguish" (65); nor was Governor Bellingham, or any of his representatives on the balcony. Indeed, perhaps, no person, "out of the whole human family . . . [was] capable of sitting in judgment on an erring woman's heart, and disentangling its mesh of good and evil" (64). To have no right also questions their authority to handle the matter. The task rightly belonged to Dimmesdale, the divine, since it was his responsibility, said the Governor to him, "'the responsibility of this woman's soul lies greatly with you'" (66). Only Dimmsdale the divine can judge the wherefore of Hester's fall.

The symbolic gist of this narration might be that the shaded light of Puritanism had neither right nor ability to pry out of nature the truth as to the goodness or evil of the creation of humankind, nor settle the paradoxes of mortality's existence: only Providence can answer the why and wherefore of humanity's mortal nature. It seems that Hawthorne is therefore saying that only some decision or act of Heaven could resolve the paradox, that Dimmesdale is its divine representative to work out that resolution, "the accountability under which I labor" (67). Hawthorne may have purposefully and particularly referred to Dimmesdale as "the divine" to figure a representative of Deity who was responsible for the creation of the "mystery of a woman's soul, so sacred, even in its pollution" (66).

This sacred pollution is an oxymoron that may signify a coupling of the divine with mortal nature; it may imply that Hawthorne may envision mortality as a combination of two entities, one good, and the other, in the minds of the speculators, as an evil one, because of its passionate and corruptive tendencies; and it may raise in the mind of the reader the question of the value and purpose of such a co-mingling. Represented by Pearl, humanity, as "many children" (90) of the Divine, yet living in a degenerative state, appears to be the offspring of that union.

Hawthorne posed another kind of oxymoron on the scaffold, where the reader may find many answers, to explain the mystery of the mixture, when Dimmesdale says, "Heaven hath given thee an open ignominy, that thereby thou mayest work out an open triumph over the evil within thee, and the sorrow without" (67). Perhaps to Hawthorne, Hester's ignominious triumpth is a visage of earth life, an open ignominy, later to be transmuted into an open triumph by patiently enduring and working it out, through yielding to the intimations from the universal heart. Perhaps this statement by the divine implies that Adam and Eve, in their simple innocence, could have achieved no triumph over evil without coming face to face with it in a mortal body, that goodness can neither be known or achieved without the presence of its twin, evil.

The disentangling of the "mesh of good and evil" (64), in the heart of human nature, may not be fully accomplished in his tale, but Hawthorne's allegory seems to frame the hopeful resolution of the paradox as one of its major themes. This paradox seems but a corollary to the short essay, at the end of the book, on the subject of how love and hate in humanity may be "the same thing at bottom," with "their earthly stock of hatred and antipathy transmuted into golden love" (261). To Hawthorne, perhaps the likelihood of this transmutation of hate into love, of evil into good, is his Anti-transcendental take on the resurrection, wherein the mortality of nature may be transformed into an immortality of nature.

Nevertheless, at this time, neither could Dimmesdale resolve the mystery of Hester's soul. Though he is described by Hawthorne in glowing terms–" childlike . . . with a freshnesss, and fragrance, and dewy purity of thought, "a white, lofty, and impending brow," and "speech of an angel"—for different reasons, he could not, indeed, would not, have Hester identify him as the father of Pearl, at this particular time. Until the right time for this resolution, the judgment inherent within, and under the hand of him who was responsible and capable to disentangle this sacred pollution,

Hawthorne indicated that the crowd was more worthy to judge her because "whatever sympathy she might expect lay in the larger and warmer heart of the multitude" (64), which warmth was evoked by the moving speech of Dimmsdale. Love, revealed in compassion and sympathy for the sinner, is contrasted with the condemnation of the sinner by the Puritan fathers. Perhaps it is only the embodiment of compassion and mercy that capacitates the power of rendering judgment. Puritanism was influenced too much by the dark side, and too little by the radiant light of the spiritual realm, ever to conduct the soul through the gates of Paradise.

That Hawthorne, however, does seem to give recognition to some progress that has been made over time in the reformation of Christianity is also indicated in Hawthorne's comment by the townsman in reference to the Massachusetts magistracy:

> [T]hey have not been bold to put in force the extremity of our righteous law against her. The penalty thereof is death. But, in their great mercy and tenderness of heart, they have doomed Mistress Prynne to stand only a space of three hours on the platform of the pillory, and then and thereafter, for the remainder of her natural life, to wear a mark of shame upon her bosom. (63)

This tidbit of faint praise, unless Hawthorne is simply being sarcastic, may betoken his timid link to the soil of Salem as well as a watermark in the gradual transformation of society he envisioned.

THE RIGHT OF JUDGMENT

Reverend Dimmesdale is recognized by the Governor as the one to extract a confession from Hester, as a gesture of repentance, and presumably as a means of redemption, as to who the father of Pearl is. The Reverend did not wish to pass judgment upon or exact a confession out of Hester, as do the "prying multitude;" but given the charge, he tremenously made an earnest and heart-felt appeal to Hester to reveal the name of Pearl's father.

Simple and childlike, intelligent and sensitive, pure in thought and angelic in speech, Dimmesdale finds himself in a predicament much like the man of Nazareth, who was called upon by the ruling Pharisees of his time to judge an adulterous woman caught in the act. As the Nazarene claimed not to have come to judge but to redeem his creation, so perhaps Dimmesdale does not wish to judge Hester. From Hawthorne's perspective, the situation may appear similar: the Creator and Author of humankind, who set up the fall of Adam and Eve's civilization, will be its judge later; Dimmesdale (the divine) has assumed responsibility for Hester (Nature) and her child (humankind), and has been asked to judge Hester in deference to the crowd, who indicate they would prefer Dimmesdale than the Reverend Wilson.

The Reverend Wilson had suggested that Hester's naming the father might remove the scarlet letter from her bosom, to which she replied,

> "Never! . . . It is too deeply branded. Ye cannot take it off. And would that I might endure his agony, as well as mine! . . . And my child must seek a heavenly Father; she shall never know an earthly one!" (68)

Besides the issue of the right of judgment, there may be three other allegorical allusions in this quotation: the sharing of the agony of life's pains, the issue of how redemption is achieved, and the idea of never knowing an earthly father.

Not only does the Reverend Wilson not only have the right, but Hester has implied that neither does he have the power; that is, perhaps it is not within his office to remove the brand, as though that brand were an agony so deep that only an heavenly Father might be able to remove it. The agony symbolized in that which Hester and Dimmesdale share might be the identical or similar travail, as common to humanity's mortal nature, as that which the Nazarene is said likewise to have taken upon himself as the Son of man, as a kind of condescension. Besides enduring her own suffering mortality, Hester is likewise willing to share vicariously and reciprocally that of the divine's, should it be required.

Perhaps in Hawthorne's perusing of ancient documents, he sought to metaphorize the words of Isaiah in this peculiar relationship between Hester and Dimmesdale:

> Surely he hath borne our griefs, and carried our sorrows; yet we did esteem him stricken, smitten of God, and afflicted.

> But he was wounded for our transgressions, he was bruised for our iniquities: the chastisement of our peace was upon him: and with his stripes we are healed.[3]

Within the scope of that Christian creed, in regards to how mortalilty is redeemed, redemption does not come by simply removing its consequences, as possibly symbolized by Reverend Wilson's offer to remove the scarlet letter, but lies at the very heart of the Christian hope. Since mortality is branded too deeply in death for any mortal being to remove or change it, although in the Christian creed by one man mortality came for all, it begs an infinite and merciful pardon, from an immortal Being who has that blanket power to remove the effects of the fall. The promise that the effect of the Fall, as symbolized by the scarlet letter, cannot be merely lifted, is due to the fact that redemption is embedded in an Atonement to be suffered by a divine personage, as possibly symbolized by Hester's intuitive artful embellishment of the same token.

Pearl herself seems instinctively to have sensed somewhat some close connection to the divine Dimmesdale, something about him that only twice attracted her affectionate closeness, for she raised her arms out to him as an answer to his plea for Hester to reveal the identity of Pearl's father (67). This gesture by Pearl is interpreted by one of her inquisitors, Reverend Wilson, as a plea to reveal her father's identity; and though it may only be Pearl's instinctive warming to his appeal, it may reflect the intrinsic nature and desire of mankind, especially her better part, to want Deity to make its relationship to her known. As one actor upon the stage of life, Pearl's role seems that of making sure this relationship is declared, as we see her time and again prompting Hester and Dimmesdale toward some foreknown destiny

Nature typified, Hester is willing to endure the stigma of sin and looks to another to redeem her. Hence, Hester therefore looks to Dimmesdale the divine to assist in Pearl's quest for a heavenly Father to remove the pollution from the sacred soul. This Act must be made by a heavenly and not an earthly father. Dimmesdale appears to represent that divine agent who will yet confess his role and responsibility in that regard in due time. The plan of Providence must be achieved, and the scaffold yet awaits for Dimmesdale.

This allusion to a Heavenly Father, by implication, seems to relate the destiny of humankind, for which end Hester endures, to the beginning of humankind. If Pearl shall never know an earthly father, the implication is that she has never known one. Again, we may be confronted with the allegorical significance of the birth of Pearl, a mystery perhaps as relevant as the "Divine Maternity" (56), or the birth of Adam and Eve. Perhaps Hawthorne is simply agreeing that the beginning of humankind began other than by an earthly creation.

THE SILENCE OF THE LAMB

For the Romantic, the human being can entreat nature in the hope to perceive intuitively a reality of the truth surrounding that nature, a reality that lies more in the realm of the spiritual than in the physical. But nature cannot authoritatively declare in and of itself who the father of mortal nature is. Perhaps a knowledge of the Creator of mortal nature cannot be deduced by earthly reasoning; and Pearl must look to a heavenly Father to authoritatively identify her Creator. Hawthorne may be speaking for a divine father; but he also seems to be asking and quasi-answering the questions allegorically, "who is responsible for the mortal nature of mankind, what destiny is in store for her, and what justification is there for the silence of heaven concerning the problems of mortality?"

In the short run, Hawthorne may simply be stating that a rational or earthly philosophy will not explain the beginning or future destiny of humanity, but that any authoritative explanation is better than none, in order to be true to one's nature, even if the worse is declared in giving answer to such a question (260). Hawthorne's novel itself may be his own truthful response to his own curious and natural sensitivities.

Perhaps Hawthorne is implying not only that nature is bound more to the will of Providence that it realizes, that humankind's destiny is laid out, but also that the "Universal Father" might allow the revelation to these questions to those individuals who pry intuitively for them rather than relying on rational explanations. Representing the willed destiny of

Deity, Dimmesdale does not really want this revelation to be untimely or openly made, since a premature acknowledgement of responsibility in the mystery would hamper his ministry. For the Nazarene to have made it publicly and more openly known that he was the Creator of humankind, and a cause of their mortality, before his ministry was finished, might have limited his unhindered ministry by motivating the Pharisees to end his mission earlier than they did. He might have had to perform more miracles in his behalf, which he did not appear to care to demonstrate very often, and only as needed, for the sake of continuing his ministry unemcumbered by any greater degree of Pharisaic antagonism.

Likewise, if Deity boldly and openly claimed, as Hawthorne seems to believe, that he was responsible for the conditions of mortality, its pains and miseries, this knowledge might have modified the effects of the Redemption. It seems reasonable to conclude the corollary that, as a man of Christian tendencies, Hawthorne might also have thought that the silence of heaven was justified by the rational nature of humankind, who may need to believe that they are responsible for their own sins. Otherwise, by holding the Creator himself responsible for them, we might fail "the truest test of a life successful to such an [happier] end." Besides heredity, environment, and circumstance, we might have a fourth scapegoat upon which to hang our accountability. Perhaps to Hawthorne, that sense of responsibility has been quietly shared by Deity, in contrast to its lack as fairly demonstrated openly by humankind.

This exchange upon the scaffold subtly dimly implicates Dimmesdale, and likely foreshadows his later confession, as being involved in Pearl and Hester's predicament. His inquiry of Hester may have been earnest because it was a truth that needed revealing, even though to him the time was not ripe for this knowledge to be made public. Hester's transformation, and Pearl's destiny, seem to depend upon this redemption of human nature, in want of some recognition of its connection with Deity.

IN WANT OF CONNECTION

In the young Reverend's appeal, we may have an example of the Romantic's inquisition into nature to discover truths of the spiritual realm; that is, by prying into our nature, we may sense some connection with the divine and discover its manifestations. Some philosophers claim that inherent in humanity's nature is an unconditional concern, the "numinous" sense–deep innate sensitivity to something sacred, an underived feeling for the holy, with responses of wonder, awe, and reverence . . . a given fact of human consciousness that cannot be traced to rational or empirical sources. (Madsen, 72)

In other words, something deep inside the human soul intimates something larger that itself, and begs for some confirmation, some recognition, some confession, some assurance of humankind's connection with Deity. Hawthorne's allegory, perhaps symbolized by Dimmesdale's Election Sermon, may be his philosophical deposition on the matter.

THE BLACK FLOWER OF PURITANISM REJECTED

True to the Puritan posture that Hawthorne anathematized in his novel, Mr. Wilson's anticlimactic discourse on sin brings out the hellish hues imagined to reside in the scarlet letter, as though the human race is destined for the "flames of the infernal pit" (69), which the letter presumable symbolizes, from one point of view. To accept this point of view, the dark side of Puritanism, with its stern emphasis on justice for the slightest deviation, is to doom oneself to a life of hopeless gloom. To reject this point of view was diabolic to the Puritans, and probably also to Chillingworth, whose influence upon both savage and civilized society seems insinuated by his costume. That the Puritan ecclesiaticals quickly accepted him as a servant of the people may represent his influence over civilized society, especially as it recognized him as a man knowledgable in medical science.

To this dark discourse by Mr. Wilson, Hester, who "had borne, that morning, all that nature could endure," was insensible, "while the faculties of [her] animal life remained entire" (69.) These passages seem to identify Hester more openly as Nature herself incarnately resigned to her state. Hester acquiesced to the condemnation of Mr. Wilson's speech, and in the end of the tale, stayed in Boston: but Pearl, empathizing with her mother's suppressed feelings, screamed out her rejection of the condemnation and later leaves to another part of the country. Pearl, whom her mother clasped closer to her bosom when she recognized Mr. Prynne, and who empathetically "writhed in convulsions of pain" (70), did escape from Chillingworth's clutches into another brighter world, so to speak.

Hawthorne's message may be, then, that, although nature cannot lift itself from its own mortality, humanity may obtain a higher state of being than that preached by Puritanism.

Hester's refusal to accept the shame, although she is resigned to its consequences, and Pearl's reactions both seem to highlight the view that rejects the idea of the depravity of human nature. Hawthorne's allegory rejects the Puritanic interpretation of Christianity, promising in the elaboration of the scarlet letter, from another point of view, merciful relief for all who are gracious, merciful, and compassionate. To identify with those qualities of Deity, in time, may remove the pains, the agony, and the conditions associated with the fall, and provide escape from the "flames of the infernal pit."

The worth of the human body is therefore connected to the nature of its creation, which, at the seat of its curiosity, solicits some recognition of that creation. Hawthorne will next engage in a conversational flashback, between Hester and her ex-husband, Master Prynne, to relate the main cause of the black flower of mortality.

CHAPTER 4

THE INTERVIEW

Now the serpent was more subtil than any beast of the field which the LORD God had made. And he said unto the woman, Yea, hath

God said, Ye shall not eat of every tree of the garden?

And the woman said unto the serpent, We may eat of the fruit of the trees of the garden:

But of the fruit of the tree which is in the midst of the garden, God hath said, Ye shall not eat of it, neither shall ye touch it, lest ye die.

And the serpent said unto the woman, Ye shall not surely die:

For God doeth know that in the day ye eat thereof, then your eyes shall be opened, and ye shall be as gods, knowing good and evil.

And when the woman saw that the tree was good for food . . . and a tree to be desired to make one wise, she took of the fruit thereof, and did eat, and gave also unto her husband with her; and he did eat.[1]

Perhaps the unveiling of Hawthorne's allegory begins seriously in this chapter in the exchange between Chillingworth and Hester. The interview may be logically out of sequence in the plot of the tale to symbolize the particular allegorical exchance above, but its flashback to a previous time is in fair keeping with the sequence of historical events, although a Romantic allegory may not be confined to such. Nevertheless, as a conversation referring to a former relationship in a former time, the inteview between Hester and her ex-husband, Master Prynne, seems a historical reminiscence of the scene in the Garden of Eden, where Lucifer in the form of a snake seduces Eve successfully to partake of the tree of knowledge of good and evil. This earlier relationship had occurred before her fall, seems to be responsible for it, and becomes a crucial sub-plot in the allegory. Once the details are fully grasped, their allusion is practically inescapable, and provides a key that opens the tale to the rest of the allegorical story, barring the reader's prejudice against its religious nature or, contrarily, its seemingly profane aspersions.

It should be noted that in any allusion to the creation of humankind, that reference is aimed at the creation of the mortal being, for most references to that event have in mind the advent of mortal nature in the sphere of humankind's existence. Although the creation of humanity first began, from the Christian's perspective, as an immortal being, the general conception of the creative scene appears to focus chiefly upon the creation of the mortal or fallen state of being. Therefore, the terms, humanity, humankind, mankind, the human race, and others refer to the mortal existence. The term, early humankind, specifically is a reference to humankind's immortal state of being. Hawthorne does not specify such a distinction in his tale, but this chapter does address the issue in a subtle and obscure manner in the conversations between Hester and Master Prynne.

Master Prynne posed as the physician, Roger Chillingworth, who is called into the prison to treat Hester and her ailing baby, which seems to be insubordinately upset and rebellious against her mother's moral agony. Pearl's "illness" was a full empathic reaction to the anguish her mother had experienced, and may very well reflect Hawthorne's own moral sentiments about Puritanic or similar retribution. Roger, appearing to be rather objective and non-judgmental toward his wife, or ex-wife, Hester, is, however, later in the tale transformed from an apparent angel of medical mercy into a Satanic figure, of whose visage Hester is intimately fearful.

The interchange between Hester and Chillingworth in the interview is a review of a previous interchange between them that seems highly analogous of a legendary interchange that began the history of humankind. That earlier interaction, seemingly initiated in innocent ignorance on her part originally, and rejected shortly afterwards, perhaps because knowledge was such a poor purchase for the price, discernibly may symbolize the impact Old Scratch had upon the world through his scheming in the Garden of Eden.

REVENGE REVEALED

Roger was lodging in the prison, "the most convenient and suitable mode of disposing of him" (71), a suitable place for the personage he represents, and offers her a mixture that she suspects may kill her. He has apparently already sedated Pearl with some concoction that has put her fast to sleep, and her objections out of mind. Hester is suspicious, perhaps because she was beguiled or deceived before by him. His potion to her does not put her to sleep, but may have made her even more amenable to his deceptive ploys. His scheme at present, as the reader discovers, is not to seek revenge so much upon Hester, at the moment, as upon the father of Pearl, once he discovers who it is; and then he can claim both Hester and Pearl as his own, to warm himself by the warmth their presence might make in the innermost chambers of his cold heart.

> "Hast thou enticed me into a bond that will prove the ruin of my soul?"

> "Not thy soul," he answered, with another smile, "No, not thine!" (77)

Nor does he seek to harm the child, he says; it is the child's father he claims he seeks to identify and to claim as his. However, once he discovers who the father is, then he will claim all three, neither of which can escape the end result of that claim. When Hester refused to reveal the identify of Pearl's father, Chillingworth responded, "'Thou wilt not reveal his name? Not the less he is mine,' resumed he, with a look of confidence, as if destiny were at one with him'" (75). Contradicting himself, true to the chief characteristic of the character he figures, Chillingworth stated,

"'Thou and thine, Hester Prynne, belong to me. My home is where thou art, and where he is'" (76).

As a probable Satanic image in his "refined cruelty" (73), Chillingworth sought to find some hidden evil in Dimmesdale in order to lay claim to their souls, thus possibly symbolizing the historical parallel of Satan seeking, by way of temptation, to find some flaw of character in the man of Nazareth, thus nullifying the Redemption. Then nature and humankind would belong to him, "as if destiny were at one with him." The use of this phrase, "at one with him," may be an ironic twist upon the spelling of "at-one-ment," thus indicating Satan's ill-conceived confidence of victory over Deity, and the subjection of humankind under his power. Chillingworth lies again when he says, "Think not that I shall interfere with Heaven's own method of retribution," because that is his singular intent, as we see later when he tries to prevent Dimmesdale's confession upon the scaffold. That confession itself is a destiny that Providence seems to have planned, and Hawthorne may have symbolized, as the act of retribution for humankind.

CHILLINGWORTH'S CONFESSION

Chillingworth admitted, perhaps with a small facade of humility gracing a large measure of pride, to making the first wrong by tempting Hester with gifts that led to her infamy. In their reacquaintance, Chillingworth reminisced about his unhappy state of mind prior to the time he met Hester and seduced her with knowledge: "It was my folly! I have said it. But, up to that epoch of my life, I had lived in vain. The world had been so cheerless!" (74) Whether the admission was a moment of truth, or a boast, may not be clear in the text; but his devious smiles and convoluted confession—that the knowledge he shared with her led to the loss of her youth and beauty (analogically the transition from immortality to mortality)—implies that he is responsible for Hester's fall. This confession apparently absolves Dimmesdale, with whom Hester enters into a relationship later, perhaps in search of redemption, as responsible for her fall, although the reader is led to believe he caused her fall by fathering Pearl, whose birth is shrouded in ambiguity, if not in mystery itself. This confession, like his twisted mind and body, is a masterpiece of disguise and deception, and is quoted at length to pinpoint its details.

"Hester," said he, "I ask not wherefore, nor how, thou hast fallen into the pit, or say rather, thou hast ascended to the pedestal of infamy, on which I found thee. The reason is not far to seek. It was my folly, and thy weakness. I,—a man already in decay, having given my best years to feed the hungry dream of knowledge,—what had I to do with youth and beauty like thine own! Misshapen from my birth-hour, how could I delude myself with the idea that intellectual gifts might veil physical deformity in a young girl's fantasy! Men call me wise. If sages were ever wise in their own behoof, I might have foreseen all this. I might have known that, as I came out of the vast and dismal forest, and entered this settlement of Christian men, the very first object to meet my eyes would be thyself, Hester Prynne . . . . Nay, from the moment when we came down the old church-steps together, a married pair, I might have beheld the bale-fire of that scarlet letter blazing at the end of our path!" (74)

Hawthorne here reveals Chillingworth's double-minded deviousness cleverly as Milton does in "Paradise Lost," some of the themes of which are paralleled in Hathorne's allegory. If Satan were to have met Eve a second time some time later after the fall of human nature, much of this passage appears to be Hawthorne's conception of what the gist of their conversation might be like. In a disclosure that seems to parallel what transpired in the Garden of Eden between Eve and the serpent, Chillingworth feigned but did not seem ignorant of "the idea that intellectual gifts might veil physical deformity in a young girl's fantasy!" (74); but he later admitted to falsity, folly, and a betrayal of Hester's "budding youth into a false and unnatural relation with [his] decay" (75). However, in Roger's own mind he absolved himself from the condition in which he found Hester. In other words, their former relationship seems to represent the historical contract wherein the youth and beauty of immortal life was exchanged for the knowledge of decadent mortality. The intellectual gifts Chillingworth shared with Hester concealed the consequencea of an eventual degeneration of her beauty and youth.

Human nature, having been changed in the Garden, in exchange for a little knowledge, from immortality to mortality, be it so far removed from its former paradisiacal state of purity, does not wish to honor any contract or identity with Old Scratch, but seeks redemption from past mistakes and reconciliation with the divine. Although mortal nature resulted from a kind of contract between Eve and Old Scratch, mankind has mostly aligned itself with her Creator rather than with his antagonist. Thus, Hester's relationship with Dimmesdale may be as much, if not moreso, one of seeking redemption from her fall, as a sinner seeking reconciliation, than as one seeking something more.

It seems intended by Hawthorne that the reader catch Chillingworth's Freudian slip when he rephrased his reference to Hester's falling into a pit to her ascending to the "pedestal of infamy" (74), the scaffold, where he found her. In and of itself, the slip possibly poses an irony signifying how Satan, aspiring to the throne of his Rival, fell into the bottomless pit instead. It also might suggest that Hester's fall was a kind of ascension to some pedestal of high position, though that position has an infamous sting. We will explore the symbolism of the scaffold later in regard to this oxymoron.

Chillingworth smiled twice during the interview, "with a smile of dark and self-relying intelligence" (75), that itself becomes a clue or signal to the reader that he intends to practice his sophistry upon Hester's introspective nature. His self-relying intelligence is characteristic of the pride and arrogance which led to Lucifer's downfall into a bottomless pit, in the Christian theology, as symbolized later by Chillingworth's own diminishment and death. As a Satanic figure, who glories in his own self-deception, we can surmise that he, like Satan, believed he was wise, therefore knew the consequences for sharing his knowledge with Hester, and was mixing both lie and truth to manipulate her again according to his hostile intentions.

Chillingworth openly connected Hester's fall to his folly and her weakness as he rationalized his part in her infamy. Roger even suggested to Hester that he might have known or foreseen the consequence to himself, as well as to Hester, for his actions. He implied that his folly for sharing knowledge with her was unknowing of the consequences of decay, a loss of her youth and beauty. Yet, though he is "a book-worm of great libraries," several times he says, "I might have foreseen . . . . I might have known . . . . I might have beheld" all, even "I might have beheld the bale-fire of that scarlet letter blazing at the end of our path!" (74)

Indeed, twice in the novel Chillingworth beheld his destiny, in connection with the scarlet letter, with a horror that made him shrink.

The innuendo possibly suggests that Satan, besides having foreseen the fall of Nature as the effect of the "intellectual gifts," might also have beheld the destiny awaiting him for his rebellious opposition. This momentary beholding in horror of the scarlet letter upon Hester's bosom, when first he saw her upon the scaffold, may represent the bale-fire damnation into which his soul is to be cast. Chillingworth will once again envision that horror, when Dimmesdale is upon the scaffold, before Hawthorne is through with him, and the reader will see him fading in power and confidence.

One might wonder if Eve's greatest temptation was boredom with the perfection she enjoyed in the Garden. Perhaps, to Hawthorne, her weakness was the fantasy that she could gain the intellectual gifts of a knowledge of good and evil, becoming like the gods, without experiencing the death, or physical deformity, promised by her Creator. Such a fantasy might presuppose that ultimate joy was not a product of the creation of the paradise in the Garden of Eden, and therefore that mortality itself was an experience necessary for an ultimate joy to be achieved later. That one cannot know the sweet without knowing the bitter is suggested later in the tale.

A MISSHAPEN BODY, A TWISTED MENTALITY

In disclaiming knowledge that her fallen state would ensue if she applied the knowledge he gave her, Chillingworth reasons: "Misshapen from my birth-hour, how could I delude myself with the idea that intellectual gifts might veil physical deformity in a young girl's fantasy!" This semantically contradictory statement, as well as the passage in which it is contained, cleverly suggests the twisted psychological difficulty the Christian concept of Satan must have in dealing with truth. Eve's fancy was to gain the knowledge of the gods, which quest might perhaps necessitate rationalizing in her gullible innocence that partaking of the forbidden fruit might not result in her "physical deformity," death, or loss of youth, beauty, and innocence. But such a rationale could hardly be conceived sensibly without a knowledge of what death meant. This rationality, the first of its kind in the innocent mind, imbibed from the alleged master of it, introduced mortality into humankind's perfect world, and according to Hawthorne, may possibly account for "the mesh of good and evil" that plagues the best of us, that is, if a perfect world could exist without a knowledge of both.

The physical deformity of Chillingworth, as a Satanic figure, with the left shoulder a trifle higher than the right" (58, 60), is figured as an outward expression of his internal deformity, and possibly indicates Satan's lack of spiritual integrity, or a psychological incongruity and inability to deal with the truth, thus casting his conversation as a mixture of truth and lies to serve his devious designs. The character of Chillingworth, and possibly other characters in the story allied with him, suggests that Lucifer may be out of touch with reality, believing what he chooses to believe, and confident that he can attain the unattainable. Like Satan, who is confident he can destroy the souls of many, Chillingworth and Mistress Hibbins are confident they can win the souls of Hester, Dimmesdale, and Pearl. At the same time, perhaps any person who tells lies habitually and often enough may soon begin to believe them, and have difficulty discerning between truth and falsity. So misshapen from his "birth-hour," Chillingworth indeed might question whether or not he knew he was deluding himself.

Mentally warped as he was physically deformed, it would have been easy for Lucifer to have deluded himself with any idea, especially with the idea that Eve would not really die. Apparently Hawthorne thought that Satan lied, or had a twisted concept of death, when he said, "Ye shalt not surely die . . . and shall be as gods, knowing good and evil." Death could be defined as cessation of existence, but that is apparently not what the Creator meant when he promised that Adam and Eve would die if they partook of the forbidden fruit, or even touched it[2]. Immediate physical death was not forthcoming, as they died later within the thousand years, or the day that the Lord promised them they would die[3].

HESTER'S PHYSICAL DEFORMITY

The physical deformity experienced by Hester when she was young and beautiful seems to reflect the promised death Eve innocently chose to ignore, when she chose to gain the knowledge of the gods by partaking of the forbidden fruit. In the cannons of Christianity, death has two meanings. There are two types of death, one is physical and the other is spiritual. The former is the separation of body and spirit, wherein the body returns to earth, and the spirit lives on in another sphere of existence. The latter is conceived by a few Christian religionists as a separation from the presence of the Creator, and not as a cessation of existence. So our first ancestors died immediately spiritually when they were kicked out of the Creator's presence, and their bodies began decaying as mortals, either by being cast out of that life-sustaining presence, or by partaking of forbidden element, or both.

Both types of death in the Christian code can be overcome upon certain conditions; and, in his allegory, Hawthorne may be alluding to both the resurrection and a period of enlightenment for humanity, should they return from whence they came. As it was, Adam and Eve experienced both types of death, as promised in the Garden of Eden, "in the day thereof," or within the year of the Lord's time. The allegory may use this equivalency as the time-frame of the tale: a thousand years of earth life equals one year of Pearl's life, who attained the age of seven years in the tale.

Representing the civilization of mortal beings from the time of the creation to the end of mortality, Hester in her youth appears to represent the nature of Adam and Eve, both of whom were beguiled into a contract with death. Cast out of the Garden of Eden, they were cast out of the Lord's presence and therefore died spiritually instantly, which is similar to Satan's expulsion from heaven, and is a kind of spiritual death, or decay, in the words of Chillingworth.

A MAN ALREADY IN DECAY

The fall of humanity was effected when Eve contracted an "unnatural relation with [Satan's] decay" (75). It is possible that Hawthorne referred to Chillingworth's decay to represent Satan's spiritual degeneration rather than a physical one because, in the Christian's theology, Satan has no physical body, only a spirit. That decay possibly began at the time he was cast out of heaven, when he aspired to the throne of his Creator and his Creator's glory[4]. Being cast out of his presence, that spiritual degeneration continued, and had an unnatural effect upon the immortal youth of creation when he shared his knowledge deceptively with Eve in the Garden.

Chillingworth also stated that Hester was the first to meet his eyes when he came out of "the vast and dismal forest" into Boston. Biblical text purports that Eve was apparently the first person Lucifer spoke to when he appeared upon the scene, presumably from outer darkness, where he had been cast, to tempt her in the first settlement in the Garden of

Eden. He did so in the form or body of the serpent, which was the most subtile beast created by its Maker: "close the serpent sly Insinuating, wove with Gordian twine His braided train, and of his fatal guile Gave proof unheeded." (Milton, in Harrison, et al., p. 479)

TO THWART THE PROVIDENTIAL PLAN

Perhaps Roger's quest for revenge began with his sight of Hester, as Lucifer's opportunity came as early as the morn of creation in the Garden of Eden, when he entertained the thought of disrupting its occupants' happy estate:

> "Ah gentle pair, ye little think how nigh
> Your change approaches, when all these delights
> Will vanish and deliver ye to woe,
> More woe, the more your taste is now of joy . . . .
> League with you I seek,
> And mutual amity so strait, so close,
> That I with you must dwell, or you with me."
> (Milton, ibid.)

Chillingworth's desire to claim Dimmesdale's soul, "Sooner or later, he must be mine,"(75) and that of Hester's and Pearl's, "Thou and thine, Hester Prynne, belong to me," (76) perhaps figures part of Lucifer's plan to thwart the plan of the Creator as an act of revenge for being cast out. Chillingworth, who sought to make his home with Hester, Pearl, and Dimmesdale, claimed that he and Hester had been "wronged" by each other and by Dimmesdale. Sorting out the allegorical meanings of the concept of "wrong," from a discussion between a liar and one who is easily deceived, might be a formidable task left to another student's efforts. Suffice it to say here, in summary, that Roger apparently wronged Hester by beguiling her with a contract for knowledge, by which she lost her youth and beauty; and she "wronged" him for abandoning him, or breaking a covenant of marriage, when she experienced the consequences of the deception. Being susceptible to logical deduction, and therefore perhaps easily deceived, Hester was probably acquiescing to his accusation of her wrongness. Perhaps any wrongness on Hester's part in this exchange, from

Hawthorne's point of view, might reside in her acquiesing to his interests on the basis of logic rather than passion.

The divine probably has wronged Hester, possibly from the viewpoint of Hester, the distorted view of Chillingworth, or the conclusion of the reader, by abandoning her with child; and he has possibly wronged Roger by winning Hester's loyalty. Referring to the possible Biblical analogy, the Creator "wronged" Lucifer, according to the latter's irrational point of view, when he thwarted Lucifer's ploy by reclaiming his creation in a covenant after its fall, and promising a way out of their new dilemma. Or perhaps the question of the wrongness of the divine, as representative of Divinity, is the same as echoed by Milton in the words of his Satan, for being cast out of heaven: "Thank him who puts me loth to this revenge On you who wrong me not, for him who wronged." (ibid.) Also, in being cast out of heaven, he was denied the prospects of ever owning a warm body like that of Adam and Eve's.

After Eve's seduction by her thirst for knowledge, which brought about the fall, Satan may have summoned more hope in wrecking revenge upon the Creator who had exiled him to darkness, as in the case of Chillingworth's attempt to prevent Dimmesdale's confession upon the scaffold. Old Scratch himself may have known somewhat of the plan to redeem humankind from his fallen state and schemed to thwart it. This knowledge is evident in the declarations of his angels, or evil spirits, who were reported to recognize the Nazarene as the Son of God, when he cast them out of the bodies of individuals possessed by them.

> And, behold, they cried out, saying, What have we to do with thee, Jesus, thou Son of God: art thou come hither to torment us before the time?[5]

> What have I to do with thee, Jesus, thou Son of the most high God?

> I adjure thee by God, that thou torment me not . . . . And he asked him, What is thy name? And he answered, saying, My name is Legion, for we are many.[6]

According to Christian theology, the temptations of Jesus of Nazareth in the wilderness, when he fasted forty days and nights, prior to beginning his ministry, is cited as another Biblical record of Satan's attempt to thwart the plan of the Atonement. If he could succeed in tempting the sinless one to sin, then the plan of Redemption would have been frustrated. This attempt seems figured in Chillingworth's constant and prying companionship with Dimmesdale.

Therefore, after cozying up to Hester in order to seduce her into naming the father of Pearl, Chillingworth proclaimed and asked, "Hester, the man lives who has wronged us both! Who is he?" (75) Her refusal to tell him may reflect the difficulty for intellect alone to pry out of nature the truth, Hawthorne's secret truth, of who is responsible for the birth of humankind. When Hester refused to tell Roger who the father was, Master Prynne asserted himself as a master in prying into the soul, and, notwithstanding her refusal, would still be able to discover the dark secrets of any sin he assumed lay in the man. The "prying multitude" may not uncover the truth, but Chillingworth declares that he will detect it by the shudder of his foreshadowing fears. These fears may be the horrors he senses as the ultimate outcome of his spiritual degeneration.

> But, as for me, I come to the inquest with other senses than they possess. I shall seek this man . . . . There is a sympathy that will make me conscious of him. I shall see him tremble. I shall feel myself shudder, suddenly and unawares. Sooner or later, he must needs be mine! (75)

The "prying multitude" (75) may refer to the efforts of earth's inhabitants to uncover the truth about Deity's relationship with man. That relationship is to be revealed or confirmed in time through the symbolic confession of Dimmesdale upon the scaffold. (Whether intended or not by Hawthorne, the prying multitude may also speak to the generations that have not been able to decipher the meanings of the scarlet letter.) As Satan sought to thwart Providence's plan by preventing the Redemption, so Chillingworth sought to prevent that revelation, or act of retribution, destined by Providence to be fulfilled by Dimmesdale. As Satan schemed to sit upon The Creator's throne and possess the bodies of humankind, so Chillingworth likewise hoped of warming himself from the household fires of many guests, for which he claimed his cold and lonely heart had room enough for habitation.

To Possess a Body

Referring to a previous time when he had lived a vain, cheerless life, from a twisted viewpoint, Chillingworth, solicited Hester's sympathy:

> "My heart was a habitation large enough for many guests, but lonely and chill, and without a household fire. I longed to kindle one!
>
> It seemed not so wild a dream,—old as I was, and sombre as I was, and misshapen as I was,—that the simple bliss, which is scattered far and wide, for all mankind to gather up, might yet be mine." (74)

Again, we hear the echoes of Milton, in the thoughts of his Archdemon, as he gazed wistfully upon the blissful pair in Paradise:

> "Hell shall unfold,
> To entertain you two, her widest gates,
> And send forth all her kings; there will be room,
> Not like these narrow limits, to receive
> Your numerous offspring." (ibid.)

At one level, Chillingworth seems to be saying he wants home life; at a deeper allegorical level, the meaning seems to mirror Satan's desire to possess a warm body like all mortals. The allusion conjures up the Christian belief that Old Scratch and his angels desire the bodies possessed by humankind scattered far and wide in the earth, as though these bodies provide warmth from the cold, dark, loneliness of the nether world into which he and his legions have been cast. Wandering alone and cold without a body to warm himself in, unlike all the inhabitants of earth, what else could Hawthorne have been proposing here but that Satan hoped the downfall of humankind would provide him with the blissful habitation of a household fire like unto theirs, once he can lay claim to them all? For Chillingworth to claim the souls and bodies of Dimmesdale, Hester, and Pearl, may also allude to the Christian doctrine of a literal resurrection, in some denominations, wherein possession of one's soul includes the possession of one's resurrected body as well. Whereas Milton believed in materialism being eventually transmuted into holy spirit (Harrison, et. al, Vol 1, p. 483-484), Hawthorne appears questionably to speak for a literal restoration, but perhaps, of course, likewise of a higher order.

The probably basis of this longing for "a household fire" by unembodied spirits is, of course, only Biblical. Believing in a physical resurrection, some Christians refer to the account where evil spirits, who have no body, are eager to claim one, even if it were the body of swine. Chillingworth's longing may refer to that eagerness in the incident when the man of Nazareth met two persons possessed with devils in the country of Gergesenes[7]. He casts them out, and they beg him to allow them to possess the bodies of swine feeding at some distance. With his consent, they do, and the herd of swine, confused and crazed by that embodiment, ran directly into the sea and drowned. This scripture has been used by some Christians to show the value of the resurrection, the possession of a material body, just as Paul tried to convince the Sadducees at Corinth that the resurrection was real and literal.[8]

Hawthorne may have had these references in mind when he wrote the passage quoted above, and he added his personal touch to this allusion at the very end of his tale. The possibility of these allusions imply a beneficial purpose the Creator may have in mind when he created bodies out of the elements of the earth and breathed into them their spirits. These and other symbolic references, possibly alluding to the value of the human body and some transformation or resurrection of it by a divine touch, mentioned later, also suggest Hawthorne's possible rationale for confuting the Puritan concept of the depravity and ignominy of the flesh.

MR. PRYNNE'S CLAIMS

Hawthorne reveals how the character of Chillingworth diminishes in the eyes of the reader as his thoughts become personified in diabolical deeds of hatred and revenge. Seemingly calm, cool, and collected, Chillingworth begins to unravel his hostile and diabolical plot to possess the soul of the protagonist, Dimmesdale. In the confidence of his pride, Chillingworth vows, "he must needs be mine!" (75)

In such a pompous outburst, reflective of another Biblical reference, Mr. Prynne reveals a sense of self-importance "with a look of confidence, as if destiny were at one with him," as though he thinks he is equal in power to the task he has set before him. The term, "as if," is one of Hawthorne's cues to the reader to check for allegorical parallels, but, in this case, may refer simply to his grandiose image of himself.

The reason may not be very clear at this point in the tale as to why Chillingworth (Satan) claims that Hester (nature) and her child (humankind) belong to him. Mr. Prynne may intend to make that claim as soon as he discovers the father of Pearl. Satan could only make that claim only if he can defeat or thwart the Redemption. It is clear that Roger and Hester had "so close a relation between himself and her" (71), as indicated by Hester bearing his name, that some measure of belonging is warranted. In some cases, a name connotes taking upon its bearer certain properties or characteristics. Like Mr. Prynne, who was "a wanderer, sorely against my will" (61), Hester was estranged from society. Like Lucifer, who was cast out of the presence of God, defined in the Christian code as a spiritual death, humankind, because of its mortality, a physical degeneration toward death, was cast out of the Garden of Eden, which was likewise a spiritual death, and was re-quartered in a lone and dreary world. And, like Roger, Hester has fallen, and her youth and beauty is deteriorating. Humankind has fallen into mortality, and become a castaway, by a falsified contract of knowledge with a castaway.

Hawthorne refers to this allegorical relationship in the words of Chillingworth:

> "Here, on this wild outskirt of the earth, I shall pitch my tent; for, elsewhere a wanderer, and isolated from human interests, I find here a woman, a man, a child, amongst whom and myself there exist the closest ligaments . . . . My home is where thou art, and where he is." (76)

The woman may refer to Hester, the fallen nature of humankind; the child, to Pearl, the civilization of all humankind, through whom succeeding generations will yield a better tomorrow; the man, to the divine Author of humankind, whose mission it is to redeem Hester and Pearl; and the wanderer, to Roger, who would claim triumphantly, not only the earth as his home, by reason of the effects of his contract with the woman, but also wherever the man is. Or the three, man, woman, and child, may refer simply in general to members of the human race, under the spell of physical death, who may come under the spell of his spiritual death, in "closest ligaments."

Roger's claims are reminiscent of a Biblical prophet who understood the nature of the fallen angel, who thought he could be equal with Deity:

> How art thou fallen from heaven, O Lucifer, son of the morning!

> How art thou cut down to the ground, which didst weaken the nations!

> For thou hast said in thine heart, I will ascend into heaven, I will exalt my throne above the stars of God: I will sit also upon the mount of the congregation, in the sides of the north:

> I will ascend above the heights of the clouds; I will be like the most High.

> Yet thou shalt be brought down to hell, to the sides of the pit.[9]

The last line of the last verse is included because there has been at least two instances foreshadowing that event in the allegory. The first time occurred when Mr. Prynne's penetrative insight beheld with writhing horror the scarlet letter upon Hester's bosom (61). At that time he exercised control over this feeling by casting it out of his mind. He is even able to touch the scarlet letter later with a smile, one of three in the interview. Later in the tale, he again shrunk in horror when he beheld the scarlet letter upon Dimmesdale's chest.

It must also be noted that, at this point, in this face-to-face interview with the antagonist, fearful of such a penetrating boast that the prying Master Prynne could read the name of Pearl's father (Arthur) in it, Hester covers the scarlet letter A. This is likely another clearer unveiling of one of Hawthorne's meanings of the letter upon Hester's bosom: it may stand for Arthur, or the Author of Creation, as well perhaps as the agony of the Atonement.

A Second Contract

To give us one more clue to the relationship of the four main characters and their representations, Hester asks Chillingworth, "Art thou like the Black Man that haunts the forest round about us? Has thou enticed me into a bond that will prove the ruin of my soul?" (33) Chillingworth's previous comments, and his answer, tie both questions together in the affirmative, "'Not thy soul,' he answered, with another smile. 'No, not thine!'" (34); indirectly, by lack of denial, Chillingworth identified himself with the Black Man, who lived also on the outskirts of the wilderness. From the text of the interview, the reader realizes also that Roger is lying about not wanting her soul also.

For Hester to contract silence as to Chillingworth's identity, even though or especially since she does not know what Chillingworth's plot is, seems morally wrong. She intuitively senses she has entered into another misaligned contract, possibly by deception again, that could again affect her soul. Her silence, however, seems justified at the surface level of the story on the basis of a reciprocal agreement: she will not divulge to Dimmesdale Chillingworth's identity, if he will not divulge his relationship with Hester to Dimmesdale. At the allegorical level, nature and evil seem naturally silent, just as Providence seems silent about its relationship with humankind. Yet, Hawthorne himself, later in the tale, appears to indicate that this silence at the allegorical level may be perhaps a greater error than the relationships into which the parties have entered.

Thus we find in this chapter that Hawthorne begins to unravel the mystery of his tale to the penetrative insight of the reader, who should at this point begin to recognize who the antagonist is at the allegorical level, and therefore, axiomatically, wonder who the protagonist is.

CHAPTER 5

HESTER AT HER NEEDLE

Come now, and let us reason together, saith the Lord:
though your sins be as scarlet, they shall be as white as snow;
though they be red like crimson, they shall be as wool.[1]

J ust as scarlet sin can become white as snow, this chapter of the allegory
addresses the paradox of how the fall into mortality, though a long
burden which nature must endure, is actually a blessing promised at
the end. Whatever the needlework Hester wove may mean to symbolize, it
at least betokens the intricate method by which Hawthorne wove his tale
to change the readers' affections for the main characters. The intimations
of her needlework are posted around about her in the society that is as
oblivious to them as perhaps to the readers of Hawthorne's tale.

IN THE SUNSHINE OF TRUTH

The tale continued with the end of Hester's confinement as she exited
the prison "into the sunshine, which . . . seemed . . . as if meant for no
other purpose than to reveal the scarlet letter on her breast"(78). The light
of natural day is a clue to the reader to focus upon this beautified symbol,
and perhaps, by way of the Romantic within, seek to discover its greater
truth. The term, "as if," again alerts the insightful reader to pry intuitively
for deeper meanings, especially in conjunction with the metaphor of
sunshine that illuminates the subject. That particular truth, embellished
around the scarlet letter, Hester will turn into a "lurid triumph" (78)
over the lifetime of ignominy she must endure. She will loyally look to
Dimmesdale to achieve that triumph.

But now, as she emerged into the light of common day, "She could no longer borrow from the future, to help her through her present grief," which she must endure to the end of her life (79). She had been sustained in prison by the vigor of support of an iron arm that had given the "very law that condemned her." The "vital strength" of this iron arm that had held her up was probably "the sole portion that she retained in the universal heart," (84), the hope for which on Sundays she went "to share the Sabbath smile of the Universal Father" (85). Perhaps the embellishment of the letter in prison had borrowed from the future the vital support of the promise of a brighter day and had given her a sense of "passionate and desperate joy." But now she must prove she can sustain that strength "by the ordinary resources of her nature" (78) throughout the duration of it. The law that made the promise had been interpreted by its present carekeepers to condemn her.

The needlework she wove, perhaps inspired intuitively in the routine course of her life, wherein she served her fellowmen without judging them, perhaps likewise betokens the hope of that future triumph, as we may see later, the hope for a transformation to be effected by a one and only unto whom she looks for redemption. In other words, mortality must endure its human nature until the end of time, with what ordinary resources lay within Hester, in hope that some ghastly triumph will solve the problems of common day.

As seen by this purveyor, Hawthorne has figured Hester as a personification of human nature, as seen in the eyes of her Puritan ministers. Throughout all her days, in their judgment,

> she would become the general symbol at which the preacher
> and moralist might point, and in which they might vivify and
> embody their images of woman's frailty and sinful passion . . .
> as the figure, the body, the reality of sin. (79)

Their perspective on the value of human nature would forever see human nature as depraved and worthless. She, who had been "the child of honorable parents," she, "who had once been innocent," she, who was "the mother of a babe, that would hereafter be a woman," would be imaged to the last days of her life as the embodiment of sin (79).

But the reader will find that Hester's resources include kindness and compassion toward her vilifiers, which help transform them as well, as the reader's view begins to be changed about Hester herself. Representing mortal nature, Hester in her needlework, by which she fancied others as she did herself, and which perhaps represents the best use of each human's natural resources, showed "how sacred love should make us happy, by the truest test of a life successful to such an end!" (263). It is perhaps fitting that this preachment should be included at the conclusion of Hawthorne's tale, and mentioned here as the possible meaning symbolized by her needlework. To Hawthorne, her needlework may constitute the exemplary life of the hopeful enduring to the end, despite eccleasistical aspersions. Perhaps Hester's transformation also may reflect a transformation of that particular raw view of the worth of human nature, its "glow of passion" and "tenderness of sentiment" (34).

Hester's public spectacle upon the scaffold earlier had made her a "common infamy." Not just Puritanism, but "all mankind was summoned to point its finger" at this infamy, which is common to all humankind, not simply to Hester alone. She was "the figure, the body, the reality of sin . . . the type of shame" envisioned by the dark heart of Puritanism, into whose soil her roots were struck, her home where she must stay. Hester appears to represent a symbol of the mortality of nature, seen as depraved and ignominious in the eyes of Puritanism, which visage is reflected in Hester's own consciousness and cannot be broken until death. But not so in the eyes of Hawthorne and those who hold a sympathetic view of human nature, perhaps by some communion with the universal heart. That communion may be symbolized by the warm rays of sunlight, like the "smile of the Universal Father" she would seek, but find naught but vilification instead. Hawthorne will convert this token of shame into a halo as the people begin to behold another refined view of Hester and Dimmesdale.

"RABBI! RABBI!"

Hawthorne contrasts Hester's misery in New England with her former life in rural England, "where happy infancy and stainless maidenhood seemed yet to be in her mother's keeping" (80). The Romantic would see the rural setting as closer to nature, closer to the ideal beginning of life, and the city as farther away from it. That is to say, perhaps, that there was happiness and purity while she was kept within the innocent care of her young years before her fall from "her mother's keeping." Though she is resigned to her distress, yet there is one "passionate and desperate joy," a kind of recompense which Hester instinctively anticipates at the end of her long ordeal. It would be a gruesome victory which she seems to worship by the manner in which she embellished her own scarlet letter, Pearl's attire, and her neighbors, with her needle work.

> There dwelt, there trode the feet of one with whom she deemed herself connected in a union, that, unrecognized on earth, would bring them together before the bar of final judgment, and make that their marriage-altar, for a joint futurity of endless retribution. (80)

This sentence singularly bonds together several themes that can open the intuitive eyes of the reader to the main allegorical testament of Hawthorne's beliefs. That one particular person referred to can be no less than Dimmesdale, who possibly represents the divine redemptive element of the Providential plan that will connect nature forever with its spiritual counterpart through an endless retribution, though that union not be recognized by the likes of jaundiced Calvinistic interpretations. Until that time, nature is chained to a mortality that galls its inmost soul. There is therefore the strongest connection between Hester, as a figure of mortal nature, and Dimmesdale, as a figure of Divinity. He is her spiritual Rabbi, and she looks to him for relief from her ordeal. This spiritual relationship explains and justifies the mystery of her unremitting loyalty to him. It also justifies the denial of her contract with Chillingworth and her desires to be with Dimmesdale, who also has a Master to whom he looks for guidance in fulfilling the role ordained for him.

Hester's needlepoint wove the threads of that future connection, not only between herself and Dimmesdale, but also among members of the community. She had intuitively woven the scarlet letter upon her breast to signify something more triumphant than the lurid, something more holier than the dismal countenance of Puritanism, by which she is both oppressed and depressed.

Hester then is perhaps weaving the hope of a union in most of the apparels she makes for the people of her community, a union "not recognized on earth," or at least among the majority of its inhabitants, that will be consummated at "the bar of final judgment" in an "endless retribution." Although a glorious day will occur when the resurrection of the body and spirit (at "their marriage-altar") is accomplished through the medium of an everlasting redemption or retribution, perhaps Hawthorne would have us wonder, as he wondered, that since there is a sense that the whole Divine arrangement might be suspect, then some answer should be forthcoming to address the suspicion. Presumably, he has begun to nourish the seed of another philosophical urge, to interweave and address the unique theme of heavenly silence.

Should the union referred to above be alluding to the resurrection of natural element with the divine spirit within man, then, as a correlary theme, Hawthorne may be suggesting therefore that flesh must not be evil and depraved, if it is destined to be joined in an eternal union with its diviner element, which idea is somewhat reinforced later.

THE TRANSFORMATION

Hester's instinctive urge to seize upon the idea of this saving connection is counteracted by the logical impulse to cast it off, possibly because its momentary joy exacerbates or compounds her misery, a misery brought on by the aspersions of Puritanism toward her fallen nature, which she allowed to squelch her joyful hopes. Her needlework "might have been a mode of expressing, and therefore soothing, the passion of her life. Like all other joys, she rejected it as sin" (84). Her logical faculties, therefore, contrive a state of mind that is half truth and half self-delusion:

> What she compelled herself to believe,— . . . as a motive for continuing a resident of New England,—was half a truth, and half a self-delusion.
>
> Here, she said to herself, had been the scene of her guilt, and here should be the scene of her earthly punishment; and so, perchance, the torture of her daily shame would at length purge her soul, and work out another purity than that which she had lost; more saintlike, because the result of martyrdom. (80)

The above quote has a curious notion: Hester is posed possibly to become a martyr worthy of sainthood, because of enduring the torture of her earthly shame. Hawthorne is early pointing toward a transformation, a purging of her soul, another purity, to which she was looking forward.

The half truth of her hopeful thought may have come from that intuitive part of her senses that as likely intimated the truth. The half part of self-delusion appears to be the logical result of Puritanic indoctrination she has been compelled to accept.

In this constant battle between Hester's intuition and her logical speculations, the reader seems to be prodded by Hawthorne to deduce some divine hope of redemption from mortality, a transformation forthcoming. But the transformation appears to be, at the allegorical level, a retransformation: immortality, transformed into mortality, would be changed back into another kind of purity like unto its earlier state. The character of Pearl points to this promise always, and the zeal of Dimmesdale plots the way.

Notwithstanding, Hawthorne seems to have identified Hester in this passage more as a victim than as a party to the act of her infamy. Like the Redeemer who cried out upon the cross in perhaps his greatest moment of loneliness and pain, "Eloi, Eloi," Hester is doomed to cry out in misery for the rest of her life because of one particular act of passion, the passion of the creation, as we have postulated. The exact details of this act are never disclosed, but are left to the imaginative deduction or intuition of the reader. Most readers assume adultery at the level of the tale itself, but the allegorical overtones indicate that she, as a representative of a fallen civilization or type of Mother Nature, is indeed a victim in some way, a kind of sacrificial lamb in the process of dying.

The perspective of Hester's community focused upon the deplorable aspect signified by the scarlet letter. The unspoken word in their minds was spoken by their children in derision as she passed, and its effect upon her formed a self-perception that held her apart from the world she lived in, though not entirely cast off.

> In all her intercourse with society . . . there was nothing that
> made her feel as if she belonged to it . . . . as if she inhabited
> another sphere, or communicated with the common nature by
> other organs and senses than the rest of human kind . . . like a
> ghost that . . . can no longer make itself seen or felt" (84),

and, though searching to share its "forbidden sympathy," conjures up in others only the emotions of terror and repugnance.

This is one of the most difficult analogies Hawthorne has used in his tale: how is human nature like a ghost? Perhaps it has something to do with a kind of sacred pollution (67, 163) which Hester senses within herself, but to which the society about her is not tuned in. All humankind have the same organs and senses, but not all give ear to the intuitive impulses of the sacredness of mortality, its divine purpose and hallowed destiny. Perhaps Hawthorne is depicting Hester as that best part of human nature that cannot communicate, like a ghost, to the rest of humankind what it is experiencing.

Deep within Hester was "a taste for the gorgeously beautiful," which she could only exercise by symbolic means in her needlework (83). She sought out the poor "to be the objects of her bounty," but like a ghost, seeking forbidden sympathy, awakened only bitter scorn from her patrons. Her feelings of isolation from her society, framed by the perspective of the world into which she was cast, and abandoned, "seemed to be the sole portion that she retained in the universal heart" (84), wanting to share its sympathy with the common sinner, but hampered in doing so by the image projected by her scarlet letter. Such was that experience that made her feel she did not belong.

But once in a while, she sensed a sympathetic eye. Another passage may connect Hester's transformation with Dimmesdale's role so early in the tale, but not as clearly developed as later:

> But sometimes, once in many days, or perchance in many months, she felt an eye—a human eye—upon the ignominious brand, that seemed to give a momentary relief, as if half of her agony were shared. The next instant, back it all rushed again, with still a deeper throb of pain; for, in that brief interval, she had sinned anew. Had Hester sinned alone? (86)

The sympathetic "eye" may refer to those few who looked upon her empathetically, because they were also humbly aware of their own fallen nature. Seeing in the embellished scarlet letter the same message, they may have felt the same hope, perhaps as a kindred spirit, of the ultimate end of joy. It does not appear to be a companionship of misery that gave her temporary relief, but a companionship of hope. And since this was a rare incident, Hawthorne may be saying that only a few may have sensed the deeper significance of her refinement of the letter.

However, the single "human eye," might be Dimmesdale's, he who sympathetically shares her agony. But how would his human eye give Hester a full but only momentary relief? It seems mostly a Romantic notion that the simple gaze of a human eye could fully relieve another's suffering, or for that matter, create it. Hawthorne made sure to contrast the positive effect, or relief, of this one single human eye with the negative effects of the eyes of Hester's community that created it, whether the accustomed eye or the eye of a stranger (86).

What connection, then, might Dimmesdale represent that can give real relief? Is this temporary relief of Hester, by the gaze of Dimmesdale, or some other, meant to be symbolic of the promise inherently endowed within his mission, which both he and she intuitively feel, of which he later comes to be fully conscious? And is this promise purposefully and elaborately embedded in the scarlet letter not only upon Hester's breast, but also upon Dimmesdale's chest and Pearl herself? Is the human eye the eye of an anthropomorphic Deity, whom Dimmesdale may represent, in whose image He created humankind flesh and bone, thus sharing responsibility in humanity's misery? Does the sympathetic eye—whether Dimmesdale's or his Master's, or the center of the universal heart—which gives temporary relief to Hester in her present state of agony, suggest that there is a promise of complete relief in the future, by some union and purging retribution at the bar of final judgment?

Life is in the throes of death itself, and whether its sense of a destined afterlife is real or imaginary doesn't appear to be that much of a questionable issue in Hawthorne's allegory, which points in the direction of an afterlife as a probable reality. He seems to believe that Nature, in the figure of Hester, was a product of divine creation, that, through some deceptive contract, achieved the fallen state of mortality, and, in context of the setting of the tale, was subjected to society's interpretation as depraved and evil. The definition of matter itself as intrinsically evil predates Calvinistic doctrine back as far as Greek and Oriental thought, and Hawthorne seems opposed to this definition in his description of Hester.

Therefore, innocent before the act that reduced her immortal creation to one of mortal corruption, Mother Nature, as figuratively alluded to in one of the passages above, seems to be proclaimed as a martyr destined to sainthood following the sacrifice. That paradise, "which she had lost" in the Fall, may be regained, which gain Hawthorne may refer to as Hester's transformation. Yet, ill-accused by contemporary religion, Nature silently accepts the mislabel of shame played out upon her as an expression of the instinctive sacrifice worthy really of sainthood. For the most part, she endured the beleaguered self-perception imposed upon her in the insignia planted upon her bosom by the eccleastical magistrates. She even suppressed the joy of hope by consequence, and perhaps as a part, of that imposition. Though she intuitively sensed something sacred in the emblem, she yielded to the reasonable interpretations by her ministers.

By implication alone, Dimmesdale, the divine, shares Hester's agony in his own sensitive way. But does he also share the sin? The reader assumes so by reason alone, but not by any explicit statement by Hawthorne as to what that sin might be, as nowhere in his allegory are the words "adultery," "adulteress," or "adulterer" used. Hawthorne seems to ask questions, for which the answers may seem obvious to the reader, but for the purpose of eliciting the reader's questioning of the obvious answer, as though to pose an alternative answer in the midst of his allegorical allusions. It appears to be a technique designed to puzzle the reader enough to seek for that allegorical message.

The answer to the question, "Had Hester sinned alone?" is therefore too obvious at the surface level of the tale. But at the allegorical level, the answer approaches a possible philosophical question Hawthorne may have been contemplating himself: did the part that Providence played in the creation and fall of human nature constitute something that may be considered wrongful? As will be noted shortly, Hawthorne may be implying that something seems wrong about the chemistry of mixing the essence of beauty, Hester's inherent and latent nature, with the self-consciousness of her mortal nature. The idea of mind embodied in matter, especially a passionate matter, might seem suspect. But contemplating such a conclusion does not seem as heretical as to state that it might be.

It may also be Hawthorne's intent to indicate that time and the fruits of Mother Nature's labors will eventually transform the negative perspective of nature conceived in the eyes of the Puritan community, and perhaps in the minds of humankind in general in his day, into a more enlightened one through the eye and mission of another. In the sunshine of our present generation, this prophetic hope has been partially realized: the majority of contemporary religions of Christianity no longer dwell upon the sinful nature of mortality or the depths of its depravity. Unfortunately, a present view of some pockets or our American way of life may suggest a pendulum swing farther than ever a Puritan prophet, or even Hawthorne himself, could have imagined.

THE WEAVING OF A MEANING

The rich and spiritual adornment with which she embellished the scarlet letter became attractive to members of the community. Although "sumptuary laws forbade these and similar extravagances to the plebeian order," they nevertheless paid her to

> add the richer and more spiritual adornment of human ingenuity to their fabrics of silk and gold . . . . Deep ruffs, painfully wrought bands, and gorgeously embroidered gloves, were all deemed necessary to the official state of men assuming the reins of power . . . .

By degrees, nor very slowly, her handiwork became what would now be termed the fashion. (81-82)

Hawthorne has her society being somewhat transformed slowly by her handiwork among the people. This change in the community may figure a movement toward a more compassionate society that is carefully threaded throughout the tale, perhaps connected to a change of insight about the scarlet letter, and seems a theme that lies predominantly at the base of Hawthorne's allegory. Even Pearl's apparel, woven with Hester's "fantastic ingenuity," exhibited a semblance of the refinement with which Hester had outlined the scarlet letter upon her own bosom, as though it "appeared to have also a deeper meaning," which Hawthorne tells us he shall address further (83). This deeper meaning may have to do with a spiritual refinement.

Hester's needlepoint, and her actions in the community, began to reidentify the infamy of the letter as something more noble in nature. Her handiwork with the needle seemed to embellish the clothing of the Puritan community, and their minds, with brighter embroidery than theologically hitherto allowed, much as she had elaborated her own scarlet letter, all perhaps as a token of the prophetic hope of a brighter day coming.

True to the Romantic notion that truth can be found to emerge from the heart of nature, the innocence of nature may unfold its brightness and beauty and become more the fashion or custom than the black cloth or customs of contemporary religion, "fashions which it might seem harder to dispense with" (82). Hester's weaving, combined with her humanitarian services, may symbolize this unfolding transformation in the hearts of the people, and the allegory seems to narrate the process of a spiritual refinement of the community. Her needlepoint "really filled a gap which must otherwise have remained vacant" (82). This gap may represent the void in the lives of the followers of contemporary religion because the heart and centerpiece of its faith was missing. The love, mercy, and compassion for one's fellowmen was not the central theme of the current-day Christian's devotion and worship. Her compassionate actions in the community, like a sainted and cloaked Anne Hutchinson, began to modify the attitudes of its residents. This merciful motif, though hidden beneath the tenets of Puritanic justice, is much the same motif that is being fostered by Dimmesdale's image, and perhaps the gist of Hawthorne's own conclusions.

A KIND OF LURID TRIUMPH

It is highly significant, therefore, that Hester turned the spectacle on the scaffold "into a kind of lurid triumph" (78). Her needle continued to combat the assumed ignominy of the fall and sought to reveal to all the "joint futurity of endless retribution," which had some connection with Dimmesdale's mission. She sensed her mission, instinctively, rather than knowledgeably, as that of making the connection between the mercy manifest in the universal heart and the community of her fellow Puritans. Though she carried out the primary duty of her office in Boston—to suffer her ignominy with resignation—according to the justice of the law under the control of Providential destiny, she did it because of that merciful, blood-red hope of joint futurity worthy of her seven-year sacrifice, and despite the compelling logic and enforcement of the Puritan code. What Hester's destiny might be, in view of her hope and sacrifice, is shadowed in the mind of the reader as to what that very puzzling end might be.

So Hester's needlework upon the scarlet letter pinned to her chest, upon the fashions of dress preferred in the community, and upon the clothing of her child in fanciful or fantastic ingenuity, has a deeper meaning that seeks, though dimly, to connect humankind with divinity, justice with mercy, and the present with the future. It may be said that her handiwork could represent Hawthorne's attempt to secretly embellish the religion of his own time with the spirit of the law by directing his tale at the heart and center of Christianity, the future Redemption of humanity from the mortality of this world.

THE MORBID MEDDLING

At the same time she was being oppressed by the Puritanic view, Hester is also depressed so much by the Puritan concept of human nature, which forbids even the hope of joy, that her intuition and her logical reality are in conflict. Hawthorne posed this conflict between her desire, or intuitive sense, to be with her true love, and the darksome spell which Puritanism had cast upon the likelihood. The spell logically rejects this hope, in the which logic Hawthorne, in a manner of double-speak, directs or tokens the reader's attention to another corollary theme of the allegory:

> This morbid meddling of conscience with an immaterial matter betokened, it is to be feared, no genuine and steadfast penitence, but something doubtful, something that might be deeply wrong, beneath. (84)

One of the more complex commentaries by Hawthorne, this statement lacks other supportive references, unless it pertains to a conflict between basic intuition of human nature and a learned, perhaps oversocialized, conscience, a controversy between the mind and the heart. Perhaps its complexity is marked by a question posed in the mind of the reader, "What is the immaterial matter referred to?"

The context of the statement may suggest a mixed conflict between her natural sense of the beautiful, perhaps posed by the immaterial nature of the spirit, identified elsewhere probably as intuition, its resulting sensation of joy, and the consciousness of a rejection of that joy, as conjured by Puritanic indoctrination. To Hawthorne, it seems he feels that one's conscience, rather than signaling penitence within the human soul, poses instead an incongruity in it that betokens something is wrong, perhaps even to the point of doubting the value of a morbid conscience. At the surface level, the mixing of Hester's conscience, as programmed by the Puritanical fathers, with the immaterial substance of her intuitive or spiritual inner nature, wherein she would express the beauty of her creation, if she were allowed to, projects the idea that the mingling thereof may be inherently wrong. Perhaps, to Hawthorne, logical deduction and intuition should operate in harmony. Today's psychology might agree that conscience may be overlearned just as it can be underlearned.

The use of the word, "meddling," has two meanings Hawthorne may have meshed or mixed together. One meaning is "to mix," and the other, "to interfere." The "morbid meddling of conscience with immaterial matter," in this case, may possibly refer allegorically to the infusion of a divine spirit within the human body, which has intimations of beauty and a splendid destiny, with its counterpart, the mental consciousness about our mortality, that has been invoked by the logical deductions of institutional philosophies. What may be "meddling" about this combination of Puritan conscience with spiritual intuition may be the morbidity of the former. What may be perhaps "morbid" about this meddling is the Puritan labeling of human flesh as depraved. Or it may refer in general to our puny and viral efforts to enforce some standard of moral conduct on the part of others.

Perhaps beneath the surface of the tale lies a philosophical conclusion of Hawthorne's that hints at something wrong about the whole aspect of human nature itself; and the statement above may reflect the distorted views of society about the creation gone amiss, as will be discussed in some detail later.

THE EFFECT OF THE SCARLET LETTER

The scarlet letter Hester beautified seems to have another effect upon her other than that cast by the Puritan perspective, about which effect Hawthorne again asks the reader questions to deduce the connections between the scarlet letter and the community of mankind:

> the scarlet letter had endowed her with a new sense . . . . it gave her a sympathetic knowledge of the hidden sin in other hearts. She was terror-stricken by the revelations that were thus made.

> What were they? Could they be other than the insidious whispers of the bad angel . . . that, if truth were everywhere to be shown, a scarlet letter would blaze forth on many a

bosom besides Hester Prynne's? Or must she receive those intimations—so obscure, yet so distinct—as truth? (86)

Again, Hawthorne, in teasing intimations from the reader by his questions, is highlighting the greater accuracy of intuition as a bearer of truth. Hester has apparently tapped into two impressions, one from the dark side, and another from the natural side. A new sense of the scarlet letter has seemingly embued her with a sympathy for the consciousness of shame shared by humankind. "Sometimes, the red infamy upon her breast would give a sympathetic throb," or assert "a mystic sisterhood" she sensed in common with her fellows (87). These intimations, the reader may answer, are not entirely "the whispers of the bad angel," but suggest that the letter, for the better part, stands for the connection between the Atonement and the sins of all humankind. The scarlet letter A is the symbol that makes that connection, with two meanings. Redemption for the penitent is one of those meanings.

The other meaning seems disclosed in a kind of parable, or legend with which Hawthorne concludes this chapter. He refers to "a terrific legend," or the fire and brimstone of hell so many ministers love to preach:

> The vulgar, who, in those dreary old times, were always contributing a grotesque horror to what interested their imaginations, had a story about the scarlet letter which we might readily work up into a terrific legend. They averred that the symbol was not mere scarlet cloth, tinged in an earthly dye-pot, but was red-hot with infernal fire . . . .
>
> And we must needs say, it seared Hester's bosom so deeply, that perhaps there was more truth in the rumor than our modern incredulity may be inclined to admit. (87)

"Red-hot with infernal fire," the scarlet letter seems to signify, at least to the vulgar, the pains of hell, as preached by many a minister of old, and may be reflected in one of the various reactions of the people to Dimmedale's revelation in Chapter 23. Perhaps "the vulgar," rather than referring to the bold sinner, were those ministers who reacted with such awful imaginations as to the meaning of the scarlet letter, as though they were the voice of Old Scratch himself: "O Fiend, whose talisman was that fatal symbol, wouldst thou leave nothing, whether in youth or age, for this poor sinner to revere?–Such loss of faith is ever one of the saddest results of sin" (87). Perhaps faith in, and reverence for, the One in whom forgiveness resides, was diminished or swallowed up in the fear of hell, which may have been thought to be a stronger motivator to the many than was the attraction of love to the faithful. Though the emphasis on hell fire and damnation by the Puritan ministers seemed to be the trademark with which Hawthorne brandished his forefather's religion, he did indicate that that legend may contain more truth than our incredulity permits. This legend, however downplayed, may be the baggage of Puritanism Hawthorne retained within his own theology, and may have tinged the scarlet letter therewith.

CHAPTER 6

PEARL

What is man, that thou art mindful of him?
And the son of man, that thou visitest him?
For thou hast made him a little lower than the angels,
and hast crowned him with glory and honour.[1]

Pearl is thought to represent the best of the civilization of humankind, in contrast to a rejection of the black and negative aspects of Puritanism, or contemporary religion. She seems to personify that breed of humanity nursed toward some advanced transformation, in some other location, upon some other soil richer than that of New England. She appears to signify the destined purpose of the creation of the human race, a child developing into a woman through the beneficial experiences of her childhood. In the process of her development, Hawthorne seems to philosophize metaphorically upon the nature of humanity.

A PEARL OF GREAT PRICE

Hester's art, therefore, is also fastened upon the clothing she designs for her daughter. Pearl is named to represent the only treasure that Hester has.

> [S]he named the infant "Pearl," as being of great price,—purchased with all she had,—her mother's only treasure! . . . God, as a direct consequence of the sin which man thus punished, had given her a lovely child, whose place was on that same dishonored bosom, to connect her parent for

ever with the race and descent of mortals, and to be finally a
blessed soul in heaven! (89)

Of all the creatures created or organized out of the elements of nature,
mankind was the crowning glory because she was fashioned in the image
of her Creator. In the history of the world, for the most part, it doesn't
appear to matter what pool we come from, but what this thought may pass
upon our mind in some fleeting instant, despite or because of what agonies
may have engendered the mood. Referring most obviously to the Biblical
parable about the pearl of great price, and specifically to the merchant man
who sold all that he had to buy the pearl[2], Hawthorne has Hester willing
to invest all she had to bring forth the child, and this in order, perhaps,
through Pearl, to bring Hester and Dimmesdale to "their marriage-altar,"
to transform mortality into immortality. Indeed, Hawthorne appears to
state above, and not in the doubtful mind of Hester, a direct, strong, and
positive answer to the questions formed for the reader in the previous
chapter. Those questions point to where Pearl came from, that she was
not a demon offspring, but a gift of God, whose purpose was "to connect
her parent for ever with the race and descent of mortals, and to be finally
a blesssed soul in heaven!" (89)

That parent may be Hester: wherever Hester went, so went Pearl; and
wherever Pearl may go, she embodied the best of Hester. Symbolic of
nature, Hester appears to be the mother of humankind, Pearl; and Pearl,
developing into a woman, seems to represent her future. Symbolic of a
civilization of humankind living a more prosperous and benign order,
Pearl, as a companion to Hester, who must learn and benefit from Hester's
experience, appears to be that best part of Hester that becomes the future,
connecting Hester's mortal nature forever with an immortality at her later
transformation. She is a "lovely and immortal flower" that grew in beauty
and intelligence "out of the rank luxuriance of a guilty passion" (89),
perhaps the passion of the human creation, though presently imbued with
impending death, still a splendid and luxuriant creature.

Hester,then, may represent the antecedent from which an advanced
species will emerge with an improved attitude toward the Creator's
handiwork and mature at some future date in some other clime. Hester
is to Pearl what the caterpillar is to the butterfly: the child is mother of
the woman. Perhaps Pearl herself is the transformation by which Hester,
as nature, is connected to the human race. Symbolic of the cause of that

transfiguration is the divine, Dimmesdale, whose ascent to the scaffold seems to represent the redemption that effects that transformation, perhaps somewhat suggested in the conclusion of Hawthorne's tale, by being buried next to Dimmesdale's sunken grave.

On the other hand, perhaps Dimmesdale may also be "her parent" referred to. In other allegorical terms, Pearl is the object of the creation that emerges out of the fallen nature of the world, connects mortal nature forever with her divine parent, and is destined to become "a blessed soul in heaven!" (89) Christian doctrine holds that the best destiny of humanity, as the offspring of Deity, created in his image, is to return home as "a blessed soul in heaven" following this mortal life. It is perhaps no less than the doctrine of the election, which, in a quick flashforward, might conceivably be the allegorical subject of Dimmesdale's election sermon, the intent of which was to show "the relation between the Deity and the communities of mankind" (249). In a way, the triangle of Dimmesdale, Hester, and Pearl may signify the connections between mortality, immortality, and heaven; and Pearl, as a blessed soul in heaven, may be destined to bring both parents together at the "bar of final judgment."

We may even surmise that what Hawthorne had in mind with this trio was to give his own election sermon, his own philosophical confession upon a scaffold, in the middle of a night that surrounds it.

A PEARL OF GREAT PRICE

More openly and summarily stated, Hawthorne, in meditating on the problems humankind faces with its origins, may be professing his own personal conclusions, that Deity (Dimmesdale, as a divine), as the father of humankind (Pearl), has breathed into the earthly elements of nature (Hester) the offspring of a lovely child, who will share for a while the same aspersions of ignominy as she, but eventually connect nature forever with the race of humankind, so as to become a blessed soul in heaven. Stated differently, in the Christian perspective, the Creator has arranged for the souls of humanity to be embodied with the elements of nature in a plan that, through the Fall and the Atonement, enables the human race to be raised in the resurrection, body and spirit, and live a higher order of life in heaven. Thus, Hawthorne possibly and subtly may have stated his belief in a literal resurrection of the natural body.

In the passage below, for another example of a positive and strong statement by the narrator, Hawthorne seems to be speaking of the human tabernacle itself, as the offspring of Adam and Eve, rather than of Pearl herself.

> By its perfect shape, its vigor, and its natural dexterity in the use of all its untried limbs, the infant was worthy to have been brought forth in Eden; worthy to have been left there, to be the plaything of the angels, after the world's first parents were driven out . . . . Pearl's aspect was imbued with a spell of infinite variety; in this one child there were many children . . . . (90)

Pearl's "aspect," or symbol, appears to be that she represents all or many of humankind, or particularly, a singular future and maturing generation. She may figure that generation of humanity worthy to have remained in Paradise, a generation for which the Creator created the world. Christian theology purports that, as the Creator moves and molds his creation toward that perfection, which resides in his own person, he appears to honor that creation with a plan to reinstate those conditions that originally existed in the Garden of Eden. We see later in Pearl's child play a prophetic foreshadowing of those conditions, as depicted by Isaiah, wherein a child plays harmlessly with the animals[3.]

Though Hester rationally feared the worse to be revealed in Pearl's nature, Pearl appears, in the mind of Hawthorne, to reflect the opposite. Though Hester is not so fully convinced about Pearl's real nature, because the instincts of her mortality are confused by her rationality, Hawthorne's inmost Me seems hopefully imbued in the subtle commentaries that idolize her. As it was for Hester, to whom her only treasure, Pearl, meant every thing, so often does a parent at times pause to wonder. Hawthorne had probably done no less many times as he gazed upon his own child, Una. In such rare moments of tranquility, as he peered fondly into her eyes, could he have supposed what the Creator, as a Father, might have felt himself in looking upon his own in their happiest moments? Could Hawthorne have sensed a bit of heaven's purity there that made him ponder awhile about the purpose of such a creation? Perhaps many a parent has conjectured whether gazing into the eyes of innocent childhood may be as close to heaven as one may get while still earthbound.

THE MUTABILITY OF HUMANKIND

So Pearl, possibly as a representative of many children, upon which the Creator, like a benevolent Father, may look down upon with high aspirations, is adorned by her mother with the best that money can buy, arrayed in the "richest tissues that could be procured." Perhaps, to Hawthorne, the best that lies within the nature of humanity does seek to give this intervening lot the best of care, as it looks down the long road to its promise of immortality.

In addition, Pearl's entire aspect comprehended "the full scope between the wild-flower prettiness of a peasant-baby, and the pomp, in little, of an infant princess." From prettiness to pomp, Pearl's scope of "outward mutability" seemed to be matched by "the various properties of her inner life," that possessed depth as well as variety (90), as does the individuality of the human family. Her moods were "illuminated by the morning radiance of a young child's disposition, but later in the day of earthly existence, might be prolific of the storm and whirlwind" (91). Besides figuring Pearl as a principle representing the breadth or spectrum of the human race, these descriptions of her may refer also to the depth and variety of its inner properties. Her various moods might signify the general mien or disposition from one generation to the next, wherein the last generation of humankind, in the Biblical text, may experience some greater turbilence of nature[4].

IN WANT OF DISCIPLINE

Like a young child's disposition, from radiant light to stormy weather, the impulsivity of humankind, like Pearl's, has always been in want of discipline. As lavishly as possible, human nature, from the dawn of life throughout its existence, is disposed to brandish its intervening substance of mortality with whatever grace it can. Hawthorne seems to note that the question of how to discipline humanity's impulsivity seems to vary from one generation to the next. Hester's care of Pearl was more lenient than that of her day, which, to Hawthorne, was harsher than that of his own time; and she imposed "a tender, but strict, control over the infant immortality that was committed to her charge" (91-92). Pearl is being nurtued by a firm control, but with a tenderness perhaps unlike the children of parents who subscribe to the discipline of the Puritan code.

As to the purpose of Hester's discipline, in the preceding quote, Hawthorne has possibly given another clue to the reader, who may wonder what he mean by referring to Pearl as an "infant immortality" placed in the care of Hester. The reader may question what might be her prospect as a full-grown woman, or adult immortality.

THE NATURE OF HUMANKIND

Pearl is allowed "to be swayed by her own impulses," perhaps because, to Hawthorne, passion seems to be too innately rooted, human nature so endowed with it, that suppressing it might be futile, or even destructive.

> Throughout all, however, there was a trait of passion, a certain depth of hue, which she never lost; and if, in any of her changes, she had grown fainter or paler, she would have ceased to be herself;—it would have been no longer Pearl!" (90).

It is perhaps this theme of sacred passion that characterizes Hawthorne's divergence from institutionalized religion. Its existence in the nature of humanity juxtaposes a paradox that questions the varied attempts of the world to control it: "lacking reference and adaptation to the world into which she was born . . . [the passionate depth of] the child could not be made amenable to rules" (91), or the rules of contemporary religion. The Romantic in Hawthorne seems to say that it is in the true nature of humankind to be out of place in a mortal world given to a Puritanic moral code, to which it has been subjected, and by which it has been wrongly judged and condemned. Hawthorne sources this passionate nature or disposition of Pearl as a result, while Pearl was in Hester's womb, of that momentous period when she was

> imbibing her soul from the spiritual world, and her bodily frame from its material of earth. The mother's impassioned state had been the medium through which were transmitted to the unborn infant the rays of its moral life; and, however white and clear originally, they had taken the deep stains of crimson and gold, the fiery lustre, the black shadow, and the untempered light, of the intervening substance. (91)

Hawthorne may be indicating that Pearl's soul came from the spiritual or divine world, a higher form or more noble breed before humankind's creation, and that her body is of the elements of the natural or mortal world, a dualistic principle. A possible interpretation of Hawthorne's Romantic tongue might propose that Hester's "impassioned state" is a reference to the natural nature of mortality, or her human womb, into which Pearl entered as an unborn spirit or soul. Coming from the spiritual world, Pearl's moral life was white and clear before entrance; and upon entrance into the intervening substance of mortality, had taken upon herself the tinges of mortality—the deep stains of crimson sin, the black shadow of the Puritanical (or contemporary religious) environment, the fiery lustre of mortality's impassioned nature, and the untempered light of common day experience. Perhaps, to the Antitranscendentalist, the untempered light is the ability to see without influence from other sources, black or white, dim or clear, which light begins to act upon the creature so born.

The use of the term "gold" is also intriguing: what is so golden about earth life? If the "intervening substance" with which Pearl is endowed is the resulting element of mortality intervening between the antemortal life and the life following mortality, perhaps the stains of gold represent a derivation of the divine or royalty invested in humanity's creation. At the very beginning of his special characterization and imaging of Pearl, Hawthorne has pictured her as a "little creature, whose innocent life had sprung, by the inscrutable decree of Providence, a lovely and immortal flower, out of the rank luxuriance of a gulty passion" (89). He has again symbolized her as a figure of immortality, springing from an innocent life into the guilty passion of mortality, though lovely and luxuriant in its rankness, "worthy to have been brought forth in Eden," and destined "to connect her parent forever with the race and descent of mortals, and to be finally a blessed soul in heaven!"

Possible Christian implications of these images—and the kind of Christianity to which Hawthorne subscribed may be as debatable as the obscurity of his book—is that humanity may be the literal spirit offspring of Deity; that for some divine purpose, humankind (Pearl) is embodied with element, "beautiful and brilliant," that was not meant to be disposed of later; and that, after exiting this intervention of mortality, she perhaps shall return back to the original state of being "white and clear." But, while mankind is dwelling in this intervening phase of existence, she must endure the black shadow of its religious orders in an unrefined light because, of necessity, she must partake of the nature of her mother.

It appears that Hawthorne's "intervening substance," tempered with a mixture of intervening influences, was caused by some mistake or broken law, perhaps "something doubtful, something that might be deeply wrong," which may allude to the Fall.

> In giving her existence, a great law had been broken; and the result was a being, whose elements were perhaps beautiful and brilliant, but all in disorder, or with an order peculiar to themselves, amidst which the point of variety and arrangement was difficult or impossible to be discovered. (91)

Thus Hester was incapacitated to tell whether Pearl was a human child or an "airy sprite" (92). To interpret the same briefly: because the intervening substance of mortality, though it be beautiful and brilliant, is a combination of substance from the spiritual world, and from the black shadows of untempered light, human nature is not disposed to ascertain the point or divining line by which these various elements can be sorted and identified by their source. So impossible to be discovered by human reasoning, that Hawthrone, as the reader shall see later, predicts a forthcoming prophet or prophetess to enlighten the human race.

The quotations above may be Hawthorne's description of the nature of humankind in a nutshell. Though mankind is rebellious, often impish, and yields to the temptations of the flesh, yet there awaits a better destiny for her if she recognizes, accepts, and follows a merciful and compassionate ordering of life.

Pearl is seen as an entity that does not identify so much with the mortality of this world, or its ecclesiastical prescriptions of conduct, as does Hester. Pearl seems finely tuned to a spiritual world which whispers whithersoever it will, "like a glimmering light that comes we know not whence, and goes we know not whither;" and she appeared often to be unsympathetic, with "a strange remoteness and intangibility," to Hester's plighted consternations (92). Hawthorne may have been rephrasing a Biblical text, and another corollary analogy, to show a different characteristic or representation of Pearl, and is quoted to question further his possible intended meanings by the allusion:

The wind bloweth where it listeth, and thou hearest the sound
Thereof, but canst not tell whence it cometh, and whither it
goeth; So also is every one that is born of the Spirit.[5]

Perhaps Pearl was moved in her moods like one "born of the Spirit," and was not always responsive to Hester's dilemmatic frettings. However, rather than comparing Pearl to the wind itself, suggesting she might represent the finer quality residing in humankind, he may be simply associating Pearl's intuitive moments with such wisps and whispers of the wind. In the interaction of the two characters, the concept of dualism—wherein Hester might represent the material element of matter, and Pearl its mental or spiritual counterpart, the two parts operating as cause and effect upon one another—is not configured in this analysis. Although Hawthorne may have placed some such value on the relationship between the two, whereas Pearl went wherever Hester went, this layman favors their relationship as representing the continuity between the present state of mortality and its future transfiguration, which relationship is more consistent with other themes in the novel.

Pearl's defiant moods, born of uncontrollable "new and incomprehensible intelligence" (93), seem to reflect a spiritual sense that resists the labeling of life as one of gloom and despair, to deplore the treatment of her mother and herself as ill-begotten, and to harbinger the destiny of a loftier society. Toward this destiny, Pearl, perhaps as the best or better part of Hester, instinctively guides her mother's decisions. It is this special sense, with which Pearl is endowed, that one might suspect that Hawthorne has figured her to represent a particular number of "many people," who, "by the truest test of a life successful," might be those among the "communities of mankind" who had some special relation or connection with Deity because they were attuned to the universal heart.

PEARL'S BLACK FIELD

Pearl's relationship with other children confirmed her lack of identity with the Puritan society, "disporting themselves in such grim fashion as the Puritanic nurture would permit" (94). These children surround and scorn her; and with a fierce temper borne of "intelligible earnestness" (94), she rejected the revilements heaped upon her mother and herself. It is interesting that Hawthorne, in the metaphorical description of Pearl's play, a parable within the allegory, candidly identifies the analogies of her play:

> The pine-trees, aged, black, and solemn, and flinging groans and other melancholy utterances on the breeze, needed little transformation to figure as Puritan elders; the ugliest weeds of the garden were their children, whom Pearl smote down and uprooted, most unmercifully. (95)

The identity of the aged, black, and solemn pine trees, as symbols of the Puritan elders, who fling the painful tales of their tenets into the air, serve as a more obvious clue to the meaning of the black field of the engraved escutcheon: "On a field, sable, the letter A, gules" (264). To elongate this analogy, black is to Puritanism as Puritanism, or contemporary religion, perhaps from Hawthorne's point of view, is to Pharisaism. If the symbol of black is so obviously associated, this "herald's wording" leaves the "curious investigator" with questions about the other symbols: Then what do the letter A and the gules represent? What message of worth and dignity is being heralded by Hawthorne's legend? The answers seem related to Pear's origin and destiny.

WHENCE COMETH PEARL?

Through Hester's various moods and thoughts, Hawthorne continues to frame questions for the reader: Is Pearl an angel or is she an imp of evil? One passage compares Pearl's wrath and incoherent exclamations to that of a witch.

> If the children gathered about her, as they sometimes did, Pearl would grow positively terrible in her puny wrath, snatching up stones to fling at them, with shrill, incoherent exclamations that made her mother tremble, because they had so much the sound of a witch's anathemas in some unknown tongue. (94)

Following descriptions of Pearl's behavior, as observed by Hester, Hester exclaims to her Father in heaven: "what is this being which I have brought into the world!" (96) This question may pinpoint the Romantic clash between logic and intuition in Hester's mind as well as it may project the curiosity of the reader to seriously investigate every analogy Hawthorne may be using in his tale. Hester does not seem to know since her mind is clouded over by the Puritan stamp of darkness, "a dismal labyrinth of doubt" (99).

Thus Hawthorne has Hester questioning Pearl to provoke and focus the reader's inquiry, possibly to whet one's intuitive inclinations for some answer: what are you? Where did you come from? What are you meant to be? For the reader, symbolic of her name, Hester Prynne seems to be prying into the nature of humankind, as human nature is inherently and instinctively inclined to do, to derive the answer to these questions. To help the reader answer them, Hawthorne gives clues in symbolic and parabolic form.

One such clue in this chapter is Pearl's identity with the scarlet letter. Hester remembered an occasion when Pearl's first awareness of her surroundings seems to have been the scarlet letter.

> [P]utting up her little hand, she grasped at it, smiling, not doubtfully, but with a decided gleam that gave her face the look of a much older child. Then, gasping for breath, did Hester Prynne clutch the fatal token, instinctively endeavoring to tear it away; so infinite was the torture inflicted by the intelligent touch of Pearl's baby-hand. (96)

Pearl identified with the scarlet letter by seeming to recognize its higher meanings by an ability intuitively beyond her childish years. Hester's own instinctive recoil perhaps may signal human nature's reactive and sometimes tortuous awareness of our own present unworthiness, "with still a deeper throb of pain" (86), the nearer a bit of heavenly foreboding touches us. Besides the personal pain of which human nature might be instinctively knowledgeable, perhaps the "infinite" torture may refer to the infinite nature of the Redemption that promises to consume all torment. The gleam in Pearl's face may reflect what Hester sensed unknowingly of the promise inherent within the scarlet letter A. Hester's rational mind, conflicted in a maze of doubt, often conjured up misconstructions that grapple with her intuitions on more than one occasion. That the gleam made Pearl's face look older is perhaps an instinctive, prophetic, and more sure knowledge, or foreshadowing, of what is to be in her later years, when she is finally a woman, transported to another clime and far better habitat.

Another child-play riddle is a behavior that astonished her mother. One summer day, Pearl gathered wild-flowers and delighted in throwing and hitting the scarlet letter with them (97), perhaps as a mockery of the aspersions of depravity placed there by the Puritan fathers. Perhaps the play is as well a prophetic recognition of the real meaning of the scarlet letter to which Pearl is directing Hester's confused attention.

The discussion between Hester and her child also pointed towards Pearl's origins as issuing from a Heavenly Father, including Hester. Pearl had asked a question about her progenitry, and Hester had given the more obvious answer, from a Christian perspective, which was probably not the answer Pearl is seeking:

> "Thy Heavenly Father sent thee!" answered Hester Prynne . . . .
> "He sent us all into this world. He sent even me, thy mother. Then, much more thee! Or, if not, thou strange and elfish child, whence didst thou come?" (98)

The use of the word "sent" may be designed to imply a former life, from which one is sent, as a kind of transition from one place to another. So the question, "Whence didst thou come?" is one of those questions Hawthorne seems to be wanting the reader to ask in order to understand his allegory. Pearl instinctively threw the question back to Hester, whom she knew knew the answer: "'Tell me, mother!'" said the child seriously . . . . 'Do thou tell me!" Hester, still in a puzzling quandary, cannot "resolve the query."

As to its origins, the nature of humankind is still befuddled, torn between the logic of science and the contradictory claims of current religious customs. As Hawthorne's readers contemplate what the answer might be to the question of Pearl's allegorical origin, they should eventually conclude that humanity's nature is identified more with good than with evil because the fatherhood of Pearl is likely the divine. If so, does the reader detect some connection between Dimmesdale and the "Heavenly Father?"

It appears, at this point in the allegory, neither does Hawthorne seek to resolve the query for the reader, at the surface level, as to whom Pearl's earthly father may be, or, at the allegorical level, whether the Heavenly

Father is her creator. He, like Pearl, is just pointing his finger, and may be echoing the two voices of mankind about her origin. Such, it is interesting to note, so seems the case, that when Pearl points to the scarlet letter, in the midst of this query, she proclaimed seriously, "'He did not send me!' cried she, positively. 'I have no Heavenly Father!'" (98) It is as though the letter A to which she is pointing has been identified by her as a person, who has not SENT her, and, therefore, she has no Heavenly Father. Whether or not Hawthorne is cleverly pointing to Arthur as the person who did not SEND her, and is insinuating, in Pearl's quest to know her earthly father, that Arthur may somehow nevertheless be involved in the matter, is not clear but as puzzling as Pearl's query.

A REFORMATION IN THE MAKING

Hawthorne concluded this chapter leaving the question in the mind of the insightful reader to be resolved later as the representations of his characters become clearer by other symbolic references. Nevertheless, one additional clue is given in the last paragraph.

Pearl's defiance and impish delights were atypical of Puritan behavior. At the end of the chapter (99), the gossip of the townspeople, typical of the attitude of established religion toward reformative actions, have circulated the talk that compared Pearl to "a demon offspring," a term used by Catholics of old, in their day of unclouded sunshine. But, Hawthorne relates, so likewise did the Catholic monks consider the reformer, Luther, "a brat of that hellish breed," much like the Puritans considered other reformers in their day. Pearl's actions are rendered comparable to that of Luther, whose antinomian efforts at reformation resulted in castigation. Hawthorne seems to be posing an analogy: as the Reformation was to Catholicism,. so is Pearl's representation to Puritan interpretation. In other words, the view of the nature of humankind, as seen by Hawthorne, beautiful and destined for joy, is seen by Puritanism as a hellish concept, because their view is that the flesh is depraved and a worthless impediment to heaven. The implication to the contrary here may be that the human body, in the mind of Hawthorne, in connection with Pearl's origin and destiny, is likely to be more significantly worthy than contemporary religion proposes. She may therefore be presented as a figure whose philosophical behavior is opposed to the present image of how mortality is to be redeemed.

The pondering reader will soon understand that Hawthorne seems to be looking forward to a refinement or replacement of Puritanism by casting off its black shadow and restoring a view of life as a thing to be enjoyed, since joy seemed to have been sacrilegious to the Puritan code of worship. The reader may even conclude that Pearl may represent the outcast prophetess of a new generation, one that will eventually escape the gloominess of life imposed by the morbid interpretation of contemporary religious institutions. Perhaps, when Christianity has undergone a reformation suitable to cultivating the true Christian character, this other generation is destined to live in a clime, at some future date, other than under the Bostonian morbidity.

CHAPTER 7

THE GOVERNOR'S HALL

Forasmuch as this people draw near me with their mouth, and
with their lips do honor me,
but have removed their heart far from me,
and their fear toward me is taught by the precept of men . . . [1]

The symbolic meanings of Bellingham's mansion may be more strained in this chapter than in any other, but the Governor's hall appears to represent a mixture of religion and state that reflects a somewhat degenerate attempt of the Puritan fathers to reform the Reformation. Both Governor Bellingham and John Wilson, veritable historical figures, were in meeting together when Hester and Pearl arrived. John Winthrop, who died later in the tale, was the present governor of the colony, and Bellingham was a former governor who was an honorable member of the society, with much influence still, and perhaps chief among those who think that Pearl should be taken from Hester and put in the care of better Puritan upbringing. Mr. Wilson, a clergyman born in Windsor, England in 1588, who came with John Winthrop in 1630 to colonize Massachusetts, actually was in Salem at one time, and was consort with John Winthrop in the antinomian controversy over Anne Hutchinson's ministry. Of a good reputation, his characterization is favored by Hawthorne over that of Bellingham's.

Armed with the "sympathies of nature" (101), Hester and Pearl go there to plead her case before him in an attempt to solicit his support for not separating them. At the allegory level, perhaps she goes to argue that human mortality should not be separated from the human race. It is this minion's opinion that the controversy over the separation of Hester from Pearl symbolizes the philosophical controversy over the value of a mortal body, therefore whether or not the resurrection will be a literal union of body and spirit. In some Christian perspectives, this reunion shall in some way materialize in a better fit of the physical characteristics of mortility with the spirits of humankind. Hawthorne seemingly only alludes to the possibility of this reunion in connection with the solution of the dilemmas of life.

The decay evident in the Governor's hall seems to symbolize the inability of Puritanism to handle the problems of life, perhaps as a consequence of their focus upon the depravity of humanity, and their rejection of grace, perhaps as demonstrated by their expulsion of Anne Hutchinson. We therefore see traces of the theme of a present need still for a transformation of the contemporary religions order.

ENDOWED WITH LIFE

Arrayed in a "crimson velvet tunic . . . embroidered with fantasies and flourishes of gold thread," Pearl, who "seemed the unpremeditated offshoot of a passionate moment" (101), was first to be seen dressed in a garb that "made her the very brightest little jet of flame that ever danced upon the earth" (102). Pearl is described in more detail in such a way in this chapter as to identify her clothing as "the scarlet letter in another form; the scarlet letter endowed with life!" Several references to Pearl as immortal seem to figure her as humankind endowed with life everlasting, though an offshoot of a moment of passion, perhaps to personify the prophetic promise of two Passionate moments in time, the Creation and the Redemption of humanity.

The chief effect of the Redemption is the endowment of life promised apparently to those whose life, "by the truest test," becomes "successful to such an end!" (263) At the same time, the little flame of fear Pearl's visage seems to conjure, especially in the minds of the vulgar and hostile, may relate to an absence of grace, as contained in Anne's ministry, and therefore may be used as a figure of speech to refer to the pains of "hell fire and damnation" preached by the Puritans. Hawthorne apparently did not completely dissociate this particular tenet from his belief system, which seems somewhat embedded likewise in the meanings of the scarlet letter.

The characteristic of angelic life with which the crimson velvet tunic is endowed is supported by the symbolism of gold thread that hold Pearl's shroud together. Gold in the tale seems to represent royalty, or divine appointment, or a hallowed office. This connection also, then, associates the scarlet letter with a divine endowment of life. Destined to be an angel, or playmate with the angels (90), whose life should have been in the Garden of Eden, she seems a messenger of life for the sensitive few who are redeemed, and a messenger of death and hell for the insensitive many who are unredeemed by their hostility, or absence of compassion. Pearl appears then to be both a harbinger of hope and a foreboding of fear. She seems to shadow the judgment to one state of being or the other as she dutifully focuses Hester's and Dimmedale's attention to the office of the scarlet letter.

That Pearl "seemed the unpremeditated offshoot of a passionate moment" is the seeming appearance of adultery at the first level of meaning. At the second level of meaning, we have seen that that appearance is changing into another form endowed with life; and the reader may conclude that humanity's mortal creation, though perhaps unpremeditated, was the result of either Eve's passion for knowledge or the passion of Deity usurped. Again, we may have the implication that the mortal creation was not planned, but an act of passion. As well also as her prior immortal creation, though planned, was perhaps also an act of passion. The mortal creation, in the eye of Hawthorne, according to the eye of this beholder, may have seemingly been the unfortunate result of a plan of Providence gone awry, or else propitiously purposed. If we can accord the mystery of Pearl's birth with the same degree of mystery with which Hawthorne has safeguarded this act of passion, then there should be some reasonable doubt in the mind of the reader as to a judgment call of adultery.

If Hawthorne's tale is an allegory depicting his understanding about the fall of mankind and her redemptiion, then we must consider the implication of some other kind of act of passion as a possible implication for the birth of mankind. Hawthorne himself has alluded to an immaculate conception to highlight that mystery. This may not suggest that humankind was born as is reported of the Nazarene, but may suggest a creation of humankind just as mysterious as was that of Adam and Eve. And whereas Hester may not be an historical figure so much as a principle representing human nature, Pearl may be seen as a principle also, representing human mankind, an offshoot of the passionate moment of her unexplained creation.

An Analogy

Hawthorne has openly posed an analogy for the reader to ratiocinate. Pearl's dress has been fashioned in an elaborate similitude of the scarlet letter A that Hester wears on her bosom. This crimson tunic is

> an analogy between the object of her affection, and the emblem of her guilt and torture. But, in truth, Pearl was the one, as well as the other; and only in consequence of that identity had Hester contrived so perfectly to represent the scarlet letter in her appearance" (102).

In both senses as object and emblem, Pearl, as the object of Hester's affection, in her glorified attire, appears to represent an endowment of blessed immortal life; and, as emblem of guilt and tortue, may also signify otherwise.

But more than that, in another sense, Pearl may not be the only object of Hester's affection. She has another parent, and some sense of connection thereto. The reader also may sense some connection between the scarlet emblem and Dimmesdale, to whom not only does Hester's loyalty and devotion seek for some resolution from her dilemma, but also of whom Pearl expects some redeeming outcome. As a principle of the Redemption, which Dimmesdale' mission may represent, Hawthorne may be relating his character to the agony of the sacrifice that effects it. Or pehaps he is merely contrasting the two messages embodied in the letter A, the one of sanctification of the elect, and the other of retribution for the vulgar.

Hester intuitively had contrived a perfect representation of the letter A in her daughter's attire because, and only in consequence of that perfect identity, Pearl seems to be that representation of perfection in humankind as achieved through the sacrifice of mortality. If Pearl, dressed in her red tunic, is the analogy itself that Hester has created, both person and fabric, then the object of Hester's affection may be Dimmesdale, or the Promise inherent in his mission, either to redeem the compassionate from guilt and torture, or to consign the insensitive and antipathetic to them. Pearl and her attire symbolically may represent the likeness of the two effects—the effect of the Promised Redemption and the effect of the Fall. Pearl, as a child of Dimmesdale and Hester, may connect Dimmesdale's mission with the infamy of Hester's fall. As Dimmesdale's mission is to Hester's infamy, so is the Redemption to the Fall. We see later, at the brook-side, more about Pearl's office that guides the pair toward their unity or union.

As an allegorical offshoot of another act of passion, the Atonement, Pearl then may represent redeemed mankind as the Creator intended her to be, and the analogy between the characters and the emblem may forecast Hawthorne's take at disentangling life's "mesh of good and evil" (64). Or we may simply say that the abstraction is too complicated an implication for the mind of any writer, or too far-astray from Hawthorne's philosophical bent to be authentic. It is only polite, at the least, to leave some room for the nay-sayers, though this plebian is sure that, given one's motives, other alternative explanations can very well be created to negate this one. However, in honor of logic, as a measure of truth, it is only fair to propose that any explanation is better than none.

A HALF-FLEDGED ANGEL OF JUDGMENT

In one way, Pearl is half-fledged because she has not developed fully into the woman she is to become. The maturity of her womanhood is perhaps the perfection of the civilization of humankind she represents. That maturity will not, and perhaps cannot, be nourished upon the soil of Puritanism:. Mankind has elsewhere her destined abode and another time for her complete development.

As an half-fledged angel, Pearl is close to three years old in the time frame of the tale. Humankind likewise is a half-fledged angel not yet immortalized. In the time frame of the allegory, the "three years" may indicate the advent of the Nazarene in the meridian of times, with the promise that mortality would take on immortality at the end of the world's time, or the seven thousand years of mortal existence.

In addition, beside her portrait as a messenger of hope, on the way to the Governor's hall Pearl displayed the other image as a messenger of fear, when the children of the town decide to throw mud at her and Hester. This metaphor commonly means casting some derogatory aspersion, and may signify the vilification of nature by the Puritans, or their persecution of others with different religious understandings. As do the elders, so do their children, in miniture form. Hawthorne may have chosen the object of mud, rather than some other, perhaps to imply the repugnance and the wrongness of the act, in keeping with the theme of the sacredness of human nature. Pearl, however, instantly puts them to flight with a fury that resembled, in her fierce pursuit of them, an infant pestilence,—the scarlet fever, or some such half-fledged angel of judgment,—whose mission was to punish the sins of the rising generation. (103)

Hawthorne seems to cast Pearl also as a half-developed judge or judgment, as though, if representing a righteous breed to be, or a higher commission, she may stand to judge the unrighteous at some future time, or, at least, stand as a standard by which they are judged. Perhaps implied in the passage is the notion that the future generation of a more advanced religious order and perspective, symbolized by Pearl, in some way may be involved in the judgment of those who are insensitive to the universal heart. Christian theology may have supplied Hawthorne with this theme: "Do ye not know that the saints shall judge the world?²" But since the "rising generation" would include only a portion of humanity, the reference above may apply only to the surface level; that is, Pearl, as an infant, is a pestilence only to the children of her day, although the "rising generation" might signify a greater inclusive.

This imagery of judgment, however, may be supported by the metaphor of Pearl as "the very brightest little jet of flame that ever danced upon the earth" (102). Christian theology claims that the wicked, or tares of the earth, perhaps the rising generation of the last days, will be consumed by fire. Pearl may represent this temporal aspect of the judgment at that time, wherein the worldly elements of the earth are destroyed by fire, as well as its spiritual aspect, wherein the worldly minded presumably reap the rewards of their labors for failing "the truest test of a life successful" to some joyous end.

LOYALTY TO THE END

What is the love and loyalty that binds Hester to Dimmesdale? Hester never divulged the identity of Pearl's father in the tale, if she had one, and seeks to establish or reestablish their relationship with the divine. Some critics have focused blindly upon their unrepentant desire to maintain an assumed illicit relationship as a slap in the face of their Christian posture. Because these critics may have Puritanized their literary views, and rendered surface judgment before probing insight, they have failed to sound the allegorical depths below the tale and may have been caught up in the same Puritanic mud-slinging of Hester's generation.

Whereas Hester appears more devoted to the young divine, or the redeeming one, Pearl appears more prophetically faithful to the destiny of the threesome. In Christian theology, humankind is endowed with divine life, therefore has an awareness of the forces of good working upon its nature, and has been bequeathed with either the embryonic gift to be redeemed from the Fall, by sensitivity to its Redemption, or the embedded fate to be thwarted by insensitivity to it. Perhaps the passion of Hester's pain helps redeems humanity from its mortal nature according to "sacred love . . . by the truest test of a life successfujl to such an end!" Hester's love and Pearl's loyalty may represent no less than that faithful obedience all nature seems predisposed to accord its Maker and its Redeemer, and probably would, were it not for the influence from the dark side of reality, as Hawthorne has suggested elsewhere in his narrator's commentary (160).

INTUITION VS. REASONING

The reader is also directed to the Romantic slant that explains why Pearl is more intuitively faithful than Hester to Dimmesdale's mission. In describing how Pearl has been lavishly dressed, Hawthorne uses one of his similes, "as if," to show the destructive influence of reasoning upon the intuitive sense.

> The mother herself–as if the red ignominy were so deeply scorched into her brain, that all her conceptions assumed its form–had carefully wrought out the similitude, lavishing many hours of morbid ingenuity, to create [the] analogy. (102)

Hester as been so brainwashed by the Puritan fathers to the point that she conceptually believes in her ignominy; nevertheless, she senses something more sacred in the ingenuity of her handiwork as an analogy. One of the conflicts in Hawthorne's novel is that between reason and intuition, wherein the two are counterposed with opposite effects, although Hawthorne does not seem to pose them so much as mutually exclusive of each other as companions better suited when equally matched.

A SEVEN YEAR'S SLAVE

Seven years is a redundant theme that occurs most often in three consecutive chapters following Hester and Pearl's walk in the forest to be reunited with Dimmesdale. Reference to this time frame is given in another analogy of the Governor's bond servant, who will be a slave for seven years, although he was free-born; that is, he was meant to be free. This servant admits Hester and Pearl into the hall of entrance.

> Hester Prynne gave a summons, which was answered by one of the Governor's bond servants; a free-born Englishman, but now a seven years' slave. During that term he was to be the property of his master, and as much a commodity of bargain and sale as an ox, or a joint-stool. (104)

The metaphor or short parable of the bond servant is possibly an analogy that supports the theme of the time frame. Although being born free possibly indicates that he wasn't always a slave, at the end of the seven year period, or bond-service, he will go free. Though freely born to immortality, mortality is a kind of bond-service to impending death, the release from which appears to be the focus of Hawthorne's allegory. The freedom acquired at the end of the seven thousand years of life's mortality is the one for which Hester is constrained to hope.

That the slave was "as much a commodity of bargain and sale as an ox, or a joint-stool," both interesting choices as object to typify slavery, or possibly lack of free-will, is an analogy that parallels the one Hawthorne used in comparing life as a stage upon which actors perform assigned roles for some destined end or purpose. Perhaps the focus upon the servant's freedom is designed to signify a hope for redemption from such slavery at the end, for which day both Hester and the bond-servant wait patiently. Until that end-time, the servant seems to be little more than a pawn to be moved around at someone else's pleasure. Hester herself seems to feel bound to that same endurance, as though that were her present destiny serving the purpose of a kind of retribution.

Hawthorne is probably not being too cynical in the case of either analogy, but simply casting life as it may seem to be to him. Hawthorne doesn't seem to show too much more cynicism in his novel than to suggest that humanity may be treated like an ox or a joint-stool. The serf's servitude may likely represent mankind's mortality as a bond-servant to materiality for a period of her seven thousand years. This materiality is subject to degeneration and eventual death, after which time, death and its slavery shall be swallowed up in the victory over the grave, according to Christian theology. In the meanwhile, humankind has been bought and sold, yoked, and acted upon at will as their master or neighbor close at hand has pleased. From the way empires have risen and fallen, either from internal corruption or external, it could even be said, as the Christian claims, that this entire show of life may be subject to the machinations of a master puppeteer. We will meet a pinion of that master at the end of Hester's visit with the Governor.

A MUSEUM OF THE PAST

The Governor's house seems to be another but lengthy parable within the allegory that treats the changes in traditional religious governments. In its earlier days there was a freshness in the hall's exterior and a cheerfulness that radiated from its windows "of a human habitation into which death had never entered" (103). Now the mansion is crumbling to decay in an air of melancholy, and the sunshine only reflects from the mansion, "as if diamonds had been flung against it by the double handful" (103), perhaps to indicate a measure of waste in the Govenor's grandiose attempt to restore it.

A hint of the degeneration of Puritan Christianity, if not the Protestant Reformation itself, or fall from the freshness of light and truth, and its ensuing melancholic effects, seem evident in the symbolism represented in the descriptions of the mansion and hall. The hall may symbolize what once was the Garden of Eden, where no death had entered its habitation, until the Fall, and/or a time prior to the apostasy of the Christian church, or whatever it was, for which a reformation was thought crucial. In general, the symbolism of decay appears to reflect a failing attempt to restore or replace its original grandeur.

> This was a large wooden house, built in a fashion of which there are specimens still extant in the streets of our elder towns; now moss-grown, crumbling to decay, and melancholy at heart. (103)

The hall is decorated and furnished from relics, or "heirlooms, transferred hither from the Governor's paternal home . . . the whole being of the Elizabethan age, or perhaps earlier" (105). These furnishings may represent the artifacts or articles of religion passed down from one age or place to another to indicate an attempt to retain the splendor of the original; nevertheless, a lack of substantial change for the better is marked by the decaying aspects of the hall.

The armor of the Governor also reflects the same absence of joy and glorious destiny in the Puritanical attitude toward life's purpose: it yields a distorted and exaggerated picture of the scarlet letter Hester wears. Pearl is the one who points out to her mother this exaggeration in a good-naturedly, scoffing manner (106). This metaphorical reflection may allude to the distortions of original truths as reflected by contemporary religions.

STRAINING ON A GNAT

The portraits of Bellingham's lineage carry an air of pretentiousness inherent in the vestiges of Puritanism that may cover up a draft of hypocrisy, "like the large pewter tankard, at the bottom of which, had Hester or Pearl peeped into it, they might have seen the frothy remnant of a recent draught of ale" (105). That the tankard was seen on a hall table instead of a dinner table seems to flavor the incident of discovery somewhat. Its placement suggests a casual or customary usage rather than as a formal necessity at dinnertime, and this attitude is contrasted by row of portraits in the hall way.

> On the wall hung a row of portraits, representing the forefathers of the Bellingham lineage . . . . All were characterized by the sternness and severity which old portraits so invariably put on; as if they were the ghosts . . . of departed worthies, and were gazing with harsh and intolerant criticism at the pursuits and enjoyments of living men. (105)

To Hawthorne, these portraits of the forefathers of Puritanism, hanging on the walls of their decaying kingdom, reflected the spirit of intolerance for activities focused on enjoyment, which their current leaders were nevertheless pursuing earnestly, and without too much concern for their obviousness, as though position and status gave these notable worthies license to forego application of their tenets to themselves.

There are a couple of examples of hypocrisy that parallel another time in history now commonly known and associated with a single word, Pharisaic. In an allegory containing Biblical content, it would be a natural connection for the reader's mind to relate these examples to that historical past, were one mindful of the disparity between the Puritan articles of faith and their practice. Whether or not Hawthorne intended for the Puritan religion to symbolize that segment of history, as a background for his allegorical allusions, is a possibility that can hardly be ignored.

Further, it appears that Governor Bellingham and other "statesmen of eminence" would involve themselves in "matters of even slighter public interest, and of far less intrinsic weight than the welfare of Hester and her child" (101). Matters involving public participation, however small, as though the appeal of public attention was a primary motive, seemed to be of greater importance than that of deciding the fate of mankind. Hawthorne included an example of this disparity in a controversy that engulfed the entire legislative body of the colony, over the trivial matter of the ownership of a pig. Perhaps Hawthorne intended to associate the leadership with "another social state" in Biblical history, in the meridian of time, whose supposedly spiritual guides would strain at a gnat, and swallow a camel[3].

As a symbolic example of the decadence of the Puritan religion, Hawthorne uses the symbol of light again, this time in the Govenor's hall. Perhaps the significance of its occurrence in the hall, a place to gather guests, and therefore impress them while they wait, also has some bearing on the illustration. Pearl wanted to strip the sunshine reflecting from the hall and play with it, but Hester told Pearl that she must gather her own sunshine, since Hester has none to give her. In other words, perhaps, there are only simulated or distorted truths reflected in the dogmas of the Puritanism, and mankind can only play with borrowed light from its mansions, "moss-grown, crumbling to decay, and melancholy at heart." Or, perhaps, since cheer no longer comes from the Governor's hall, mankind must make her own sunshine, without the aid of institutional customs, which contain only tainted appearances of light and have little value in and of themselves.

Hawthorne may be hinting here, in connection with the description of the hall, as he elaborates later in Hester's prophecy, that a reformation of the past will not do, that humankind must start anew with new light and revelation. In our current or succeeding dispensations, if there should be a religion whose claims for such a renewal could be found veracious, then Hawthorne himself might be deemed as a prophet of such to come. Or perhaps Hawthorne is simply saying again that, since the customs of contemporary religion offer no doorway into Paradise, the new world, as a distant departure from the religious despotism of Old England, like as it were no gateway to India, was not the Garden of Eden expected by its seekers of truth and freedom.

THE GARDEN LOST

Even the garden outside the mansion is a failure, possibly suggesting symbolically the failure of the New England experiment in Puritanism to restore that which was lost. The walkway was "bordered with some rude and immature attempt at shrubbery," and "the effort to perpetuate on this side of the Atlantic . . . the native English taste for ornamental gardening" was considered hopeless (106). The Atlantic Ocean may symbolize the time-gulf between the Garden of Eden, with its previous perfect code of conduct for a glorified life, on the one side, and mortality, with its imperfect interpretations of that code, on this side of the Fall. Or the sea may simply represent the theological schism between the last two attempts to reform Christianity. The latter allusion seems more appropriate to the theme of hopeful improvement over time in the religious character of its institutions and people.

The "rude and immature attempt at shrubbery" may refer to the Puritan attempt to restore on this side of the Atlantic, not so much the glory of a lost garden paradise, but "the native English taste for ornamental gardening" that may represent the English version of the Reformation. The American experiment possibly survived as long as it did because "there were a few rose-bushes, however, and a number of apple-trees" (107). These rose bushes may symbolize the remaining vestiges of hope for redemption from the Fall that still survive in contemporary Christianity. Pearl's pleas for one of its roses seems to echo the craving of the human family for the promise for a more cheerful life, perhaps based upon a more accurate perspective of nature, as encrypted in the Redemption.

The apple trees may reflect the proverbial apple Adam ate that is now planted throughout the New England earth. Hawthorne tells us that the apple trees were

> probably the descendants of those planted by the Reverend Mr. Blackstone, the first settler of the peninsula; that half mythological personage who rides through our early annals, seated on the back of a bull. (107)

Stretching the parable a little further, or imposing one parable upon another, Hawthorne might be saying that the apple-trees are possibly symbolic offshoots of the alleged forbidden fruit of the tree of knowledge of good and evil, or the various temptations introduced to the "communities of mankind" by Satan, who was possibly the first settler in the earth after being cast out of heaven. Perhaps the Black Man of the Forest, then, if not one and the same, is a close relative of the Reverend Mr. Blackstone!

In any sense, Hawthorne makes one more attempt in this chapter to label the religious experiment in America as practically unsuccessful, again using fruit, and the cue, "as if," as a symbolic reference. Cabbages, and a pumpkin vine,

> rooted at some distance, had run across the intervening space, and deposited one of its gigantic products directly beneath the hall-window, as if to warn the Governor that this great lump of vegetable gold was as rich an ornament as New England earth would offer him." (107)

Perhaps the Romantic humor in Hawthorne empowered the lump with some gift of lengthy, directional movement, and non-verbal speech, to be dumped before the view of the Governor, or the reader, in hope he is intuitively listening, or noting that the garden of Puritanism may produce little profitable commerce in the market square.

Note that Hawthorne has closed this chapter, as he did in the preceding chapter, and in others, with a reference to the dark side. He refers to Mr. Blackstone as "half" mythological, as though there are records or annals of humankind indicating he may be thought as much to be real as to be mythical. This brief parable seems to recognize the theological dispute over the reality of Old Scratch. Nevertheless, though the Biblical Satan did not plant the tree of knowledge of good and evil in the Garden of Eden, yet he used it to bring about the Fall of Adam and Eve; and the poor apple tree ever since has been nominated to bear the infamous fruit that did them in.

Perhaps the apple trees symbolize the continuing presence of temptation inherent in mortality, while the rose bushes symbolize the hope and promise of mortality's redemption from such. And the pumpkin perhaps speaks for something else that is needed before the twain shall meet.

CHAPTER 8

THE ELF-CHILD AND THE MINISTER

> What advantageth it me, if the dead rise not? . . .
> But some man will say, How are the dead raised up?
> And with what body do they come? . . . [1]

The purpose of this chapter in the tale seems to be to elaborate the allegorical relationship between Pearl and the young minister, Dimmesdale, as well as to weave other related themes into the allegory. One theme seems to deal with the decay and decline of the religious order of the day, of which a form of hypocrisy was seemingly one of its characteristics, as a background for an informal tribunal on Pearl's destiny. But the main theme of this chapter, symbolized by the proposed removal of Pearl from Hester's care, is more difficultly deduced than the first, but appears to relate to the plot of the tale, and to the Biblical text above.

If there is an allegorical meaning underneath the tribunal discussion about what to do with Pearl, it seems to be an extension of the allegory treating the controversial theme of whether or not humanity is to be resurrected with a physical body. In other words, to remove humankind from nature because nature is evil, denies the value of the physical body, and obviates the necessity of a resurrection. On the other hand, to allow mankind (Pearl) to continue to live in the care of a natural world (Hester) suggests the value of the physical dimension and its compensatory destiny.

Hawthorne's use of parables to detail the allegory is confirmed also at the end of this chapter by his reference to using the parable as a means of communicating (117). The short interchange between Hester and Mistress

Hibbins also relates to the diabolical plot to win the souls of Hester and Pearl as a conjunctive consequence of winning the young divine's soul. Hawthorne continues to cast Puritanism in the dark, and to hold them responsible for the black shadow over New England.

AN INFORMAL TRIBUNAL

The magistrate, ex-Governor Bellingham, representing the legal order, thought of Pearl as one of the "children of the Lord of Misrule" (109), and he invited Mr. Wilson to examine Pearl for traces of Christian nurture provided by her mother. That he was a brother to the witch, Mistress Hibbins, who consorted with the Black Man of the forest, and was later executed as a witch, allies witchcraft with the legal system of the Puritan experiment: they live under the same roof! To Hawthorne, both may spring from the same source. Ironically, the ex-Governor, perhaps still representing the legal voice of Puritanism, declared Pearl "equally in the dark as to her soul, its present depravity, and future destiny!" (112)

John Wilson, the oldest cleric of Boston, representing the religious order of the times, is perhaps more objectively rational than his contemporaries because he is older and does not assume the child to be "one of those naughty elfs or fairies, whom we thought to have left behind us, with other relics of Papistry, in merry old England" (110). This statement seems a clear enough reference to the departure of Puritans from England when they failed to reform the English Church. Like Hester, Mr. Wilson would like to know what Pearl really is and who her father might be. Though his concern properly seems to represent humankind's rational quest for knowledge about the nature and origin of man, as a minister having doubts about Pearl's nature and her origin, he seems to represent a less biased Puritan's perspective that, nevertheless, in its intellectual darkness, was a little shy of the red-rich, spiritual essence of compassion, human or divine, that bolsters the Christian hope. Though Mr. Wilson was not initially convinced that Pearl was a product of evil, neither was he sufficiently attuned, as was Dimmesdale, to Pearl's true merits, and concluded she was a young witch. Hawthorne sees him possessed with a genial benevolence that was greater than his contemporaries, though not as well developed as his intellectual prowess. To Hawthorne, it seems that intelligence without empathetic benevolence is degenerative.

It seems fitting that Dimmesdale and Chillingworth are also both present at this judgment call to vie for the care of Pearl. Dimmesdale, as a defender of faith in humankind, eloquently and passionately pled that they should "leave them as Providence hath seen fit to place them!" (115) His argument was for the truth of what Hester claimed, the sacredness of their relationship, and the blessing of goodness each might be for the other. On the other hand, Master Prynne, though apparently only a bystander, nevertheless, prying only for the evil he might joyfully find, seems in accord with the Puritan inquisition, as rendered by Mr. Wilson when he misconstrued Pearl's moods. "'The little baggage hath witchcraft in her, I profess,'" said he to Mr. Dimmesdale. "'She needs no old woman's broomstick to fly withal!'" (116)

Though Hester and Pearl had gone to ex-Governor Bellingham's estate to plead her case to him for keeping Pearl, the meeting had become a trial of sorts, in which it seems Hawthorne invites the reader to participate. A question asked later by Roger, as a bystander, seems addressed more to the reader than to the tribunal.

'Would it be beyond a philosopher's research, think ye, gentlemen, to analyze that child's nature, and, from its make and mould, to give a shrewd guess at the father?' (116)

The task before the reader, who likely would agree that Hester and her child should not be separated, is to analyze the nature of Pearl within the entirety of the tale, and to reason with Hawthorne as to the allegorical value and purpose of that relationship. Knowing or believing that Pearl is of holy origin leads to the conclusion, by this interpreter, that Hawthorne is suggesting a divine reason for the union of flesh and spirit, in order to justify the mesh of good and evil in the world, which reason is rendered by Hawthorne later.

THE GOVERNOR'S FRILLS

Hester also was delivering a pair of fringed and embroidered gloves for the Governor to embellished his body, however contrary to the expectation of Puritanism that one dress plainly and simply. The Governor was "showing off his estate," which is in the midst of being imperfectly improved, "and expatiating on his projected improvements" to three other visitors (108). Such ostentation was also a contradiction within the Puritanical perspective of old, and serves as another demonstration of practice out of accord with preachment. However, as shall be noted, such reflects small changes in heart that is happening through Hester's compassionate services.

> The impression made by his aspect, so rigid and severe, and frostbitten with more than autumnal age, was hardly in keeping with the appliances of worldly enjoyment wherewith he had evidently done his utmost to surround himself. (108)

Hawthorne states that although the creed—depraved, the body should be deprived—was not taught by the Puritanical forefathers, yet their theological custom "to speak and think of human existence as a state merely of trial and warfare" suffered them no pain of conscience when they contrarily availed themselves of the comforts of life (108). This rationalization suggests either or both an apparent form of hypocrisy or an attitudinal precusor for the reformation Hawthorne seems to project. Along with the Governor's "frostbitten" aspect, and Mr. Wilson's beard, "white as a snow-drift," Hawthorne is coloring these ministers with unworthy qualifications, as though their ministry is in stalemate despite their efforts at reformation. He seems to question their hopefulness that the fruits of their labors "might yet be naturalized in the New England climate," and "compelled to flourish" against the garden wall (ibid.). Perhaps compelling anything to flourish, whether against a wall, in an open field, or in a house of worship, might be considered, in the end, an act of vanity. Perhaps there is the slight indication that successful growth is not fostered by a compulsive soil from without, but motivated by some self-driving force from within.

A FORERUNNER

Also reminiscent of the background of Pharisaism, reference is made to John the Baptist, an Essene whose religious practice was consistently ascetic.

> The wide circumference of an elaborate ruff, beneath his gray beard, in the antiquated fashion of King James's reign, caused

his head to look not a little like that of John the Baptist in a charger. (108)

This comparative description of the ex-Governor Bellingham may suggest he shared some affined tastes with the governor of Judea who beheaded John, or simply remind the reader of Hawthorne's decapitation from office. At the same time he is compared to a dead prophet, he is also identified with the old customs during the reign of King James, whose death ended the influence of Puritanism in England. This reference may also call to mind the contrast between the ascetic Nazarene, John the Baptist, and the Puritan leaders, the carekeepers of the King James version of the Bible, who loved worldly cares more than the congregation they taught. Or they may merely be a manner of introducing the character of John the Baptist.

In either or both senses, as the forerunner who prepared the way for the coming of the Redeemer, upon whose shoulders a new government was to be placed, the reference to John may be a foreshadowing of Dimmsdale's mission upon the scaffold. Dimmesdale gave the Election sermon at the election ceremonies honoring the inauguration of the new governor prior to and in connection with his confession upon the scaffold, and may have a symbolic connection with the same ceremony. After Dimmesdale gave his electrifying sermon, as destined by Providence, and quasi-confessed his relationship to Pearl, he seems to have voluntarily given up his life.

These references seem, therefore, to foreshadow a forthcoming change or reformation of Puritanism, unless they dare go further and proclaim a decapitation of the old, a tearing down of the whole system of society, and beginning all anew, as will be postulated further later in Chapters 13 and 17. However, in connection with the thrice mention of a time frame at this time in the plot, as suggesting the meridian of time, the tearing down and beginning anew might allude to the division between B.C. and A.D, the disenfranchisement of the Pharisaic Judaism and the building anew of Christianity.

Introduction of John the Baptist into the allegorical plot, in conjunction with three references to the time-frame again (109, 111, and 112)—when Chillingworth is noted as having been around about three years in the settlement, the same as the lifetime of Pearl—likely represents a symbolic time and place setting at the allegorical level. The advent of the Nazarene, as measured from the beginning of humanity, places the reader in the meridian of time. In Christian theology, the Nazarene came to reconnect the communities of humankind with their Creator by the resurrection; and it is notable that Dimmesdale, as a redeeming image, should be the mediator to plead passionately for that plan—that the mortal element (Hester) should remain connected with mankind (Pearl) (113-116). Whereas Puritanism, from the point of view of a few faiths who may still hold to the Calvinistic doctrine of total depravity, would deprive humankind of such a reunion, as an impediment to the wishes and intentions of the Creator, others declare the union of spirit with the physical to be the very purpose of the Creation, as well as of its reunion in the resurrection, which appears to be a part of Hawthorne's inmost Me.

The reader may also be reminded of Surveyor Pue's "decapitation" as a type of forerunner for the good news of Hawthorne's tale, when Hawthorne fortunately lost his head as a surveyor prior to finally being able to write his story of Hester. Whether or not Hawthorne was hinting at some comparison with his own situation may be more hypothetical than he intended. Nevertheless, the reference to John the Baptist again recasts the same historical setting, and intuitively poses the thought to the reader that Hawthorne's parabolic message may rely upon these castings to forecast Dimmesdale as a type of redeemer himself.

THE PROTAGONIST AND THE ANTAGONIST

The two ministers, Roger Chillingworth and Arthur Dimmesdale, in a "close companionship," may remind one of the short essay on love and hate at the end of the book. That these two should be together at the tribunal to decide Pearl's fate is allegorically fitting. In the symbolic investiture of the divine (the Creation) and in the gift of mortality (the Fall), both have had a hand in the process of Hester's (nature's) infamy. Their presence completes the allegorical or controversial background for the informal tribunal in which the Governor has invited his visitors to take part in judging as to whether Pearl should remain in her mother's keeping. In considering what to do, the tribunal seems to turn upon what Pearl is and where she came from: is her cheerful and childishly flitting playfulness derived from evil, or is it good distilled from the divine?

Pearl told the assemblage that "she had not been made at all, but had been plucked by her mother off the bush of wild roses, that grew by the prison-door," again a possible allusion to both aspects of Pearl's soul, as interpreted by the Puritanic Governor, "its present depravity, and future destiny!" (112) Hawthorne has cued the reader to relate Pearl's paternal genitor to the symbolic meaning of the red rose, and supported that relationship by reference to other instances of the use of that red symbol, the rose bush by the prison, and the Govenor's red roses. That Pearl may not have been made at all, in the ordinary fashion, but has been plucked from the red rose bush by the prison, again addresses allegorically the mystery of her birth. This reference may be easily overlooked by the reader, who may have already determined logically that Dimmesdale has fathered the child, in the ordinary fashion of fatherhood, and is loathe to see anything sacred in Pearl's creation.

At this point in the tail, neither Chillingworth's evil intentions nor the reasons for Dimmesdale's silence are addressed for the reader's prying ponderance. However, Hester noticed that Chillingworth's features have changed, "how much uglier they were . . . his dark complexion . . . grown duskier, and his figure more misshapen" (112). One of the possible themes throughout Hawthorne's tale is that, what a person feels about what he focuses his attention upon determines what he becomes, possibly reflecting another Biblical passage: "As a man thinketh in his heart, so is he.?" Because Roger is intent upon discovering evil within Dimmesdale's soul, with a hostile attitude, his character is degenerating further toward the darkest end of the love-hate continuum.

Hawthorne seems to be addressing the controversy of the resurrection in his tale, giving equal ground to both, and allowing slight hints as to his leanings. He makes several references to Hester's transfiguration back to her original beauty, from which it was changed by the fall, to her reunion with Dimmesdale, and to the immortal Pearl's "future destiny;" these references not only suggest Hawthorne's allegorical intentions, but leans into some cause to effect such. The confirmation of those considerations seem to occur at Dimmesdale's confession, a symbolic revelation for which the scarlet letter, and other symbols of redness, portend some sacred aspect. Later, to address the theme of Dimmesdale's silence on the matter, Hawthorne appears to add to that destiny the correlary theme of Divinity needing to be true to itself by declaring its worse, or showing some trait thereof, in the creation of humankind (260).

A SCARLET VISION

To discover who the father of Pearl was, Mr. Wilson, upon learning her name, invoked her yielding to Puritan instruction, if she were ever to wear the pearl of great price in her bosom. Connecting Pearl with the gospel of Christian instruction, to be worn within her bosom, is very close to Hawthorne's reference to her as "the scarlet vision" (110). But, as we have entertained, Hawthorne believed that Puritanism provided no road to heaven, and next turns the reader's attention to his rebuttal of their right to judge Hester or Pearl.

In Pearl's refusal to answer Mr. Wilson's question, with but a large measure of contempt, something more seems meant here that casting Pearl as a discerner of motives, who, like most children, seems to differentiate intuitively between darkness and light. This deeper inference goes even further than her contemptible attitude toward the Puritanical castigation of her mother, Governor Bellingham's biased judgment, and Mr. Wilson's unworthy inquisition. For example, discerning Mr. Wilson's intent in his question as to who made her, Pearl seems to have resented his assumed right to question her creation, or to judge whether she should remain with her mother or not, and refused to cooperate, with a spirit of perversity, even though Hester may have made known to her who her father was (111).

Allegorically, as a scarlet vision, she appears to be a kind of prophetess who intuits a promise embedded in the scarlet letter's greater meaning. The metaphor of the red rose and the scarlet letter consistently throughout the tale seem to refer to the promise of immortality as part of Pearl's (mankind's) destined nature. She appears to embody a scarlet vision that is bound up in an act of grace, as an apparition of Hester's compassion, as though Hawthorne intended to use the symbol of redness to reflect the Christian promise, that though our sins be as crimson as scarlet, they shall be as white as snow[3].

MEDIATOR OF THE SACRED PLEDGE

When the Governor's mind seemed to be made up, Hester furiously defended her right to keep her child and pled for the young divine to intercede for her as her pastor. In other words, as a redeemer, Dimmesdale appears to be a symbolic mediator for and in behalf of mankind. In defending Hester's right of ownership of Pearl, Dimmesdale declared that there is "a quality of awful sacredness in the relation between this mother and this child" (114). That quality of awful sacredness in their relationship seems to allude to the divine purpose of the Creation, the Fall, and the Redemption, which are bound up in the relationship between the Creator (represented by the divine, Dimmesdale) and the communities of mankind (represented by Hester and Pearl). It seems a sacred relationship between nature and humankind, as between mother and child.

As Dimmesdale—whose "large dark eyes had a world of pain in their troubled and melancholy depth" (113), perhaps as though he bore the weight of the sins of humankind—pled for the sacred union of Hester and Pearl, he justified their continued relationship as

> the solemn miracle which God hath wrought, in the existence of that child . . . . for the one blessing of her life . . . for a retribution too; a torture . . . an ever-recurring agony, in the midst of a troubled joy! . . . . [S]he hath an infant immortality, a being capable of eternal joy or sorrow, confided to her care,—to be trained up by her to righteousness,—to teach her, as it were by the Creator's sacred pledge, that, if she bring the child to heaven, the child also will bring its parent thither! (114-115))

Twice Hawthorne has used the term "infant immortality" with metaphorical reference to Pearl in the solemn miracle of her relationship to Hester. Hawthorne poetically seemingly has compressed the Christian code into a few lines: In its infancy, mortal life, a retribution for the Fall, and a consequent torture, flourishes with its mixture of trouble and joy, but has an immortality capable of either eternal joy or sorrow, by the sacred pledge of the Redemption, "if she bring the child to heaven." In conjunction with other Hawthornean themes, perhaps, if mortal nature should yield intuitively to the teachings from the universal heart, it will bring her inward child to heaven, and thereby herself be transfigured into the beautiful woman she was created to become.

Hawthorne seems to recognize the solemn miracle of the Creation of humanity, perhaps especially in a moment of Hester's passion: "See ye not, she is the scarlet letter . . . and so endowed with a million-fold the power of retribution for my sin?" (113). Although Hester's struggle to bring her child to heaven appears to rely heavily upon her ability to resolve the conflict between the pressures of intellectualism, and the consequent red ignominy so deeply scorched into her mind, Pearl herself seems to personify the promise of the Redemption of mortality to a million-fold, a number that allegorically might signify those that are so redeemed. Hester's mental faculties are so overwhelmed by the infamy of the scarlet letter, she is often bewildered by the child; and later, in the absence of Pearl, influences Dimmesdale to give in, through his own mortal impulses, to her reasonable argument. It must be noted that in the one instance of Hester's separation from Pearl, she presents an argument that appears to overwhelm the divine's own sense of destiny and mission. However, though distracted by her reasons, he finally recovered and yielded intuitively to his own extraordinary sense of self.

To Hawthorne, when intuitive knowledge is overwhelmed by the preponderance of intellectualization, the spiritual realities may not be so obvious. To the Puritan, the reasonable argument is: why should the body be reunited with the spirit if the body is depraved and ignominious? Hawthorne's answer seems to be: why not, since the Almighty created both? If Hawthorne is discussing the controversy over the resurrection of the physical body, that is, whether the spirits of mankind (Pearl, as a representative of all mankind) should remain with the natural physical body, or the element of nature (Hester), he seemingly favors the union.

Briefly summarizing the passage above, the Creator's sacred pledge appears to be the Promise of the Redemption, that if the nature of mortality is endured in humility and compassion, as Hester demonstrated, it may be transfigured and brought into heaven with humankind. To Hawthorne, the relationship between nature and the spirit of mankind, seems to shore up some hallowed purpose for a re-embodiment of the body with its spirit. Perhaps much like, to Wordsworth, "the child is father of the man," to Hawthorne, the daughter is mother of the woman. As Pearl is the mother of Hester, so to speak, the infant immortality sensed within is the parent of the body, and both work together to bring them both to heaven. As mortality is a schoolmaster to its immortality, so is Hester to Pearl, and each relies upon the other. As to the benefits of Hester's training of Pearl, perhaps the nature of humankind is goodly designed enough to educate the divine essence of men and women, and vice versa; and both, through divine intervention, may be restored from the effects of the fall.

An Intuitive Knowledge

For the Romantic, nature carries an instinctive knowledge to guide humanity like no other carekeeper. "God gave her the child, and gave her, too, an instinctive knowledge of its nature and requirements" (114). The Romantic in Hawthorne seems to proclaim that mortality is embued with a sense of what is required of it, and by its guidance can lead it back to heaven. So endowed by the Creator, he holds mankind in holy regard and plans for her a golden destiny, by way of Hester's retribution.

Redemption, however, in the Christian text, is passionately a two-edged sword: It cuts one way in that one Man vicariously experienced the pains of those who are intuitively sensitive to the purity of that way. Or it cuts another, through the souls of all those who are not so compassionately or mercifully attuned. The scarlet letter appears to encase both promises. According to basic Christian theology, and seemingly to Hawthorne, mankind, like Pearl, is "an infant immortality, a being capable of eternal joy or sorrow," destined to inherit immortality and experience one side of the sword or the other, perhaps depending mostly upon one's sensitivity to the universal heart.

The Creator and the Created

Dimmesdale concluded his earnest mediation by proposing that, for both their sakes, Hester and Pearl remain "as Providence hath seen fit to place them!" (115) Following his successful passionate appeal, Pearl, in a most tender caress, displayed love for him, a love that "mostly revealed itself in passion . . . by a spiritual instinct, and therefore seeming to imply in us something truly worthy to be loved" (115-116). There are only three instances, perhaps the most touching moments in Hawthorne's story, where Pearl shows her affection for Dimmesdale, each progressing toward the moment of climax at the end. Earlier, when Dimmesdale pled fervently for Hester to break her silence, for his sake as well as hers, Pearl "directed its hitherto vacant gaze towards Mr. Dimmesdale, and held up its little arms, with a half-pleased, half plantive murmur" (67). When he pled for Pearl, at this time, to remain in the care of Hester, and Pearl took his hand softly in both her own and "laid her cheek against it; a caress so tender . . . ," he hesitantly kissed her brow (115). And later, when Dimmesdale, in recognition of their affinity and relationship, asked if she was now ready for a kiss, Pearl allowed him to kiss her lips to break the pall of silence. As Dimmesdale remains loyal to his destiny, as sensed by Pearl, and nears the scaffold voluntarily, her affections deepen by their display. These progressively sweet exchanges seem to deal with the relationship between Dimmesdale and Pearl, the minister and the elf-child, the Creator and the created. Perhaps this maturing intimacy shows that, as the Creator evidences his responsibility for his creation, mankind may respond tenderly, and become worthier of the Creator's love or favor. At this point, the reader might conclude that Chillingworth may have intuitively sensed some special relationship between Pearl and the minister, and may suspect Dimmesdale's involvement.

So Dimmesdale's strong argument prevailed, Mr. Wilson conceded "to leave the mystery as we find it," and the tribunal is satisfactorily ended. But Hawthorne has given a clue to the reader, in the words of Mr. Wilson, that may possibly suggest how Hawthorne has arrived at his own conclusions on the matter.

> "Better to fast and pray upon it; and still better, it may be, to leave the mystery as we find it, unless Providence reveal it of its own accord." (116)

As Hawthorne suggests that perhaps Providence knows best, and not institutionalized religion, as to the destined relationship between mortality and humankind, he hints of the value he may have accorded intuition as a better source of knowledge than the speculation of logical reasoning.

Hawthorne may be also alluding to the possibility that revelation from Providence may yet address the problem of mortality, and thus may be setting the stage for Chapter 23. At the end of his tale, Hawthorne indicates that the revelation of the scarlet letter may signify that Providence, "of its own accord," through the action of his divine representative, has revealed the mystery of mankind's origin in Pearl's affinity and relationship with Dimmesdale. In that chapter, Dimmesdale, upon the scaffold, passionately displays the ultimate of his love by revealing himself covertly as responsible for Pearl. This revelation is made in a cloaked confession that also identifies the scarlet letter Hester wears as his own personal agony. However, the revelation is seen differently by those who witnessed Dimmesdale's confession, perhaps in similitude of the various reactions to the Nazarene's mission. Most readers assume that the confession is an obscure acknowledgement by Dimmesdale as being Pearl's father; but not every reader may consent to that assumption, and see nothing in it at all. And that varied reaction to Dimmesdale's confession seems to symbolize Hawthorne's projection of the controversy in society over the creation of humankind.

Pearl instinctively sensed a better destiny for humankind than that contrived by the Puritan interpretations. Perhaps that better sense is a progressively intuited conclusion Hawthorne unfolds in the conflict between the Puritan perception of the human being and the argument presented by the minister, thus calling this chapter, "The Elf-Child and the Minister." The designation "Elf-child" seems to represent the Puritan view of human nature, and "the Minister" seems to reflect Hawthorne's.

If the allegorical connections are understood at this point in the novel, then the answer to Hawthorne's question for the reader, whence cometh humankind, becomes clearer, and the answer is revealed later in Pearl's destiny: mankind's origin is divine in nature because her destiny has a glorious end.

FOILED AGAIN!

As has been pointed out, it is Hawthorne's style to say one thing and mean another, a kind of double speak. The parable or analogy at the end of this chapter, an interchange between Mistress Hibbins, is an example of this strategy to reveal and cover up at the same time. As implied in the supposition, "if we suppose this interview betwixt Mistress Hibbins and Hester Prynne to be authentic, and not a parable," Hawthorne is probably inferring that the interview is a parable, but also a representation of authentic history. He may also be alluding to the whole tale of the scarlet letter as a contrivance of his own invention.

Hawthorne may have thought that the reader would need a stronger clue in deciphering and relating the meaning of this parable to the allegory. He seems to surmise that superficial readers will only get the first level of meaning of the tale, unless they analyze the parable with reference to the allegorical representations of the characters in relation to one another. So it may be likely that he explicitly suggested the possibility of the Mistress Hibbins' scene as a parable to those inclined to think it through for its relevancy.

In this brief "interview," Mistress Hibbins, who wanted Hester to come with her to the forest to consort with the Black Man, was checking out Hester's state of mind or being. Hester implied that if she had lost Pearl, whose daughterhood was interpreted by Dimmesdale as a Providential design, she would have accepted death willingly and sold her soul to the Black Man in the forest. So "even thus early had the child saved her from Satan's snare" (117). Hester's statement, the narrator's comment, and Mistress Hibbins' frown, suggest that Hester had not sold her soul to the Black man in the forest, nor intended to. Yet the confidence of the witch, who rebutted, "we shall have thee there anon!" though matched by that of Chillingworth's, is swallowed up later in the confession and death of Dimmesdale upon the scaffold.

In the parable of the witch's quest, Hawthorne appears to acknowledge the struggle between the forces of good and evil over the possession and ownership of the souls of humankind, and to consider the plausibility of the elements of the physical world also being joined with their souls by divine intent. It possibly relates to the destiny of humanity over the issue of the right of ownership, as contained in some Christian theologies, which may need some elaboration.

Perhaps Hawthorne was familiar with this issue in the obscure book of Jude and other Biblical references.

> Yet Michael the archangel, when contending with the devil he
> disputed about the body of Moses, durst not bring against him
> a railing accusation, but said, The Lord rebuke thee[4].

Whether the dispute over the body of Moses was one of ownership or some other is not clear in the context of Jude alone, although he does refer to the angels "which kept not their first estate, but left their own habitation," like Roger and his savages, who came to Boston to peddle their wares. But much like Old Scratch's, or those of the legion of spirits who wanted to possess the bodies of swine when they were cast out of human bodies, the desire to possess a body of any kind by unembodied spirits seems such a viable force as to suggest some magnificence in owning one. Some variations of Christian theology have held that he and his legions cannot possess a body of their own, because of their former rebellion in heaven, but may acquire habitation with those whose owners have been vanquished by them, perhaps in the day of judgment, as well as, in some reported cases, here on earth.

Thus, Mistress Hibbins' boast to Hester, who represents the physical side of nature, may imply, in the conclusions of Hawthorne, this hope of those legions cast into outer darkness. And the age old conflict, in the Christian's world, between the forces of good and evil vying for the souls of humankind, and possibly their bodies, seems to lie at the roots of Hawthorne's allegorical inferences about the problems of mortality.

To further elaborate, specifically to the Biblical text, the conflict over the souls of humankind, between the fallen angels, led by Satan, and the angels of heaven, perhaps led by Michael, might seem to be of greater significance to Hawthorne if the issue of the physical resurrection is as important as the mastery of the spirit. Since, in the Christian faith, all are resurrected, the right of ownership may also be part of the great controversy in this struggle. Whatever Moses' sin was that seemed to give the devil some claim to his body, if we can take any of his claims to heart, considering Moses was a pretty good chap, Satan's claims might be fairly more inclusive. And equally victorious, should his attempts to thwart the plan of Redemption have been successful. Thus, Chillingworth's claim to Hester and Pearl seems to rest upon his victory over Dimmesdale, which victory might thereby ally humankind's destiny with the Black Man of the forest.

In conclusion, to take Pearl away from Hester, then, may imply, at the deeper level of the allegory, a separation of mankind from her human nature, or perhaps, in terms of the Biblical text, a separation of body and spirit. That Dimmesdale's mediation has dimly assured the union possibly speaks for the value of a literal resurrection in Hawthorne's philosophical ruminations. Thus this chapter on the elf-child and the divine may illustrate the common Christian concept of humankind being saved "from Satan's snare."

Hawthorne usually corroborates a specific implied meaning with other events, a kind of cross referencing, like latitude and longitude pinpointing a specific location. If the issue of Hester's transfiguration plays to this same theme, then perhaps, later, after we get another view of Hester, "We shall see whether Hester Prynne were ever afterwards so touched, and so transfigured."

CHAPTER 9

THE LEECH

How art thou fallen from heaven, O Lucifer, son of the
morning!
How art thou cut down to the ground, which didst weaken
the nations!
For thou hast said in thine heart, I will ascend into heaven,
I will exalt my throne above the stars of God . . . .
I will ascend above the heights of the clouds:
I will be like the most high[1].

The blood-sucking leech is the designation Hawthorne has given
Roger Chillingworth, who is draining the life out of Dimmesdale,
and is perhaps a fitting metaphor for Old Scratch. Doctors once
used leeches to bleed their patients, and that methodology seems to have
become a label for their profession in earlier times. Hawthorne's use of
that term may possibly be a little expressive of his differences with the
physicians of his day.

Roger's Origins and Implications

Hawthorne wanted the reader to labor for the answer to the question
at the symbolic level, "Where did Pearl come from?" But he less obscurely
tells the reader, more directly than for any other character, whence Roger
Chillingworth hails.

His first entry on the scene, few people could tell whence,
dropping down, as it were, out of the sky, or starting from

the nether earth, had an aspect of mystery, which was easily heightened to the miraculous. (121)

[H]e chose to withdraw his name from the roll of mankind, and, as regarded his former ties and interests, to vanish out of life as completely as if he indeed lay at the bottom of the ocean. (118)

Probably, Hawthorne has allegorized the historical or Biblical figure, Lucifer, in the character of Chillingworth from the writings of Isaiah above and John below.

And there was war in heaven: Michael and his angels fought against the dragon; and the dragon fought and his angels,

And prevailed not; neither was their place found any more in heaven.

And the great dragon was cast out, that old serpent, called the Devil, and Satan, which deceiveth the whole world: he was cast out into the earth, and his angels were cast out with him . . . . for the accuser of our brethren is cast down, which accused them before our God day and night.[2]

It becomes fairly clear at the end of this chapter, from the full text of the chapter, that Roger is a figure symbolic of that old serpent himself, who, according to Biblical history, before time on earth began, by his own rebellious actions, chose to be cast out of heaven. From the sky to the nether earth seems an appropriate metaphorical description of his fall from grace; and his disguised influence upon earth, from the depth of the bottomless pit, seems likewise a parallel for Chillingworth.

Another reference is made to Chillingworth's claim of Indian captivity (127), when it seems he is, if indeed not their leader and Medicine Man himself, at least their consort and comrade in savagery. Rather than being a captive of the Indians who came to Boston to ransom him, the Indians are probably his minions because they do his bidding. We see them in the background, but only Chillingworth—who comes and goes as he pleases, unlike one who is kidnapped and held for ransom—speaks to the characters in the story. Hawthorne possibly may have included the Indians in his tale, and linked Chillingworth's exploits to them, to represent those rebellious souls, who, with Lucifer, were cast out of heaven into the nether earth, or the forest where the knowledge of good and evil is not restricted by the laws of civilized society.

HIS ATTACHMENT TO DIMMESDALE

To the town of Boston, from the wilderness of the savage to the wilderness of New England, Chillingworth the leech came, and quickly attached himself, as a constant companion, to Dimmesdale, the divine. Perhaps Hawthorne has devised another parallel to the beginning of the ministry of the Nazarene, who has been noted to have had some close companionship with Old Scratch for some forty days and nights, if not continuously thereafter. Chillingworth, Master Prynne, is in disguise as a physician, whose "previous period of life, had made him extensively acquainted with the medical science of the day," and "a brilliant acquisition" to the community (119), or so the townspeople thought at first.

> Heaven had wrought an absolute miracle, by transporting an eminent Doctor of Physic, from a German university, bodily through the air, and setting him down at the door of Mr. Dimmesdale's study! (121)

At first, Chillingworth is perceived by less insightful inhabitants of Boston as a gift from heaven. To balance this initial high opinion of Chillingworth held by the Boston community, Hawthorne, perhaps sharing his opinion of physicians a little less obscurely, contrasted the spiritual sensitivity of the early emigrants to America with that of the physician. He also qualified that gift to their community as likely to be only a medical blessing.

> They seldom, it would appear, partook of the religious zeal that brought other emigrants across the Atlantic. In their researches into the human frame, it may be that the higher and more subtle faculties of such men were materialized, and that they lost the spiritual view of existence amid the intricacies of that

wondrous mechanism, which seemed to involve art enough to comprise all of life within itself. (119)

Hawthorne appears to think that the warm and wondrous mechanism of the body seemed, to the physician, to have so enthralled that profession as to be considered marvelous enough to contain the very power of life in itself, and thus may have lost touch with the spirit within, and the spiritual realm without. Their intuitive faculties, it would appear, were so focused on the material aspects of the human body itself as to be spiritually oblivious to the idea that the power of life might have elsewhere its source; and we see the contrasts between the two aspects of spiritual oblivion and material transcendence in the conversations between the physician and the minister.

Later, some of the townspeople, with less materialized perspective, began more astutely to suspect some adversarial conflict in their relationship.

> A large number–and many of these were persons of such sober sense and practical observation, that their opinions would have been valuable, in other matters–affirmed that Roger Chillingworth's aspect had undergone a remarkable change . . . especially since his abode with Mr. Dimmesdale. At first, his expression had been calm, meditative, scholar-like. Now, there was something ugly and evil in his face . . . . According to the vulgar idea, the fire in his laboratory had been brought from the lower regions, and was fed with infernal fuel. (127)
> To sum up the matter, it grew to be a widely diffused opinion, that the Reverend Arthur Dimmesdale, like many other personages of especial sanctity, in all ages of the Christian world, was haunted either by Satan himself, or Satan's emissary, in the guise of old Roger Chillingworth. This diabolical agent had the Divine permission, for a season, to burrow into the clergyman's intimacy, and plot against his soul. (128)

Hawthorne has again perhaps used the word, "vulgar," as though the idea of hellfire and damnation might be itself a vulgar idea spawned by some contemporary ministers. He appears to associate that vulgarity with the ugliness and evil in Chillingworth's face, as though he might embody its source. While Dimmesdale is perhaps prying for the good that is contained within the human soul, Chillingworth is seen as prying for the evil that he believes dwells there, to some benefit of his own. He also believes, in a fashion Hawthorne describes later, that he can detect such by prying into their intimacy, and exploiting such for some dubious reason of his own, which reason of ownership has been explained previously.

In the typical narrative above, Hawthorne has juxtapositioned both protagonist and antagonist, and more obviously, has labeled Chillingworth as a Devil figure attempting to exploit the divine. To so easily ascertain the representation or principle characterized by Chillingworth, the reader might just as quickly identify his counterpart at the allegorical level, but for the nagging mystery of Pearl's origin. That mystery, in the outreach of a reverent Christian conscience, forbids an analogy with the most likely historical candidate, and must itself first be resolved compatibly with one's belief system before the larger mystery can be fathomed. When Hester is envisioned also as a personification of principle, nature, more than simply as a person, and Pearl likewise is seen as a representation of future humankind, then it becomes possible to figure Dimmesdale, in a Judaistic setting, as representative of the principle of Redemption as hosted in the Nazarene.

Dimmesdale appears to be cast as a divine representative of Deity, who created humanity, with a particular sore mission to perform on earth, which would require a mortal agony before eventual triumph. Many of his parishioners have sensed Chillingworth's adversarial influence upon the one person to whom he has become inseparably attached, but they hope, with some measure of confidence, that Dimmesdale will be victorious at the end.

> No sensible man . . . could doubt on which side the victory would turn.

> The people looked, with an unshaken hope, to see the minister come forth out of the conflict, transfigured with the glory which he would unquestionably win. Meanwhile, nevertheless, it was sad to think of the perchance mortal agony through which he must struggle towards his triumph.

Alas, to judge from the gloom and terror in the depths of the
poor minister's eyes, the battle was a sore one, and the victory
any thing but secure! (128)

The above passages depict Dimmersdale as a personage of especial
sanctity to be transfigured in glory, but who is subject to the prying and
plotting efforts of Master Prynne. They lay the groundwork for a later
chapter that unfolds the intensity of that mortal agony, a cup of which he
is want to escape, and the victory over which he is all but secure. The use of
the term, "sensible," in keeping with Hawthorne's perspective on intuition,
may refer to the sensible man's use of all his senses, biological, mental, and
intuitive. Perhaps to him, the sensible man might unquestionably perceive
the mission of the Nazarene, though filled with mortal agony, as being
triumphant, the end of which, though not secure at present, would be
a transfiguration of glory. Hawthorne might be speaking for the faith of
Dimmesdale's parishioners, perhaps in light of their intuitive sensibilities,
as well as for the divine, in projecting what might be in store, not only for
the Nazarene, who spoke of a return to glory[3], but also for his followers[4].

A PERSONAGE OF ESPECIAL SANCTITY

The young divine's fasts and vigils "to do as great deeds for the now
feeble New England Church, as the early Fathers had achieved for the
infancy of the Christian faith" (120), pose possibly as another analogy
of Dimmesdale's mission to the beginning of the Christian faith in the
meridian of time. The analogy parallels the infancy of the Nazarene's
ministry in Jerusalem to redeem Judaism from the apostasy of the scribes
and Pharisees. Perhaps Hawthorne has figured the feeble New England
Church of Puritanism as a type of Judaism, and the young minister, an
image of a personage of especial sanctity, as a representation or extension
of Providence "to perform its humblest mission here on earth" (120).

When the readers intuitively explore the descriptions of Dimmesdale
throughout the tale, perhaps much in fashion like many of the Nazarene's
followers intuitively sensed something sacred in him, then their sensitive
inward ears may lead them to some inference at the allegorical level.
But they must suspend the idea for a while, without some rational or
Puritanic rejection of it as though it were some antinomian's heresy. They
must hold with the idea until they can discern what principle Hester's

character represents at a deeper level—the principle of human nature itself, rather than merely an historical personage. Once their relationship at the allegorical level is understood, then the figure of Pearl can be seen, in a relevant regard, as a community of many, either as the multitude of humankind, or a large portion thereof.

So at this point in the tale, Hawthorne indirectly attunes the reader to use intuition to ascertain the representation of the character, Dimmesdale, as discussed later in more detail. That Hawthorne has fairly and obviously figured Chillingworth as an antagonistic Satanic image, then it should require no great leap of reason or intuition for the reader to conclude, at the allegorical level, that such a historical figure in the tale presupposes the existence of a contemporary protagonist in his tale also. Chillingworth's obsessive attachment to and machinations upon Dimmesdale becomes a finger post for the reader to divine who the most likely candidate is.

Hawthorne again makes this association when he characterizes Dimmesdale as the divine who "was considered by his more fervent admirers as little less than a heaven-ordained apostle" (120), "like many other personages of especial sanctity." These admirers may have constituted that portion of the multitude that "forms its judgment, as it usually does, on the intuitions of its great and warm heart" (127). Dimmesdale's compassionate appeals, by which he seems to identify with the agonies of his parishioners, are a departure from the invective incriminations used by his fellow Puritan clerics, in much the same way the Nazarene's followers noted an authoritative difference and compassionate appeal in his teachings in contrast to the keepers of the Mosaic law. Indeed, Dimmsdale's preachments engender a loyalty and devotion from his parishioners, who are starving for compassion under the auspices of ill-focused Puritanism, or so it seems from Hawthorne's point of view. In gaining his parishioners loyalty through his heart-felt pleas, Dimmesdale is clearly seen as a divine with an exceptionally spiritual appeal, opposed by the presence of Chillingworth.

But , from the beginning of the tale, the reader has a reasonable, if not knowledgable, bias that forbids such a hallowed opinion, a bias that feeds upon other inexplicable implications that oppose such a distinction. However, the difficulty in discerning Dimmesdale's representation rests as much in the obscurity with which Hawthorne has shrouded his inmost philosophical leanings as in the prepossessions of the reader. Even the gist of Dimmesdale's victory, wherein he eventually transcended self and fulfilled what he deemed to be his special mission, is cloaked and dispersed in various reactions of his parishioners, perhaps relevant to their level of belief and intuition. What Hawthorne has configured, at the end, as varigated responses to Dimmesdale's confession and revelation, he has similarly left to his readers to discern by their different gifts of imagination, but not without some coaching, what allegorical meanings he may have written into his novel.

THE VALUE OF INTUITION

Hawthorne uses the word, "faith," or various morphic forms thereof, only about fourteen times in his tale, and more often then as a manner of speech rather than as an implication of any further significance. Yet he seems to have definitely played upon the reader's intuitive senses by underscoring its value in the interplay between his characters, and in his narrator's commentary. His emphasis upon intuition may have some connection with the faith of his characters, but it does not appear that he used intuition as an equivalent of faith, for he seemed to have had some difficulty in defining it for the reader: "a nameless something more,—let us call it intuition" (124).

Perhaps a person's belief system, or faith, forms the basis for which one's inclinations interpret what he chooses to make out of what has been observed. But intuition itself, to Hawthorne, appears to be the name he has given to what others, given also to philosophical ponderings, have called the numinous sense, or the sacred sense, which may have something to do with the universal heart, or the collective unconscious. Perhaps gifted with a measure of introspective self-analysis, some of these writers surprisingly agree on one common conclusion:

> It is recognition of a wholly unique spread of awareness in man—that is called, by Otto, the "numinous" sense—deep innate sensitivity to something sacred, an underived feeling for the holy, with responses of wonder, awe, and reverence. This, it is claimed by many, is primary, a given fact of human consciousness that cannot be traced to rational or empirial sources. We do not learn it. It is somehow, and strangely, innate. (Madsen, 72)

As noted before, Hawthorne has cued the reader to the value of intuition in Dimmesdale's parishioners, and is likely posturing the same, not to the reader's logical mind only, but to the reader's intuitive sensibilities. Hawthorne expounds on the principle of intuition, as reflected in the divine's parishioners, who are able to see the conflict between Dimmesdale and his antagonist, and to hope for the divine's victory. The Romantic bias valuing intuition over reason alone is revealed in several passages, one of which discredits the reasonableness of the Reverend's friends who think that it is the hand of Providence that has led to the physician's boarding with Dimmesdale.

> When an uninstructed multitude attempts to see with its eyes, it is exceedingly apt to be deceived. When, however, it forms its judgment, as it usually does, on the intuitions of its great and warm heart, the conclusions thus attained are often so profound and so unerring, as to possess the character of truths supernaturally revealed. (127)

In this remarkable passage, Hawthorne, in contrasting the rationality of experience through use of the physical senses alone, with that of a more penetrative sense, seems to alert the reader also to a need for an intuition of the heart in order to render accurate judgment on the characters of his story, if they are to discover the profound and unerring truths they represent at the "supernatural" level, or, we might interpolate, at the allegorical level.

Just as Hawthorne has reversed the reputation of the character of Chillingworth in his tale, he also appears to have planned for the reader to use intuition to pry into and identify the truths or principles all his characters represent. For example, in discussing Hester's name, Prynne, which she obtained from her husband, Master Prynne, and in explaining its pronunciation and meanings, we have already noted the Romantic's tendency to pry into nature to discover superscripted truths, "so profound and so unerring," that transcend the reality experienced solely through the physical senses.

The relationships between the characters seem a portrayal of principles much more than they are representative of historical figures; and Hawthorne's ambiguous lack of definitive identity of their representation seems to rest mostly upon his dependence upon the reader's intuitive sense to discover them. Therefore, there may be three levels at work in Hawthorne's tale: the surface tale of the fictitional characters' relationships, the allegorical level of the historical figures' relationships, and, for lack of a better term, the "supernatural level" of corollary principles. As these principles interrelate, they seem to formulate a number of themes that purvey certain conclusive explanations about life Hawthorne may have entertained. It becomes the task of the reader to pry a little deeper into the tale and link these three levels together.

The master of this prying attempt, Master Prynne, in his disguise as a physician, has attempted to discover Dimmesdale's true identity by prying into his soul, but to no avail.

> So Roger Chillingworth–the man of skill, the kind and friendly physician–strove to go deep into his patient's bosom, delving among his principles, prying into his recollections, and probing every thing with a cautious touch, like a treasure-seeker in a dark cavern. Few secrets can escape an investigator, who has opportunity and license to undertake such a quest, and skill to follow it up. (124)

By so attaching himself to Dimmesdale, it is likely that Chillingworth may have already suspected the young divine as a person of some significance, with some hidden sorrow, for which he seeks the cause as a means to destroy him. But it is not clear at all, or even hinted, that this suspicion includes Dimmesdale's relationship with Hester and Pearl, which knowledge he does not seem to discover until the end of Chapter 10. Hawthorne relates the attributes needed, along with certain necessary skills, for an investigator to discover those truths that are transcendental to what appears. Chillingworth had some of these attributes, but could not find what he expected.

> If the [physician, investigator, or reader] possess native sagacity, and a nameless something more,—let us call it intuition; if he show no intrusive egotism, nor disagreeably prominent characteristics of his own; if he have the power, which must be born with him, to bring his mind into such affinity with his patient's, that this last shall unawares have spoken what he imagines himself only to have thought; if such revelations be

received without tumult, and acknowledged not so often by
an uttered sympathy, as by silence . . . then, at some inevitable
moment, will the soul of the sufferer be dissolved, and flow
forth in a dark, but transparent stream, bringing all its mysteries
into the daylight. (124)

Thus Hawthorne qualified what he meant by intuition, and other
qualities of character that help forage a successful flow of transparent
truth. In the case of "dissolving" the soul or representation of Dimmesdale,
Hawthorne may be telling the reader that he may also need such qualities
to understand the mystery of Dimmesdale's suffering, and, as far as it
pertains, the mystery of the scarlet letter.

Chillingworth possessed the prominent characteristic of native
sagacity and intuition, and restrained his egotism in an accommodating
agreeableness; but his vengeful nature lacked any affinity with his patient,
and his native sagacity and intuitive senses could not fathom the secret of
Dimmesdale's heart. He had to resort to a direct and disagreeable ploy to
make this discovery, which, to his wonder and horror, he does so in the
following chapter.

So Dimmesdale's waning strength and vitality had been linked, by his
more observant parishioners, to Chillingworth's ploys. The physician had
also been seen "in company with Doctor Forman, the famous old conjurer,
who was implicated" in the murder of Sir Thomas Overbury some thirty
years past, and is rumored, during his supposed Indian captivity, to have
participated in their savage incantations, and possibly imbibed of their
black art (127). Hawthorne has left little room for the reader to see
Chillingworth otherwise than as an evil influence presently focused upon
one particular personage, and consumed with a hostile motive far from
the center of some warm, cosmic heart.

GOD'S WILL

In this chapter, we have another insight into both characters, and
especially a glimpse into the motives of each, in one brief conversation
between Chillingworth and Dimmesdale. As Chillingworth is seeking
to practice his medicine upon Dimmesdale, Dimmesdale's motive and
mission is subtly revealed, though cloaked :

"Were it God's will," said the Reverend Mr. Dimmesdale . . .
"I could be well content, that my labors, and my sorrows, and
my sins, and my pains, should shortly end with me, and what
is earthly of them be buried in my grave, and the spiritual go
with me to my eternal state, rather than that you should put
your skill to the proof in my behalf." (122)

This utterance by Dimmesdale is interpreted mockingly by
Chillingworth in plainer words: "And saintly men, who walk with God
on earth, would fain be away, to walk with him on the golden pavements
of the New Jerusalem" (122). That Dimmesdale would rather die than
follow Chillingworth's counsel, in regard to improving his weak, physical
condition, seems a parallel to the weakened condition of the Nazarene,
following his rather lengthy period of fasting, when he indicated it was
his Father's will that he chose to follow instead of Satan's[5]. Dimmesdale
seems to describe his mission on the earth in such a way as to describe the
mission of the Nazarene, whose purpose, he stated, was to end all suffering
and pain by his death and divine sacrifice, burying all earthly things in the
grave, while all things spiritual ascend with him into heaven.

Yet, "the gloom and terror in the depths of the young ministers eyes"
foreshadowed a "mortal agony through which he must struggle towards his
triumph" (128). This terror may reflect the anguish the Redeemer knew he
had to experience before his ministry would be gloriously finished. It may
be the same wonder and horror that Chillingworth discovered, in Chapter
10, when he saw the symbol of Dimmesdale's inmost secret suffering,
which may have forecast for him his own suffering, in an unparalleled
moment of truth, in precognition of Dimmesdale's victory, despite his
rational attempts to suppress its reality in his own mind.

THE SPIRITUAL AFFECTS THE PHYSICAL

It must also be remembered that Chillingworth is the same scholar
who had shared his scientific knowledge with Hester, whatever that was.
(Metaphorically that knowledge may be the "science" or "medicine"
which Eve applied in the Garden of Eden and changed all nature from an
immortal state to a mortal one.) Dimmsdale declared that he did not need
the physician's medicine; he apparently knew that his physical condition

related to his spiritual suffering, even as Chillingworth also sensed as he watched Dimmsdale carefully.

> Wherever there is a heart and an intellect, the diseases of the physical frame are tinged with the peculiarities of these. In Arthuf Dimmesdale, thought and imagination were so active, and sensibility so intense, that the bodily infirmity would be likely to have its groundwork there. (124)

This intense sensibility of the divine to his inner suffering—whether for his sinful nature as a mortal or the vicarious sins he may be suffering for others—may be an indication of the extraordinary sensitivity to the smallest sin. This sensibility may also lay the groundwork later for associating Dimmsdale's spiritual suffering with his need to confess. That confession appears to be a kind of atonement for the burden of sins he seemed to have taken upon himself, which burden is exacerbated because of his singular and intense sensitivity to sin, about which we learn more later.

WHY HITHER?

So we get a small glimpse into the nature of both the protagonist and the antagonist, the latter of which we see most clearly as a Satanic figure, if not the Devil himself incarnate. The townspeople had asked, before they knew Roger better, "Why, with such rank in the learned world, had he come hither? What could he, whose sphere was in great cities, be seeking in the wilderness?" (121) Hawthorne shrouds the allegorical answer to the questions in a thicker cloud of mystery, but the questions point to the significance of the relationship between the physician and the divine. Perhaps the pulsations of Hawthorne's own inner self, in answer to that question, start to unfold in the peculiar companionship of the physician and the minister, one which the physician maintained with devious intent, and which the minister seemed to tolerate, for lack of choice, and entertained, not because of any sentimental affinity, but because of its intellectual depth and scope (123).

If Hawthorne really believed in the account of Lucifer being cast down to the earth, he may have asked, along with many other students of Biblical history, "Why would Deity have allowed Lucifer and his angels to inhabit "the nether earth" and from thence, arise to harrass humanity with his vengeful machinations? What principle of truth can be learned from such a placement?" Hawthorne's allegory only implies an answer in a trail of hints left here and there.

Chillingworth's desire to enjoy the same thing all humankind enjoys—"the simple bliss, which is scattered far and wide" of that "wondrous mechanism"—seems motivated by his former domain, which was "lonely and chill, and without a household fire" (74). The most obvious "wondrous mechanism" that humankind enjoys is the human body, a warm refuge from the presumably colder, previous domain. Perhaps his life in the wilderness, dropping down into the New England settlement, and seeking a housefire of his own, relate to that one particuar antinomian, who has a plan to prevent humanity's redemption from the mortal world he helped contrive, by which prevention he may claim possession of those wondrous mechanisms. Thus he came to town for revenge, and developed a plan to claim the souls of Dimmesdale, Hester, and Pearl.

Most of the entirety of Chapters 9 and 10, wherein Chillingworth has openly stalked the minister, burrowed into the clergyman's intimacy, and plotted against his soul," may be interpreted as a capsule of the temptations the Nazarene might have experienced, in the wilderness, on the seashore, or wherever he went. Perhaps Hawthorne, puzzled over the Divine permission granted to Old Scratch to tempt the man from Nazareth, if only for a season, might have pondered over the same predictament for the rest of humankind. The questions posed at the beginning of this chapter might presuppose that Hawthorne was equally puzzled about the presence of evil, the problems of life allegedly consequent, the resolution thereof, and the seeming silence of heaven on the matter. *The Scarlet Letter*, therefore, appears to be a treatise, an autobiographical impulse, arising from questions in his alleged study of the Biblical text; and his conclusions are difficultly discernable only in a thorough study of the remaining half of his tale.

CHAPTER 10

THE LEECH AND HIS PATIENT

> And I will put enmity between thee and the woman,
> and between thy seed and her seed;
> it shall bruise thy head,
> and thou shalt bruise his heel.[1]

The worst of Chillingworth's crafty character is unraveled before the reader in this chapter, while Hawthorne elaborates more on Dimmesdale's character in the next. But, in doing so, besides revealing the physician's devilish nature to the reader, and Dimmesdale's true identity to Chillingworth, Hawthorne begins to give the reader better insight into the interior of Dimmesdale's heart. The physician has become uglier and more sinister in nature as he probes into Dimmesdale's identity in search of something that is corruptibly common to mortality. He is obsessed in finding some wicked treasure buried in the heart of the young divine so as to claim him his own. As he prys for some confession from the minister, he is disappointed to discover the opposite, until he underhandedly discovers a "dark treasure." In the very beginning of this chapter, Hawthorne foreshadows that discovery; and at the end, when Chillingworth beholds the jewel within the bosom of Dimmesdale, "the apple of his eye," it filled him not only with joy, wonder, but also with horror, "alas for his own soul" (129).

JEWEL ON A DEAD MAN'S BOSOM

Again, calm and kind Old Chillingworth is related as once having been a "pure and upright man" (129), much in the same way, using a

Biblical analogy, as Lucifer himself, in a twilight time before the creation, had attained the status of son of the morning before being cast out for rebellion. As Lucifer, in response to his banishment, had sought vengefully to destroy the souls of humankind, Chillingworth has begun to pry into the soul of Dimmesdale for some treasured evil, perhaps because of perceived "wrongs inflicted on himself. But, as he proceeded . . . like the reflection of a furnace," or a ghastly fire, a glimmering light gleamed from his prying eyes (129), perhaps symbolic of the burning fires of Hades, an analogy used in Biblical text to compare with its forecasted actuality. The reader sees Chillingworth in the midst of his transformation, wherein

> a terrible fascination, a kind of fierce, though still calm, necessity seized the old man within its gripe, and never set him free again, until he had done all its bidding. He now dug into the clergyman's heart . . . like a sexton delving into a grave, possibly in quest of a jewel that had been buried on the dead man's bosom . . . . Alas for his own soul, if these were what he sought! (129)

This simile is the first of two regarding a sexton, or grave digger, perhaps symbolizing the allegorical relationship between Chillingworth and Dimmesdale. Chillingworth examines Dimmesdale's soul like a sexton digging a grave in search of a treasure, a jewel lying upon the bosom of a dead man. Allegorically, the sexton may represent Old Scratch's attempt to steal from humankind the jewel of the resurrection, the pearl of great price, or the gift of eternal life. On the suspicion that Dimmesdale "hath inherited a strong animal nature from his father or his mother" (130), Chillingworth probed, like a thief "with purpose to steal the very treasure which this man guards as the apple of his eye;" but, alas, instead of finding, as he expected to find, a glimmer of evil, which was growing ravenously within Chillingworth himself, he disappointedly found, perhaps with wonder, in the minister's interior, something unusually rich and divine,

> many precious materials, in the shape of high aspirations for the welfare of his race, warm love of souls, pure sentiments, natural piety, strengthened by thought and study, and illuminated by revelation . . . invaluable gold . . . . (130)

We might ask, as Chillingworth is revealing himself moreso to the reader as the epitomy of evil, is the representation of Dimmesdale's character likewise becoming more evident? What is the jewel upon Dimmesdale's compassionate bosom, the treasure he guards cautiously from common knowledge? Does the emblem of suffering upon Dimmedale's breast represent some treasure many a dead man guards "as the apple of his eye?" Is the jewel upon the dead man's chest a symbol of the promise of the resurrection, and/or of eternal life, that the Redemption assures? Do not Arthur's aspirations for the welfare of his parishioners, brightened by revelation from Providence, seem symbolic of the Redeemer's pure and sentimental quest to extend to all humanity the one singular blessing regarded as the pearl of great price? What connection does this jewel have with Pearl herself? These are the kinds of questions Hawthorne seeks to raise in the mind of his readers to assist them in discerning the allegorical meanings of the symbols, and perhaps arriving at a particular understanding of Deity's relationship with the "communities of mankind."

FREEDOM FROM A BROKEN LAW: A PRINCIPLE OF BEING

When Hester and Pearl are seen outside by the minister and the physician as they pass by the window, Chillingworth again poses the questions, as Hawthorne poses for his readers to ask themselves: What is Pearl? "Hath she any discoverable principle of being?" (134) In other words, what principle of being does she represent allegorically? Dimmesdale's answer, "as if he had been discussing the point within himself," appears to contain Hawthorne's allegorical response within Dimmesdale's representation: "None,—save the freedom of a broken law" (134).

The divine within Dimmesdale is answering a question Hawthorne wants the reader to ask at the allegorical level, a question his characters have asked more than once about Pearl; and now Hawthorne has provided a great clue to what principle of truth her character represents. She appears to represent an enlightened breed of humankind imbued with a sense of freedom that was lost by breach of a particular law.

> In giving her existence, a great law had been broken; and the result was a being, whose elements were perhaps beautiful and brilliant, but all in disorder; or with an order peculiar to

themselves, amidst which the point of variety and arrangement was difficult or impossible to be discovered. (91).

Since we are examining Hawthorne's tale from the perspective of Christian theology implied in his metaphors, perhaps the greatest freedom humankind can acquire, according to its records, is freedom from the slavery of mortality, its thirsts, its hungers, its limitations, its eventual death. Since the law that was broken brought about the fall from immortality to mortality and enslaved all nature to its consequences, there yet remains, in the breast of the optimist, a hope that nature can be freed from this enslavement, a way to redeem humankind from the fall.

To the ardent Christian, that freedom cannot happen without divine intervention. By the broken law, Pearl, the child of fallen nature, who, by the maturing affinity she experienced from her mother's sufferings, and by the redemption signified in Dimmesdale's confession, is figured as being free from all earthly law by becoming a law unto herself. This destiny, of which Pearl is confident throughout, seems bound up in the fulfillment of the office of the scarlet letter. That office was not done in Chapter XIII, when the reader gets a clearer view of Hester as representing mortal nature (166). As the readers may see, or not, that the office of the scarlet letter is being fulfilled by Dimmesdale when he, in a sense, reconciled or redeemed himself and Hester and Pearl by his confession upon the scaffold, and by his voluntary death, they may see, or not, a parallel with the Redemption, wherein the Redeemer ransomed himself for mankind, perhaps in recognition of the fact that he was also her Creator.

But Hawthorne said, "Freedom of a broken law," not freedom from a broken law. If there is a difference, it may imply that the law, in the first place, would have provided freedom; but having been broken, the law could not provide it; and to seek that freedom would require some object worth seeking. The logic leads to the same conclusion at the allegorical level: a redemption is required to alleviate the fallen conditions; a power infinite enough to consume all the consequencs of the broken law, in order to satisfy the demands of justice, must bring about that redemption. Perhaps symbolic of redeemed humankind, Pearl may represent the future principle of a promised restoration of that freedom, to be secured only by Dimmesdale fulfilling the duty of the office of the scarlet letter, the mission which the oracle signals.

In Chapter XXIV, upon the voluntary death and confession of Dimmesdale, Hawthorne tells us that the scarlet letter, "at last manifesting Heaven's dreadful judgment by [its] presence . . . has done its office," though "long meditation has fixed it in very undesirable distinctness," or dimly so (258-259). By his confession, the Providence of Heaven has finally answered, in the symbol etched upon Dimmesdale's breast, by the agony of the burden of sin he bears, the question that dominates the tale of woe: is there to be relief from Hester's plight? Will she be transfigured back to the delightful beauty of her youth? Dimmesdale's mission, though long fixed "in very undesirable distinctness," as the redemption of Hester and Pearl, appears to represent the principle of the Redemption of humanity's mortal nature from the broken law; Pearl, the principle of the Redeemed. Some Christian theology holds that the two roles of Creator and Redeemer are performed by the same divine being. In that doctrine, as the Holy One of Israel, Christ is also identified as the Creator of the world.

This redemptive connection seems demonstrated by Pearl in the paragraphs before and after the question above posed by Chillingworth, and appropriately answered by Dimmesdale. Pearl, dancing in "perverse merriment" upon the grave of a departed worthy—one of whom might be one of Boston's earliest founders, Isaac Johnson—was asked by Hester to "behave more decorously." She did so promptly by more delicately picking some prickly burrs growing by the grave and placing them decorously around the scarlet letter on Hester's bosom. In other words, contempt, or lack of respect for the founders of Puritanism, is replaced by an higher aspiration, an emphasis on the symbol that may represent a day when humankind is freed from its Puritanic heritage, or from the graveyard of a narrow mentality.

From the black shield to the scarlet gules, Pearl intuitively remained focused upon the one object that seemed to possess her thoughts. At the same time, when Pearl saw the young divine in the window, where he is philosophizing with Chillingworth, she throws one of the burrs at him. Such possibly signifies to the reader some connection between the prickly burrs she was tossing, the scarlet letter, and the minister, thus perhaps identifying the Arthur of the scarlet letter as well as interjecting a reminder of his mission.

A LAW UNTO HERSELF

Noticing that she and her mother have been seen by the minister and the physician, Pearl identified the latter as the Black Man of the forest: "Come away, mother! Come away, or yonder old Black Man will catch you! . . . But he cannot catch little Pearl!" (134) Perhaps Pearl cannot be caught because she likely represents the promise of a better world inherent in the redemption that she cheerfully foreshadowed, seems always intuitively to be pointing toward it, and appears to be above the worse the world can throw at her,

> like a creature that had nothing in common with a bygone and buried generation, nor owned herself akin to it. It was as if she had been made afresh, out of new element, and must perforce be permitted to live her own life, and be a law unto herself, without her eccentricities being reckoned to her for a crime. (134-135)

The passage above seems most remarkably a parallel description of the resurrection itself, its life of new element, which is no longer associated with its past, its former laws, or its labels, according to the Christian perspective. Perhaps Hawthorne had in mind a similitude of one of Isaiah's prophecies: "For, behold, I create new heavens and a new earth: and the former shall not be remembered, nor come into mind[2]." It may be equally a reference to the millenial era, when, under a new Govenor, perhaps with different laws to govern its existence, mortal nature has been "transfigured" into an immortal nature. Either theological state of being would have little if anything in common with its buried generation because it would be comprised of new material elements of a higher nature. Nor would the differences be considered evil or reckoned as criminal in nature, as has Hester's nature been so considered by those who have misunderstood and mislabed it so. The freedom from the broken law yields the freedom of a new law.

ON DIMMESDALE'S SILENCE

The interchange between Chillingworth and Dimmesdale in this chapter is a theoretical bout in which the two scrimmage over the wisdom of confessing what the source of the young divine's pain and infirmity might be. Although Dimmesdale expressed his want of confession, but seems bound to a code that forbade it, at least until an appropriate time, readers might side with Chillingworth's argument against silence, that confession is the remedy for his agony. It notably is the object of the young divine's silence about the source of his suffering that some critics have earmarked as the greater sin of Dimmesdale. The long and inexplicable absence of confession seems to bother them more than his relationship with Hester, the fatherhood of Pearl, or the mystery of the scarlet letter itself. But in this chapter, Hawthorne has disclosed the reason for his silence, which, at the surface level, may reek with "undesirable indistinctness," but at the allegorical level, seems justifiable.

Still pursuing his case for Dimmesdale's confession, Chillingworth answers the young minister's question about some unsightly plants the physician was examining.

> "They grew out of [a dead man's] heart, and typify, it may be, some hideous secret that was buried with him, and which he had done better to confess during his lifetime." (131)

> "Perchance," said Mr. Dimmesdale, "he earnestly desired it, but could not . . . . [I]t may be that [such men] are kept silent by the very constitution of their nature. Or . . . guilty as they may be, retaining, nevertheless, a zeal for God's glory and man's welfare, they shrink from displaying themselves black and filthy in the view of men; because, thenceforward, no good can be achieved by them; no evil of the past be redeemed by better service." (132)

Dimmesdale gives two reasons why the hypothetical man or men might not confess: the constitution of their nature may dictate it, or they may decide that the good they might do otherwise may achieve better results than the display of their sins so openly. Perhaps the first reason justifies the silence of heaven, at the allegorial level, and the second, perhaps a little more weakly, excuses Dimmesdale at the surface level of the tale. However, we have noted that Dimmesdale's argument does not seem to be for complete silence, but for a timely confession that does not impede the betterment of humankind, even though he, and perhaps Hawthorne as well, perceived the act of confession as not essentially a requirement for retribution, a term that might be synonymous with redemption:

> The heart, making itself guilty of such secrets, must perforce hold them, until the day when all hidden things shall be revealed. Nor have I so read or interpreted Holy Writ, as to understand that the disclosure of human thoughts and deeds, then to be made, is intended as a part of the retribution. (131)

Perhaps veiled in the quote above is Hawthorne's own private opinion, from his study of the Bible, as to the relevance of confession in the plan of repentance. To him, retribution might entail the harboring of such guilt until the day all is to be revealed and released in a moment, or eternity, of joy.

Another point Hawthorne makes for the character and representation of Dimmesdale is the statement that "it must needs be better for the sufferer to be free to show his pain, as this poor woman Hester is, than to cover it all up in his heart" (135). Dimmesdale appears to long for such an open confession as Hester has made, but does not seem to consider himself free to reveal the reason for his pain, as though it was not within the constitution of his nature or calling to do so.

> "Many, many a poor soul hath given its confidence to me, not only on the death-bed, but while strong in life, and fair in reputation.
>
> And ever, after such an outpouring, O, what a relief have I witnessed in those sinful brethren! Even as in one who at last draws free air, after long stifling with his own polluted breath." (132)

Summarizing these last three passages, it appears that humankind cannot retain their "zeal for God's glory and man's welfare," in a premature confession that blackens them in the view of others; for "no good can be achieved by them" (132). Dimmesdale's very constitution of his nature may not permit its disclosure before the appointed time because of the indelible damage it will do to his followers' faith. Likewise, the Nazarene did not openly wish to reveal his role as the Creator of humanity, the

Jehovah of the Old Testament, whose suffering would encompass the sins of humankind, before it was necessary to bring about the sacrifice that would assure his mission. The call for an end of the silence of Dimmesdale, which is the novel's suspenseful linchpin, is possibly the confession the Pharisees sought from Jesus so they could slay him for blasphemy.

FORESTALLING THE CONFESSION OF A SECRET

Seeking to find some deplorable sin or hideous secret, Chillingworth finally got Dimmesdale to consider that his physical malady might lie somewhere in the torment of his soul. Reason convinces the reader that Dimmesdale is tormented by the sin of his relationship with Hester. Something else might whisper that the sin symbolizes something else more sacred, more intense and extensive. One of the torments the minister experienced is the anguish of wanting and needing to identify his responsibility for Hester's child. The symbolic torment of the divine nature Dimmesdale embodies, and his super sensitivity to the burden he carries, by the very nature of that constitution, appear to represent the need of Providence to declare authorship of humanity, to confess staging the necessary fall into mortality, and the responsibly to set things right. At the same time, at the allegorical level, the confession of that truth should not have been made specifically unto the Pharisees, but to the people themselves, who might instinctly sense it. Paraphrasing the words of the Nazarene: one does not vainly cast jewels or pearls before swine[3]. That confession could only come at the proper time, to the proper people, and in the right way, according to Providence.

That the silence of Dimmesdale is dependent upon certain conditions or expectations other than those of the Puritan ministers or Pearl or, especially, those urgings of Mr. Chillingworth, becomes evident in the interchange between Dimmesdale and Chillingworth. Dimmesdale declared his committment to silence as dependent upon one factor. Upon one person alone will he rely for guidance, to that one Being only will he turn for own redemption, and he will never lay open "the wound or trouble in [his] soul . . . to an earthly physician!"

> No!–not to thee! . . . Not the thee! But, IF [my italics] it be the soul's disease, then do I commit myself to the one Physician of the soul! He, if it stand with his good pleasure, can cure; or he

can kill! Let him do with me as, in his justice and wisdom, he shall see good. (136-137)

Everything depends upon the will of Him alone to whom he listens. In this declaration (note the exclamation marks), Hawthorne may be comparing Dimmesdale to one figure alone, in the annuls of Christianity, who was committed from day one to the end to do the will of the Father. Perhaps the Redemption was etched into the constitution of the Nazarene from the day of his birth, and Hawthorne internalized that expected agony in the character of Dimmesdale more intensely as the nearness of its time approached. Dimmesdale seems to be waiting intuitively upon that one voice alone to communicate to him the cure for the wound or trouble of his soul, even if and when that solution includes death. This utterance seems the foreshadowing of his impending death upon the scaffold, just as the man from Nazareth knew at some point in his mission that his own death was part of that mission. Dimmesdale's death, as was his confession, seems therefore part of the cure, both of which perhaps symbolize, to Hawthorne, features of the Atonement: the promise of a resurrection, the redemption of humankind, and a compensation and answer to the silence of Heaven on the reasons for mortality, the dark problem of this life.

In the quote above, Dimmesdale also questions the physician's assumption that the wound, or the trouble his soul experiences, is his soul's disease. It may be that that wound is something else, at the allegorical level, other than some personal sin, which is the most logical conclusion to the reader. The pain in Dimmesdale's heart may represent the vicarious suffering for all the sins of humanity, from which the soul of the Christian's Christ vicariously experienced to redeem them.

References are made to the passion expressed by Dimmesdale, who rushed out of the room without waiting for an answer to his question. When Chillingworth asked Dimmesdale to confess his spiritual pain, the young minister made the passionate declaration as a matter of integrity and not as a matter of cowardice. The word "passion" is used four times on one page, as though Hawthorne is using repetition as a device to cue the reader for a connection. Talking to himself, as he contemplated prying into Dimmesdale's soul, Chillingworth says,

"But see, now, how passion takes hold upon this man, and hurrieth him out of himself! As with one passion, so with

another! He had done a wild thing ere now, this pious Master
Dimmesdale, in the hot passion of his heart!" (137)

The passion of the "wild thing [done] ere now," which may refer
allegorically to the passion of the Creation, may be related to the passion
with which Dimmesdale maintains his silence, as though the cause of his
malady seems to be divinely instilled in the same integrity in which the
passion of the Creation resides, "as with one passion, so with another!"
Hawthorne may be saying that the two passions are related, if not the
same. The cause of his physical suffering, and, therefore, its redemption,
is not to be healed by the powers of the adversary, nor at that time, but by
some other power, "the one physician of the soul!"

To Hawthorne, the passion associated with the Creation may also
be related to the passion of the Redemption. Perhaps Hawthorne may
have secretly harbored the rationale, that by masterminding the Creation,
as well as the Fall, Providence needed a sinless being, infinite in nature,
perhaps the Creator himself, to confess that responsibility as well as to
make the infinite Redemption therefor. Hawthorne has used the term
"actors" often to describe the role of his characters, as if Providence might
be their playwright; and destiny seems bound up in the roles of his four
main characters. To Hawthorne, perhaps confession of responsibility
may be implied in the act of the Redemption, as might be Dimmesdale's
confession upon the scaffold; and his voluntary death at the end of his
ministry in Boston, the climatic fulfillment of the plot of the tale, implying
an emphatic seal of the promise inherent within.

Symbolically, then, Dimmesdale's silence could represent the reluctance
of the Nazarene to reveal his identity, until the right time, as the Creator,
who would also be the Redeemer of humankind. Like Dimmesdale,
he made utterances to infer his identify, and eventually confessed that
identity, as reported in records noted as a New Testament of the same,
as the great I AM, the Creator of the human race, who lived before the
Abraham of the Old Testament.[4] It was the voluntary confession of this
identity that served the Pharisees with the evidence they sought to get rid
of their antinomian.

However, this possible representation of Dimmesdale as a reflection
of the Nazarene seems limited to the want of confession at this point,
and does not include any similitude of his persecution by the Jewish
leaders. Indeed, the ministers of Puritanism appear to show no ill will

toward the divine, but rather a high and almost deferential regard, which itself suits the analogy. The one exception, which Hawthorne may have deemed respectfully sufficient, was a statement that might imply far and wide knowledge of evil intent toward Dimmesdale by his fellowmen. It is quoted here to support the discussion of the analogy.

A shipmaster seemed aware of some friction between Dimmesdale and his acquaintances when he referred to the divine, "he that is in peril from these sour old Puritan rulers!" (235). It may be that Hawthorne did not deem it necessary to develop the analogy to any further extent. Perhaps it would have been less obscure, or too obvious an analogy, to have included the dramatization of this conflict in his tale; or, for financial reasons, he needed to publish his novel without further embellishment of this particular issue. Or, to agree with the naysayers, in order to salvage the mystery, Hawthorne may have never intended such allusions in the slightest.

THE DIVINE ELEMENT IN DIMMESDALE

In his interrogation of Dimmesdale, Chillingworth expected to find an animal nature, and some spiritual malady, that was the cause of the minister's physical suffering. Instead, Chillingworth found nothing in Dimmesdale but what attributes, as described more thoroughly in the following chapter, might constitute the substance of what was missing in the effects of Puritanism. In the Biblical parallel, Satan likewise found the Nazarene not only impervious to temptation or manipulation, but true to the destiny for which his character, or "the very constitution of [his] nature," prepared him.

Dimmesdale had "a zeal for God's glory and man's welfare," and had a mission that was imprinted upon his bosom, like a jewel, of which Hester's scarlet letter seems only a reflection. Perhaps his agonizing pain reflected the price of that pearl as a foreboding or impending Providential mission for the welfare of his race, that in time he knew he would have to fulfill. Although the divine was "[a]t the head of the social system," he was "only the more trammelled by its regulations, its principles, and even its prejudices. As a priest, the framework of his order inevibably hemmed him in" (200). This dilemma parallels the same situation experienced by the Nazarene, a High Priest, who, along with his fellowmen, was beleagured by the Pharisaic regulatory interpretations of the Mosaic law. Perhaps

Puritanism was to Dimmesdale what Pharisaism was to the Nazarene. The nearer the man of Nazareth approached the Garden at Gethsemane and the cross at Galgotha, he seemed to become more resigned to his fate, though, like Dimmesdale, who was momentarily unwilling to undergo its agony, he was still reliant upon Providence's will to complete his particular mission.

So Dimmesdale, to the Romantic, seems to represent a being whose attributes reflect an extreme sensitivity of heart to intimations from the spiritual dimension. As a religious figure, he appears to represent a Redemption for those who possess similar sensitivity, and, contrary to other opinion, may indeed be the hero in Hawthorne's tale.

THE DARK PROBLEM OF LIFE

In Chapters 10 and 11, Hawthorne seems to be centering on the core of his allegory, Dimmesdale's representation. In the theoretical interchange between Chillingworth and Dimmesdale, the conversation focused upon whether or not the need for confession resolves one's burden of sinfulness. Chillingworth would have the sinner fling his sinfulness openly to the world to obtain "unutterable solace" (132). That is, his remedy for the sins of humanity would include confession alone. Dimmesdale's point of view held that no ultimate good is derived from humankind "displaying themselves black and filthy in the view of men," for they cannot rid themselves of their iniquities; it was what resided in their hearts, which "will yield them up, at that last day, not with reluctance, but with a joy unutterable" (132). On that day, "the dark problem of this life [will be] made plain," and a "knowledge of men's hearts will be needful to the completest solution of that problem" (132). In these passages, Hawthorne may be enlarging Chillingworth's limited "unutterable solace" to Dimmesdale's more comprehensible "unutterable joy," to reflect the full effects of the Redemption that only the power of Divine mercy can effect.

> "There can be, if I forebode aright, no power, short of Divine mercy, to disclose, whether by uttered words, or by type or emblem, the secrets that may be buried with a human heart. The heart, making itself guilty of such secrets, must perforce hold them, until the day when all hidden things shall be revealed." (131)

In other words, the dark problems of this life, not only will be plainly understood in a day to come, but shall be resolved by a power of Divine mercy, perhaps that dark treasure, that jewel in the bosom of a dead man's grave, that is typified by the scarlet letter embellished upon Hester's bosom, and etched upon Dimmesdale's. The confession, death, and the sunken grave of Dimmesdale may all be types signifying that particular Divine mercy by which nature and humankind may be united with the Divine.

Perhaps, to Hawthorne, humanity may see the solution to the dark problem of life only somewhat dimly at present, but more clearly on the day of judgment, as heralded by Christianity, when humankind not only may rid themselves of their dark secrets, but also undergo a redemption, or transfiguration, of nature. In the next chapter, this redemption may be shown to reside in the interior of each human heart, as Hawthorne prepares the reader to understand the nature and extent of the interior of Dimmesdale's heart, which indicates that something else might be required other than his simple confession.

THE SECRET UNCOVERED

Later, unable to obtain the confession he wanted, and suspecting that the minister's "'sickness, a sore place, if we may so call it, in your spirit, hath immediately its appropriate manifestation in your bodily frame'" (136), while the minister slept, the leech opened his vestment, "that, hitherto, had always covered *it* [my italics] even from the professional eye" (138). What Chillingworth saw, what the parishioners see later, and what the reader sees, is in the eye of the beholder. Each one sees the meaning that *It* contains for them, as is noted by Hawthorne in Chapter 24. What Chillingworth saw is left for the reader to imagine.

In this last episode, Hawthorne leaves no doubt in the reader's mind that the leech represents the epitome of evil in the spiritual dimension. The physician comported himself riotously when he made the discovery upon the minister's bosom, as would Satan "when a precious human soul is lost to heaven, and won into his kingdom" (138). Chillingworth not only is ecstatic because he possibly thinks he has discovered either some weakness of Dimmesdale, and/or his true identity, but is also horrified possibly because of the impending consequence the manifestation foreshadows for him personally, as we see more clearly later in the last two chapters.

The meaning which "the manifestation" in Dimmesdale's bodily frame has for Chillingworth, a revelation one might say, is implied in the "wild look of wonder, joy, and horror" upon the leech's face (138). He marveled perhaps because he did not know, until this discovery, the true and full character of the divine. What Chillingworth could have seen upon Dimmesdale's bosom might symbolically include the wonder of the intense infinity of humanity's sins harbored in one individual's soul, his unspeakable joy at the vastness of them, his utmost horror in the redemption of them, and the terror of the inescapable pains and agonies to be heaped upon himself by them. That judgment may be the possible horror Chillingworth seems to have twice intuitively envisioned, and shut out of his mind as quickly as he rationally could, until he experienced, at the scaffold, the utter failure of his exploits upon Dimmesdale. It is a horror that Hawthorne may have conceived as being experienced by those whose lack of compassion rendered them unattuned to the universal heart, and perhaps rendered them prey to their own hostility, as we find happening in the character of Chillingworth. However, upon this occasion, Chillingworth's experience of horror, although but momentary, required a greater struggle to return to his own self-deceptions; and he focused upon his estacy in order to proceed with his diabolical plot. As though thought has the power to exceed the reality or forestall its inevitability,

"There is nothing either bad or good but thinking makes it so" (Hamlet, Act II).

On the other hand, perhaps what the reader thinks he/she sees in what Chillingworth saw, may constitute the variegated chimera Hawthorne has posed for his readers, much as what the parishioners saw when Dimmesdale, upon the scaffold, bared his chest to them. Most often our observation of events are tinted by our value systems; and what Chillingworth saw upon the chest of Dimmesdale Hawthorne has left to the intuitive imagination of the reader. Chillingworth's joy in what he saw did not signify he had won the minister's soul, but perhaps only the hopeful prospects of it. We later see his failure to prevent the confession, which, in all appearances, coincide with Dimmesdale's redemption, and we evidenced Roger's diminishment at the end of Hawthorne's tale.

The reader may very well at this point in Hawthorne's tale have answered for himself the question: what discoverable principle of being, then, hath Chillingworth? The Romantic element of evil existing in the spiritual dimension, side by side, with the divine, with access to the human soul, is seemingly also identical to a Biblical preachment, which may form the foundation for it.

> For we wrestle not against flesh and blood, but against
> principalities, against powers, against the rulers of the darkness
> of this world, against spiritual wickedness in high places.[5]

We refer again to Hawthorne's short Romantic essay on love and hate at the end of his novel as an attempt to philosophize his comprehension of the existence of good and evil on the same plane, or in the same dimension, perhaps even to fulfill the same Providential purpose. Perhaps then, in Hawthorne's perspective, Chillingworth appears to represent the result of one end of the continuum of evil, hate, while Dimmesdale appears to represent the other of good, love; and the adherents of all religions, in transformation from one to the other, may lie somewhere in between, depending upon what desires may be found in their hearts, what rational thoughts distort their intuitive signals, and what they do with their moments of truth. For example, both Dimmesdale and Chillingworth are noted, in the beginning of this chapter, as experiencing intuition. The divine's "sensibility of nerve often produced the effect of spiritual intuition," wherein he sensed "something inimical to his peace" in the presence of Chillingworth. The physician, "who had perceptions that were almost intuitive," could just as quickly camaflauge his inimical thoughts to allay the minister's suspicions (130). The difference in what transformation seems to be taking place in these two characters seems to depend upon the interior of their hearts, and the use toward which they employ their intuitive gifts.

CHAPTER 11

THE INTERIOR OF A HEART

Surely he hath borne our griefs, and carried our sorrows: yet
we did esteem him stricken, smitten of God, and afflicted.
But he was wounded for our transgressions, he was bruised
for our iniquities: the chastisement of our peace was upon
him; and with his stripes we are healed . . . . and the LORD
hath laid on him the iniquity of us all.
He was oppressed, and he was afflicted, yet he opened not
his mouth . . . . for the transgression of my people was he
stricken . . . .
Yet it pleased the LORD to bruise him; he hath put him to
grief . . . .
He shall see the travail of his soul, and shall be satisfied: by
his knowledge shall my righteous servant justify many; for
he shall bear their iniquities . . . . he hath poured out his soul
unto death: and he was numbered with the transgressors;
and he bare the sin of many, and made intercession for the
transgressors.[1]

The chambers of this chapter seem to be the very walls of hell
within which Dimmesdale is suffering, and to contain a
characterization of Dimmesdale as unlike any mortal being,
and preeminent among them. His pain is enlarged by a change in his
relationship with the physician because of the "revelation, he could almost
say, [that] had been granted" (140) to Chillingworth, who is now filled
with a "depth of malice" (139).

THE PAINS OF HELL

It appears that the revelation was granted Chillingworth by Providence, which used "the avenger and his victim for its own purposes" (139). Chillingworth could therefore now "play upon him as he chose" (140). Not only has Providence set the stage for its actors but now has given rein to an avenger to do his worse, for whatever purposes it has in mind.

> All that guilty sorrow, hidden from the world, whose great heart would have pitied and forgiven, to be revealed to him, the Pitiless, to him, the Unforgiving! All that dark treasure to be lavished on the very man, to whom nothing else could so adequately pay the debt of vengeance! (139)

In assuming the world has a great and compassionate heart, whether Hawthorne might have simply been using poetic license to contrast the malice of Chillingworth with some universal heart or "collective conscience," is matter for some other more worthy to consider. The purpose of this purview focuses upon the extent to which the dark treasure, in some inexplicable or vicarious way, pays for some indebtedness. What dark treasure has Chillingworth seen; what debt needs to be paid; for what purpose does Providence use the adversary upon the stage it has set; for what plot do the actors perform; and how can this dark treasure pay to Chillingworth a debt of vengeance?

To Hawthorne it appears that Deity has allowed the Adversary to see that dark treasure, perhaps as a payment for a debt that satisfies his hunger for revenge, however ill-conceived his hunger might be. All that dark treasure and guilty sorrow, as we have heretofore suggested, as representing the sins of the world, which have been heaped upon the divine, whose sympathetic heart is forgiving, has now been witnessed by the one being, who is unforgiving, pitiless, and vengeful. And the wonder and joy of its vastness may be his payment for all his efforts at vengeance upon the souls of humans, to satisfy the demands of justice, as exacted by eternal law, "but alas for his own soul!" Some Christian doctrine, holding that the cost of the rebellion by Lucifer and his angels was the missed opportunity to come to the earth and obtain a body of flesh and bone, also suggests that the success of his exploitations here might offer the only possible way to inhabit a warm and comfortable home, to kindle "a household fire" therein

(74). However, although the above quote is the narrator's commentary, Hawthorne may only be speaking from the perspective of Chillingworth, and not his own. If commenting on what Hawthorne thinks may be a reason why Providence allowed Lucifer such free reign over the hearts of humankind, he may be suggesting that Old Scratch's success in his thirst for vengeance is a kind of fitting compensation for his losses, or, since nothing else will do, a measure of justice demanded by a broken law.

Symbolically, and ironically, a revelation of Dimmesdale is shown to the one being who seeks revenge for "wrongs inflicted on himself," and we might add, by himself, a revenge that in time will bear the same effect upon himself as he has devised for Dimmesdale, Hester, and Pearl. These pains are identified in association with Old Scratch, the Pitiless, the Unforgiving. In a "quiet depth of malice," the physician became an active persecutor in heightening the awful shame felt within the interior of the clergyman's heart, perhaps the shame of millions heaped upon his soul, all pointing to his role in their redemption. At a wave of the Tempter's wand,

> uprose a grisly phantom,—uprose a thousand phantoms,—in many shapes, of death, or more awful shame, all flocking roundabout the clergyman, and pointing with their fingers at his breast!" (140)

Hawthorne may be saying that shame and guilt are part of the pains inflicted by the Avenger. So much so, perhaps, that the divine conceived of himself as "utterly a pollution and a lie!" (141). Perhaps, in the throes of Hawthorne's Christianity, Dimmesdale's pain of shame and guilt seem to metaphorize the pains of hell for which the Redeemer suffered for humankind, and Hawthorne may be emphasizing that internal, or eternal, conflict in the character of Arthur. That vicarious suffering may be the dark treasure Dimmesdale saw, the jewel on the dead man's chest, the horrorful self-fulfilling sight which ignited the Master of Prying's malicious and hateful attempts to steal or thwart. Perhaps, as a license of the allegory, Hawthorne elongated the pains and agonies of Dimmesdale as a way of demonstrating the intensity of the Redemption itself. In Chillingworth's role as a chief actor in intensifying that pain, perhaps Hawthorne is insinuating that the misery of hell itself is under the power of Satan. Hawthorne does not seem to make any implications, however, as to the dimensions of that misery, whether it is accumulative in their effect, or rather a specifically fixed experience, limited and equal to that which each hostile and uncompassionate person may suffer. And the chief victim, "ever on the rack," for whom the Avenger was now no longer an observer, but a participating and chief actor, was the sensitive and intense divine, whom Hawthorne characterizes, epithetically, in a broad range of virtues.

A DIM SHADOW

Hawthorne has Dimmesdale asking the reader this proverbial question again: what is the identity of the young divine? "Then, what was he?–a substance?–or the dimmest of all shadows?" (143) Hawthorne seems to use the metaphor of "dimness" in several ways: one, as a reference to Dimmesdale's vague perception of the Chillingworth's evil influence upon him; two, as an obscure revelation of God's relation to mankind; three, as the opposite of real substance; or four, as the method of teaching Arthur used, which appears to be parabolic.

In the first case, most obviously, Dimmesdale "had constantly a dim perception of some evil influence watching over him" (140). Being suspicious of Chillingworth, but more suspicious of his own "bad sympathies" for the man, he "thus gave him constant opportunites for perfecting the purpose to which . . . the avenger had devoted himself" (141).

A second way Hawthorne seems to use "dimness" as a metaphor addresses the silence, or dimly shadowed revelation Dimmesdale received from heaven. Hawthorne's veiled perspective of Providence's responsibility for the Fall, which we have mentioned somewhat already, makes Dimmesdale's dimness very akin to Hawthorne's abstruseness, who never disclosed openly the meanings of his most remarkable allegory. It may be a matter of opinion as to whether Dimmesdale or Hawthorne was more true to himself by showing "freely to the world, if not your worst, yet some trait whereby the worst may be inferred!"

Thirdly, Dimmesdale, like the Nazarene, apparently also taught sermons with the use of parables, shadow-like representations of high principles of being: "It was his genuine impulse to adore the truth, and to reckon all things shadow-like, and utterly devoid of weight and value, that had not its divine essence as the life within their life" (143).

A fourth particular kind of dimness, might represent the Nazarene's lack of knowledge as to the depth and extent of the burden he had to suffer. In the Christian's text, at some point in time, the Nazarene knew that he must undergo the pains of guilt and agony for the sins of humanity, but, Hawthorne might have thought that the depths of hell may not have been fully known until the time the Agony of the Redemption was experienced. This dimness, resulting in Dimmesdale's yielding to his mortal nature's weakness and acquiesing to Hester's speculative escape plan, might be Hawthorne's rationale for the Nazarene's one moment of self-willingness, or wish to escape or shorten his suffering. Thus Dimmesdale is a fitting name for a character who endures the deepest valley of inexplicable suffering without knowing fully beforehand whence its source or thence its magnitude.

Dimness, to Hawthorne, may therefore be an analogy to the unknown depth of the Atonement, "the burden, whatever it might be, of crime or anguish, beneath which it was his doom to totter" (142). As a shadow of truth, Dimmesdale's character seems to hint of the compassionate introspection that intensified his sensitivity to "the sinful brotherhood of mankind," whose pain was a burden received into his own heart (142). In addressing this unknown depth, Hawthorne may have had in mind the Nazarene's question upon the cross when he lamented, "Why has thou forsaken me?[2]" According to more modern Christian rationale, hell might be that complete loneliness; the absolute separation from all light, truth, and heavenly influence; the great abyss unknown to all those who escape its chains, the agony of which is metaphorically compared to the pains inflicted by fire. The abandonment the Nazarene apparently felt may have reflected the necessary depth of the Redemption he must experience upon his own, alone, without the aid of his Father's presence within him, in order to fully satisfy the burden. Before that utterance, he apparently had always felt the presence of his Father in a kind of in-dwelling relationship[3]; that is, he may have sensed his thoughts and will.

Additionally, "the dimmest shadow" may refer to the idea that the promise of the Redemption had little substance in Puritanism, or, for that matter, in the minds of those given more to scientific or intellectual logic.

Further, dimness, as the opposite of something clearly substantial, might represent an ideal seen imperfectly, as through a dim looking glass. Dimmesdale asks himself if he is real substance or only "the dimmest of all shadows" (143). Was the Nazarene really who he claimed to be, as an instrument of Providence, or was he purely a figment of his own imagination?

WHAT PRINCIPLE OF BEING?

Perhaps the question which the young minister asks himself, as to what he is, is much like the question Chillingworth asks Dimmesdale of Pearl: "Hath she any discoverable principle of being?" (134) The reader should be led to ask this question of each of the four main characters of the allegory: what principle of truth do each represent? It is likely asked for the sake of the reader to contemplate at the allegorical level. What discoverable principle of being does Dimmesdale represent? Is there any substantial principle of being represented by the character of Dimmesdale?" In other words, does Dimmesdale, like Pearl, represent some essential principle, or being, or is he only a creation of his own imagination and no more? Is Hawthorne also prompting the reader to ask the question: "Was the Nazarene the principal being he claimed to be, or just a product of his own thinking?" Believably, as proposed in this interpretation of Hawthorne's allegory, Dimmesdale represents more than a fictional character because Hawthorne, before analyzing the "dim shadow" side of Dimmesdale, explored the more favorable aspects of Arthur's comparative stature, in connection with the interior of his heart. Hawthorne's description of the divine'a nature and character all but places a label of the name he represents.

A BURDEN OF THE HEART

Ironically, Dimmesdale's popularity increased in brilliance due to the intensity of his sorrows that are inflamed by Chillingworth's vengeance.

> While thus suffering under bodily disease, and gnawed and tortured by some black trouble of the soul, and given over to the machinations of his deadliest enemy, the Reverend Mr. Dimmesdale had achieved a brilliant popularity in his sacred office. He won it, indeed, in great part, by his sorrows . . . . His fame, though still on its upward slope, already over-shadowed the soberer reputations of his fellow-clergymen. (141)

The greater the Avenger's influence, the greater number of parishioners turned to his compassionate appeals. In other words, perhaps, the greater the influence of Old Scratch upon his subjects, the greater their demands for a redemption therefrom. The increase in intensity of sorrows due to this influence may then seem to speak for the Redemption being an accumulative effect rather than a single, limited experience. But such an implication may never have occurred to Hawthorne, or may have been of little concern, should it have; or he would have typically made other references to it.

The young divine's fame, then, which overshadows that of his fellow clergymen, is a parallel to the ministry of the Nazarene. Hawthorne also appears to compare some of these "true saintly fathers" to the twelve disciples of the Lord before the Day of Pentecost.

> All that they lacked was the gift that descended upon the chosen disciples, at Pentecost, in tongues of flame; symbolizing, it would seem, not the power of speech in foreign and unknown languages, but that of addressing the whole human brotherhood in the heart's native language. These fathers, otherwise so apostolic, lacked Heaven's last and rarest attestation of their office, the Tongue of Flame. They would have vainly sought–had they ever dreamed of seeking–to express the highest truths through the humblest medium of familiar words and images. Their voices came down afar and indistinctly, from the upper heights where they habitually dwelt. (141-142)

These clergymen, like the Twelve apostles, could vainly have addressed humanity in the language of parables, which comprised words and images from the lowest walks of life, perhaps because they were not as humble as Dimmesdale. His "burden, whatever it might be, of crime or anguish, beneath which it was his doom to totter . . . kept him down, on a level with the lowest" (142). The burden of pain he carried, or embodied, identified him with them. Whereas the twelve disciples at times squabbled among themselves as to who was the greatest in the kingdom of God, whose thoughts often descended "from the upper heights where they habitually dwelt," the Nazarene is said to have descended below all humankind as the servant of all, and therefore, the humblest.

However, the allusion to the twelve apostles, as a distinction between them and the man of Nazareth, focused upon the Tongue of Flame, or the Holy Ghost, and the disciples' lack thereof. Perhaps Hawthorne was equally aware that the Nazarene's apostles, unlike himself, upon whom the Holy Ghost had already descended, did not receive this gift until after their leader's death.

Hawthorne notes that when most clergymen achieve high recognition, they aspire to political office, as though their hearts are not set so much upon the glory of their Master as upon their own. Dimmesdale, however, had no such aspirations but to bear his burden and give his life, and death, for the sake of his parishioners.

Perhaps the most striking description of Arthur's interior that parallels the Nazarene's is given in one particular paragraph on him,

> the man of ethereal attributes, whose voice the angels might else have listed to and answered! But this very burden it was, that gave him sympathies so intimate with the sinful brotherhood of mankind; so that his heart vibrated in unison with theirs, and received their pain into itself . . . ." (142)

This passage seems to address the one power of Divine mercy, infinite in its vicarious comprehension of receiving the pains of humankind into itself, the one power capable of resolving the problems of humanity. This sympathetic reception of humankind's pains, then, seems to be the vicarious kind of pain in Dimmesdale's heart. It is the one link that most clearly portrays Dimmesdale's agony as symbolic of the Nazarene's, whose voice both good and bad angels obeyed, whose heart, burdened with the sins of humankind, was intimately connected with them, and vibrated in compassionate unison with theirs. Their pain, in all actuality, was his pain.

As an essential substance, Dimmesdale—whose "genuine impulse to adore truth" imbued his teachings with the metaphoric weight or value of "divine essence as the life within their life" (143)—seems to characterize the man from Nazareth, who was reported to be the essential life within the life of humankind: "In him was life; and the life was the light of men.[4]"

Dimmesdale, like the Nazarene, was the man who took "upon himself to hold communion, in your behalf, with the Most High Omniscience" (143). He strongly appears to represent the Mediator, who held communion with his disciples and asked them before his crucifixion to continue the practice with believers as a means for their salvation. According to Christian theology, the Nazarene was the link between the Most High Omniscience and "the communities of mankind" by authoring the resurrection of the flesh with the spirit, and, most essentially, their redemption to a better world. He took it upon himself to be the mediator of the new covenant of the Last Supper, the memorial sacrifice which effectuates humankind's eternal communion with Deity. Like Dimmesdale, he accepted a mission to be the shining example "whose footsteps . . . leave a gleam along [his] earthly track, whereby the pilgrims that shall come after [him] may be guided to the regions of the blest" (143). He was the connection or "relation between Diety and the community of mankind," upon whom the burden of the sins of the "brotherhood of mankind" fell, a burden with "a thousand phantoms,—in many shapes, of death, or more awful shame" (140).

The number, thousand, may be perhaps symbolic of millions of hearts looking to and dependant upon that suffering in their behalf. Perhaps the appeal of Christianity is the thought that its Author's suffering was so personally connected with each of those hearts that they are drawn towards him, a similar element that drew Dimmesdale's parishioners to him. Whether as a compassionate appeal, or some more enigmatic connection, as he received their pain into his own heart, they felt in their hearts the pain of his own,

> that sent its own throb of pain through a thousand other hearts, in gushes of sad, persuasive eloquence. Oftenest persuasive, but sometimes terrible! The people knew not the power that moved them thus. They deemed the young clergyman a miracle of holiness.

> They fancied him the mouthpiece of Heaven's messages of wisdom, and rebuke, and love. In their eyes, the very ground on which he trod was sanctified. (142)

In this attraction to Dimmesdale, some similitude to the mission of the Nazarene seems likely, as defined in another Biblical text: "And I, if I be lifted up from the earth, will draw all men unto me.⁵" These analogies seem to be a parallel track of the Nazarene's own character, mission, and influence, and predominately presuppose a representation of him.

Besides this parallelism, in the passage above, Hawthorne appears to personalize the Passion of the Atonement as a sympathetic, intimate burden of humankind's sins which the Nazarene took upon himself, whose heart, according to the Biblical prophet, Isaiah, "hath borne our griefs, and carried our sorrows." The languages of Hawthorne and Isaiah are different, but the meanings are the same. The experience of the Redemption, along with the temptations in a life of mortal flesh, was the burden, "which it was his doom to totter" (142), that perhaps also made the Nazarene sympathetic with the common sinner. At the same time, this depth of sorrow may have capacitated his heart to be that much more compassionate and open to forgiving those burdened with sin. That pain and compassion, and the spirit that accompanied it, has drawn to him millions upon millions of the hearts of humankind. On the other hand, or at the same time, that "throb of pain through a thousand hearts" may be a symbolic measure of those millions who shall bear that pain because of a lack of a compassionate heart, perhaps much in the Biblical sense, "Keeping mercy for thousands, forgiving iniquity and transgression and sin, . . . that by no means will clear the guilty.[6]"

Likewise, as in the eyes of Dimmesdale's parishioners, "the very ground on which he trod was sanctified" (142), is a possible reference to the veneration accorded the places where the Son of Man walked. Moreover, the divine is even venerated by the virgins of the young minister's church, who become

> victims of a passion so imbued with religious sentiment that they imagined it to be all religion, and brought it openly, in their white bosoms, as their most acceptable sacrifice before the altar. (142)

This passage seems a dim reference to the nuns of the Catholic Church, who dedicate their virginity (white bosoms) and vow at the altar of marriage to the Christ to live lives of service to his cause. Other allusions to that former generation of believers may indicate Hawthorne's own veneration for those with such dedication, as he did similarly with some of the Puritans who appeared to have such empathies of the heart.

It does not appear, from the entirety of the novel, that Hawthorne actually conceived of such devotion as a victimization of his parishioners. The only evil Dimmesdale apparently ever conceived in his heart were moments of temptation, to which he never indulged, in contemplating the abandonment od his mission. It would be regarded as a great misunderstanding to regard him as the earliest prototype of an Elmer Gantry.

A POLLUTION AND A LIE

In the pulpit the young minister often tried to confess by vaguely vilifying himself.

> They heard it all, and did but reverence him the more . . . . He had spoken the very truth, and transformed it into the veriest falsehood. And yet, by the constitution of his nature, he loved the truth, and loathed the lie, as few men ever did. Therefore, above all things else, he loathed his miserable self! (144)

After building up Dimmesdale, and lauding him above those of his fellowmen, Hawthorne half way into his novel throws a monkey wrench into the analogy. Dimmesdale is depicted, in his own words, as "a pollution and a lie . . . the worst of sinners, an abomination, a thing of unimaginable iniquity" under "the burning wrath of the Almighty" (143-144).

So, after possibly having an epiphany as to Chillingworth's and Dimmesdale's representations, is the insightful reader being pushed by Hawthorne into another paradigm shift, possibly to uncover further philosophical inclinations that may be unorthodox and questionable? Is he now using hyperbole for effect to focus on another paradoxical message? The reader has been taken from the mystery of Pearl's birth through the mystery of the scarlet letter and the mysterious pollution of the divine to yet another mystery of The Lie! It may be more than simply an Hawthornian image of internal upheaval due to conflicting emotions in Arthur, and more than an hypothetical reflection of a highly sensitive soul, whose purity has to assimilate and embody the presence of a multitude of heinous and soul-wrenching sins. It would seem to be another cover-up of Hawthorne's inmost Me to so completely reverse the reader's favorable opinion by such an aspersion, unless he is using hyperbole to call attention to something else, an exaggeration to emphasize another theme.

Since such a self-incriminating abasement never parted from the lips of the man from Nazareth, Hawthorne has chosen to have Dimmesdale speak of himself as a lie, perhaps, to earmark the development of a conclusion of Hawthorne's that may not have a Biblical counterpart. Hawthorne has emblazoned boldly upon the character of Dimmesdale, in addition to the anguish of pollution in his heart, the implication of a lie, for some purpose, again perhaps as another puzzle for the reader to resolve.

On the other hand, but least likely, in that pronouncement, for the sake of the incredulous, Hawthorne may be only addressing the purely logical reader. Of all the dark philosophies of religion cast falsely upon the minds of the human family, whether as dim shadows of truth, or as the paganistic ritual of worshiping idols of wood and stone, the creation of a God out of a mere man may represent the greatest falsehood of all times, to those whose logical minds cannot assimulate it. Hawthorne may have given the reader another view of humankind, which considers the Nazarene neither as a Redeemer, nor as one whose advent and life deserved to mark a division in time, but as perhaps the greatest hoax ever perpetrated upon the human mind.

Dimmesdale, in the superficial tale, seems a pollution and a hypocritical lie; at the allegorical level, for many, he may represent the same. Perhaps only the nature of the allegory, which is intended to reverse images, may redeem or qualifie this lie, by other clues provided by Hawthorne.

Or perhaps, Hawthorne, as typical for his characters, is merely projecting the same double-minded conflict of mortal nature between intuition and logic—ambivalence—upon Dimmesdale, whose dark treasure may have encompassed the pollution of all the dark blemishes of sin, including the scope of all lies, and the emotions of shame and guilt thereof. The burden of humanity's sin, thought by the devout Christian to have been carried upon the shoulders of the Nazarene, though sinless in motive and deed, yet might include an accumulation of all their lies as well as other kinds of sin. As the epitomy of purity, this embodiment of the sins of humankind, to Hawthorne, would perhaps make him feel to be the ultimate Lie as well as the ultimate pollution. Perhaps Hawthorne only intended Dimmesdale's intense internal upheaval to project a distorted emotional hologram he labeled as such.

At the same time, or on the other hand, the most obvious pollution and lie that Dimmesdale is living, however, may be his silence as to his relationship with Hester and Pearl; that is, it is a lie for as long as Dimmesdale waits to make his confession of responsibility for Hester's infamy and/or the birth of Pearl. That silence, in the absence of an open confession, might constitute a type of a pollution of truth, or lie. Or, less likely, and most highly suspect, with respect to his allegorical relationships to Hester and Pearl, that lie might refer to the heretical conclusion this author proposes Hawthorne secreted in his tale for only a few to understand. This conclusive explanation might possibly be framed in questions from Hawthorne's study of ancient documents: were there more parties to the cause of mortality other than Adam, Eve, and the serpent; was the Redemption not only a compensation, but also a dimly-shadowed confession in which the Creator of immortality admitted his responsibility as the Engineer of the Fall?

Perhaps only confirmable by the intuition of a Romantic, or some forthcoming prophetess, this possible conclusion by Hawthorne may be fostered by other questions, of which the rational mind is capable. Who planted the tree of the knowledge of good and evil in the Garden of Eden? Who knew the nature of Eve better than her Creator? Who gave two commandments, to either of which obedience seems to have excluded obedience to the other? Was the fall necessary as a part of the Providential plan? Is the dimness of Dimmesdale's confession, therefore, a silence of the Lamb?

We have partial, or dim, answers for these questions; and since we look at truth dimly, as through a looking glass, we only know in part what we see in part. Some may say, like those who claimed that Hawthorne's novel should never have been written, that the questions and answers proposed by Hawthorne, or by this foghorn, perhaps should never have been posed. Rightly so, should it be concluded that these questions impute Diety with some responsibility for the mess the world is in. Hawthorne may have only posed these questions to highlight the answers he anticipates may be forthcoming in that day when "all intelligent beings, who will stand waiting, on that day, to see the dark problem of this life made plain" (132).

If the fall into mortality was a dark necessity Providentially designed for a future state of happiness that could not otherwise be experienced, neither heresy nor blasphemy may be imputed to Hawthorne, nor any incongruence imputed to Deity. If the Creation, Fall, and Atonement were tied together in the role of one Deity, and if that Redemption was also an act of justice as well as mercy, whether or not heaven was responsible and silent as to the possible paradox staged in the Garden may matter only to those who are perplexed by it.

At the same time, Hawthorne's reliance upon expected revelation to clarify the matter treats the subject of silence that bothers many readers. His endorsement of intuition suggests that some prophetess, or some other Daniel, may yet come forth with supportive explanations. Perhaps Hawthorne was aware of Biblical texts assuring the perplexed Christian that such answers come, but not without some effort on their part. Since revelation about the truth of historical and present matters seems most often associated with close communication with the Christian's Deity, silence on heaven's part would seem to be not so much an undersight on his part as it might be on humankind's; that is to say, if no one has ever asked him if he held himself partially liable for the fall into mortality, who's to blame for the silence and the lack of information on the subject? Or, if Deity's representatives, like Dimmesdale, have spoken, or attempted to penetrate the density of humanity's receptivity, has there been anyone there to glimpse through the opaqueness, and then been allowed by his fellowmen to interpret it?

TO THY OWN SELF BE TRUE

The seeming falsity of Dimmesdale might then appear to be his silence, or the long delay in communicating his responsibility, or the dimness with which he attempted to communicate it, for an act for which he was responsible. The lie that Dimmesdale is living in silence seems to relate to his last statement upon the scaffold:

> Among many morals which press upon us from the poor minister's miserable experience, we put only this into a sentence:—"Be true! Be true! Be True! Show freely to the world, if not your worst, yet some trait whereby the worst may be inferred!" (260).

If there is any one distinctively Hawthornian moral in his novel, it possibly lies within the connection between the pronouncement of The

Lie and that one eminent passage above, which may summarize the one conclusion he has labored so ardously to keep clothed within his philosophical self. That possible connection has been elucidated heretofore, and is summarized here again for clarification of that connection: without the confession, and redemption, the dimness and silence of heaven's part in the fall of humanity, might be considered, by the most logical mind, as an absence of the truth humankind needs to understand the problems of life, its mixture of good and evil; and the Redemption possibly showed freely and voluntarily to the world, if not the worse part of it, at least a particular trait of responsibility for the matter of mortality, by the death of the Creator in the form of the Nazarene.

If Dimmesdale's silence is an analogy of the silence of Providence, then it logically follows that the Christian Deity would not exist if he is untrue to himself. Perhaps to Hawthorne, Diety, like Dimmesdale, must break silence and declare his responsibility, if he is responsible; or else he is untrue to himself, and, therefore, by exaggeration, a lie.

> To the untrue man, the whole universe is false,—it is impalpable,—it shrinks to nothing within his grasp. And he himself, in so far as he shows himself in a false light, becomes a shadow, or, indeed ceases to exist. The only truth, that continued to give Mr. Dimmesdale a real existence on this earth, was the anguish in his inmost soul, and the undissembled expression of it in his aspect. (146)

Analagously, the Redemption was therefore the one truth for which the Nazarene is said to have lived and died, a kind of confession without which, as was Dimmesdale's, he himself would have become a shadow and ceased to exist as the Principle of truth incarnate. As Dimmesdale is true to himself by his confession, Deity likewise was true by the Act of his representative, perhaps as an admission of responsibility as well as an Act of Justice, compensating therefor by an Act of Mercy, redeeming humanity from the Fall.

This possible existential philosophy, relating Deity's existence to his truthfulness, may be one of the "many morals which press upon us from the poor minister's miserable experience," and one of the few Hawthorne seems to openly declare in his novel, perhaps because it may constitute the very center of his allegory.

A more simplistic interpretation of the worst shown by Dimmesdale may be but the symbol of the scarlet letter A upon his own chest, and the means by which he was true to himself. Perhaps the worst revealed by Deity, in Hawthorne's Christianity, was the sacrifice of the man who claimed to be his Son, who suffered in the Garden of Gethsemane and upon the cross, and became the necessary means by which Deity remained true to his identity and existence.

VISIONS OF THE UGLY NIGHT

Clothed in Romantic notions, the close of the chapter seems to focus upon the dimensions of hell's diabolic falsehoods in the agony of one's imaginations. The misery Dimmesdale feels during the day haunts him at night. This agony "is the unspeakable misery of a life so false as his, that it steals the pith and substance out of whatever realities there are around us" (145).

The only truth which seems to qualify Dimmesdale's grasp on existence is the hell he willingly experienced. It appears to be the one reality or mission in life for which he is awaiting fulfillment. So he beat himself with a "bloody scourge" and fasted rigorously . . . until his knees trembled beneath him, as an act of penance" (144). Again, as in the case of his self-defamation, another detail of Dimmesdale's behavior has no identical comparison to that of the Nazarene, as likewise with his hallucinations below, but should have some symbolic significance to the analogy.

> In these lengthened vigils, his brain often reeled, and visions seemed to flit before him . . . . Now it was a herd of diabolic shapes, that grinned and mocked at the pale minister, and beckoned him away with them . . . . Now came the dead friends of his youth, and his white-bearded father, with a saint-like frown, and his mother, turning her face away as she passed by. (145)

These visions, or falsehoods of the imagination, during those ugly nights may be the author's imagination of what the mental state of a person might conjure during such a physical torment. The bloody, self-inflicted scourge may metaphorically represent the one Isaiah referred to that was used by the Romans to scourge the Nazarene, and may symbolize the stripes he bore for us, by the which Isaiah records we are healed. This mental and physical scourging may be symbolized also by the red gules upon the sable field engraved upon the tombstone shared by Hester and Dimmesdale. As in the divine's suffering, the Redemption, perhaps as projected in Hawthorne's theology, may be seen as an act of penance, willingly and vicariously experienced, for those who might otherwise experience the existential realities of hell, whatever they might be like, but for that proxical expiation.

In the passage quoted above, we hardly dare carry the allegory further than the details of the analogy were intended. It would be like pouring salt into the wounds of those who have already taken a beating with the analogy in the first place. So far be it for us to be so insensitive to those stripes to even suggest that Hawthorne may have had in mind one of the Nazarene's last utterances, "Eloi, Eloi, why has thou forsaken me?" Or even more absurdly so, to suggest that Hawthorne's philosophical self might have included not only a conception of the Nazarene being forsaken by his Father, who frowned at his suffering, but also by his Mother, the thinnest fantasy of a mother, who "turned her face away as she passed by," for whom there is no Biblical counterpart.

The scourgings and fastings and resulting ugly visions in the nights in this chapter establish the setting of the next chapter. Lost in the agony of his soul from the realities around him, Dimmesdale is struck by a new thought, and presumably goes forth into the night for a moment's peace, an escape from the reality of his misery.

CHAPTER 12

THE MINISTER'S VIGIL

And a certain ruler asked him, saying, Good Master,
what shall I do to inherit eternal life?
And Jesus said unto him, Why callest thou me good?
None is good, save one, that is, God.[1]

O f all the parables and symbols in Hawthorne's tale, those in
the minister's vigil have been the least amenable to conformity
with the allegorical interpretations, perhaps because they are
embued with a heavy dose of Anti-transcendentalism. This chapter seems
at first reading to be a a dream during one of those ugly nights following
Dimmesdale's scourgings and fastings, but there are details that suggest
intimations from the dark side of life. It is more likely that he is in a state
of mind due to his self-inflicted penance that presumbably privileges him
with intuitions boarding on revelation.

This analysis interprets the chapter as an extension of the previous
ordeal, in which Dimmesdale appears to see himself in his worst light,
possibly through the eyes of that dream. Symbolically, this dream,
nightmare, or, as it were, a trance, may represent one of the darkest hours
of the Nazarene's suffering in the Garden of Gethsemane. As a divine being
among mortals, subject to their temptations and ignominious feelings, the
man of Nazareth may have had, in the mind of Hawthorne, similar kinds
of ugly visions during his ministry, and a similar understanding of his
mortal nature, as implied in the Biblical text above. The Christian may
puzzle over the Nazarene's confession in the quote above, but Hawthorne
seems to have grasped the concept that the mortal nature of any individual
grapples to some differing measure with its sensitivity towards it. Arthur's

extreme sensitivity to his own mortal nature might pose questions to the thoughtful person, "Whose mortal sense of goodness can certify its definition more than the Author of it? Whose experiences of the weaknesses of the flesh can best describe how life itself seems to be a lie and a pollution?

The idea Dimmesdale had in the last of the preceding chapter is that he can escape from the horror of his experiences by standing upon the scaffold with Pearl and Hester in the night, when no one can see him, and that this confession will appease his sense of responsibility and give him a moment of peace, however temporarily. Whether this midnight vigil may be only wish fulfillment projected by his subconscious, or a dim representative vision of how he is to fulfill his destiny, becomes questionably evident, though other details suggest its substance as containing elements of reality.

A SLEEPWALKER'S VIGIL

There are some indications that Dimmesdale's all-night vigil is a dream, perhaps combined with sleep-walking, as an extension of the ugly visions experienced earlier.

> Walking in the shadow of a dream, as it were, and perhaps actually under the influence of a species of somnambulism, Mr. Dimmesdale reached the spot, where, now so long since, Hester Prynne had lived through her first hour of public ignominy. (147)

This statement, opening the chapter of the minister's all-night vigil upon the scaffold, strongly suggests that he is dreaming while he is perhaps also sleep-walking. The events that transpire seem to be a stream of subconscious fears and wishes to end his pain, or a weak foreshadowing of an event that must occur in the daylight at some future time. He saw Governor Bellingham and his sister, the witch-lady Hibbins, through the windows of their home; Mr. Wilson and Pearl and Hester come by; and, last of all, Chillingworth appeared, seemingly in the process of Dimmesdale's waking. The minister's all-night vigil, then, appears to be an imagined experience or anticipation in advance of the reality of fulfilling his destiny. It may have been a vision or dream during "one of those ugly nights" in which he vicariously experienced confessing his relationship with Hester and Pearl (146).

A vigil is a purposefully vigorous wakefulness or devotional watch during a period of time prior to an important event, like a fast before a festival. Holding to the representations of the characters, it may be dimly concluded that the minister's rehearsal upon the scaffold may symbolize either an unclear vision of the event beheld before its actuality, or it may symbolize his agonizing midnight vigil in the Garden of Gethsemane prior to the actual crucifixion.

Dimmesdale had been fasting and flogging himself as an act of penance; and during this one night's nightmare, the governor of the colony dies. This death historically places the setting of Hawthorne's tale three years before and four years after the death of Governor Winthrop. It is likely in the tale that it is Winthrop who died, for he is not listed in the procession with other statesmen, including former Govenors Bellingham, Dudley, and Endicott, all of whom attended the traditional Election Sermon given by Dimmesdale. The Election Sermon, therefore, might have been a customary ceremony during a transition of government at the Governor's death. Winthrop was one of the most successful founders of the theocratic government of the Massachusetts Bay Colony who defeated the ministry of Anne Hutchinson. Anne taught the doctrine of grace by faith alone, was considered an antinomian to the Puritan faith, and banished. Hawthorne spoke favorably of her in connection with the theme of grace, which seems symbolized by the red roses.

The theme possibly addressed here, in Winthrop's death, may signal the allegorical setting of a change of government, perhaps to represent the legal change in the theocracy of Judaism to Christianity in the meridian of time. Whether dream or vision, Dimmesdale's view of the experience seems to harbor Hawthorne's. Reverend Wilson, who, with a lighted lantern, was returning from his visit to Winthrop within the hour of the divine's vigil, was

> surrounded . . . with a radiant halo, that glorified him amid this gloomy night of sin,—as if the departed Govenor had left him an inheritance of his glory, or as if he had caught upon himself the distant shine of the celestial city . . . . The glimmer of this luminary suggested the above conceits to Mr. Dimmesdale, who

smiled,—nay, almost laughted at them,—and then wondered if he were going mad. (150)

Dimmesdale's near laughter at the Reverend's "conceits" perhaps reflects Hawthorne's hopeful vision of a day and time far removed from the soil of Boston and Salem. Variations and transformations then and thereafter in government, community, and religion have been found wanting and in need of further refinement, which Hawthorne hopes is forthcoming. If Puritanism considered Anne's teachings too far afield, it appears that Hawthorne at least favored movement in that direction, and seems to have centered his novel around that hope.

The quote above also may hint of a transfer of prestige and glory from the governing body to the religious body, slightly suggesting the historical rise of Christianity during the Dark Ages, perhaps a "gloomy night of sin," wherein religion became ironically oppressive. Hawthorne's philosophical self may have grimaced rather than laughed at these "above conceits."

A CRY IN THE NIGHT

The young divine imagined or experienced in his all-night vigil upon the scaffold the dark emotions of his shame, a kind of self-inflicted torment one experiences in an awareness of sinfulness,

> a great horror of mind, as if the universe were gazing at a scarlet token on his naked breast, right over his heart. On that spot, in very truth, there was, and there had long been, the gnawing and poisonous tooth of bodily pain . . . [which] he shrieked aloud; an outcry that went pealing through the night, and was beaten back from one house to another . . . as if a company of devils, detecting so much misery and terror in it, had made a plaything of the sound, and were bandying it to and fro. (148)

The several allusions in this quote seem to point to a symbolization of what Hawthorne may have conceived to represent a similitude of the Nazarene's experience in the Garden of Gethsemanie. Perhaps, in the mind of Hawthorne, the Redemption of humanity might invoke the gaze of all the universe upon his agony, as its cry reverberated from house to house, so that all should know that their pain was beaten back from them to him. Perhaps he is also ruminating that the reverberations of that Agony may be delightfully fostered by that legion of fallen angels, who exult in such pain and misery.

For Dimmesdale, Remorse and Cowardice seem to be the centers of this "agony of heaven-defying guilt" (148). The burden of sin to the sensitive heart is guilt, which breeds the Remorse that drives one to repent; thus to the scaffold for Dimmesdale. But guilt also breeds Cowardice from the fear of shame and the redeeming pain, which keeps one back from confession. Thus, ambivalence in Dimmesdale may have projected this dreamy nightwalker's midnight vigil, which, to the narrator, constituted but a "vain repentance." Both pains framed "a great horror of mind" that resulted in "the gnawing and poisonous tooth of bodily pain" located directly over his heart (148). Hawthorne does not use the word "fear" in context with this pain, but may imply it as Dimmesdale stands upon the scaffold and shrieks aloud, when the want of confessing overpowered his resistance to it. Agonizing over his struggle to make the confession he knows he must make, he wants to make, and has promised Pearl he would make, he is leery of being discovered, and identified, before his time.

Perhaps Hawthorne is echoing Biblical text, that the experience in the Garden of Gethsemane the night prior to his betrayal and crucifixion, as a foreshadowing of the experience upon the cross, was a nightmare of fear and horror, the agony of which was so intense that he prayed for the cup to pass from him. It is recorded by a physician, Luke, that in the Garden, the Nazarene sweated, as it were, great drops of blood because of the pain he suffered there[2]. One Christian belief holds that the Redemption began in the Garden, that the pain was both so physically and spiritually intense that blood actually exuded from the pores of his body, and that he would have died from the ordeal, as would any mortal, had he not had the power of life within himself.

A problem with the interpretations above is highlighted by the lack of conformity of the all-night vigil with the chronology of Biblical events alluded to. The experience in the Garden happened the night before the crucifixion on the cross, but Dimmesdale's vigil, though in the dead of night, seems to occur in no short time period prior to his confession. Nevertheless, it is a function of the art of the Romantic writer, as perhaps in this allegory, to compress time and events in such a manner, and perhaps even to reverse them. This strategy was one of the reactions against

Classicism, which focused on ordering time and space, and was used in Romantic literature in contrast to that used in earlier literature. Perhaps it can be argued that literary license may allow an author to expand a time frame as well as to collapse it in order to develop metaphorical meanings.

THE MORTALITY OF A GOD

Unlike any other character in the tale, Dimmesdale in this chapter castigated himself to a seemingly extreme degree. But then, it seems to be the nature of nightmares to worsen the outcome of fears we harbor. To continue with the allegorical meanings, it would appear, then, that Hawthorne emphasized more of the mortal aspects of the Redeemer's nature in his suffering than of his god-like or divine aspects. Then again, in some Christian creeds, the agony of hell seems to be a physical as well as a spiritual experience embodying the depths of the nether world. It may even be concluded in the Christian mind that the experience of the Redemption was the depths of hell itself.

Perhaps Hawthorne is picking up on the response of the man from Nazareth himself when he was addressed as "Good Master" by one of his would-be followers: "None is good, save one, that is, God." One possible meaning of that statement might be that perfection or complete goodness cannot be achieved in mortality, even for a mortal god, because its nature has fallen too far below that state of existence where conditions are favorable for continuous and ultimate goodness. As a mortal being, the Nazarene was also susceptible to passions and desires, conditions inferior to those in a state of existence where such passions are purged.

Thus Hawthorne appears to assume the liberty of expounding upon those passions that might have afflicted the Redeemer, but to which the Nazarene evidently never succumbed. Indeed, Hawthorne seems to exaggerate the intensity of emotions experienced by Dimmesdale because of the extreme sensitivity of the man. Perhaps the Nazarene, who identified himself as the Jehovah, the Creator come down, descending below all things, would thus have extreme or greater internal reactions to the sinfulness of the mortal nature, or the sensations of its agonies, than any other being because of the greater disparity between his spiritual purity and the composite Agony. As a vast contrast that magnifies the experience, it might be compared to the sun falling into a thick, dark hole that consumes light.

THE PROMISED MEETING

Of those that pass in the night, Dimmesdale invited only Hester and Pearl upon the scaffold. Holding hands upon the scaffold, Dimmesdale, Hester, and Pearl comprise "an electric chain." As soon as he touched Pearl's hand,

> there came what seemed a tumultuous rush of new life, other life than his own . . . as if the mother and child were communicating their vital warmth to his half-torpid system. (153)

This surge of new life seems a foreshadowing of the better life, which Pearl seems to represent, and which the future may bring when the clergyman has in actuality passed the ordeal for which he is destined. Little Pearl herself is "a symbol, and the connecting link between" (154) Dimmesdale and Hester; and the three are destined to stand together "at the great judgment day!" (153) Symbolizing humankind, Pearl appears to be the connecting link between the divine element and the material element of nature. Hawthorne may have had the resurrection of the great judgment day in mind when he had Dimmesdale promise Pearl that he will stand with her and Hester later. That promise betokens some sense of authority, which the resurrection will certainly require.

The interchange he has with Pearl is worth discussing in detail because of the symbolic meanings implied.

> "Wilt thou stand here with mother and me, to-morrow noontide?" inquired Pearl.

> "Nay; not so, my little Pearl!" answered the minister; for, with the new energy of the moment, all the dread of public exposure, that had so long been the anguish of his life, had returned upon him . . . . "Not so, my child. I shall, indeed, stand with thy mother and thee one other day, but not to-morrow!"

> Pearl laughed, and attempted to pull away her hand. (153)

Pearl is only three years old, and allegorically this age may represent the meridian of time. Intuitively she realized that the confession Dimmesdale must make must take place soon, at noontide, in the meridian of day. But the confession, the occurrence of which may symbolize the Redemption, does not seem to constitute fully the meaning of "standing together." That standing together in an electric chain might suggest a rising from a separateness, as in a resurrection, into a continuous and energetic connection toward some worthy goal. Perhaps Pearl laughed because she knew better than Dimmesdale what his destiny is, and pulled her hand away because he is not being true to the need of confession to his responsibility in the connection between them. Or perhaps her laughter reflects the gaity of the prospects of the promised being fulfilled. She persisted to remind Dimmesdale of it, of which he is equally aware and fearful, and referred again to noontide, as though that is a critical time. Hawthorne's repetition of the promise may highlight its emphasis:

> "But wilt thou promise," asked Pearl, "to take my hand, and mother's hand, to-morrow noontide?"
>
> "Not then, Pearl," said the minister, "but another time!"
>
> "And what other time?" persisted the child.
>
> "At the great judgment day!" whispered the minister . . . . "Then, and there, before the judgment-seat, thy mother, and thou, and I, must stand together! But the daylight of this world shall not see our meeting!" (153)

Perhaps the emphasis was intended to relate the "standing together" to the day of judgment, not to "the daylight of this world," but to the end of the mortal world, when the resurrection is scheduled in time to occur. However, it will not occur at all, Pearl seems to warn, unless the confession is made.

A HEAVENLY SIGN

Before Dimmesdale finished speaking, Hawthorne interjects an incident that compounds the exclamation mark at the end of his last statement to Pearl, which in and of itself seems to signify an allegorical allusion. A bright meteor, interrupting his words, appeared in the heaven to light up the night, as though heaven itself confirmed Pearl's insight, and communicated to Dimmesdale what will happen if he fails to make his confession at the designated time. Seemingly, as a kind of foreshadowing of that judgment day, or pre-enlightenment, the sign illuminated the earth

> with a singularity of aspect that seemed to give another moral interpretation to the things of this world than they had ever borne before. And there stood the minister . . . and Hester Prynne . . . and little Pearl, herself a symbol, and the connecting link between those two. They stood in the noon of that strange and solemn splendor, as if it were the light that is to reveal all secrets, and the daybreak that shall unite all who belong to one another. (154)

The singularity of that moral interpretation, as has been advanced herein, perhaps points to the allegorical significance of the symbolic union of the threesome. The daybreak may symbolize the dawning of the resurrection of the body that belongs to the spirit, in a day when all truths may be revealed. Such a revelation is a frequently occurring theme in the tale; and Pearl strongly appears to be the symbol of this reunion, when the elements of nature (Hester) are joined with the element of the spirit divine (Dimmesdale), and a glorious race (Pearl) will inherit the earth. Standing in the "noon" of that splendor may indicate that the meridian of times is the time set for the Redemption, which confirms the validity of the resurrection. Hawthorne also appears to make that Redemption inclusive of another Christian theme, of oneness, wherein like spirits are joined together, because they belong together. Whether Hawthorne is thinking of family being together, or simply referring to the concept of a division into two or more worlds hereafter, either to which the race of humankind may belong, is not clear, and does not seem to be couched by any other references.

Hawthorne then further directs the attention of the reader to the higher meaning of his allegory by highlighting the significance of this singular heavenly event, as though it contained a message involving the destiny of the world. Signs, like all meteoric appearances and other signs in those days, were commonly considered as so many revelations from a supernatural source . . . . It was, indeed, a majestic idea, that the destiny of nations should be revealed, in these awful hieroglyphics, on the cope of heaven. A scroll so wide might not be deemed too expansive for Providence to write a people's doom upon. The belief was a favorite one with our forefathers, as betokening that their infant commonwealth was under a celestial guardianship of peculiar intimacy and strictness. (154)

Following the depths of despair, self-doubt, and self-condemnation which he has experienced during the night of the last few days, the young divine seemed on the verge of waking and may be intuitively sensing a revelation from the supernatural realm in this visionary rehearsal. Perhaps, as when one, at the threshold of waking, recognizes the night's experience as a dream, and may see its relevance to his present delimmas, Dimmesdale perceived it as a revelation. The bright meteoric light seems a revelation that confirmed not only Dimmesdale's destiny and his need to confess in the light of day, at noontide, as Pearl has been indicating intuitively, but also the destiny of nations. It signals a people's doom but for some celestial guardianship that must be heeded and obeyed with strictness. This revelation, in the "awful hieroglyphics," seems to portray a doom for the people of the earth, as expansive as the heavens, unless the young divine heeds the urgings of Pearl to confess at noon day. To the Christian, under celestial guardianship, the whole world may depend upon the effects of the Redemption.

A DULL RED HIEROGLYPH

Dimmesdale sees an additional aspect within the sign, and Hawthorne appears to indicate that only Dimmesdale sees it because of a mental state of guilty imagination. But it is Hawthorne's style to say one thing and mean another

We impute it, therefore, solely to the disease in his own eye and heart, that the minister, looking upward to the zenith, beheld there the appearance of an immense letter,—the letter A,—marked out in lines of dull red light. (155)

Hawthorne has now connected the token of the scarlet letter with several themes of his allegory. This sign at the "zenith" is the same scarlet A that Hester has carried with her, into which she has fashioned the clothing of Pearl, and which is burned upon Dimmesdale's chest, the same sign that Chillingworth has stealthily discovered upon the minister's body. Just as the sign upon his chest seems psychologically induced, the sign in the sky seems also to be a configuration formed in his mind, perhaps a purely intuitive moment. Perhaps Dimmesdale alone saw the sign in the heavens because it was a Providential reminder to Dimmesdale alone that he must fulfill his destiny and make his confession. The lines of dull or dim red light of the letter A may not only signify the bloody stripes upon his back, but may also allude to and connect with the armorial legend embossed upon the tombstone over the sunken grave where Hester and Arthur have been buried. This destiny seems written "over the whole expanse of nature, until the firmament itself should appear no more than a fitting page for his soul's history and fate" (155). The Christian creed sees no less, in the Redemption, as an eternal, all-encompassing Act of Passion that embodies the history and fate of humanity.

However, out of respect for the reader, and for the varying opinions of those whose regard for common folklore may not be so intuitively digested as it is logically consumed, Hawthorne is quick to include a different view of the incident, as he does in so many other cases.

> In such a case, it could only be the symptom of a highly disordered mental state, when a man, rendered morbidly self-contemplative by long, intense, and secret pain, had extended his egotism over the whole expanse of nature . . . . (155)

Hawthorne does not let the reader forget that he is justapositioning two different values in his tale, logical deduction vs. intuition, and perhaps is leaving the reader to find his own conclusions about his allegory. Implied in the quote above is the idea that Dimmesdale's vision of his destiny, which includes the "whole expanse of nature," is simply a stroke of egotism. Either the Nazarene was whom he claimed to be, or a self-deluded lunatic. Not that that thought has not been contemplated by other minds before in regard to Dimmesdale's representation. To them, that one man could be the Savior of the human race is an egotistical claim apparent.

To back up this contrast, as the protagonist gazed upon the hieroglyphic, he was aware of the presence of none other than the antagonist, Chillingworth, at whom Pearl was pointing her little finger. He was awakened from his fancy, so to speak, perhaps as a signal that unless he fulfilled that destiny, Dimmesdale will lose his soul to him, who, "like the arch-fiend," is beholding the scene, careless "to hide the malevolence with which he looked upon his victim . . . with a smile and scowl, to claim his own" (156). Pearl was probably prophetically highlighting this fact to Dimmesdale's mind, inasmuch as she instinctively knew what the future held for her, as offspring of the divine, if he escaped his nemesis, Chillingworth. Dimmesdale sensed this evil, but still did not know as yet the part that Chillingworth plays in his mission and destiny.

It appears that Hawthorne, speaking for the Chritian ethic, is saying that the commonwealth of humankind is under the guardianship of Providence, which has written "a people's doom" and "the destiny of nations . . . in these awful hieroglyphics, on the cope of heaven." It appears to be a sign to Dimmesdale alone that the destiny of nations depends upon his fulfillment of his mission, that he must first escape the grasp of the Adversary to prevent the doom of humanity. Hawthorne may be referring to the Biblical accounts of the future, wherein warfare, pestilence, and other forebodings portray the end and doom of the world. Other signs forecast in their awful hieroglyphics in the expanse of heaven a destiny for many nations.[3]

To recapitulate, the promise of the hieroglyph is conditional: the demands of justice requires that the office of the scarlet letter be fulfilled in order that the destiny of uniting "all who belong to one another" may be accomplished: it is not so much adherence to the proscriptions of man-made law that merits this unity, but the acts of grace and compassion, of which acts Dimmesdale's plays a crucial roll. In other words, to the Christian persuasion, the Redeemer, then, is the ultimate Protectorate; and the Redemption, the high noon of humankind's history and fate.

There are other indications that the sign in the sky is not illusionary, that what Dimmesdale is experiencing is neither a dream, but perhaps a vision, elements of which were not "addressed to him alone" (155). Apparently a "gray-bearded sexton" also saw the sign, and the next day, when meeting Dimmesdale, construed the letter A to mean Angel, or the spirit of the dead governor. A parenthetical comment by Hawthorne also suggests, since others saw it, that the sign actually appeared and portended an omen, though interpreted perhaps differently by its observers, as in most portents. What the sexton saw was interpreted differently than what was perceived by Dimmesdale:

> Oftener, however, its credibility rested on the faith of some lonely eyewitness, who beheld the wonder through the colored, magnifying and distorting medium of his imagination, and shaped it more distinctly in his after-thought. (155)

Although mindful of the varying opinions formed by the imaginations of the mind, for a better fit, of those who may be witness to the same event, Hawthorne adds another comment associating the sign also in connection with the presence of Chillingworth, as though to espouse an opinion of his own.

> Certainly, if the meteor kindled up the sky, and disclosed the earth, with an awfulness that admonished Hester Prynne and the clergyman of the day of judgment, then might Roger Chillingworth have passed with them for the arch-fiend, standing there, with a smile and a scowl, to claim his own. So vivid was the expression, or so intense the minister's perception of it, that it seemed still to remain painted on the darkness, after the meteor had vanished, with an effect as if the street and all things were at once annihilated. (156)

It appears here that the sign also foretold to Dimmesdale the destruction of the earth—in connection with the presence of Chillingworth, if he could have been seen as the arch-fiend—an awfulness that awaits Hester, Pearl, and Dimmesdale on the day of judgment, if he does not heed Pearl's admonition.

THE ANGEL APOLLYON

At the same time the Arch-fiend appeared, Dimmesdale shuddering inquired about Chillingworth's identify from Hester, then from Pearl, who appeared to mock the minister for refusing to promise his confession at noon.

"Thou was not bold!—thou wast not true!" answered the child.

"Thou wouldst not promise to take my hand, and mother's hand, to-morrow noontide!" (157)

Again, the theme of being true to one's self highlights the theme of a premonitioned destiny at work behind the interrelationships of the characters. The child-like impatience of Pearl with Dimmesdale's silence appears to be an expression of Hawthorne's philosophical pondering; and Dimmesdale's later confession, when he has boldly been true to his mission, and held hands with both Hester and Pearl upon the scaffold, seems to reflect Hawthorne's conclusions about the solution to the problem of life's miseries.

Hawthorne's commentary links "a people's doom" with Dimmesdale's secret pain, as though the crimson sign in the heavens was "no more than a fitting page for his soul's history and fate" (155). This commentary possibly indicates reference to the pains of the Redemption as a possible reflection of the consequences that might befall a people who ignore "a celestial guardianship of peculiar intimacy and strictness" (155). In addition, that Chillingworth, the arch-fiend, and Dimmesdale are companions, and yet enemies, may perhaps suggest the depths of punishment into which the Redeemer had to descend in order to free humankind from the effects of its hostility.

ON WAKING UP

There is something peculiar about Chillingworth's interruption of Dimmesdale's conversation with Hester and Pearl upon the scaffold. As soon as Chillingworth speaks to the young minister, Hester and Pearl seem to completely disappear! Neither Dimmesdale nor Chillingworth address Hester and Pearl from this point to the end of the chapter. It is as though Dimmesdale is half awake and still dreaming as he sees Chillingworth approach the scaffold, and is fully awake as Chillingworth first speaks to him. The physician's address seems to comprehend Dimmesdale's sleep-walking wakefulness in the middle of a conversation that took place while he was dreaming.

"Pious Master Dimmesdale! Can this be you? Well, well, indeed!

We men of study, whose heads are in our books, have need to be straitly looked after! We dream in our waking moments, and walk in our sleep. Come, good Sir, and my dear friend, I pray you, let me lead you home!" (157)

This comment carries the implication that Chillingworth thinks Dimmesdale has been caught walking in his sleep. It thus mitigates against the possibility that Hester and Pearl were ever present upon the scaffold, and suggests that his midnight vigil was both a somnolent reverie and wakeful visionary interpretation of the sign which he beheld in that peculiar state of consciousness. As he woke, the divine yielded himself, "with a chill despondency," to be led away home by Chillingworth. This short scenario may have another parallel to the life of the Nazarene, who, after his night's vigil in the Garden, was led away by his enemies also, perhaps with a chilled despondency likewise to betrayal by an alleged friend.

Dimmesdale doesn't really know if his night's vigil was real or only imagined in a dream, as revealed in his conversation with the sexton: "so confused was his remembrance, that he had almost brought himself to look at the events of the past night as visionary" (158). The minister's vigil, then, appears to be a sleep-walking vision of what is expected of him, and the consequences for either case of fulfilling or failing his destiny.

HANDLING SATAN WITHOUT PROTECTION

Hawthorne concludes the chapter with the second parable of a sexton, a clergyman who digs graves. The first reference was only a simile used in the chapter highlighting the relationship between the leech and his patient, wherein the former is compared to a sexton digging in a man's grave for some jewel hidden on his breast. In this chapter, a flesh and blood sexton meets Dimmesdale following a great sermon he has delivered on a Sunday, and returns one of his black gloves left at the scaffold the previous night. The entry of the parable of the sexton a second time into the tale might symbolize the reality of the impending death to which the man of Nazareth, knowing his historical fate, must submit himself, with resignation and a pure heart.

But the glove is more than evidence to Dimmesdale that he had been upon the scaffold. Referring to Satan, the sexton tells Dimmesdale he "must needs handle him [Satan] without gloves, henceforward" because "a pure hand needs no glove to cover it!" (158) The implication is that he will need both gloves, until his heart is pure, if he is to escape his nemisis. The need for the gloves may indicate the fact that Dimmesdale has not yet fully weathered the trials coming. The temptation to flee has not yet entered his head, but will, and he must meet his destiny with a pure heart and clean hands. That the gloves are black may indicate that, unless he removes them with a purity of purpose, true to his destiny, the destruction of darkness, perhaps as seen in the absence of the meteor, will be imminent.

The sexton also referred to the same letter A that had been seen in the sky the night before, "a great red letter in the sky,—the letter A,—which we interpret to stand for Angel" (158), signfying notice of Governor Winthrop's death. That others had seen the hieroglyph is indicative that the sign in the sky was an actuality. Whether the Angel signified that Winthrop's soul was taken to heaven or elsewhere is not directly commented on by Hawthorne. But his novel indirectly speaks for the angel as a harbinger of ill, a notice of the death of Winthrop, the staunch founder of a theocractic government, who had little regard for democracy or antinomian dissent. His expulsion of Anne Hutchinson from the Massachusetts Bay Colony does not seem to set well with Hawthorne in his novel.

From this point in Hawthorne's book, it might be helpful to summarize the analogy of Dimmesdale's comparisons to the Nazarene, by intermixing the two, to show the obviousness of the similitude. The Biblical text relates an angel that was released from the bottomless ocean to wreck his havoc upon the new world, probably in consequence of those who have not heeded the watchful guardianship and moral code of Providence. Out of revenge, for being cast into the wilderness, without a household fire, he would steal the pearl of great price from the bosom of the Redeemer, perhaps a treasure that assures the dead of life hereafter; but he must first thwart the divine's destiny in order to claim humankind as his own household, with its fireside warmth. It is the Christian's confidence that the Redeemer had a vision of his mission, and a knowledge of the consequences of his failure or success to fulfill his destiny, for which he was determined to do his duty, and of which his parishioners were confident of his success. That mission appeared to include an inordinate amount of pain, shame, and guilt, an ordeal to which he was steadily faithful, despite a continuous awareness of his enemy's presence. To redeem humans from their fallen condition, he must not abandon them, but own up to his relationship with the "community of mankind," and pay the penalty for his responsible part in their creation.

Having given the reader a closeup of the protagonists and the antagonist, Hawthorne turns next to a different view of Hester. He reveals the conflictful nature between her heart and mind as he examines the extent to which her intuitive sense is marginalized or overwhelmed by her Puritan environment; he insinuates a reason for her devoted loyalty to Dimmesdale, and the token of their bond; and he envisions her faint hope of some future transfiguration.

CHAPTER 13

ANOTHER VIEW OF HESTER

What profit hath a man of all his labour which he taketh
under the sun?
I have seen all the works that are done under the sun; and
behold, all is vanity and vexation of spirit.[1]

For, behold, I create new heavens and a new earth: and the
former shall not be remembered, nor come into mind.[2]

The two passages above form a contrast, seemingly analogous respectively to the first obvious view, at the surface level of the tale, and the second intended, at the allegorical level, which Hawthorne may have staged for the mind of the reader to conceive, once Hester's role as a personification of nature is deciphered. The former pictures life as a depressing state, and the latter promises a better; and both views are advanced alternately, as the warmth of intuition vies with cold speculative logic for a different, more elevated view of her signification.

The first view of Hester in the story line was the implication that she has had an illegitimate child and is doomed to a life of ignominy by the Puritan code. In her sinful state, she was shunned by society, had become a hiss and a byword, and was openly scorned and mocked. Such is the picture Hawthorne seems to portray as one view of mankind's nature, which conceives of no more purpose in her destiny than ignominy and death. Hester endured seven years in resignation to a joyless life by the stigmatization with which the religious community had publicly branded her. This cheerless life seems the life of the typical Puritan perspective, which would diminish the enjoyments of life by denying the passions of the flesh, as though their creation was, at best, a mistake, and, at worse, an abomination. Such a view of Hester as a personified perspective of nature, depicts a view of human nature as ignoble and depraved during the lifetime of the world, and, therefore, of questionable value in the hereafter. This chapter paints another view of Hester, perhaps Hawthorne's perspective of the more noble purpose of mankind's nature, and her future prospects.

Another and different view of Hester, growing out of the many good deeds she did, became that of a "Sister of Mercy" (161). The scarlet letter she wore began to lose its symbol of ignominy, and the community she served began to frame a different view of her and the icon she wore. Not only is the reader provided evidence to see a transformation of character and society, but also to see a modification or reversal of meanings as well. Just as Hawthorne is changing the minds of his readers towards his characters, so also is he changing the meaning of the scarlet letter A to reflect its greater signification. And the change has happened within a period of seven years.

LOVE AND HATE

Hawthorne begins an essay in the narrator's comments that connects the theme of the universal heart with his characters, who, over a period of seven years, have changed their view of Hester and her scarlet letter.

> It is to the credit of human nature, that, except where its selfishness is brought into play, it loves more readily that it hates. Hatred, by a gradual and quiet process, will even be transformed to love, unless the change be impeded by a continually new irritation of the original feeling of hostility. In this matter of Hester Prynne, there was neither irritation nor irksomeness. (160)

The Puritanic hatred bred by the hostility of its code is being changed by Hester's absence of irritation or hostility with her persecutor's. As a figure of human nature, her native capacity to love, by her humble and unresponsive reactions to the scorn once focused upon her, was being returned by an adoration from those she served selflessly. Thus, Hawthorne has perhaps demonstrated, years ahead of Edwin Markham, the truth of his adage, "All that we send into the lives of others comes back into our own." In his quote above, Hawthorne may also be hinting that, were it not for the constant irritating influence of the Adversary, humanity's nature might be more inclined to be loving, and more likely to rebound from moments of selfish lapses. Thus Hawthorne's later conclusion: "In the spiritual world, the old physician and the minister—mutual victims as they have been—may, unawares, have found their earthly stock of hatred and antipathy transmuted into golden love" (261).

> Hester's nature showed itself warm and rich; a well-spring of human tenderness . . . . None so ready as she to give of her little substance to every demand of poverty" (161)

Acknowledging "her sisterhood with the race of man," she visited "[i]n all seasons of calamity . . . the outfcast of society."

> not as a guest, but as a rightful inmate, into the household that was darkened by trouble; as if its gloomy twilight were a medium in which she was entitled to hold intercourse with her fellow-creatures" (161).

Hawthorne may be saying that it may be the right of mankind's nature, by the right of its creation, because of her unfortunate lapse into mortality, to be visited by a compensating gift of mercy, when troubled, in view of the fact that the inborn fallen nature of humankind is common to all. The symbol of that love and promise of mercy glimmers in "the embroidered letter, with comfort in its unearthly ray" (160-161). We note the particular significance that it is the letter "embroidered" by Hester that casts its ray of heavenly light: "The letter was the symbol of her calling," as though Hester's mercy upon the troubled few was a forebearer of Mercy yet to come to many.

THE EFFECT OF THE SCARLET LETTER

In this chapter Hawthorne comes closest to identifying what the scarlet letter really symbolizes. Although the effect of the letter upon Hester herself is opposite to its effect upon those who find only praise for her compassionate and servile nature, Hawthorne achieves this identity largely by the measure of its effects. This two-sided effect in a way is like the light of a red letter which, engraved in the center of a black field, upstages the background from whence it comes. Formerly a token of her sin, the scarlet letter to others had become

> the taper of the sick-chamber. It had even thrown its gleam, in the sufferer's hard extremity, across the verge of time. It has shown him where to set his foot, while the light of earth was fast becoming dim, and ere the light of futurity could reach him (161)

The scarlet letter has become a symbol of love and healing, a small light perhaps exceeding the limits of the short time span of earth's seven years. Perhaps it quickened the path of life, though its present guides of Puritanism were becoming dimmer. Perhaps it gave the sufferer hope "across the verge of time" before finally the bright light of futurity comes to give him/her the fullness of rest, love, and healing. In addition, besides its comforting influence upon Hester's fellow-creatures, one of its effects, though questionable at the surface level, yet favorable upon Hester at a deeper, was a strong bond between Dimmesdale and herself that could not be broken.

> Hester saw—or seemed to see—that there lay a responsibility upon her, in reference to the clergyman, which she owed to no other . . . . Here was the iron link of mutual crime, which neither he nor she could break. Like all other ties, it brought along with it its obligations" (160).

Hester has an intuitive glimmer, despite the dim sophism of Puritanic pedagogy, of some connective debt with the alleged author of her child, that could not go unpaid, a bond, with obligations, that could not be broken. This bond is the "mutual crime" that predisposed some obligations on both their parts for some future cause. The mutuality of that crime, whatever it is in the mind of Hawthorne, probably lies in the birth of Pearl, however and by whomever she was fathered. Her obligations are perhaps as evident, or as obscure, as his. In this chapter, Hester is seen as discharging hers with patience, long-suffering, and acquiescence.

We have come to understand that Hawthorne's conclusion about the fall of humankind's original nature is that its travesty appears to be a "crime," perhaps a wrong, that somehow involved Providence; and that silence on the matter may not have been a true show, that is, until the redemption was made, as posed by Dimmesdale in meeting his obligation later.

Perhaps Hester has embellished the scarlet letter out of a sense of her obligation to him, in intutive recognition of the bond the letter signifies between them. What Hester saw in Dimmesdale is probably a larger measure of what the recipients of Hester's grace saw in her, as symbolized by the "embroidered" letter. Perhaps this sens of obligation is what humankind's nature intuitively senses in the Redeemer, a promised resolution to the problem of mortality. Perhaps Hawthorne viewed the Redemption as a dutiful obligation that was encumbant upon Deity to fulfill, perhaps as a right of mortal nature due to the seeming wrongness of her fall.

The critic, focused myopically on Hawthorne's tale alone, probably thinks it is Dimmesdale who owes something to Hester; although that seems true at the surface level, at the allegorical level it appears that Hawthorne has aligned the allegiance differently and properly. Allegorically, the bond between Deity and human nature is that of the relationship and obligation of the Creator to the created, and the created to the Creator. It is probable, then, to hold to the allegorical interpretation rendered herein, that Hawthorne may be thinking that the alleged "crime" committed on the part of Deity may have been the unforeseen mistake of mortality, if it was unforeseen; and that his obligation is to reveal his responsibility and, therefore, to compensate or render justice therefor. As Dimmesdale must be true to himself, even if it means revealing the worse, so should Providence, or at least," show some trait by which the worse may be inferred!"

The effect of Hester's "warm and rich" nature, "a well-spring of human tenderness" and mercy, first changes the attitude of her fellow creatures; and then "the rulers, and the wise and learned men of the community . . . [who] were fortified in themselves by an iron framework of reasoning," begin to change. "Day by day, nevertheless, their sour and rigid wrinkles were relaxing into something which, in the due course of years, might grow to be an expression of almost benevolence" (162-163). Hostility is being changed to benevolence, hate transformed into love. Likewise, the effect of the scarlet letter itself upon Hester's beneficiaries is so great that many people refused to interpret the scarlet A by its original signification. They said that it meant Able; so strong was Hester Prynne, with a woman's strength" (161).

Perhaps Hawthorne is cueing the reader to do the same, perhaps to interpret "Able" as Arthur, Arthur as Agony, and Agony as Atonement.

> It was none the less a fact, however, that in the eyes of the very men who spoke thus, the scarlet letter had the effect of the cross on a nun's bosom. It imparted to the wearer a kind of sacredness, which enabled her to walk securely amid all peril. (163)

A self-ordained Sister of Mercy (161), Hester is the nun in this metaphor. The effect of the cross upon those who received her acts of mercy seems to be the radiance of the promise of the Redemption, which she carries upon her bosom to token the bond between them. In like manner, perhaps to signify this bond, Dimmesdale carries the effect of the cross upon his own bosom, which intensified his appeal to his parishioners. We review that appeal:

> The people knew not the power that moved them thus. They deemed the young clergyman a miracle of holiness. They fancied him the mouthpiece of Heaven's message of wisdom, and rebuke, and love.In their eyes, the very ground on which he trod was sanctified. (142)

Perhaps Arthur's charismatric appeal is the hope of the ransomed that elicits from them feelings of gratitude, reverence, benevolence, and grace itself, much the same as from Hester's venerating public. Moreover, the effect of the symbol upon others gives Hester a kind of protective power because of its sacredness.

The effect of the symbol upon Hester herself, however, is different. As a gloomy symbol of infamy–"in respect to society," a negative and erring interpretation of flesh and blood by the Puritanic transvaluation of it—it aged her, physically as well as spiritually, perhaps by reason of her constant intellectualizing about it. The Puritan society had a negative outlook on the nature of mortal flesh, and that narrow perspective had its degeneration effect upon its adherents.

> The effect of the symbol–or rather, of the position in respect to society that was indicated by it–on the mind of Hester Prynne herself, was powerful and peculiar. All the light and graceful foliage of her character had been withered up by this red-hot brand, and had long fallen away, leaving a bare and harsh outline . . . . Even the attractiveness of her person had undergone a similar change . . . . her rich and luxuriant hair . . . was hidden by a cap [so] that not a shining lock of it ever once gushed into the sunshine. It was due in part to all these causes, but still more to something else, that there seemed to be no longer any thing in Hester's face for Love to dwell upon; nothing in Hester's form, though majestic and statue-like, that Passion would ever dream of clasping in its embrace; nothing in Hester's bosom, to make it ever again the pillow of Affection. (163)

Hawthorne seems to be describing the effect of death, perhaps not so much in a physical aging, as in a mental degeneration that has browbeaten and diminished her hope. Though she had been the epitomy of compassion and worth to her community, she believed there was little within her to be loved or embraced by passion. Once a beautiful woman, who defied the customs of her time, she had been changed in nature and character by those very customs. For her, as a personification of nature, "The scarlet letter had not done its office" (166), or at least, in the time frame of mortality. Though her effect on her neighbors had brought about a kind of tranformation, Hester saw herself and the world around her in a different light. That degeneration had come about because her mind had been brainwashed by the blackness of Puritanism,; and Dimmesdale the divine, her minister, is her only hope for a transfiguration, or retransfiguration.

INTUITION VS. SPECULATION

So why is Hester so downcast? In this chapter Hawthorne reveals in his narrator's commentary a value he places on intuition, perhaps more openly than in other places. Whether "intimations—so obscure, yet so distinct" (86), "instinctive knowledge" (114), or "spiritual instinct" (116), this medium of truth seems to have an unerring effect. If native sagacity is accompanied with "a nameless something more,—let us call it intuition" (124), judgments based on this medium of light, perhaps sent from the great and warming universal heart, "are often so profound and so unerring, as to possess the character of truths supernaturally revealed" (127).

On the other hand, without that "nameless something more," to Hawthorne, conclusions drawn purely by reasoning may be suspect, and possibly even destructive. Hester's intuition, or some other nameless attribute, appears to be on the wane and is being replace by "thought."

> Some attribute had departed from her, the permanence of which had been essential to keep her a woman . . . . Much of the marble coldness of Hester's impression was to be attributed to the circumstance that her life had turned, in a great measure, from passion and feeling, to thought" (163-164).

Speculation, therefore, "an iron framework of reasoning," seems to be defined by Hawthrone as using one's intelligence, or native sagacity, without the aid of intuition, the voice of the heart, or preternatural intimations, to make one's judgments. Hawthorne may be not so much as saying that speculation ages human nature as that it diminishes or downsizes its beauty and intuitive sensabilities.

Hester lived in "an age in which the human intellect, newly emancipated, had taken a more active and a wider range than for many centuries before" (164); that is, human nature in Hester's day was under the influence of intellectualism, a phase that encompassed religious thought more actively than in former times, which perhaps may have been more under the influence of supernatural revelations.

> Men bolder than these had overthrown and rearranged—not actually, but within the sphere of theory, which was their most real abode—the whole system of ancient prejudice, wherewith was linked much of ancient principle. (164)

To the reader, it might be a matter of speculation or intuition as to what Hawthorne is saying, or to which ancient principle he may be referring; but to this purveyor, it appears that Hawthorne's inmost Me is purporting, specifically, that Puritanism had imbibed of this spirit of theoretical reasoning, and had therefore lost some of the ancient principles, or truth, linked to ancient prejudice. Perhaps to Hawthorne, the faith of early Christians has been coined as ancient prejudice, or a belief not fully supported by hard evidence. Perhaps to him these ancient principles probably go back in time to their origin, in the Biblical record, from which modern Christianity, Islam, and Judaism have currently distilled their "customs," with some various theoretical rearrangements. Consequently, theorists have proffered alternate explanations to Biblical principles that have theoretically competed with, but have not actually overthrown them. Perhaps Hawthorne believed they still existed, though dimly, but with correspondingly diminished effect.

In context with the full commentary on the matter of speculation, it may be, in general, that Hawthorne is using the term "ancient prejudice" to refer to the religious orientation that once composed one's framework or base of thought, but had been somewhat replaced in measure, or rearranged, by the paradigm of secular theorizing. The Biblical text was once the primer for learning to read and write, and education was viewed as a means of ensuring loyalty to God, and, of course, the authority of the established religious order. But, as religion was separated from the educational curriculum, perhaps due to the divergence of belief systems, scientific analysis became the primer, and education was seen as a means of ensuring loyalty to the state. In that context, and within the framework of meaning more common to Hawthorne's day, the word, prejudice, might be closer to the meaning of prediliction, or belief, than to that of bias, or prejudice, as used today. Human nature, therefore, perhaps to Hawthorne, had gradually bought into, or conformed to, this spirit of the times, and Hester, likewise, had been thereby so effected.

> Hester Prynne imbibed this spirit. She assumed a freedom of speculation, then common enough on the other side of the Atlantic, but which our forefathers, had they known of it, would have held to be a deadlier crime than that stigmatized by the scarlet letter . . . . It is remarkable, that persons who speculate the most boldly often conform with the most perfect quietude to the external regulations of society. (164)

This comment by Hawthorne perhaps pinpoints his own reservations about purely rational thought in particular, and institutional conformity in general; and is reinforced by his descriptions of his characters and their susceptibility either to intuition or speculation. At the same time, Hawthorne may be perhaps leveling his remarks not so much at scientific theory as he is at ecclesiastical speculation or interpretation, which has strayed from ancient "principle." Perhaps, to "our forefathers, had they known of it," such susceptibility would have been "a deadlier crime than that stigmatized by the scarlet letter" (164). It may be that these forefathers were the ancients who framed the "whole system of ancient prejudice" around ancient principles. Hawthorne may be referring to the historical event known in Protestantism as the Reformation, or back further before the Dark Ages.

The concluding sentence in the above quote apparently speaks against conformity to a society that would seek to regulate, perhaps with some investiture of forcefulness, the minds of others not in agreement therewith. Puritanism, specifically, exerted this control, not only over its adherents, but also over "antinomians." Had Hester not imbibed of this particular speculation, Hawthorne interjects, she might have been another Anne Hutchinson, whom Govenor Winthrop had banished from the colony,

> as the foundress of a religious sect. She might, in one of her phases, have been a prophetess. She might, and not improbably would, have suffered death from the stern tribunals of the period, for attempting to undermine the foundations of the Puritan establishment. (165)

We must not forget, however, in the seven years of her misery, that her beliefs were largely expressed consciously to the reader in a rationality that was often contrary to her actions, which more often were seemingly motivated by intuition. Hawthorne appears to check the reader's descent into this similar "iron framework of reasoning" by highlighting the necessity of intuition:

> woman cannot take advantage of these preliminary reforms, until she herself shall have undergone a still mightier change; in which, perhaps, the ethereal essence, wherein she has her truest life, will be found to have evaporated. A woman never

overcomes these problems by any exercise of thought. They are not to be solved, or only in one way. If her heart chance to come uppermost, they vanish. (165-166)

The word "womankind" appears to be a substitution for humankind, but perhaps solely in the mind of Hester. To the reader, Pearl probably represents humankind, or womankind in Hester's frame of mind. Perhaps Hawthorne seems to be saying that humanity cannot solve the problem of life by speculation alone, that since "the whole system of ancient prejudice" has been overthrown or rearranged by it, unless some infusion or reinfusion of the heart occurs, we are as hopeless as Hester; or that the problems of life can be solved only by the compassion of the heart, or by the mighty change of evaporating the ethereal essence of life from its body. In other words, perhaps, dying solves all problems of mortal life.

Hawthorne interjects an equation of what might have been squandered in the overthrow:

> It was due in part to all these causes, but still more to something else, that there seemed to be no longer any thing in Hester's face for Love to dwell upon; nothing in Hester's form, though majestic and statue-like, that Passion would ever dream of clasping in its embrace; nothing in Hester's bosom, to make it ever again the pillow of Affection . . . . Such is frequently the fate, and such the stern development, of the feminine character and person, when the woman has encountered, and lived through, an experience of peculiar severity. (163).

Perhaps by reason of being subject to the impact of age, and experiencing the peculiar severity of mortality, nature has been denied the Love and Passion needed to retain its Affectionate heart. Apparently Hawthorne thought, if his private philosophizing is really at the core of the allegory, that "the whole system of ancient prejudice" was linked to ancient principles—let's say, Passion and Love—but modified by more sophisticated speculation or theorizing, of which the Puritanic experiment is one. So Hawthorne introduces, in the midst of Hester's degeneration, an equation in capitals that might provide for her transformation. We will see these elements of Love and Passion yet unfolding as to "whether Hester Prynne were ever afterwards so touched, and so transfigured" (164).

Hawthorne may be having Hester contemplate her nature and other options in order to elaborate upon the consequences of her options, as we mortals sometimes are prone to do in moments of depression and despair. When the world gets too much with us, in our weakest moments, we calculate or speculate upon the consequences of opting out. However, Hawthorne is not remiss in implying that such speculations of unaided intellect may be assisted from the nether world, the dark side of the spiritual realm. It seems clear that Hawthorne favors this rational option no more than the option of Hester and Dimmesdale running away back to England.

In the above paragraphed quotation, Hawthorne may not only be figuring the physical effect of the fall upon mortality, but also symbolizing a spiritual degeneration of humanity during mortality. This degeneration may have occurred due to the intellectual rearrangements of ancient principles due to a loss or lack of that spiritual substance Providence imparts so subtly. Perhaps to Hawthorne, the influence of the theories of the learned, in fostering this spirit of speculation, might cast a spell, as in the spell of Puritanism, under which little in life may seem attractive enough as to be worthy of another moment of Passionate recreation.

Using the Romantic symbol of women possibly to represent civilizations, Hawthorne may be proclaiming that this fallen nature of mortality, along with the false interpretations of the value of flesh and blood, has affected all womankind (the civilizations of the earth). Like Hester, each civilization has "encountered, and lived through, an experience of peculiar severity;" but no civilzation by intellectual thought can reinfuse its physical nature with its "ethereal essence, wherein she has her truest life," after that essence has evaporated. Perhaps Hawthorne is stating that mortality is not as desirable a life for any generation as was the immortality before the fall, or the immortality after humanity is ransomed from the fall. Hawthorne may be imputing contemporary Christianity with its inability to make mortality attractive enough to appear worthy of a refined transformation, and that something else is needed.

GARY P. CRANFORD

THE VANITY OF MORTALITY

It appears then, that Hawthorne is posing another philosophical question for the reader to think about in contemplating the effect of the scarlet letter upon Hester: is mortality really worth anything after all? Is this all there is? Hawthorne probably projected this question for the purpose of getting the reader to wonder if there is anything better, so as to explore the symbolic ramifications of his allegory. His tale dimly states that there is, but may only probably arrive through a transformation of society over several generations, if accompanied by a transfiguration performed through the office of the scarlet letter.

Representing nature, Hester had been charged by Providence with the assignment of birthing, cherishing, and blossoming the womanhood of Pearl (perhaps a Romantic figure for the civilization of humankind).

> Providence, in the person of this little girl, had assigned to Hester's charge the germ and blossom of womanhood, to be cherished and developed amid a host of difficulties. Every thing was against her.

> The world was hostile . . . . Indeed, the same dark question often rose into her mind, with reference to the whole race of womanhood.

> Was existence worth accepting, even to the happiest among them? (165)

So Hester had been browbeaten by the society of Puritans to conceive of herself, speculatively, as a principle of no worth; and apparently "it is true, the propensity of human nature [is] to tell the very worst of itself" (162). As a figuration of human nature, Hester's speculative moments were often introspectively denegrating and carried her to other extremes, one of which was her attitude toward Pearl, whom, we must remember, appears to be a figuration of humankind. In other words, human nature often questions itself.

Wherever Hester went, Pearl went. Humankind was in the care of mortality, "to be cherished and developed amid a host of difficulties." But for Hester, there had been opposition in all things, without much show of the universal heart. With this state of mind, Hester often was impelled to ask,

> In bitterness of heart, whether it were for ill or good that the poor little creature had been born at all . . . . At times, a fearful doubt strove to possess her soul, whether it were better to send Pearl at once to heaven, and go herself to such futurity as Eternal Justice should provide, (165-166)

At this point, Hester's thoughts of suicide and homicide are speculative reactions devoid of any investiture of intuitive grace. It seems a notion of anti-transcendentalism that, unaided nature, left with intelligence alone, speculates destructively, as though it receives its bidding from the dark side of the supernatural dimension. "Thus Hester Prynne, whose heart had lost its regular and healthy throb, wandered without a clew in the dark labyrinth of mind" (166).

STARTING ANEW

It was this frame of mind that made her sad and contemplate "such a hopeless task before her," that Hester formed a tenative conclusion: "As a first step, the whole system of society is to be torn down, and built up anew" (165). It is as though Hester is arguing within herself for an early millennium, and an earlier Armageddon before it. The concept of separating humankind from mortality was earlier addressed in the Governor's mansion, when the magistrates contemplated taking Pearl away from Hester, and she opposed the idea vehemently. Now she is debating within herself if life is worth it.

Such a thought has entered the minds of many a disparing soul, and, in their own behalf, as well as often in the case of others disparing in their charge, have followed through with the thought. We shall see in a forthcoming chapter another thought in the form of a similar escape, "Leave this wreck and ruin here where it hath happened! Meddle no more with it! Begin all anew!" (198) The idea of starting all anew again is no new idea, and likewise has it Biblical origins.

For Hester to contemplate doing away with Pearl and herself proposes allegorically the option of doing away with nature as well as humanity. But how does the whole system of civilization get torn down and started anew?

How do you snuff out humankind and nature in one swell sweep? If there is any allegorical meaning suggested in Hester's suicidal and homicidal speculations, then perhaps Hawthorne is having the reader deliberate on the question of whether or not the pains and miseries of this life would make another option more desirable, like starting life and nature all over again. Hester, in her blackest speculation toward ending Pearl's life and her own, may symbolize other options used by Providence to solve the problems of humanity, as in the Deluge of the Great Flood, or the pre-millennial destruction of the world. Whatever Hawthorne may have had in mind, the reader may wonder if Hawthorne's vision of a better world coming had more or less reliance upon humanity's technological advances, or to some "nameless something more."

The Christianity of Hawthorne's time, perhaps not as theologically diluted as it may seem to be today, presumed that the earth will be transformed under a new government near its end. Perhaps Hawthorne is being philosophical, if not Biblical, about the future; that is, it seems needful for the human race "to start anew" to rebuild "the whole system of society" from the ground up. But hopefully perhaps not as extensively as in the days of Noah.

However, notwithstanding the Deluge was a tearing down and starting over, the nature of humankind seems to have remained the same, or has repeated itself in the generations since from civilization to civilization. Neither has there been any mighty transformation of it. Though both the past and the future of Hawthorne's present seem to have involved a transformation of people, religion, and government, only the Transformation at the end, in the Christian's world, includes a change in the elements of the earth, and all aspects of the known world, as in Hester's nature. So the tranformation Hawthorne may have figured for Hester still seems futuristic.

As with Hester, human nature diminishes with the passage of time, is subject to harsh realities, and loses all its beauty. There is inherent in the very nature of our mortality an opposition in all things that results in a diminishing world. [See C. S. Lewis, The Problem of Pain.] But, as opposition in all things natural fosters atrophy, paradoxically, sometimes the force exerted equally to match or deal with the forces of opposition may build and strengthen the ability to overcome them. However, if "the change be impeded by a continually new irritation of the original feeling of hostility," that growth might be counteracted and result in hostility, according to Hawthorne's deductions. Hester showed such a development in her inward self; nevertheless, though her attitude was fatalistic, it was not hostile. Though she despaired, she was intuitively hopeful. Thought her physical beauty deteriorated, her spiritual stamina increased.

Hawthorne therefore seems to assume there is divine purpose in the existence of a mortal world, that Providence has designed it with a host of difficulties that, by their very opposition, may lead toward the development of a better world and a life successful to such an end. Love therefore may be able to transmute Hate and hostility into an awareness that fosters its extension. This essay is threaded throughout the allegory, perhaps as its more general theme, which is acted out by the characters to point to other levels of meaning.

A Transformation of Nature

One reason Hawthorne gives for this change of attitude towards Hester seems to lie within her nature. "Such helpfulness was found in her,—so much power to do, and power to sympathize" (161), a self-ordained calling of which the scarlet letter became the very symbol. Perhaps Hawthorne is saying that nature has an inherent sympathy it shares in common with its kind. Perhaps it is the humility of its nothingness that can soften the public mind toward generosity, which opens one's heart to sympathy and inclines one towards mercy, as in Hester's example. To the Christian faith, whatever its denomination, perhaps the Redemption is the greatest manifestation of that universal heart; and this one act of passion seems to be at work in the allegory, having its effect upon the transformation of humankind, perhaps as symbolized by the wearers of the scarlet letter, only, however, when it has done its office.

Another reason, if not the same, may lie within in the nature of humanity itself. A previous quote is repeated to emphasize this point.

> It is to the credit of human nature, that, except where its selfishness is brought into play, it loves more readily than it hates. Hatred, by a gradual and quiet process, will even be transformed to love, unless the change be impeded by a continually new irritation of the original feeling of hostility. (160)

Because she had never done anything to irritate their feelings, the good deeds that Hester did for her community gave them opportunity for their hatred to be transformed into a kind of love and adoration. Chiullingworth, on the other hand, deteriorated without redemption because of his hostility. Notwithstanding, at the end of his essay on love and hate (261), Hawthorne may be suggesting that the mercy of Providence may extend to all when those irritations are removed, even to those who have been been led to hate through hostile influences. Perhaps the makeup of human nature equips humankind with qualities that enable them to overcome any perspective or frame of mind, if these qualities are left to themselves and not impeded by other continuing hostile irritations. In other words, from Hawthorne's perspective, temptations from the dark side of life, from the arch-enemy who has "set his gripe" upon humanity (167), prejudice these qualities in the selfish person, and may lead to hostility and destruction.

The opposite is also true: influence from the caring end of the spiritual dimension can operationalize a series of reactions among people whereby grace is bestowed for grace received. Hester had this influence upon all, and appeared to derive her strength from her loyalty to Dimmesdale. If there were no temptations to prejudice the good qualities within humankind's nature, then perhaps "womankind" (humankind) could overcome any complexity of life.

Another reason for the change in the attitude of the people, if not the same, may lie in the effect or promise of the scarlet letter Hester wears without, but embodies within. "Womankind" may be inspired to do her best in the hope of Infinite love, of receiving grace from the Divine beyond, for the grace and mercy she bestows upon our fellowmen here. The greater our endurance of the misery of this life, the greater our need for relief and mercy, and our allegiance to and reliance upon the One who removes our pain.

This hope in the ability of human beings to change over time, especially in their outlook on nature itself, as in the case of Hester's society, seems one of the central themes or motifs of Hawthorne's novel. The scarlet letter becomes a symbol of love out of the grace bestowed by Hester upon her community. It is likewise a symbol of the bond between Dimmesdale and Hester and Pearl,and between Diety and the "communities of mankind."

A TRANSFORMATION OF SOCIETY

Hawthorne appears to use the ideal feminine nature of tenderness, compassion, and gracefulness as a standard of measurement toward which a society is being transformed for the better. He may even be using the concept of the feminist movement to symbolize movement in that direction. However, this transformation of reforms cannot be effected by speculative genius alone, but by some mightier change that might require both death and an upper thrust of the heart:

> A tendency to speculation, though it may keep woman quiet, as it does man, yet makes her sad. She discerns, it may be, such a hopeless task before her. As a first step, the whole system of society is to be torn down, and built up anew. Then, the very nature of the opposite sex, or its long hereditary habit, which has become like nature, is to be essentially modified, before woman can be allowed to assume what seems as fair and suitable position. Finally, all other difficulties being obviated, woman cannot take advantage of these preliminary reforms, until she herself shall have undergone a still mightier change; in which, perhaps, the ethereal essence, wherein she has her truest life, will be found to have evaporated.

> A woman never overcomes these problems by any exercise of thought. They are not to be solved, or only in one way. If her heart chance to come uppermost, they vanish (165-166)

Hawthorne might simply be speculating as to what might be if women could take over and change society by the pure exercise of their thought. Perhaps he thinks too much, or allows Hester to think too much, or thinks that humankind thinks too much, that women (the civilizations of mankind) can not overcome their problems with unaided intelligence. Thus, having given herself to speculation, Hester, "whose heart had lost its regular and healthy throb, wandered without a clew in the dark labyrinth of mind" (166). Thus, so to speak, human nature is lost without the grace provided by the intimations of the heart, emanating, perhaps, from the universal one. Representing a perspective or evaluation of the nature of humankind throughout the civilizations of man, Hester's mental state might possibly symbolize what has happened to the human race in view of forgotten "ancient prejudices." Given to the scientific mind, without the aid of the truest measure of the heart, mankind may be wandering about without any clue in the dark maze of her mind as to where civilization should be headed. Hawthorne may even be suggesting that the problems of humanity may not be solved at all until that mighty change happens. That change might not occur completely in this life, but only after the heart has come uppermost and the "ethereal essence,"—perhaps the spirit embodied within the mortal substance—has departed its weary world for a new.

THE MAGIC TOUCH

Hester doesn't pine for the good old days alone, but gives herself to her intuitive sense about the future as well as about the present and past. Other than ending her life and Pearl's, there is but one single event that can change Hester back into the beautiful woman she once was, a magic touch that will bring about a transfiguration of her nature at some unknown time.

> She who has once been woman, and ceased to be so, might at any moment become a woman again, if there were only the magic touch to effect the transfiguration. We shall see whether Hester Prynne were ever afterwards so touched, and so transfigured. (164)

The reader might ask what Hawthorne meant by Hester's ceasing to be a woman. What is this transfiguration that "we shall see" whether or not touches Hester later? And what transfiguration at the allegorical level could change Nature back into its earlier beauty?

In Hawthorne's narrative on womankind, the qualities of character with which he endowed Hester Prynne are probably those intuitive feminine qualities that kept her vibrant and enthusiastic about life, but had been lost by her "experience of peculiar severity" under the hand of the Puritanic inquisition. Representing the early civilizations of mortal humankind, Hester's loss of womanhood may also refer to the loss of an immortal state of bliss prior to the fall into mortality. Mortality may again become transfigured back into immortality upon some magic touch later by some special party or event.

It is noted that in Chapter 18, "A Flood of Sunshine," Hester is transfigured somewhat back into the beauty she once was by the magic touch of a decision she and Dimmesdale made to leave Boston forever together. The decision gives both of them an "exhilarating effect" of joy and "exquisite relief" in the hope of escaping from the dungeon of their gloom and despair.

> There played around her mouth, and beamed out of her eyes, a radiant and tender smile, that seemed gushing from the very heart of womanhood. A crimson flush was glowing on her cheek, that had been long so pale. Her sex, her youth, and the whole richness of her beauty, came back from what men call the irrevocable past, and clustered themselves, with her maiden hope, and a happiness before unknown, within the magic circle of this hour. (202)

But Hester's womanhood is restored only temporarily. At the allegorical level, this transformation may only be a prophetic foreshadowing, the actuality of which seemingly could not happen without her Redemption, of which Pearl is constantly and keenly reminding Dimmesdale and Hester. The decision they have made to run away back to England seems to have a magic tough transforming their state of misery to one of hopeful relief and joy. However, it is a temporary "transfiguration" based on an anticipation or false hope that is derived from a false plan that would counteract Providential destiny. In Chapter 21, "The New England Holiday," Hester is not a woman again, but is figuratively considered dead, or has no spirit or value worthy of sympathy. Whether Hawthorne meant to foreshadow the millenium as a holiday does not seem to be supported by other references, but a change of government, at least, is at hand.

That this transformation of the whole system of society is still futuristic may be insinuated, inasmuch as Hester's transfiguration never happened in Hester's lifetime. But a kind of transfiguration, or change in nature, is foreshadowed later, in Pearl's play with wild animals, in Chapter 18, seemingly as a premonition of what she symbolically represents. The time frame of Pearl's (humankind's) seven years of age, also seems to point to this period. Hester could not bring about this change of herself, but would need the help of someone else, as we shall see later when she takes a walk in the forest.

THE OFFICE OF THE SCARLET LETTER

Besides despairing over the significance of life, Hester's speculalations lead her to conclude that

The scarlet letter had not done its office" (166).

This statement is one of the few single and short sentence paragraphs in the book, with a singular significance, and the semantic emphasis deserves attention in connection with the time frame of the allegory. Hawthorne, at the surface level of the tale, may be referring to "the foundations of the Puritan establishment" (165), or, at a deeper, to the theological remnants of Protestantism, or all institutional religions, as having not effected much change in the world. Or he may be expressing his own conclusions, through the speculative, and perhaps fatalistic, mind of Hester, that the promise of the Redemption, the scarlet letter A, doesn't seem to have done much to influence humanity's nature for the better. There may not be much of a separation between the two suggestions, but it appears that Hawthorne is allowing Hester to explore all options to lead the reader to probe more intutively for Hawthorne's inmost Me, as he links his themes and character representations together.

So, wandering "without a clue in the dark labyrinth of mind," in one of her rational and speculative moments, Hester has seemingly lost touch with the one hope for redemption from her situation. Hawthorne has puzzled the reader, either to emphasize this destructive frame of mind, or to reveal a moment of intuition wherein she began to correct a mistake made earlier by such a confused attitude.

This sentence seems to be contained in the mind of Hester, and may not be a narrator's comment on that state of mind, nor relate to the allegorical significance of the letter. As a moment of truth for Hester, the thought might be a conclusion emanating from the dismal labyrinth of confusion in which she has found herself, or an epiphany focusing her attitude on her own particular part in the role she has intuitively fashioned around the letter.

ﾠ

Or Hawthorne may be saying, as the narrator, that the hope she had placed upon the letter had failed to give her the relief she felt she needed and deserved. What more could it have done for Hester than what she had not done already in the fruits of her labors? What was the true office of this red-hot brand, if not to have withered up "[a]ll the light and graceful foliage of her character," which it had very well done? Perhaps it was the office which she had intuitively given the scarlet letter, by all the particular elaborate embroidery with which she had embellished it, to signify some significant effect yet awaiting her; and she had not done her part in the office.

So, perhaps intuitively, in recognition of the present ineffectiveness of the office of the scarlet letter, her efforts became directed toward amending one mistake she had made in a moment of confusion between her intuition and her rationality. In the following and concluding paragraph of this chapter, Hester resolved to confront Chillingworth, to redeem herself from her pledge of silence about his identity, and to inform the young minister of Roger's intentions. In Hester's determination to act well her part, Hawthorne depicts a contrast between Roger and Hester, as a reflection of his characters' positioning themselves along the continuum of Hate and Love. Hester, directed by compassion, had benefited from the seasoning effected by her long and severe ordeal; and the physician, oblivious to it, had diminished in that primary attribute Hawthorne heralds in his tale.

> Strengthened by years of hard and solemn trial, she felt herself no longer so inadequate to cope with Roger Chillingworth . . . . She had climbed her way . . . to a higher point. The old man, on the other hand, had brought himself nearer to her level, or perhaps below it, by the revenge which he had stooped for. (167)

Hawthorne has suggested that what she needed "to keep her a woman" was a tranfiguration to make her the woman she once was, in whose face once dwelt something "for Love to dwell upon," whose form once was worthy of embrace, and whose bosom once was a "pillow of Affection" (163-164). Perhaps the aging of Hester represents the degeneration inherent in mortality that needs the resurrection, not only to return human nature once again to the beauty of immortality, but also to restore it to the more fitting instrument of Affection itself. This restoration appears to be a replenishment of nature that the Lord of Love delights to look upon and is eager to embrace. About this transfiguration, Hawthorne only says, "We shall see whether Hester Prynne were ever afterwards so touched, and so transfigured." Since Hester doe not undergo in such transfiguration in the tale, it seems Hawthorne has left the resolution of this hopeful prospect entirely to the reader's own intuitive conclusions.

CHAPTER 14

HESTER AND THE PHYSICIAN

> Woe to the inhabiters of the earth and of the sea! For the
> devil is come down unto you, having great wrath, because he
> knoweth that he hath but a short time.[1]

It was in uneasy ignorance that Hester met with Chillingworth the second time following her release from prison some seven years earlier. In her first, Hester had promised not to divulge his true identity to Dimmesdale. Reliance upon her intellect was not one of her strengths; but now that she has witnessed Master Prynne's degeneration, her better, though imperfect, understanding of his motives are more in accord with her instincts about him.

Perhaps Hawthorne is saying that human nature is much like that. From time to time, if we do not ignore it through our intellectual prowess, it senses some truths within us that might guide us through this "dark necessity." The adverse influences acting upon human nature in this hostile world may then eventually become identifiable during the interplay between the intellect and the intuitive sense.

Hester, in the full strength of her character, has now therefore resolved to confront Chillingworth with a determination to expose his identity to the young and suffering minister in an attempt to save him. In this second conversation with Chillingworth, since his appearance in Boston, the disclosure of his Satanic nature has come full circle. In this chapter, the reader catches a clearer view of the fallen angel, Lucifer, and another glimpse of the horror he senses he is yet to face.

AT THE WATER'S EDGE

Dispatching Pearl to play at the water's edge, Hester found the old physician gathering herbs "to concoct his medicines withal" (167) in a secluded part of the peninsula, where the sea has made inroads into the land. This location seems parabolic, as though the sea, representing the raw forces of those nether dimensions transcending present reality, has overflowed part of the civilized mainland; and Chillingworth, as a type of grim reaper, is gathering the spoils of the overlap thereof to make concoctions for his practice. The little pool formed by the ebb and flo of the sea appears to be a portion of the great sea on the other side of life that, with "the gleam of a kind of fragmentary smile," invited Pearl into its depths: "This is a better place! Come thou into the pool!" (168). Counterfeiting her image, the little pool seemed to reflect Pearl's representative counterpart: as Pearl herself may represent the freshness of life beginning before the vastness of eternity, the little pool may represent a portion of the vastness of death to those who are seduced by its enticements "along the moist margins of the sea" (168). She "flirted fancifully with her own image" (177), but without the fear and apprehension so typical of her mother's reasoning. She is confident of the future and faithfully senses victory over what enticements may lure her otherwise Pearl's flirtation with the dark side of nature and Hester's confrontation with Master Prynne may represent a comparison or contrast between pure intuition and intuition affected by intellectualizing. Hester's difficulty with her uncomfortable situation follows in short order Pearl's assurance as the master of her fate. When it comes to differentiating between good and evil, Pearl did not seem to have as much trouble as does Hester. In fact, in the very next chapter, "Hester and Pearl," Hawthorne makes this distinction fairly clear.

> In the little chaos of Pearl's character, there might be seen emerging—and could have been, from the very first—the steadfast principles of an unflinching courage,—an uncontrollable will,—a sturdy pride, which might be disciplined into self-respect,—and a bitter scorn of many things, which, when examined, might be found to have the taint of falsehood in them. (180)

Pearl's instinctive ability to recognize falsehood, or things tainted with them, highlights one of the themes of Hawthorne's novel. Discriminating or sorting out deceptions is one of the tools with which he manipulates the intuitive reader to probe for the deeper meanings of his tale; and he purposefully perplexes the reader as he, at the same time, encourages him/her to rely on intuition more than intellectual prowess.

So, as Hester has emboldened her courage to face Master Prynne and confront him with his deceptive ploys, Pearl has been sent to play barefooted at the edge of the sea with the shells and tangled seaweed. While Hester has gone to untangle herself from her own seaweed, in face to face confrontation with the derisive visage of a smirking devil (169), Pearl in "her small white feet," has dared to step into the water. In a sense, Chillingworth's ploys beckon deceptively from the depths of a bottomless pit; and Hester has gone, armed with a knowledge of the truth, just as plainly as Pearl can behold her own white feet, to be true to the insight she has gained from experience.

Thus, Hawthorne introduces Hester's confrontation with symbolic imagery similar to that noted earlier in connection with the sexton in Chapter 12, who returned a glove to Dimmesdale, and remarked, "A pure hand needs no glove to cover it . . . . And, since Satan saw fit to steal it, your reverence must needs handle him without gloves, henceforward" (158). As Pearl confidently played in her bare feet at the water's edge, and ignored the smirking derision from the depth of the pool, Hester, in a moment of intuitive insight, has taken off her gloves to correct a past error in judgment, which she made earlier when she allowed her rationality to sway over her intuition: she has gone to bare her soul's insight to an enemy for and in behalf of Dimmesdale's sake. Pearl instinctively knew she was in no danger of being deceived, and Hester has learned from experience somewhat to trust her intuition about Roger.

Perhaps Hawthorne has used this instance of Hester's truthful confrontation to exemplify what he means later by Dimmesdale's heartfelt request, "Be True! Be True! Be! True! Show freely to the world" the truth of the matter, even if you have to admit your own worst part of it. In this chapter, she admitted a mistake she had made, and Chillingworth, bless his lying soul, in a rare moment of truth, does the same, but, of course, reflects it's consequences back on Hester.

A PROPOSITION AND REPLY

Hester told the physician that she would have a word with him, that she had something to discuss with him. In Chillingworth's response, the reader may detect a note of sarcasm or mockery: "Aha! And is it Mistress Hester that has a word for old Roger Chillingworth?" (168), as though he was reflecting upon his first association with Hester some seven years past in which she became his Mistress in trade for a word of knowledge. Hawthorne also emphasized their former relationship by three times having Chillingworth call her Mistress. Perhaps Chillingworth is ironically referring to the word he had with Hester when he shared with her a knowledge that eventually led to the effect of her fall and ignominy, as we learned in Chapter 4. Now, she returned to assure him she knows him better and planned to reveal his plan to Dimmesdale. For Hester, this "word" may constitute a revelation of seven years of experience that nature might reveal to the arch enemy had he the capacity to see his own black feet. At the level of the allegory, perhaps Hawthorne is saying that now, after seven years of mortality, nature has finally acquired a bit of wisdom, or knowledge of good and evil, repents, and wants to set things right.

But Chillingworth, instead of listening to what she came to say, as though what she was saying was immaterial, interrupted Hester with a proposition. He relayed a suggestion from a certain local magistrate that her scarlet letter might be removed in regard for the "safety of the common weal"(169). Perhaps Roger had noticed the reversed effect of the scarlet letter on the community at Boston, and would like to change it. Though this proposition might appeal to her desire to get rid of the scarlet letter, and all the misery of ignominy it has caused her, she had already once denied the authority of the Puritan official to do so at that time, and is not seduced by his offer.

Hester had sensed instinctively that the scarlet letter meant something greater than a reminder of her present state of being, and replied that

> "It lies not in the pleasure of the magistrates to take off this badge . . . .
>
> Were I worthy to be quit of it, it would fall away of its own nature, or be transformed into something that should speak a different purport." (169)

The removal of the scarlet letter may signify at the allegorical level that the resolution of the burden of life is not to be determined by anyone other than proper authority, and, apparently, that can only be accomplished by Providential destiny. Seemingly, by some mystical power, perhaps when its office is fulfilled, the symbol and the stigma will fall away on its own accord or be transformed, as foreshadowed by her embellishment of it, to signify its greater and different purpose. Faced with opposition to her moral nature, Hester's intuitive sense does not fail to compel her best to rise to the occasion.

However, later, in the forest, in a moment of intellectual weakness and false hope, when she was again speculating with Arthur to rid themselves of the letter and its consequences, Hester then threw the "badge" away, as though that was one way of getting rid of it. This inconsistency reflects again on the thematic conflict between intuition and reasoning in Hawthorne's tail. But at this time, instinctively, it appears that Hester sensed that the scarlet letter could not be removed but in accordance with the higher authority, we conclude, of some Providential plan. The office of the letter, hidden from the view of the common and present world, and clothed in a bright hope, was intended to "speak with a different purport." Perhaps that purpose was not to proclaim the depravity of mortality and the unworthiness of its nature, but to speak for the transformation of humanity's mortal nature to its former beauty.

The plan to have the letter removed, as recommended by Chillingworth, was perhaps part of his diabolical plot to thwart this destined purpose. Since the "common weal" not only have actually benefited from Hester's compassionate service, by way of the letter, (and, thus, may possibly share in this blessed transformation), such a proposition does not really provide them safety from their arch enemy, but rather provides the reverse. It instead would remove the memory of her benevolence, and the image of its symbolic promise. Thus, to have the image removed, now that Chillingworth has become aware of its beneficial effect, contrary to what may have pleased him earlier, is now his present ploy, which Hester, at this time, refuses to consider.

APPROACHING THE END

Hawthorne emphasizes the time frame of the allegory, which appears to span from the beginning of life to its near end, by inordinately referring to it three times within the first two pages of this short chapter, in the same manner he referred to Hester and Chillingworth's former relationship. The first reference occurred when Hester noticed that Mr. Prynne had changed within the **past seven years**.

> All this while, Hester had been looking steadily at the old man, and was shocked, as well as wonder-stricken, to discern what a change had been wrought upon him within the past seven years . . . . [T]he former aspect of an intellectual and studious man . . . had altogether vanished, and been succeeded by an eager, searching, almost fierce, yet carefully guarded look. It seems to be his wish and purpose to mask this expression with a smile; but the latter played him false, and flickered over his visage so derisively, that the spectator could see his blackness all the better for it. Ever and anon, too, there came a glare of red light out of his eyes; as if the old man's soul were on fire, and kept on smouldering duskily within his breast, until, by some casual puff of passion, it was blown into a momentary flame. (169)

The red glare of Chillingworth's soul, perhaps the burning of fire upon Dimmesdale's breast, and the scarlet letter upon Hester's bosom are perhaps all related. In Dimmesdale, red may foreshadow the suffering of the Redemption, a relief for those of like compassion, and a similar fate for those impervious to emanations from the "universal heart." In Hester it may embody the hope of redemption from the degenerate state of mortality, and signal the promise of that deliverance. In Chillingworth, it may signify the the defeat of humankind. To the reader, it might signify the vanity of Old Scratch's exploitations; it may signal humankind's victory over the Fall; and especially it may premonition the abyss into which he may be cast. The red glare from Chillingworth's eyes seems to be a foreshadowed promise of a smouldering fire yet awaiting him and those who join him, at his invitation.

The second reference is to the length of time Chillingworth has employed his demonic skills to "undertake a devil's office" (170). **For seven years** the physician has sought the victory over the minister, and has thus transformed himself into a devil by devoting himself, for seven years, to the constant analysis of a heart full of torture, and deriving his enjoyment thence, and adding fuel to those fiery tortures which he analyzed and gloated over. (170)

One of the themes of Hawthorne's tale seems to be that character is formed by what it feeds upon. The Puritan character is formed by the theological blackness it feeds its adherents. The satanic character of Chillingworth is formed by his desire to destroy the character and soul of Dimmesdale, and thus lay claim to Hester's and Pearl's. And the characters of Hester and Dimmesdale are formed by their sensitivity to sin and the compassion they have developed thereby.

The third reference to the time frame of **seven years** span is the length of time she has kept her promise not to divulge Chillingworth's identity to anyone.

> "When we last spake together," said Hester, "now seven years ago, it was your pleasure to extort a promise of secrecy . . . . Yet it was not without heavy misgivings that I thus bound myself . . . . and something whispered me that I was betraying [my duty to the young minister], in pledging myself to keep your counsel." (170)

Although revealing Hester's own recognition of having failed to listen to her intuitive senses in the past, whether or not this particular reference also alludes to the lack of common knowledge of Satan's identify in the world, may be only a slight possibility. Nevertheless, it is apparent that Chillingworth had discovered Dimmesdale's identity; that Dimmesdale is about to learn the identity of Chillingworth; and that it is the discovery of Chillingworth's obvious representation that clues the reader to the more difficult allegorical identity of the other three main characters.

These three references are made to the time frame of the allegory perhaps to symbolize completion, as in the completion of time. Chillingworth is now viewed by Hester as an old man with evil intent, whose steady degeneration has been rewarded by his evident hostility. He has been discovered, his work revealed, and his degeneration of character evidenced and witnessed by Hester, who, as noted heretofore, is likely a personification of human nature. As Hawthorne has allegedly proposed, all will be discovered in time, in "the day when all hidden things shall be revealed" (131), perhaps at the end of the earth's time frame.

REVERENCE, LOYALTY, AND DUTY

Hester felt bound to some honor, duty, or sacred trust she owed the minister and saw herself as his bane and ruin. Most readers assume the opposite, that it was Dimmesdale that owed something to Hester. That she felt in debt to Dimmesdale is a significant paradox that highlights the importance of the allegorical relationship between the two. Not having revealed Chillingworth's identity to Dimmesdale, and learning of his adverse influence on the divine, Hester felt that she had betrayed him, which appears to be one of her intuitive moments, and is duty-bound to redeem herself from her mistake.

> Yet it was not without heavy misgivings that I thus bound myself; for, having cast off all duty towards other human beings, there remained a duty toward him; and something whispered me that I was betraying it . . . . (170)

Without the allegorical relationship herein ascertained, Dimmesdale is the one under the heaviest obligation. But understanding the relationship between the two, at the deeper level of intended meaning, illuminates the reasons for her sense of duty to the young divine.

In other words, the Creator invested his divinity into the natural elements of the earth to make humankind a half-glorified being composed of both spiritual and natural substance. Nature is therefore obligated to the Creator for this progressive endowment, even though it is in a fallen state. Perhaps Hawthorne recognized that it is in the nature of almost all nations on earth for humans to bow to the omniscience of some Divinity, in some numinous or intuitive recognition of some greater purpose in its creation; and he thus has made Hester honor-bound to the young divine to represent such.

So Hester Prynne is duty bound to Dimmesdale, and not to her husband, Master Prynne, whose hatred, concentrated upon the young divine, had consumed him with the burning fires of revenge. This loyalty to Dimmesdale, though questionable only at the surface level of the tale, may be meant to reflect the decision of early humankind, after the mistake of the fall, to continue in their devotion to the Creator. Or it may signify the nature of humanity to cling to a faith in Deity despite its knowledge and experience with the throes of mortality, and despite its susceptibility to the influence of Lucifer's hostility. Chillingworth's devilish fixation, therefore, may symbolize Satan's awful pledge to dethrone the Creator's rule over his creation by thwarting Providence's plan for humanity.

Hawthorne could be saying at the allegorical level that Providence won back the love and loyalty that may have been briefly lost with humankind's transgression in the Garden of Eden. Perhaps the Creator won back the Christian's devotion, when he presented to Adam and Eve a plan to side-step Satan's attempt to destroy them, a plan which would redeem humanity from the fall, whereupon Satan became its arch-enemy. His spiteful revenge, and apparent successes, may be the motive that triggers his presumptious claim upon mortal humanity for that brief relapse. Thus, Chillingworth purported his claim upon Hester and Pearl, though it is contingent upon his victory over Dimmesdale.

CHILLINGWORTH'S DEGENERATION

Whatever Chillingworth represented in his youth, Hawthorne has made it absolutely transparent that "the spectator could see his blackness all the better for" his false smile that "flickered over his visage so derisively" (169), a glow of evil intention he sought to repress as quickly as possible.

> Chillingworth was a striking evidence of man's faculty of transforming himself into a devil, if he will only, for a reasonable space of time, under- take a devil's office. (170)

This transformation is effected apparently by dwelling upon the dark side of nature, or the raw and rough of unrefined inclinations one may sense in the forest of life, from whence the Man of the Forest came, bringing his savages with him.

Perhaps Chillingworth represents the furtherest digression in nature, from the ideal of love to its most degenerate level. He has become the epitome of hate in consequence of looking for the worst in human nature. His transformation feeds upon that hunger. In Christian theology, whatever Satan was before his rebellion in heaven, he had become, against all that was divine, a fallen angel, a revengeful adversary and castaway, losing his place as the son of the morning, and any prospects for either redemption or advancement.

Chillingworth's revenge hinges on his accusation that both he, and Hester, have been wronged by Dimmesdale. Confronting the physician for his evil design upon the minister, Hester obtained a confession from Chillingworth of his responsibility in Dimmesdale's suffering:

> "[i]t was the constant shadow of my presence!—the closest propinquity of the man whom he had most vilely wronged!—and who had grown to exist only by this perpetual poison of the direst revenge! . . . A mortal man with once a human heart, has become a fiend for his especial torment!" (172)

Wherein did the young minister wrong him so basely? Was it fathering Pearl's child, or winning Hester's love and loyalty? Hester never loved Master Prynne, though "he had persuaded her to fancy herself happy by his side," (176) and she had left him several years earlier. Hester had become acquainted with Chillingworth some nine years before in the splendor of his aspiring youth, had married, and then left him two years later in disillusionment. Chillingworth had only himself to blame for Hester's alienation; and Dimmesdale's relationship with Hester, first as paster, and then as the probable father of Pearl, had little to do with Chillingworth. So that accusation appears to be a miscarriage of truth. It is likewise a lie at the allegorical level, as has been explained. The truth appears to be, that as the pastor reclaimed his parishioner from her fall, so the Creator reclaimed the created, despite her fall; and humankind was born into a fallen world that may resemble a marketplace.

A VISION OF HORROR

After confessing his evil intent, Chillingworth was suddenly filled with horror, as he had a glimpse of the hateful person he had become, perhaps intuitively sensing the consequence of such a state of being. Chillingworth earlier, in an instance of truthful discovery, when prying into the bosom of Dimmesdale for the secret he harbored there, had recognized the exceptionality of Dimmesdale, in a manner that projected the young minister in almost a Divine image. Again, at this moment of his truthful confession, he perhaps saw himself, if not for the first time, more fully as the person he had become; and he experienced a moment of horror at the insight, or the consequences of such.

> The unfortunate physician, while uttering these words, lifted his hands with a look of horror, as if he had beheld some frightful shape, which he could not recognize, usurping the place of his own image in a glass. It was one of those moments–which sometimes occur only at the interval of years–when a man's moral aspect is faithfully revealed to his mind's eye. Not probably, he had never before viewed himself as he did now. (172)

The physician perhaps saw his own moral nature as never before in one of those rare moments of self-insight. But this time, in addition to the vision of horror, a feeling of gloom remains with him. This insight also possibly foreshadowed that he will lose the battle he has engaged, and the victory will not be his. The horror of this second moment of truth for the master of lies lasts to the end of the chapter, and into the next, as it seems it is taking him much longer to compose himself, by the sheer power of his rational mind, with his own self-imaginations.

Hester had beheld in Chillingworth's face, before he saw it, another ruin she associated with her burden; and when she is asked what she saw, replied, "'Something that would make me weep, if there were any tears bitter enough for it.'"(170) This answer might appear reflective of Isaiah's lamenting the fall of Lucifer: "How art thou fallen from heaven, O Lucifer, son of the morning!"[2] But the tears she would shed are probably dried up by her "experience of peculiar severity" (163). Her comment may imply that it may be in the nature of God's creation, especially those whose tears commiserate for their own bitter travail, to weep over the destruction of any soul. Perhaps Hester's insight may also carry Hawthorne's own compassion for the ruin of another being, even that of Master Prynne, as is evidenced in his liberal essay on love and hate.

FLASHBACK TO SPLENDOR

After his momentary confession and self-discovery, Chillingworth gloomily referred to a time some nine years earlier when he was a splendid fellow.

"Doest thou remember me, Hester, as I was nine years agone? Even then, I was in the autumn of my days, nor was it the early autumn . . . . [A]ll my life had been made up of earnest, studious, thoughtful, quiet years, bestowed faithfully for the increase of mine own knowledge, and faithfully, too, though this latter object was but casual to the other,—faithfully for the advancement of human welfare . . . . Was I not . . . a man thoughtful for others, craving little for himself,—kind, true, just, and of constant, if not warm affections?" (172)

Hester answered that he was much more. In Chillingworth's unguarded and extended moment of gloom, perhaps in a rare moment of truth, he has seen what he once was and now sees, through Hester's eyes, what he is now.

One of the creationist's time-concepts of the earth's creation, and of its existence, popular at the time of the writing of *The Scarlet Letter*, is a period of seven days, or seven thousand years, or seven periods of time. Nine periods of time ago, in the time frame of the allegory, places one back in Biblical time definitely before the creation. It appears to be at a time when Lucifer would have been in the prime of his status as a son of the morning, perhaps seeking to excel above his kindred, primarily for his own glory, and secondarily for theirs, the latter "casual to the other." Assuming there was life in us, as in him, before the creation of the earth and its fall into mortality, Hawthorne may be inferring that Lucifer, like Job, was known before the creation of the earth when he was in the "autumn of his days," although Chillingworth now seems to be in the winter of his discontent. The concept of a premortal life may be founded upon Biblical text, one of which is in Job:

Where wast thou when I laid the foundations of the earth: declare, if thou hast understanding . . . .

When the morning stars sang together, and all the sons of God shouted for joy?[3]

RESPONSIBILITY FOR LIFE AS IT IS

While Hester beheld the ruination of Chillingworth in his features, she felt partly responsible for it. "The scarlet letter burned on Hester Prynne's bosom. Here was another ruin, the responsibility of which came partly home to her." (170). Now Chillingworth had not directly blamed Hester for his ruination; but she had partly blamed herself, confessed that responsibility openly, and he had consented to her acknowledgment.

> "I have already told thee what I am! A fiend! Who made me so?"

> "It was myself!" cried Hester, shuddering. "It was I, not less than he.

> Why hast thou not avenged thyself on me?"

> "I have left thee to the scarlet letter . . . ." (173)

In an allegory, the reader must assume that its author has an underlying purpose for various portions of the surface tale and decide which portions are designed to convey his alternate meanings, and which solely apply to the telling of the story. That Hawthorne has had Hester confess partial responsibility for Chillingworth's ruination may have significant allegorical undertones. How is it that mortal nature may be responsible for the Adversary's destruction? Considering Hester's confused state of mind and her tendency to introspectively speculate, it may not be sufficient to simply lay the matter in the lap of her rational nature. If there be any subterranean message intended, Hawthorne may be hinting that, in the onset of a crime, the victim victimizes the perpetrator. For example, the thief blames the victim for leaving her purse alone in plain sight, and the victim feels partly responsible. That Hester was curious enough to contract an alliance for knowledge without affection, and gullible enough to trust that contract for its claims, may account for her admission of being partly responsible for the outcome of the contract. When she fled from Chillingworth, she became party to the consequences he had to face. Perhaps the nature of victimized mortality is such that it intrigues the adversary to exploit it; and in exploiting it for his own vengeful and selfish satisfactions, he fosters a degeneration he might eagerly project upon a self-abasing victim for making him thus. Hester internalized the negations of her society; and human nature consents to its general measure by a preponderance of historical evidence, perhaps as Chillingworth astutely observed, "Good men ever interpret themselves too meanly" (122).

Of course, Chillingworth quickly recoiled from his moment of truth, "permitting the whole evil within him to be written on hs features" (172-173), perhaps in the glow of having projecting upon Hester his own responsibility for his ruination. It is noted that one of Lucifer's characteristic fatal flaws, in what scant Biblical text there is on him, is that he is a liar and a false accuser of the brethren.[4] During Chillingworth's conversation with Hester, his mind vacillated between truth and lie, between denial and confession. He did not at first blame himself for what he had made of himself, but blamed Hester and Dimmesdale instead, thus perhaps revealing in himself the mind-set of an arch criminal, who characteristically focuses the blame upon others. He called their relationship a crime, yet later said they were not sinful. He claimed to have eased Dimmesdale's torment, but then confessed to have fiendishly perpetuated that torment.

However, as soon as Hester was completely absorbed in self-abnegation, and completely wrapped up in her rational and fatalistic introspection, he was "unable to restrain a thrill of admiration" and allowed himself to concede to some responsibility for her fate, perhaps conceiving himself joyfully as the cause of her misery: "Woman, I could well nigh pity thee! . . . Peradventure, hadst thou met earlier with a better love than mine, this evil had not been." (173)

That Hester acquiesced to his blaming others, admitted that he had been deeply wronged, and begged him to forgive the young divine, revealed either her simplemindedness, her conscientious introspection due to a sense of guilt in recognition of her mortality, or her mental state of abject confusion due to the conflict between her speculations and her intuitive sense. Or possibly, Hester's assent may simply imply Hawthorne's supposition about the part that Providence has played in the destiny of humanity, as noted earlier in discussing Dimmesdale's responsibility in the matter.

THE FIRST CAUSE

The "word" that Hester had for Chillingworth is that he should repent and leave off his tormenting of the young divine, or she will disclose his identify to the minister. She practically begged Chillingworth to repent of his hostility and "leave his further retribution to the Power that claims it!" (174). The physician stated that he did not have the power in himself to forgive, which may characterize Satan's inability to repent. He instead philosophized—perhaps in a gloomy moment of rare truth, either to salvage his pride, or to justify his actions as a pawn of fate—that the history of the world had unfolded due to the first step taken. Hawthorne has unloaded several allegorical implications in this short passage.

> ""My old faith, long forgotten, comes back to me, and explains all that we do, and all we suffer. By thy first step awry, thou didst plant the germ of evil; but, since that moment, it has all been a dark necessity.

> Ye that have wronged me are not sinful, save in a kind of typical illusion; neither am I fiend-like, who have snatched a fiend's office from his hands.

> It is our fate. Let the black flower blossom as it may!" (174)

The reader knows enough by now to know that Chillingworth is indeed a deceiving fiend, who had admitted to Hester earlier to being such to Dimmesdale: "Yea, indeed!—he did not err!—there was a fiend at his elbow! A mortal man, with once a human heart, has become a fiend for his espedial torment!" (172). Hester had also described him as becoming a fiend whom she could pity "for the hatred that has transformed a wise and just man to a fiend!" (173) He now has admitted to eagerly assuming the role of one, but has presented an argument that countermands the admission.

However, it cannot be forgotten that whatever Chillingworth has said cannot be taken for absolute truth. Like the half-truths it is reported that Lucifer told Eve in the Garden, his statements must be analyzed very carefully as speculations, or notions with and without substance, a mixture or posture of opinions, the truth of which he himself may not be fully apprehensive nor with which he may be concerned.

Chillingworth has declared that, though they have wronged him, Hester and Dimmesdale had sinned only "in a kind of typical illusion." Perhaps he made the statement as a prelude to negating his own admission and display of fiendishness, that neither sin nor evil can be imputed if everything has been set in motion by the first step taken. Or perhaps Hawthorne is also addressing at the allegorical level the "sin" of Hester and Dimmesdale as a symbol that appears to be sin at the surface level. Perhaps Hawthorne has chosen, in a rare moment of moral aspect, to reveal the subplot of the allegory in Chillingworth's gloomy recognition of the truth, that the "sin" of Hester and Dimmesdale is only a symbolic allusion to a deeper meaning that conveys no such breach of eternal law. The reader must not conclude that it is beneath Hawthorne to conceal his inmost me in the words of the antagonist.

In regards to the "first step awry" that Chillingworth has presumed to decide the fate of all the players upon the stage of life, or "what will be will be," we have already discussed how Hester's fall itself dates back to her contract with Chillingworth, which apparently was a kind of marriage in exchange for some enigmatic knowledge. That first step may symbolically refer to Eve's natural curiosity in the Garden of Eden to know good and evil, when she partook of the forbidden fruit, instigated the fall of nature, and perpetuated the "dark necessity" of continuing mortality, thus first "planting the germ of evil" in the newly created world. As it was probably Master Prynne who approached Hester with his proposal of a kind of marriage, it similarly was Satan who came to and seduced Eve to partake of the tree of knowledge; that was the first step, or first cause in the planting of evil as a "dark necessity."

In the matter of this cascading or domino effort of the first cause, the reader must also discern what meanings Hawthorne may be communicating by contrast: Once the seed of evil was implanted in the world, is the end result merely and completely a blossoming black flower? Is he repeating Shakespeare, "Life is a poor player who struts and frets his hour upon the stage," as though life has already been predetermined? Such is one rational view of life, and the physician seems to be preaching a predestination of total blackness, a philosophy or "old faith, long forgotten," as a logical strategy to dissipate his responsibility for his own destruction. Possibly, as he sullenly turns to buzy himself gathering herbs, Chillingworth may be spiritually tiring of facing Hester's intuitive truths, and waving her off to gain some peace of mind, or simply realizing that he cannot deter Hester from her intentions. Or, perhaps, in the first gloomy recognition of possible defeat, merely acquiescing to the vision of his own fate, and retreating wearily from Hester's confrontation.

But, by contrast to the black flower of predetermined fate, the reader may also remember the red rose bush waiting by the prison door, that "inauspicious portal . . . so directly upon the threshold of our narrative," that Hawthorne

> could hardly do otherwise than pluck one of its flowers and present it to the reader. It may serve, let us hope, to symbolize some sweet moral blossom, that may be found along the track, or relieve the darkening close of a tale of human frailty and sorrow." (p. 48).

The reader might then ponder what sweet moral gem of hope the red flower of the rose might represent to counter the argument of the black flower as our inevitable fate. Was the fall of humankind really a "dark necessity" for some brighter day? Can the black flower, the dark prison of life, be turned into a red one?

There are four references to the scarlet letter in this chapter, each of which reinforce conclusions we have heretofore discussed. They are perhaps mentioned only for that reinforcement in connection with the fatalisticl philosophy to which Chillingworth has retreated. How might this symbol relate to the sense of responsibility for the complexities of life, from the possible point of view of Hawthorne's inmost Me? We discussed the first reference in regard to with what authority the symbol could be removed from Hester's bosom. The second was made in connection with Hester's perception of Chillingworth's ruination, that apparently caused the symbol to burn upon her bosom. The burning sensation of the symbol appears to signal some relationship between the misery of life, who is responsible for the misery, and how that misery is to be resolved, the solution of which the allegory may address as a foundation for other Hawthornian conclusions.

The third reference was Chillingworth's comment, "I have left thee to the scarlet letter." He had had no direct part himself in placing the symbol upon Hester's bosom, but perhaps only an indirect part by reason or reasons whereof Hester had decided to leave him. That placement had been done by the ministers of Puritanism, although with whom Chillingworth was still conducting business. Having by the first step taken effected Hester's fall by his contract at the beginning of their relationship, Master Prynne had only to leave her in the hands of those ministers. At the allegorical level, this off-hand statement by Roger, in possibly signifying his responsibility for Hester's fallen condition, may allude to the consequence circumstances Old Scratch left for our first parents to pass on to their descendents. Having taken the first step in the degeneration of human nature, all he had to do was step back and let the consequences follow.

But, of course, Chillingworth has not simply taken a back seat to all that is going on. He was still an active and hostile participant peddling his wares and doing commerce with the residents of Boston. Moreover, his chief diabolical plot was the ruination of the one kingpin of the community, who sought to set things right, by emphasizing matters of the heart. Though Roger showed no vengefulness toward Hester, yet his design to possess not only Hester's soul, but also that of her child and Dimmesdale, is an all-encompassing enterprise.

In the midst of her loyal attempt to help free Dimmesdale from the dismal and gloomy maze of evil that she, Pearl, and Dimmesdale have been wandering in, "stumbling, at every step, over the guilt wherewith we have strewn our path" (174), the fourth reference to the scarlet letter is a parenthetical comment by Hester. She interjected that the scarlet letter had "disciplined [her] to truth . . . the truth of red-hot iron, entering into the soul . . . ." Because she considered herself as being Dimmesdale's "bane and ruin," she owed him a "long debt of confidence" (174?)

Hester seemed to sense that the bane of mortality she had endured for the seven years of ordeal had been for her own good in teaching her truth by the hot iron of experience. She had long endured in faith, with a vote of confidence in and indebtedness to the divine's care that the sad and forloin experience of her extreme severity will have a brighter end.

So it is, from the depth of Hawthorne's ruminations, according to this minion's soundings, that the guilt trip of human nature, during its long mortal existence of some period of time, has faced the red-hot iron of justice, cried for retribution vainly, and realized that all is lost, unless "the Power that claims it" is allowed to do so (174). Ever since the pall of fallen nature has brought bane and ruin to the Creator's original design, it has nevertheless looked upward, in a long debt of confidence, like Hester's embroidered hope around the scarlet letter, for some Power of mercy to redeem it from the demands of justice.

Maybe all of these are conclusions Hawthorne had considered in his not-so-obvious contemplations of the purposes of life. Or, as an Anti-transcendentalist, he may be questioning within himself as to whether or not love and hate, and good and evil, come from the same source, and whether each follows a destiny determined consequentially by the first act—that we are pawns in life and play out the roles determined by the fate ordered by the first scene. If such is the case, then, as Chillingworth claimed, there can be no wrong committed by the pawns, because they were not responsible for the first step. Chillingworth may be laying the blame at the very feet of Providence. Is he lying, or speaking for Hawthorne, if only for the sake of postulating another opinion?

A Mutual Pity

A mutual pity appeared to be shared by these two characters, whether or not this commiseration indicated anything other than what was said between the two.

> "Woman, I could wellnigh pity thee!" said Roger Chillingworth . . . .
>
> "Thou hadst great elements. Peradventure, hadst thou met earlier with a better love than mine, this evil had not been. I pity thee, for the good that has been wasted in thy nature!"
>
> "And I thee," answered Hester Prynne, "for the hatred that has transformed a wise and just man to a fiend." (173)

Nature does have great elements. Had Lucifer not met Eve in the Garden of Eden and falsely formed by deception a kind of marriage, a bond of death, who knows what better world could have existed than the one the Fall brought about. With mortality, waste exists in the degeneration and dying of all things naturally. Without mortality, evil would have been non-existent. Having earlier been touched or influenced by the wisdom of Roger Chillingworth, Hester's life was apparently transformed into sadness before she ever met Dimmesdale. Whether she can be transformed back into the beauty of her innocence is a question for which the answer is left for the reader to deduce. Whether or not human nature shall be changed from its dark necessity back to its original or better state is still a matter of debate, although Hawthorne seems to favor the possibility of the retransformation.

It must be noted that, though Chillingworth can see Hester's mercifulness only as a waste of herself, by accepting the consequences of her deeds, and by her compassionate service, Hester had in a way transformed the ignominy of her life into something noble and praiseworthy. Unable to accept the consequences for his evil deeds, as Hester and Dimmesdale do during the seven long years, Chillingworth is transformed during that same time-frame into a fiend for whom there may be no redemption; and he has, by his own scheming exploits, momentarily beheld that destiny to his own horror. Hawthorne seems to be employing the adage, "All that we send out into the lives of others comes back into our own."

In a contrived moment of speculative fantasy, still in the throes of shutting out his previous sense of horror, Chillingworth experienced a "thrill of admiration" perhaps for the majestic quality of Hester's despair. He seemed to glory in the expressed depth of her misery, as he exulted in the prospects of achieving Dimmesdale's. To Hester's appeal that he leave Dimmesdale's "further retribution to the Power that claims it," since "there could be no good event for him, or thee, or me" (174), his response, "with gloomy sternness," failed to recognize Providence's hand in the matter and denied any good purpose in life.

Whereas Hester had presumably relied intuitively upon the Power of Providential planning for a retribution from the gloominess of mortality, as a result of its problems of evil and pain, and the consequent guilt experienced along the way, Chillingworth seemed to revert back to an intellectual, or purely scientific, explanation, that all things flow from the first cause. Perhaps Chillingworth's gloomy retreat, in his inability to forgive or repent, as portrayed in the following chapter, then, from Hawthorne's perspective, serves as a rare foreshadowing of Satan's insight into his own destiny.

On the other hand, bouncing back from her moment of fatalistic despair, Hester proclaimed,

> It is not so! There might be good for thee, and thee alone, since thou hast been deeply wronged, and hast it at thy will to pardon. Wilt thou give up that only privilege? Wilt thou reject that priceless benefit? (174)

Hawthorne's essay of love and hate bears out the hope, even in Chillingworth's extreme case of hostility, that there may be mercy for the hateful, that his hostility may yet be transformed into love. To Hawthorne, it appears that Mercy might be able to claim all the demands of Justice at the end.

THE DARK NECESSITY, A BLACK FLOWER

That immortal nature was transformed by the fall into mortal nature does seem indeed a pitiful change. Much as the transformation of a son of the morning into an arch demon, by a chain of events that seem laid out in destiny by the hand of Providence, life might simply resemble a stage of actors acting out their assigned part. Told from Chillingworth's perspective of circumstantial cause, the metaphor of the black flower blossoming as it may is posed by Hawthorne perhaps only as a dark necessity. The necessity of life presupposes that the darkness of life has a purpose—that the fall into mortality was needed for a short time in order to bring about a greater state of happiness. In other words, by reason of the oppositional or competing forces brought into play by the decaying or dying of natural things, the spiritual nature of humanity may be developed and strengthened as it rises to meet the challenge. It may be an interesting parallel that Hawthorne typically has chosen to underwrite the more hopeful theme by always developing its contrast, as though life and death, light and darkness, compassion and hostility, are twins, neither being able to exist without the other.

Like Chillingworth, Satan may favor letting the black necessity of mortality blossom as it may, without any intervention or intercession from Providence. Planting the thought in Hester's rational mind—that the black flower should be left to blossom on its own accord—does not appear to have been a standard for either Hester or Chillingworth, as Hester later devised a logical plan to escape from the misery of her life, and Chillingworth is still scheming to assure that plan toward Dimmesdale's destruction.

The next six chapters play with this alternative plot, which, if fully carried out, would thwart the destined mission Providence has endowed upon Dimmesdale. While Pearl seems confident of its completion, Dimmesdale appears to be but dimly aware of how it is to be fulfilled, and Hester senses only the promise of its end results. That subplot, with encouragement from Chillingworth, would prevent the divine's confession and result in the loss of his soul. Without that confession, the black flower would indeed blossom out of this dark necessity, and there would be no rose bush at the exit of life's prison. Hester, Arthur, and Pearl would be claimed by Roger; and allegorically, for lack of a redemption, humankind would belong to Old Scratch.

ONLY ONE SO SENSITIVE

There is a hint in Chillingworth's attitude of a rational approach to dealing with problems, especially those created by wrong doings: come what may, I will deal with it later, as though they might fly away with the wind. On the other hand, a higher order of response to such, according to one's sensitivity, might be immediate introspection and a proneness to admit responsibility, even when their portion is the smaller part, no matter how terrible it might be, or what trait may be shown to infer the worse. That sensitivity is a central theme in Hawthorne's tale in the development of his characters and what they represent. Whether Hawthorne was exploring all points of view, but slightly indicating his preference in the matter, is left open for reader intuition, providing one's rational inclinations do not push it completely off the catbird seat.

We must not pass from this chapter until one significant comment by Hawthorne is analyzed, in regard to this theme. Dimmesdale was so sensitive to Hester's condition, for which he silently assumes some responsibility, that it tainted everything that he thought, felt, and did. Hawthorne notes this parenthetically in the passionate confession of Chillingworth that he is a fiend. It is a singular remark, in the midst of Chillingworth's one pure moment of truth, that characterizes Dimmesdale like no other mortal. In an outburst of unrestrained intelligence, and true confession of his worst, Chillingworth declared:

> Never did mortal suffer what this man has suffered. And all, all, in the sight of his worst enemy! . . . He knew, by some spiritual sense,—for the Creator never made another being so sensitive as this,—he knew that no friendly hand was pulling at his heart-strings. (171)

This glimpse into Dimmesdale's character is another disclosure of what he may represent. The young divine is so sensitive and introspective that he is repulsed by the slightest hint of wrongdoing, and burns in the burden he seems to be taking vicariously upon himself. As a parallel, to the Christian, there has never been a mortal so sensitive and compassionate as the Redeemer, never a mortal who suffered as he suffered in taking upon himself the sins of humanity. Perhaps Hawthorne, in the character and dialogue of Chillingworth, had in mind the Biblical text wherein even the devils recognized that the Nazarene was the Son of God.[2]

Loyal and dutiful, Hester left Chillingworth and went speedily to find Dimmesdale to disclose her previous husband's identity to him in attempt to alleviate some of his suffering. She had left him once before, and perhaps had come to Boston to seek something she knew not what. Chillingworth resumed his "employment of gathering herbs," as though to continue his goodly role of physician; but, as we find him in the opening page of the next chapter retreating despondently from the reality of his moment of truth, with his gray beard almost touching the ground, he may be gathering herbs to nourish the black flower of life, and not letting it blossom as it may.

Hester and Chillingworth have declared their worst. The question still remains as to when or whether Dimmesdale will declare his.

CHAPTER 15

HESTER AND PEARL

For he that toucheth you toucheth the apple of his eye.[1]

A s Chillingworth "went stooping away along the earth," like a snake slithering away from discovery, with his gray beard almost touching the ground, not quite defeated but aptly put in his place by Hester's truthful confrontation, Hawthorne begins this chapter with some questions in Hester's mind about Roger's destiny, such as, "would he spread his bat's wings and flee away, looking so much the uglier, the higher he rose towards heaven?" (176) The possible answer to that question is not fully suggested until the essay on love and hate puts Hawthorne's touch on it.

Chillingworth has already started to get his come-uppance. He has beheld again the horror awaiting him, and has not as quickly rebounded therefrom. Now the reader needs a clearer view of the relationship between Hester and Pearl, and their relationship to Dimmesdale, and to contrast those relationships to that with Chillingworth.

A MIGHTIER TOUCH

After her confrontation with Master Prynne, Hester realized she hated him because he had betrayed her into marrying him and "has done me worse wrong than I did him!" (176) She had allowed herself to trade some magnificent unfolding of her womanhood for a lukewarm fancy or semblance of happiness with him. The "calm content, the marble image of happiness" of their tepid relationship had robbed her of a life that could possibly have been far greater had she not been beguiled by him. Hester had been touched by the connivings of Master Prynne, and, as we shall see in the forthcoming chapters, this moment of hatred will have a mighty touch of its own. But perhaps she hates him more for his machinations upon the divine in his effort to steal the apple of his eye (130). Hawthorne seems to be referring to what could have been if "some mightier touch . . . may have awakened all her sensibilities" (176).

There seems to be some connection between the apple of Dimmesdale's eye, which Master Prynne seeks to steal, and this "magic touch . . . a still mightier change," that Hawthorne worries the reader to ponder "whether Hester Prynne were ever afterwards so touched, and so transfigured"(164, 165). Figuratively, this touch seems to be that of "some other man," or divine being, who may have "awakened all her sensibilities" to the spiritual dimension, perhaps finding other ways presumably to make early humankind progressive in nature, had it, instead, not been touched or mortalized by the act that led to the fall. Touched as she was by Master Prynne instead, which touch caused Hester to lose her beauty and, as it were, become somewhat "actually dead"(226) at the end of her seven years ordeal, she looked to the one person by whom she was duty bound, to "the only man to whom the power was left [her] to be true" (171) to that mightier touch. She patiently awaited for a transfiguration to awaken all her sensibilities, for which her Puritan conscience forbad her to hope. Master Prynne's claim on Hester and Pearl hinges upon his success in rising "out of some nether region,—to snatch back his victim from what he sought to do!" (252). His object was to steal the apple of Dimmesdale's eye, to prevent him from fulfilling the office of the scarlet letter. Could Hester's transfiguration, perhaps to be realized in her daughter, Pearl, be the apple of Dimmesdale's eye?

The momentary realization of what she had missed in her present state of being throws "a dark light on Hester's state of mind" (177), sparks her hatred of Chillingworth, and causes her to wonder if the seven long years of her miserable ignominy has had any effect upon her ability to repent: "What did it betoken? Had seven long years, under the torture of the scarlet letter, inflicted so much of misery, and wrought out no repentance?" (177) Has the mortal nature of humankind, in the seven thousand years of earth life, reaped no benefit from the misery of its existence? What did this long period of "calm content, the marble image of happiness," presage? The two questions she asked herself are questions whose allegorical ramifications the reader seems summoned to explore. It may be that Hawthorne is saying that Hester's hatred is fostering speculative considerations that may lead to another wrong decision, that her spirit of fatalism may be conjuring up thoughts that may have a thwarting influence later. The reader will be confronted with the prospects of this speculation in this and the next five chapters.

Hawthorne may have already answered these questions, in a more positive note, with another exclamation mark, before he had Hester ask them: "Let men tremble to win the hand of woman, unless they win along with it the utmost passion of her heart!" (176) Chillingworth had not won Hester's hand because he had not won it by a passion of the heart, but had only seduced it by offering to share his knowledge. That is, perhaps, without the passion of heart, the nature of humanity is doomed to experience only a contented mirage of happiness, or worse. That passion of the heart, as heretofore interpreted, is perhaps the impassioned hope of the heart, reflected in one's compassionate love for one's fellow beings, as exemplified by Hester, and is yet to be demonstrated by Arthur. It dwelt within the bond of loyalty between Hester and Dimmesdale, and required a mightier touch. Her transfiguration itself hinges upon this bond.

Therefore, touched, as by death, as she was in her marriage to Master Prynne, Hester had fled from the contract by leaving him and coming to Boston, perhaps in search of some redeeming touch.

> She marveled how she could ever have been wrought upon to marry him! . . . And it seemed a fouler offense committed by Roger Chillingworth, than any which had since been done him, that, in the time when her heart knew no better, he had persuaded her to fancy herself happy by his side. (176)

Hester alludes to the time of her innocence, when she knew no better, as the time this marriage was contracted. Allegorically, as we have discussed in chapter 4, "The Interview," that age of innocence may represent the innocence that expired in the Garden of Eden, when Eve partook of the tree of knowledge of good and evil, at Satan's bidding. He had persuaded her with his lies, and her immortality was transformed into mortality. Just as Satan was allied with death, so became the civilization of humankind allied with the misery of the same consequences of mortality, from which there is no escape, but for some passion of the universal heart. Hester's relationship with Chillingworth betokened a kind of alliance, or marriage—a contract that closed out all other options open to her. But Hester was now loyal to and devoted to Dimmesdale, looking for a relationship with the divine, having learned to despise the false promises of Master Prynne.

Hawthorne appears to be saying in his allegory that, if nature had not been seduced in the Garden of Eden by the essence of evil to partake of the fruit of the tree of knowledge of good and evil, perhaps her immortal sensibilities could have been developed in other ways more magnificently than they were now being developed under the challenges of mortality. As it is, mortal nature has to endure the effects and consequences of her fallen state. She must learn to deal with the problems of a state of being that requires both physical and spiritual maintenance, just to live, perhaps at best, a mere contented, "marble image of happiness," or, at worst, "the miserable fortune, as it was Roger Chillingworth's."

So Hester's mind may again have been given to the dark side of reasoning, having been touched as she was by the mind and wisdom of Master Prynne, and fostered by her Puritan background; and she wondered if there had been any purpose to the misery she had endured. Having traded what could have been for a lukewarm fancy with which she became disillusioned, whether or not she can be touched again and retransformed back into her original beauty, is a question Hawthorne seems to have posed for the reader. It seems that every time Hawthorne raises a question, he is expecting the reader to seek an answer within the context of the symbolism.

PERCEPTION OF A GREATER REALITY

Hester's gullibility and seductibility by her logical notions is contrasted to that of Pearl's intuitive ability to discern between deception and reality. The difference appears to be the difference in their intuitive sensibilities to a greater reality than what exists. Introspective intuition, and its accompanying compassion of the heart within, might forecast a brighter future. Because of Pearl's self-assured sense of a greater destiny than what mortality offers, the reader should be led to ponder the reasons for that confidence. Let the child lead.

So Hawthorne returns the reader to Pearl, who was left in the preceding chapter playing by the side of a pool that had found some course inland from the sea.

At first, as already told, she had flirted fancifully with her own image in a pool of water, beckoning the phantom forth, and—as it declined to venture—seeking a passage for herself into its sphere of impalpable earth and unattainable sky. Soon finding, however, that either she or the image was unreal, she turned elsewhere for better pastime. (177)

The pastime to which Pearl turns seems to be the contemplation of a greater reality than the present one. Often her play symbolizes a greater beyond: perhaps there is more purpose in life than seeking aluring but false phantoms. Realizing that the image in the pool is unreal, or not representative of that spiritual dimension or reality that is greater that mortality, she is not lured by its deathly invitation. This pastime to which she turned may represent a civilization given more to compassionate conquest than that figured by Hester, whose view often appears to reflect the view of a community of humanity that sees the flesh as unworthy. Pearl's heritage, therefore, is not the same as Hester's. Both have a sense of compassion, but the difference might be that Pearl can see her own white feet in the pool of life, and Hester is lost in a labyrinth of mind.

One little gray bird, with a white breast, Pearl was almost sure, had been hit by a pebble, and fluttered away with a broken wing. But then the elf-child sighed, and gave up her sport; because it grieved her to have done harm to a little being that was a wild as the sea-breeze, or as wild as Pearl herself. (177-178)

This passage may be a small foretaste of Pearl's representation that is given bredth and color at the end of Chapter 18, when she plays with the animal kingdom in peaceful adoration. Or perhaps Hawthorne is simply inserting a comment of his own concerning the human race's lack of reverence for life, as in the case of even the smallest of living things, as an example of "the utmost passion of the heart."

Representing perhaps a more insightful, and therefore, a more benevolent civilization, and realizing there is a greater reality to pursue, Pearl turns her play toward what seems to be the center of her fixation by creating an imitation of the letter A her mother wears, but she makes it freshly green, instead of scarlet! The child bent her chin upon her breast, and contemplated this device with strange interest; even as if the one only thing for which she had been sent into the world was to make out its hidden import. (178)

If Hawthorne's readers are as intuitively insightful as he hopes them to be, then they may be sensitive to the signs and clues Hawthorne gives them to address the allegory in his tale. Both the exclamation mark and the suppositional phrase, "as if," are clues to the hidden import of the scarlet letter. These two devices are used repeatedly throughout his tale to guide the apprehensive reader to the message within.

To the author, one of Pearl's roles appears to be intuitively focused upon the fulfillment of the office of the scarlet letter, which, as we shall see later, connects Deity with the "communities of mankind." The green letter A may stand for the freshness of a new life after the scarlet letter has done its office. It may signify the one and only singularly great deed that transforms the civilizations of humanity into a better world, one which glories in peace and joy, without the slightest tinge of misery and despair characteristic of the present reality. Seemingly, then, according to this interpretation of Hawthorne's allegory, that "one only thing" of which the civilizations of humankind may have been sent here to distill from the dews of earth might be the message of a redemption slightly hidden from common sight.

The implications of the phrase, "sent into the world," have too few supporting references in Hawthorne's tale for us to render an interpretation of what it could signify with any great degree of certitude. The phrase may suggest Pearl's existing elsewhere before being sent to earth for a particular reason, and may be meant to imply a premortal life for humankind. Because there are only a few Biblical references to such an idea, and even then mostly by implication, perhaps Hawthorne, even if intentional, likewise has only rarely alluded to it, as though the idea hung intuitively by a thread at the far periphery of his belief system. But the indented quote above evidently is another reference to the greater meaning of the scarlet letter from the perspective of what Pearl herself may represent.

A Magnificent Obsession

Pearl, though her undeveloped sensibilities may not accurately have comprehended it, obsesses about the scarlet letter upon Hester's bosom, which she wears to symbolize some of the consequences of her fall. Pearl seems to sense that there is a relationship between the symbol upon her bosom and the sign of the minister placing his hand over his heart. There is a relationship configured at the surface level, but the allegory signals a deeper relationship with questions to direct the reader's intuitive sensibilities.

> "Dost thou know, child, wherefore thy mother wears this letter?"

> "Truly do I!" answered Pearl, looking brightly into her mother's face.

> "It is for the same reason that the minister keeps his hand over his heart!" (178-179)

At other times, there have been indications that Pearl instinctively sensed the value of the connection and desired to tease both Hester and Dimmesdale with her intimations, perhaps intended by Hawthorne as a type of foreshadowing of a greater meaning in the scarlet letter. Surely Pearl's obsession with the scarlet letter signifies something greater than the physical (or shepherding) relationship Hester had with the divine minister! Hawthorne is probably addressing the promised or destined reality of a new life, in behalf of humankind, after the token has fulfilled its office in the present reality. Pearl's

> inevitable tendency to hover about the enigma of the scarlet letter seemed an innate equality of her being. From the earliest epoch of her conscious life, she had entered upon this as her appointed mission. Hester had often fancied that Providence had a design of justice and retribution, in endowing the child with this marked propensity. But never, until now, had she bethought herself to ask, whether, linked with that design, there might not be a purpose of mercy and benevolence. (180)

Slowly, with numerous references, Hawthorne seems to build toward a picture of mercy and benevolence that is linked to the representations of the characters' relationships. The elf-child, flitting about with a cheerful and confident aspect, had a somber moment or three in which she focuses the reader's attention of the link between Hester's scarlet letter and the reason the divine often places his hand over his heart. Three times Pearl asked her mother what the connection might be: "What does the letter mean, mother?–and why dost thou wear it?–and why does the minister keep his hand over his heart?" (180-181)

Pearl instinctively knew there was a connection. Her enigmatic mission seems to be to link Providence's design of justice and retribution with the plan of mercy and benevolence, connecting Hester (nature) with Dimmesdale (the divine). The child's repeated questioning near the seashore takes on a different "unwonted aspect" for Hester. Her appointed mission is unfolding as Hester's intuition may be tuning in to those spiritual realities. Hester's fancy has now conceived perhaps what her subconscious was telling her when she peculiarly and elaborately embellished the scarlet letter, as though there was more to it than the Puritan perspective of justice and retribution. "Such were some of the thoughts that now stirred in Hester's mind, with as much vivacity of impression as if they had actually been whispered into her ear." (180). Hester is listening to her heart, and not her mind.

Hester wondered if the child, as a "spirit-messenger," had an errand "to establish a meeting-point of sympathy" (179), "to soothe away the sorrow that lay cold in her mother's heart . . . and to help her to overcome the passion [there]" (180). That mercy and beneficence are linked with the scarlet letter is the insinuation or discovery Hester finally makes due to Pearl's inquisitive prompting and prying rather than Hester's own native sagacity.

It would appear that the constant questioning posed by Pearl is purposed by Hawthorne to conjure up in the reader's mind the same question over and over again, "What does the letter mean?" as though there is some mysterious answer far deeper in meaning than simple justice and retribution for flawed mortality. As already explained within the interpretation given by the author's analysis, that link is the hope of mercy and benevolence provided by the Redemption, symbolized dimly in the confession of Dimmesdale upon the scaffold. That bright red hope, betokened by the embellishment of the scarlet letter on Hester's bosom, is matched and tied to the same scarlet letter being etched upon the divine's breast. The two symbols are linked together purportedly as a promise of redemption of mortal nature from this dark necessity, a redemption that may be fulfilled in Hester's future by a singular event for which the symbols speak.

THE PRYING NATURE OF HUMAN NATURE

Hester Prynne's prying into and understanding her own nature, much like that of Master Prynne's prying nature, seems less developed than Pearl's in helping her to see the redemptive beauty of her own nature. It is as though Hester represents a civilization or population whose nature is overshadowed with a perspective that limits its ability to hope and see beyond its dismal and dreary aspect. On the other hand, Pearl, as a representation of a more advanced portion of humankind, seems to be imbued with a greater instinctive sense of truth, or more sensitive line of discovery, perhaps because of the divine investment in humanity's creation, or her refusal to be burdened by the Puritan complex. If Hawthorne's readers weigh Hester's doubtful thoughts in context with her rational speculations, they may see Pearl endowed with qualities which may blossom into a noble character. As a "half-fledged" figure, Pearl seems to embody certain embryonic qualities that may ennoble her womanhood later.

> In the little chaos of Pearl's character, there might be seen emerging—and could have been from the very first—the steadfast principles of an unflinching courage,—and uncontrollable will,—a sturdy pride, which might be disciplined into self-respect,—and a bitter scorn of many things, which, when examined, might be found to have the taint of falsehood in them. She possessed affections, too, though hitherto acrid and disagreeable, as are the richest flavors of unripe fruit. With all these sterling attributes, thought Hester, the evil which she inherited from her mother must be great indeed, if a noble woman do not grow out of this elfish child. (180)

Apparently, as numerous the times this purveyor has harangued the reader to do the same, so the numerous times Pearl asks her mother the questions–"what does this scarlet letter mean?–and why dost thou wear it on thy bosom?–and why does the minister keep his hand over his heart?"–are intended to prompt the reader to pry into the cryptic meanings, to analyze the symbols and parables, and to read between the lines. Hawthorne closes the chapter with these same questions, unrelentingly pressing his readers for an answer, with a brief clue; while at the same time, he does not let them forget the seven year time frame of his tale, which he mentions twice in this chapter, as he has done so inordinately in others:

> "Silly Pearl," said she, "what questions are these? . . . What know I of the minister's heart? And as for the scarlet letter, I wear it for the sake of its gold thread!"

> In all the seven bygone years, Hester Prynne had never before been false to the symbol on her bosom. (181)

Having borne the severity of the gloomy maze of life, with a heart most often true to the purpose of the scarlet letter, Hester's devotion of indebtedness to and confidence in the divine's ministry has been fairly constant to this point in time. She has worn the symbol faithfully, not only for its stigmatic intent, but also for the sake of the promise of its golden threads. And she has cared for Pearl with no less constancy.

That Pearl, who may also signal Hawthorne's hope for his own daughter, Una, represents any evil whatsoever is most doubtful. As any father would hope for his daughter, it is highly likely that Pearl, on the basis of scorning every falsehood that seeks to thwart her destiny, represents the embronic form of a noble womanhood, which will develop and be disciplined in time. Pearl, Hawthorne, and perhaps most of humanity, seem to hope that the civilizations of humankind may unfold progressively from generation to generation, as a wild flower blossoms from season to season in greater profusion.

To Hawthorne, it appears that a transformation may be in the making, that at some future date a transcendental restoration may yield a better crop of humankind than has been advanced by either traditional or contemporary religious philosophies. If the intimations of the heart give sway over cold logic, because of the divinely impregnated nature of humanity, this transfiguration may come more from within than from without. At that time, the message of the scarlet letter may have fulfilled its office and left no duty unperformed. The controversy as to whether humanity is basically evil or good in nature may be swallowed up with the flowering; and perhaps the true nature and identity of humankind may later become known by its fruits. Like a rose bush blossoming at the door of the blackest prison, compassion and mercy within us may compass justice and retribution and unfold the kingdom without. Or it may require yet some mightier touch.

CHAPTER 16

A FOREST WALK

Whereby the dayspring from on high hath visited us,
To give light to them that sit in darkness and in the shadow of
death, to guide our feet into the way of peace.[1]

F ollowing the footpath that "straggled onward into the mystery of the primeval forest" (183), the reader strolls with Hester and Pearl deeper into the darker aspects of transcendentalism. Perhaps to Hawthorne, life itself is but one dimension of reality, the apprehension of which may be often overshadowed and obscured by the "moral wilderness" of society's conventions and customs, a dark shadow dimly lit with fleeting flickers of light evasive of grasp. Spotted with flitting rays of sunshine that illuminate the free spirit along its way, the path of life may be opened to those spiritual dimensions that transcend the common experience.

THE FOREST

The forest, the shores of the peninsula, the wooded hills of the country, the open sky—these settings—where the raw nakedness of nature's truths may be intuited by the inquisitive and sensitive mind—are often the study of the Romantic. To Hawthorne, it seems that the forest represents the raw and uncivilized nature where intuition is not hampered by rational speculation or the conventional "customs" of civilized society. In this case, "the vast and dismal forest" may also represent that vast and dismal dimension beyond the dimension in which we live, outer darkness, from which the Anti-transcendentalist receives intimations of both light and darkness, and into which Hawthorne's characters come and go in the course of their daily activities. Intuition may serve them with impressions of transcendental truth, unless they are suppressed by presumptuous logical deductions or speculations. To the Transcendentalist, the forest may be alive with emanations from which one can extract meanings of the spiritual that transcend the realities of the physical. To the anti-Transcendentalist, those emanations may reveal dimensions of truth from the lower regions as well as the higher of the spiritual realm.

So it is to the forest Hawthorne takes his readers to listen to some melancholy voice of a little brooklet. It seems his intent to take his readers on a forest walk with Hester and Pearl, and to cast upon them the spell of anticipation of a momentous event about to happen, a sad event, which seems to relate to something that has already happened, of which the brooklet whispers. However, it seems that the role of the forest itself is to overshadow and squelch the sad song of this meandering streamlet. The road was so narrowly hemmed in by the forest that it had become only a footpath the solitary pilgrim must search for in near darkness. The forest

> stood so black and dense on either side, and disclosed such imperfect glimpses of the sky above, that, to Hester's mind, it imaged not amiss the moral wilderness in which she had so long been wandering. (183)

Hawthorne has labeled the "mystery of the primeval forest" as a moral wilderness into which Hester has been wandering for some seven years. It would appear, then, that the Puritanism of Hester's day represents another outgrowth of the moral wilderness in which human nature (Hester) has been wandering since the beginning of life (Pearl). This wilderness has crowded both the road and the stream, perhaps due to a loss or corruption of "ancient principle" brought about by the various interpretations. Perhaps the "freedom of speculation," entertained by Christian thought, or for that matter, all religious opinion, since the beginning of time, has overgrown the straight and narrow path laid down through this primeval forest.

A HEAP OF MOSS

Preferring to meet the minister beneath the open sky, Hester and Pearl find a spot "deep into the wood," far from the narrow path and hidden from the sky. They stroll from the habitations of the mainland into the dark and dismal forest, and sit upon a heap of moss to await Dimmesdale, who is expected to appear on his return from a visit with "the Apostle Eliot, [who was] among his Indian converts" (183). That is all Hawthorne has to say, in this tale, about John Eliot, one of the first of Puritan ministers whom Hawthorne seemed to have admired, and who shared similar characteristics as Dimmesdale. But we are syntactically left to hang with the question: "Were the Indian converts Eliot's, or were they Dimmesdale's through his Apostle, Eliot?" It appears that Hawthorne may have purposefully referred to the apostolic ministry to allude again to some historical setting.

Because it apparently relates symbolically to the fall, the reformations of religious thought, and the disparaging perspective of Puritanic or like creeds, throughout the seven year period of the life of the earth, a rather lengthy quote is included to help define the symbolism of the moss, the pines, and the little brook.

> Here they sat down on a luxuriant heap of moss; which, at some epoch of the preceding century, had been a gigantic pine, with its roots and trunk in the darksome shade, and its head aloft in the upper atmosphere. It was a little dell where they had seated themselves, with a leaf-strewn bank rising on either side, and a brook flowing through the midst, over a bed of fallen and drowned leaves. The trees impending over it had flung down great branches, from time to time, which choked up the current, and compelled it to form eddies and black depths at some points; while, in its swifter and livelier passages, there appeared a channel-way of pebbles, and brown, sparking sand. Letting the eyes follow along the course of the stream, they could catch the reflected light from its water, at some short distance within the forest, but soon lost all traces of it amid the bewilderment of tree-trunks and underbrush, and here and there a huge rock, covered over with gray lichens. All these giant trees and boulders of granite seemed intent on making a mystery of the course of this small brook; fearing, perhaps, that, with its never-ceasing loquacity, it should whisper tales out of the heart of the old forest whence it flowed, or mirror its revelations on the smooth surface of a pool. Continually,

indeed, as it stole onward, the streamlet kept up a babble, kind, quiet, soothing, but melancholy, like the voice of a young child that was spending its infancy without playfulness, and knew not how to be merry among sad acquaintance and events of sombre hue. (185-186)

The profuse heap of moss upon which Hester and Pearl sit, and where Dimmesdale will later sit during their forest rendezvous, for four chapters, is a spot Hester has chosen to discuss a plan of escape from the reality they suffer. That heap of moss may represent either a fanciful insulation from reality, or the plane of existence whereon Hester lives, or both. It may also hint of some suspension from the reality of the spiritual dimension, the path from which they have strayed during their speculative moments, to a plane of pure fantasy. Periods of severe pain may conjure up such figments of the imagination in the mortal mind, as it seems to have done in Hester's.

But the most parsimonious interpretation might view the moss, the lichens, and other symbols of decay simply as the remnant of past institutional "customs." A possible analogy of the moss may represent the luxuriant remains or traces of original Christianity upon which speculation vies with intuition.

The gigantic pine, which once stood with its head once open to the inspiration of the heavens, while its roots and trunk were engulfed in the "darksome shade" of the regions below, may represent the original grandeur of that faith, perhaps towering over the other trees with "ancient principle." The great branches flung down may signify the several religions who have broken away from their mother tree, and choked the stream into contrary eddies and dark depths. The other trees may represent the several divisions of religious institutions, and the "fallen and drowned leaves" may represent those disciples of such whose fate has succombed to their speculative ventures. Or, the contemporary religion that has branded Hester may be the particular moss that feeds upon the religious decadence of the preceding ages.

There is a strong suggestion in this short allegory of the dismal forest, within the general allegory, of the Puritanic failure to transform or restore Christianity back to its original vivacity due to the fruits of speculative reasoning without intuitive assistance. The metaphors of the tree-trunk and moss could be graphic description of the attempts of current Christianity to survive in a world given more to intellectualism than to that something Hawthorne called intuition. To the dark romantics, perhaps conventional speculations may be influenced by emanations from the dark side of nature. While in the dismal forest, Hester, brainwashed by the speculative stigmas of Puritanism, has influenced Dimmesdale, far from the narrow path, to intellectualize on the same plane as she. Whatever destroyed the pine, and reduced it to the remains upon which they sit, may be responsible for providing these two with their moment of commiseration, and their decision to make a hasty retreat therefrom.

Much like the parasitical moss feeding upon the fallen tree, there is perhaps no heavier burden for the earth to bear than that of a dying world, which necessitates its inhabitants to fend for themselves, and to feed upon what has gone before. The fate for Nature (Hester) seems the gloom and melancholy the fall has produced. The fate for the divine (Dimmesdale) seems the painful Redemption which Deity's emissary on earth must endure as an essential element of the plan which Providence has responsibly provided to compensate for that fall. Hawthorne seems to be stating that the spiritual world, decaying right along with the physical world, needs redemption, a destiny perhaps which Providence has planned to provide.

"VIVACITY OF SPIRITS"

To find Dimmesdale, into this "moral wilderness" Hester with Pearl straggled along a footpath, narrow, hemmed in on both sides by the black and dense forest. The flitting cheerfulness of the flickering sunshine, always "at the farther extremity of some long vista through the forest" (183), seems just beyond Hester's grasp. This light of day appears to offer the quest of these solitary pilgrims some intuitive revelation. Though the rays of that emanation appear elusive to Hester, they are not to Pearl, who senses some affinity with the light.

> "Mother," said little Pearl, "the sunshine does not love you. It runs away and hides itself, because it is afraid of something on your bosom. Now see! There it is, playing, a good way off. Stand you here, and let me run and catch it. I am but a child. It will not flee from me; for I wear nothing on my bosom yet!" (183)

Pearl absorbed the sunshine, "all brightened by its splendor, and scintillating with the vicacity excited by rapid motion" (184). She seemed to share a kind of kinship with the sunlight, perhaps a better sense of intuition that maintained her high spirits. But sunshine, perhaps as a figure of the light of truth, hath no affinity with darkness; so whenever Hester tried to merge with the sunbeams, they vanished. Perhaps this "sportive sunlight—feebly sportive, at best, in the predominant pensiveness of the day and scene" (183), had difficulty in penetrating through the canopy of speculative Christianity.

Through the sportiveness of the sunlight, Hawthorne contrasts Hester's dark mien with the spirited nature of Pearl, who is free from the troubles caused by the stain and disease of Puritanism.

> There was no other attribute that so much impressed her with a sense of new and untransmitted vigor in Pearl's nature, as this never-failing vivacity of spirits; she had not the disease of sadness, which all children, in these latter days, inherit, with the scrofula, from the troubles of their ancestors. (184)

Pearl is not influenced by the mournful past, and looks brightly to the future. Though she benefited vicariously from Hester's experiences, Pearl did not inherit the scrofulous troubles of Hester's Puritanic generation, nor their predecessors', or any of nature's gloomy and joyless way of life. She had a newness and vigor of spirit that baffled Hester, who was mired in the everglades of Puritanic elucidation. Perhaps mortality's makeup may offer little other choice to its mournful existence. Perhaps to Pearl, who frequently teased Hester for her perspective, much as we sometimes tease one another of our own past troubles and worries, the prospects of immortality smiles down upon its mortal past in full view of its forthcoming redemption.

And perhaps this "infant mortality" needs to share vicariously the experiences of mortality. Evaluating what Pearl needed, Hester indicated that "[s]he wanted—what some people want throughout life—a grief that should deeply touch her, and thus humanize and make her capable of sympathy" (184). This comment is one of few rare insights into what may be Hawthorne's understanding of why mortality is fraught with pain and suffering. Pearl"–who was necessarily the companion of all her mother's expeditions" (183), was always at Hester's side and had shared in her sorrows. Hawthorne's commentary, through the mind of Hester, seems to underline the principle that suffering is what is needed in this mortal domain to transform our nature in its infancy into a mature sympathetic "womanhood." So humankind is apparently humanized by the grief of mortality in order to be transformed by some magic touch into a worthy benediction.

The reader must remember that Hester was not capable of judging herself because her intuitive sense had been marginalized by Puritan indoctrination. Pearl, on the other hand, because she was more intuitively wired and therefore less confused, resisted that dark perspective with all the spirit she could muster. Since Hester's mind was harrowed up in moral confusion, her perspective was perhaps true for mortal nature; but not so for Pearl, who possibly images a future world without a life of such pain and suffering. Hester often spoke from downcast despondency due to the past from which she could not escape. Pearl spoke brightly without morbidity and seemed to represent something positive in the future. Hester's gloominess seemed a symptom and sign of the spiritual plague of contemporary religion and its failure to transform humankind. Pearl's unrequited, vivacious, and determined spirit appears to represent humankind's (and Hawthorne's) rejection of this spiritual scrofula, a morally contaminating disease, at the same time it signals the hope of realizing some transcendent replacement later. It is this bright world that possibly may be reflected in the elusive "gleam of flickering sunshine" which, every now and then, broke through the cloud of shadows cast by the dark trees, stirred by some intuitive breeze (183).

THE MELANCHOLY BROOK

Hawthorne compares Pearl with the whispering brooklet, whose current of life "gushed from a well-spring as mysterious, and had flowed through scenes shadowed heavily with gloom. But, unlike the little stream, she danced and sparkled, and prattled airily along her course" (186-187). She encouraged the little brooklet: "'Pluck up a spirit, and do not be all the time sighing and murmuring!'" Pearl, speaking possibly for a future humankind, intuitively in tune with her sacred sense, may be that inward voice that picks up on the brightness of the scarlet letter's full and future promise. However, the brooklet babbled onward, not so much for Pearl's sake, as perhaps for the reader's, about past mournful happenings, and about another sad event yet to happen.

As Pearl is contrasted to the streamlet, perhaps as a source of some sad truth, so also is Hester's life compared with the tone of its message. Light reflects from the stream, perhaps as a sad narrator of life, and tells Hester about her own sorrowful fate.

> But the brook, in the course of its little lifetime among the forest-trees, had gone through so solemn an experience that it could not help talking about it, and seemed to have nothing else to say . . . .

> "What does this sad little brook say, mother?" inquired she.

> "If thou has a sorrow of thine own, the brook might tell thee of it," answered the mother, "even as it is telling me of mine!" (186-187)

In this passage, Hawthorne appears to key the message of the brooklet to one of the themes Hester's life seems to represent, which is connected with the message of the scarlet letter she displays so openly upon her bosom. Its speech was "kind, quiet, soothing, but melancholy, like the voice of a child that was spending its infancy without playfulness, and knew not how to be merry among sad acquantance and events of sombre hue" (186). The brooklet may have spoken of its childhood's lifetime without joy, possibly because its message was transformed into a mystery by the giant trees, underbrush, and huge rocks, or possibly because those sad (Puritanical) acquaintances had not known how to teach joy nor had allowed it to be taught.

In the course of the stream, Hawthorne may by symbolizing the annuls of history, whereby a bewildering maze of events have all but closed in and hedged up the waterway of the straight and narrow path, hemming it in on both sides by bouldered barriers, and forcing it into its circuitous route towards its destined end. Browbeaten by the forest, the streamlet seems to whisper the melancholy of something lost in the process of time, to lament the course of its meandering, and to echo the resulting gloom. To Hawthorne, perhaps it intimates the bewildering and ambiant intellectual vascillations of previous religious interpretions of ancient prejudice, the remains of which the dark forest is wont to smother.

The brooklet appears to be short-sighted in its sadness, while Pearl'a vision seems unequivocally sagacious in expection of brighter things yet beyond. Indeed, though the melancholy in Hawthorne's novel does seem to center around the darkness of society's past interpretations and the dimness of Providential light thereon, there is yet another sad whisper of the brooklet the reader may be inclined to hear. The brooklet also seems mournful of something futuristic.

> [T]he little stream would not be comforted, and still kept telling its unintelligible secret of some very mournful mystery that had happened—or making a prophetic lamentation about something that was yet to happen—within the verge of the dismal forest. (187)

The streamlet seems to foreshadow some future happening, although it focuses upon the sad aspects of it, and may not choose, as Pearl would have it, to consider the brighter aspects of that happening. Not only does the brooklet appear to be a sad commentary on history, but also a prophet that "mirrors its revelations on the smooth surface of a pool" (186) to those who can see or hear its soft message. This voice was counterbalanced by that of Pearl's, whose brightness should have some portent to Hawthorne's readers.

THE EMPATHY OF NATURE

To the Romantic Hawthorne, Nature seems most sympathetic to the solemn events it has witnessed or anticipated experiencing, and whispers its truths to those whose intuitive sense have not been hampered by speculative ruminations. And Hawthorne seems to personify Nature's voice as a means to alert the reader to hidden meanings within his tale.

Perhaps the mournful tale of the little brook is the sad story of humankind since the fall, and especially the failure of religion to address the event, its consequences, or reasons therefor. Perhaps its tale also includes the prophetic anticipation of the ill-fated decision Hester and Dimmesdale will shortly make to escape their destined suffering, as they sit upon their moss-covered plane in the dismal forest. It is as though the divine element in Dimmesdale, in a moment of weakness, has been invited by his own mortal nature off the beaten path, concerning an anticipated event to which he has committed himself.

Or perhaps the mystery about which the booklet prophetically whispers is similarly reflected by a Romantic Georgia poet, Sydney Lanier, and may parallel the same empathetic, "kind, quiet, soothing, but melancholy" Romantic voice of the brooklet.

A Ballad of Trees and the Master

Into the woods my Master went,
Clean forspent, forspent.
Into the woods my Master came,
Forspent with love and shame.
But the olives they were not blind to Him,
The little gray leaves were kind to Him:
The thorn-tree had a mind to Him
When into the woods He came.

Out of the woods my Master went,
And He was well content.
Out of the woods my Master came,
Content with death and shame.
When Death and Shame would woo Him last,
From under the trees they drew Him last:
'Twas on a tree they slew Him–last
When out of the woods He came.
(Mary Lanier, ed., Poems of Sidney Lanier)

This act of suffering, reflected in Nature's empathetic sadness, might be the myopic message of the streamlet through the dismal forest.

Just as the despairing Hester was a contrast to the vivacious Pearl, the sad little brook was a contrast to the flitting sunlight, and Pearl sought elsewhere for playfulness that perhaps reminded her of the brightness of some forthcoming event. She, having

> had enough of shadow in her own little life, chose to break
> off all acquaintance with this repining brook. She set herself,
> therefore, to gathering violets and wood-anemones, and some

scarlet columbines that she found growing in the crevices of a
high rock. (188)

THE SCARLET COLUMBINES

Pearl's turning from the brook to gather the scarlet columbines
suggests that, as a scarlet enigma herself, but dressed in green, she had
more meaningful business than dwelling upon the morbidity of the past or
present. This turning from one activity to another may remind the reader
of a similar event, in which Pearl, having danced upon the grave of Isaac
Johnson, was told to "behave more decorously;" so she turned instead to
placing prickly burrs around the scarlet letter on Hester's bosom, perhaps
to emphasize its decorous and painful purpose. Once again, as a harbinger
of brightness rejecting the gloom of the past, Pearl turn's the reader's
attention from blackness to redness. The imagery of red is repeatedly kept
before the mind's eye of the reader to highlight its significance to the
central theme of the allegory.

That the scarlet columbines were found in the crevices of a high
rock possibly indicates Hawthorne's choice of words to infer Pearl's
higher purpose. That the columbines were growing in the crevices of
this split-open rock may also be in keeping with the allegory: rock, as a
forceful barrier to the streamlet, has been rent asunder by the promise of
some divine and mysterious purpose. Or perhaps, more strenuously, the
scarlet columbines may signify that the promise is to issue from some rock
of redemption that has been split asunder.

That Pearl broke away from the sadness of the murmuring brooklet
may indicate that Pearl did not identify with the mournful tale of the
forest but had her mind and heart set on something beyond which
contained a little more cheer. It possibly might foreshadow her breaking
away from or dwelling apart from Hester's kind of life at the end of the
tale. The sunshine itself that breaks through the canopy and plays upon
the brooklet might be the light of a bright promise to justify and redeem
the whole of its experiences.

Hawthorne's narrative conjures several questions that appear to guide
the sensative and prying reader down the streamlet's course as clues to evade
the diverting overgrowth of customs and codes of conduct proscribed by the
forest trees. Is the little stream only lamenting its witness of a scene shortly
to happen, when Dimmesdale sits with Hester upon a moss-covered bed

of decaying debris, while she plans their evasion of destiny? Or is this sad foreshadowing, whispering only the sad tale of humanity's philosophical history and predicting the symbolic redemptive confession and death of Dimmesdale? Does Pearl's dancing vavacity and columbine gathering look to the promise that overshines this sad history?

One may conjecture that Anne Hutchingson, for whom Hawthorne may have had litte misgiving, might have helped the stream course a little livelier on its way, had she not been crowded out by the giant pines of her day. Or any other antinomian since, or in our day, that may give us a brighter picture of tomorrow. Perhaps, with any present day enlightenment, for which Hawthorne seemed to hope, the stream still flows with livelier passages through a swifter channel-way, and the sunshine reflects more brightly from the surfaces of some of its pools and eddies.

These contrasts of light and dark, sadness and joy, intuition and intellect, suggest that the essence of truth whispered by the brooklet had managed to circumnavigate, for the most part, the scrofulous theology of the moral wilderness; and, if Hawthorne be prophet, may weave its course a little straighter, with a little more cheer charting the way.

In our walk through Hawthorne's forest, none of mysteries of the contrasts may have yet revealed to his readers the mutual and ultimate destiny his four main characters will experience in relation to each other. This destiny seems linked to the fulfillment of the role of the scarlet letter, the impact which the Black Man of the Forest has played in Hester's and Dimmesdale's life, and how that impact is about to be played out center stage in its influence upon their destiny. By way of introduction to the next chapter, Hawthorne concludes his walk in the forest by expounding upon that parable, in connection with the symbol of the scarlet letter, and perhaps in connection with Hester's influence upon Dimmesdale.

THE BLACK MAN OF THE FOREST

Hester plays up to Pearl, who has heard the superstition, and tells her part of the answer of what the scarlet letter is: "'Once in my life I met the Black Man!' said her mother. 'This scarlet letter is his mark!'" (185) Hester may be referring to her marriage contract with Master Prynne, and/or both the first and second interviews with him, the latter of which she finally recognized him as a hateful fiend. His mark may represent the dark condemation of mortal nature because of its fall from a period of grace, which fall appears to have happened in consequence of that contract. It is the asssumption of the casual reader that Hester has fallen because of her birthing of Pearl; but it is studiously clearer in Hawthorne's tale that Hester's fallen nature was a direct consequence of the knowledge Master Prynne shared with her in this contract.

But Hester's meeting with the Black Man was not in the forest, where many go willingly. She had not sold her soul to Old Scratch, so to speak, like one of the many "that meets him here among the trees . . . [and] write their names with their own blood" (185). Her meeting the Black Man, and receiving his mark, does not claim her or place her in the book of the Black Man because, though desparing, she has not given up but is determined to be true in her devotion to the one man in whom her hope resides.

Hester previously had told Old Miss Hibbins that she would have given her soul to him had she lost custody of her child, indicating that her soul was still secure, even though her life was resigned to despair and gloom. Though she had intellectually speculated and contemplated both suicide and homicide, she had not committed a deed that consigned her soul to the Black Man of the Forest. Loyal and devoted to Dimmesdale, like Mistress Hibbins is to the Black Man, she had been true to her destiny despite her sidetracking, rational tendencies. That one's willing signature in blood is required in selling one's soul to the Black Man may indicate that one must willingly give himself, and his life's blood, to the dark side. Neither Hester's speculative ignorance in contracting with Master Prynne a kind of marriage, her agreement not to divulge Master Prynne's identity, or her forthcoming misguided suggestion to Dimmesdale to flee destiny, appear to qualify her as having sold herself to anyone else other than Dimmesdale.

This loyalty poses a paradoxical question to the reader that can only be answered by understanding the mystery behind the embellishment of the scarlet letter, and in its connection with Dimmesdale. Alhough Hawthorne may have been referring exclusively to Eve's contract in Hester's answer to Pearl's question, we have noted that he has also implicated the role of Providence in that fall of nature, in the character of Dimmesdale, wherein the divine in him was nevertheless true to his nature by later responsibly accounting for his silence. We can understand her loyalty when we picture Eve, following her intellectual compromise of a direct dictate of Providence, as having thereafter remained loyal to her future Re-creator.

As we have heretofore speculated before on the subject of how Nature (Hester) could be disposed of, or how Nature could dispose of humankind (Pearl), we concluded that such a feat would have to be perpetrated by some force of power other than Hester's. To Hawthorne, human nature seems a pawn in the hand of Providence that is nevertheless subject to being acted upon by intuition as well as native sagacity. Perhaps he perceives the rise and fall of civilizations, amid the various transformations of society, as relegated by its religions institutions, as an indication of their inherent or natural tendencies. Shorn of the medium of intuition by which to receive divine guidance, nature apparently self-destructs, perhaps by not so sagacious thought. Perhaps Hawthorne concluded that the remedy to the problems of this mortal dark necessity appears to necessitate the office of some scarlet mission completing its full and destined duty of "disentangling its mesh of good and evil."

CHAPTER 17

THE PASTOR AND HIS PARISHIONER

Not my will . . . . [1]

This single chapter, an intriguing clue to the allegorical relationship between Dimmesdale and Hester is the simple fact that Arthur Dimmesdale's full name is inordinately mentioned eleven times, or twelve, if we include the mention of his first name alone. Does Hawthorne intend to make a point with this inordinate number? Is he seeking to connect the two initials together, A. D., to suggest the term, *anno Domini,* thus attributing to Dimmesdale some similitude of meaning?

The reader may note a peculiar twist of this interpreter's fancy as he slides easily from the surface tale to the allegory, and, from time to time, intermixes them, with some little compunction, as though it were becoming more difficult to separate the two. It is not intended to confuse the reader, but to manifest the parallels.

SPECULATION AND INTUITION IN THE DARK FOREST

Hester and Dimmesdale met and sat down upon the same heap of moss where Pearl and Hester sat before, in perhaps a kind of time-out from reality. We must remember that they are still in the dark forest, where they are subject to intimations, or intimidations, from the dark side, and where everything becomes symbolic. They are far from the beaten path of life's rugged course and susceptible to errant speculations; and their conversation in the forest, given better allegorical perspective in the next chapter, is a type of Hawthornian flashback to help keep the intuitive reader on track.

As an outsider outlawed from society, but harangued by its "human institutions," Hester "had habituated herself to such latitude of speculation as was altogether foreign to the clergyman" (199); and, according to the Romantic notion, the mortal nature of humankind is such as to be more easily influenced by its environment in the dismal forest. Dimmesdale, therefore, though theretofore steady in pursuing his destined mission, is to be influenced by a spirit of speculation coming from Hester, or mortal nature. In a moment of weakness, he will entertain the willful thought of wanting the cup to pass from him. This moment of weakness is extended through the next few chapters, until he exits the "mortal maze," successfully conquers himself, and remains true.

A COLLOQUY OF SPIRITS

The seven-year time frame is mentioned again prior to a passage in which one of two possible meanings seemingly deals with an encounter of these two characters as unembodied spirits at some place similar to the world beyond the grave.

> It was no wonder that they thus questioned one another's actual and bodily existence, and even doubted of their own. So strangely did they meet, in the dim wood, that it was like the first encounter, in the world beyond the grave, of two spirits who had been intimately connected in their former life, but now stood coldly shuddering, in mutual dread; as not yet familiar with their state, nor wonted to the companionship of disembodied beings. (189-190)

That Hawthorne may be alluding to a previous state of unembodied spirits prior to the creation of an embodied existence, whether that embodied existence was immortal or mortal, seems less likely a proper interpretation of the above passage than that of life after life. The reference to Hester and Dimmesdale "not wonted to the companionshp of disembodied beings" seems to refer instead to that space of life following death, when the body is laid in the grave, and the disembodied spirit goes elsewhere for companionship.

The simile has the appearance of indicating one of three possibilities, or all three. They are out of touch with reality, they are together in a world of fanciful imagination, or they are, for a while, suspended on the same intellectual plane. In other likely words, Dimmesdale has descended to Hester's level, and is temporarily rationalizing their dilemma.

> The grasp, cold as it was, took away what was dreariest in the interview. They now felt themselves, at least, inhabitants of the same sphere. (190)

The coldness of their touch, as in the absence of the heat of either passion or mortal flesh, seems to symbolize a state of existence out of touch with the destiny of the passion of the Redemption, or out of tune with the reality of their Providential roles. Sitting on the green moss in the dark forest, they seem to be inhabitants of the realm of fancy, suspended from the reality of what must be, and perhaps under the influence of dark emanations from the spiritual realm, which, though deceitfully uplifting for a while, temporarily divert them from their destined missions.

In the forest, Hester and Dimmesdale commiserate on the effect of their act and compare what they did to Chillingworth's vengeful ploy. Hester's penance in wearing the scarlet letter and doing good deeds do not remove the dreariness from her life. Because of the great disparity between the high plane of the young divine's spirituality, and his extreme sensitivity to the lowness of his mortal nature's tendencies towards sinfulness, Dimmesdale condemns himself as the worse of sinners. Arthur claims he has no substance because he

> should long ago have thrown off these garments of mock holiness, and have shown myself to mankind as they will see me at the judgment-seat" (192),

instead of cheating them with his silence, while they were "crushed under this seven years' weight of misery" (198). It is interesting to note that Hawthorne, again referring to the time frame of seven years at least four times in this chapter, had Dimmesdale seemingly referring to the whole of humanity, rather than the few parishioners in Boston, who might be the audience of his confession.

There are two possible allegorical ramifications implied by this admission. One is a form of hypocrisy wherein one appears to be less than what he is. It is the reverse of the kind wherein one seeks to appear better than he really is. At the surface level, the reader sees Dimmesdale as the latter. At the deeper level of meaning, in regard to Dimmesdale's representation of the Nazarene, Hawthorne could be referring to the former type, wherein the Nazarene appeared to be only a man, but eventually proclaimed himself to be, in the Christian persuasion, the promised Messiah, and later gradually led his followers to believe that he was Jehovah, the one who had given the Mosiac law to Israel in the first place, and the one who would meet them "at the judgment seat." In some Christian circles, it is held that he had condescended to be born in a mortal world as Jesus of Nazareth, but, until the proper time, to be unknown to the world he had created as the Creator, the One who has been its manager for the "seven long years" of its existence. Perhaps to Hawthorne it was a kind of falsity to his holiness not to clearly identify who he really was, and appeared less than he was in order to work out his plans for the Redemption of humanity. Dimmesdale had claimed indirectly that it would defeat his purposes should he reveal his identity before it became necessary. Thus Dimmesdale longed to be true to his identity, but could not, until the right moment in time. And such might be Hawthorne's message in what might be the one major moral, or preachment, in his tale: "Be true!" as we will explore later. However, for the present, if not forever, the reader may prefer to be completely satisfied with only the surface level of meaning, that Dimmesdale is simply tired of hypocrisy.

The other possible implication of the above quote, in regard to cheating humanity for seven years, also may pertain allegorically to the silence of heaven. That is, perhaps from Hawthorne's point of view, mankind, throughout her seven years of existence, may have been "cheated" by the silence; that is, wherein the existence and identity of the Creator of mankind has been kept covered by a veil and is but dimly known to them.

Of course, as weak as Dimmesdale's excuse might have appeared to some readers, it likewise is not easy to accept the Christian's claim that heaven's silence on the matter exists simply for the purpose of proving humanity's faith in, rather than a knowledge of, that existence and identify. Perhaps the Christian's emphasis on faith is similar to Hawthorne's emphasis on intuition.

A Consecration of Its Own

Hester and Arthur agree before they reluctantly leave the forest that what the physician was doing to Arthur was blacker than Arthur's sin. In contrasting their deed with Chillingworth's, an interesting comment is made about their deed seemingly at the allegorical level.

> "[Chillingworth] has violated, in cold blood, the sanctity of a human heart. Thou and I, Hester, never did so!" . . . .
>
> "Never, never!" whispered she. "What we did had a consecration of its own. We felt it so! We said so to each other! Hast thou forgotten it?" (195)

What? Hester and Dimmesdale never violated the sanctity of a human heart? At the surface level of the tale, wherein we assume an adulterous relationship between them, had no human heart been violated? Perhaps Hawthorne is speaking either in defiance of custom, or hinting at the allegorical level that there was no violation of any human heart in the creation of humankind. On the other hand, the Adversary (Chillingworth), at that same level, desecrated the human heart in the very moment he seduced Eve, in the midst of her glorious immortality, to partake of the forbidden fruit in order to acquire knowledge, at which point in time, human nature fell into a mortal state of being.

And what was it about their deed that constituted a kind consecration of its own? At the surface level, Hawthorne is clearly defying conventional thought, that two would dedicate themselves to each other out of wedlock. At the allegorical level, however, he may be indicating that the act of creation signified no less than the divine element investing itself in nature so as to endow the human soul with the gift of infant immortality. That would be a kind of sacred consecration, of its own, at a different level of meaning, of course.

That Hawthorne has noted that they, for a short time, exist on the same plane (190), suggests that, before and after their rendezvous, they were on different levels of existence. Theretofore, one seems to have existed at an earthly level for some earthly mission, and the other at an heavenly level for some Providential one. Though Hester—as a perspective of gloom embodied in the Puritanic interpretation—belongs to those of the seven years span of time on earth, she may represent the civilizations of mortality whose sufferings qualify them for some higher divine purpose. Though Arthur—as a sensitive representative of Providence—belongs to those who are sensitive to the Good and True, he may represent those who are reconciled from the throes of mortality, for which he may be partly responsible. His mission may be dedicated to those who are compassionate, repentant, and reformed creatures of service to others; and the scarlet letter burning upon his chest may signal that mission. It may also signal the suffering of those who experience "eternal alienation from the Good and True," a kind of earthly madness (193).

Both Hester and Arthur, at the least, seem a consecration for and in behalf of the better destiny of Pearl, whose intuitive foresight may envision an Act of Passion that redeems all. She is a product of them both, by the design and grace of Providence. Pearl, who embodies both the divine and natural elements, may represent those whose truthful perspective of life envisions a superior theology at some future, beyond the seven thousand years of earth's mortal time. Such a vision of a better destiny ennobles their conduct of life and frees them from the bondage of current civilized conventions and customs. Perhaps Hawthorne's novel may have projected this vision as his "mode of glorifying God, or being serviceable to mankind in his day and generation."

That Hester and Dimmesdale would seek to hide from such a destiny would be tantamount to a grievous violation of human sanctity. Such was her proposal, as Hester reasons with Dimmesdale against his better senses. She asked, "Is there not shade enough in all this boundless forest to hide thy heart from the gaze of Roger Chillingworth?" (197). The intention of this question seems directed more to the reader than to Dimmesdale, for why would he wish to hide in the forest? It is perhaps an allusion to the metaphorical meaning of the forest: of all the speculative philosophies interpreting the situation of humanity's mortality, surely there would be some way to rationalize avoidance of Dimmesdale's miserable destiny. Dimmesdale's sad reply is likewise, in the same metaphorical reference, a remarkable allusion to the consequences of such a tragedy: "Yes, Hester, but only under the fallen leaves!" His fate would perhaps be worse than that of those who had fallen prey to the sophistication of other errant religious or rational justifications: he would lie beneath them, perhaps under the complete "seven years' weight of misery." Indeed, at the allegorical level, from Hawthorne's possible Christian perspective, it would appear that all humanity would be lost without the redemption, perhaps another reason for Hester's devoted willingness to "gladly have lain down on the forest-leaves, and died there, at Arthur Dimmesdale's feet" (193).

Thus, Chillingworth, as an embodiment of evilish vengeance practiced mainly upon a solitary and central figure, has violated that human sanctity, and claims all those whose insensitivity alienates them from the Good and True. Lucifer's motive likewise was one of destroying souls for his own revenge. The Creator's motive in engineering the creation, and the fall was, perhaps as a "dark necessity," a godly consecration of life which, as Hester deemed wise for Pearl's experience, "needed this grief to develop her sympathetic nature" (184).

"ALIENATION FROM THE GOOD AND TRUE"

> Roger's design upon Dimmesdale was, not to cure by wholesome pain, but to disorganize and corrupt his spiritual being. Its result, on earth, could hardly fail to be insanity, and hereafter, that eternal alienation from the Good and True, of which madness is perhaps the earthly type. (193)

The reader must not forget that by the destruction of Dimmesdale, in the thwarting of his mission, he also lays claim to Hester and Pearl, as though that victory is vicariously inclusive. One might ask, how could Dimmesdale's destruction render "eternal alienation from the Good and True"? Is Hawthorne only singling out Dimmesdale as experiencing the result of Chillingworth's machinations? Or is he referring in general to the Adversary's influence on all humanity, that all madness on earth is a type of this alienation afterwards?

Hawthorne does not address in the allegory the issue of how the experience of mortality is a "consecration of its own," or why their act was, in the words of Chillingworth, a "dark necessity," but simply offers the claim upon its own not-so-obvious merits, with some explanations in the comments of, and in behalf of, his characters. But when Dimmesdale leaves the forest, having entertained a measure of his own will, he found himself diminished, perhaps "disorganized and corrupted," as though he were a different individual experiencing a glimpse of madness.

GARY P. CRANFORD

IDENTIFYING JUDAS

It may be only a coincidence, as likely it may be claimed of all the symbolic interpretations advanced herein, but one of the few this expounder might admit to, that the only time Arthur's first name is used alone in this chapter—an exception to the eleven other times when his full name is used—is in the passage wherein Hester passionately appealed to Arthur for forgiveness of her betrayal, and identified Arthur's Judas as her husband, the physician and Arthur's companion. As a type of Judas Iscariot, one of the twelve apostles who betrayed the Nazarene to those who planned to kill him, Chillingworth feigns supportive companionship to Dimmesdale, but plans diabolically to destroy and claim his soul.

Perhaps the historical time element was considered secondary, or collapsed, as a Romantic device, in Hawthorne's coverage of events leading up to Dimmesdale's betrayal. Or perhaps the reference to the minister's name is shortened to represent the reduction of the Twelve to eleven when Judas hung himself on a tree. In other words, Dimmesdale learned that Chillingworth was a Judas dedicated to his destruction perhaps similarly as the the Nazarene learned that one of the twelve, Judas Iscariot, was his betrayer. It is a minor point, so nothing of substance is lost if these details are only extraneously coincidental. At the same time, however, in support of the major premise of this text, so many coincidences betray their fortuity. It is the consistency of these innumerable coincidences which seem to cement the meanings of this purveyor's analysis. Then again, the crumbs one might pick up from another's droppings might be put back together in a disorganized and corrupted pattern.

THE QUALITY OF PASSION

The question of the value of passion in the mixture of mind and matter poses a problem in the matter of ethics, but it appears that Hawthorne values passion only as it is composite with the tenderness of sentiment. To Hawthorne, passion seems to flow from the warm vibrations of one's intuitive senses rather than from the cold fluctuations of the rational mind. From the beginning of his allegory to its end, he has therefore sought to imbue his characters either with this warmth or this coldness, which apparently he could not do while distracted by the duties of the custom house.

• 386 •

The characters of the narrative would not be warmed and rendered malleable, by any heat that I could kindle at my intellectual forge. They would take neither the glow of passion nor the tenderness of sentiment, but retained all the rigidity of dead corpses . . . . In short, the almost torpid creatures of my own fancy twitted me with imbecility, and not without fair occasion. (34)

Passion void of a tender sensitivity appears to violate "the sanctity of the human heart seems to lead to enmityAs a passionate divine, sensitive to the sentiments of his parishioners, Dimmesdale is more in tune with reality than Chillingworth, and, for that matter, Hester. However, notwithstanding Dimmesdale's integrity, Chillingworth apparently would lay claim to the young divine's soul simply for the sake of the passionate nature of the body itself. When Hester identifies her husband to Arthur,

The minister looked at her, for an instant, with all that violence of passion, which—intermixed, in more shapes than one, with his higher, purer, softer qualities—was, in fact the portion of him which the Devil claimed, and through which he sought to win the rest. (194)

The language of this passage from which the quote is taken could be construed also to contain an equivocal meaning: if Old Scratch could claim a portion of the Nazarene's soul—or that physical part of passion, which was intermixed with the divine attributes of the spiritual—then he might claim all of it, and more. In other words, if one sin could have been found in the Redeemer's soul, because of the passionate nature of mortality during his torment on earth, then perhaps he might claim all the rest of the souls of humankind, perhaps on the basis that the root of evil resides in the violent quality of passion, a passion that turns to hatred, and feeds the acts that damn it. There is one particular Biblical text, along with others we have previously similarly associated with the subject of body possession, which Hawthorne might have considered in advancing this theme. In like manner, Old Scratch tried to claim Moses' body on the basis of an infirmity for which Moses was refused entrance into the promised land.[2]

Through Dimmesdale's passionate sense of guilt, for some act or acts in the past, however inexplicable they appear to be, Chillingworth would seek to wrest from him the rest of his soul, on the one tenuous premise, to him, that passion can be disorganized and corrupted. The passion of Dimmesdale is mixed with higher qualities of his divine spirit, which, though suspended for a while, triumph later in leading him to his destiny. Dimmesdale to the end was a passionate person, highly sensitive, for the most part, to his destiny, and fulfilled his destined mission by focusing his passion upon it later.

It is a destiny that haunts both Hester and Dimmesdale intuitively; and the shadowed forest, though unemcumbered by the customs of civilized life, yet itself a moral maze, appealed to their natural inclinations, like ghosts one to another, on the same mortal level. Though possessed with a spiritualized passion, Dimmesdale's suspended consciousness, momentarily caught by a spectre of thought, beheld the earthly features of his mortality, and entertained the speculation proposed by Hester.

> It may be, that his pathway through life was haunted thus, by a spectre that had stolen out from among his thoughts . . . . Each a ghost, and awe-stricken at the other ghost! They were awe-stricken likewise at themselves; because the crisis flung back to them their consciousness, and revealed to each heart its history and experience, as life never does, except at such breathless epochs. The soul beheld its features in the mirror of the passing moment. (190)

It is this one moment's thought far from the narrow path in the forest, extended allegorically in time to divulge the full ramifications of the spectre, that perhaps reminded them of the fearful aspects of their destiny. For Hester, mortal nature anticipates death throughout its history and experience, and, but for the rare moments in settings that seep into one's consciousness, squelches its aspects as "[e]arth fills her lap with pleasures of her own" (Wordsworth, in "Ode," Harrison, p. 99). For Dimmesdale, the divine in the man, for one brief passing moment, while dwelling on the same plane of earthly moss with Hester, perhaps sensed the dark side of his mission, and fain would have passed it by, were it solely up to his own will, and not to the will of him that had sent him.

Failing to convince Dimmesdale to hide in the moral maze of the forest, Hester tried another ploy, as though his loyalty was fixated on his fellow ministers: "And what hast thou to do with all these iron men, and their opinions? They have kept thy better part in bondage too long already!" (197) Heretofore, these "iron men" have seemed as companions who have honored him as a master teacher. However, we have mentioned that Dimmesdale's Puritan colleagues, like the dismal forest that squelched the whisperings of the brooklet, may be representative of the Pharisees and Sadducees with which the man of Nazareth rubbed elbows; and now, in the eyes of Hester, and by Dimmesdale's response, we see them as a fettering impediment to the influence of his better part. Dimmesdale acquiesced to Hester's criticism of his colleagues by responding to and directing his answer only to her request to flee across the sea.

AN ALTERNATE PLAN

Hester pleads with the young minister to leave the wreck and ruin of life behind, to cross the sea with her and start anew, and to make himself a higher name than Arthur Dimmesdale, because there are possibilities of other trials and success.

> "Leave this wreck and ruin here where it hath happened! Meddle no more with it! Begin all anew! Hast thou exhausted possibility in the failure of this one trial? Not so! The future is yet full of trial and success. There is happiness to be enjoyed! There is good to be done! Exchange this false life of thine for a true one." (198)

Hester's rationale was relentless, as is mortal nature's when it begins to weaken. It may be, as we have discussed earlier, that Hester's appeal to begin anew is the appeal of nature, in a moral wilderness, begging for the divine within to leave the wreck and ruin of mortality behind and to begin humankind all over again elsewhere. She may be arguing rationally that the success of their escape can be compensated for by other creations and greater successes. This singular moment of speculative escape, "into the themes that were brooding deepest in their hearts" (190), is much like the one earlier when, in a depressed state of mind, Hester, questioning the value of life and thinking to kill herself and Pearl, reasons about transforming society: "As a first step, the whole system of society is to be torn down, and built up anew" (165). That earlier moment of speculation has conjured up an alternate plan to the one Providence had laid out for them. For Hester and Dimmesdale to cross the sea back to England might possibly symbolize Deity taking Mother Nature elsewhere, possibly back to a former state, and starting a new race all over again, which may be the plot of the next chapter.

LET THIS CUP PASS

Perhaps the voice of Hester is also the voice of the flesh speaking to the soul of the divine to find a way to escape the agony of the scaffold. Dimmesdale's determination to fulfill his destiny, despite this one moment of mortal reflection, could be the carpenter's answer to that excruciating moment in the Garden of Gethsemane when he pled in prayer, "let this cup pass from me." The rest of that plea, "nevertheless, not as I will, but as thou wilt," Dimmesdale perhaps figures later when he recovers from his madness. Perhaps their elopement comprises Hawthorne's equivalent to a passing of the cup.

But still Dimmesdale continued to echo his determination to carry out the Providential plan exacted of him, despite the promptings from his own mortality.

> "The judgment of God is on me," answered the conscience-stricken priest. "It is too mighty for me to struggle with!" . . . . I am powerless to go. Wretched and sinful as I am, I have had no other thought than to drag on my earthly existence in the sphere where Providence hath placed me. Lost as my own soul is, I would still do what I may for other human souls! I dare not quit my post, though an unfaithful sentinel, whose sure reward is death and dishonour, when his dreary watch shall come to an end!" (197)

But for a couple of phrases, this passage is a remarkably transparent comparison with Dimmesdale's counterpart. The extremely sensitive minister, wretched because of the hell his soul experiences under the burden of sins he carried upon his shoulders, was determined to do what he had been destined to do by Providence, for the sake of other human souls. What Hester had proposed will not happen on his watch. Though he had temporarily stepped down to Hester's earthly level, as an unfaithful sentinel, he must continue though death and dishonor befall him, and, we might add, until he has finished his mission upon the cross, I mean, scaffold.

Dimmesdale replied to Hester's appeals that he does not have the strength or courage "to venture into the wide, strange, difficult world, alone," that he must die, to which Hester whispered, "Thou shalt not go alone!" Elaborated in the succeeding chapter, Hester meant that she and Pearl would go with him if he would leave his flock and start anew elsewhere. For Dimmesdale to abandon the destiny that Providence has laid out for him may mean to him that wherever he would go, thereafter he would be alone or cut off from the rolls of humanity. Perhaps Hawthorne is referring to the isolation of the damned who are consigned to the regions of Sheol.

THE REDEMPTION OF OTHER SOULS

Perhaps, as Dimmesdale sensed that the loss of his soul was tied to the salvation "for other human souls," his loneliness might represent the loss of souls if the Nazarene had chosen not to undergo the Redemption, but to lie instead "under the fallen leaves." Hawthorne reinforces this possible theme. In a moment of mortal despair, Dimmesdale asked Hester a question, possibly for the sake of the reader to ponder the office of his calling, "What can a ruined soul, like mine, effect toward the redemption of other souls?–or a polluted soul, towards their purification?" (191) How can his polluted soul redeem the souls of others? It seems that the consciousness of guilt and misery is focused upon the soul of this man's extreme sensitivity, like no other, and he wonders if there is a connection between his own wretched soul and the souls of humankind. How can he, so polluted [with their sins], bring about their redemption? To what destiny is Providence driving him? There are perhaps no better or clearer allusion to the vicariousness of the Atonement than this, although Hawthorne has cleverly framed them within the context of this one doubting moment. And it is one of the few rare moments in which the reader might intuitvely gaze beyong the veil to see Dimmesdale's true representation. Or, one might easily conclude that this purveyor has only been dropping crumbs along the way, and the poor reader is but standing facing a candy house of delusional fantasy, which is as much a fairy tale as Hawthorne's fiction.

Perhaps Hawthorne is simply engaging the reader by projecting the thought, "how can one man's suffering vicariously redeem the souls of mankind," rather than suggesting that such a doubt ever entered the Redeemer's mind. In a moment of reflective relief from too much empathy with Dimmesdale's plight, one familiar with Biblical themes might revert, for a comparison, to the ancient prejudice of Isaiah,

> Surely he hath borne our griefs, and carried our sorrows: . . . .
>
> But he was wounded for our transgdressions, he was bruised for our iniquities . . . and with his stripes we are healed . . . .
>
> Yet it pleased the Lord to bruise him; he hath put him to grief.[3]

and be "relieved only by [the] one ever-glowing point of light gloomier than the shadow" (264). Perhaps Hawthorne may have envisioned a measure of relief from the problems of life, by that one ancient principle, the act of which was doubtlessly gloomier than the shadows cast by the dismal forest.

NOT TO GO ALONE

The statement from Hester that he would not go alone carries the implication that she and Pearl will go with him. The idea of Hester's willingness to go with him opened up a whole new perspective for the young minister, who had never thought of such an option, and becomes the subject of the next few chapters. Up until this statement, Dimmesdale's mind has been set on doing what he senses to be the will of Providence despite the burden he carries. He has refuted all other arguments presented by Hester

We must remember that Hester and the young minister are still commiserating on that "luxuriant heap of moss." That they may be together forever is a kind of impatient predilection, perhaps acceptable to the rational mind, but not indicative of the reality that might justify or assure it. The likelihood of their being ever together is framed in a question at the end of the tale, the answer to which is left for the reader to see what he or she prefers to see.

For a short time, then, the moss insulated these two lovers from the reality of that fated destiny. Dimmesdale's pathway, "by a spectre that had stolen out from among his thoughts," had been haunted thus in Hester's relentless speculation.

In the next chapter, they will elaborate upon their speculative venture, embibed from their surroundings; at worst, experience a brief moment of solace in their impetuous time-out; and, at best, perhaps foreshadow some future real relief.

CHAPTER 18

A FLOOD OF SUNSHINE

O my Father, if it be possible, let this cup pass from me.[1]

In the forest, the dark romantic may meet with and sell his soul to the Black Man for some black magic, or possibly be illuminated by a flood of sunshine from the spiritual world. The flood of sunshine in the forest in this chapter may represent what it is like to be free from the governing regions of all conventional law, and perhaps only a foreshadowing of the promise of freedom from the bondage of mortality, as it is freed from all sense of earthly law. It might crudely be analogized as perhaps similar to the relief of deliverance from the throes of false labor. Less crudely and more conjectural, it might be compared to the exhilarating thought of being released from a painful body at death into the region beyond "the scope of generally received laws," where one may freshly think to devise his own set of rules and decorum to a new life, that is, until the law that is reappears.

Suspended upon the same surrealistic plane of pure speculation, far from the beaten path of reality, the divine in Dimmesdale has given in to the rational argument of his mortal companion, on the pretext that they can abandon all, including foregoing the Confession, and still be together. Perhaps the single implication of this false hope, possibly willed by the carpenter's son in his one moment of self-will, is that, even without the Redemption, the resurrection could still happen, at least for him. In a wild moment of dark speculation, which Hawthorne identifies clearly in the second paragraph, both Dimmesdale and Hester throw off the regions of law, as though they can escape its effects, at least during the brief interval of their time-out from reality.

Whereas Hawthorne takes three consecutive chapters and a day to dwell upon the momentary weak-mindedness of Dimmesdale in considering a rejection of his destiny, the weakness of the mortal flesh of Joseph's son may have been, at the least, less than a split second, as an impulse he immediately constrained, or, at the most, may have extended throughout the duration of his ordeal in the garden of Gethsemane. Again we have possibly the allegorical technique of expanding time in the development of a theme. Chronology and duration of events are logical structures, and may be altered to explore Hawthorne's Transcendentalistic style, possibly upon the premise that truth purportedly transcends them both in the transmission of its message.

THE HUMAN STRUGGLE

For seven long years Hester had struggled against the human institutions of a society, established by priests or legislators, that had outlawed her; and her point of view, perhaps from a developing sagacity, has become highly critical of her care-keepers, "with hardly more reverence than the Indian would feel for the clerical band, the judicial robe, the pillory, the gallows, the fireside, or the church" (199). Perhaps Hawthorne is sharing his own point of view somewhat in Hester's, especially to note that, having "habituated herself to such latitude of speculation," her state of mind "was altogether foreign to the clergyman." Dimmesdale's mind was always focused upon the law, and now he is being confronted with the natural man within him; having "been broken down by long and exquisite suffering . . . his mind was darkened and confused by the very remorse which harrowed it" (199).

Hawthorne seems to be building a case to justify the Nazarene's momentary focus upon his human self, in which he willed to escape the ordeal in Gethsemanie.

The suggestion or temptation to flee came from Hester, who appears to represent mortal nature; and Dimmesdale, who may represent the divine nature, has entertained, for the first time, an idea that, at first, struck him with fear and horror, perhaps because he is still embedded in the reality of facing his intended destiny. For Hester, after seven long years of "outlaw and ignominy," of being browbeaten with Shame, Despair, and Solitude, mortal nature has entered a region of her own. Though these teachers "had made her strong . . . [they had] taught her much amiss." And the young divine, for the moment on the same speculative sphere, thought

> that it was human to avoid the peril of death and infamy, and the inscrutable machinations of an enemy; that, finally, to this poor pilgrim, on his dreary and desert path, faint, sick, miserable, there appeared a glimpse of human affection and sympathy, a new life, and a true one, in exchange for the heavy doom which he was not expiating. (200)

Perhaps this speculative perspective, or point of view, seems typical of weary-worn human nature to Hawthorne, especially when it has been castigated by the proscriptions of misaligned clergymen. Whereas Hester's distress may be physical and emotional, it is mostly for herself that she suffers; for Dimmesdale, it appears that his spiritual suffering is an expiation for a heavier doom that vicariously is more extensive. Yet, the spirit of freedom entertained fleetingly by both appears to be derivative from a moral wilderness, especially since that maze has offered no relief of "human affection and sympathy." Though the idea of being together with Hester might bring a new life, the reality that it was not really a true one will not come till later when the minister exists his moral maze. But the thought of the warmth and comfort of Hester, and the devotion of Pearl, is the coup de grace to Dimmesdale's resistance. Dimmesdale rationalized that if he had had "one instant of peace or hope, [he] would yet endure, for the sake of that earnest of Heaven's mercy." (201) Here he seems to be thinking of himself, not of the plan of mercy for the sake of others, and is wrestling with the inclinations of his flesh.

Heretofore this temptation, it has been contrary to Dimmesdale's Providential destiny to abandon his flock: "Lost as my own soul is, I would still do what I may for other human souls!" (197) It appears contrary to the avowed omniscience of Deity that the Man of Galilee would act according to his own human will, but would pursue Providence's. To abandon the plan of the Redemption would constitute abandonment of the Redeemed. Hester, as the spirit of nature, is not bound to these rules of conduct, as is Dimmesdale, the spirit of the divine. Outlawed from society, Hester has been freed by the license of her scarlet letter to wander where she will; and now she was counseling the divine also to think likewise of escape into the lawless regions.

His spirit indeed was willing, but his flesh weak; and at the crucial point of his relinquishment, Dimmesdale makes one final plea, "O Thou to whom I dare not lift mine eyes, wilt Thou yet pardon me!" This plea appears to be Hawthorne's wording of the same humble plea the Galilean made in the Garden to pardon him from the burden under which he intensely agonized, as noted at the beginning of this chapter.

At the allegorical level, one far-fetched possible meaning of this new idea—that the divine will not go alone into the "wild, strange, difficult world," but will be together with mortal nature—might suggest that the Son of Man could have abandoned the cross, taken mortal nature with him, begun his ministry in some other clime, and raised his seed in a new way of life. Or it might, less dramatically, insinuate the unrealistic prospect that his spirit, rendered free by a frenzied imagination, would not go alone into the cold, strange, and different world, but would be accompanied by the passionate warmth of a natural tabernacle.

The minister's experiences have never led him "beyond the scope of generally received laws," except for the one "sin of passion, not of principle, nor even planned" (200). Perhaps that unspecified act of passion was not a breach of divine principle, nor the sin of a rational plan, but an act of passionate caring, or creation, for which he had assumed responsibility. Perhaps to Hawthorne, as it was for Michaelangelo, the creation of humankind was an epoch of passion by the touch of the finger of the Creator; that is, the Creator possibly created humankind in the flesh, in a moment of passion, to capacitate his being with passion itself, which therefore could not be evil in and of itself. The Re-creation, or Re-transformation, might also occur by the same mighty touch.

Nevertheless, in the forest, or the raw, moral wilderness, tempted by nature and struggling as a priest within "the framework of his order [which] inevitably hemmed him in . . . the clergyman resolved to flee" (200 and 201), to escape from the mission of suffering, and to avoid the confession he had dreaded for those same seven years. Perhaps it was the physical nature of the Nazarene that appealed to his spirit in want of a way out of drinking the bitter cup, if it were possible. Dimmesdale's spiritual being, however, as we shall see in a later chapter, had the power to relinquish this inclination of the flesh, but only by careful analysis of his thoughts and feelings after his unique experiences following his exit from the forest.

Glow of Strange Enjoyment

In an elongated moment of decision, the divine had yielded to the appeal of his partner in crime, and experienced

> a glow of strange enjoyment [throwing] its flickering brightness over the trouble of his breast. It was the exhilarating effect—upon a prisoner just escaped from the dungeon of his own heart—of breathing the wild, free atmosphere of an unredeemed, unchristianized, lawless region. (201)

The hope and joy both Dimmesdale and Hester feel, at the prospect of fleeing justice and mercy, seems more human than divine. It seems merely the temporary exhilaration of a thought or idea that will only flicker for a while, for its brightness will expire, even as the prisoner, though free for a moment, is yet subject to answer the end of the law. At worst, it seems to be a sphere or strange world of false hope, where exists no Christian ethic, no law of justice or mercy, and, therefore, no real redemption from the dungeon of his heart. At best, it might foreshadow some semblance of the joy that comes from real relief. But Hawthorne quickly assures the reader that the problems of humanity will not be solved by this alternate plan. Shortly, Pearl will appear to signal to them, as a kind of prophetess, that something is amiss.

A Lost Jewel

Hawthorne again refers to the emblem of the scarlet letter upon Hester's bosom, and its deeper symbolic meaning, as a jewel, but in this case, a lost jewel, as she tosses it among the withered leaves, perhaps to symbolize that the loss of the pearl of great price means no transfiguration for withering mortality.

> With a hand's breadth farther flight it would have fallen into the water, and have given the little brook another woe to carry onward, besides the unintelligible tale which it still kept murmuring about. But there lay the embroidered letter, glittering like a lost jewel. (202)

The plan her rational mind has devised might have burdened the brook with another woe, had it landed in the brooklet. That additional woe might likely be no other than the attempt to escape the destiny inscribed within the emblem of her suffering. Perhaps "[t]he mystic token alighted on the hither verge of the stream," and not in the stream, to signify that the decision is on the verge of the stream of history, not yet a matter of reality, but still a figment of their imagination near fruition.

Having ridden herself of the emblem, at least in her mind, she has, for the while, been released from the stigma placed upon her by Puritanism. Perhaps, in the imagination of her heart, Hester experienced a temporary transfiguration, the description of which is quoted at length, as it might foreshadow the forthcoming light for which she has for seven long years hoped.

> The stigma gone, Hester heaved a long, deep sigh, in which the burden of shame and anguish departed from her spirit. O exquisite relief! She had not known the weight, until she felt the freedom! By another impulse, she took off the formal cap that confined her hair; and down it fell upon her shoulders, dark and rich, with at once a shadow and a light in its abundance, and imparting the charm of softness to her features. There played around her mouth, and beamed out of her eyes, a radiant and tender smile, that seemed gushing from the very heart of womanhood. A crimson flush was glowing on her cheek, that had been long so pale. Her sex, her youth, and the whole richness of her beauty, came back from what men call the irrevocable past, and clustered themselves, with her maiden hope, and a happiness before unknown, within the magic circle of this hour. And, as if the gloom of the earth and sky had been but the effluence of these two mortal hearts, it vanished with their sorrow. (202)

Is this the transfiguration she hoped would give back her beauty as a woman? Is the magic circle of this moment "the magic touch to effect the transfiguration?" As Hawthorne promised, "We shall see whether Hester Prynne were ever afterwards so touched, and so transfigured" (164), is this the particular fulfillment of that promise? The answer lies interpretatively in a few clues, or thoughts, contained in the passages above, and in the events that follow, as if to expose to the reader this "as if" affluence, and to highlight by contrast the substance of destined reality.

In the first place, part of the richness of her womanhood returning contains a "shadow" as well as "light," suggesting possibly that the return is a foreshadowing of a real relief, and not the reality of it. The phrase "seemed gushing from the very heart" seems to make her joy a semblance. All that is restored gathered around her "maiden hope," implying an anticipation rather than an actual fulfillment of the return. The clue, "as if," may indicate that "the gloom of earth and sky" they had endured only vanished as an outflow from them, the substance or conditions of which may yet remain. Perhaps this gloom is both earthly and heavenly, like that which redeems it. In the spirit of speculation, the mind might easily rid itself temporarily of earthly gloom; but the gloom of both earth and sky may really only be disposed of if their true destinies are intact.

However, these minor clues are not as concrete as the events that naturally followed to show whether or not Hester was forever, or "ever afterwards," so touched. That her beauty returned temporarily is not symbolic of the transfiguration of which Hawthorne is figuring perhaps to be everlasting. It is simply the unknowing, unlawful, effusion of sympathetic Nature, as Hawthorne, checking the reader's gleeful assumptions, explains shortly after the bursting sunlight.

> All at once, as with a sudden smile of Heaven, forth burst the sunshine, pouring a very flood into the obscure forest . . . . The course of the little brook might be traced by its merry gleam afar into the wood's heart of mystery, which had become a mystery of joy.

> Such was the sympathy of Nature—that wild heathen Nature of the forest, never subjugated by human law, nor illumined by higher truth—with the bliss of these two spirits! Love, whether newly born, or aroused from a death-like slumber, must always create a sunshine, filling the heart so full of radiance, that it overflows upon the outward world. (203)

Human nature, without the divine element, is wild and heathen, hardly submissive to human law, "nor illumined by higher truth," perhaps because its flesh and blood truths are raw and unregulated and need illumination by higher truths. It can easily be flushed by the aspects of Love, which, though suffering from a death-like slumber, can overleap the boundaries of the real world, and presage that ultimate joy to its cherished objects. In this exceptional instance, it seems as though a flood of sunshine, empowered by Love, illuminates the darkness of the forest as a kind of omen prefiguring some mystery of joy, or higher truth, that may yet follow.

Resting on the same physical or speculative plane of nature, these two spirits, of the divine and of nature, out of touch with reality, rejoice together in the flickering glow of a strange joy in the forest, the realm of simulated truth free from the proscriptions of civilizations, as well as from the law of justice. However, Nature, of its own accord, sympathetic with its own children, may not be completely or accurately "illuminated by higher truth." Perhaps the hope and joy they experience speculatively is a sylvan deception that, if one doesn't heed intuitions from the spiritual dimension that reflect a greater reality, could lead them awry. Pearl soon appears upon the scene to cast doubt upon their imaginative wonder.

The brooklet seems to be the spokesperson for this greater reality of the spiritual sphere that transcends the vicarious experience Hester and Dimmesdale momentarily glimpse for themselves. For a brief moment, while they exult together in the light of speculated bliss, Nature, in sympathy with both joy and misery, responded with a flood of sunshine that appears, at best, briefly to premonition relief from the darkness and gloom of their suffering. The mystery of this summary joy can be traced by the brook's merry gleam far back into the wood's heart of mystery. In an environment devoid of law, the mystery of sadness has become a mystery of joy during this wild moment entertained by the two spirits.

BUT NOT TO BE DECEIVED

Pearl, at the same time, and on the other hand, was not so deceived by any need to speculate. She ate the partridge-berries "now red as drops of blood upon the withered leaves" (204), possibly to signify her intuitive faithfulness to the promise of the blessings contained in the redemption, or the resurrection of the dead, the effect of which may be uniformly symbolized in red, as blood upon withered leaves. Likewise, "the great black forest—stern as it showed itself to those who brought the guilt and troubles of the world into its bosom—became the playmate of the lonely infant" (204), because she was not confused by its darkness, nor impervious to higher truth, and did not buy into earthly whelms.

Despite the troubles and guilt brought into the world by the fall and the transgression in the Garden of Eden, the denizens, partridge, pigeon, squirrel, fox, and wolf are Pearl's gentle and fearless playmates, and may remind the reader of a similar Biblical setting during a future promised time.

> The wolf also shall dwell with the lamb . . . and the weaned child shall put his hand on the cockatrice' den. They shall not hurt nor destroy in all my holy mountain: for the earth shall be full of the knowledge of the Lord.[2]

Pearl is in perfect harmony with the wilderness, and nature seems to be under her will. Her nature is therefore gentler. She adorns herself with the flowers of nature, "or whatever else was in closest sympathy with the antique wood" (205), as though to presage some destiny of humankind's unity with nature. If there is any mystery of the forest, she is it, a mystery of joy, a spirit of the future that is mindful of the past. This scene with the animals seems a pretaste of those better times Hawthorne may have forecast in hope and joy, "but with fear betwixt them" (199). Between the hope of humanity for a resolution of its problems, and the reality of the promise, is a moment or so of fear. What that fear might refer to symbolically seems left to the reader to surmise, as few references clue it's possible meanings. But the green scarlet letter she made for herself may represent a new life elsewhere, when the red scarlet letter has fulfilled its dutiful office.

Therefore, the joy the two spirits of Hester and Dimmesdale imagined was strange, the brightness was flickering, and the atmosphere around them breathed of unchristian unredemption, suggesting possibly to the reader's mind that their plan to escape is only an illusory flicker that does not reflect a higher truth. The little brook at their feet, into which Hester almost threw the scarlet letter, doth the same tale repeat,—or would have, if the emblem had fallen into it—of another woe added to its burden, the uncomprehending woe of a nullified redemption. But the scarlet letter only landed at the border of the stream, and is to be retrieved only in the next chapter.

So Pearl was called back to join with Hester and Dimmesdale. Pearl reentered the scene, "standing in a streak of sunshsine, a good way off, on the other side of the brook" (203), to reprimand and remind them of their destiny for and in behalf of her sake. She does not wish to join them, on perhaps the wrong side of the brooklet. "[I]n closest sympathy with the antique wood," she perhaps is in tune with the mystery of the fallen trees, though not in sympathy with its present melancholy. Perhaps the reader has noticed that the forest, perhaps a little more intimidating at first, appears to be much more empathic now that Pearl has made it her playground, as though her presence has enfused something of her own nature into it.

Standing in sunshine, she seems to sense the rapture of the mystery long lost in the melancholy of the decaying wilderness. The forest seems to long for a return of something associated with the confident, the peaceful, and the loving spirit of Pearl.

> The truth seems to be, however, that the mother-forest, and these wild things which it nourished, all recognized a kindred wildness in the human child.

> And she was gentler here than in the grassy-margined streets of the settlement, or in her mother's cottage. The flowers appeared to know it; and one and another whispered as she passed, "Adorn thyself with me, thou beautiful child, adorn thyself with me!" (205)

The flowers seem to speak to a future time, when, in the Christian faith, the regenerate beauty of mankind will take upon herself the regenerate beauty of the mortal element. In a way, Pearl appears to represent Hawthorne's outlook on life's prospects brighter than that of his Puritan heritage, or perhaps any generation given to philosophical speculations. She is Hawthorne's voice in allegory, that speaks aloud in spirit to the inferences of his "as if" commentaries. As we see in the next chapter, she is the "bright-apparelled vision, in a sunbeam" (204), of a higher truth, that, speaking to Hester and Dimmesdale from the other side of the brook, checks the speculative nature of Hester's plan to escape the destiny that Providence has laid out before them.

CHAPTER 19

THE CHILD AT THE BROOKSIDE

And a little child shall lead them.[1]
Walk not after the flesh, but after the Spirit.[2]

This chapter offers many more clues that tie the allegorical relationships of the main characters together. Pearl seems to be the kingpin, the clasp that hold the scarlet letter to Hester's bosom, the connection between Hester and Dimmesdale, and "the visible tie that united them" (206). Intuitively she guided or reminded Hester and Dimmesdale of the destiny that must unfold by their suffering.

SHE IS MOSTLY THINE!

As Hester and Arthur momentarily imagine what it would be like to be free of the burden they share, Pearl slowly is walking back from her rendevous with the forest, slowly perhaps because she saw Dimmesdale in his present state of mind. Hawthorne displays her in the fulness of her allegorical wonder, "a splendid child," whose features seem to mirror her as the offspring of the divine and the glory of nature. Hester and Dimmesdale remark about two aspects of her appearance, one of which is whom she is most like. Hester began, "She is a splendid child! But I know whose brow she has!" Perhaps Nature, at its best, would identify itself more like the divine. To which comparison, Arthur replied,

> Dost thou know, Hester, . . . that this dear child, tripping about always at thy side, hath caused me many an alarm? Methought—

O Hester, what a thought is that, and how terrible to dread it!—that my own features were partly repeated in her face, and so strikingly that the world might see them! But she is mostly thine!" (206)

Perhaps this exchange, with all the exclamation marks highlighting its allegorical significance, again points to the controversy about the true nature of mortality. Hawthorne seems to declare, loudly enough, once these three characters are recognized for what they represent, the Biblical concept that humankind is a composite, an off-shoot from two quarters, one comprizing the divine element, as the off-spring of Deity, and the other, that of the earthly element, as a creature from the dust. So concisely does he seem to say that humankind embodies the quality of shunning that which is wrong, the "brow she has," and was so strikingly created in the image of Deity, that it is terrible to dread the thought of it. Nevertheless, perhaps from heaven's point of view, humankind has been the cause of much alarm to that quarter, and therefore is mostly earthly, at least at present, and heaven may not be readily inclined as yet to claim too close a resemblance.

Hester had the last word on the matter, "No, no! Not mostly! . . . A little longer, and thou needest not to be afraid to trace whose child she is" (206). This prediction may contain some allegorical ambivalence, but Hawthorne may be referring less to Hester's speculative plan to run away together—to escape their fated destiny—than to her intuitive sense that those destinies shall be fulfilled as designed by Providence.

The second aspect of Pearl's appearance Hawthorne seems to address might relate symbolically to what "our dear old England" might represent, and what might be a forecast of Pearl's destiny. In Hester's concluding comment on the subject, she remarked,

But how strangely beautiful she looks, with those wild flowers in her hair! It is as if one of the fairies, whom we left in our dear old England, had decked her out to meet us. (206)

Again, the "as if" switch is on, perhaps as if to alert and enlighten the reader to the other side of Hawthorne's tale. It almost seems as though Hawthorne is saying that old England might represent a former life, the other side of the veil from whence an angel has attired Pearl in a symbolic beauty, strange to their present perspective, with which to meet the couple.

Perhaps to signify the relevance of both arguments, Hawthorne interjects his own commentary as a fitting resolution thereof:

> In her was visible the tie that united them. She had been offered to the world, these seven years past, as the living hieroglyphic, in which was revealed the secret they so darkly sought to hide,—all written in this symbol,—all plainly manifest,—had there been a prophet or magician skilled to read the character of flame! And Pearl was the oneness of their being. Be the foregone evil what it might, how could they doubt that their earthly lives and future destinies were conjoined, when they beheld at once the material union, and the spiritual idea, in whom they met and were to dwell immortally together? (207)

Perhaps in no other passage does Hawthorne strive to reveal to the reader the principles that these three characters seem to represent: Pearl appears most strongly to be the future of humankind incarnate, bedecked in all the radiance bestowed by the intimations of the kindred forest, apparelled in a sunbeam of prophetic light, tokening the oneness of the earth and the divine. Hawthorne has cast her as the living symbol, the "character of flame," and perhaps as the promise of the redemptive At-one-ment, by which material and divine element may "dwell immortally together," not in spite of but by the cause of the kind of consecrated act performed by her creation, "be the foregone evil what it might." Whatever caused the fall into mortality, and the consequent evil inherent, "offered to the world, these seven years past," Pearl is the hope of the world for the duration of it, the promise embedded in the mystery of the scarlet letter, all inscribed and plainly manifest to the reader, or any other psychic, who can "read the character of the flame!"

Where Pearl had stopped near the stream, "a pool, so smooth and quiet . . . reflected the image of her little figure . . . more refined and spiritualized than the reality" (208), as though perhaps to premonition a better image of what the future holds for mankind.

Perhaps Hawthorne appears to believe that that future will have more investiture of the spiritual idea than the earthly in the union of the two. Perhaps he may be indulging part of his philosophical self, that in the resurrection of the body with the spirit, the result would be more spiritualized and refined that the present reality.

Whether Pearl is this prophetess or magician, or whether Hawthorne is referring to some other Daniel to interpret the "character of flame," is a question left for one's imagination. But who can question, or doubt, along with Hester and Dimmesdale, the "feeling[,] which neither of them had ever before experienced, . . . that their earthly lives and future destinies were conjoined . . . and were to dwell immortally together?" (207) This passage and question, perhaps posed by Hawthorne to the mind of the reader more than to the minds of Hester and Dimmesdale, may be the greatest clue "the curious investigator may still discern, and perplex himself with the purport" thereof (264).

THE DIVIDING LINE

Hester calls to Pearl by the brookside, but she will not cross over the brook to her mother, who feels estranged from her. It was not Pearl, but Hester and Arthur, who "had strayed out of the sphere in which she and her mother dwelt together" (208)—they, who had lost their sense of reality, they, who had agreed to hide from their destinies. Nevertheless, the young divine seemed intuitively aware that Pearl is trying to tell them what she perhaps only intuits, that they cannot live in both the world of fantasy and the real world.

> "I have a strange fancy," observed the sensitive minister, "that this brook is the boundary between two worlds, and that thou canst never meet thy Pearl again." (208)

The brook appears to divide these two spheres between what is and what could be, and may reflect a "more refined and spiritualized" image of Pearl's intuitive apprehension of what must be. Dimmesdale sensed that Hester can not be joined with Pearl, as the matter stands at present, but does not seem to know exactly what it is that separates them. Since Hester and Dimmesdale seem to be in a fantasy world, betokened by a spirit of speculation, that puts them on an equal plane apart from reality, their speculation possibly symbolizes an effect that would change the future in a way that is not in harmony with the foreordained destiny of humankind. This future destiny cannot be achieved if destined events do not occur as fate seems to have decreed them. Pearl may the prophetess that senses this foreordained destiny, and the brook the sympathetic natural witness of the forest.

Pearl's experiences on the other side of the brook seem to represent, as noted in the preceding chapter, the destiny of the world, an ideal state of nature and humankind, beyond the seven thousand years of its gloomy existence, that is, if things proceed as planned; which apparently means that Dimmesdale must join with Hester and Pearl and acknowledge his responsibility to Pearl and her mother, in order, allegorically, to bring about the fulfillment of a sacred promise. That confession constitutes a redemption, not just for Dimmesdale, but for Pearl and Hester. And allegorically, it appears to represent a redemption for all humanity.

THE PROPHETESS

Seeking "to detect and explain to herself the relation which they bore to one another" (209), Pearl finally and authoritatively points her finger to her mother's empty breast, from which she had flung away the scarlet letter earlier. The brooklet does the same, with an emphasis on the "flower-girdled and sunny image," as if to confirm the truthfulness and destiny of the scarlet letter inherent within her gesture.

> At length, assuming a singular air of authority, Pearl stretched out her hand, with the small forefinger extended, and pointing evidently towards her mother's breast. And beneath, in the mirror of the brook, there was the flower-girdled and sunny image of little Pearl, pointing her small forefinger too. (209)

Hester's empty breast, where the scarlet letter was previously clasped in place, and at which Pearl's finger is pointing, likely represents "the alternate plan" she and Dimmesdale have devised to rid themselves of their sorrowing lives. Her glance at the young minister likely reminded him of the agony festering in his heart and needing to be purged by confession, as "his hand—with that gesture so habitual as to have become involuntary—stole over his heart." Pearl's pointing finger, her soul-piercing glance, and the brooklet's spiritualized reflection seem to communicate to both her parents that the scarlet letter must do its office, or have its effect, and that only the confession can seal their unity.

"[A]ll glorified with a ray of sunshine, that was attracted thitherward as by a certain sympathy" (208), Pearl, signaling a higher truth, could not accept or give recognition to a solution that was not within the destiny she apprehended. As the brook pictured Pearl more refined and spiritualized, it may appear that Pearl is figured as a prophetess who senses their true and significant relationship, and what must transpire to bring about a better world in which the human race might live. A new life, a new beginning cannot happen without the confession-redemption. Human nature, nor the nature of the world, can change unless the scarlet letter A has fulfilled its office for the sake of all humanity. Hester may be transfigured, not by any rational approach, but only by some mighty tough of a mightier hand.

Still pointing her little forefinger, Pearl's piercing shrieks, in rejection of the speculated solution shared by Hester and Dimmesdale, are reverberated by the woods, "as if a hidden multitude were lending her their sympathy and encouragement" (210). If at any time Pearl is the prophetess Hester envisioned earlier, it is at this crucial time when Dimmesdale has been tempted to run away from the office of his destined calling. Perhaps these shrieks, resounding a multitude of echos throughout the forest, may represent, unless we are carrying the analogy too far, the wailing of the damned and decaying forest crying out for relief in agreement with the true destined plan. Indeed, as Hawthorne has implied earlier in his tale, Pearl's single voice represents many voices of humanity, as she is many children in one (90). To Hawthorne, perhaps the needs of humankind demand a resolution to the problems inherent in mortality.

The Redemption presupposes death; and recognizing Pearl's rebuke, Hester wields "a crimson blush upon her cheek . . . and then a heavy sigh; while, even before she had time to speak, the blush yielded to a deadly pallor" (210). Perhaps, much like "the partridge-berries . . . now red as drops of blood upon the withered leaves" which Pearl had picked in the forest earlier (204), death precedes their alleged revival. The crimson blush may reflect Hester's recognition of Pearl's higher truth; the sigh may signal the resumption of resignation to her destiny; and the deadly pallor presupposes the necessity of the death of mortality, and no escape therefrom before.

Hester confessed her error in dispensing of the scarlet letter, but has not yet grasped the fullness of Pearl's rejection:

"But, in very truth, she is right as regards this hateful token. I must bear its torture yet a little longer,—only a few days longer,—until we shall have left this region, and look back hither as to a land which we have dreamed of. The forest cannot hide it! The mid-ocean shall take it from my hand, and swallow it up for ever!" (211)

This statement is an extraordinary moment of insight, or far sight, for Hester, but for Hawthorne, perhaps only an unusual or common perception. At the surface level of the tale, Hester is comtemplating that she must endure her torment until the three of them flee their plight across the ocean. Neither she nor Dimmesdale at this point has comprehended the incompatibility of their speculated plan. However, at the allegorical or intuitive level, the passage might be alluding to the interval of time and space after death, the mid-ocean between the region of this life and the next, that swallows up mortality forever, wherein we look back on earth life only as a dream.

Hester, then, not only retrieved the scarlet letter but also resumed, in her appearance, submission to her mission of endurance a little longer.

There was a sense of inevitable doom upon her, as she thus received back this deadly symbol from the hand of fate . . . . As if there were a withering spell in the sad letter, her beauty, the warmth and richness of her womanhood, departed, like fading sunshine; and a gray shadow seemed to fall across her." (211)

Having left the mossy plane, and returning the scarlet letter to its rightful place, Hester's quasi-restored womanhood faded as she reentered the world of reality. Pearl then bounded across the pond, kissed her mother's brow and cheeks, and then kissed the scarlet letter too, proclaiming, "Now thou art my mother indeed! And I am thy little Pearl!" (211) Once again, perhaps we hear immortality claiming mortality as her mother, with a kiss of the scarlet letter to certify its due office.

But for that relationship to exist, Pearl sensed something else had to happen, on the part of Dimmesdale, as typified by three intelligent questions she asks her mother, three clues that strike to the core of the allegory: "Does he love us?" "Will he go back with us, hand in hand, we three together, into the town?" "And will he always keep his hand over his heart?" (212) Perhaps these questions could be rephrased at the allegorical level: Does the Creator love humankind enough to reconcile the problems of the world? Will he take us, humanity and nature, hand in hand with the divine, out of this dismal forest, back into a law-abiding society? And will he fulfill his destiny and remove the burden upon his heart?

Hester answers the first two question in the affirmative, intuitively, in apparently confident hopefulness.

> "Not now, dear child," answered Hester, "But in days to come he will walk hand in hand with us. We will have a home and fireside of our own; and thou shalt sit upon his knee; and he will teach thee many things, and love thee dearly. Thou wilt love him." (212)

"Only a few days longer" has become "days to come." But whether or not Hester's picture of their happy-fireside-togetherness bespeaks the fulfillment of their speculated plan in just a few days longer or the fulfillment of Providence's plan, in yet further days to come, may be the ambiguous double-speak of the allegory. whereas this happy reunion may represent a literal resurrection to a different kind of world.

The third question was dismissed lightly, and apparently left Pearl still not completely satisfied, for she does not kiss Dimmesdale, who is afraid of her at this time, inasmuch as he has not yet returned to the reality of his destiny. Perhaps Hawthorne chose not to address the thematic answer to this question at this point so as not to relieve the tension that builds in the following chapter, and climaxes in the remaining. Neveretheless, this third question may have been answered earlier, inadvertently at the allegorical level, while Hester was still thinking erroneously of escaping by ship: "yet a little longer,—only a few days longer" (211), and Dimmesdale will no longer be afraid to claim Pearl as his own, nor "always keep his hand over his heart."

Dimmesdale noted that only twice has Pearl shown any acceptance of the young minister (207). Her acceptance of him seems to progress the nearer he approaches his destined duty to the office of his divine calling. Once, when before the Govenor he defended the right of Hester to claim the child, Pearl caressed his hand, and he kissed her brow. The other was earlier when, in a half-hearted attempt to obtain a confession from Hester, as to who was the father of Pearl, he cloaked his desire to come down from his station and reveal himself as the father. At that time, Pearl had intuitively reached out to him "with a half pleased, half plaintive murmur" of acceptance, as though his intercessory plea in their behalf was nearer the truth.

There was also a probable third time, later, during the minister's vigil, when he anticipated the Confession upon the scaffold, held hands with both Hester and Pearl, forming "an electric chain," and felt "a tumultuous rush of new life, other life than his own, pouring like a torrent into his heart" (143). Pearl's full acceptance of Dimmesdale is fulfilled even later on, when she willingly kissed him most intimately upon his lips, after his confession upon the scaffold. The time element, "in days to come," at the allegorical level, may extend beyond the redemptin-confession, to the time of the resurrection, if and when the Divine finally reclaims his child.

Hawthorne's comment, as the narrator of the story, concerning the return of gloom to Hester, as she was brought back to her destined lot, is an interesting insight that may allude to the typication in his tale: "So it ever is, whether typified or no, an evil deed invests itself with the character of doom" (211). Perhaps, in reference to the deed that brought about the evil in the world, this bit of wisdom portrays Hawthorne's perspective, that no evil deed goes unpunished, and that the problems of life must be addressed and compensated for, as though an absolute law demanded this kind of justice.

It is this purveyor's view that Hawthorne's tale typifies the principle that the demands of justice must be met, reveals his understanding of how they were met, and adds some conclusions of his own about the matter. Perhaps his commentary here may suggest more than Hawthorne's reluctance to cast off his religious heritage completely: that is, that the gloom in the world may harbinger some deed invested with evil in the making of it. Such a statement might allude to Hawthorne's own personal philosophical slant as to what true absolute justice demands, which is, as we have hitherto postulated, that mortality needs a confession-redemption to justify the plight and vicissitudes thereof.

AN ADDITIONAL BURDEN

Although Hester had already signaled her submission to fate, at least knowingly for a while, Arthur as yet had had no such intimations. When he kissed Pearl, she washes it off in the brook, perhaps because it was not given in a state of truthful affinity. "Pearl would show no favor to the clergyman" (212), perhaps because Arthur had not been willing, at that time, to go back with them, "hand in hand, we three together, into the town." With Hester's attrition, destiny, or the plan of eternal life, is getting back on track; what remains is for Arthur to find his way out of fantasy land. This unfinished quest seems part of the burden resting upon the little heart of the stream. Perhaps it is also the burden still of a weary world yet awaiting the full effects of the Redemption.

ANOTHER SAD TALE

While Hester and Dimmesdale sat "upon a heap of moss" and together made

> such arrangements as were suggested by their new position, and the purposes soon to be fulfilled . . . the melancholy brook would add this other tale to the mystery with which its little heart was already overburdened, and whereof it still kept up a murmuring babble, with not a whit more cheerfulness of tone than for ages heretofore. (213)

Apparently Hester had not completely given up the plan, though contritely aware that she was not fulfilling her office of the scarlet letter. The arrangements made, on Hester's part, seem to be the one aspect of integrity not addressed by Hawthorne, as though perhaps her unquestionable devotion and loyalty to Dimmesdale obviated it. The agony of the Atonement is not a cheerful message, but to plan to thwart the destiny of humanity, a destiny which only this agony can bring about, is perhaps an additional burden of sorrow, about which the prophetess of the wilderness may babble to intuitive ears.

Perhaps Hester and Arthur's fantasizing about escaping to Old England may represent, as a speculative far-cry from reality, the philosophical speculations of religionists who wonder why life could not have been arranged differently, or what might happen should there be no redemption. And perhaps, to Hawthorne, the religions of his day and earlier had not done their office with any more cheerfulness than the brooklet in bringing their messages to the world, because they had forgotten the very center, or the heart, of their message.

CHAPTER 20

THE MINISTER IN A MAZE

And he went a little further, and fell on his face, and prayed.[1]

D
immesdale had been sidetracked from his duty-bound destiny
by the speculation proffered by Hester that he might escape it.
Heretofore he had never considered the thought, having been
dedicated to one purpose of a calling greater than his own will. In this
chapter, Hawthorne mirrors or foreshadows the character Dimmesdale
could become if he yielded to his own will and was not true to the
Providential plan. Until he relinquished his own will and again relied
upon the will of Deity, the young divine seems to have lost himself in an
unfamiliar world, one that was turned upside down and opposite to the
one he knew. He sensed himself transformed into a different person by
his brief visit with Hester in the dark forest, and was under the spell of a
foreign and hostile influence.

PARASITIC CHRISTIANITY

Glancing back at Hester and Pearl, whom he saw where he left them
by the brookside, he realized that the time spent in the forest with Hester
was not a dream. Hester had been left standing by a dead

> tree-trunk, which some blast had overthrown a long antiquity
> ago, and which time had ever since been covering with moss,
> so that these two fated ones, with earth's heaviest burden on
> them, might there sit down together, and find a single hour's
> rest and solace. (214)

The metaphor of the tree trunk appears again to address the decaying world from the time of some great blast. The event of the blast seems to signify some great catastrophic occurrence. In keeping with the allegory, it might refer either to the loss of a living world, as in its pristine paradisiacal glory, or the loss of some long antiquity of truth, as heretofore suggested. In the first case, the mortal world is now in decay due to the transformation. In the second case, the cessation of the living water of original Christianity gave way to the dark ages, wherein most ministers thereof declare the heavens are closed to revelation, "an age in which the human intellect, newly emancipated, had taken a more active and a wider range than for many centuries before" (164). Such a long antiquity ago may extend to more than the black idea of the dilapidated nature of current Puritan Christianity. We have noted before that the parasitic moss on the tree trunk likely represents the feeding of contemporary religions upon the remainder of the gigantic tree of pristine truth.

We have also alluded to the possibility that their "single hour's rest and solace" may be a time out from the reality of their destiny. Dimmesdale's time out may demonstrate an elongated moment: whether one moment, one hour, one day, or "a lapse of years" (217), there was a time when the mortal nature of the carpenter's son communed with his spirit and willed to forego the fate for which he had been prepared; yet, according to Biblical records, he never committed a wrongful act. Although Dimmesdale was racked with an empathetic awareness of the sins of others, such that their pain and their shame was vacariously his, yet Dimmesdale's "deeper sense" had kept him from any wrongful act of intentional sin, according to his own understanding. Perhaps Hawthorne has stretched out the one moment of the Nazarene's own will so as to entertain the reader with his conception of the possible psychological ramifications of such an errant thought which occur in this chapter.

TO ALTER FATE CHANGES ALL

Without the divine commitment and intent to carry out his destined fate, Dimmesdale discovered that, not only did the familiar objects of his environment seem to have undergone some mutability, but that also his very nature had changed. As his mind vacillated between two ideas—remaining true to himself or fleeing—the pathway through the woods back to town seemed "wilder, more uncouth with its rude natural obstacles" (216). He discovered that his natural tendencies to do good had been transformed so strangely and abruptly that his thoughts became unholy. Even his intuitive nature had been deceived by his indulgence in the thought that flight was the best escape from his suffering, and that there was no better time than the present to do it.

> Nevertheless, to hold nothing back from the reader,—it was because, on the third day from the present, he was to preach the Election Sermon; and, as such an occasion formed an honorable epoch in the life of a New England clergyman, he could not have chanced upon a more suitable mode and time of terminating his professional career. "At least, they shall say of me," thought this exemplary man, "that I leave no public duty unperformed, nor ill performed!" (215)

The possible significance of the time factor stated in the above passage is that Dimmesdale died on the third day just after he preached the Election Sermon and made his confession. Unthinkable that Hawthorne would hold anything back from his readers, the passage above may refer to the three days the Nazarene hung on the cross before his death that followed his ordeal in the Garden of Gethsemane.

However, the minister, still in the maze of rationalizing his will to sidestep the mission he had theretofore sensed, is still miserably deceived because he is still contemplating, after he preached the Election Sermon, to terminate his career by flight, thus, contrary to his rationalization, leaving the public duty of confession unperformed, and the office of the scarlet letter undone. Hawthrone's narrative, following this fit of speculation, epitomizes this internal conflict between Dimmesdale's divine sense of mission and his own will, perhaps because it relates to the main theme of being true to oneself.

> Sad, indeed, that an introspection so profound and acute as this poor minister's should be so miserably deceived! . . . No man, for any considerable period, can wear one face to himself, and another to the multitude, without finally getting bewildered as to which may be the true." (215-216)

Nevertheless, true to his destiny, Dimmesdale terminated his career by confession and death on the third day, and not by flight. It may or may not be Hawthorne's intention to hypothesize the experience of the minister in his maze as an analogy symbolically alluding to the Nazarene's one moment of self-mindedness in the Garden of Gethsemane.

The plan he and Hester had speculated to act upon entailed sailing upon the sea in a ship to the Old World, one that "roamed over its surface with remarkable irresponsibliity of character" (215), perhaps to reflect upon Dimmesdale's character, if he should carry out the irresponsible plan. As long as the plan was in his heart, he found that his feelings had become almost unresponsive to moral law, that the man returning from the forest was not the same person. If he should meet some friends on his way home, he felt he would say,

> "I am not the man for whom you take me! I left him yonder in the forest, withdrawn into a secret dell, by a mossy tree-trunk, and near a melancholy brook!" . . . . In truth, nothing short of a total change of dynasty and moral code, in that interior kingdom, was adequate to account for the impulses now communicated to the unfortunate and startled minister. (217)

Dimmesdale discovered that his divine nature had been subdued, his compassion for his parishioners and others had been diminished, and an extreme amount of self-control was necessary to prevent injury to them. His extreme sensitivity to the universal heart had rendered him an especial awareness of the conflict he was experiencing, and opened his eyes to the consequences of not being true to his higher instincts.

> "Have I then sold myself," thought the minister, "to the fiend" . . . . He had made a bargain very like it! Tempted by a dream of happiness, he had yielded himself with deliberate choice, as he had never done before. And the infectious poison of that sin had been thus throughout his moral system. It had stupefied all blessed impulses, and awakened into vivid life the whole brotherhood of bad ones. (220, 222)

LOST IN TIME AND PURPOSE

"Yielding to natural impulses borne of speculation, rather than following the higher intuitions of the heart, can make devils of us all," seems to be the message of the maze into which the young minister had found himself, reflects the conflict Hester experiences from time to time, and possible is meant to be a moral coined for the reader's consumption. Lost in a labyrinth wherein he was torn between two paths to follow—his intuitive nobleness or his rational deception—he was nevertheless loyal to his intuitive sense of duty despite his impulses.

> At every step he was incited to do some strange, wild, wicked thing or other, with a sense that it would be at once involuntary and intentional; in spite of himself, yet growing out of a profounder self than that which opposed the impulse. (217)

The young minister seemed to have two selves talking to him. While his rational self told him deceitfully that following the impulse would be involuntary to his divine nature, his intuitive self told him that it would be intentional. Yet, perhaps deeper than his own intuition, was a profounder self revealing to him both his rational and intuitive senses gone astray. He seemed to be experiencing a kind of schizophrenia, a dissociation of two personalities, but was however endowed with a higher sense that enabled him to perceive both.

BACKWARDS IN TIME

By way of interjection, it must be noted that Hester's engagement of a ship to take them back to England might also represent a movement backward in the revolutionary efforts of Puritanism to reform the English church, or a throwback to the attempts of contemporary religion to reform Christianity. When the Puritan movement concluded it was impossible to reform the Church of England, some Puritans had come to settle in the New England coasts, one of which was the Massachusetts Bay Colony. The voyage back to England, therefore, might symbolically represent to Hawthorne another failure in the attempted advancement of Christianity. Perhaps the errant remedy would be to return to a former stage rather than to rely upon the destined future. However, allegorically, Hawthorne clearly labels this alternative, in one of the above passages, as deceptive.

THE POWER OF WILL

This backward movement also is reflected in the reversal of Dimmesdale's natural tendencies, all due to submitting to his weaker nature and deciding to follow his own will. While in this state of conflicted senses, Arthur Dimmesdale encountered no less than five temptations or impulses. These impulses revealed to him a tendency within himself, like one of the sea-faring vessels heading back to Old England, "which, without being absolutely outlaws of the deep," yet roamed over the surface of the deep with an "irresponsibility of character" (215).

Nevertheless, his higher self forced him to be true to his divine nature despite these new evil feelings and tendencies. Dimmesdale had given in to a moment's weakness of his mortal nature's speculative inclinations, and Hawthorne explicitly states the cause of this vicissitude of character: "The minister's own will, and Hester's will, and the fate that grew between them, had wrought this transformation" (217). Up until this moment, the minister had been devoted to the will of Providence, not his own, and Hester had accepted her fate with resignation. But it is the nature of the flesh to seduce the divine within to escape the inevitable. Thus, the idea to flee came from Hester, and not from Dimmesdale. The carpenter from Nazareth himself had fallen upon his face and willed not to have to undergo his Gethsemane; yet he was able to yield himself unto the will of the Supreme Being with whom he was still in communion. We find that Dimmesdale, also by a higher sense than himself, was able to resist the temptations, the yielding to which would have thwarted his confession upon the scaffold.

FIVE TEMPTATIONS

His first temptation, interestingly and appropriately enough, was the impulse to blaspheme the sacrament of the Lord's supper in an interchange with one of his deacons, one of whose duties in the church was probably to pass the bread and wine to the congregation. Although the kindly old gentleman addressed the young minister with "paternal affection" and "worshipping respect . . . as from a lower social rank and inferior order of endowment, towards a higher,"

> [I]t was only by the most careful self-control that [Dimmesdale] could refrain from uttering certain blasphemous suggestions that rose into his mind, respecting the communion-supper. (218)

Why did Hawthorne select this subject as a point of departure from the nature and destined fate of Dimmesdale? This selection is surely no coincidence, but may reveal Hawthorne's remarkable insight into the meaning of the Atonement. The institution of the sacrament of the communion-supper, by representing the body and blood of the Savior, symbolizes the carrying out of the Atonement as designed by Providence. As a figure of the Nazarene image, Arthur's blasphemy of the sacrament would be the perfect cynical or devilish slur in some subliminal realization of his intended failure to carry out the destined confession. Such blasphemy might even be considered the greatest sin Dimmesdale could commit, seeing that he symbolically would, in a sense, be crucifying Christ to himself afresh, and put him to an open shame, which, in the Christian code, would be unforgiveable.[2]

No less insightful is Hawthorne's selection of the second temptation, to whisper into the ear of a devoted parishioner some heretical "unanswerable argument against the immortality of the human soul" (219). Without the Atonement doing its office, there could be no immortality, an argument against which there could be no answer.

Following the temptations of blasphemy and heresy, the third temptation could be likewise properly ordered in terms of gravity of consequences. The young divine is tempted to destroy the soul of a virgin sister with a look that communicated seemingly a message of sexual impurity. But Dimmesdale, by some higher instinct, covered his face to prevent this disaster.

Hawthorne selects little children as the fourth choice of subjects which Dimmesdale was tempted to offend with a barrage of wicked words. Perhaps they were chosen in the sense that this sin would be so grievous that it would have been better for Dimmesdale to have been tossed into the sea with a millstone around his neck.[3]

The fifth temptation was the longing to utter some "heaven-defying oaths" to a drunken seaman. All of these temptation he resisted because of a higher self with which he is still in communion, despite himself.

> It was not so much a better principle, as partly his natural good taste, and still more his buckramed habit of clerical decorum, that carried him safely through the latter crisis. (220)

These fiend-inspired temptations during Dimmesdale's period of fasting may call to the mind of the Christian the temptations of the Nazarene in the desert, or wilderness, in which he fasted for forty days, and then thereafter began his ministry to his own. That they occurred close to the end of Dimmesdale's ministry rather than at the beginning, as in the case of the Nazarene, may not necessarily be a parallel as significant as the other elements of the analogy, which may be free from the constraints of sequence.

In a holistic view, it appears that Hawthorne seems to have fused three Biblical events together—the temptations the carpenter suffered in the desert at the beginning of his ministry, the prayer in the Garden near the end of that ministry, and his short three year ministry between these events. This fusion of events and collapsing of time may be typical strategies used by the Romantics that is markedly different from the realism of the Classicists. It is also a technique used in the development of an allegory.

SELF-AWARENESS AND THE NATURE OF PASSION

Arthur came to his better senses when he realized that these temptations had come from the arch-fiend, or Old Scratch, and that he had been victorious in squelching them. When he communed with his better self, he realized that his decision to follow his own will in the forest would have constituted a contract with the fiend, or Black Man of the forest. He admitted to himself that, in being tempted by Hester's proposal, and in consenting to it, "he had yielded himself with deliberate choice, as he had never done before, to what he knew was deadly sin," and that he had shown "his sympathy and fellowship with wicked mortals and the world of perverted spirits" (222).

But wait a minute. Has Hawthorne made a terrible mistake and contradicted himself? Has Dimmesdale never before "yielded himself with deliberate choice . . . to what he knew was deadly sin?" Has not the reader been led to assume that the young divine committed adultery with Hester? Unless Hawthorne has made a profound error, this paradox could be explained only by questioning the assumption that Dimmesdale is the physical father of Pearl. At the same time it harbors the mystery of Pearl's origin, it perhaps most fittingly, at the allegorical level, mystifies the creation of humankind. Another rational explanation, from Hawthorne's point of view, is that the act of Pearl's creation, whatever it was, that made him feel responsible for Hester and Pearl, was not a deliberate choice, or a deadly sin, but a spontaneous impulse of passion. And since passion dwells at the center of our mortality, perhaps its creation cannot be considered a deadly sin.

In this case, readers must examine the nature of passionate impulses in Hawthorne's tale. We have addressed this nature only briefly, and wish only to summarize it now. There are impulses from the dark side of the spiritual realm, which happen during moments of rational speculation, especially when pressed upon a person by the dark and erroneous interpretations of the age. There are impulses that occur intuitively from the light or truthful side of that realm, which happen during moments of transcendent insight. It appears that passion itself, to Hawthorne, since it comes with the package of creation, may not be considered so inglorious, for he has focused upon two momentous events as acts of sacred passion, the Passion of the creation, and the Passion of the redemption. Perhaps it is in the deliberation that matters, wherein when speculation vies and wins against the intuitive motive of the heart, the outcome may be hostility.

Hawthorne, then, seems to be saying that the act, whatever it was, was an impulse from the intuitive side of his divine nature, not a deliberate choice, and, perhaps, then, not a deadly sin. In keeping with the author's interpretation of the allegory, is Hawthorne suggesting that the Creator created humankind (Pearl) out of an impulsive passion and not out of any deliberate choice? Is he looking upon Michaelangelo's masterpiece of the creation and interpreting the creation as an impulsive moment of passion? Doe Hawthorne, in his philosophical ruminations, propose that Deity needs therefore to make a confession, if not for the best, then, at least, a show for the worst, of his responsibility in the creation of mortality? Or we may simply say that Hawthorne may have overlooked a contradiction to occur within his allegory.

Hawthorne does not appear to make a distinctive connection between Hester's fall, as conceived by Chillingworth, and Dimmesdale's alleged fathering of Pearl. But he does make a clear distinction by implicating Satan as responsible for the fall, and Deity as responsible for the creation of mortality, which is a kind of mother to its prospective immortality, and thus, an elevated form of humankind. It is as though Hester represents not only mortal nature but all of humankind in their mortal state, and as though Pearl represents the future outgrowth from that mortal state, as a destiny intertwined with the office of the Redemption. Perhaps Hawthorne is not stating anything at all, but merely pondering and wondering himself, at the least, or, at the most, counting on a future answer as to what the connection is between the purpose of the fall and the future destiny of humanity. Perhaps Hawthorne has therefore shrouded Pearl's fatherhood in a mystery and invoked questions or explanations of his own about the nature of mortality in relation to its creation, both points yet to be solved by future revelation.

Such an analysis leads to another question that resounds heavily upon the mind of the reader, which we have addressed somewhat before: why does Dimmesdale feel the shame of the act as though it were an abomination, that he is the vilest of all sinners, if he is indeed an image of the Nazarene? The answer, in keeping with the nature of Dimmesdale character and the allegorical meanings of Hawthorne's tale, seems to be that Dimmesdale's experiences may symbolize or reflect the shame and abominations the Nazarene may have felt in assuming vicariously those of humanity as an act of compensation, even though he himself was innocent and pure. Dimmesdale is so introspectively and intuitively sensitive to this burden that his agony strongly appears to be a reflection of that possible experience. Even his rational mind is full of doubts about himself, though intuitively he steadily moves toward the scaffold and his destiny.

> "Am I mad? Or am I given over utterly to the fiend? Did I make a contract with him in the forest, and sign it with my blood? And does he now summon me to its fulfillment, by suggesting the performance of every wickedness which his most foul imagination can conceive?" (220-221)

At the very moment of his comprehension, he "struck his forehead with his hand" (221), as though he had finally come back to his true senses. Perhaps to demonstrate his return to the office of the scarlet letter, Mistress Hibbins, who was the fiend's servant, entered the scene at the close of his temptations. This encounter apparently indicates to the reader that the minister had realized his experiences as temptations from the netherworld, and had momentarily comtemplated acting upon his own will deliberately.

These last encounters of the young divine—perhaps to symbolize the last full measure of the depths to which the Son of Man might have believably descended below all things, in order to rise above all thing—help strengthened him with a resolve that was full of energy and life, which he possibly had not possessed during his entire ministry. Hawthorne notes that by the time Dimmesdale exited the forest and entered his dwelling, that

> [a]nother man had returned out of the forest; a wiser one; with a knowledge of hidden mysteries which the simplicity of the former never could have reached. A bitter kind of knowledge that! (223)

A heightened sense of self has refocused his new insights upon the one act of passion he must yet perform to be free of his burden, and remain true to himself. These insights, though based upon bitter experiences, contain hidden knowledge that the simplicity of his former person could not have acquired without Old Scratch's influence. From this point in the tale, Dimmesdale no longer has a dim view of his future, but a much clearer one, privately entertained, that seems to include a vision of what he must do.

Hawthorne seems to be saying, in the interplay among his characters, that experiencing both good and evil, or the temptations thereof, whether as an elf-child or a God-child, if the knowledge doesn't make us hostile, as in the case of Chillingworth, the result may be an enlightenment that might not be achieved in any other way.

FAREWELL, OLD FRIEND

When Dimmesdale's antagonist and bitterest enemy next visited him at home, now a shelter from the storm of life, the young minister had fully recovered himself. He could now handle Satan "without gloves, henceforward" (158), because he was no longer in a maze, and had obtained full knowledge, with bitter experience, that will assist him in fulfilling his destiny. He could even regard his enemy as a friend, perhaps without whose influence he could not have acquired his present wisdom. Having "borne a hundred thousand agonies" in the town of his ministry (222), he was now ready to prepare for the last final act of passion. At this visit, Chillingworth was fully aware of Dimmesdale and Hester's former plan to flee to England with Pearl; and he was aware that Dimmesdale also knew his inimical identity. If they followed through with their plan, Chillingworth knew that he would have won their souls. So he encouraged Dimmesdale to continue on and prepare himself for the Election Sermon by availing himself of the physician's knowledge.

> "Were it not better," said he, "that you use my poor skill to-night? Verily, dear Sir, we must take pains to make you strong and vigorous for this occasion of the Election discourse. The people look for great things from you; apprehending that another year may come about, and find their pastor gone."

> "Yea, to another world," replied the minister, with pious resignation. "Heaven grant it be a better one; for, in good sooth, I hardly think to tarry with my flock through the flitting seasons of another year! . . . . I thank you, and can but requite your good deeds with my prayers."

> "A good man's prayers are golden recompense!" rejoined old Roger Chillingworth, as he took his leave. "Yea, they are the current gold coin of the New Jerusalem, with the King's own mint-mark on them!" (224)

Chillingworth flattered himself that his services to the young minister would lead Dimmesdale to continue his commitment not to confess his relationship with Hester. He seemed assured that the good man Dimmesdale will only use prayer as the recompense required of him, and patronized him with some worldly sense of the value of prayer by describing prayers as the God-approved coins that can pay a person's way into heaven. As knowledgable of his Bible as Hawthorne appears to be, perhaps he used the proverb that even Old Scratch can quote scripture if it serves his purposes. Chillingworth did not want the young minister to own up to his responsibility for Hester and Pearl, encouraged their departure from Boston, and later planned to accompany them, perhaps to further their departure from destiny, and thus to qualify his claim to their souls. However, Dimmesdale led the physician on, double speaking as though he planned to leave New England. What Dimmesdale had in mind, however, does not appear to be his departure from New England to Old England, as devised by Hester, but from life itself, as he seemed to have anticipated his death shortly after a true recompense.

After his enemy left him, the young minister supped ravenously, for his fast and vigil were over; he now knew what he must do, and he hungered "with earnest haste and ecstasy" for the task he saw clearly before him.

> Then, flinging the already written pages of the Election Sermon into the fire, he forthwith began another, which he wrote with such an impulsive flow of thought and emotion, that he fancied himself inspired. (225)

He spends the rest of the night rewriting what "Heaven should see fit to transmit the grand and solemn music of its oracles" to him; "and at last sunrise threw a golden beam into the study, and laid it right across the minister's bedazzled eyes." The common symbol of light often appears to suggest a revelation is occurring, and the symbol of gold perhaps stamps it as genuinely divine in nature.

So Dimmesdale is now a new and complete man, fully endowed by proven experience and heavenly ministration, and enthusiastically committed to the destiny he perceives Providence has made absolutely clear to him. That the Election Sermon may be a time-pressed alllusion to the Sermon on the Mount, which followed the Nazarene's season of fasting and temptations, and culminated in a similar exit as Dimmesdale's, seems to be supported by the next two chapters that refer to two other comparable events in proper allegorical sequence.

CHAPTERS 21 AND 22

THE NEW ENGLAND HOLIDAY AND THE PROCESSION

> And the multitudes that went before, and that followed, cried,
> saying,
> Hosanna to the Son of David: Blessed is he that cometh in
> the name of the Lord; Hosanna in the highest.[1]

C ombining these two chapters of Hawthorne's tale perhaps symbolizes a duality of two preeminent roles within the time frame of the allegory—that of a new Governor coming into office, and that of Dimmesdale in giving the Election Sermon. The procession into the capital of Massachusetts for both events occurred on a holiday declared to celebrate the election of a new governor. The name of the new governor, which historically was John Endecott, is not specified, but only named among the statesmen in the procession, perhaps significantly to indicate that the office is yet to be filled.

The Governor was elected to political office to officiate in a temporal kingdom, while Dimmesdale had been selected, as chief among the clergymen, in his ministry of a spiritual kingdom, to give the Election Sermon. Rather than a nomination by the Puritan leaders, but more a matter of the popularity of Dimmesdale among the people, he was selected to begin the election proceedings.

Symbolically, the two roles of govenor and minister are possibly melded into one at the allegorical level. The change of governors and the procession may presage the significance of a timely event, which, whether at the end or beginning of the seven thousand years of the earth, may be chronologically immaterial to the Romantic. In the chronicles of

Christianity, the millennial era itself is to be inaugurated by a change of governorship, when the King of kings shall come to reign, whose kingdom was inaugurated over his own at his Atonement. Perhaps, at the allegorical level, this transition of govenors may represent not only the diminishment of the reign of Judaism, and all such similar prototypes that have lost their original vigor, but the final formation of a new. At the end of "this seven years' weight of misery," perhaps Hawthorne anticipated humankind leaving "this wreck and ruin here where it hath happened!" to "Meddle no more with it!" and to "Begin all anew!" (198). "Such a spiritual seer [as he] might have conceived . . . seven miserable years as a necessity, a penance" (227), worthy to qualify Pearl and her offspring for such a particular day.

Therefore, the holiday and procession seem highly reflective of the Nazarene's entrance into Jerusalem, where he is thought by many people to be going to claim or proclaim his right as king of Israel during the Feast of the Passover. Since he himself had declared his kingdom only a spiritual one, his entry into the capital of Judah only symbolized, for the Christians, a future time when he would become King, of a kingdom both spiritual and temporal. Likewise, no event was more central to Judaism than the Passover, wherein a lamb was sacrificed as a sin offering for the forgiveness of the sins of Israel. The Passover was celebrated, like a holiday, at the same time the Nazarene offered himself as a sacrifice for the sins of the people.

It appears to be no coincidence that a parade or procession into Boston occurred on the same day the Election Sermon is to be delivered, as though the procession might represent the Nazarene's triumphant entry into Jerusalem, the name from which Salem may be derivative. Why Boston was chosen as the setting for Hawthorne's novel instead of Salem is probably a proper analogy: as Boston was the capital city of Massachusetts, and the chief center of Puritanism, perhaps characterizing "the incomplete morality of the age" (233), so was Jerusalem the capital city and center of Judaism, whose Mosaic law, according to the Christian code, the Nazarene came to fulfill and end because of its vapidity and meaningless hypocrisy. He was therefore opposed by them, as was Dimmesdale by his peers, "he that is in peril from these sour old Puritan rulers!" (235) This opposition was downplayed by Hawthorne, but nevertheless mentioned, possibly so as to strengthen the analogy.

HESTER'S TRIUMPH

In these two chapters, the time frame of the "seven years past" (226) is mentioned at least twice, in conjunction with the new holiday to be celebrated, as though its celebration demarcated a special event in Hester's life, and in the life of all those who had come to celebrate this one particular day. As a Romantic device to collapse the chronological order of past events, perhaps Hawthorne has melded two Biblical events together—the redemption of humankind, and the end of earth's time—and has left it to the reader's intuition to deduce the open-ended conclusions to his allegorical message.

The redemption-confession was near at hand, and Hawthorne signifies "that Hester was actually dead, in respect to any claim of sympathy, and had departed out of the world with which she still seemed to mingle" (226). This symbolic death may serve to finalize Hester's representation of mortality at the end of time, and may also represent the "incomplete morality," or spiritual lifelessness, embodied in Puritanism, "which undoubtedly characterized the mood and manners of the age" (230).

Hawthorne seems to have imbued Hester with two opposing aspects, one perhaps to represent the spiritual conditions of the time. Her exterior "was like a mask; or rather, like the frozen calmness of a dead woman's features" (226), perhaps to reflect the face of Puritanism that is now seen in the market-place as a sombre and lifeless form. In the make up and disposition of the people gathering there, the reader can now behold this religious form to be the sham that it was. To note this particular aspect of deterioration, at the time of this holiday, there appears to be a breakdown in the sway of Puritanic influence among all those who have come to witness the inauguration of the new governor. "The persons now in the market-place of Boston had not been born to an inheritance of Puritanic gloom" (230). For example, Hawthorne contrasted the somber aspect of the Puritans with the gaiety of the sailors, who "transgressed without fear or scruple, the rules of behaviour that were binding on all others; smoking tobacco under the beadle's very nose;" and the double standard "remarkably characterized the incomplete morality of the age" (232-233). As we have noted before, the market-place may symbolize the make up of Puritan converts, adherents, and their ministers pedaling their wares and enforcing their economy upon others. However, the people gathering for the holiday "were countenanced, if not encouraged, in relaxing the severe and close application to their various modes of rugged industry" (231). The most conspicuous was no less than Chillingworth, who "was by far the most showy and gallant figure, so far as apparel went, anywhere to be seen among the multitude" (233).

The other aspect Hawthorne addresses in Hester's frame of being is that of the interior of her heart, that is reflected more openly and dramatically in Pearl's demeanor. Though she still mingles with the people in her symbolic gray attire, yet Pearl, who "owed its existence to the shape of gloomy gray . . . was decked out with airy gayety" and "betrayed, by the very dance of her spirits, the emotions which none could detect in the marble passiveness of Hester's brow" (228). Hawthorne introduces this aspect of Hester in such a fashion as apparently to alert the reader to the paradox composed in Hester's countenance, which may hardly be discernable.

> It might be, on this one day, that there was an expression unseen before, nor, indeed, vivid enough to be detected now; unless some preternaturally gifted observer should have first read the heart . . . .

> Such a spiritual seer might have conceived, that, after sustaining the gaze of the multitude through seven miserable years as a necessity, a penance, and something which it was a stern religion to endure, she now for one last time more, encountered it freely and voluntarily, in order to convert what had so long been agony into a kind of triumph. (227)

This "spiritual seer," prophet, or Daniel, to Hawthorne, might include some insightful reader who is strangely and inexplicably gifted enough to conceive in Hester's countenance what is intuitively contained in her heart. Though Hawthorne appears parenthetically to focus on the intuitive nature of Hester, he has her speak from the intellectual side, interpreting her intuition in the light of their anticipated, speculative voyage. To her, that triumph is escape from Puritan castigation: "A few hours longer, and the deep, mysterious ocean will quench and hide for ever the symbol which ye have caused to burn upon her bosom!" (227). Although her intellectual side is still harrowed up in the prospects of freedom by default, her intuitive nature may reflect, fully in the mien and countenance of

Pearl, an expression that inconceivably marks more truly the significance of the day at hand at the allegorical level—a release from the miseries on this side of the ocean of life, to some haven on the other. Hawthorne is perhaps telling the reader that the celebration of the change in governorship is related to that "expression unseen before," in that she anticipates converting her long agony "into a kind of triumph," and perhaps relishes that anticipation with a last show of her subdued fate. This special occasion of victory seems related to another metaphorical conversion in which Hester intuitively anticipates no longer drinking out of a mixed cup of grievously bitter and purgative tonic. That intuition seems portrayed in the narrator's commentary.

> Might there not be an irresistible desire to quaff a last, long, breathless draught of the cup of wormwood and aloes, with which nearly all her years of womanhood had been perpetually flavored? The wine of life, henceforth to be presented to her lips, must be indeed rich, delicious, and exhilarating, in its chased and golden beaker; or else leave an inevitable and weary languor, after the lees of bitterness wherewith she had been drugged, as with a cordial of intensest potency. (227)

Perhaps this cup of purgative wormwood, from which Hester seems to have imbibed all her life, represents the breath of life by which one purges oneself; and perhaps her last quaff of it is the last deep breath of life one takes in hopeful anticipation of partaking from the cup of wine hereafter. Perhaps the last breath of mortality is inhaled in memory of its mixture of wormwood and aloes with which its years have been perpetually flavored.

What wine of life does Hester intuitively anticipate to be henceforth drinking? Intuitively, and allegorically, mortal nature, as in Hester's, so long endured in agony, and once viewed as depraved and ill-begotten, may be hopeful of undergoing a triumphant transfiguration. The time frame of the allegory suggests that the promise and hope of the redemption from the dark necessity of mortality, and/or possibly a spiritual regeneration as well, is about to be fulfilled. This hope perhaps anticipates "the great judgment day" (153) that, in the annuls of Christiandom, is to follow an era of peace and unity with nature. That future cup may indeed be either rich and delicious; or it instead may offer but a weary languor of intense

Gary P. Cranford

efficacy, and seems reminiscent of the cup of which the Nazarene prayed he would not have to drink, and which, in some religious philosophies, many may fear of having to partake.

It may also represent the same cup of the sacrament of wine the Nazarene introduced in remembrance of the blood of redeeming life. The wine of life, metaphorically consistent with the imagery in this complex allegory, then, in the Christians' world, appears to be no less than that eternal or immortal life promised by the Nazarene. The act of partaking becomes perhaps as a witness, if need be, to follow his example, or to recognize his place in their lives; otherwise, not to partake thereof, would leave a bitterness to their taste from the drugs of life's sinfulness, from which one has not been so redeemed.

Hester, as a representation of nature, and particularly its Puritan depiction, likewise has, with all due and proper resignation, drank fully from the cup of her seven year's travail. Now she intuitively hopes on this special occasion to drink the wine of life from a golden beaker, which may allude to the legend of the Holy Grail itself, or perhaps to a transfigured splendor of youth and beauty that Hawthorne would have us anticipate, for Hester's sake. Hester does not seem to be able to intellectualize this anticipated sacred transformation, only to sense it, while Pearl seems able to give it physical or manifest expression.

Pearl's bright and sunny, effervescent flitting about like a bird reflected this intuitive aspect of Hester's hidden emotions.

> On this eventful day, moreover, therr was a certain singular inquietude and excitement in her mood, resembling nothing so much as the shimmer of a diamond, that sparkles and flashes with the varied throbbings of the breast on which it is displayed . . . . and therefore Pearl, who was the gem on her mother's unquiet bosom, betrayed, by the very dance of her spirits, the emotions which none could detect in the marble passiveness of Hester's brow. (228)

Pearl seems to be the voice and object of Hester's hope, as displayed upon her breast, owing its exhilarating existence to Hester's plight, though it contained a stigma which she disdained to condone or partake. So, again, Hawthorne appears to proclaim that mortality is the mother of immortality, that special civilization of humankind Pearl may represent.

It is perhaps to Hester's seven long years of suffering and travail that Pearl owes her future prosperity, and Pearl herself may be the promised transfiguration of Hester; or, as a prophetess, she may embody the spirit of hope and confidence in the office of the scarlet letter to bring it about.

CHASTE HESTER

The two aspects Hawthorne seems to have presented in Hester's nature—the external resignation and the internal exhileration—perhaps characterizes the best that might be expected of mortal nature. Though sinful, and given to the fancies of its imagination, it has an inward sense that nevertheless could draw it to the divine, as marked by a compassionate heart attuned to the universal. Thus, though bedecked with passion, or because of it, what might be considered a deplorable state of being might be transformed into a degree of triumpth, if faithful to "the truest test of a life successful to such an end."

It is also interesting that Hawthorne would use the word "chased" in reference to the golden beaker from which Hester hoped to partake of the "wine of life." The term "golden," as used in other passages, seems always connected with a revelation of royal or divine truth. But the word "chased," homonymic to the word "chaste," seems selected also to serve the insightful seer with the message that Hester's infamous deed either was not unchaste, or was about to become transformed into a holy victory for her. Its use suggests that whatever the coadunated consecration of her first meeting with Arthur was, in view of the many references to its hallowed aspect, Hawthorne may be now calling it chaste. Perhaps the penance of her seven long years, from Hawthorne's point of view, hallows the purpose of mortal life, and converts it to a kind of sacred triumph, as in the case of the Christian promise wherein mortality will take on immortality, the corruptible become incorruptible.[2]

Though the scarlet letter Hester wore typically isolated her from others physically, (and also spiritually), by forming about her

> a small, vacant area—a sort of magic circle . . . so changed was Hester Prynne's repute before the public, that the matron in town most eminent for rigid morality could not have held such intercourse [with a seaman] with less result of scandal than herself. (234).

Hester was now seen in such a light as to suggest that Hawthorne has now formed a halo around her, as he intended to do, by showing "how her beauty shone out, and made a halo of the misfortune and ignominy in which she was enveloped" (52).

A NEW REIGN

Pearl had caught the spirit of the procession from her mother, which many have come to see on the occasion of the change in rulers. The blacksmith had cleaned himself, the oppressive jailer was nodding and smiling at Pearl, and the Indian and sailor had come to witness the event. As in Hester's suppressed feelings, there was a measure of "unwonted jollity" in the air, somewhat compressed, but nevertheless "dispelling the customary cloud . . . for the space of a single holiday" (230).

This crowd perhaps represents a spectrum of humanity witnessing an event promissory of a day in which a new Protectorate's rule may bring greater joy to the world. From Hawthorne's seedbed of imagination, it may also represent the makeup of Jew, Gentile, and heathen in the city of Jerusalem at the Feast of the Passover, among whom may have circulated possible high expectations for a change in the Jewish government. The Passover was celebrated to remind the Israelites of their escape from Egyptian bondage, and the descendants of Judah were expecting a king to come through the lineage of David, perhaps to deliver them from the Roman empire. Perhaps the spirit of the celebration of the holiday also was tinged with gratitude for deliverance from the oppressive governance of the old world.

Hawthorne makes a remarkable comment about such festive celebrations that

> give, as it were, a grotesque and brilliant embroidery to the great robe of state, which a nation at such festivals, puts on . . . . The dim reflection of a remembered splendor, a colorless and manifold diluted repetition of what they had beheld in proud old London,—we will not say at a royal coronation, but at a Lord Mayor's show,—might be traced in the customs which our forefathers instituted, with reference to the annual installation of magistrates. (230)

It appears, in this narrator's commentary, that Hawthorne is looking with some slight askance at the pretension with which political offices are assumed, as though trying to recapture, in the grotesque and diluted customs repeated by our forefathers, some previous splendor of a Lord's show. For example, Old England's monarchies, and others theretofore, may represent the attempts of humankind to duplicate the dignity and honor due a real Lord. Perhaps, in the description of the details of the holiday and the procession, there is a mixture of both substance and façade.

The popularity of the young minister, Dimmesdale, in Boston is noted by Hawthorne as a possible preliminary rise to political power, the same kind of power the Nazarene's believers hoped he would display to throw off the Roman yoke.

> His was the profession, at that era, in which intellectual ability displayed itself far more than in political life; for—leaving a higher motive out of the question—it offered inducements powerful enough, in the almost worshiping respect of the community, to win the most aspiring ambition into its service. Even political power—as in the case of Increase Mather—was within the grasp of a successful priest. (238)

Perhaps it was the intellectuality of Dimmesdale's peers, "these sour old Puritan rulers," whose motives of service were not only beyond reproach but also competitively put his more appealing and popular services in peril. Notwithstanding, Dimmesdale saught no political office, but wished only to deliver a sermon that would have a significant spiritual effect upon his parishioners. Afterwards, he sensed that he would die, perhaps as a seal upon the truths in his sermon, as well as a fitting end to his confession, a kind of redemption for Hester and Pearl. Though Hawthorne has displayed in the divine only the highest of motives, what happened later upon the scaffold had a varied effect upon his audience, much as the carpenter's death was an unexpected reverse to the wishes of his followers.

Hester explains the purpose of the festivities to her daughter, whose first impression of the event is that it is "a play-day for the whole world." Perhaps the Passover was a kind of play-day, a memorial celebration of the day when the elect, like the Egyptian slaves, would be passed over by the pall of death.

Perhaps Pearl's play in previous chapters, especially on the other side of the brook, was a kind of memorial for the same triumphant end.

> "For, today, a new man is beginning to rule over them; and so—as has been the custom of mankind ever since a nation was first gathered—they make merry and rejoice; as if a good and golden year were at length to pass over the poor old world." (229)

That good and golden year may refer to the millennial era of peace and prosperity that is to transform the "poor old world;" and the change in the governorship in Massachusetts metaphorically may allude to the Christian's faith of the Protectorate's personal reign during that period of time.Again, a metaphor of "a good and golden year" is introduced by the phrase, "as if," as a clue to some double meaning at play in the tale. The new man may not refer so much to the governor as to the new man prefigured by Dimmesdale. The alleged analogy ends with the contrast between the intellectual and spiritual motives of the minister and his competitors, and does not extend itself to any other allusion to the Nazarene's political kingdom.

> It was the observation of those who beheld him now, that never, since Mr. Dimmesdale first set his foot on the New England shore, had he exhibited such energy as was seen in the gait and air with which he kept his pace in the procession . . . . Yet . . . his strength seemed not of the body. It might be spiritual, and imparted to him by angelic ministrations . . . . but the spiritual element took up the feeble frame, and carried it along, unconscious of the burden, and converting it to spirit like itself. (238)

Dimmesdale's attitude and strength foreshadowed not only the Election Sermon he is about to give but also his confession upon the scaffold. He now knew his destiny and was determined to carry it out to the end, his mind "busying itself, with preternatural activity."

BACK AGAIN TO REALITY

To Hester's chagrin and speculative thoughts, Dimmesdale was oblivious of her and Pearl, as though he had forgotten their plans to vacate the New World for the Old; "he seemed so remote from her own sphere, and utterly beyond her reach" (239). The divine was no longer subject to his mortal nature, no longer ruled by his speculative will; and, sensing a renewal of his earlier convictions, she again speculated.

> Her spirit sank with the idea that all must have been a delusion, and that, vividly as she had dreamed it, there could be no real bond betwixt the clergyman and herself. (239-240)

Gazing upon him, Hester "felt a dreary influence come over her, but wherefore or whence she knew not." Initially, she sensed her destiny returned as she eyed the minister, whose mind was so preoccupied with so much" preternatural activity," not so much only for the message soon to be spoken, but perhaps also in conjunction with the confession he may also have been planning to make upon the scaffold, that he was beyond her reach. Hester was still given to natural conjecture and presumed, because Dimmesdale did not glance in her direction, that he will not recognize the bond between them. She did not realize that he intended to recognize that relationship in a very dramatic way upon the scaffold, not on her suggested terms, but on those of a higher order; and her hope is revived later upon the scaffold.

Mistress Hibbins, however, who sensed a relationship between them, made a remarkable comment that forecasted an ironic reversal of results contrary to her understanding of her Master's intent, who will attempt to prevent Dimmesdale's confession rather than encouraging it.

> When the Black Man sees one of his own servants, sighed and sealed, so shy of owning to the bond as is the Reverend Mr. Dimmesdale, he hath a way of ordering matters so that the mark shall be disclosed in open daylight to the eyes of all the world! (242).

As we shall see later, that is what the Reverend will do, but not to the triumpth of the Black Man, as expected by Witch Hibbins. We shall see that the confession was made and the "mark" shown, as Hibbins proposed, but to Chillingworth's defeat by the very disclosure of that mark upon Dimmesdale's chest. Master Prynne had already seen the mark, and, though he knew the relationship between them, he had been terrified, in a rare moment of truth, possibly by intuiting his own defeat and destruction in it.

At this point, Hawthorne turns the tale back to a contrast, in which he describes the inability of the Puritan code to embrace fully the spirit of joyfulness, perhaps as anticipated in the occasion being celebrated. This reversal seems a common and frequent occurrence in Hawthorne's allegory, perhaps to keep the reader constantly aware of what could be by focusing upon what is wrong with what is.

Not gaiety but sadness is the lot mapped out for the life of the Puritan settlers, whose religion has cast its shadow over succeeding generations, perhaps even to the end of time.

> Their immediate posterity, the generation next to the early emigrants, wore the blackest shade of Puritanism, and so darkened the national visage with it, that all the subsequent years have not sufficed to clear it up. We have yet to learn again the forgotten art of gayety. (232)

This gayety is what Hawthorne has highlighted in the celebration of the New England holiday and in the procession, perhaps in symbolic anticipation of some forthcoming momentous event. But perhaps it is not the present to which humankind must look for joy, but to the future.

At least, it does not appear to Hawthorne that a return to the past would be a better solution. To evade their destiny by a backward move to the old world, from which the new world of the American experiment thought to escape and upon which to improve, may not be the solution to the problems at hand. To Hawthorne, that improvement by the Puritan venture, or contemporary religion, was not the answer to the needs of humanity, nor does it appear Hawthorne would favor a return to the old ways of handling the problems of a mortal world.

Hawthorne ends the chapter on the New England holiday with a foregone conclusion for Hester: neither she nor Dimmesdale can escape or alter their destiny without a price. To her dismay, Hester learns that the divine's enemy, Chillingworth, has planned to depart with them on the same voyage back to the Old World, perhaps to assure his victory by seeing to the success of their scheme to return to Old England.

> But, at that instant, she beheld old Roger Chillingworth himself, standing in the remotest corner of the marketplace, and smiling on her; a smile which . . . conveyed secret and fearful meaning. (235)

Perhaps this smile would have assured her that their plan would not achieve the desired result, but for the sound of the procession that captured her attention instead.

PRETERNATURAL DETEMINATION

Hester, before she "could call together her thoughts" (236), did not seem to be fully intellectually aware of the ramifications of her and Arthur's plans to alter their shared destiny. Hawthorne has interrupted her instinctive nature with the thought of the procession. On the other hand, the young minister, following the dignitaries of the procession, seemed not only to have regained cognizance of his divine instincts but to have become fully determined to pursue the destiny he sensed Providence had laid upon him. Although he was no longer sympathetic to the weakness of his mortal nature, "in that far vista of his unsympathizing thoughts" (239), he was now in full accord with Pearl's intuitions concerning his destiny; and he stepped to it with a spiritual energy that transported his feeble frame with uncanny strength to the particular place where he was to deliver the Election Sermon. In the forest he was human and free to own his natural feelings. Back from the maze of a world gone awry, he returned to his destiny, enlightened and renewed, with the vigor of divine purpose.

Pearl also recognized that the young minister passing by had changed and was not the same man whose kiss she repulsed in the forest. Whereas Hester was distraught at the recognition, Pearl seemed further invigorated by hers, as though the change in Dimmesdale seemed in approximate accordance with her sense of destiny.

"I could not be sure that it was he; so strange he looked," continued the child. "Else I would have run to him and bid him kiss me now, before all the people." (240)

Pearl's feelings for Dimmesdale had changed because he was a new man determined to fulfill his destiny, much as she intuitively foresaw. Perhaps picking up on the reasons for Hester's depression, her restless vivacity performed a tiptoe dance among the crowd, playing upon and vibrating "with her mother's disquietude," perhaps as if to audaciously forecast the end result of her vision (244). Perhaps representative of the promise of humankind's redemption, her feelings of some affinity with the divine, though perhaps not yet completely assured, overflowed to those around her, as evidenced by a group of mariners, who "gazed wonderingly and admiringly at Pearl" (244). This affinity she felt for Arthur was similar to the same loyalty Hester intuitively demonstrated towards the young minister, despite his seeming remoteness at the moment. That affinity may represent the attachment the redeemed Christian has formed to the Author of eternal life, and may be sealed by Dimmesdale's confession upon the scaffold and his death thereafter.

LOYAL TO THE LAST

From her depressing thoughts, Hester was moved by her conversation with Mistress Hibbins, Old Scratch's advocate, to speak honorably of the young reverend, as she stood irresistibly near the scaffold, which was an extension of the meeting house into the marketplace. There she listened intently to the minister's Election Sermon. She was spell-bound with the tones of the sermon, which, apart from its words, had a spiritual sense and meaning for her with which she sympathized so intimately. The tones of the sermon also touched the sensibilities in the bosom of all the listeners with its pathos of human suffering. With

> an atmosphere of awe and solemn grandeur . . . majestic as the voice sometimes became, there was for ever in it an essential character of plaintiveness . . . of suffering humanity, that touched a sensibility in every bosom! . . .

The complaint of a human heart, sorrow-laden, perchance
guilty, telling its secret, whether of guilt or sorrow, to the great
heart of mankind; beseeching its sympathy or forgiveness,—at
every moment,—in each accent,—and never in vain! It was this
profound and continual undertone that gave the clergyman his
most appropriate power. (243-244)

Hawthorne may have attempted to depict in the tone of the Election
Sermon the same appeal of the Nazarene's to those who felt his empathy
for their misery; and it appears that his suffering, in the Christian's behalf,
evidenced in the many relics worn and displayed by them, has had that
same connectivity with the great heart of humanity. Perhaps it was the
intensity of the Redeemer's human pain and sorrow, along with his divine
purity and engaging words, that stirs the sympathy and wins the worship
of those who "could detect the same cry of pain" as in themselves (243).
Analagously, the unanimity of appeal in Dimmesdale's Election Sermon
seems similar to the universal appeal embodied in the message of the
sermon preached in the brief span of the Nazarene's three-year ministry.

But Hawthorne throws a shadow over the analogy with an aspersion:
Dimmesdale's heart is "perchance guilty," and telling its secret, "whether
of guilt or sorrow." The Christian does not conceive of any guilt
committed by the carpenter. Is Hawthorne allegorically again suggesting,
by casting a shadow of doubt about Dimmesdale's guilt, that their might
be some possible sorrowful responsibility in Deity's relationship with the
creation of the "community of mankind?" This undertone of sinful and
sorrowful pathos, in seeking out the elect, might imply such a questioning
presumption on Hawthorne's part. Should the general analogy hold true,
Hawthorne again seems to be putting his own twist on the reasons for the
Redemption.

"THE RELATION BETWEEN THE DEITY AND THE COMMUNITIES OF MANKIND"

Hester, as a representation of the spirit of human nature, was held to
the spot, or time and place, at the foot of the scaffold, by an inevitable
intuitive magnetism that seems to comprehend her history, or the history
of the mortal world. An indescriptive sense, "too ill-defined to be made a
thought, but weighing heavily on her mind," told her that "her whole orb

of life, both before and after, was connected with this spot, as with the one point that gave it unity" (244). This one point that gave her whole sphere of life unity, and connected it with the spot where she stood, might be the forthcoming confession she anticipated intuitively, the revelation, so to speak, if we may get a little ahead of the story, that confessed the relation between the one Deity and all of humanity.

While Hester listened by the scaffold, where Dimmesdale nearby is preaching from the "sacred pulpit," Hawthorne in the last three sentences of the chapter, "Procession," connects the two, with the insignia of the scarlet letter, highlighted with exclaimation marks and a question, as possible clues to cue the reader's intuitive awareness of his double-speak:

> The sainted minister in the Church! The woman of the scarlet letter in the market-place! What imagination would have been irreverent enough to surmise that the same scorching stigma was on them both? (247)

The reader might sense, "conceiving, perhaps, that the wearer of this brilliantly embroidered badge must needs be a personage of high dignity among her people" (246), that Hester may be connected to something higher than just to her mortal element, that her whole nature, before and after the fall, before and after the redemption, is united to a higher dimension of life by some sacred intervention. This unity with the divine element appears to be the message of Christianity that, perhaps to Hawthorne, might be missing from the religions of the Old World, and from the New England experiment. He may himself have felt some significance in a relationship with the Author of our humanness, which, like Hester and Pearl, defies condemnation and anticipates some compassionate redemption from our infirmities as mortals. This affinity and bond with the divine seems to hallow our material element, and, to Hawthorne, to resent, as in the dynamism of Pearl's repugnance, the coinage of its depravity and infamy. In his tale, Hawthorne seems to challenge the imagination of the reader to see beyond the irreverence of their alleged infidelity, to behold some better destiny of humankind that is connected to Deity in a sacred union.

Perhaps, like a scarlet letter engraved upon a sable field, Hawthorne is telling the insightful reader that the destiny of humanity may have a more noble end than even our religions have recognized since the dimming of ancient principle. Pearl appears to be the embodiment of that destiny, the unity of being that defines humankind's relationship with Deity. As Hester's child, she is seen by her present-day religionists as a demon offspring, not in spite of but because of the "indescribable charm of beauty and eccentricity that shone through her little figure, and sparkled with its activity" (244). In the Puritan perspective, anything so vivacious and delighted by life must be the offspring of Old Scratch. For this perspective, Hawthorne may have held some slight contempt, but perhaps with some compassion for those caught up in it.

THE LINEAGE OF PEARL

Before Dimmesdale revealed himself upon the scaffold, Hawthorne makes one more pass at the fatherhood of Pearl, perhaps to position in the mind of the reader once more the question from whence she came; that is, whether the mortal nature of humankind is entirely devilish, or whether it has a divine destiny that glorifies it's creation. In a conversation between Hester and Mistress Hibbins, the witch-lady confidently gloated over the supposed victory of the Black Man of the Forest, presumptively affirming "a personal connection between so many persons ([Hester] among them) and the Evil One." (241)

> "What is it that the minister seeks to hide, with his hand always over his heart? Ha, Hester Prynne!"
>
> "What is it, good Mistress Hibbins?" eagerly asked little
>
> Pearl. "Hast thou seen it?"
>
> "No matter, darling!" responded Mistress Hibbins . . . . "They say, child, thou are of the lineage of the Prince of the Air! Wilt thou ride with me, some fine night, to see thy father? Then thou shalt know wherefore the minister keeps his hand over his heart!" (242)

The term, "Prince of the Air," probably comes from a Biblical passage in reference to Old Scratch, called Satan or Lucifer in the same volume.

> And you he hath quickened, who were dead in trespasses and sins;

> Wherein time past ye walked according to the course of this world, according to the prince of the power of the air, the spirit that now worketh in the children of disobedience.[3]

The witch would convince the reader that Satan will be the father of humankind, but Dimmesdale is to disclose the mark upon his breast shortly in an act that identifies him as Pearl's father, and then to expend his life willingly, perhaps as a seal thereof. That act is the subtle and dim confession that he is responsible for Hester's condition and the creation of Pearl. Humankind's lineage, then, as perhaps Hawthorne would have it, may have more connection with Deity than with the Prince of the Air.

Pearl's nature had been so rebellious and antagonistic to the stigma placed upon her mother's chest, and the people that tormented her mother so, that she had been identified by them as a witch-baby, demon offspring, or such as indicates a lineage from the Evil One. But the reader may now have a true perspective of Hawthorne's Pearl, perhaps as he envisioned for his own child, Una, and may now see Pearl not as a child of disobedience, but more a child of light and truth holding to the destiny laid out for the many she may represent. Because of the confession that is to be made by Dimmesdale, which to some few of his parishioners may only dimly reveal the true fatherhood of Pearl, she will not be claimed by the dark side of eternity. To Hawthorne, perhaps neither will the human race be wholly claimed by our chief Adversary, because of the redemption-confession.

In the next chapter, Hawthorne appears to affirm, somewhat dimly, the true "relation between the Deity and the communities of mankind." Hawthorne ends the chapter, "The Procession," by tying the significance of the scarlet letter to the relationship between Hester and Dimmesdale.

> At the final hour, when she was so soon to fling aside the burning letter, it had strangely become the centre of more remark and excitement, and was thus made to sear her breast

more painfully, than at any time since the first day she put it on. (246)

Hester was still contemplating leaving by ship, not knowing the preternatural intentions of the divine. Perhaps to signify the error of her speculations, as the crowd gathered strangely around her, the letter burned more painfully than ever. Perhaps the focus of their inexplicable excitement and remarks signaled their complicity in its significance, and perhaps Hawthorne is building toward the climax of its revelation.

CHAPTER 23

THE REVELATION
OF THE SCARLET LETTER

For in him we live, and move, and have our being; as certain
also of your own poets have said,
For we are also his offspring.[1]

This chapter is the centerpiece of Hawthorne's allegory. If, up to this point in his novel, the reader has not understood his allegorical representations, the revelations in this chapter might provide the keys to unlock the mystery of *The Scarlet Letter*. Indeed, the Election Sermon itself seems to provide the primary theme of the red hieroglyph. Hawthorne may even have possibly conceived this chapter as his own sermon to his readers, or those who are "elect" enough to understand its meanings as his friends. Nevertheless, just as varied as were the responses of Dimmesdale's audience to his revelation upon the scaffold, so have been the responses of Hawthorne's readers to his tale, and so will they be to this author's interpretation of the same, [and undoubtedly, just as varied in their opinions of the editor's liability in resurrecting it].

THE ELECTION SERMON

None of the words contained in the Election Sermon are quoted. Indeed, it would appear that the allegory itself is that sermon the reader is to sense intuitively. It is the premise of this author's interpretation that if the words of the sermon were to be given the reader, and the meanings clearly delineated, they probably would be somewhat identical to his analysis.

Therefore, Hawthorne may be telling the reader that the subject of Dimmesdale's Election Sermon delivered in the meeting-house is the very allegorical theme of his novel:

> His subject, it appeared, had been the relation between the Deity and the communities of mankind, with a special reference to the New England which they were here planting in the wilderness . . . . [I]t was his mission to foretell a high and glorious destiny for the newly gathered people of the Lord. (249)

Though Hawthorne is the narrator of the story, if he should identify with any one of his characters, it would seem to be Dimmesdale. It is this author's hindsight that Hawthorne's novel has clothed significant Biblical events in the dress of an allegory in order to share with his friends his thoughts on the reasons for the mess the world is in, not just to be a writer of a book, but with the particular purpose of serving mankind and glorifying his Maker in his own quiet way (10). In so doing, he has treated the subject of Deity's relation with his special creation, its mortality, with a reference to humanity's feeble efforts to address its problems, and the means to redemn it. Perhaps, as it was for Dimmesdale, he had a philosophical urge, in using the Biblical text, to point to a happier world for those who have newly gathered "by the truest test of a life successful to such an end!"

There are critical elements in understanding Hawthorne's tale, and this chapter communicates the theme that Dimmesdale's mission was "to foretell a high and glorious destiny" for those who gather under the wings of the Lord. To Hawthorne, that destiny seems to have entailed not only a redemption, but also a confession, of a sort, revealing, if not the best, then a show of Providence's responsibility in the process of that transformation back to immortality.

Dimmesdale personifies that means of restoration; Hester, that mortality which is to be transfigured; Pearl, that particular childlike destiny unfolding; Chillingworth, the efforts to thwart that destiny; and the scarlet hieroglyph, the symbol that represents the sacrifice which establishes the immortal relationship between Deity and the communities of mankind. That transformational process may have required the dark necessity of mortality typified in the tale by Hester's tribulations, which are due to the heavy influence of the black background of America's gloomy Puritan experiment. Thus, Hawthorne sketches in the mind of his readers the hieroglyphic artwork of a letter A in scarlet stripes upon a sable field to symbolize the prospects of such a hope against the shadows of the transformation process.

The many inexplicable and obscure passages and the unanswered questions the characters pose for the reader may be understood when Hawthorne's allegory is seen from the perspective of a Romantic, or Anti-Transcendentalist. The questions or comments Hawthorne seems to be making about the origin of sin, the fall of nature, the parties responsible, and the plan to compensate humankind by an act of redemption, are revealed in the relationships between the main characters and the various metaphors or parables used to develop the deeper meanings of the tale.

HAWTHORNE'S CONCLUSIONS

There are many parallels between the actions of the characters and those of certain historical figures. For instance, Dimmesdale is seen as a kind of intuitive prophet with a distinctive mission as he comes to the end of his prepared speech, which, according to the united testimony of the people, "never had man spokein in so wise, so high, and so holy a spirit, as he that spake this day" (248).

> And, as he drew towards the close, a spirit as of prophecy had come upon him constraining him to its purpose as mightily as the old prophets of Israel were constrained; only with this difference, that whereas the Jewish seers had denounced judgments and ruin on their country, it was his mission to foretell a high and glorious destiny for the newly gathered people of the Lord . . . . Thus, there had come to the Reverend Mr. Dimmesdale . . . an epoch of life more brilliant and full of triumph than any previous one, or than any which could hereafter be. (249)

The passage above associates Dimmesdale with the prophets of Israel, but with one distinction that associates him more with the Nazarene, who wished to reform the Jewish nation and redeem a fallen people. Like Dimmesdale, he opted for a higher destiny, "brilliant and full of triumph," which seems to lie at the heart of the message of the Election Sermon, as it does at the core of the mission of the Galilean. His revised Election Sermon, which originally may have been about the election of the new governor, presumably may have addressed the gathering of those who are to be connected with Deity, perhaps at the day when a new Governor is to be installed over the earth.

The agony suffered by the divine, his confession, death, and possible resurrection, point to one singular act that would gather the people. The Election Sermon itself, perhaps more than other aspects of Dimmesdale's ministry, possibly capsules, in a nutshell, that "shower of golden truths" which he shared with his parishioners, and may likely represent allegorically the words spoken by the man from Nazareth.

> But, throughout it all, and through the whose discourse, there had been a certain deep, sad undertone of pathos, which could not be interpreted otherwise than as the natural regret of one soon to pass away. Yes; their minister whom they so loved–and who so loved them all, that he could not depart heavenward without a sigh–had the foreboding of untimely death upon him, and would soon leave them in their tears! This idea of his transitory stay on earth gave the last emphasis to the effect which the preacher had produced; it was as if an angel, in his passage to the skies, had shaken his bright wings over the people for an instant,—at once a shadow and a splendor,—and had shed down a shower of golden truths upon them . . . . He stood, at this moment, on the very proudest eminence of superiority . . . a reputation of whitest sanctity. (249)

Dimmesdale is figured in this passage like an angel who has come down to earth for a particular mission and, after a "transitory stay," is about to return to the heaven from whence he came. The passage seems to project the Nazarene's short, three-year ministry, whose whole discourse was marked likewise with an underlying pathos, perhaps not so much in regretful remorse of an anticipated horror, but as in a compassionate remorse for the pains of humankind's mortal sins he claimed to take upon himself.

The divine's predicted death seems likewise an allegorical replication. as does the analogous description of his angelic ascension into heaven after a "transitory stay on earth." The use of the word, "transitory," perhaps as opposed to "temporary," interestingly highlights the earth more as a time and place of transformation than as simply a waylay station from one place to another, as in a journey whose particular quest is defined by the transitional changes made there.

Hawthorne's use of the phrase, "as if," again focuses attention to another allegorical parallel, as if Dimmesdale's sermon, death, and "passage to the skies" left a blessing of his wings upon the people. The golden truths he had spoken, perhaps both a shadow and a splendor, during his transitory moment, seemed to herald him as preeminently purest and holiest among ministers.

It must be noted, and perhaps agreeable to most Christian scholars, that their scriptures hallow the Nazarene as having effected the most important events in the history of the world, in the shadow of the cross, and in the splendor of a marvelous resurrection. It is said that this personage, who condescended to stoop upon his mortal footstool, descended below all things temporarily in order to spread his wings over all who would gather beneath them. His unexpected crucifixion cast an initial black shadow upon his followers, but was thereafter seen as a miraculous gift in the promise of a resurrection for all. The healing within his wings, as "a hen gathers her chickens under her wings,"[2] is a metaphor often used in the Bible to express the bredth of his compassion for his followers.

THE HOSANNAH SHOUTS AND THE FEAST OF THE SACRIFICIAL LAMB

In two other examples of parallelism, Hawthorne next, possibly having congealed the teachings of the Nazarene into one Election Sermon, ushers the procession of readers toward the town-hall, "where a solemn banquet would complete the ceremonies of the day" (250). The crowd, in childlike loyalty, utter a shout in veneration of the preacher.

> When they were fairly in the market-place, their presence was greeted by a shout. This–though doubtless it might acquire additional force and volume from the childlike loyalty which the age awarded to its rulers–was felt to be an irrepressible outburst of the enthusiasm kindled in the auditors by that high strain of eloquence which was yet reverberating in their

ears . . . even that mighty swell of many voices, blended into one great voice by the universal impulse which makes likewise one vast heart out of the many. Never, from the soil of New England, had gone up such a shout! Never, on New England soil, had stood the man so honored by his mortal brethren as the preacher! (250)

The crowd anticipated a change in the governorship of the land, that perhaps the preacher might aspire to their expectations, but Dimmesdale seems to have envisioned a different course. Their universal shout is reflective of the shout given the Nazarene upon his entrance into Jerusalem, as recorded by several accounts of the Biblical text.

And the multitudes that went before, and that followed, cried, saying, Hosanna to the Son of David: Blessed is he that cometh in the name of the Lord; Hosanna in the highest.[3]

And they that went before, and they that followed, cried, saying, Hosanna; Blessed is he that cometh in the name of the Lord:

Blessed be the kingdom of our father David, that cometh in the name of the Lord: Hosanna in the highest.[4]

And when he was come nigh . . . , the whole multitude of the disciples began to rejoice and praise God with a loud voice . . . .

Saying, : Blessed be the King that cometh in the name of the Lord: peace in heaven, and glory in the highest.[5]

On the next day much people that were come to the feast, when they heard that Jesus was coming to Jerusalem,

Took branches of palm trees, and went forth to meet him, and cried, Hosanna: Blessed is the King of Israel that cometh in the name of the Lord.[6]

Hawthorne seems to have been familiar enough with these passages to suggest that some "universal impulse" had blended their many voices into "one great voice" as it made "one vast heart of the many," in childlike loyalty, perhaps reminiscent even of "the children crying in the temple, and saying, 'Hosanna to the Son of David.'" This man from Nazareth seemed to have comprehended the "loyalty," or whatever could have caused such an "universal impulse, which may have compelled children, mere babes and sucklings, as well as adults, to perfect praise.[7]

In the passage above, Hawthorne may also have given his definition of the "universal heart" (84). It may compose summarily all the sympathy and sorrows that flow from the "great heart" of the world (139), "unite all who belong to one another" (154), and connect with "the Universal Father" (85). Perhaps this was Hawthorne's Romantic way of explaining how a crowd of many people, by some "universal impulse," as "one vast heart of the many," could unanimously shout with "one great voice" in honor of the one man whose teachings had touched their hearts. Perhaps the passage, in Hawthorne's unique way, also demonstrates how Deity connects with the communities of mankind.

The solemn banquet given in honor of the new governor, to finalize the purpose and ceremonies of the day, also reminds us of the Feast of the Passover that was being celebrated by the Jews at the time of the Nazarene's death. Of that feast, he was cast symbolically as the sacrificial Lamb slain for the sins of those for whom spiritual death would pass over in the day of judgment, whose sacrifice would "complete the ceremonies of the day" as the Lamb of the feast of the Passover, who would in time become the new Governor of the land.

The man of Nazareth, however, to the disappointment of many, did not wish to ascend to the throne at Jerusalem as King of Israel at that time. Neither did Dimmesdale wish to become a political power, which Hawthorne states was often the favored opportunity for successful clergymen. But his triumph or victory was to be achieved by fulfilling his office, for the children of humankind, to which he earnestly believed he was called by Providence. To the disappointment of Hester and his parishioners, Dimmesdale passed to the skies and to a saintly reward. His confessional message to the many was ambiguous by intent and therefore, possibly by design, misunderstood, perhaps as well as was the Nazarene's, and, no less, Hawthorne's, all of which may remain so until some antiquary of days appear and presume to set the record straight.

The Office Fulfilled

Whereas Dimmesdale was deluded heretofore, in assuming he would have fulfilled his office well after having given the Election Sermon, we see that thereafter he subdued his own will, in the final apex of his agony, and had in all truth possibly fulfilled the office of his inspirational mission.

> The energy—or say, rather, the inspiration which had held him up, until he should have delivered the sacred message that brought its own strength along with it from heaven—was withdrawn, now that it had so faithfully performed its office. (251)

The office that was performed faithfully appears to include that of the inspiration Dimmesdale received in the transmission of his message, but the office of the scarlet letter was not completely performed in its delivery. Whether or not Hawthorne considers Dimmesdale's mission complete without the confession is not made clear at this point, nor has there been any implication of a resurrection to "the immortality of the human soul" (219), no union at the marriage altar "for a joint futurity of endless retribution" (80), no maturation of the "infant immortality" (91, 115), save in the hint of an anticipated transformation of Hester, as heretofore prefigured. Apparently, from the context of the passage above, Dimmesdale's essential duty seemed performed. Perhaps Dimmesdale's Election Sermon only represents the short ministry of the humble Nazarene and the importance of his message in general. Perhaps the divine's suffering throughout his ministry represents the pains of his redemption.

Once the sermon was finished, the light now shared, the flame sunk low, the young minister is left hardly alive; but the crowd looked on with continued wonder and awe.

> This earthly faintness was, in their view, only another phase of the minister's celestial strength; nor would it have seemed a miracle too high to be wrought for one so holy, had he ascended before their eyes, waxing dimmer and brighter, and fading at last into the light of heaven! (252)

One here might say that Hawthorne is again compressing and rearranging time and events by possibly comparing Dimmesdale's departing to the alleged ascension of the Nazarene into heaven. That Dimmesdale's death comes almost immediately after this foreshadowing, as the curtains close upon each of his characters, is therefore perhaps immaterial to this technique.

Yet Hawthorne adds efficacy to the Election Sermon, perhaps as a seal to the significance of its truthfulness, by adding another act of passion to his tale. Without the confession and the power of the "magic touch," it would appear that all would have been but an exercise in vanity on the part of Hawthorne's performers. Perhaps Dimmesdale's own predicted death highlighted this significance as yet another corollary to the prophetic promise of retribution.

THE CLOSING SCENE

Perhaps similarly as in any play, Hawthorne brings his four main characters together for the grand finale, perhaps to indicate there is a connection between them in the allegorical meanings of his tale of guilt and sorrow. Having delivered his sermon in an energy born of inspiration, Dimmesdale weakly left the meeting-hall and moved with the procession toward the banquet hall. He paused at the scaffold, where still stood Hester and Pearl. Here, with these two, he had one duty left to perform before he died. He tenderly and triumphantly beckoned for Hester and Pearl to join him upon the scaffold. Apparently, Old Roger Chillingworth's presence also was needed in the scene upon the stage of Dimmesdale's union with Hester and Pearl, as the spectators, silent and inactive, watched

> the judgment which Providence seemed about to work . . . . Old Roger Chillingworth followed, as one intimately connected with the drama of guilt and sorrow in which they had all been actors, and well entitled, therefore, to be present at its closing scene. (253)

We have reference again to Hawthorne's characters as actors upon a stage, this time as appearing most fittingly in the last scene of his drama. Acting out the role of the Adversary—known more commonly on earth as the Devil, or Satan, and less commonly as Lucifer in a pre-earth existence—perhaps Roger Chillingworth, not going by the name of Master Prynne, is intimately connected with the whole problem of guilt and sorrow in the earth, which situation has been dramatized by Hawthorne's characters. Inasmuch as the transformation from immortality to mortality is a very intimate connection, his presence upon the stage of life should be included in the last scene. Hawthorne, as possibly slightly intimated in this quote, may be well pleased with his drama and his characters, all of whom have been well titled, and well entitled to end the drama together.

> At this instant old Roger Chillingworth thrust himself through the crowd,—or, perhaps, so dark, disturbed, and evil was his look, he rose up out of some nether region,—to snatch back his victim from what he sought to do! (252)

These passages may not appear to be a parallel in the life of the Galilean, for it could be assumed that his adversary did not attempt to thwart but to speed the death of the Nazarene. However, it is not his death but his resurrection that empowers the Christian's hope for humanity's "glorious destiny." Hawthorne seems to have symbolically projected this victory over death simply by Chillingworth's defeat at the scaffold. The magic touch by which the "infant immortality" of Pearl matures at the transfiguration of Hester is yet to be intimated in the last chapter of Hawthorne's tale.

THE ONE REFUGE

The Black Man of the forest acknowledged that Dimmesdale had escaped from his destruction by ascending the scaffold and making his confession, the one act in the one place only by which Dimmesdale, Hester, and Pearl could form their "electric chain" forever (153).

> "Hadst thou sought the whole earth over," said he, looking darkly at the clergyman, "there was no one place so secret,—no high place nor lowly place, where thou couldst have escaped me,—save on this very scaffold!" (253)

In another rare moment of truth, perhaps Master Prynne's admission of defeat is designed for the reader to assimilate, with all other possible allusions, as a victory for the other characters, and the principles they might represent. The cross upon which the carpenter finished his life's purposes, and by his death initiated the resurrection, seems fairly represented by the scaffold upon which Dimmesdale ascended; and perhaps was the only place, high or low, that humanity through this redemptive act could have escaped Old Scratch. It was the one place prepared for the "judgment which Providence seemed about to work."

Dimmesdale declares to Hester, "For thee and Pearl, be it as God shall order . . . . God is merciful! Let me now do the will which He hath made plain before my sight" (254). The will of God for Hester appears to be that she must wear the scarlet letter for the duration of her mortal existence. Whereas Pearl is destined for some more gracious state of being, so does humanity yet await that destiny. Dimmesdale's fate is to make his connections with Hester and Pearl known to his parishioners—or perhaps in other words, to reveal "the relation between the Deity and the communities of mankind" (249)—and apparently to seal that revelation with his life. That office was fulfilled as he ascended the scaffold and accepted the judgment of Providence.

A LITTLE PAST MERIDIAN

What the young minister did seems deemed by Hawthorne as a kind of inevitable fate or redemptive judgment which the world needs to compensate for its long mortal sufferings since its creation. Perhaps to him, that mortal creation also seems to stand in need of a certain confession, which Dimmedale is now determined to do, in behalf of Deity.

> "Hester Prynne," cried he, with a piercing earnestness, "in the name of Him, so terrible and so merciful, who gives me grace, at this last moment, to do what—for my own heavy sin and miserable agony—I withheld myself from doing seven years ago, come hither now, and twine thy strength about me!" (253)

Again Hawthorne makes another reference to the time frame of the allegory, which seems to say that the heavens have been or will be silent about some particular truth until the end of the seven thousand years of the earth's existence. The "heavy sin and miserable agony" may refer to the Redemption that in some way may also represent a confession for

Providence's responsibility in the earth's fall from immortality to its "dark necessity."

When Dimmesdale told Hester he should have done this seven years ago, Hawthorne could be implying his conclusion that Deity would have liked to acknowledge his responsibility in the creation and the fall into mortality at the first or beginning of the seven thousand years, but chose not to, as Dimmesdale explained to his adversary, to render his work more efficacious. Perhaps Hawthorne concluded philosophically that the Redemption was not only the solution to the problems mortality presents, but also a dim show of the worse of Deity's involvement in them. Like a drama acting out a foreordained plot, with antagonist and protagonist competing for some desired end, his tale is not a perfectly clear picture explaining what that show was entirely all about. Elsewhere, Hawthorne gave some justification for Dimmesdale's silence or ambiguity, but by this interpretation, perhaps a little less clearly than Providence's. He likewise gave meager cause for his own ambiguity, as we have heretofore explained. Thus, Dimmesdale, as the foremost character, possibly representing Hawthorne's most philosophical self, is properly titled.

At this point, the time frame of the allegory seems again to collapse as the tale refers to both the seven year period and the meridian of times at the time of Arthur's confession, or revelation. It is as though he is allegorically compressing two events together, typically as some authors of the Old Testament did in their double prophecies; that is, the Redemption itself, in the meridian of times, may forecast the judgment at the end of the millennium, as though the two events, if not inexplicably the same in effect, are at least connected.

> The sun, but little past its meridian, shone down upon the clergyman, and gave a distinctness to his figure, as he stood out from all the earth to put in his plea of guilty at the bar of Eternal Justice. (254)

ETERNAL JUSTICE

Dimmesdale is distinctively figured as a Christ image in many ways by Hawthorne in this chapter, a kind of kingpin to the allegory. But there are two basic problems entailed in so doing, as this purveyor has tackled heretofore, that universally pitch themselves against the analogy.

The first is his relationship with Hester, and the second is his declaration of sinfulness and extreme sense of guilt. However, when the insightful readers put the pieces of his metaphorical puzzle together, and beholds those problems as part and parcel of the explanation of life's experiences, the picture holds up to the reader a statement that seems inescapably to say, as implied in the passage above, "It is only Eternal Justice that there be a Redeemer of mankind from her mortal nature because he was chiefly her creator." Perhaps to Hawthorne, not only was it an act of passionate Mercy for Providence to provide a way out of mortality, but it was also a matter of Divine Justice.

But this statement or conclusion is not Biblical; it is an implication that Hawthorne seems cleverly to have couched in a tale through the meanings of metaphors connected in context with the main characters' Romantic allegorical representations. It is the substance of the quasi-heterodoxy this antinomian proposes may lie at the heart of Hawthorne's allegory, as though Hawthorne wanted to reveal his understanding of why the Creator would allow sin, pain, misery, death, and all those consequences of mortality to flow out of the Garden of Eden. This problem of an all-knowing Deity who is all loving, yet who allows the occurrence of all kinds of pain and misery in a world he has created, is one of the foremost philosophical paradoxes that has fretted the minds of many great men, and, somewhat evidently, as well as Hawthorne's. That he should have a response of his own to this paradox is nothing new. But what is new is the conclusion that may be inevitably drawn from the pieces of the puzzle he leads the reader to surmise.

Hawthorne's literary genius treats this paradox with a conclusion all his own that may seem heretical in content to his time, and possibly in our own time. Although Hawthorne seems less clearly to connect the creation with the fall, he more clearly, though still obscurely, connects the fall with its redemption. He also connects the Redemption with some "glorious destiny" against a background of, or with a special reference to, contemporary religious interpretation. He makes these connections through metaphors symbolized by a bright red letter on a black field, with a brilliance of imagery true to the complexity of intellect with which Melville credited his contemporary.

THE BURDEN OF RESPONSIBILITY

At the climax of Dimmesdale's confession, again we have allusions to the Nazarene. With reference to the "brand of sin and infamy" for which he is responsible, Dimmesdale referred to himself in the third person, but probably with the intention of referring allegorically to the person he represents, as responsible for the burden:

> "It was on him! . . . God's eye beheld it! The angels were forever pointing at it! The Devil knew it well, and fretted it continually with the touch of his burning finger! But he hid it cunningly from men, and walked among you with the mien of a spirit, mournful, because so pure in a sinful world!—and sad, because he missed his heavenly kindred! Now, at the death-hour, he stands up before you!" (255)

In what way did Dimmesdale miss his heavenly kindred in coming to earth? There is no text in Hawthorne's novel giving any foundation for such an assertion. In what way was Dimmesdale "so pure in a sinful world!"? Hawthorne has Dimmesdale apparently alluding to someone other than himself, but then identifies that third person as himself. This bold statement seems therefore to have less meaningful reference to Dimmesdale himself, at first, than to the historical figure and principle he may represent, before he declares himself to be that personage. It seems an apparent identification of Dimmesdale's mirrored representation in the analogy Hawthorne has poised, and becomes another clue in unraveling the mystery of his allegory.

The passage above also implies, in reference to himself as a type, that Dimmesdale was a pure being in a sinful world. This statement again questions the assumption that he ever committed any grievous sin. Yet, for many superficial readers, the purity of Dimmesdale is overshadowed by an implication of adultery in the tale, that is, until they realize that the tale itself is only a vehicle or framework for the allegorical messages Hawthorne has so cunningly woven therein. Dimmesdale's highly sensitive and introspective reactions to the burden of sin, themselves, possibly reflect Hawthorne's images of a divine being's sensitivity to his mortality, and possibly as well to the burden of the sins of humanity borne vicariously upon his shoulders.

A HEART FULL OF SYMPATHY

The mysterious horror Dimmesdale revealed upon his breast, of which he said Hester's scarlet letter was but "the type of what has seared his inmost heart" (255), may be the fulness of the pain of the Redemption, for which the pains of mortality itself are but a mere image or taste of that greater horror. Hester carried only the symbol of that horror, and the castigations consequential thereto, throughout the seven year period, whereas that horror was etched into the very flesh of Dimmesdale. Perhaps Hawthorne pictured the burden of that agony, burning mournfully upon the Nazarene's heart throughout his ministry, as an embodiment of the sins he would take upon himself. Nature itself, bearing the miseries of mortality (in the form of Hester), especially as heaped upon it and its partakers by the interpretations of contemporary religion, shares in that burden.

Dimmesdale, "in the crisis of acutest pain, had won a victory" (255), and forgave Chillingworth for his part in his torment, much in the same way as the Nazarene, perhaps at the height of his pain upon the cross, extended forgiveness to his tormentors. "'May God forgive thee!' said the minister" (256). A spell was broken when Pearl kissed him; and she appeared to undergo a change, wherein all her sympathies were developed by the grief in which she had taken part.

> Pearl kissed his lips. A spell was broken. The great scene of grief, in which the wild infant bore a part, had developed all her sympathies; and as her tears fell upon her father's cheek, they were the pledge that she would grow up amid human joy and sorrow, nor for ever do battle with the world, but be a woman in it. (256)

The reader is reminded that Hester said earler that Pearl needed this grief to develop her sympathetic nature (184). That grief may be the part that all humanity develops by the experiences of mortality; but the tears of grief Pearl shed may represent those shed by those who commiserate in the pains of the suffering Redeemer. Her kiss seems a seal and confirmation that Dimmesdale, in claiming his own, had been true to his fatherhood, and the mission for which he had been destined. Her nature, therefore, is confirmed to have divine parenthood in origin, and thus perhaps to be worthy of a "glorious destiny" in the future by that act of ownership.

Pearl will forever bear herself off well as a woman in a world given to human joy and sorrow. Perhaps the sympathies of mankind, developed by the experiences of mortality, in recognition of the sacrifice that redeemed her, are to be transformed into a similar love and regard for the divine. True womanhood, to Hawthorne, seems to contain the essence of compassion and grace; and that humankind which identifies with the Divine Being is claimed by him as his own, as his seed, upon whom he places his name, perhaps as they become like him in compassion and grace.

THE BROKEN LAW

In his last breath, his farewell to her seems to reflect the triumphant fulfillment of his mission. Despite the law they broke—perhaps either in the creation of humanity's mortality, or in their speculative thought to escape their detiny—and despite the consequences of fear, pain, temptation, and death, he declared his loss but temporary. To Hester, who pled for immortality with Dimmesdale, the dying minister promised but one thing–mercy.

> "Hush, Hester, hush!" said he, with tremulous solemnity. "The law we broke!–the sin here so awfully revealed!–let these alone be in thy thoughts! I fear! I fear! It may be, that, when we forgot our God,—when we violated our reverence each for the other's soul,—it was thenceforth vain to hope that we could meet hereafter, in an everlasting and pure reunion. God knows; and He is merciful! He hath proved his mercy, most of all, in my afflictions. By giving me this burning torture to bear upon my breast! By sending yonder dark and terrible old man, to keep the torture always at red-heat! By bringing me hither, to die this death of triumphant ignominy before the people! Had either of these agonies been wanting, I had been lost for ever! Praised be his name! His will be done! Farewell!" (256)

Of all the scenes and symbols addressing the allegory, the passage above appears to be the pivotal challenge to the reader's discernment of whether Dimmesdale could be an image of the Nazarene. Those who have given Hawthorne's novel only a cursory reading may most heartedly deny the possibility. Although the reader may have gotten past the implication of alleged adultery, and sensed something pushing from beneath the surface level of the tale, this scene—with which he/she comes boldly face to face with Dimmesdale's admission of sinfulness, of the law he broke with Hester, and of some violation of reverence between them—becomes the greatest barrier to understanding the full implications of the allegory.

In this passage, Hawthorne is probably not confusing the two incidents in Hester and Dimmesdale's relationship which relate to this admission. He more than likely is referring to the second incident in the forest, wherein they planned to escape their ignominy by evading their destinies as laid out by Providence. Their first act, whatever it was (and however obscurely it has been addressed in the tale) had not "violated the sanctity of a human heart. Thou and I, Hester, never did so!" It had been treated as a kind of "consecration of its own" (195), perhaps as though the passionate nature of the creation was a sacred act. But the second act, a deliberate and rational planning to thwart the Providential plan, is treated worse by far than the first. It was this second deed that was indeed a violation of their reverence for each other's soul, and the first apparently was not. The passage, "when we forgot our God," probably refers to the second act and not the first, and may imply that they presently have remembered their true duty to each other. Had they betrayed these destinies as they had planned, it would have been vain for them to hope for an everlasting and pure reunion. That that reunion is even possible implies that their union, from the beginning, not only may be forgivable, but also a part of merciful approval; indeed, perhaps to Hawthorne, a "dark necessity."

The young divine asked Hester to remember only two things, the broken law and the dreadful consequences contingent thereupon. The law they broke, if not reference to their betrayal of reverence, may refer allegorically to the one in the Garden of Eden, when Eve partook of the forbidden fruit of the tree, planted there by no other than Deity himself, thus resulting in the birth of mortal humankind; and the "consequences" may refer to the sinful nature of mortality and the agony of the Redemption needed to compensate for the fall. Whatever Hester's relationship with Master Prynne and Dimmesdale was that resulted in Hester's fall is considered a sin by Dimmesdale, a sin which, as her minister, he appeared to take upon himself. Whatever it was and whoever was responsible for the deed that caused Adam and Eve to break the law in the Garden of Eden, Deity, perhaps only from Hawthorne's own intutive ruminations, seems to have assumed a portion of the responsibility therefor. "[T]he sin here so awfully revealed," in other words, may refer to the consequences of humanity's sinful nature, so awfully revealed in the world by its universal presence, for which a Divine Being needed to answer universally in order to finalize Eternal Justice.

The implication of the passage as to whether they shall be together hereafter, however, is not clear at this point either. Hawthorne appears to be somewhat more ambivalent on this issue in this scene, as though to leave Hester's question open, "Shall we not spend our immortal life together? Surely, surely, we have ransomed one another, with all this woe!" (256) It is perhaps the one open-ended question left for the reader to ponder in Hawthorne's open-ended allegory.

However, the implications thus far, and in the last chapter, appear to point allegorically to the hopeful union of both to represent the resurrection of the physical body with the spiritual body, the mortal with the divine. Whereas Hester believes surely that they have ransomed each other's soul by the suffering they have shared, and should therefore "spend immortal life together" (256), Dimmesdale says that he does not know, but that there is hope in God's mercy for an "everlasting and pure reunion." Hawthorne may be saying, in the words of Dimmesdale, that he himself does not know, bu is relying upon the mercy of his Creator to resolve all misunderstandings and difficulties life offers.

There is a clash even among Christians about the resurrection. Various Christian interpretations of Biblical scripture assert that mortality, flesh and blood, which Hester symbolically seems to represent, cannot return to live in the presence of holy Deity, since no unclean thing can enter therein; but resurrected, immortal flesh, which no longer is sustained by blood, may have some other power of sustained movement.

The apparent contradiction in these interpretations may account for the allegorical ambivalence or indefiniteness Hawthorne leaves in Dimmesdale's response to Hester's soul-searching inquiry. Or perhaps he is reflecting the controversy in Christendom itself as to whether the physical body is to be resurrected with the rising spirit. This hope for an everlasting reunion then, transcendentally speaking, appears to be discerned only intuitively and dimly by Dimmesdale and Pearl.

The tone and imagery of the allegory, however, to this student of Hawthorne's novel, speaks not only to the one general destiny of the resurrection, or the transfiguration of the human body into an immortal state, but also particularly to a greater awaiting unity and ownership with the Divine. At the same time, there is a shadow and a horror that seems to await those who identify more with Chillingworth's nature. Both of these destinies appear to be part of the message of the scarlet letter. Both seem reflected "by one ever-glowing point of light gloomier than the shadow" (264). This varied destiny is possibly viewed by Hawthorne in the intimations of the scarlet letter against the black and gloomy perspective of the New England experiment in America, which maintained a very restrictive and narrow focus on sinfulness, to the exclusion of its proper absolution.

It Is Finished

At Dimmesdale's farewell and death, the silent crowd let out a sound that reflected the reverence with which they beheld their minister, and may contain some hint of earthly elements carrying the sound after his departing spirit, perhaps as a voice united with nature.

> That final word came forth with the minister's expiring breath. The multitude, silent till then, broke out in a strange, deep voice of awe and wonder, which could not as yet find utterance, save in this murmur that rolled so heavily after the departed spirit. (257)

The words, "His will be done!" and the voice, or "murmur that rolled so heavily," which does not seem to come exclusively from the crowd, "which could not as yet find utterance," seems reminiscent of the voice of nature, in the Biblical record, that is reported to have echoed after the Nazarene's departing. Perhaps, to the Christian, those few followers who witnessed that death were not able to offer the full sympathy due the dying of their divine, perhaps because they were dismayed at his unexpected death. Later, however, his followers understood, in review of all that he had taught, and gave utterance in full sympathy.

But the elements of nature itself, at the instance of his death, from the review of the witnesses of the scene, are reported similarly as having vibrated and rolled a great murmur of sympathy heavily heavenward. Perhaps it was more this testimony of nature itself, than the dying of the Nazarene, that seemed to fill those at Golgotha with awe and wonder. For the Romantic in Hawthorne, the awe and wonder of Dimmesdale's multitude, and the worshipful aspect toward their dying minister, perhaps signifies the holy distinctiveness with which Hawthorne treated the character of Dimmesdale in his allegorical tale. This analogous quality of the crowd, and the distinctive reserve Hawthorne has given the closing scene, singularly embellishes Dimmesdale, like the scarlet letter A engraven upon a black shield, with an awe that begs repetition of a previous passage that focuses upon the uniqueness of Dimmesdale's character and representation:

> The sun, but little past its meridian, shone down upon the clergy- man, and gave a distinctness to his figure, as he stood out from all the earth to put in his plea of guilty at the bar of Eternal Justice. (254)

The sun seems to represent an affirmation of Providence smiling down upon the young divine, a "little past its meridian," giving him a distinctiveness apart from all others. Perhaps, standing out above all of the earth's inhabitants, the distinctive name of the Nazarene, has minded Hawthorne, in his own quiet way, and peculiar "mode of glorifying God," to give subtle reverence thereto. Perhaps his one novel, that has so mystified the world with its abstruseness, has been enveloped in a form of communication that has befuddled its readers as much as the parables and the dim messages of the Nazarene mystified his audiences. Possibly, in addition to proclaiming his philosophical self on the matter, Hawthorne may have related the ministry and mission of the Galilean not only as an act of Infinite mercy, but also as an act of universal justice, in which the Creator may have expressed his own accountability.

GUILTY

If, from all the preponderance of parallels between the tale and the allegory, as thus depicted in this analysis, we can deduce that Dimmesdale is a representation of the historical figure of the Nazarene, as a principle of the Redemption from the Fall, one of the most intriguing parts of the analogy lies in the picture of guilt Hawthorne has painted into Dimmesdale's experience. The above passage states that Dimmesdale's Confession was "his plea of guilty at the bar of Eternal Justice." The stain of Dimmesdale's guilt is a recurring theme, and is one of the two primary problems this analysis must confront, and has confronted, in order to make it more amenable to public credulity. That Hawthorne has possibly juxtaposed one of his characters with a revered historical figure, who notably was personally guilty of no mean or unholy comportment, the word, "guilty," wears wearily as much upon the Christian reader as the juxtaposition itself does to the literary liberal, who would have none of it.

Perhaps the word "guilty," and all aspects of and references to that term, is likewise a metaphor in itself, with a parallel meaning not equal to its surface meaning, as is the case with most of the symbolism in Hawthorne's tale, but an expression associated with the vicarious nature of the burden of sin he may have been taking upon his ministerial shoulders. That guilt, and its fraternal twin, shame, might be the feelings associated with that vicarious burden. Or perhaps Dimmesdale's plea of guilt at the bar of Eternal Justice represents Deity's final admission of responsibility for the earth's creation, inherent in the Redemption, that may voice its role more clearly in the day of judgment, according to Hawthorne. On the other hand, just as much as it may symbolize the sins of humanity and their consequences, guilt and pain, borne by the Redeemer, the "sin" or act that he agonizes over may reflect the Biblical instances wherein the Lord of Israel was noted, if correctly translated, to have repented that he ever made humankind[9].

A REVIEW

For those not familiar with it, perhaps a brief synopsis of the history of the Nazarene might show its parallels with the details of Dimmesdale's character, particularly as mentioned in this chapter. The knowledgeable Christian may conceive the full context of the Old and New Testament as pointing to the condescension of a Deity, who, as the Creator, gave up his preeminence among his kindred there, stepped down from his heavenly kingdom in the meridian of earth-time, and took upon himself the nature of that mortal tabernacle. There he walked among his creations unbeknown to them, "so pure in a sinful world," and then sealed the purpose of his mortal ministry by voluntarily giving his life at the death-hour. That context holds that the angels knew and spoke of the Atonement of the Anointed One coming, history itself pointing to the meridian of times. Old Scratch knew it also: "Thou believest that there is one God; thou doest well: the devils also believe, and tremble;"[8] and vainly tried to stop it with his burning fingers. Though the angels heralded it, and Old Scratch sought to thwart it, yet the Nazarene seemed to have hidden from the eyes of all, for a while, his true identify as the one chosen to redeem his own creation. It was hidden in the humble manner of his birth, his life as a carpenter's son, and revealed only at the right time to effect his destined mission.

The entirety of Hawthorne's tale seems to lead up to a possible conclusion that he may have thought the reason the Nazarene was chosen to be the Redeemer of the world might be because his own sensative sense of justice might have importuned some show of accountability for its creation, as its Creator, and that Eternal Justice can only be met by an Eternal admission of that responsibility. It seems that Hawthorne may have considered the Atonement to contain inherently that admission, by implication, and that he picked his characters to demonstrate dramatically his particular philosophical conclusions, as mysteriously as he could, in the form of allegory.

CHAPTER 24

CONCLUSION

Blessed are the meek: for they shall inherit the earth.[1]

The drama of the play is over, the portent of the scarlet letter "has done its office" (259), and the readers now file with the audience into the foyer to discuss their reactions to what they have experienced. Of the several accounts of what the multitude at the scaffold saw upon the minister's breast, the question in the mind of the reader might be, "What is Hawthorne trying to communicate as to what the revelation to the divine's parishioners meant?" Often he advanced various and diverse perspectives, then appears to lead the reader to guess or intuit the view towards which he leans.

As the readers congregate to review their own intimations received from the drama posed by Hawthorne, Hawthorne will have the audience, who witnessed Dimmesdale's Confession, relate their varied reactions to their own individual experiences. The question of what Hawthorne may have intended, at least, might support the premise that he wished to couch his allegory in a quasi-open-ended fashion, with insinuations that touch on his philosophical self.

As to the case of Dimmesdale's confession, revelation, and death, Hawthorne has left more to the imagination of the reader as to what significance the event has in the allegory. As in the case of Hester's anticipated transfiguration, the purely rational knowledge of whether it really happened, or may be yet to happen, at the allegorical level, may not have been meant to be experienced by the reader, that is, until, or if and when, it may actually happen in the future, and may only have been meant by Hawthorne to be an anticipation, as a function of his open-ended allegory. At best, perhaps it begs the reader to look closely for clues yet even more subtle.

THE VARIETY OF INFERENCE

Not all the parishioners conceived the same understanding or derived the same message from the minister's revelation of the mark upon his chest. "As regarding its origin, there were various explanations, all of which must necessarily have been conjectural" (258). To appreciate Hawthorne's use of varigated responses to an event, a quote is repeated from an earlier most significant incident that parallels that of Dimmesdale's confession upon the scaffold, with Hester and Pearl again at his side. On the night of the divine's vigil, in Chapter 12, while Dimmesdale was in the midst of simulating such a confession, and forming "an electric chain" with Hester and Pearl, who were standing by him on the scaffold, a sign of bright light was beheld in the night sky; and Hawthorne, as the narrator, notes a certain peculiarity associated with the observation of such an extraordinary event.

> Oftener, however, its credibility rested on the faith of some lonely eyewitness, who beheld the wonder through the colored, magnifying, and distorting medium of his imagination, and shaped it more distinctly in his after-thought. (155)

So the credibility of what was seen by the eye-witnesses to Dimmesdale's confession, which were divided in their report into four groups, rested upon the faith, the imagination, and the rationale of the eye-witnesses, perhaps each according to their own inclinations. Perhaps that is the reason Hawthorne preferred the allegory as the vehicle to cast his philosophical play upon his public. Rather than boldly declaring himself, he might rather have had his readers assume what they would according to their own particular propensities; and he might have classified as his friends those who might intuit by choice what his own inclinations were, which, he probably surmised, would be only a few. At the same time, he probably knew that the writer might obtain a greater audience by not being so direct, while dimly addressing the few whom his work favored (3-4).

The first account, or explanation, of the origin of the scarlet letter, as related by some parishioners of the incident, claimed that, although they admitted Dimmesdale may have been carrying out his own penance in his relationship with Hester, that though there was a scarlet letter, it was imprinted into Dimmesdale's flesh by Dimmesdale "inflicting a hideous torture on himself" (258). In other words, there was nothing supernatural or miraculous about the token. Should Hawthorne again be comparing Dimmesdale to the Nazarene, he would be recognizing those who see nothing extraordinary about his Redemption in that it was perhaps simply a result of his own contriving.

The second account held that Chillingworth caused the sign by "magic and poisonous drugs." Yes, there is always the crowd, in the face of an idea or sign, who might rather ascribe the supernatural to the work of the nether regions than to heaven's; and in many cases, perhaps rightly so, since epistemological discernment of the source is sometimes a difficult venture.

A third account of those who actually saw the sign—by

> those best able to appreciate the minister's peculiar sensibility, and the wonderful operation of his spirit upon the body,—whispered their belief, that the awful symbol was the effect of the ever active tooth of remorse, gnawing from the inmost heart outwardly, and at last manifesting Heaven's dreadful judgment by the visible presence of the letter. (258)

This third account, of the three who actually saw the letter upon his chest, seems to be the response that addresses the revelation from which Hawthorne seeks to whisper his philosophical conclusions connecting Deity's relationship with the communities of mankind. It is voiced by those who appreciate the "minister's peculiar sensibility," sense some heavenly power working upon him, and discern the judgment of Heaven that was manifestly gnawing within his heart. Perhaps Hawthorne may view these as those who share some sympathy with him, understand the value of intuition in observing the affairs of humanity, and therefore may appreciate some of the peculiar sensibilities of the author himself.

The use of the word "wonderful" might be puzzling to readers who may still be hung up at the surface level of the tale. They may hardly see anything wonderful about the operation of Dimmesdale's spiritual suffering, however manifestly it appeared upon his body, or anything remarkable about his dim confession. Whether or not Hawthorne chose this word for its ambiguious meanings may warily be explicable. "Wonderful" may mean, formally, surprising or astonishing, and not, informally or colloquially, splendid. To Hawthorne, it may be meant to communicate both.

This third account, as reported by some of Dimmesdale's parishioners, appears most representative of Hawthorne's allegorical intentions, for one primal reason. It is in keeping with Dimmesdale's character, and his representative principal, who both were sensitively responsive to both the nature of their mortality and their intense spiritual or moral intuitiveness. Even Chillingworth recognized, as we have heretofore mentioned, in one of his rare moments of truth, the uniqueness of Dimmesdale's sensitivity: "the Creator never made another being so sensitive as this" (171). In the field of Christian folklore and testimony, it perhaps could be said by some more familiar with the subject, that there has never been a being proclaimed to be so sensitively compassionate to the ills and woes of humanity as has been the Galilean, who reportedly healed many, bore the pains and agonies of the repentant, and, in a larger measure, served all humankind. The "tooth of remorse, gnawing from the inmost heart outwardly, and at last manifesting Heaven's dreadful judgment," may be Hawthorne's representation of that vicarious and universal sacrifice the Nazarene is purported to have rendered.

In the final analysis of the three accounts, the third, at least, recognizes some connection between Deity, the token that burned outward from his heart to his body, and Heaven's judgment of the communities of mankind. To this group of eye-witnesses, the acuteness of feelings, with respect to his highly developed conscience, points to the depth and height of Dimmesdale's delicate morality, so much so that his physical body manifested that intense sensibility. According to the Biblical record, the agony of the Redemption must have been excruciating, inasmuch as the Nazarne's "sweat was as it were great drops of blood falling down to the ground."[2] Such an exudation, were it blood indeed, and not merely sweat, might readily involve the supernatural and substantiate the second and third account, but hardly the first.

It is neither perhaps of slight significance that Hawthorne's choice of the color red might have been intended to represent symbollically that particular agony. Living in the same sphere with Hester, Arthur's extreme sensitivity to his "sin," essentially transcribed upon his chest, from his heart inside to the outside, the same symbol as the letter A she wore. The same agony-confession that bonds Hester and Dimmesdale seems to lie in the claim that the Atonement, in much similar fashion, bonds both the natural and spiritual elements of humankind. Perhaps Hawthorne meant for the transcription to be like some mysterious writing on the wall, a message portending consequence for humanity's sinfulness, or a redemption from mortality.

Hawthorne may have conjectured that, had there been any other way for the Creator to fulfill his purposes for the ultimate destiny of the human family, he would have chosen that alternative path. Though Hawthrone proposed an alternative course, of a sort, symbolically, by Hester to Dimmesdale, which the latter sensibility considered and ultimately rejected, Hawthorne seems to maintain the integrity of Providence by holding to the destiny that is laid out for humanity, according to the Christian code. That is to say, in the last summary on the matter, that this destiny may require humankind's long, miserable patience with mortality, as in the case of Hester's seven year infamy, and the condescension and agony of a Deity, as in the analogy of Dimmesdale's indemnification, to atone or compensate for that misery. Thus, Dimmesdale (as a manifestation or representative of the Divine) confessed his relationship with Hester (representing the material element of nature). In an implied mysterious act, he was responsible for the birth of Pearl (the residue of humankind for whom a better world is intended); died to confirm this special interrelationship; and thus the office of the scarlet letter was executed as designed.

FAITH VERSUS DOUBT

Others witnesses, a fourth view, reported having seen no mark whatsoever.

> It is singular, nevertheless, that certain persons, who were spectators of the whole scene, and professed never once to have removed their eyes from the Reverend Mr. Dimmesdale, denied that there as any mark whatever on his breast . . . . Neither, by their report, had his dying words acknowledged, nor even remotely implied, any, the slightest connection, on his part with the guilt for which Hester Prynne had so long worn the scarlet letter. (259)

In this fourth report, perhaps Hawthorne is saying that, just as some of his parishioners saw no divinity in Dimmesdale, nor heard him acknowledge any connection with the guilt Hester had borne all her life, there are "certain persons" in the throng of humanity who look upon the Nazarene as merely a man, and not as a Redeemer of humankind's guilt and mortality. Further, their explanation of the event was that the divine had only expressed

> to the world how utterly nugatory is the choicest of man's own righteousness. After exhausting life in his efforts for mankind's spiritual good, he had made the manner of his death a parable, in order to impress on his admirers the mighty and mournful lesson, that, in view of Infinite Purity, we are sinners all alike. It was to teach them, that the holiest among us has but attained so far above his fellows as to discern more clearly the Mercy which looks down, and repudiate more utterly the phantom of human merit, which would look aspiringly upward. (259)

This is to say, then, in this regard, that the episode of the Nazarene's voluntary sacrifice, despite all the efforts by which he exhausted his life for humanity's sake, had no such connection with the miseries of mortality. The event was only a show that he and all the rest of the mortal race were but sinners; and that the life and death of the divine was but a gesture recognizing that Mercy from above looks down, as it chooses, without regard for humanity's feeble and vain efforts to pursue any course of merit. This view might be similar to Chillingworth's justification of his actions, and is repeated here to highlight the significance of Hawthorne's treatment of the fourth account.

> My old faith, long forgotten, comes back to me, and explains all that we do, and all we suffer. By thy first step awry, thou didst plant the germ of evil; but, since that moment, it has all been a dark neccessity . . . . It is our fate. Let the black flower blossom as it may!

Hawthorne's peculiar arrangement of the first three explanations, held apart from the fourth, may divide Dimmesdale's audience between those who saw and those who did not see the transcription or manifestation of the letter. He may have set this fourth group apart as an intended demarcation between those who have sensitively intuited intimations from the spiritual realm and those who may only see what their intellect alone has revealed to them. Perhaps he may also associate with this group those who sense no allegorical meanings in his ordinary tale, no "deep meaning in it, most worthy of interpretation," that escapes the analysis of the mind.

It is also interesting to note Hawthorne's comment about the first three reports: "The reader may choose among these theories" (259), as though he may deem the fourth group of "certain persons" a class by themselves. The tone of the passage describing the fourth report seems to cast the perspective, in an overconfident mien, that any degree of a mortal's righteousness is in effect worthless. It might be argued that the fourth point of view might be Hawthorne's, that the scarlet letter is therefore only a story and has no deeper allegorical meaning. Or one might conclude that Hawthorne is simply reflecting his own bias against the purely scientific approach to life's problems.

Hawthorne doesn't make any comments parenthetically about the first two reports, indicating that they possibly have a bearing upon the allegory. But he appears to discredit the fourth report by using the royal "we," perhaps to include his friends.

> Without disputing a truth so momentous, we must be allowed to consider this version of Mr. Dimmesdale's story as only an instance of that stubborn fidelity with which a man's friends—and especially a clergyman's—will sometimes uphold his character, when proofs, clear as the mid-day sunshine on the scarlet letter, establish him a false and sin-stained creature of the dust. (259)

In other words, some of the viewers maintained their conclusions with a staunch fidelity to their former opinions, even though the event heralded some momentous truth. The royal "we" does not dispute the truth revealed in Dimmesdale's momentous revelation, but is gracious enough to recognize that others may hold stubbornly to their notions, despite evidence to the contrary that is as clear "as the mid-day sunshine on the scarlet letter.". In possibly slighting the fourth report, Hawthorne may also be refuting the rationale for its view that we are all sinners equally. On the other hand, perhaps what Hawthorne is merely saying is that it is neither Mercy nor human merit alone that lifts one upward, but simply being true to oneself, as his tale demonstrates.

Perhaps Hawthorne hinted at his preference in his reference to some epistomological verification that perhaps justified his view, as presented in his book.

> The authority which we have chiefly followed—a manuscript of old date, drawn up from the verbal testimony of individuals . . . fully confirms the view taken in the foregoing pages. (259-260)

Hawthorne seems to be saying that the view which he has presented in his tale, however obscurely and dimly drawn up the reader may consider it, is based upon the authority of some ancient manuscript and is confirmed by the testimonies of contemporary witnesses of the event. Based upon the premises established by the author's interpretation of Hawthorne's tale, that authority allegorically would appear to be no less than the Biblical records of eye-witnesses to the life, the teachings, and the purposeful death of the Nazarene, a few of which are alluded to in his book. The tale of the scarlet letter upon Hester's bosom and Dimmesdale's chest, then, at the allegorical level, might simply be authenticated by reference to that text, which, of course, would outrule the validity of the fourth report.

Hester's life of service despite her shame, Dimmesdale's devotion to his mission despite its agony, and Chillingworth's damnable deterioration, despite his former honor: these merits are no phantoms without consequence or destiny in Hawthorne's tale. Nor was the act, whatever it was, in which both Hester and Dimmesdale colluded, without direct consequence. As "a false and sin-stained creature of the dust," Dimmesdale's role, as an actor upon the stage of life, may suggest that the Nazarene may have answered responsibly for himself, as well as for Hester and Pearl, in exacting due justice for the world, as Providence's manner of "disentangling its mesh of good and evil." As a mortal, the Nazarene inherited a sin-inclined or "sin-stained" nature, therefore was subject to temptation, and proclaimed, in less dramatic honesty than the minister, when addressed as Good Master, "Why callest thou me good? There is none good but one, that is, God."[3] Dimmesdale's sense of guilt and sin might be Hawthorne's perspective of the Nazarene's sensitive view on the nature of mortal life. Whether or not he commiserated throughout his three-year ministry with the expected agony of the cross, may be more conjecture than even this layman's analysis, although Dimmesdale's figure may have projected an elongated and intensified version of the same.

Allegorically, Hawthorne also seems to undermine the fourth view that faith and hope alone are adequate, that our works or merits do not need to justify our beliefs. But what is more clear and obvious about his tale is that Mercy and Love at least claim the merciful and compassionate sinner, without which the test of life is not successful to the end of happiness. At the same time, to Hawthorne, if not so apparent to the reader, it seems possible that Mercy, as efficacious a part as it may play in the Providential plan of life, may not rob the demands of Eternal Justice, not even for the Creator.

Other than posing a possible simple contrast between Puritanism and Christianity, or Hawthorne's concept of what it was intended or ought to be, the varied reactions to the divine's confession may possibly represent the differing explanations for the Nazarene's ministry, much as perhaps Hawthorne anticipated a varigated respons to his tale. More than likely, Hawthorne was probably cognizant of the fact that the same is true for each of the religions of the world, that for whatever the original may have been, the varied interpretations thereof, over time, may have led to several ineffective applications thereto. Even though his qualitative rebuke of Puritanism may evidence his discouragement with contemporary religion, Hawthorne opted for a positive outlook for the future.

THE FALSEHOOD OF SILENCE

Perhaps to dramatize the significance of confession he thought needed in the Redemptive plan, Hawthorne once more addressed the theme of heaven's silence, and uses a series of exclamations before a particular sentence that may underscore the main moral he wished to expound in his tale.

> Among many morals which press upon us from the poor minister's miserable experience, we put only this into a sentence:—"Be true! Be true! Be true! Show freely to the world, if not your worst, yet some trait whereby the worst may be inferred!" (260)

The paragraph in which the quotation was made appears to summarize Hawthorne's tale in a nutshell. Using the royal "we," Hawthorne's exclamations marks highlight the narrator's personal statement concerning the divine's experience, and may puzzle the reader as to its allegorical significance. Of all the morals pressed upon the readers in his story, this one singularly pinpoints Dimmesdale's confession as crucial to the allegory: be true to the best or the fullest extent of what you are, even if that means revealing the worst within you, or at least inferring it by some quality of character. His confession, coupled with the disclosure of the symbol etched upon his breast, showed to the world his worst, or at least inferred it, by the integrity of his sacrifice.

Hawthorne may have been saying, thereby, that the Redemption, symbolized by the agony and the portent of Dimmesdale's suffering, was the outward expression or confession of responsibility for the action that led to the fall, which might be perhaps the worst that can be said for Deity's possible involvement therein. The mournful agony of the Galilean's life and death as a mortal, perhaps as personified by Dimmesdale and tokened in his own scarlet letter, was possibly the outward trait manifesting the worse part of Deity's collusive or clandestine participation in engineering the existence of mortality. That is to say, from either Hawthorne's view or this purveyor's, perhaps the passion of taking upon himself the same mortality he created, and bearing the pains and miseries of his creation, was the worst show, by inference, of that responsibility.

Perhaps the silence of Providence, therefore, as to the ultimate cause of the fall, and perhaps the reasons therefor, may in Hawthorne's mind have required some answerability, if not accountability, to satisfy his sense of justice in the matter of the Creation seemingly gone awry; and Dimmesdale's agony and confession, along with the other actors on stage, could have been his configuration to resolve his own philosophical dilemma with Christianity. Moreover, whether or not this particular dilemma and resolution posed for Hawthorne any other difficulty, one further implication may be suggested in his allegory: just as Deity seems to hold us responsible for the consequences of our actions, He also may share a keen sense of responsibility for the consequences of his own actions, actions that apparently required the dark necessity of mortality to achieve his divine purposes. Thus, only an eternal divine can exact an eternal payment for the necessity therefor.

Perhaps one of the "sins" of "Infinite Purity" Hawthorne may have surmised, then, may be the seven thousand year period of silence Providence has maintained concerning his party to the act of mortal creation; therefore, stained with the sins of the world, the Nazarene redeemed Deity from the seeming lack of integrity, or, at worst, the appearance thereof embedded in that long period of silence: Therefore, Dimmesdale, finally, was true, true, true to himself, his mission, and perhaps to Hester and Pearl, by word, by trait, and by an ultimate testimony.

CHILLINGWORTH'S DISINTEGRATION

Quick to counterpose destinies, Hawthorne follows up Dimmedale's with his antagonist's. "[H]e positively withered up, shriveled away, and almost vanished from mortal sight, like an uprooted weed that lies wilting in the sun." Since

> there was no more devil's work on earth for him to do, it only remained for the unhumanized mortal to betake himself whither his Master would find him tasks enough, and pay him his wages duly" (260).

These passages may be allegorically alluding to the legendary dragon of the Biblical record, who, as an unembodied spirit, had lost all feeling for humankind, and, in payment for his evil deeds, is to be bound for a thousand years elsewhere by the powers of Deity, with no more work to do at present:

> And I saw an angel come down from heaven, having the key of the bottomless pit and a great chain in his hand.

> And he laid hold on the dragon, that old serpent, which is the Devil, and Satan, and bound him a thousand years.

> And cast him into the bottomless pit, and shut him up, and set a seal upon him, that he should deceive the nations no more.[4]

Whether or not the Adversdary is also seen by Hawthorne to be a pawn of Providence to be used to bring about its purposes, or whether he wondered if the existence of evil is necessary for the development of good, may be left to an examination of this particular lead into his essay on love and hate.

ON LOVE AND HATE

We deferred a discussion of some questions asked in Chapter 15 by Hester, pertaining to Chillingworth's possible destiny, as a reference to Hawthorne's possible conclusions concerning humanity's destiny:

> Did the sun, which shone so brightly everywhere else, really fall upon him? Or was there, as it rather seemed, a circle of ominous shadow moving along with his deformity, whichever way he turned himself? And whither was he now going? Would he not suddenly sink into the earth, leaving a barren and blasted spot . . . . ? Or would he spread bat's wings and flee away, looking so much the uglier, the higher he rose towards heaven? (176)

In the passages above and below, Hawthorne seems to have lubricated his rendition of justice by moralizing on the possible future destiny of Chillingworth and his companions, whether they have lived a compassion life, as Hester and Dimmesdale, or a life of hostility, as Chillingworth. The unanswered questions above also precede his short essay on love and hate.

The first two questions appear to address the worth of Chillingworth's past. Was he of such a character that the sun really once shone upon him? Perhaps, to represent some principle or figure of the past, Hawthorne may be asking, "Was Lucifer, the son of the morning, really more noble than he hence became, or was he always casting his shadowy character as a pall over all wherever he went?" That Hawthorne may be referring to another Biblical text, wherein Lucifer is called the son of the morning, is not unlikely, for Chillingworth's decline is seen throughout his novel.[5]

The second two questions seem to address Chillingworth's future, as would the projections of the allegory, as a whole, for all of humanity: "Will Lucifer himself, the caldron of hate, as any other so inclined, really be confined forever to the bottomless pit of the earth, or, possibly because of his worthy past, be allowed to rise heavenward, from hate to love, despite the ugliness of his character?"

It is most likely that, while Hawthorne is conjecturing about Chillingworth's possible karma, he is also echoing a more compassionate Christian message for the fate of humankind. Only by inference does Hawthorne project Chillingworth's fate onto the rest of us. Less we judge harbingers of good and evil amiss, Hawthorne therefore treats us to a short essay in his last chapter with this introduction:

> But, to all these shadowy beings, so long our near acquaintances,—as well Roger Chillingworth as his companions,—we would fain be merciful. It is a curious subject of observation and inquiry, whether hatred and love be not the same thing at bottom . . . . Philosophically considered . . . the two passions seem essentially the same, except that one happens to be seen in a celestial radiance, and the other in a dusky and lurid glow. In the spiritual world, the old physician and the minister—mutual victims as they have been—may unawares, have found their earthly stock of hatred and antipathy transmuted into golden love. (260)

This passage seems a climatic continuation of the theme initiated earlier, and a quote is repeated again as another reference to relate the essay as a general theme to his tale:

> It is to the credit of human nature, that, except where its selfishness is brought into play, it loves more readily that it hates. Hatred, by a gradual and quiet process, will even be transformed to love, unless the change be impeded by a continually new irritation of the original feeling of hostility. (160)

Acquainted with the spirit of good and evil, and the disposition of human nature, we have addressed Hawthorne's probable philosophical insights, and likely his preferred leanings, concerning the destiny of sympathetic and compassionate humankind. In the questions above, we could say that Hawthorne was not catechizing so much as he was ruminating about the destiny of those as well whose lives are filled with hatred. Perhaps the characters of Hawthorne's tale seem but shadowy representations of the effects of love and hate upon the hearts and minds of the human family—depending upon their sensitivity to the kingdom within—for whom we should suspend judgment, because their nature may belong to and spring from the same stock. Perhaps an implication of this thought is that, in the spiritual world, without the impact of mortal nature, without the influence of hostile forces, or their counterparts, and without the objects of their hatred, the hostility of humankind may be changed into celestial love. Hawthorne's "Good Master," then, might indeed be a Merciful Master, who defines mercy as he defines justice. However, in this essay on love and hate, which postulates both as possibly coming from the same stock or source, perhaps he was inclined to believe that it is what one learns from his environment, and not one's genetics, that differentiates between the two in time; and that that learning may be ultimately unlearned.

This essay helps to clarify the representations of the minister and the physician as principals or principles of being: the first, the epitomy of love, and the second, the epitomy of hate. But the idea that both positions of earthly manifestations may become "transmuted into golden love" is to say, for Hawthorne, that good might be the ultimate end for all our differences, whether caused by different degrees of intuitive sensibility to the higher principles of life, or by the degree to which we base our conclusions on the value of life solely upon the intellect alone. In its implication that the spiritual world around us may transmute the material experience of this life into an ultimate reality that transcends our common existence, this brief essay seems to be strictly anti-Transcendental in substance, as it addresses the evil side as well as the good side of spiritual reality.

A NEW WORLD

Hawthorne introduces a "matter of business" to the reader, or the news of a better world to which Hester has transported Pearl before she returned to Boston. It is perhaps fitting to the allegory that Hester should transport Pearl to the new world: the only avenue to immortality is through the experience of mortality.

Leaving this discussion apart, we have a matter of business to communicate to the reader . . . . [Roger Chillingworth] bequeathed a very considerable amount of property, both here and in England to little Pearl . . . .

So Pearl—the elf-child,—the demon offspring, as some people, up to that epoch, persisted in considering her—became the richest heiress of her day, in the New World. (261)

Indeed, Pearl has inherited all that Chillingworth has left behind, and much more on the other side of the sea, much like the Christian hope of the meek inheriting the earth, and heaven, during a period of peace and plenty, following Satan's banishment therefrom. She goes to some other distant land, perhaps to signify that her present state of existence will not know or identify with the Puritan interpretation of life's purpose and meaning, or likewise, with any of the inadequate attempts of society to address the problems of mortality, or, for that matter of business, with anything pertaining to mortality, on this side of the sea. Her life seems to have been transmuted into a golden sphere apart from the gloomy earthiness of Hester's, although she has not forgotten her mother's experiences and sacrifice for her.

Letters came, with armorial seals upon them, though of bearings unknown to English heraldry . . . . Hester was seen embroidering a baby-garment, with such a lavish richness of golden fancy as would have raised a public tumult, had any infant, thus apparelled, been shown to our sobre-hued community . . . . In fine, the gossips of that day believed . . . that Pearl was not only alive, but married, and happy, and mindful of her mother. (262)

The "armorial seals" upon Pearl's letters to Hester may indicate a coat of arms that heralds a new era or kingdom to be ushered in and enjoyed by those not burdened by the gloominess which Hester had inherited from her English descendants. Perhaps that is why the bearings are completely different to the English age. Perhaps it is this difference, as well as the distant relationship between Hester and Pearl—the life present as the related precursor of the life future—that endows Hester with a greater ability to comfort others, and an assurance of a happier state of existence on the other side of the sea.

> [T]he scarlet letter ceased to be a stigma which attracted the world's scorn and bitterness, and became a type of something to be sorrowed over, and looked upon with awe, yet with reverence too . . . .

> She assured them, too, of her firm belief, that, at some brighter period, when the world should have grown ripe for it, in Heaven's own time, a new truth would be revealed, in order to establish the whole relation between man and woman on a surer ground of mutual happiness . . . .

> The angel and apostle of the coming revelation must be a woman, indeed, but lofty, pure, and beautiful; and wise, moreover, not through dusky grief, but the ethereal medium of joy; and showing how sacred love should make us happy, by the truest test of a life successful to such an end! (263)

This passage, perhaps more than any other, shores up Hawthorne's religious philosophy in contrast to the perspective of his Puritan past, or contemporary interpretations of the Christian experience. It appears he anticipated a forthcoming revelation of new truths, during a brighter period, when a future generation, lofty, pure, beautiful, and wise, through the experience of joy, will testify of a way of life that assures happiness by its truths. Transformed through the earth's darker periods, wherein the body is no longer looked upon with scorn and bitterness, this prophetess will apparently evidence how the truest test of life lived to the end of joy, effected by the sacred love of Providence, may determine that destiny. Whereas the scarlet letter that Hester wore, as she had emblazoned it upon her bosom, now only may token the promise of that day, that day may bring a messenger that will "show how" the message, inherent in the token of the scarlet letter, is a surer ground for effecting joy for all.

Moreover, Hawthorne has repeated again the purpose of the message of the Election Sermon, but with a different use of intriguing wording. Simply declaring "the relation between the Deity and the communities of mankind," has been modified to establishing "the whole relation between man and woman on a surer ground of mutual happiness." By justapositioning this difference so, it is difficult to escape the impression that Hawthorne might be symbolizing Deity as a man and the communities of mankind as a woman or women. It shores up previous assertions that Hawthorne may have used the image of womanhood as a refinement of the generations of humanity; that is, Hester, as the best mortality can offer, and Pearl as the more refined offspring of mortality. It likewise could be conjectured that Hawthorne may subscribe to the Christian belief that Deity is a glorified man. This assertion may be just as lofty as picturing the Nazarene as a de-glorified Deity condescending to earth to accomplish a particular mission.

THE PROPHETESS

Perhaps the reader, at this point, is puzzled about Hawthorne's reference to prophetesses in conjunction with what his women might symbolize. "Earlier in life, Hester had vainly imagined that she herself might be the destined prophetess" (263). Now that the scarlet letter has done its office, she can assure others of a brighter day, but only as a woman "bowed down with shame . . . burdened with a life-long sorrow" (263). But Hester's brainwashed perspective of the mortality she represents was that of a "dusty grief," perhaps a fair comparison to the Biblical metaphor of the woman, "being with child cried, travailing in birth, and pained to be delivered."[6]

There are hints in Hawthorne's tale that Pearl might be the other prophetess, the generation in which the new truth is coming. In the same Biblical text from which Hester might have been conjured, another feminine parallel to Pearl might have been extracted: "And there appeared a great wonder in heaven; a woman clothed with the sun, and the moon under her feet, and upon her head a crown of twelve stars."[7] However, the woman in both verses are the same woman, and it would greatly belabor the comparison to further detail the analogy. But it can be said, that Hester delivered her child from the throes of New England to a better world. Representing a distant kingdom and prosperous New World, Pearl may be the destined prophetess who was delivered from the pain of mortal labor; her voice that of the new revelation (church or kingdom); and Pearl's own child that advanced generation of the future.

Master Prynne, who we have previously indicated may represent the Master of this present world, had left her an inheritance in a new world. Hawthorne seems to have had in mind that, according to Christian theology, the meek shall inherit the earth, and may have implied it so, when "little Pearl . . . became the richest heiress of her day, in the New World." So Hawthorne appears to have joined ranks with other Utopian writers, who indicated, more explicitly than he, their belief in a coming restoration or revelation to bring about a better way of life.

WHAT REMAINS

Hester dies and is buried among many monuments with armorial bearings, one of which is also engraved upon the tombstone she and Dimmesdale presumably share together, perhaps to herald some royal significance of their grave site. The King's Chapel was built next to the burial grounds later, perhaps to symbolize its hallowed spot in the scheme of life and death. By implication, Hester is buried next to Dimmesdale, with a space between, "as if the dust of the two sleepers had no right to mingle. Yet, one tombstone served for both" (264), apparently to show some connection between them, though there might be a space between them for awhile, as though, perhaps, after all, they may have a shared destiny together in time. Side by side, bonded together in the same sphere, what each represents together may forecast the realization of their faith in the future, perhaps made possible by their mutual sacrifices.

Upon that tombstone, and the last words ending Hawthorne's tale, was "the semblance of an engraved escutcheon . . . the curious investigator may still discern, and perplex himself with the purport." This armorial shield "bore a device, a herald's wording of which might serve for a motto and brief description or our now concluded legend; so sombre is it." The somber message of the allegory appears to be encrypted in a riddle for the curious reader to encipher: "On a field, sable, the letter A, gules," which message is "relieved only by one ever-growing point of light gloomier than the shadow" (264). The word "gules" may take on the connotation of action as a verb, rather than simply as a noun, to form a complete thought. Equipped with an interpretation of Hawthorne's allegory, the reader now has all the clues necessary to solve the riddle, as he or she sees it.

The sable field is apparently the shadow of Puritanism, or any off-color religious institution, that casts a somber pall over its own as upon their neighbors. Against this shadow stands Hawthorne's symbol of the message of his legend, perhaps a relief therefrom which may cast nevertheless "an ever-growing point of light" that, despite the gloomy aspect of its starting truth, like the sad voice of the brooklet, continues to increase in the brilliance of its effects.

The effects of this relief seem futuristic, as in the symbolic promise for which his red insignia proxies. Perhaps the motto symbolizes the particular transformation or transfiguration Hawthorne pitches for Hester, embodies in Pearl, and apparently projects for the many children who may become united with the universal heart, or the "Universal Father." Perhaps the gloominess of the ever-growing point of light refers in particular to the symbolism of Dimmesdale's agony, a gloominess that projects a point of light or enlightment that may be forthcoming through an "ever-growing" transformation of humankind. Or perhaps it may refer to the destiny for those whose hostility is greater than the shadows of humankind's forests.

Perhaps Hawthorne's heralded wording summarizes the central theme of his novel: a people, a generation, a dispensation, a civilization, perhaps the childlike meek of the earth, may hopefully exist in another world where all, even hostility and hate, is transmuted into a golden love beyond Pearl's seventh year. But Hawthorne has added a subtle touch to the transformation he seems to anticipate hopefully in the interaction of his characters.

THE SUNKEN GRAVE

Perhaps that hope is embedded in the sunken grave by which Hester has been laid. In conclusion, we must raise the reader's eyebrow once more to Christian theology from the probable perspective of Hawthorne's.

> And, after many, many years, a new grave was delved, near an old and sunken one, in that burial-ground beside which King's Chapel has since been built. It was near that old and sunken grave, yet with a space between, as if the dust of the two sleepers had no right to mingle. Yet one tombstone served for both. (264)

The question in Hawthorne's novel of whether the mortal body will rise with its divine counterpart, from "infant immortality" to fully developed "womanhood," hinges upon the final sign or symbol cleverly poised by Hawthorne in the use twice of one word, "sunken," in reference to the divine's grave. Perhaps the most intuitive implication of this one word is that it is sunken because "He is not here, but is risen."[7] Arthur Dimmesdale apparently has already been resurrected, and perhaps symbolizes the resurrection of its Author. Perhaps to Hawthorne, the sunken grave symbolizes the empty tomb.

Hawthorne leaves the reader to his own surmises; but in context with his tale, as an allegory, with many allusions to the Christian text, this student, as with every student of life who may see what he prefers to see, considers Hawthorne as a possible apologist for Christianity, in his own quiet and intelligent way. Sometime, in the seventh thousand year period of humankind, perhaps a union of the divine with his twinkled bride will bring a time of hallowed joy to its transfigured state. Maybe she will be as beautiful as Hawthorne has imaged Hester, before her fall.

Since humanity today has progressed beyond the Calvinistic principle of the body being depraved and unworthy of association with its divine counterpart, it is probably more acceptable now than in Hawthorne's day, like "an ever-growing point of light," for the common Christian to believe that divinity and nature, in the form of spirit and body, may forever be joined together. Perhaps the promise of this transformation of life, or transfiguration, makes the present one a little gloomier than it might otherwise be without the promise. Or the promise points to the gloomier end of those who fail to understand how sacred love, and a life devoted to it, bestow a future life of greater joy.

Thus Hawthorne ends his novel with a sad note, as though his faith in a brighter day is still weighed by the gloom of what remains. Or perhaps he is saying that the union promised by the Atonement, in a resurrection of the body beautiful with its spirit divine, has been tenderized and hallowed by the gloom, like relief after pain, or love following hate, as though one cannot be experienced without the other. As in the case of Dimmesdale, whose sense of destiny and divine purpose seemed to be hallowed by his experiences with his adversary, so might Hawthorne have weighed in on the side of hope for the rest of humanity.

In the final analysis, perhaps what Dimmesdale's parishioners heard, in their varied perceptions, is meant to reflect the various responses of Hawthorne's readers to his novel. Although his last words in this open-ended allegory, where one may perhaps see what one chooses to see, give no definite clue as to his own leanings, yet the insinuations within the tale forecast a better view of, and a more worthier future for, mortality, and strongly point to the finer attributes of Hawthorne's Christianity. Can we not say, then, that this writer of story books, in the tale of the scarlet letter, has indeed created a special "mode of glorifying God," and may have been serviceable to some segment of the communities of mankind?

EDITOR'S EPILOGUE

Perhaps by now a higher perspective of Hester, Pearl, and Dimmesdale, as discerned through their allegorical relationships, has overshadowed or ameliorated the narrower and superficial view of their narrative relationships in the tale. Perhaps a different view of Hawthorne's characters has embued his readers with a sense of the sacred love these Romantic icons may symbolize, and has advanced a greater appreciation for his ingenius mastery of the allegory. That love does seem to represent Deity's relationship with the communities of humankind, a love story that yet may hopefully become the focus of future artistic and more representative interpretations.

And as to poor Mr. Bayinhund himself, who has given life to an old manuscript, perhaps as a Daniel of sorts, we may say that, at the least, he has been lifted from the ignominy under which he has long been buried these many years. Hopefully, moreover, no mean regards may be accorded his editor for bringing forth his posthumous handiwork, unless it be for the long delay in honoring the demands of conscience. In that respect, he must plead companionship with Dimmesdale, step up upon his own scaffold, and likewise make amends in the public eye for his timid deliberations. He would hope that some "new eye" might gaze down mercifully and favorably upon these old pumps, at least, until the whole matter is laid a little more clearly before their understanding.

Perhaps Hawthorne's readers can now accord his greatest piece of literature with more appropriate treatment, in view of the proposition that the real beauty of this great American novel has not been fully credited by the carekeepers of American art. If his editor could chance appear not too sacreligious, he might dare say, that perhaps Brother Bayinhund has not been too far amiss in claiming that we have worshiped too long at the altar of obscurity, and that it is time to declare the real Hawthorne to his intended public.

Perhaps, at the least, it may be said that Hawthorne's noble work was not intended to appeal to the prurience, nor to the sensationalism with which so much of our modern art seems preoccupied. Instead of the black, lurid act of passionate adultery that has been somewhat cinemated and glorified into some sordid chronicle, this masterpiece does seem to address, as Hawthorne may have declared, the more meaningful relationship between Deity and humankind. Its spiritual essence is probably the central attraction that has captivated, somewhat at the intuitive level, the multitudes of insightful readers who have fallen in love with this remarkable tale, perhaps without knowing fully why. That there is a "glorious" destiny for humanity is the message that should be heralded from the four corners of his work, not the inexplicable affair of its two main characters, or the sordid misery of each.

Those who may have been offended by the unexplained silence of Dimmesdale, or who may have thought ill of Hester for her loyalty to him despite her lifelong suffering, may now understand how this tale does indeed glorify God, in Hawthorne's own mysterious way, as he seemed to have intended (10). And—like as it was for Pearl, who ceased to live among the gloom of an erroneous perspective, and for Hawthorne, who rejected that part of his ancestral past—perhaps it can be said someday, for the more enlightened future readers, that "the scarlet letter ceased to be a stigma which attracted the world's scorn and bitterness, and became a type of something to be sorrowed over, and looked upon with awe, yet with reverence too" (263). Its symbol, like the rose plucked for the reader at the portal of the prison from which Hester emerged, "may serve, let us hope, to symbolize some sweet moral blossom" and "relieve the darkening close of a tale of human frailty and sorrow" (48).

A FALSE OR TRUE CHRIST

We must close our query now, for that is only what an analysis can ultimately be; and I do so with the last words of Mr. Bayinghund that I have managed to keep in my mind; They may very well account for his motive in writing this manuscript:

> Ever since a young man years ago discovered the beauty and goodness of Christianity, he has held this question in his mind: why was Christ the one chosen to wring out the Atonement?

The answer he was given—"because Jesus was the only perfect and sinless one"—never settled his gnawing curiosity. He has always felt that there was something more, something untold in the scriptures, something more significantly so. Perhaps Hawthorne had the same hungry appetite for something more substantial. Perhaps his intuitive senses never rested until, in the wee hours of the night, struggling over his studies of Biblical text, he was led to conclusions he regarded as too sacred to utter, let alone to publish openly before the world.

It is this thirst for truth that drives some minds to the edge of knowledge, that compels them to penetrate the depths of the earth and the heights of the stars, sometimes at all costs to themselves, leaving some of them destitute and penniless, never to achieve recognition for what they did during their lifetime. Perhaps *The Scarlet Letter* has cast its Hawthronian spell upon this young man and provided an explanation that makes a little more sense of this world's mesh of good and evil.

EDITOR'S CONCLUSION

We now cast the ashes of Bayinhund's vision upon Hawthornian waters, which, be they living or stagnant, may meander within some primeval forest, whisper another message not so sad, and eventually force itself again through the old town pump in Salem. Whether he or Hawthorne may have been redeemed from the graves of misunderstanding, and this work, by some miraculous resurrection, become a definitive explanation of a great mystery, may depend upon the very intuition of the reader, a tenacious appetite to understand, the elasticity of imagination, and a few other unmentionables left unsaid.

Perhaps in the back recesses of the hidden mind, the question may also be raised: "if such a weak-minded fellow as Daniel could have verbalized it, could not a fairer-minded bard as Hawthorne first have conceived it?"

If, wherewithal, should future readers opt not to give simple and cursory attention to the details Daniel has so painstakingly laid out, perhaps the two of us, were he ever to be found out, could be accorded some pretentious claim to brotherhood, and be buried vicariously side by side, despite the chanting, divided segment of Hawthorne's public which this analysis may surely find. Perhaps some sympathetic Romantic would be so kind as to mark our interment, the ignominy of our schizophrenic labor, with only one black tombstone, and no less some clear scribbling of the epitaph, "a red C in gules upon a sable field."

It is finished. This antiquary commends Hawthorne's Redemption into the hands of those who may presume to have the final word on the matter. Nevertheless, whether student or professor, we will still only grovel together at the feel of Hawthorne. Whether we desire to think freely, or to echo at the shrine of obscurity, "We have a Shrine, and we need no more Shrine!" the mystery may remain a mystery always. Or, at least, until the bright day come and we find our differences transmuted into golden agreement.

APPENDIX 1

REFERENCES

Article 4
[1]Psalms 8: 3-6
[2]Revelations 12: 10

Article 5
[1]Revelations 21: 2

Article 6
[1]Romans 2: 6-9

Article 9
[1]Isaiah 53: 5

Custom-House—Introduction
[1]Proverbs 23: 6-7
[2]Matthew 23: 15

Chapter 1-2
[1]Jeffersons Complete Works, Vol. 7, pp.210 and 257

Chapter 3
[1]2 Corinthians 11: 13-14
[2]Revelations 12: 10
[3]Isaiah 53: 4-5

GARY P. CRANFORD

Chapter 4
[1]Genesis 3: 1-6
[2]Genesis 3: 3
[3]2 Peter 3: 8
[4]Isaiah 14: 12-14
[5]Matthew 8: 29
[6]Mark 5: 7-9
[7]Matthew 8: 28
[8]I Corinthians 15
[9]Isaiah 14: 12-15

Chapter 5
[1]Isaiah 1: 18

Chapter 6
[1]Psalms 8: 4-5
[2]Matthew 13: 45-46
[3]Isaiah 11: 6-9
[4]Matthew 24
[5]John 3: 8

Chapter 7
[1]Isaiah 29: 13
[2]1 Corinthians 6: 2
[3]Matthew 23: 24

Chapter 8
[1]1 Corinthians 15: 32, 35
[2]Proverbs 23: 7
[3]Isaiah 1: 18
[4]Jude 1: 9

Chapter 9
[1]Isaiah 14: 12
[2]Revelations 12: 7-10
[3]John 7: 39; 11: 4; 17: 1
[4]Romans 8: 30
[5]Matthew 4: 10

Chapter 10
[1]Genesis 3: 15
[2]Isaiah 65: 17
[3]Matthew 7: 6
[4]John 8: 58
[5]Ephesians 6: 12

Chapter 11
[1]Isaiah 53: 4-12
[2]Matthew 27: 46
[3]John 14: 10-11
[4]John 1: 4
[5]John 12: 32
[6]Exodus 34: 7

Chapter 12
[1]Luke 18: 18-19
[2]Luke 22: 44
[3]Matthew 24

Chapter 13
[1]Ecclesiastes l: 3, 14;
[2]Isaiah 65: 17

Chapter 14
[1]Revelations 12: 12
[2]Isaiah 14: 12
[3]Job 38: 4, 7
[4]Revelations 12: 10

Chapter 15
[1]Zachariah 2: 8

Chapter 16
[1]Luke l: 79

Chapter 17
[1]Matthew 26: 39
[2]Jude l: 9
[3]Isaiah 53: 4-10

Chapter 18
[1]Matthew 26: 39
[2]Isaiah 11: 6, 8, 9

Chapter 19
[1]Isaiah 11: 6;
[2]Romans 8: 1

Chapter 20
[1]Matthew 26: 39
[2]Hebrews 6: 6
[3]Matthew 18: 6

Chapters 21-22
[1]Matthew 21: 9
[2]1 Corinthians 15: 42
[3]Ephesians 2: 1-2

Chapter 23
[1]Acts 17: 28
[2]Matthew 23: 37
[3]Matthew 21: 9
[4]Mark 11: 9-10
[5]Luke 19: 37-38
[6]John 12: 12-13
[7]Matthew 21: 15-16
[8]James 2: 19
[9]Genesis 6: 6

Chapter 24
[1]Matthew 5: 5
[2]Luke 22: 44
[3]Matthew 19: 16-17

[4]Revelations 20: 1-3
[5]Isaiah 14: 12
[6]Revelations 12: 2
[7]Revelations 12: 1
[8]Luke 24: 6

APPENDIX 2

EXTRACTIONS

Of the few critical analyses I have studied, so as to discern the validity of Bayinhund's analysis, if I may make a slight judgment on the basis of a few inquiries, one analysis stands out that strongly supports his deductions or, that is, at least provides a solid foundation for them. I have excerpted Becker's analysis in parts as a foundation upon which Daniel's analysis could have been based, had he been aware of Becker's work; indeed, some parallels are so remarkable that one might suspect plagerism, if indeed Daniel had had knowledge of Becker. I have critiqued Becker's work in an appendix to Daniel's interpretation because of its heavily scholastic style, and, perhaps, for lack of any better place to put it. I apologize for including such a laborous bit of scholarly abstraction in what I have proclaimed from the beginning to be a text written for the layman. It may be a tiresome imposition in which only the most vigilant student may wish to sink himself, and its value lies only in the bridge it forms between the scholar and the layman.

Given the complexity of Hawthorne's allegory, Becker is one of the few critics that has offered a detailed and near-complete analysis of it. He has not advanced the cursory comments to which others have reverted, perhaps for either lack of time or interest or, for that matter, for some overwhelming abundance of dismay. Hawthorne would probably call him a friend, if not one of his closest. His analysis is the most thoughtful and insightful that I have had the pleasure of comparing with Daniel's conclusions, and I owe Professor Newberry my most humble gratitude for referring me to his work on the subject.

D. K. Bayinhund's analysis had no references to Becker's own, so we can assume he knew it not. Had he known it, using Becker's work to add validity to his conclusions would have greatly served him. As Daniel's interpretation took him beyond the analysis of Ragussis, whom he quoted to support a premise or two, so it also exceeded Becker's, although the latter was published, and completely unknown to me, before my discovery. Nevertheless, Daniel's editor must confess that his memory of Bayinhund's manuscript might possibly be tinged with some slight reflections from Becker's analysis, but only to the extent of circumstantial concordance after the fact.

Whatever the case, Becker's work appeared upon the scene about the same time as the discovery of Daniel's manuscript in its resting place, where many shall probably say it should have remained. Being only a student, Daniel appears not to have been as restrained in relieving the ambiguity from Hawthorne's tale. Becker came close to interposing a religious orientation but appears to have remained cautiously within the intellectual domain that is unaccustomed to intuitive conclusions. On the other hand, Daniel, as ignorant as any student is in comparison to the professors of academia, did not hesitate to intrude upon their hallowed halls but dared, if ignorance shows any courage at all, to envision Dimmesdale as an image of the Nazarene.

Heaven might forbid. The fuzzy skies of academia may fall, and the scourge of blasphemy may drive more than one of us to the scaffold. Be that as it may, Hawthorne's intentions, whether valid or not, within or without the walls of this analysis, have been tossed into the winds of the public's imagination, which may be the only vehicle capable of penetrating that lofty wall of the scholars. In time, perhaps other Beckers may not halt midway, nor toss the genius of their profession into the pit of ambiguity. If any might seize upon some intuitive epiphany similar or identical to Daniel's, he or she may nevertheless have to be so bold as to defy the brotherhood and desecrate the holy altar of obscurity now enthroned upon Hawthorne's genius. Notwithstanding, it is the claim of this purveyor that the image of Hawthorne has not been diminished one iota by this analysis but raised to the higher level that may have been the heart of his nobler aspirations.

On the other hand, it might appear to the more lenient of us, or the more impious, to say most graciously that Becker himself may have been a kind of Daniel in the making, if we could raise the latter to so erudite a position in the literary world without being demeaning to the former. It might even be questionable as to which might be the forerunner of the other, considering both to be worlds apart, or whether either or both might be that Daniel of which Hawthorne spoke, or the first of such to be. Whereas Becker wisely may have seen fit to abase the full implications of own analysis, which the annuls of refined literature might otherwise have disdained or discredited, without the aid of more popular support, Daniel has dared to go where no one else has apparently gone.

However spacious and far out Bayinhund's analysis may appear to those quite affrighted with such heights or too faint-minded to the transport, one might nevertheless still prefer the clothing of night, or some semblance thereof, to approach the truth of the matter, or simply await hearing from the mouth of the the old Town-Pump himself.

As Daniel's posthumous editor, I have taken the liberty below in excerpting from Becker's work in order to show that all Daniel's conclusions are not absolutely spineless, and should, were they not overdone, therefore stand proudly erect, deserving of each pound of flesh added thereto in its resurrection. Since it is only a rare few who prefer dessert before the entrée of their choice, I am also assuming that the reader will not seek to digest Becker until after he has had his fill of Daniel. However, Becker himself deserves to be a main course, and should be relished separately and completely.

Whereas Becker's analysis focused mostly upon Hawthorne's style and methods of calling the reader's attention to some deeper allegorical meanings but did not thoroughly seek to disclose what he thinks the characters represent or what their connections and interactions mean, on the other hand, Bayinhund focused mostly upon those connections and upon the meanings in the symbols and analogies of the tale. He lacked the conciseness of Becker, perhaps because of the numerosity of symbols and such that he undertook so painfully to fathom. Notwithstanding, a little commentary by the editor may follow each excerpt for the sake of clarity, on the presumption that Daniel's exposition has not supplied sufficient elucidation heretofore to surfeit any one's taste for it. At the same time, the reader, we feel confident, should be able to relate the excerpts to Daniel's conclusions, with or without much assistance from his editor, whose comments, for the sake of brevity, are couched in Bayinhund's behalf.

* * *

In the excerpts below, as Bayinhund's editor, I have referred to Daniel's conclusions that either concur or differ from Becker's in order to take the reader beyond Becker's experience of *The Scarlet Letter*. Where there is no comment, we might consider Daniel ecstatically in agreement. Whereas any agreement may show some enthusiasm in his editor's comments, it must be admitted that an editor can hardly be wholly unattached from his work when it comes to a match between esquire and yeoman.

For the sake of brevity, this editor's references to John Becker's analysis are taken from his book, *Hawthorne's Historical Allegory: An Examination of the American Conscience*. Kennikat Press: Port Washington, NY, 1971. His references to Hawthorne's novel, by page number only, are referenced to the Centenary Edition, Volume 1 (Nathaniel Hawthorne. *The Scarlet Letter*. Ohio State University Press, 1962). It needs to be added that Becker's references to *The Scarlet* Letter, by page number only, are referenced to the same volume of the Centenary Edition of Hawthorne's novel. We begin with Becker's introduction to his book.

Introduction

> The Puritans exercised their allegorical bent chiefly in the interpretation of history, and history is also Hawthorne's favorite arena of fictional speculation. This conjunction of history and allegory suggests the possibility that some form of biblical typology, that is, the interpretation of historical events in terms of past events and future expectations rather than abstract concepts is the literary characteristic which binds Hawthorne to his Puritan ancestors and distinguishes him from the traditional allegorists (Becker, 4).

This comment supports Bayinhund's interpretation of Hawthorne's allegory as a reflection upon historical events and figures as they relate to future events. However, below that historical level appears to be a deeper level involving abstract concepts, or "principles," as Hawthorne called them, interacting with one another. His allegory takes us back in time, past our Puritan fathers, even to the beginning of life and, perhaps, to the principles for its formation.

Bayinhund concluded that Hawthorne did indeed use a form of typology in his alleogry, and identified the historical figures thereof as no less ancient than Eve, Lucifer, and the Nazarene himself. However, as a Romantic, given to more generalized concepts, rather than simply recasting history to repeat some moral, Hawthorne appeared to have formulated a principle of truth around each allegorical character and his or her interactions with other characters, to develop new, philosophical insights of his inmost Me.

THE CUSTOM-HOUSE

> The fact that the story of *The Scarlet Letter* seems to have no intrinsic dependence on its introductory essay has caused many critics to reject it . . . But there is an increasing body of criticism which finds that "The Custom-House" adds important dimensions to the whole (Becker, 61).

Bayinhund made the connection between the "The Custom-House" and Hawthorne's tale by identifying the "introductory essay" as a backdrop to the story of Hester. The characters, their environment, and its surrounding structures epitomize the various effects of Puritanism upon its adherents, presumably according to their intuitive insights into the spiritual domain. These officials of a fading Christian experiment represent something more functional in the allegory than simply a background to Hawthorne's own past, from which he sought to distance himself; they may be phantoms of philosophical underpinnings, much further in the past, aimed to shore up the foundations of that faith.

> Hawthorne himself throws us off the track by disclaiming any structural function for "The Custom House" . . . But Hawthorne's modest authorial disclaimers and surface apologies are not to be trusted any more than his claim to be merely the editor of the story of *The Scarlet Letter* . . . (Becker, 62).

> Hawthorne, then, does not write a traditional preface to a traditional allegory to tell us what he intends to do . . . All he will say is that he is laying himself on the line and doing so with

a full awareness of his own serious commitment. He will say something significant, in spite of all that may be adduced by himself or by others against that possibility . . . (Becker, 70).

At the beginning of "The Custom-House" Hawthorne invites us . . . to commune with his soul. Hawthorne was a romantic, and he would like us to be among "the few who will understand him, better than most of his schoolmates and lifemates" . . . Hawthorne is concerned to keep "the inmost Me behind its veil," and to do this he allows us the strictly defined role of "friend, a kind and apprehensive, though not the closest friend" (Becker, 72).

It is a tragedy that so few friends have come forward to express their understanding of his allegory. But perhaps their greater regard lies in the popularity of his novel, as though, intuitively, his readers were able to commune with his soul and sense something worthier than what the more vocal voice of his critics have managed.

As the world of the Custom-House was totally unwilling and unable to take account of the rich sensibilities of an artist like Hawthorne, so the world of the Puritans was unwilling and unable to take account of the rich femininity of a woman like Hester . . . Hawthorne was stifled by this indifferent world, and it is not at all surprising that his experience of that world should project itself as a major theme of the story which evolves out of his Custom-House experience.

Perhaps there is an allusion to the same tension between the sensitive individual and the insensitive official world in the allegorical vignette which intrudes itself into the description of the Custom-House . . . (Becker, 72).

At this point, Becker quotes from Hawthorne the description of the eagle over the entrance to highlight this lack of sensitivity or compassion. It is this piercing, harsh, and most fitting allusion that underwrites the dark background of the tale. It contrasts with the universal heart and connects with all the symbols and metaphors, of which the scarlet letter becomes the redeeming focal center. To Hawthorne, this intuitive sensitivity is often challenged by the intellect, or the reasoning that might oppose it.

> To place oneself, however, as Hawthorne does, clearly and boldly before the reader is to create a different kind of relationship between the reader and the story than the one established by the techniques of realism or by traditional narrative in general. . . . The author, by insisting upon his own presence, keeps us outside the story world he creates, in order to keep our interpretative faculties alert for the more explicitly intellectual task he has put before us (Becker, 74).

Bayinhund purports that that intellectual task for the reader also includes an intuitive interpretation of Hawthorne's insinuations, as a function of one's sensitivity.

> The second phase of the Custom-House essay consists of two somewhat extended character sketches . . . The two figures are at opposite ends of the scale of humanity (Becker, 75).

Bayinhund also noted this "scale of humanity" among the Custom-House officials, as a result of the impact of Puritanism upon society. He discussed it in relation to Hawthorne's essay on love and hate and the general sweep of his themes aimed at the purposeful meaning of the embellished scarlet letter.

> Hawthorne creates two still-living links with the Puritan past, each of whom manifests qualities of that past which are important in the story of Hester Prynne. One represents the final reduction to animality of Puritan materialism and insensitivity to human feeling. The other represents the dying fire of the nobility and idealism which was the inspiring motive behind the whole Puritan enterprise. What Hawthorne sees around him, in this dull and moribund world of Custom-House veterans, is the crumbled remains of a world which was once able to hold these qualities in tension so that moral issues, at least for some, were as deeply serious as they are for him (Becker, 77).

Daniel described this scale as a kind of continuum of effect, relative to the presence of compassion or hostility in the individual, and relative to the intuitive sensibilities of each. He believed that the Custom-House itself represents the established order of Puritanism; that the Custom-House officials represent the powers within that order; and that its customs represent the theological interpretations, practices, and effects of that Christian institution and, perhaps as well, current interpretations. The adherents of Puritanism fall along that continuum, perhaps more schewed to the left, from materialistic insensitivity to spiritual sensitivity to matters of the heart. Though Hawthorne may appear to be detached from the historical figures of his tale, as the editor, he occasioned to make bold statements showing attachment to the themes his characters and their interactions project, as a representation of his own philosophical self.

> There is, then, a kind of ultimate irony which inspires Hawthorne to place the discovery of *The Scarlet Letter* within this backwater of decay and death . . . Within a society of decaying human spirits amid its piles of useless bureaucratic scribbling, Hawthorne comes upon a symbol which will carry him back into the intense vitality of its past (Becker, 77).

Bayinhund carried the allusion of a decaying society back in time to the degeneration of the Mosaic law in the hands of the scribes and Pharisees, which society was a backdrop to the need for a redemption or transformation of it and, thus, the role of the Nazarene. It would not be surprising to discover that historians have noticed similar groups of naysayers in every society they have studied in detail, especially in our own.

> Hawthorne constructs the fictitious narration of his discovery of the letter to arouse suspense . . . We are first diverted by Mr. Pue, his commission, and what was left of him when his body was exhumed . . . When we finally perceive that [the faded, red cloth] is the letter A, we are again side-tracked by Hawthorne into thinking of it as a badge of honor. We are left with a final mystery-making puzzle—the burning sensation which Hawthorne felt in his breast when he placed the letter there (Becker, 77).

What Hawthorne has elicited here is a clear demand for interpretation of the letter. And this demand for interpretation which he himself has placed in the reader is his way of alerting us to the fact that in reading *The Scarlet Letter*, we are reading an allegory . . . As he tells the story of the discovery of the letter, he himself plays with its possible meanings and induces us to do so by the sense he gives of freedom to indulge in such a play of the mind. There is no predetermined meaning. We contemplate it with him (Becker, 78).

Hawthorne seems to have designed his novel so that that this contemplation will include the reader's intuitive insight and eventually a reversal of the reader's perspective. It is as though Hawthorne is depending upon the sensitivity of the reader not to pass a puritanical judgement upon his characters until they have the full picture of his allegory.

However, rather than strictly a sidetrack, Hawthorne begins the creation of two images and meanings to the scarlet letter—the one the rational mind assumes and the other which a sympathetic friend might intuit. He then expands upon the allegorical image within the body of his allegory until a reversal of the assumed image becomes nearly irresistable. It is this reversal of images and meanings that is characteristic of Hawthorne's allegory, and the scarlet letter does indeed become a "badge of honor."

Hawthorne does not present us . . . with an invitation to solve an allegorical puzzle to which he himself knows the solution because he constructed it. There is more than an intellectual puzzle here. There is, he suggests, a connection so deep and so intimate between himself and what the letter represents that the touch of the symbol creates a burning sensation, causes an involuntary shudder, involves him and us in a process which is deeply personal, for all its contemplative detachment. Hawthorne's own experience of the scarlet A in "The Custom—House" is an integral part of the allegorical structure which he creates (Becker, 78).

Perhaps Becker makes no connection more crucial to the main theme of his tale than this connection between Hawthorne and the symbol, as though it perhaps bears some significant connection between the tale and the reader as well. It is this connection that figures in "the relation between the Deity and the communities of mankind" (Hawthorne, 249), which appears to be the subject or main theme of Hawthorne's allegory.

> Hawthorne achieves, by . . . measured steps into the past, more than just the desired aura of romance . . . He emphasizes that the movement back in time is a part of the meaning of his story, a part of the structure of his fiction. Again, it is Hawthorne's own experience of the parallels and the contrasts between that distant time and his own present world which constitutes the allegory. This is to say again what has been said before, that Hawthorne is the hero of *The Scarlet Letter* (Becker, 79).

Becker may credit Hawthorne as the hero, perhaps solely upon Hawthorne's reaction to the scarlet letter A. Perhaps Bayinhund would agree on the basis of the philosophical intimations which the allegory communicates to him. But as a resurrected character of the posthumous Surveyor Pue, who allegedly recorded the story of Hester, and as the editor of the tale, Hawthorne is placing himself outside the tale and looking back at it with reserved detachment—presumably years later—when in all actuality, he is the very author of the tale itself and not one of its characters.

Hawthorne can be the hero without any doubt if the whole purpose of the tale, as Bayinhund purports, is to expound, however stealthily, Hawthorne's own philosophical thoughts in an elaborate analogy. But according to Daniel's intimations, he may account Hawthorne as only one of the many of humankind, referred to only in general in his novel, who have such a similar connection with the scarlet letter.

The one person symbolizing that connection between "Deity and the communities of mankind" is Dimmesdale. However, because he besets himself so intensely with the burden of "sins," of which he feels the weight upon his own soul—in some kind of mysterious expiation for some undisclosed act of passion—and is silent about the whole issue, he strikes at the very core of that sense of Puritanism remaining in us; and we cannot see beyond what the Pharasees, by comparison, saw in the upstart Nazarene of their day.

Because of the failure of Becker's and other scholarly attempts to analyze fully the significance of Dimmesdale's representative role as a possible image of the man from Nazareth, Bayinhund would agree that these scolars cannot, therefore, fully accord Dimmesdale the honorary merit of the status as the hero in Hawthorne's tale. Since most published critics, therefore, have not regarded Dimmesdale's extreme sensitivity to his "sin" as a symbolic reflection or projection of the agonies and miseries of humankind suffered by the Christians' Christ, they have failed to see, perhaps by reason of their own prepossessions, that far beyond the surface tale.

THE SCARLET LETTER

For the purpose of analyzing "The Custom-House" we have assumed that it is the introduction to an allegory. The test of that assumption is the present examination of the novel proper. The method of testing, however, is not *apriori*; it is not an attempt to show that a certain previously discovered allegorical interpretation works when it is applied to the story. Such approaches have tended to drift away from the texture of the story . . . . [I]t seems much more valid in dealing with Hawthorne, in the light of what he was doing with the form, to let the concept of allegory form as the story develops. Consequently, the method here is to suppose that there are certain techniques which can be called allegorical techniques . . . . Held close to the story by the examination of its techniques, we have a better chance of arriving at that allegorical interpretation which the story itself suggests while at the same time perceiving the originality of the Hawthorne's recreation of the allegorical form. The only strategy that seems appropriate to such an analysis by techniques is that of a running commentary (Becker, 88).

Although Becker suggests that the reader allow Hawthorne to develop the allegory form as the story develops, he is undoubtedly not suggesting that the reader allow Hawthorne to do so without regard to any presupposed interpretation that Hawthorne had in mind. The system of typology in play in his novel is aimed toward a reversal of views about each of the main characters, and by design metamorphs the themes at work: the end is clearly created as an intended reversal of its beginning.

> Hawthorne concludes his opening chapter with a self-consciously gallant offer of a rose from his bush. In doing so he draws attention to his presence as narrator . . . It works, as do the other techniques we have examined, to alert the reader to the allegorical genre . . . He is induced instead to reflect with the author on these elements as symbols which demand thought rather than as objects which make for verisimilitude. With this same purpose in view, Hawthorne reminds the reader of his allegorical intent. The rose "may serve, let us hope, to symbolize some sweet moral blossom, that may be found along the track, or relieve the darkening close of a tale of human frailty and sorrow" (48). Because *The Scarlet Letter* is an open-ended allegory whose meaning is not presupposed but to appear gradually, it is not necessary for Hawthorne to specify the moral here . . . (Becker, 90–91).

Becker's interpretative efforts focus mostly on a running commentary showing the allegorical nature of *The Scarlet Letter*, but regrettably, he is not compelled to advance an interpretation of the allegory. Although his analysis provided him opportunity to do so, he seems to have closed his eyes on much of the allegorical symbols and figures of speech, as though he was focused more upon the aspects of allegory than interpretation. These other contextural symbols and analogies suggest that Becker has only touched upon the second layer of the richness and depth of Hawthorne's allegory. Why Becker stopped in midcourse, in so brilliant an analysis, is a mystery in itself. Perhaps because he was puzzled by the various symbolic meanings, he preferred to focus his examination upon the early American conscience.

> Hawthorne . . . established the reader clearly within the context of meaning—centered fiction and [gave] him a pair of visual symbols on which to anchor the thematic ideas as they arise . . . .

Hawthorne reflects on the capacity of such a people [the crowd gathered around Hester] to treat a sinner with sympathy. He asks whether they respect the principle which for him is at issue in the story, the principle of the sanctity of the human heart (Becker, 91).

Becker has stated his interpretation of the main theme of the allegory—"the principle of the sanctity of the human heart." Bayinhund would agree that that theme seems a little too frail of substance and too vapid of motive around which an author would alone create such a complex and intricately woven form of work as Hawthorne has. You don't build a four-lane bridge just to allow a rickshaw to pass over, unless, we might add, you may be anticipating other, greater traffic to follow. The reader should expect more from such an elaborate matrix of symbols and analogies and become intent on discerning such from intuitive intimations cast around the characters' representations and their interactions. That was the purpose for which Hawthorne selected his method of communicating to his public, which Becker explains later.

The principle of the sanctity of the human heart is therefore obviously understood at the surface level of the story. What is left for the allegory to represent if that's all there is? Bayinhund would ask whether the rosebush, Hester's scarlet letter, Pearl's whole attire in the like aspect of a scarlet letter herself, the red berries Pearl eats, and the bloody stripes Dimmesdale inflicts upon himself stand for something mysteriously more that what is obviously understood. Why all this sanctity about the obscurity of the deeper meanings of the tale? Becker has built a good bridge and, hopefully, provided the means for other traffic to follow, provided his peers do not set up a roadblock thereto. He appears to be staging the readers for something, and does quite well in setting up an interpretation for them; but his analysis is apparently not designed to explain the mystery and, thus, creates another in the process by whetting the reader's appetite for an explanation. But perhaps he went as far as he could, or dared to go, in interpreting the principle for which Dimmesdale's character represented. That interpretation should begin with an examination of what principle of being Hester represents.

The drift of the dialogue which follows illustrates the paradox which Hawthorne has been considering . . . [W]hen the ugliest and most pitiless female demands that Hester die: "Is there not law for it?" (51), [t]he allusion here suggests the words of the Pharisees in St. John's story of the woman taken in adultery (Jn. 8:5); and Pharisaism is the perfect characterization for the Puritanism we see here. But again there is a counter-statement, this time from a man in the crowd. He, like the young wife, insists on the importance of the interior: "Is there no virtue in woman, save what springs from a wholesome fear of the gallows?" (Becker, 52)

Remarkably, Becker has penetrated a representation and alluded to its historical precedent, Judaism, perhaps as a symbolic reflection of the Puritan background; but, whereas Dimmesdale is poised as the antithetical figure to Puritanism, whose sensitivity of heart contrasts most other Puritan characters, Becker did not seem to grasp, or choose to disclose, whom the primary figure was that opposed the iron-clasped erosive effects of the Pharisaic law upon their own "prisoners." Was Becker only hinting and unwilling to make the connection between what Puritanism represented and what Dimmesdale represented? This one possible suggestion of a specific historical representation is as far as Becker appears eager and willing to go. That may be because he was not insightful enough, or perhaps he dared not counter the age-old opinion—as proclaimed boldly by Henry James, for example, and shared by his retinue of critics—that there is no Christ image in Hawthorne's tale. Nevertheless, Becker did refer to the Biblical text; he did expose one aspect of historical background; and he thus opened the door for scholars to explore the impact and effect of Hawthorne's several references to the same.

Although Becker's analysis seemingly was only meant to analyze Hawthorne's style and methods of allusion, rather than to reveal those allusions, their connections with each other, and the meanings of their interactions, his analysis, has, however, established a precedent for further explorations of those connections and meanings. Whether or not that has been done does not seem yet to have come to the public's attention, which is what Daniel's editor intends.

This initial dialogue is arranged into a neatly dialectical pattern, a pattern characteristic of allegorical structure . . . . [Richard Poirier, A World Elsewhere (New York: Oxford

University Press, 1966, p. 32] Hawthorne's dialogue, then is not realistic. It functions to illustrate rather than to dramatize. What it illustrates is the tension we have already begun to see within the heart of Puritanism. We may relate this tension to the contrast between the prison door and the rosebush. The Puritan people as a whole are more in sympathy with the iron social discipline symbolized by the prison door; but among them there are voices which, because of their respect for the interior of the heart, will be drawn to the mercy symbolized by the rosebush (Becker, 92–93).

To explain this tension within Puritanism, Becker references Yvor Winters:

"Whereas the wholly Calvinistic Puritan denied the value of the evidence of character and behavior as signs of salvation . . . it became customary in Massachusetts to regard as evidence of salvation the decision of the individual to enter the Church and lead a moral life." (*In Defense of Reason,* Third Edition, paper; Denver: Alan Swallow, n.d., p. 159)

Becker then explained, quoting Hawthorne [upon the appearance of the town-beadle escorting Hester], "Hawthorne is careful again to make explicit the fact that we are reading an allegory." 'This personage [the town-beadle] prefigured and represented in his aspect the whole dismal severity of the Puritan code of law . . . On the threshold of the prison-door, she repelled him, by an action marked with natural dignity and force of character, and stepped into the open air, as if by her own free-will" (52) (Becker, 93).

Thus Becker has clearly portrayed Hester's rejection of the Puritanic code, and has come close to figuring what her beauty and dignity represent to Hawthorne.

Hester appears in direct antithetical contrast to the beadle. Her action is a free act signifying her interior rejection of the role of sinner which is being forced upon her . . . Hester stands forth in defiance of that [Puritan] society. She has taken the symbol which was to make her another allegorical figure in the Puritan allegorical world and by force of an almost violent art, has turned it into an expression of her own defiant individuality. Her entrance is the refusal to submit to the allegorical role of adulteress in which she is cast by Puritan society . . . Hawthorne obviously does not see Hester as the Puritans do. What he sees is her beauty and dignity. He even suggests a certain sanctity—her beauty makes a "halo" of her misfortunes . . . Hawthorne stands at that point in American intellectual history when what was once a small voice raised among the Puritans in favor of the individual conscience has become a dominant voice [Perry Miller, "From Edwards to Emerson," *Errand into the Wilderness* ("Harper Torchbooks," paper; New York: Harper and Row, Publishers, 1964, p. 192)]. In his story Hester is a figure like the sainted Ann Hutchinson under whose footstep the rosebush had sprung to life. Somehow then in some as yet unclear way, she represents Hawthorne's rejection of Puritanism. We will see, as the story develops, how far Hawthorne is willing to go in making Hester the representative of his own principles (Becker, 93–94).

Becker later distinctively projected Hester as representing nature, which projection is a crucial element in considering what principles his other main characters represent in his allegory. However, Becker did not seem quite able to see her as representing Hawthorne's own view of the beauty and dignity of the human form, in contrast to the Puritan's rejection of it as depraved and unworthy of creation. Unclear to Becker, this projection is elucidated by Bayinhund as a contest of views regarding the value of the human body and, thus, the whole purpose of mortality. Hawthorne has presented both views of human nature, and appears to have left it to the intuitiveness of the readers to discern his own preferences.

As a further grasp of this conflict, Becker quotes Hawthorne's strongest condemnation of the Puritan view of the mortal body in its use of the pillory:

> The very ideal of ignominy was embodied and made manifest in this contrivance of wood and iron. There can be no outrage, methinks, against our common nature,—whatever be the delinquencies of the individual,—no outrage more flagrant

than to forbid the culprit to hide his face for shame; as it was the essence of this punishment to do. (55)

He makes us see her for a moment through the eyes of a hypothetical Papist in the crowd. To such an observer she would seem an image of the Virgin Mary, though, Hawthorne is quick to tell us, she is the very opposite of Mary in her role as the betrayer of motherhood and the antithesis of salvation . . . It is a favorite technique of Hawthorne to force us to view Hester from alien viewpoints . . . This is Hawthorne's way of periodically calling our attention to an allegorical dimension beyond the Puritan allegory . . . (Becker, 97).

It must be noted, on page 56 of Hawthorne's novel, that, although the reader is getting only an initial view of Hester, Hawthorne already is at work reversing Hester's image to point at her representation and connection to the central theme, as purported by Bayinhund. I believe that Daniel, who has named that allegorical dimension, would not agree that Hawthorne was quick to assure us that Hester was "the very opposite of Mary" in the role of "betraying motherhood." However, Hawthorne did provide the reader various viewpoints of his characters, but with the allegorical intention of reversing these views in the minds of his intuitive readers. For example, he used the parenthetical phrase, "but only by contrast" (56), and then soundly proceeded in the same paragraph to note so well the reverential similarities. Just as Mary was probably held suspect of some foul deed by her public and moved away to avoid what Hester refused to avoid in her public, so has Hester not only been suspected but condemned for her fallen nature, though she stayed in Boston and weathered it out.

Just as Mary was vindicated, so was Hester in the destiny of their child. Just as Mary was the mother of a special person, who had a mission to perform (note how carefully Becker deigned not to mention the Nazarene's name), so does Hester's child, Pearl, at the allegorical level have a destiny to fulfill. Her comparison to the historical figure of Mary, despite Hawthorne's seemingly mild reluctance to make it, is another reference to the same historical time frame of the Pharisees.

So Bayinhund would not concede that Hester is an "antithesis of salvation" but assert that she is an essential part of it in the allegorical dimension. Once the readers establish in their minds that Hester represents the principle of nature, they might ponder what principles the other main characters in Hawthorne's allegory represent. To Bayinhund, Hester seems the very vehicle upon which salvation is focused, the substructure of the life for which Hawthorne anticipated a reformation. As a representation of mortal nature, she is the forerunner or focal point of salvation, and the very heart and mind of it. She is conflicted motherhood hoping for a redemption of herself and her child, and she looks to Dimmesdale for that redemption.

> What Hawthorne gives us, is more than just allegorical characters. He constructs an allegory about a world which crudely and naively tries to make men over into allegorical figures. The resulting distortions of their humanity make them the vehicles he needs for the expression of his own deeply psychological allegorical vision (Becker, 101).

Having recognized the principle of nature represented by Hester's character, Becker appeared to get lost in an entanglement with the psychological ramifications of that recognition. Though Becker may have analyzed Hawthorne and his characters from a psychological perspective, Bayinhund would believe that Hawthorne created his allegorical figures mostly by hyperbole, perhaps to make them more recognizable as allegorical characters. Bayinhund seems to have examined Hawthorne's novel in view of the internal conflicts within humankind, between reason and intuition, love and hate, compassion and hostility; in terms of the religious motives and missions that drove each character within a Puritan environment; and with regard for his readers connective involvement in the same conflicts.

Bayinhund has also examined Hawthorne's own motive and mission for writing his allegory; and though Becker, and Hawthorne himself, may have alluded to the psychological aspects in the interactions among his characters, Bayinhund has emphasized more the spiritual ramifications of the mortal world into which humankind has found itself conflicted.

Lost in the psychological mire that contorts the American conscience, Becker focused upon another favorite theme of psychological realism.

> The hint of diabolic possession through a bond with Satan plays about all the characters of *The Scarlet Letter* [William

GARY P. CRANFORD

Bysshe Stein, *Hawthorne's Faust: A Study of the Devil Archetype*
(Gainesville: University of Florida Press, 1953)] (Becker, 103).

Daniel would say that only two characters have such an obvious bond
with Satan, Chillingworth and Mistress Hibbins. This bond is at the
extreme end of a continuum between hate and love, which Hawthorne
discusses at the end of his novel to summarize in general the base principles
for the philosophical theater of his characters. Other characters have a
relationship with Chillingworth, who represents the epitomy of evil and
who, as the Black Man of the Forest, consorted with his captives, the
Indians, and sought to do the same in the civilized world of the Puritans.
But both Hester and Dimmesdale never made such a bond and, therefore,
escape the clutches of Chillingworth. Their psychological state is only a
reflection of their spiritual state mixed with the consciousness of mortality,
Hester's more by puritanic conditioning, Dimmesdale's more by his unique
spiritual sensitivity to the burden of silence than to the burden of "sin" he
shares in the creation of Pearl. Pearl seems never to have been influenced
at all by either Hester, Dimmesdale, or Chillingworth. She stands apart,
though a companion, like the future is a part of the past.

The relationships of these four characters play to the main theme
of the tale; but neither Pearl, Hester, or Dimmesdale are demonized by
their relationship with Chillingworth, or by Hawthorne. They but react
to the influence of the dark side of life and eventually escape it. Daniel
would say that Hester's mental state was not twisted but perplexed by her
puritanic abasement. Nor did this abasement twist Dimmesdale's mental
state; rather, his was confused by the influence of the conflict between his
physical and spiritual proclivities.

So between Becker and Bayinhund's analysis, we see the psychological
orientation of the scholar and the religious skew of the plebian. Though
Hawthorne himself seems to set himself apart from the play of characters
he has created, the narrator of the story often inserts himself within the
tale to reinforce the allegorical themes and move them toward the thematic
climax at the end.

It is Hester, finally, who sees Pearl as demonic . . . Of course, the
Puritan world reinforces Hester's imposition of an allegorical
role on Pearl (Becker, 107).

In the first place, Daniel, as others have projected, viewed Pearl as an image of Una, Hawthorne's own daughter. Would Hawthorne see his own daughter as demonic? Would he have the same view of her as the Puritan magistrature? Of course not. This conclusion, perhaps extrapolated from the dominant characterization of Chillingworth, is strained from Becker's inaccurate generalization that all Hawthorne's characters are demonic.

In the second place, as Daniel has explained, Hester is wishy-washy in her thinking because it is influenced by both intuitions of truth and the self-deceptions induced by the logical indoctrination of Puritanism. Therefore, Puritanism does not "reinforce" Hester's questions about the nature of Pearl but, rather, frames and hammers the logic that opposes her intuitions about Pearl's angelic nature. Hawthorne would have us listen to our intuition intimations rather than contrive some logical conclusion that negates them.

When seen as Hawthorne's views of the creation, the fall, and the redemption, the interpretation proposed by Bayinhund suggests differentiated allegorical roles for each of the main characters, as well as for many other of his characters, according to the degree to which they are sensitive to matters of the heart more than they are given to materialism and other self-centered motives. Hawthorne's play on the conflict between reason and intuition, quickened by his own parody of questions to the reader, unfolds in his characters an allegory that addresses moral questions that have, perhaps, been around since Adam and Eve. These views, for a Romanticist, are aided by intuition and hampered by reason, as evidenced by his characters' use of them.

Philosophers of all kinds have questioned the meaning of life; the sources of good and evil; and the purposes of sin, pain, and misery in a world we can hardly understand. To Hawthorne, at least as Bayinhund saw him, such a world cannot be as clearly seen without that intuition of a higher order which senses a futuristic redemption of humanity from its own pitiful machinations. That Hawthorne, a much deeper thinker than we suppose, could do less is a rash supposition, much as the rash judgment imposed on Hester by the Puritans.

So Pearl is no demon, according to Daniel's perspective.

Hester's questioning about her nature plays to the allegorical purpose of leading the reader to intuit what she really represents. It is a strained logic that hastily declares all four characters to be either twisted or demonic. Hawthorne has designed his allegory for the insightful reader to see below the surface tale of appearance, to get a reversed and more highly ordered perspective of what each character represents, and to discern what philosophical conclusions the play of their interactions may compose for the reader. Perhaps to extrapolate more boldly, if Pearl is to be cast as a reflection of Hester, she is Hester after her retransformation—the child is mother of the woman. Hester is fallen and conflicted nature, Pearl becomes redeemed nature, and Dimmesdale authors that redemption. As a divine, his ministry among his parishioners gears them toward the same goal, as does Hester's devoted service.

> We have seen the Puritan people more or less at one with their Puritan officials in their interpretation of people and events. However, as the story progresses, they begin to manifest a kind of wisdom, which, though wrong, is more merciful and open than official thinking. Hawthorne begins to speak of a natural sympathy of mankind in the mass which, in spite of the pressures of official thought, begins to arrive at its own conclusions (Becker, 115–6).

Bayinhund and Becker proposed that Hester became a kind of Anne Hutchinson (who was cast out by the Puritans earlier) within the rank and file of Puritanism and that she helped them, in her generation, move toward greater sensitivity to things of the heart and demonstrated the mercy figured in the scarlet letter she wore. Dimmesdale's role is the catalyst for that generational shift. Hester's is to endure her fallen nature in her generation until her transformation is effected in another And the reader sees even her generation changing, as Becker noted, quoting Hawthorne:

> While human nature may be ready to forgive, the officials of the society which had determined Hester's role were slower to bend:

> "The rulers, and the wise and learned men of the community, were longer in acknowledging the influence of Hester's good qualities than the people. The prejudices which they shared in common with the latter were fortified in themselves by an

iron framework of reasoning, that made it a far tougher labor to expel them" (162).

What we see here is that nature, symbolized by the rosebush . . . has been at work among the people setting up a division between them and their rulers. The theme of nature against society is working itself out slowly and surely. Is Hester, then, a kind of standard bearer or personification of benevolent nature? (Becker, 120-21)

Becker had answered this question somewhat earlier: "Hester seems to be taking on a role as the human embodiment of a natural force at work within the heart of Puritanism" (Becker, 111-112). Daniel would agree that Hester does, indeed, personify nature, both immortal nature before the fall, which is referred to briefly and only in flashback, and mortal nature after the fall, which is subject to the flaws of reason or intellectualism. Becker seemed to grasp this common flaw of nature by quoting and explaining Hawthorne's symbolism of it:

"All the light and graceful foliage of her character had been withered up by this red-hot brand, and had long ago fallen away, leaving a bare and harsh outline, which might have been repulsive, had she possessed friends or companions to be repelled by it" (163).

Here, the metaphor for her is that of a dead tree, a clear contrast to the natural richness of the rosebush . . . Hawthorne is not saying that life is gone from her but that it has been unnaturally repressed and springs forth in twisted shapes . . . Hester is infected with the essentially anti-feminine fault of intellectualism; and her intellectualism can lead only to self-defeat, because "a woman never overcomes these problems by any exercise of thought. They are not to be solved or only in one way. If her heart chance to come uppermost, they vanish" (166) (Becker, 121–22)

Thus, Hester is a dying tree by the change in her immortal nature before her fall to that of a mortal one afterwards. Becker, in posing the question of whether Hester personified nature, was one step closer to understanding the allegorical relationship between her representation and Dimmesdale's and, thus, to the religious ramifications of other principles at play.

In addition, Becker has recognized the interplay between intellectualism and intuition that Hawthorne has puppeted before the reader, although Becker may not have been aware of Hawthorne's intent to project that recognition as a model for the reader in understanding his allegory. He also nearly unfolded Hawthorne's view on the purpose of mortality.

> What we see in Hester, then, is a woman whose thoughts have led her astray but whose suffering has led her aright, to a new sensititivy, to a deepening of her respect for the human heart. She has not been able to grasp this new perfection intellectually . . . Chillingworth, on the other hand . . . has arrived at a point of total dialectical opposition to Hester . . . Hawthorne sees, however, that his own deeper moral principle is what is at work in the lives of these two people . . . We have, then, an almost complete moral reversal of two characters, which serves Hawthorne's allegory in clarifying the moral principle about which they pivot, respect for the human heart (Becker, 122–24).

That moral reversal, according to Bayinhund, seemed designed by Hawthorne's allegory as a catalyst to facilitate the reader's intuitive interpretation of Hester's real nature and mission, to discern "that mystery of a woman's soul, so sacred even in its pollution," whose purpose was, from the "open ignominy" given her by Heaven, to "work out an open triumph over the evil" within her (66-67.)

Quoting Hawthorne, 172–74, Becker summarizes Hester's symbolism, but seems unable to fathom what principle of truth Dimmesdale's character represents.

> Hester, at first a symbol of resistance, then the representative of the elemental force of nature, here appears to have won through as the representative of Hawthorne's fundamental moral principle: respect for the sanctity of the human heart (125) . . . .

Though Hester has become the symbol of Hawthorne's basic value, Hawthorne now goes beyond that principle . . . As the story moves . . . to its climax in the forest, the question of Hester's truth becomes as important as the question of Dimmedale's truth.

However it is important to note, as the question of truth begins to move into the forefront of the play of moral questions, that truth here is a far deeper and more complex thing than *reason*. Hawthorne never goes back on the heart. He is not neo-classic, but romantic. As Hugo McPherson says, for Hawthorne:

The realm of imagination is the realm of night, of moonlight and magic; it is in this realm that one truly "sees." Reason belongs in the daylight realm of empirical action, and is concerned with law measurement, and mechanism . . . In Hawthorne's personal vision . . . we have not a bipolar Head-Heart conflict but a tableau in which the Heart is central, flanked by two suitors—the empirical, daylight faculty of Reason and the nocturnal, magical power of imagination. [Hugo McPherson, *Hawthorne as Myth-Maker.* "University of Toronto Department of English Studies and Texts," 16, University of Toronto Pressss, 1969, p. 11] (Becker, 125-26)

Recognizing the conflict between Reason and imagination, or rather, as cast by Hawthorne, the opposition of intellect to intuition, Becker is puzzled by the forest scene and views the forest as a kind of hell.

Bayinhund would agree that Hester represents the mortal nature of humankind fallen from an earlier immortality, but that the forest itself may represent the nature of the world in its rawest form, or the anti-transcendental side of Hawthorne. Theretofore, Dimmesdale's vision had been straightforward; but in the forest, wherein he and Hester were subject to the dark side, his sense of destiny was overwhelmed and, for a moment, compromised by Hester's rationalization.

Hawthorne has recreated the world of Dante in the American forest. The meeting in the forest is a meeting of souls in hell, souls frozen in the eternal state of a decisive earthly choice.

The question that naturally bedevils the critic is why he has placed this all-important and climactic meeting between the lovers in such a setting. Did he create a hell in order to make the heaven that appears in a flood of sunshine only the more real? Or is he telling us that that flood of sunshine is illusory, a deception of the Black Man in whose kingdom it is merely a cruel way of redoubling the sorrow of hell? . . . What Hawthorne is illustrating here is what he has told us so many times before. Hester is confused. Her loyalty to Dimmesdale is all-powerful. It would make her a moral paragon perhaps in a world where the supreme moral principle is respect for the sanctity of the human heart. But for Hawthorne, that principle is not enough.

For the moment neither Hester nor Dimmesdale has grasped fully the need for truth (Becker, 130).

Yes, Daniel would say, Hester's confusion is our confusion—the battle between pure reason and pure intuition, the conflict between the weaknesses of the flesh and the spiritual dimension. Her destiny lies in the confines of mortality, whose logical deductions are misled in the forest of life. But Daniel would forebear to call the forest a representation of hell, only a region uncharted and uninhabited by man, the naked and raw edges of nature unclaimed by conventional customs and institutional lockdowns, where the Romantic can go to receive emanations of truth and light, and where the anti-transcendentalist may be influenced by the dark side as well as the other. In Hawwthorne's tale, the forest seems to be the place where Dimmesdale was led by Hester's logical conclusions to consider an illusory and unacceptable way of escaping or relieving the pains of life in conventional Boston.

To Dimmesdale, to Hawthorne, and to Daniel, the principle, the value of the sanctity of the human heart, is not enough. He sensed he had a profound mission given him by providence that he must fulfill, and though he was temporarily sidetracked by Hester's rationality, the downside of mortality, he recovered instinctively, intuitively, by and through his encounters with other realities coming out of the forest on his way homeward. Through that experience in the forest of life, Dimmesdale was empowered to withstand and handle his archenemy without gloves.

From the beginning Hester has followed an instinct telling her to stay where the scarlet letter was placed on her . . . And when she returns to the settlement after long years of absence, she resumes it again, not in conventional Boston, but at the edge of the seashore, another place closer to uninhabited nature, in the little cottage where she had previously dwelt. Her destiny is mortality's destiny. It remains behind. But her investiture in Pearl, whom Hawthorne described as an "infant immortality," and who eventually dwelt on the other side of the sea, resides in Pearl's mature immortality. However, as Hester resided on this side of the sea, so is mortality still with us. Hester's transfiguration did not happen in Hawthorne's tale, and humankind's final fate is still futuristic.

> Her one great moral gift, her love and loyalty, her desire to shield the heart of Dimmesdale from injury, is at war with the truth . . . A conflict of basic moral principles, respect for the human heart and respect for a kind of total truth is unresolved in her. She is, Hawthorne has told us over and over, in a moral maze (Becker, 131–32).

Bayinhund describes this conflict as a confusion between intimations of the heart and the rational reasonings of intellect. Intuition, or intimations of the heart, point to the reality of humankind's true destiny, Becker's "kind of total truth;" and the intellect alone reasons against that destiny, plies for an easier solution, and temporarily creates discord. Dimmesdale is temporarily caught in that conflict as his own human nature leans towards Hester's intellectualizing, but his intellectual and intutive awareness of the consequences for such weakness soon recoil with a renewed, intense, and enhanced power, a power that propels him more clearly and resolutely towards the destiny he had but dimly viewed theretofore. But it was not his weakness, but his recovery from that weak moment, that ignores Hester's plans.

> It is not merely Dimmesdale's weakness which makes Hester's plan come to nothing in the end. It is the inexorable pressure of reality. Pearl, the only character in the book who achieves a kind of salvation, is, we shall see, the only one who insists that reality be respected (Becker, 132–33).

Bayinhund explains that "the kind of salvation" Pearl achieved in the end represents the future of humankind, the child possibly becoming a kind of transfiguration of the mother. As a result of the reality finally achieved by Dimmesdale upon the scaffold, and the long ordeal of mortality endured by Hester, Pearl matures as an advanced civilization or generation of mankind. Pearl, who represented many people, inherited a kind of destined well-being because of the roles Hester and Dimmesdale performed. True to their destiny, the role of suffering nature created a more compassionate heart in Hester, and the role of redemptive confession stamped Dimmesdale's claim upon Hester and Pearl. That redeeming claim defeated Chillingworth, who sought to own not only Dimmesdale's soul but those of Hester and Pearl as well.

> We have returned to the theme of nature which has run like a thread through the story . . . Nature in man is the "great heart of humanity" which forgives. Inanimate nature is the sub-human symbol of humanity's merciful heart. Nature exists throughout the book as the salvific counter-force at work eating away at the rigidities of Puritan Pharisaism . . . In other words, the society-nature conflict, important as it has been, has only a limited thematic value, just as respect for the human heart has only a limited value as a moral principle within the allegory. *The superior force which transcends the rival forces of nature and society is difficult to name* [italics mine]. Perhaps it is best called the force of reality. But what is clear is that the only adequate moral response to this force is truth (Becker, 152-53).

Daniel dares to put a name to that superior force that bridges the rival forces of nature and spirit. Whereas knowledge and reason are the gifts of mortality to humankind, intuition, like the infrequent and fleeting bursts of sunshine through the forest canopy, is the gift from that superior force that can steer us aright as humankind travels through it. He has proposed that the universal heart of providencial design, whose emanations are perceived by those of more compassionate mien, arches in the character and role of Dimmesdale, as an image of the Nazarene's promise, whose stated mission was to redeem humankind from his fallen state of mortality.

Perhaps Reconciliation to society was achieved by the confession-redemption of Dimmesdale upon the scaffold, as an admission of responsibility or involvement in the creation of humankind. The truth and hope of Hester's salvation or transformation, in union with Dimmesdale, is to be passed on to Pearl, who may represent lost paradise regained, or, at least, a more advanced stage of humankind's transformation one step closer to that ultimate goal. Dimmesdale appears to be the vessel of that hope, which may be carried on presumably by Pearl's own child. Pearl's marriage, more than likely, may therefore represent a yet more advanced civilization than the present, destined to enjoy the salvation promised in the embellished scarlet letter.

> Pearl is the symbol of the love of Hester and Dimmesdale, but of the whole truth about it, its sinfulness as well as its natural beauty. In the context of the meaning—drive of the allegory, Hester must resume the letter and Dimmesdale must publicly acknowledge his love. This is what Pearl's actions say. There is no evasion of the truth (Becker, 135).

Of course Pearl is more than the symbol of love to Bayinhund; she is the offspring of nature and providential design, destined to enjoy the promise of the embellished scarlet letter. So her mission is more focused on the fulfillment of its divine office than upon its Puritanic labeling. Her role, like one's super-ego, is to encourage Hester's continued endurance to the end and Dimmesdale's redemtive ownership.

Becker then presents a case against Dimmesdale being the hero of the book, a chief argument of which is an erroneous conclusion of Hawthorne's disapproval of him.

> [S]omewhere between the forest and the scaffold, Dimmesdale underwent a radical conversion which gave him the strength to confess. This often leads to the conclusion that Dimmesdale is the hero of the book since he is the only character who undergoes a dramatic change. It seems to me that a close following of the text leads to none of these conclusions . . . [T]he shift is never as to elevate Dimmesdale into the hero's role . . . Hawthorne keeps up the same ominous rhythm of

disapproval of Dimmesdale as he had at the moment of Hester's "triumph . . ." (Becker, 136-37).

Here Becker quotes the narrator's derogatory comment on Dimmesdale's desire to conclude his career at the end of his sermon.

> "Sad, indeed, that an introspection, so profound and acute as this poor minister's should be so miserably deceived! We have had, and may still have, worse things to tell of him; but none, we apprehend, so pitiably weak; no evidence, at once so slight and irrefragable, of a subtle disease, that had long since begun to eat into the real substance of his character. No man, for any considerable period, can wear one face to himself, and another to the multitude, without finally getting bewildered as to which may be the true." (215-216)

> There is no ambiguity here about the fact that the sermon itself is no sign of salvation (Becker, 137-138).

But Becker has taken this quotation out of context with the central message of the allegory and thus has ignored all other narrator and character comments placing Dimmesdale on a higher plane than any other character. True, Becker's criticism highlights two other themes at play, Dimmesdale's personal involvement in his relationship with Hester and Pearl, and the mystery of Dimmesdale's silence about that involvement. But the reader of this allegory must not misconstrue the intermixture of these themes to speak too soon about Hawthorne's final message.

Daniel holds to the view that Dimmesdale is the hero, not because of the dramatic change he experienced, but because of his allegorical representation as a vital part of the central theme of redemption that moves all the players in the drama. He explained that, once we envisioned Dimmesdale as the historical figuration of the Nazarene, as a providencial vessel, the answers to all questions fall into place, as the pawns of providence move toward their destiny according to their feed into the universal heart. Bayinghund contended that Dimmesdale is the hero because his mission, as an emissary of providence, is to fulfill the office of the scarlet letter, to claim responsibility for the birth of Pearl (humankind), and to redeem Hester (human nature) from her ignominious state, by admitting ownership upon the scaffold.

The reader may also remember that Hawthorne presents different views of each of his main characters. The above narrator's comment favors the unheroic, perhaps to highlight two other themes at play in the allegory, as mentioned above: In Hawthorne's concluding chapter, he repeats the same idea: to be true to oneself, one must "Show freely to the world, if not your worst, yet some trait whereby the worst may be inferred!" (260) Bayinhund's interpretation resolves the unfavorable aspects of Dimmesdale's character by revealing the allegorical principles of Hawthorne's characters in relation to the mysteries of Dimmesdale's involvement in and silence about his relationship to Hester and Pearl.

Becker has misconstrued one of Hawthorne's parenthetical comments by overlooking one other critical aspect of Dimmesdale's short trip through Dante's world, as Becker called Dimmesdale's forest experience. That experience began the maze in which Dimmesdale the divine found himself once he allowed his intuitive insights to be compromised by the intellectual reasoning proffered by Hester. In that maze Dimmesdale was confronted by every phantom demon that a hero must face. His thinking is befuddled, and Hawthorne's narrator comment is disparaging Dimmesdale's false resolution to preach his sermon before he vacates the premises with Hester, according to her plans disclosed in the forest. That hypocrisy is the wrong recourse; he is deceived by Hester's logic, and Hawthorne is agreeing with Pearl—he must stay, make his confession, identify himself as the author of Pearl, and complete the plan providence has laid out for him.

Another conclusion drawn hastily in error is Becker's quasi-cynical comment about the sermon Dimmesdale is to deliver. The sermon he was going to give, at this point, is abandoned later as he emerged out of the maze and returned to his true sense of destiny as a divine better equipped to deal with it. The new sermon *is* the election sermon, the election of a new governor in the land, and the subject of the connection between deity and the community of humankind, which is possibly the very essence of salvation, as Bayinhund explains, relating the two subjects.

From this point on, Becker's analysis of the American conscience quickly descends into a denigration of Dimmesdale's character, thus weakening the impact of his dim confession upon the scaffold and the full meanings of Hawthorne's allegory.

Dimmesdale's perverse desire to do moral hurt to his parishioners is not a mere psycho-mimetic portrayal of symptoms. It is also a systematic sweep of Puritan society. The people Dimmesdale meets are arranged in a descending order of Puritan respectability: deacon, eldest female, youngest female, children, seamen, Mistress Hibbins. The coverage is intentionally complete. It says that Dimmesdale is driven toward the moral perversion of every member of his parish and even those outside his parish. The climax comes when Hawthorne touches once more on the theme of diabolic possession [after his meeting with Mistress Hibbins] . . . The inability to face up to himself is still basic to Dimmesdale's moral attitude. This is what he shows in his desire to preach the election-day sermon . . . Dimmesdale has reached no moral heights. He is morally as weak as ever. He is merely a prey to the sinner's fleeting moment of exaltation (Becker, 137-38).

While in his maze, Dimmesdale was experiencing the consequences of his logical persuasion as he interacted with his parishioners. It is as though Hawthorne is depicting what a divine being might experience in a mortal world. He was a changed character by the seduction to his logical side; but later, when he came to his right senses, he carried out the mission he had been intuiting all along; and he carried it out with a determined resolution. The test of that resolution is shown in Dimmesdale's interaction with Chillingworth following his recognition of the person he was becoming because of his previous false reasoning.

The climax in the development of Dimmesdale's value is not at this point in the story. A hero is not completely developed until he has experienced all the barriers and obstacles raised up to prevent him from his heroic task. Having left an election sermon two days earlier only half finished before taking his trip to visit the Apostle Eliot in the forest, Dimmesdale met Hester in the forest; and from the point of this meeting to the time of his return to his house, Dimmesdale went through a temptation that showed him the depths of hell.

The climax of Dimmesdale's ordeal ends with the visit of Chillingworth. We sense only by intuition that he had become a different person, not a demon, but, having come face-to-face with all the demons of his day, including his own mortality, a more divine creature, now equipped to write the election sermon for his parishioners prior to his departure. He had taken off his gloves, no longer needing their protection from lesser beings, and handled this visit from Chillingworth with finese, and without Hawthorne's comments.

Dimmesdale instinctively had in mind another departure other than the one he led Chillingworth to believe he was about to make. "Yea, to another world," replied the minister, with pious resignation. Heaven grant it be a better one" (224). Hawthorne does not elaborate what that departure was, but he had Dimmesdale probably anticipating an intuitive foreshadowing of his death within a short time after he delivered the election sermon.

It is from this point on in his story, that Hawthorne quietly intimated how Dimmesdale became the hero of his allegory, and he did it mostly without analogies until the very end. He had an energy that no longer required the medications Chillingworth had concocted from earthly herbs at the edge of the sea, which medicines may represent Old Scratch's temptations to the mortal man. It was now "a new kind of animal vitality" (Becker 1971, 139) because the moral victory had been won. There was no more evidence of wishing to put off the crowning ordeal he had yet to face. It was the energy of a divine finally committed and fully resigned to the purpose of his mission, and he proceeded from this point on with a vitality of intuited or revealed knowledge. There were no longer any self-doubts, and he no longer needed gloves to handle his adversary.

But Becker is puzzled about Dimmesdale's confession upon the scaffold because of its seeming ambiguity; it is not clear to him what allegorical meaning it plays in the story.

> Is this the self-centered individualism so characteristic not only of Puritan material culture, but especially of Puritan spirituality? Or is it the psychological freedom of a man who realizes that the deepest and fullest love cannot intrude between God and another soul, that love has to recognize this limit inherent in the solitude of every human person? Does Dimmesdale, at the very moment when he has the courage to acknowledge his love for Hester and Pearl, renounce them out of fear for his own salvation, or stand free of them with the clear—sighted love of a man who knows the limits of love? It seems an unresolved question which leaves the meaning of Dimmesdale's character

ambiguous with precisely the ambiguity that is at the heart of
Puritan faith (Becker, 143) . . .

Dimmesdale remains the ambiguous representative of the
Puritan world. The vitality which came to him in the forest was
not, in terms of the book, a vitality rooted in freedom, Christian
or pagan. Perhaps there is no mimetic, that is, psychological
explanation for Dimmesdale confession. It remains tainted
with ambiguity (Becker, 144).

So Becker genuflected at the altar of obscurity and called for a
psychological explanation for Dimmedale's confession because he could
not, or would not, extrapolate one. What we do not understand, or refuse
to understand, we tend to label as ambiguous. When discussing an issue
for which we have not yet obtained a clearer understanding, labeling
anything ambiguous or obscure seems merely a sophisticated apology for
that lack of insight.

Dimmesdale is definitely not a representative of the Puritan world.
Whereas Puritanism breeds hostility toward the sinner, Dimmesdale's
sensitivity and compassion for the sinner places him at the other end of the
hate-love continuum. Of all the characters in TSL, he is rather the highest
representative of the divine element in the mortal man. His sensitivity, by
a continuing intuition, and not by educated or knowledgable reason, gives
him best access to providencial design, to the realities that transcend the
obvious. He, thus, represents the finer elements of Christianity because
his compassion and symbolic redemption lie at the center of it.

Daniel's interpretation does not rely upon any psychological
explanation because the confession is traditionally symbolic, as every
other allegorical device Hawthorne used in his novel. Any psychological
rumination of his characters, or of Hawthorne himself, should be aimed
at the core of his allegory—to show the relationship between the divine
and the material element in an explanation for the material-moral state
of humankind from its origins, through Puritanism, and to its destined
future.

Becker cannot make any sense out of Dimmesdale's confession
because he has not deciphered Dimmesdale's allegorical representation.
The interpretation Daniel has advanced clears up the ambiguity of
Dimmesdale's silence and dim confession. If there is a defense or apology

for a seeming veil of ambiguity, it might be that the veil is in place only as a filter against logical deduction; that is, it is left to the individual (even to Hawthorne's readers) to intuit what is good and sacred to the human heart. There is no clear-cut answer to the state of man's existence other than what he chooses to believe intuitively on faith. And that seems to be what Hawthorne is asking his readers to do. From all the alternative reasons expostulated by his characters, the reader, as the individual in society, must wend his or her own way to find the answers to the riddle of humankind's dilemma. And hopefully, to Hawthorne, generation upon generation will come closer to the answer, as humanity becomes more sensitive and compassionate in nature, and eventually achieves the Utopia that humankind wants.

That is, perhaps, the moral value which Daniel has deciphered from *The Scarlet Letter*: the inherent promise in the Christian philosophy inherited by Puritanism, to which the Puritans were blinded by their worldly leaders, that there is a day of peace and tranquility coming for humankind and that a prophetess (perhaps a nation or a more kindly and loving people) will yet arise to either announce or possess it. Dimmesdale's sacrifice upon the scaffold and his impending, voluntary, and destined death, heralds the promise implicit in humanity's material relationship with the divine element in humankind's nature—that there may be a reunion in which all the corruption of the material element will be transformed and that the mixture of good and evil, love and hate, whatever its source, may be commuted or consumed by the compassion of the universal heart.

So the destined shame that Dimmesdale took upon himself does not represent either the "self-centered individualism so characteristic . . . of Puritan material culture . . . and spirituality" or "the psychological freedom of a man," or a renouncement of his relationship with Hester and Pearl. It represents the opposite—a universal expiation and freedom for all humankind bound up in the mess of mortality, showing deity's true relationship and involvement in our own makeup. The kiss Dimmesdale placed upon Pearl signifies the creator's ownership of his creation, mankind, and seals the promise of that better world. The kiss he gave, and Pearl accepted without cringing, symbolized the spiritual reunion the three of them craved. Though Hawthorne addressed the material reunion later with a similar dimness of clarity, he did not leave the reader without substance for intuitive intimation.

However blind to these central values of Christianity Hawthorne's critics may have been, Bayinhund has added a new dimension to the study of Hawthorne that may renew the spiritual life many have thought was distorted by his novel.

> Perhaps, after our own critical journey through the novel and the forest of criticism which continues to grow up around it, we may be forced to return to the words of one of Hawthorne's earlier and better critics for our conclusion. George E. Woodberry finds Hawthorne almost as blind to the positive values of Puritanism as Hawthorne finds Puritanism blind to the values of the human heart. In emptying Puritanism of its Christian values Hawthorne has distorted "not so much the Puritan ideal—which were a little matter—but the spiritual life itself" (Woodberry, George., *Nathaniel Hawwthorne*. Boston: Houghton Mifflin Company, 1902, p. 202-3.) (Becker, 147).

Missing the central theme of Hawthorne's novel is misunderstanding Hawthorne at his best. Bayinhund would contend that Hawthorne has not emptied Puritanism of its Christian values nor distorted its spiritual life but, instead, indicated to his friends its emptiness and signaled what was missing in it. He has reminded us, by the scarlet letter we all wear, that our focus should not be on condemning the sinner for his sinfulness, as the Puritan experiment did, but to focus on the hope that can deliver us from it "by the truest test of a life succcessful to such an end!" (263) He has extended the hope that, as painful as life may be, perhaps even the vilest of sinners, like Chillingworth, may have their destiny, in time, transmuted from its temporary state of hate to a more lasting one of love.

So one erroneous conclusion can lead to others, as Becker demonstrates in his final review.

> Hester dies in sorrow and is buried separately from her love "as if the dust of the two sleepers had no right to mingle" (264) (Becker, 147).

Quoting Hawthorne out of context, especially the following sentence, Becker has overlooked the pattern of equivocalness Hawthorne used to juxtapose two opinions side by side, at the same time using surrounding text and inferences to point in the direction of his philosophical self. Bayinhund hangs his interpretation heavily upon the inferences in Hawthorne's concluding remarks as the narrator of his "as if" allegory. He would therefore conclude his own venture with Hawthorne's novel by focusing upon the text that Becker omitted, in particular the sentence that Becker has slighted for lack of understanding.

> And, after many, many years, a new grave was delved, near an old and sunken one, in that burial ground beside which King's Chapel has since been built. It was near that old and sunken grave, yet with a space between, as if the dust of the two sleepers had no right to mingle. *Yet one tombstone served for both* [my italacs]. (264)

Why would Hester be buried next to a grave so that one tombstone marks both their grave sites? Would Hawthorne place her beside someone that was not a character in the story? Why not bury her in another graveyard far distant, rather than next to Dimmesdale's? And is the space between them intended to be interpreted as distance rather than time? Bayinhund has asserted that Hawthorne has addressed the issue of a material reunion, to occur in a better time, for Hester's burial comes too closely on the heels of the question: Will Hester and Dimmesdale be together again hereafter? The mystery is intended as an open-ended question, the answer to which is left to the reader's preference, or perhaps preferably (to reflect Hawthorne's openness) for some future time to answer.

Hawthorne twice referred to the sunken grave next to hers. That may be Hawthorne's subtle way of attaching his own hope to the dismal spot. It may not be too far-fetched an interpolation to add, if indeed not also the most logical, that the sunken grave site beside Hester's suggests some removal of its contents. The reader may assume deterioration or resurrection, but the latter is more consistent with the tone and substance of the allegory. And we will leave the question to the next Daniel as to why Hawthorne chose the burial place next to the King's Chapel.

But Becker has given us a key to further explore the mind and matter of Hawthorne's great mystery: if Hester truly represents Nature, what might be the ramifications of each configuration of her relationship with his other characters? Let Becker and Daniel, if we are not being too inclusive, be the beginning of such an exploration.

*   *   *

This extrapolation can only be justified on the basis that Hawthorne's allegory purports to indicate that the mortal body is a splendid creation; has it purposes; and, because of intervening providencial design, may undergo a transfiguration "in an everlasting and pure reunion" (256).

The framework of his allegory then, according to Daniel, is that the story appears to be an "as if" sirenian seranade of death, the subtle echoes of which are instead a refrain that glorifies God and exalts the life beyond. Bayinhund would close his comments with the question that Hawthorne seems to address more to the reader than to his hero character, Dimmesdale:

> Shall we not spend our immortal life together? Surely, surely,
> we have ransomed one another, with all this woe! Thou lookest
> far into eternity, with those bright dying eyes! Then tell me
> what thou seest? (256)

To Daniel, then, Hawthorne's novel appears to be an invitation to his readers to share his intimations on immortality, though dimly as he may have perceived them. Perhaps his descendants and his readers may now wonder a little less, as he surmized his ancestors might, whether or not he was "serviceable to mankind" and not merely a writer of storybooks.

APPENDIX 3

AN APOLOGY

Indeed, perhaps the entirety of this volume composes an apology. Because we live in a changing America whose traditional values and prejudices seem to shift from generation to generation, as Hawthorne anticipated for the better, it appears inevitable that some of one's readership will be offended by an openness of attitude. In his own time, perhaps in his seemingly obscure way, Hawthorne was being careful not to offend or disturb his readership by keeping his "thoughts . . . frozen and utterance benumbed" (4). In seeking communion with Hawthorne's true nature, perhaps Bayinhund's openness has unfrozen those thoughts and uttered a "scarcely decorous" interpretation that might be reasonable objectionable to many; and in his attempt to peek behind the veil of Hawthorne's inmost Me, he may have stepped on quite a few toes. His editor has therefore attempted to soften the impact of Daniel's interpretation of Hawthorne's allegory.

Although he may feel somewhat hypocritical, he believes he has been a discreet apologist standing in for both Hawthorne and Bayinhund. For example, his discretionary use of the title, Nazarene, for the man from Nazareth, one of the hundreds of names and titles that have been used to describe his impact upon the world, is a compromise I have made with some reluctance. But like Hawthorne, if he has done nothing else, he at least has finally completed his own circle of existence in honoring his conscience and pledge to a little known student. May he and Daniel now rest in peace.

BIBLIOGRAPHY

The following bibliography references only those works that were cited in this book. A list of all other references provided by memory would be more unnecessarily tedious.

PRIMARY

Hawthorne, Nathaniel. *The Scarlet Letter.* The Centenary Edition of the Works of Nathaniel Hawthorne, Vol. 1. Ohio State University, 1962.

Becker, John E. *Hawthorne's Historical Allegory: An Eamination of the American Conscience.* Port Washington, N.Y.: Kennikat Press, 1971.

SECONDARY

Anderson, Robert, et al. *Elements of Literature, Fifth Course: Literature of the United States.* New York: Holt, Rinehart and Winston, Inc., 1989.

Bell, Michael Davitt. "Arts of Deception: Hawthorne, 'Romance,' and *The Scarlet Letter,*" pp. 29-56, in *New Essays on The Scarlet Letter,* Michael T.Colacurcio, Ed. New York: Cambridge Univ. Press, 1985.

Bloom, Harold, ed. *Modern Critical Interpretations: Nathaniel Hawthorne's The Scarlet Letter.* New York: Chalsea House Publisher, 1986.

Bloom, "Introduction," 1-8.

A. N. Kaul, "*The Scarlet Letter* and Puritan Ethics," 9-20.

Michael Ragussis, "Family Discourse and Fiction in *The Scarlet Letter*," 59-80.

Evan Carton, "The Prison Door," 97-120.

Brownson, Orestes. "A Story That Should Not Have Been Told," in *The Scarlet Letter*, by Nathaniel Hawthorne. New York: Bantam Books, 1965.

Charvat, William, et al, Ed. *The Centenary Edition of the Works of Nathaniel Hawthorne,* Vol. *1*. Ohio State University Press, 1962.

Evans, G. Blakemore et. al, Ed. *The Riverside Shakespeare*, 2nd ed. Boston, New York: Houghton Mifflin Company, 1997.

Ford, Paul Leicester, Ed. *The Works of Thomas Jefferson*, Federal Edition, Vol. 7. New York and London: G. P. Putnam's Sons, 1905.

Harrison, G. B., et al., Ed. *Major British Writers*, Vol. 1. New York: Harcourt, Brace & World, Inc., 1959.

Harrison, G. B., et al., Ed. *Major British Writers*, Vol. 2. New York: Harcourt, Brace & World, Inc., 1959.

Hawthorne, Nathaniel. *The Scarlet Letter*. New York: Dell Publishing Co., 1979.

James, Henry, Jr. *Hawthorne*. New York: Harper & Brothers, 1879.

Lanier, Mary,Ed. *Poems of Sidney Lanier*. Macon, Ga: Middle Georgia Historical Society, Inc., 1967.

Madsen, Truman G. *Eternal Man*. Salt Lake City: Deseret Book Company, 1966.

Porte, Joel. "Introduction," in Nathaniel Hawthorne's *The Scarlet Letter*. New York: Dell Publishing Co., 1979.

Spector, Robert Donald. "Part Three. How the Novel Took Shape," in *The Scarlet Letter*, by Nathaniel Hawthorne. New York: Bantam Books, 1965.

Spring, Joel. *The American School 1642-1993*. New York: McGraw-Hill, Inc., 1994.

Woodberry, George E., Ed. *American Men of Letters: Nathaniel Hawthorne*. Cambridge, Mass.: The Riverside Press, 1902.